James Turner Johnson AND THE Just War Tradition

SELECTED ESSAYS

EDITED BY
Eric Patterson, Gina G. Palmer,
and Timothy J. Demy

STONE TOWER PRESS

James Turner Johnson and the Just War Tradition: Selected Essays

Edited by Eric Patterson, Gina G. Palmer, and Timothy J. Demy

Stone Tower Press
7 Ellen Rd.
Middletown, RI 02842
stonetowerpress.com

Paperback ISBN: 979-8-9868172-2-4

Formatting and cover design by Amy Cole, JPL Design Solutions.

Cover art: *Niccolo Mauruzi da Tolentino unseats Bernardino Della Ciarda at the Battle of San Romano* by Paolo Uccello, painting date uncertain, ca. 1435–1455, Galleria degli Uffizi, Florence. Public domain image.

Printed in the United States of America

CONTENTS

Foreword 1

Introduction 3

Acknowledgments 19

Personal Reflections on My Life and Work 21

CHAPTER 1
What Guidance Can Just War Tradition Provide for Contemporary Moral Thought About War? 33

CHAPTER 2
The Just War Tradition and the American Military 45

CHAPTER 3
Historical Roots and Sources of the Just War Tradition 83

CHAPTER 4
Just-War Idea and the Ethics of Intervention 119

CHAPTER 5
The Question of Preemption 145

CHAPTER 6
The Broken Tradition and Question of Whether Force Can Be Used Justly 163

CHAPTER 7
Can Force Be Used Justly? 183

CHAPTER 8
Jihad and Just War 207

CHAPTER 9
Aquinas and Luther on War and Peace: Sovereign Authority and the Use of Armed Force 215

CHAPTER 10
Just War Theory: Responding Morally to Global Terrorism 241

CHAPTER 11
Catholic Just War Thinking: The State of the Question 267

CHAPTER 12
The Just War Idea: The State of the Question 295

CHAPTER 13
Torture: A Just War Perspective 337

CHAPTER 14
Thinking Historically About Just War 343

CHAPTER 15
Just War and Jihad: Two Traditions on the Use of Force 365

CHAPTER 16
Holy War 385

CHAPTER 17
Ad Fontes: *The Question of Rebellion and Moral Tradition on the Use of Force* 407

CHAPTER 18
Contemporary Just War Thinking: Which Is Worse, to Have Friends or Critics? 419

CHAPTER 19
Religion, Violence, and Human Rights: Protection of Human Rights as Justification for the Use of Armed Force 447

CHAPTER 20
The Erosion of Noncombatant Immunity in Asymmetric War 467

CHAPTER 21
The Just War Idea and the Contemporary Security Environment 487

CHAPTER 22
Getting It Right: Changes in Just War Thought on Sovereignty, Just Cause, and Right Intention from the Classic Just War Idea Till Today 501

CHAPTER 23
Christian Ethics & the Realm of Statecraft: Divisions, Cross-Currents, & the Search for Connections 515

CHAPTER 24
Reading Augustine 529

CHAPTER 25
Paul Ramsey and the Recovery of the Just War Idea 545

Appendices 565

Appendix A 567

Appendix B 575

Chapter Sources 619

About James Turner Johnson and the Editors 625

FOREWORD

It is a pleasure to offer a few comments in connection with this collection of articles and lectures by James Turner Johnson. Intended to serve as a companion to a previously published volume of essays on Johnson's work, the items included here will serve to acquaint scholars interested in the ethics of war with his distinctive approach and wide learning. All those presently working in this area are indebted to the editors for their work in bringing these pieces together, and I am certain that I speak for many in expressing gratitude to them.

In this connection, I also consider it fitting to say thanks to Jim Johnson himself. I met Jim in 1987, when I was a participant in his National Endowment for the Humanities Summer Seminar for College Teachers. At the time, I was preparing for a move to Florida State University, where I would begin work that fall as an assistant professor in the Department of Religion. Jim organized the seminar around his recently completed book, *The Quest for Peace: Three Moral Traditions in Western Cultural History*. Along with the other participants, I learned a great deal from Jim's account of the development of just war tradition and various forms of pacifism. More importantly, however, Jim helped me to sort out some ideas about the Muslim analogue to just war tradition. This assistance proved invaluable in the development of an early article comparing just war and jihad traditions; further, when I told Jim of my aspiration to encourage conversations between scholars knowledgeable about the just war tradition and people working in Islamic Studies, he responded with enthusiasm and suggested we work together on the project. Over the following months, we wrote a proposal and, with the support of a grant from the U.S. Institute of Peace, put together a series of seminars which led to two edited volumes. Thus began a collaboration which continues to this day, with Jim not only serving as a colleague and friend, but as a mentor. For this I owe Jim a great deal; but my story is hardly unique. Over his long career, Jim's encouragement, guidance, and scholarly acumen have been important to many, and it seems important to acknowledge that.

Of course, this collection of Jim's work also provides an occasion to express gratitude for his many contributions to our understanding of the ethics of war. Jim is well-known for his emphasis on the just war tradition as an historical and cultural phenomenon. As the present volume makes clear, however, this does not make for an arcane approach of interest only to academics. Jim always strives to make connections between the historical tradition and contemporary issues. Whether these have to do with questions posed by new developments in the technology of war or by conflicts like the Gulf War or the post-9/11 response to jihadist groups, Jim's analyses are always clear and helpful. In terms of the modern development of just war thinking, he is fond of describing the work of Paul Ramsey, Michael Walzer, and the 1983 pastoral of the U.S. Conference of Catholic Bishops as the "three pillars" of the conversation. Given the breadth and depth of his many contributions, I think we might put Jim's work in that same league.

I shall close with mention of Jim's dedication of *Just War Tradition and the Restraint of War* to "those who have gone before and those yet to come, in the hope that the tradition of restraint in war will never be lost." In the interest of that goal, Jim Johnson has already done more than his part—and he is not yet finished.

John Kelsay, Ph.D.
Distinguished Research Professor
Department of Religion
Florida State University

INTRODUCTION

In August 2011 the entire world seemed to be wondering how to think about the tenth anniversary of the 9/11 attacks and subsequent Global War on Terrorism. The Obama Administration's first two years in office had been controversial, to say the least. On the international front, the Administration clearly wanted to disentangle itself from Afghanistan and Iraq, cut a nuclear deal with Iran, and avoid fighting another international terrorist organization (in this case, ISIS, or Islamic State). How does a country, with tens of thousands of troops on the ground and close relations with allied governments, actually disentangle itself from its many responsibilities, not the least of which is limiting future violence by dealing with criminals, detainees, and long-term captives held in the prisons of Iraq and Afghanistan? One critical dilemma in August 2011 was what to do with the countless murderers and terrorists held in Iraq's jails and prisons. The U.S. Central Command's commanding general, General James Mattis, brought together a small group of experts to provide counsel on the ethics of detention. The real issue was policies of "catch and release" and the Iraqi penchant for releasing the worst offenders. How could it be ethical for the U.S. to capture murderers and terrorists, only to release them or hand the keys over to the Iraqis, when the U.S. withdrew from Iraq? Among those who General Mattis invited to brief him at CENTCOM headquarters in Florida was James Turner Johnson.

Whether in the classroom, in print, or briefing a flag officer, James Turner Johnson exemplifies the academic who sees his work as service: service to the academy, service to students, service to the discipline, service to one's country, service to others, and service in the pursuit of peace and security. His testimony to General Mattis reflected this. Indeed, James

Turner Johnson has substantially contributed to and cultivated the continued development of the tradition. His pioneering work in the "historical-moral" methodology takes into account influences from theological and canonical works as well as military, legal, and political praxis of each historical period. He recognizes the give-and-take between the needs of diplomats and warriors on the one hand, and philosophical contemplation on the other. This stands in direct contrast to those who impose today's sensibilities onto past eras or who refuse to reckon with the real-world commitments and needs of those serving the public trust.

Like the just war tradition itself, Johnson's work has one foot squarely in the lessons and arguments of the past, with the other foot stepping forward to encounter the latest issues of the day as they relate to this ever-broadening tradition. He has written on everything from weapons of mass destruction to great power conflicts to irregular warfare. He remains a critical figure transmitting an important moral tradition to new generations of scholars, soldiers, and statesmen, based upon the foundational writings of great ethicists, philosophers, and purveyors of faith and reason that include the likes of Ambrose, Augustine, Aquinas, Vitoria, Grotius, Lieber, among others.

Moreover, as opposed to the artificial boundaries of the academy, Johnson represents trans-disciplinary academic scholarship on just war thinking spanning philosophy, history, law, theology, ethics, international relations theory, political science, comparative religion, and military ethics. Johnson and his works are just as welcome at the International Studies Association as at the American Academy of Religion.

This book is a collection of some of James Turner Johnson's works, primarily taken from outside his book volumes. Many have come to know Johnson through his books and, thus, this book is designed to introduce readers to a selection of his other works such as his articles, essays, and unpublished speeches that exemplify the arc of Johnson's career. This book is also designed to be a companion volume to the recent volume about his writings, *Responsibility and Restraint: James Turner Johnson and the Just War Tradition*. *Responsibility and Restraint* brings together top scholars who critically examine Johnson's legacy: his engagement with Catholic scholars and the Catholic Church, his work alongside that of Michael Walzer and Paul Ramsey, as well as his analysis of Islamic thinking on war and peace, and other topics. When one combines this volume with *Responsibility and Restraint,* one has an excellent, though not exhaustive, overview of the key contributions Johnson made for more than half a century.

FROM MEMPHIS TO RUTGERS: A CAREER OF ACHIEVEMENT

James Turner Johnson was born in 1938 near Memphis, Tennessee. A descendant of Scottish and Swedish immigrants who came to North America during the Colonial Era, he grew up in Crockett Mills, named for Davy Crockett, and his early life was like that of many Americans during that time: having been educated in local public schools; having relatives and grandparents who lived nearby; having been part of a family disrupted by World War II when Johnson's dad worked as a welder at various defense installations along the East Coast; and having experienced the rhythms of farm life, school, church, and the four seasons in pastoral Tennessee.

Johnson reports that his public school education "served him well." A personal biographical statement by Johnson can be found in this book, but suffice to say that he transitioned away from interest in physics and math and after graduating from Brown University (A.B.) in 1960, he determined, "I made up my mind that what I really wanted to do was to study human ethical thinking." After graduating from Brown, he returned to Tennessee for a period of intense academic study, earning a degree from Vanderbilt University (B.D.) and then matriculating to graduate studies in New Jersey at Princeton University (M.A., 1967; Ph.D. with Distinction, 1968).

For nearly half a century (1969–2015) Johnson served in the Department of Religion at Rutgers University. He taught undergraduate and graduate courses on religion, ethics, comparative religious ethics, the ethics of war and peace, political ethics, ethics and international affairs, just war tradition and international Law of Armed Conflict (LOAC), and Western and Islamic traditions on statecraft and war. He was ever generous with his time and was considered by his students to be an outstanding teacher and mentor. Reflecting on the experience of working with Johnson to advise a senior student on her honors thesis, one of his colleagues noted:

> Johnson met with the student every week, and every week he surprised me with the depth and breadth of his knowledge. Most of all, however, as an adviser, he managed to challenge the student, to push him to do more, and yet never discourage him. As someone who still feels like she's learning to juggle the blend of encouragement and critique, cheerleading and pushing, that advising a thesis demands, I felt like I was sitting at the feet of a master. The student in question, by the way, won a Henry Rutgers prize for his thesis. I'm not saying that was all Jim's doing—of course it wasn't—but he was a model adviser.

While at Rutgers he served in a variety of roles, including department chair, director of international programs, senator, as well as on various dissertation and university committees. He represented Rutgers University to various outside agencies, including the Atlantic Council and National Association of State Universities and Land-Grant Colleges. Due to his outstanding record, Rutgers awarded Johnson its prestigious Daniel Gorenstein Memorial Award for "both outstanding scholarly achievement and exceptional service to the university." Johnson's Gorenstein Lecture was delivered on September 29, 2015 and is reprinted in its entirety in *Responsibility and Restraint.* Johnson's Gorenstein Lecture chronicled the way that his career developed at the same time that the academic study of religion was evolving, with widening distance between theology and religious studies. The lecture also argues for the continuing relevance of historical moral inquiry on peace, security, and war, both as an academic enterprise and in the formation of the next generation of decision-makers.

Johnson also served the wider academy. He was an active member of numerous scholarly societies, including the American Academy of Political and Social Science, American Academy of Religion, International Studies Association, Society of Christian Ethics, and the American Association of University Professors. During these meetings, he was ever available to meet with old friends as well as young professors and graduate students. One young scholar remembered, "I can't believe that James Turner Johnson is asking me to tell him about my dissertation and hopes for an academic career. He seems to take seriously my goals. He listened. He gave me a little bit of useful advice, but, mainly, he listened."

Some of his support from the National Endowment for the Humanities was for summer faculty seminars, a sort of in-depth summer school bringing together university faculty from across the country. He has served on the editorial boards of a number of journals, including *Religious Studies Review*, *The Journal of Law and Religion,* and *Providence: A Journal of Christianity and American Foreign Policy.* He served as the General Editor of *The Journal of Religious Ethics* (1981–1991) and as an editor of *Studies in Religious Ethics* (1985–1991). Perhaps most importantly for expanding serious scholarship on just war thinking and military ethics, he co-founded the *Journal of Military Ethics*, serving as its co-editor from 2001–2010. He was also one of the founding contributing editors of *Providence: A Journal of Christianity and American Foreign Policy.*

Over the years, Johnson received recognition as a nationally-renowned scholar. He has been awarded grants from the most prestigious foundations, including the National Endowment for the Humanities, the Earhart Foundation, the U.S. Institute of Peace, the Guggenheim Foundation, and the Rockefeller Foundation, among others. He is the author or editor of eighteen books and well over one hundred scholarly articles.

Johnson has been invited to give lectures to the U.S. military academies and war colleges, senior leaders at the Pentagon and combat commands, and consulted with the Council on Foreign Relations, as well as a number of other organizations. In overseeing student groups in more than a dozen countries, he has lectured in Canada, Malta, Oman, Norway, Belgium, the United Kingdom, the Netherlands, and elsewhere. He is truly a scholar and teacher with an international impact.

JOHNSON'S LITERARY ACHIEVEMENTS: THE INTELLECTUAL HISTORY OF A CAREER

The "Just War History" Trilogy

One would probably not guess that James Turner Johnson's dissertation topic was seventeenth-century English Puritan marriage ethics. That project, which became Johnson's first book, documented Puritan attitudes on family and marriage, with an eye to how those views influenced later English and American Protestant thinking on sex and marriage. Following his first book's publication, a fellowship to the Huntington Library in Pasadena, California, with its outstanding collection of early English-printed books, brought Johnson to the topics of "just war" and "holy war" in English literature.

The next few years were extremely productive as Johnson published three major books on the history of the just war tradition. A look at these important early works provides a foundation for understanding recurring themes and approaches over the subsequent three decades of Johnson's scholarship. His first book on just war thinking, *Ideology, Reason and The Limitation of War* (1975), focused on the issues at the nexus of religion and conflict during that era. The second, *Just War Tradition and the Restraint of War: A Moral and Historical Inquiry* (1981 and later editions), carried the historical analysis through the eighteenth, nineteenth, and twentieth centuries. The third, *The Quest for Peace: Three Moral Traditions in Western Cultural Tradition* (1987), focused on contrasting visions of peace and security.

While serving as a fellow at the Huntington Library in 1973, Johnson uncovered a trove of materials from English language sources reacting in real-time to the Continental Wars of Religion, the Puritan Revolution in England, the Irish Rebellion, and similar subjects. The language employed was often that of "holy war," i.e. religiously justified or spiritually understood approaches to politics and conflict. This was not really the type of totalizing holy war that we associate with jihadism or historical wars that justified ethnoreligious "cleansing" of others on behalf of purifying a land-based upon faith. Rather, the language was more akin to traditional, albeit muscular, just war narratives that brought into focus not just restraint but also justice, self-defense, and avenging the moral standards of the community. This study resulted in another book: *Ideology, Reason, and the Limitations of War: Religious and Secular Concepts, 1200–1740* (1975), which laid the basis for Johnson's later works.

It is noteworthy that Johnson was writing during a period of conflict and American soul-searching. The Vietnam War was at its height during his time in graduate school and was coming to a conclusion as his academic career began. He began writing as America was reflectively looking at important anniversaries, most notably the fiftieth anniversary of the treaties ending World War I and the twenty-fifth anniversary of the end of World War II. Americans, and others, were comparing those "good wars" with what they were seeing of the Vietnam War on their television screens. Not surprisingly, his next book, *Just War Tradition and the Restraint of War: A Moral and Historical Inquiry* (1981), dealt not only with the past but also engaged with two contemporary books that were specifically rooted in those wars. The first, Michael Walzer's *Just and Unjust Wars*, used many examples from World War II, from the killing of individuals to the use of atomic weapons. The second was Paul Fussell's *The Great War and Modern Memory*. Johnson, who says that his *Just War Tradition* book is a favorite among his works, reflects that his 1981 book set the stage for much of his later works. Two key themes from just war tradition that occur again and again in his work are the way that cultural and religious traditions reconcile the dilemma of regulating violence, and the importance of natural law reasoning.

In correspondence with the authors, Johnson reports that the purpose of the third book of his historical trilogy, *The Quest for Peace* (1987), was both to round out the history of moral tradition on war in the West and to honor the basic idea that just war should have the aim of peace and reconciliation (tracking this back to Augustine's writings). Rooted in classical political theory inherited, in part, from Cicero and Greco-Roman thought and practice and later work by Augustine and Ambrose, it was assumed when the just war tradition fully came together in the twelfth and thirteenth centuries that politics was defined by three goods or ends: order, justice, and peace. These were considered inseparable from one another: Good order is the sum of justice and peace in the community; justice is the sum of order and peace; and peace is the sum of order and justice. The three requirements for a just resort to force, put in place by the canonists and summarized by Aquinas in his Question "On War" in *Summa Theologica* were *sovereign authority*, *just cause*, and *right intention*; and these corresponded directly to the three ends of politics itself. So, the classic idea of just war reinterpreted and rephrased the goods of politics as requirements for the use of armed force in the context of the responsibilities for government of a political community, a *res publica*. "*To make this point was the fundamental purpose of that book*" [emphasis by Johnson]. Johnson lamented that his fundamental purpose in writing *Quest for Peace* failed, evidenced both by the fact that the people who bought his first two books generally ignored this third one and, more essentially, those sympathetic to pacifism who did read the book were hostile to hearing anything about how the use of armed force could contribute to peace—as they still are.

Johnson's Applied Just War Thinking

The 1980s and 1990s saw the flowering of Johnson's impact. As noted previously, he served as a journal editor, co-founded a journal, and served in leadership roles at Rutgers and in various academic societies. He became a frequent consultant and speaker on the morality of force in religious bodies and military institutions. He gave addresses in more than two dozen countries, from China to South Africa, from Oman to Morocco, and Slovakia to the United Kingdom. Many of Johnson's books and articles from this time took a more applied approach to just war tradition, including *Can Modern Wars Be Just?* (1984). This book deals with the moral dimension of headline topics from the height of the Cold War: strategic nuclear weapons, tactical nuclear weapons, terrorism, and unconventional warfare by guerrilla and revolutionary movements. In fact, Johnson delved deeply into then recently developed weapons systems, including cruise missiles and the neutron warheads. The book also addressed a perennial just war issue and one that is increasingly salient to democratic societies: decisions by individuals. Johnson gave special attention to "obedience to orders" and conscientious objection as they apply within larger Western frameworks for understanding the relationship of the individual to the state. It is not surprising that nearly forty years later, *Can Modern Wars Be Just?* continues to be featured on course reading lists and as a solid introductory text on just war or military ethics more broadly.

The applied character of some of Johnson's work coincided with dramatic changes in the international landscape, notably the rise of Islamist terrorism, greater U.S. military involvement in the Middle East, and the end of the Cold War. The latter spawned numerous destabilizing conflicts, resulting in a need for just war literature applied to an unstable international system, rogue states (e.g. Saddam Hussein's Iraq), insurgencies and civil wars, and the never-ending problem of weapons of mass destruction. Johnson wrote extensively about the responsibility that governments have to provide political order at home and abroad. One example is his co-authored book with George Weigel on the moral imperative of the Persian Gulf War, *Just War and the Gulf War* (1991). Johnson and Weigel described the importance of buttressing international law through protecting vulnerable states and consummating the intent of international covenants, such as the U.N. Charter, when facing outlaw regimes like Iraq as well as destabilizing conditions in failing states. Johnson's monograph *The Just War Idea and the Ethics of Intervention* (1993) was written after the restoration of Kuwait, while the United States was grappling with what to do in Somalia, post-Soviet Afghanistan, and to counter the Balkan genocide. In order to advance thoughtful approaches to peace, he simultaneously co-edited a book addressing best practices for transitional justice and conflict resolution in *Beyond Confrontation: Learning Conflict Resolution in the Post-Cold War Era* (1995).

It was during this time that Johnson began to consider comparative just war and holy war traditions, especially those associated with Islam. He also developed a long-standing intellectual partnership with University of Florida professor John Kelsay, co-editing two books with him. In the late 1980s Johnson participated in four conferences at Rutgers University comparing Western and Islamic religious and cultural traditions on war, peace, and statecraft. The objective was to bridge the gap of knowledge and understanding between the study of the West and the study of Islam. The resulting book, co-edited with John Kelsay, was *Cross, Crescent, and Sword: The Justification and Limitation of War in Western and Islamic Tradition* (1990). A companion volume, also co-edited with John Kelsay, came out a year later and was of immediate interest due to the Persian Gulf War: *Just War and Jihad: Historical and Theoretical Perspectives on War and Peace in Western and Islamic Traditions* (1991).

Six years later Johnson published another book on the historical development of the idea of holy war in the Christian West and Islam: *The Holy War Idea in Western and Islamic Tradition* (1997). The work offers a comparative study of how these two cultural traditions historically have defined the interrelationship of religion, statecraft, and war. Johnson would go on to write numerous other articles and book chapters assessing Islamic ideas as they related to contemporary topics such as "Debates Over Just War and Jihad: Ideas, Interpretations, and Implications Across Cultures" in a 2009 edited volume on the then controversial topic of a "war of ideas" between the Islamic East and the Judeo-Christian, democratic West.

For the subsequent two decades, Johnson continued to balance a deep, scholarly approach to the just war tradition alongside an applied approach useful for statesmen, scholars, and military professionals. Perhaps his most widely read book comes from this era, *Morality and Contemporary Warfare* (1999). The book received outstanding reviews across the board. *Theological Studies* called it "a most excellent work." The *Journal of Military History* stated that the book "exudes wisdom." Catholic theologian J. Bryan Hehir, a key contributor to the 1983 pastoral letter, *The Challenge of Peace*, praised the book:

> In *Morality and Contemporary Warfare*, Johnson offers a synthetic summary of the just-war ethic and engages new issues of politics and strategy. This book...will enrich the normative analysis of politics and war. I recommend it highly.... This is a very good book on an important topic.

Sir Lawrence Freedman, the "dean of British strategic studies," commended the book in the *Times Literary Supplement,* stating:

> In his latest book, James Turner Johnson, one of the great American exponents of the just-war approach, demonstrates its values by applying it with sustained rigour to the conflicts of the past decade, starting with the 1991 Gulf War.... Johnson['s analysis] exudes wisdom.

As Johnson was in wide demand as a speaker to military audiences during this era, he recalled of his books at that time:

> I focused on drawing out the implications of the historical tradition of just war and the values it defined; I still began every one of them with a historical summary review of the tradition. This shift also reflected my increased involvement (by invitation) in dialogue with professional military and policy people, and they were less interested than I in the historical antecedents and underlying values there: they wanted to focus on practical contexts and ethical guidance for action in those contexts.

Johnson continued to impact the academy and the applied realm of national security and military ethics in the wake of the September 11 attacks, including his 2005 book, *The War To Oust Saddam Hussein: Just War and the New Face of Conflict.* He went on to deal with some of the most pressing issues of an unstable world during the global war on terrorism: noncombatant immunity, armed military intervention, weapons of mass destruction, the weaknesses of international institutions, and the evolution of customary and treaty-based international law. Moreover, he continued to encourage the next generation of just war scholarship through personal mentoring, involvement in scholarly associations and advancing the opportunities of rising scholars, most notably through his major co-edited collection, *The Ashgate Research Companion on Military Ethics.*

Johnson continued his engagement with the key issues of the day through his final decade at Rutgers, including his sole-authored book, *Sovereignty: Moral and Historical Perspectives* (2014). The reader may not think of "sovereignty" as the most alluring topic, but at the time the issues surrounding sovereignty and government legitimacy resulted in major books by world-class scholars. Among these were Daniel Philpott's *Revolutions in Sovereignty*, Jean Bethke Elshtain's *Sovereignty: God, State, and Self*, and Francis Fukuyama's *The Origins of Political Order.* Elshtain and Philpott began their books with the Peace of Westphalia (1648) and describe how this set the foundation for international relations today, whereas Fukuyama's work takes an anthropological approach to structures of political order deeply rooted in history. Johnson's book was complementary, but also sharply contrasted these works. Johnson locates the notion of "authority" in the Western just war tradition and traces it over two millennia, charting changes at the end of the Middle Ages and throughout the modern period. Most importantly, Johnson's is not simply a history: it instead elucidates what all of this means for today and what we perhaps can learn from the past. When one considers that the book looked back on the failings and failures of states (e.g. the Balkans, Iraq, Sudan, Afghanistan, and the Democratic Republic of Congo), the weaknesses of the United Nations and the UN's Responsibility to Protect (R2P) Doctrine, as well as hinted at new debates over the legitimate foundations of Western democracies (e.g. the democracy-integralist controversy), Johnson once again contributed a voice of wisdom and reason.

JOHNSON'S "HISTORICAL-THEOLOGICAL" METHODOLOGY

Johnson developed a distinctive methodology in his historical and philosophical works, which he outlined as early as 1979 in an article in the *Journal of Religious Ethics.* Johnson argued for a "historical-theological" approach to understanding and applying key moral concepts. In correspondence with the authors, Johnson wrote that his early scholarship at the Huntington Library and elsewhere convinced him that the development of just war thinking resulted from the "interaction" of theory and practice: "The just war idea...originally result[ed]...from military, political, and legal praxis and reflection on it as well as from canonical and theological work." Such an approach was particularly apropos in the late 1970s as both the study of ethics and security studies had become increasingly abstract and syllogistic. Johnson writes, "So I shifted my methodological attention to the religious ethics scholarly community."

John Kelsay, in an analysis of Johnson's methodological approach in *Responsibility and Restraint*, praises Johnson's "historical casuistry," describing it as the "interdependence of practical judgment and historical knowledge." According to Kelsay, Johnson perceives history as a fruitful, even obligatory, conversation with past generations that stimulates our moral perceptions and expands the horizons of our moral imagination—it's the Burkean parlor in which we encounter people of different times and places who share the same questions that preoccupy us. Kelsay suggests that Johnson's conversation with the past proceeds from his belief that "engagement with history has relevance for the present, in the sense that learning to think with the leading developers of just war tradition provides guidance for those attempting to sort the rights and wrongs of war in contemporary cases." We are just looking over our shoulder, as Kelsay tells us: "Johnson's approach is founded in the hope that by 'thinking with' Aquinas and other interpreters of just war tradition [i.e. contextually], we might find the wisdom to navigate current circumstances." Such forward-looking benefit is found, for instance, when we uncover neo-scholastic just war thinkers' judgments regarding noncombatants caught up in siege warfare and consider more contemporary dilemmas about armed humanitarian intervention and strategic bombing.

By recognizing that moral dilemmas—even those that center on technological advances such as nuclear weaponry—are nothing new and that ethical debate did not begin, nor will it end, with us, Johnson's approach to historic inquiry, Kelsay notes, is marked by deep humility. In turn, his historic approach marks Johnson as a moralist. This explains why we suggested above that Johnson's historical approach is fruitful for scholarship and prudential ethics. Kelsay cites Johnson's essay "Historical Tradition and Moral Judgment: The Case of Just War Tradition," where Johnson asserts that the task of the Christian ethicist, as it is with any moralist, is to speak from within the moral tradition out of which moral analysis arises. This responsibility implies two additional ones: one that is educational and a second that is critical. The educational function is to serve as a curator of the historical knowledge vouchsafed to the Christian community; the critical function is to understand the meaning and interrelations of its various elements and to reintroduce this accumulated wisdom to the contemporary community, clarifying how it bears on present concerns. As Johnson puts it, it is not enough to ask, "What God is doing in the world." He asserts that we also need to grasp what God has been doing from the beginning and "to keep faith with those generations of persons in the past who discerned moral and theological values in their reflection on the meaning of the divine activity." Johnson reminds us that this is what being a part of tradition means.

Johnson increasingly put this methodology into action in the then newly developing (1990s) sub-field of military ethics. Johnson says that his dialogue with military professionals in a variety of contexts was modeled, in part, on the experience of his Princeton professor, ethicist Paul Ramsey. Johnson reflects:

> My model here was Paul Ramsey, who before and during the period when he first engaged the idea of just war read closely in the work of the civilian nuclear strategists, attended conferences with them, and carried on dialogue with some of them. He became particularly close with one of them, Albert Wohlstetter, and put me in touch with Wohlstetter when I began to work on just war. About half of both his books from the 1960s are extended critical dialogues with some of these theorists. When he turned to the subject of medical ethics he spent a period of leave at Georgetown, where he was able to attend the daily meetings of the hospital doctors in which they discussed current cases, sometimes accompanied staff doctors on their rounds, and did some of the same at Johns Hopkins. His effort to get inside the thinking and practice of the professionals in both these fields contrasted sharply with how other Christian ethicists at the time operated, keeping a distance from the world of praxis and engaging the thinking there either not at all or only at arm's length. The dialogue I was able to have with both military and policy professionals over my career was my attempt to follow Ramsey's model, and in my case as well as his, it contrasted sharply with not only the failure of most others in my field who wrote on just war to do so but the outright avoidance of some to have contact with anything close to the military profession.... But my historical work on the just war idea convinced me that this was originally a result of influences from military, political, and legal praxis and reflection on it as well as from canonical and theological work, and I consciously sought to reflect this in my own approach to the subject.

This book ends with a set of resources useful to scholars and students who want to investigate Johnson for themselves. The chapters that follow this introduction were chosen in order to demonstrate the widest possible relevance of Johnson's just war thinking while emphasizing works that many scholars may never have seen. One thing that will strike the reader is how often Johnson's titles draw attention to a question, *the* question, or *the state of the question*:

- Can force be used justly?
- Just war tradition: the state of the question
- The question of rebellion and moral tradition in the use of force
- Roman Catholic just war thinking: the state of the question

Johnson continues to be courageous in taking on the big questions and judiciously providing answers. We trust that this volume will assist you beyond simply getting to know James Turner Johnson: it will help you answer, for yourself, crucial questions about the morality of warfare.

ACKNOWLEDGMENTS

This project would not have been possible without the gracious contributions and support of James Turner Johnson. We have been inspired by his scholarship and leadership in this field, and are honored to edit this volume.

With minor edits, all chapters are reproduced as originally published. The editors are appreciative of the assistance provided by several students and graduates who helped us proofread the book. We are grateful to Spencer Burress (Baylor University), Linda Waits-Kamau (Regent University), Abigail Lindner (Regent University), Eleanor Campbell (Taylor University), Addison Hollomon (John Cabot University), Meg Huber (Southern Virginia University), Bethany Mendeke (LeTourneau University).

PERSONAL REFLECTIONS ON MY LIFE AND WORK

JAMES TURNER JOHNSON

I was born in 1938 in my grandfather's house in Crockett Mills, Tennessee, a small farming community in West Tennessee. My mother had come there from Memphis, 95 miles away, to have me in the context of her family's support. My father came up on weekends from his own Memphis job, and for my birth.

My grandfather was the town postmaster. He had grown up in a not much larger town not far away, Friendship, and moved to Crockett Mills when he married my grandmother. I found out when I got older that my grandfather, Edward Swanson, was descended from another Edward Swanson, who had been a member of the military exploring party that had founded Nashville and established a fort there during the Revolutionary War. His family line, in turn, traced to yet another Edward Swanson (or Edvard Svanson), a sergeant in the armed force that protected the seventeenth-century Swedish settlements on the Delaware River.

My grandmother's maiden name was Dean, the name of a sub-clan of the Scottish Davidson clan, and her forebears had been among the Scots who immigrated to the Carolinas during the late colonial period and settled in the Carolina piedmont. After American Independence, as western migration began to take hold, both the Swansons and the Deans had moved west into Tennessee, eventually settling in Crockett County (named for Davy Crockett). Dean relatives made up a large portion of the population around Crockett Mills.

The Crockett Mills Christian Church stood next to the regional school on a hill dominating the lower area where the business section of the town lay. My grandparents' house was directly across the gravel road from the school and church, and when I became old enough I began school there and a year or so later joined the church. Churches of other denominations ringed the town, located at country crossroads, and where one lived in relation to these churches determined one's denomination: the local options, besides Crockett Mills' Christian Church, were Baptist, Methodist, and Cumberland Presbyterian—all denominations that traced to the Cane Ridge Revival ("the great revival in the southwest") named after a small creek running by present-day Lexington, Kentucky. The relation among these different churches was close but competitive, and as a boy I heard many discussions of the relative merits of their various theologies.

My father's background was generally similar. His mother's maiden name was Gregory, another Scots name carried by a family that had settled in the North Carolina piedmont and moved to West Tennessee about the same time as the Deans. Her father and mother owned a farm in the very northern part of Shelby County, where Memphis is located. Not far away, just over the county line in Tipton County, my paternal grandfather, whose name was Johnson, lived with his parents and two sisters on a somewhat larger, more prosperous farm owned by his parents. While the Gregorys attended the local Presbyterian Church, about three miles away down the dirt/gravel roads in the area, the Johnsons attended a larger Methodist church nearer Covington, the Tipton County seat. Just as the Dean family makes up a large section in the Crockett Mills cemetery, so the cemetery of the Gregorys' Presbyterian church includes a large number of Gregorys, and the cemetery of the Methodist church the Johnsons attended includes a large group of Johnsons. From my great-great grandfather's headstone I discovered that he had been born in Albemarle County, Virginia (Jefferson's county) before moving to West Tennessee as an adult. Other headstones in this cemetery belonged to people of about the same age who had been born in the same area of Virginia, suggesting that they had all migrated as a group to West Tennessee and settled near one another. My grandfather Johnson's farm differed from the Gregorys' in two important ways: it was enough larger to qualify as a plantation, and my father's grandfather owned slaves prior to the Civil War and Emancipation, while the Gregorys farmed with the help of their large family of children. This established a social difference which lasted after the war and through the marriage of my paternal grandparents, with my father favoring the Gregory relatives and his sister my aunt favoring the relatives on the Johnson side.

Not until I was an adult and became interested in American history did it occur to me that on both the paternal and maternal sides my ancestry traces to the American colonial period. I never heard anything about this while growing up. All my relatives and everyone my family knew could make the same claim; so it didn't matter much to them.

After my birth my mother and I moved to Memphis, the site of my father's job, and lived there until the beginnings of World War II, when my father, a welder, was classified as an essential worker, removing him from the military draft pool, and began a string of war-related assignments in various locations around the eastern part of the country. Most of these were relatively short-lived, and so Mother moved back to Crockett Mills with me. She joined my father for longer-term jobs from time to time, with me in the care of her unmarried sister, but most of the time she was there with me. I started school in Crockett Mills, and at the end of the war my father moved there too, setting up a business. We lived together in my grandfather's house with him and my mother's unmarried sister; my grandmother had died. When I was midway in seventh grade we all moved to Memphis: my grandfather had retired as postmaster; my uncle, who had been drafted and spent the war in the army post office in New York, had gotten a job in Memphis after the war, and now my father had gotten a job in Memphis as well. So from mid-seventh grade through high school graduation I was educated in the Memphis public school system. It served me well.

I don't remember thinking of myself as intellectually particularly special during the early grades, though my mother had read to me regularly in my early years and taught me to read before I started school, until the fall of my seventh grade, still in Crockett Mills, when I had a relatively young teacher who would single out homework done by me for particular comments and praise. She did the same for a girl in my class, but not as often for a few others, and never, so far as I know, for most of the class. In Memphis my intellectual awakening took place in eighth and ninth grades, where Fairview Junior High School had excellent teachers in American history, English, spelling, and math. I remember especially the history class, which I completed with the highest overall average by a couple of points. In tenth grade I moved to Central High School, Memphis's preeminent academic high school, where I started in French (winning a prize in a state contest in my third year) but spent more time and effort in math and the sciences. I graduated as one of a dozen or so who had achieved all-A records. We were acknowledged at graduation, but there were no designated valedictorian and salutatorian; the student speeches were from students selected for that purpose.

Memphis's Central High School was not only academically preeminent in the city but also in the state, and this translated into its being a target for recruitment by top colleges and universities. At the same time, the teachers in my classes made no secret of their expectation that those at the top of our class year would go on to these colleges. Among my friends in the all-A group two attended Columbia, one went to Yale, one to MIT, one to Cornell, two or three to Princeton, and I entered Brown in Fall 1956 with a full scholarship and a declared major as a bachelor of science (Sc.B.) candidate in physics. The Sc.B. track included distribution requirements in the humanities and social sciences along with the math and science requirements that were the core of the major. Thus along with physics and calculus I studied philosophy, history, sociology, and economics, while also continuing French. While I did well in physics, I had trouble with calculus freshman year, reflecting one lack in Central's education. Central's math offerings included no calculus, but the freshman science-oriented math track at Brown was a year-long course in calculus, and nearly all the other people in the class had been introduced to calculus in high school. I made it through somehow, and the next year's course, modern algebra and solid geometry, built on types of math with which I was familiar. But by beginning of junior year I found that the non-science distribution courses I had been taking had reshaped my sense of what I wanted to learn about and the career path I wanted to follow. So that semester I withdrew from the Sc.B. track. This required that I designate an A.B. major, and I chose a new joint major in mathematics and economics, which allowed me to transfer my math credits, add my economics ones, and complete the major with a designated mathematical economics course and upper-level economics courses, all of which allowed me to graduate with my class in June, 1960. I did well in this major. In my math-econ course, with my background in the more advanced science-math classes, I was at the top of the class. Mathematical economics was then a new discipline, and Brown was one of only a few colleges to offer a major in it. I have often reflected that if I had continued along that trajectory I would have become a "quant" and taken part in the extensive reshaping of economics and finance that quantitative analysis and predictive mathematical models introduced. I would have had a very different life.

But I had already decided on a different course for further study and the course of my career. My non-science distribution courses had opened up to me the study of normative issues in human behavior. There were two possible directions to take to pursue this: one through the field of philosophy, and one through that of religion. My year-long history of philosophy course had had little to say about ethics, and indeed, at that time ethics was at a low point in the concerns of the academic discipline of philosophy. Both because of this and because of my background I looked into the study of ethics in the frame of religious studies, where I encountered a vibrant, intellectually broadly reaching, and socially involved kind of study that was much more like what I hoped to do in my professional life.

At that time entry into a Ph.D. program in religion required either an M.A. or a B.D. (the kind of degree today generally called an M.Div.). The B.D. took a year longer but was cheaper, and financial subsidies were also available. From the divinity schools I applied to, I chose to enter the program of Vanderbilt Divinity School in the fall of 1960, also observing that after seven years in New England and New Jersey, this would give the South another chance at me and me another chance at the South. My family, of course, were all only four hours or so away in Memphis and West Tennessee.

The VDS faculty in the years I was there—1960–63—included some members well established at the top of their respective fields (I think here of Philip J. Hyatt in Old Testament and Kendrick Groebel in New Testament) along with an exceptional group of younger scholars just reaching the peak of their intellectual creativity: Gordon Kaufmann in theology, Langdon Gilkey in historical theology, Bard Thompson in church history, Walter Harrelson in Old Testament, Leon Keck in New Testament, and James Sellers in Ethics. Within two or three years after my receiving the B.D., Hyatt and Groebel had retired and all the rest had moved to more prestigious positions except for Harrelson, who chose to stay at Vanderbilt.

The education I received in all these fields not only taught me more than I had ever earlier known about Christian tradition and its development, including the various kinds of interaction between Christianity and other elements in culture over its two thousand years of history. This has stayed with me, shaping how I think about the place of religion in society and culture and also my conception of the importance of history for this. This education was so thorough and so detailed that I found myself often consulting my course notebooks in connection with my later teaching at Vassar and Rutgers.

In my last year at Vanderbilt I took a seminar on Augustine with Langdon Gilkey. This seminar left me with a lifelong fascination with Augustine's thinking, his life, and his historical impact. I also met another member of the seminar who was on leave from Newberry College to finish his Ph.D., and through him I came to teach two years at Newberry as a sabbatical replacement before going on to graduate school at Princeton for my doctorate.

In James Sellers' ethics course at Vanderbilt I encountered for the first time the work of Paul Ramsey, and it was Ramsey's presence as the lead ethics person in the Department of Religion at Princeton University that led me to apply there, to be accepted, and three years later, to complete my Ph.D. Ramsey by that time (1965–68) had already published his first book on just war (*War and the Christian Conscience*, 1961) and his second was in press (*The Just War*, 1968), and he was intellectually gearing up for his later work in medical ethics. I had two seminars with him, one each year before my comprehensive exams, and neither had anything to do with just war. The second seminar was on Christian understandings of sexuality (a running interest of his), and my seminar paper was an examination of English Puritan thinking and practice on sexuality and marriage during the late sixteenth and early seventeenth centuries, when the Puritan movement was just beginning and getting established. Later, at Ramsey's suggestion, I wrote my dissertation on this same topic. It was accepted "with distinction"; I received my doctorate, and the dissertation became my first book.

The Princeton program also required two seminars in a cognate field that differed for each Ph.D. candidate. I chose the Department of Politics, with the result that one of my seminars was with Michael Walzer, who the following year moved to Harvard. I got to know Walzer better later, when he had moved back to Princeton's Institute for Advanced Study and I was getting started on my academic career as a member of the Rutgers faculty.

When the book based on my dissertation was in press I began to think about what to do next—specifically, whether to do more on the topic of sexuality or to stay with the Puritans—and I was fortunate to receive a fellowship to spend a summer at the Huntington Library in San Marino, California, a major portion of whose holdings are printed copies of English books from the beginning of printing until the end of the seventeenth century. There, I was casting about in this literature looking for a new subject I could explore and write about, and I discovered the enormously rich body of writing dealing with England's departure from the Church of Rome, its war with Spain, and its relation to the wars of religion that raged for more than a decade on the European Continent. English writers—political, religious, and other—contributed much of the literature produced on this topic during this period, but English presses also translated and published works from Continental scholars and churchmen over religion and war. (Among such works were the first English versions of Hugh Grotius's *On the Laws of War and Peace.*) This subject became the focus of my work at the Huntington, and it led to my first book on just war tradition, *Ideology, Reason, and the Limitation of War* (1975). Since then I have continued as the main theme of my writing to focus on the just war idea, the tradition that defines it, and its contemporary implications.

I followed that same method in my second book on the historical development of the just war idea, *Just War Tradition and the Restraint of War* (1981), and my expansion of this approach into my study of pacifism and its relation to just war tradition, *The Quest for Peace* (1987). Between them, though, was a book of a somewhat different kind, *Can Modern War Be Just* (1984), one rooted in the historical tradition but which sought to draw out the implications of this understanding of just war for the policy and practice of contemporary warfare. Since then most of my writing, including several books but also numerous articles, chapters, and talks, has followed this pattern.

As I began to enter the realm of applied ethics I became associated with Georgetown University professor and Chair of the Department of Government, William V. O'Brien. Bill wrote on international policy and international law, and as a retired Army colonel (he had served in WWII) he also had a close relation with military officers doing advanced studies in and around Washington. He was also a committed Catholic, and he was early drawn into the debates that heated up over the drafting of the U.S. Catholic bishops' 1983 pastoral letter, *The Challenge of Peace.* He brought me into those debates as well, and for a year he and I worked together speaking at a broad variety of Catholic colleges and universities on this topic. Through Bill I also met George Weigel, with whom I co-authored *Just War and the Gulf War* (1991) and who later (2004) involved me in discussions of Catholic thought and policy on international affairs at a seminar in the Vatican and a conference held at the Gregorian University in Rome.

More broadly, my work was drawing me into connections to the military service academies and war colleges, and in the year after the terror bombing of the U.S. Marine barracks in Lebanon I was asked to join the team of "subject matter experts" who conducted the Naval Chaplains Professional Development and Training Course at sites around the world. These connections helped to shape my thinking and writing about ethics and war for the rest of my career. In a sense this period of my work was bookended by my serving as founding co-editor (with Norwegian military chaplain Baard Maeland) of the *Journal of Military Ethics* for nine years beginning in 2002, up to my last book, co-edited with Eric Patterson, *The Ashgate Research Companion to Military Ethics* in 2015, the year of my retirement from the Rutgers University faculty. During this same period my work broadened to include comparative study of the Islamic tradition of *jihad* of the sword and its relation to statecraft, a study whose beginning was marked by my getting to know the work of John Kelsay on Islam and war when he was a member of the NEH Summer Seminar for College Teachers I directed in 1987. John and I later collaborated on a number of projects, producing two books. Later I expanded this comparative interest to include the work on Chinese ethical traditions on war spearheaded by Hong Kong scholar Ping-Cheung (PC) Lo and John's Florida State University colleague Sumner B. (Barney) Twiss.

There is much more I could say about the development of my life and work and especially the people I met in the course of it and the insights I drew from them, but there is no more space for this here. For interested readers, these are all chronicled in my CV.

Looking back and reflecting on the history described above, I have often remarked to myself how much its contours have been the result not of planning on my part but of fortunate placement at various inflection points and my actions in response to opportunities presented to me. I could have become a mathematical economist but decided to go in another direction. I could have pursued the theme of sexuality and its ethics over history in various contexts, but for the Huntington Library grant that opened up the study of just war tradition and the ethics of war to me. I recognize now, on reflection, that my happy experiences in studying history from the eighth and ninth grades through college and divinity school have deeply shaped my approach to scholarship: the historical focus and method I used in that seminar paper under Ramsey and in my dissertation have remained at the core of my seeking to understand the nature and development of the just war idea. As mentioned earlier, my interest in Augustine dates to the Gilkey seminar at Vanderbilt, though I have since moved in various directions away from that taught by Gilkey in that context, and I believe I have learned much more about Augustine and the Augustinian tradition in the course of my writing on it in connection with the just war idea than could ever have been imagined by me or anyone else in that seminar—including the teacher—when I took it.

The message I take from this is the importance of being open to experiences, issues, and approaches as they arise and doing one's best to respond to them as creatively as possible, while also keeping an eye on the main direction in which one wants to go. What I have hoped for in my writing, and what I hope for in the present book, is that it will present readers with new ideas, issues, and possible ways toward fuller appreciation and understanding that merge with the readers' own concerns and personal directions in ways that complement each other.

James Turner Johnson

ABSTRACT

This early article (1982) by Johnson argues that just war tradition and moral theorists can adequately provide guidance for contemporary discussions of *jus ad bellum, jus in bello,* and the development of moral warfare technologies.

CHAPTER I

WHAT GUIDANCE CAN JUST WAR TRADITION PROVIDE FOR CONTEMPORARY MORAL THOUGHT ABOUT WAR?

In the original topic put to me, I was asked to comment on the adequacy of "the just war doctrine." This is a misleading way of stating the issue. What we encounter when we look for just war ideas in western moral thought is a plurality of doctrines within a single recognizable tradition. If we concentrate on the former, then we must ask, "Whose doctrine?" and be confronted with a bewildering multiplicity. We may reasonably differ about which particular contributors to the tradition we may choose to emphasize, but we may not, I think, reasonably put in dispute the adequacy of the overall moral tradition to which the name "just war tradition" has become attached.

Another familiar misconception is to think of just war ideas being the more or less exclusive property of Christian—and more specifically, Catholic—moral thought. In fact, though, the twin themes of just war tradition—justification of some uses of force in the protection of values, along with restraints on the application of such force—have been nourished as much from non-Christian as from Christian sources. It is certainly correct to think of Christian moral tradition on war, but this is only one aspect of the broader western cultural tradition on the restraint of war. In my own usage, "just war tradition" generally refers to this broader phenomenon rather than to the component part represented by Christian moral thought.

Let me pursue this matter a bit further. If just war tradition is not narrowly Christian, it is even less rightly thought of as an exclusive product of moral theology—or, indeed, of moral philosophy. While I often use terms like "moral thought" and "ideas" as a kind of shorthand, in reality just war tradition has developed as much or more out of practice as from theory. In the Middle Ages the Christian component included both a theoretical element from scholastic theology and a practical element from canon law; the scholarly consensus today is that the latter was, in its own time, the more significant. The secular component was, in this period, even more weighted toward the side of practice: chivalric customs, established patterns of relation among princes, the civil law. In the sixteenth and seventeenth centuries theorists like Victoria (also, Vitoria) and Grotius made an undeniable contribution to conceptualizing the tradition within which they both worked; yet the changing face of war at the dawn of the modern period also shaped their thinking, as well as the further development of the moral tradition. In the eighteenth century significant contributions to the developing tradition came both from theorists—principally men like Emmerich de Vattel and John Locke—and from the practice of limited war in the so-called "sovereigns' wars" of this period. In the nineteenth and early twentieth centuries international law carried and further developed the tradition and blended theory and the practice of states. It is really in this century, and more particularly in the debates that have emerged in this country since the end of World War II, that theoretical moral analysis has been recaptured as a mode of contributing to our cultural tradition on war and its limitation.

This said, I must still hold that critical and constructive moral thought provides an indispensable balance to the practical side of just war tradition. Only the theorist can take the long view; only the theorist can analyze, summarize, cut through dead wood, identify wrong turns, and draw out the implications of positive elements in the developing tradition. The need for moral theoretical input into the process of development was substantially forgotten through much of the nineteenth century, and I believe this is one reason why in World Wars I and II western culture came to accept the rightness of unlimited means of war—the shelling of cities and gas warfare in World War I and in World War II the obliteration of population centers by conventional explosives, napalm, and finally atomic weapons. That our culture has come to accept such an intentionality as this concept of "total war" is directly counter to the meaning of the entire tradition that treats warfare as sometimes justifiable yet always to be practiced with restraint. A significant part of the role of the contemporary moral theorist dealing with war is to remind the larger culture that, in terms of its own highest values as expressed over history, the turn toward total war has been a wrong turn; war does not have to be total; it is possible to think again of justified force that must be applied with restraint.

A question as to the adequacy of any system of moral guidance, whether on war, sexuality, economics, or whatever, is really three separate but related questions:

1. Is it "right"? That is, does this system correspond to the moral values of the culture or community within which it has come into existence?

2. Does the system in question provide an adequate conceptual framework for moral analysis and judgment?

3. Does this system represent a bridging of the gap between the ideal and the possible? That is, does it produce practical moral guidance as well as identifying the relevant moral values for the situation at hand?

In terms of the just war tradition rightly understood, that is, as representing a cultural consensus on whether war is justified and what limits should be imposed on the use of force in the service of statecraft, the *prima facie* answer to all the above questions must be positive. As to correspondence, yes, just war tradition does correspond to the moral values of our culture. Indeed, we must say more: it is through examination of just war tradition that we find out what those values are. As to whether the tradition provides an adequate conceptual framework, I will simply say at this point that people in our culture cannot really escape thinking about morality and war in terms of the ideas and standards developed and preserved in just war tradition. This is by no means to say that conclusions from such thought must always be the same, whether from one historical period to another or from one individual to another. But it is to affirm that we begin with a generally common set of moral perceptions and share a common language of moral discourse. As to the question of practical moral guidance, of bridging the gap between the ideal and the possible, in this brief discussion I doubt that I can do better than point to the interpenetration of the theoretical with the practical over the history of development of the just war tradition. The world of this tradition is the world of practical realities in the relations among states; yet the moral values it embodies also represent a window to the ideal. Together they produce a tradition that is capable of judging a particular decision to employ force either justified or unjustified, a particular use of force either right or wrong. This is what I understand to be practical moral guidance.

Let us now turn to this question of adequacy in a more concrete way. Just war tradition has coalesced around certain major ideas, some having to do with whether the resort to force is justified or not (in classic terminology, the *jus ad bellum*), and some having to do with limitations on the use of force even after the *jus ad bellum* decision has been made. (These latter ideas form the tradition's *jus in bello*, or "law of war.") I wish to examine briefly three of the former sort of ideas and two of the latter, asking what content the tradition has given them and what is the relevance of these notions to contemporary issues.

1. The requirement that every use of force be in a just cause is possibly the most inclusive idea within just war tradition. Historically at least four separate and somewhat different contents have been assigned to it. In Augustine's discussion of defense of the neighbor an interventionist

conception of just cause is at work: it is the Christian's duty (and, by extension, the duty of any just state) to intervene on behalf of innocent neighbors who are the object of aggression. Thomas Aquinas expanded this concept by reflection on a Pauline passage referring to the duties of those who rule: "(The prince) is minister of God, to come in wrath to punish evildoers." On this conception the principal justifying cause for use of force is punishment. Third, there is the notion that defense always constitutes a just cause; this idea is as old as the ages and is, at least in theory, the only legitimate case for resort to war allowed in contemporary international law. Finally, there is the concept that all "holy" wars are just, which has its secular counterpart in the various concepts of ideological war, "national war," "people's war," war for "supreme emergency," and so on. This is really a limiting case of the just cause concept, and it differs from the other three causes mentioned in legitimating unrestrained use of force. Ironically, a persistent major theme in American attitudes in this century has been that this is the only justifying cause worth taking seriously, and it has led us into policies mandating all-out war against any nation that might challenge us. But the self-righteousness this implies is hard to justify, and the weight of the just war tradition points the other way, toward justifying limited uses of force for limited causes.

The international law component of the tradition has increasingly reduced the possible just causes to one, defense against aggression, and subsumed the others under this head. But from the point of view of moral analysis, this is perhaps too much of a reduction. In particular, I wonder whether it is not necessary to keep in mind what Augustine saw clearly: that it is a moral duty for those who have power to protect those who are relatively impotent but who are being threatened by another more powerful than they. This means, I think, that we have a duty to construct our alliances so as to manifest our readiness to become involved in the defense of other peoples; it also implies that some cases may arise in which we have a duty to intervene in the absence of specific treaties of alliance.

2. The requirement that every use of force be undertaken by right authority has traditionally served to legitimize the use of force by princes and, later, by states. Perhaps more than any other just war concept this one may seem irrelevant to an age when much cynicism exists about state power and in which, by contrast, popular revolutionary movements have in some quarters taken on the presumption of legitimacy that formerly attached to the state. It is well to recall that the history function of the requirement that force be used by a "right" authority was chiefly to limit exactly the kind of unrestrained general violence and indiscriminate destruction that characterizes civil war. That is, this notion of right authority came into being as a way of defining the police function of a coherent community of people bound together under a commonly recognized authority, in opposition to the depredations of lawless persons or bands who challenged not just the ruling authorities but the peace of the community itself. This is the way the late medieval canonists (for whom the criterion of right authority was clearly the preeminent just war category) used this idea, and for them it was unambiguously a means of restricting resort to force and the destruction that use of force inevitably brings upon the lives and livelihoods of peaceful people. At the very least this traditional notion requires us today to apply the same standards to all uses of force, whatever their ostensible justifying cause: to inquire whether there is an authority who can control the use of force so as to restrict its effects to morally legitimate purposes, and to inquire as to the breadth and depth of popular support this authority possesses.

3. The traditional requirement that use of force be the last resort, after everything else has been tried, seems to me to bear particularly pointedly on contemporary affairs. We do not have a world government and are unlikely to have one in the foreseeable future, but we do have an international system manifesting a great deal of stability and—at least so far—durability. In such a stable international environment the emphasis must be on relationships that do not involve the resort to forceful means. Fortunately, the tools of such relations—diplomacy, economics,

intellectual and cultural exchange—flourish in such an atmosphere, while the presumption is strongly against the initiation of a major war, which would by definition mark the end of this era of stability. The same consideration does not apply to uses of forceful means at lower levels and in the service of diplomatic or other fundamentally non-forceful undertakings. But the key concern is that the game must be worth the candle, and even in such cases force must be the last step, not taken till other steps have been tried. On the other hand, the criterion of last resort reminds us that the use of force may be a legitimate resort, when there are no other ways to protect values that require to be preserved. Just war tradition points toward neither militarism nor pacifism, but to a state of affairs in between.

4. The requirement of proportionality has two forms, depending on which is the issue: the decision to use force or the decision to employ such force as is available. In *jus ad bellum* terms, the aim is to ensure that the overall damage to human values that ensures from resort to force will be at least balanced by the degree to which human values are preserved or protected. This "counting the costs" requires thinking into the future, and while such projection is notoriously risky, it must be done.

In reflection on the proportionality of contemporary warfare in this *jus ad bellum* sense, it is important to distinguish between the destructive capability of modern weapons and the intentionality that determines whether the most destructive means will be used and, if so, in what contexts. These are distinguishable questions, and it's necessary for moral analysis to make the distinction. World War II offers ample examples of an intentionality aimed at producing indiscriminate mass destruction; the death camps and counter-city bombing predated, after all, the atomic bomb. Without the precedents of Dresden, Hamburg, and Tokyo the obliteration of Hiroshima and Nagasaki would have not been thinkable. Thus when we think of contemporary occasions when the use of force might be justified, consideration of proportionality requires that we think not only of the foreseeable results of unlimited use of whatever weapons are available—including chemical and biological weaponry as well as the nuclear arsenal; it requires us to think about how limits may be imposed to allow the use of forceful means to protect values that are otherwise not able to be preserved.

This consideration leads naturally into the *jus in bello* meaning of the traditional concept of proportionality. At the very least, I would suggest, those persons are right who have advocated counterforce targeting of strategic nuclear weapons. The presumption against chemical and biological weapons is also rightly aimed; such weapons are inherently indiscriminate and, perhaps even more than nuclear weapons, produce long-term effects that endanger human lives and values long after a war in which they might be used. This is the essence of disproportionality. In general, considerations of proportionality point us toward utilization of conventional weapons, and beyond that they point to the need to develop means of war that may be used more proportionately than those now available. A moral obligation to use restraint in the protection of values implies the need to develop means of war that can in fact be employed restrainedly, in the service of human intentions. Thus the just war concept of proportionality requires two things: first, that we forget the intentionality that has conceived war as necessarily total and has nourished the development of means of war that serve that conception, and second, that we foster development of weapons that lend themselves to use in the service of a non-totalistic human intentionality.

5. I have kept till last the wisdom preserved in the just war conception that noncombatants should be protected from the ravages of war. Since the Middle Ages this has been one of the strongest and most recurrent themes in the developing tradition, though it has not always been understood the same way. Paul Ramsey's argument that noncombatants must be immune from direct, intentional attack is not identical, for example, with the eighteenth-century notion that damage to noncombatants was to be kept limited by limiting the theater of war. This latter concept has surfaced again in some contemporary limited-war thought, while humanitarian international law, like Ramsey, concludes that certain classes of persons must be protected no matter

where they are located. What is important, I believe, is that we not forget that noncombatants are morally different from combatants, and that warfare in which combatants are perceived and treated as if there is no difference is inherently against the major moral tradition on war our culture has produced. Yet powerful forces in the modern world have tended to suppress the memory of this moral obligation to protect noncombatants, and nowhere is the result of this more evident than in a strategic nuclear policy that threatens population centers rather than the military forces that (I should think presumably) would be the real enemy in wartime. The evil is not limited to nuclear strategy, however; when terrorists choose noncombatants as their preferred targets—and the more disconnected such victims are from the structures of power that are the ultimate target, the more successful the terrorism—then we have at least as glaring a case of the immorality of a conception of war that does not recognize that noncombatants and combatants are different and are owed different treatment.

Finally, in this connection, I would observe that, as in the case of the concept of proportionality, the moral requirement to protect noncombatants implies the development of weapons usable in ways that satisfy legitimate military functions without corollary damage to noncombatant lives, livelihoods, and property. This has important implications for the debate now in progress over the neutron bomb, the cruise missile, MX, and other components of United States military policy.

To sum up, I have been arguing that just war tradition provides us with three fundamental moral reminders: first, that sometimes the use of force may be necessary to protect or preserve values that would otherwise be damaged or lost; second, that both the resort to force and the use of force must be subject to a searching intentionality of restraint; and third, that means of war should be developed so as to serve its morally legitimate goals.

BIBLIOGRAPHY

Best, Geoffrey. *Humanity in Warfare*. New York: Columbia University Press, 1980.

Ford, Harold P. and Francis X. Winters, ed. *Ethics and Nuclear Strategy.* Maryknoll, NY: Orbis Books, 1977.

Johnson, James Turner. *Ideology, Reason and the Limitation of War*. Princeton: Princeton University Press, 1975.

Johnson, James Turner. *Just War Tradition and the Restraint of War*. Princeton: Princeton University Press, 1981.

O'Brien, William V. *The Conduct of Just and Limited War*. New York: Praeger Publishers, 1981.

Ramsey, Paul. *The Just War: Force and Political Responsibility*. New York: Charles Scribner's Sons, 1968.

Ramsey, Paul. *War and the Christian Conscience*. Durham, NC: Duke University Press, 1961.

Walzer, Michael. *Just and Unjust Wars*. New York: Basic Books, 1977.

ABSTRACT

Taken from the opening chapter of a co-edited book published in the aftermath of the Gulf War (1991), Johnson addresses the war in light of the just war tradition. He argues that with respect to *jus ad bellum*, military intervention was justified. So too, with respect to *jus in bello,* was the war justified—especially in light of the use of then-new "smart weapons."

CHAPTER 2

THE JUST WAR TRADITION AND THE AMERICAN MILITARY

Much moral debate in American society takes place in arguments over politics, economics, social policy, the application of technology, and other such subjects. This is as it should be, since moral concerns, properly understood, relate to all arenas of human activity. Of particular relevance to this book is the fact that, despite the efforts of political realists to dissociate the practice of statecraft from ethics, American political debate over the use of military force is full of arguments and appeals rooted in moral concerns. Indeed, far from being irrelevant to the political process, such concerns have historically played a major role in American political life. Americans want their nation's actions to be moral; it is part of the legacy of that tradition by which this country is "a city set on a hill," a model for other nations to follow.

Exactly how the moral element should express itself in political policies, decisions, and actions is the stuff of abundant discussion and the motivation for much activity in the public sphere. For the moral element is not a seamless web; it is expressed through a variety of types of claims drawn from diverse sources and supported by a multitude of reference points. It is no less powerful for that; rather, this variety simply testifies to the freedom and independence Americans enjoy within their social and political structures. To acknowledge such diversity is to say that we cannot make distinctions among the merits of various moral claims and arguments. Indeed, making such distinctions, and thereby adding to the moral clarity of the issues at stake, is itself part of the contribution that ethical analysis has to make to the exercise of statecraft.

This essay examines one particular element in the moral debate over American use of military force against Iraq in the Gulf War: the justifiability of that action in terms of the just war tradition of Western culture. This tradition has deep roots in both the ancient Hebraic and the classical Greek and Roman foundations of the West. It has developed over history in both religious and non-religious strands and takes contemporary form in religious doctrine, in international law on war, in codes of military conduct, and in underlying values regarding human rights and the rights of nations.

THE LANGUAGE OF MORALITY

Just war claims were much in evidence in the debate over American involvement in the 1990–91 Gulf War. "This is a just war," President Bush told the convention of the National Religious Broadcasters. "I fear that...the undertaking of offensive military action [by the United States against Iraq] could well violate [just war] criteria," declared Archbishop Daniel Pilarczyk, president of the National Conference of Catholic Bishops. His colleague, Archbishop John Roach, spelled out before the Senate Foreign Relations Committee the criteria for a just war as understood in Catholic teaching. The *Christian Century* published a debate on "Just War Tradition and the War in the Gulf," and the American Society of Christian Ethics adopted a resolution on the war that explicitly invoked Christian just war reasoning. The religion editor of the *New York Times* wrote several columns on this subject, which was also a focus for treatment in other newspapers, television and radio commentary, and the national news magazines.

These were some of the direct references to the idea of just war. But clearly articulated concepts of what makes the use of military force justified or unjustified were also evident in the debates that took place within the United Nations Security Council and the U.S. Congress. Both the explicit and the implicit reliance on the language of justice and morality reveal the vigor of a moral tradition whose roots go deep into Western cultural history, but whose modern development has extended to the moral traditions of other cultures as well. Every culture has a moral tradition that addresses the justification and limitation of war. Though the specific terms and structures of what has come to be called just war tradition are those that have taken shape in the West, their ideas represent a far broader concept of the moral uses and limits of military force.

For our present purposes, we will remain within the framework of just war ideas as they have taken shape in Western cultural history, for this is the context within which the American debate has developed. This tradition provides us with categories for moral reflection about war, peace, and statecraft. It also gives us tools to evaluate the contents of those categories: notions of right and wrong, justice and injustice in international affairs; of the justified use of force within the purposes of statecraft, including peace as an ultimate goal; and of limits on justified use of force.

There is a classic, systematic form of just war theory, and I will return to it below when I outline my own moral judgments on the use of military force against Iraq. But since just war ideas are also employed in looser, less systematic ways in American moral and political discourse, I will turn to these first.

Just War and Pacifism

Just war claims in the American tradition are often set over against arguments drawn from some form of pacifism; frequently the two issues are mixed, with just war reasoning used to support a pacifist rejection of the use of force as an instrument of national policy. Some theorists impute to just war theory a presumption against violence, a view that would align it with certain kinds of contemporary pacifism. Yet historically just war tradition rests on a different presumption, a fundamental rejection of injustice. The use of violent force may be right or wrong depending on whether it serves justice or injustice: hence the idea of "just" or "justified" war. Nor do all forms of pacifism stem from a rejection of violence; the sectarian pacifism of the earliest Christians, medieval monasticism, and the radical pacifist groups of the Reformation era arose out of an animus against secular society as a whole, not just its violent aspects. Just war theory and pacifism are thus distinct moral traditions, and pacifist arguments must be assessed on their own terms, not confused with just war reasoning.

"The use of power, and possibly the use of force, is of the *esse* of politics," wrote Paul Ramsey, whose works on Christian just war theory in the 1960s were a major contribution to contemporary moral reflection on military issues in American politics. Ramsey noted:

> At the same time the use of power, and possibly the use of force, is inseparable from the *bene esse* of politics...inseparable from politics' *proper* act of being politics, inseparable from the well-being of politics, inseparable from the human pursuit of the national or the international common good by political means. You never have good politics without the use of power, possibly armed force.

In a later essay, Ramsey turned the matter around, stressing the inseparability of ethics from politics:

> Ethics are not logically, externally related to politics. These two distinguishable elements are together in the first place, internally related. Our quest should be for the clarification of political ethics in its *specific* nature, for the ethical ingredient inherent in foreign policy formulation, for the wisdom peculiar to taking counsel amid a world of encountering powers, for—as a subset—the laws of war and of deterrence so long as these are human activities properly related and subordinated to the purposes of political communities in the international system.

It is just this connection between the possibility of good politics and the possibility of the use of force that just war tradition presumes in theory and seeks to establish in fact; pacifism rejects out of hand the possibility of such a connection. The inherent nature of this connection is apparent in the various strains within the just war tradition—religious elements, including both theology and canonical rules of conduct; secular elements, including theoretical, customary, and positive international law, political philosophy, military codes of conduct, and the historical practice of limitation in war; and other lines of development of lesser scope and importance.

A Varied and Complex Tradition

The historical development of these various carriers of just war tradition resembles the changing waterways of a river delta: now the major streams flow apart, now they mingle their waters, now they part again and recombine with other streams. In this way each of the distinguishable elements within the larger tradition is related to all the others and to the whole, while manifesting its own particular perspective on justice in the use of military force. The just war tradition, understood as encompassing all these streams of development, constitutes the major Western cultural effort to define and explore the ethical justifications and limitations of the use of military force as a proper tool of political activity. As James Childress argues, it establishes the categories of moral reason when considering the use of force and lays down *prima facie* duties to be observed in that use. It is thus not surprising that Americans debating the morality of American involvement in the Gulf War should have had recourse to this tradition in seeking to understand their country's obligations and rights and in seeking to justify their conclusions about the proper course of action for the United States to follow.

In American public life, then, there is both a history of the application of moral concerns to political questions and a deep moral tradition addressing the notion of just use of force in the service of statecraft. More specifically, during the Gulf War the terms and conditions of just war thinking were set by developments that took place within three major carriers of just war tradition in recent history. Each of these needs to be sketched out in turn: developments in Christian just war doctrine in debate over nuclear arms and deterrence and over U.S. involvement in the Vietnam War; developments in international law regarding efforts to outlaw aggression, to prevent crimes against humanity, and to strengthen the law of war; and developments in American military doctrine and capabilities as they may be applied to limiting and making more discriminate the destructiveness of war.

CHRISTIAN JUST WAR THINKING

Paul Ramsey's 1961 *War and the Christian Conscience* provides a major benchmark for understanding the recent development of Christian just war thought. In this work, which sought to counter what Ramsey perceived as growing Christian contextualism as well as a widespread argument that Christianity is inherently pacifist, Ramsey argued that Christian just war theory is based on the moral duty of love of neighbor. The obligation to protect the neighbor who is being unjustly attacked provides justification for Christians to resort to force; at the same time, love also imposes limits on such force, requiring that no more be done to the unjust assailant than is necessary to prevent the evil he would do, and that no justified use of force ever can itself directly and intentionally target the innocent. Christian just war theory, argued Ramsey, is thus "twin-born," with limitation accompanying justification of resort to force. At the same time, the specifically Christian character of the just war idea as developed by Ramsey led to a focus on issues that classic just war tradition has called *jus in bello*, those having to do with right conduct in the *use* of force, and a general neglect of the other aspect of the classical tradition, the *jus ad bellum*, regarding the justification of *resort* to force.

The Challenge of Nuclear Weapons

Focusing especially on the *jus in bello* principle of discrimination—the requirement that noncombatants not be directly and intentionally attacked—Ramsey in the latter part of *War and the Christian Conscience* developed a powerful argument against nuclear deterrence by counter-population (later called "counter-value") targeting. At the same time, he did not oppose nuclear weapons in principle, stating that counter-force uses of such weapons, observing the principle of discrimination, were not morally objectionable. In essays later written and collected in *The Just War* he extended this argument, taking into account developments in both nuclear weapons and strategic thought and, as the American involvement in the Vietnam War deepened, moral issues in the conduct of that war.

These two works by Ramsey were genuinely seminal. At the time these books were being written, the heirs of Reinhold Niebuhr's Christian realism were fighting over its implications for the nuclear age, and except for these there were no other Christian ethical theorists besides Ramsey addressing in specifically Christian terms the justification and limitation of the use of military force in the service of statecraft. Ramsey's emphasis on an absolutely binding ethical requirement of love as the basis for Christian thinking about war effectively countered his contextualist adversaries, making it necessary for them to consider moral issues related to the use of force in other than merely prudential terms. Simultaneously, his insistence that in certain circumstances Christian love imposes a positive requirement of resort to force also provided a strong rebuttal to the Christian pacifist position that love mandates that one never participate in violence. Thus Ramsey gave Christian just war thinking a new and forceful dimension that has decisively shaped, for good and for ill, subsequent debate by both just war theorists and pacifists.

An Overemphasis on Discrimination

An unfortunate side of Ramsey's reconstruction of just war thought was his avoidance of *jus ad bellum* issues. This was not accidental; he regarded them as matters of practical political judgment and thus outside the sphere of competence of Christian moral theorists like himself. The problem with this line of thinking is that, when coupled with Ramsey's stress on the absoluteness of the principle of discrimination, it had the effect of introducing a new *jus ad bellum* based on the test of discrimination alone, rather than basing justification for force on the need to serve an innocent neighbor under unjust attack. Ramsey never addressed the dilemma posed by the possibility that his "twin-born" bases of Christian just war theory might conflict: how does the Christian respond to the love-based obligation to protect the neighbor when the only way of doing so would require action that violates the requirement of discrimination?

Nuclear pacifists such as the British theorist Walter Stein and, more recently, John Finnis and others resolved this dilemma in favor of the principle of discrimination. Arguing that nuclear warfare could never satisfy this absolute moral requirement, they reasoned backwards that war in the nuclear age is not justified: the absence of compliance with the *jus in bello* thus became a denial that there could ever be a *jus ad bellum*, a justification for resort to force in the service of the ends of statecraft. Others, especially during the Vietnam era, extended this reasoning still further to the position of "modern-war" pacifism, arguing that the nature of warfare in the contemporary age is to be inherently indiscriminate and disproportionately destructive in its effects. This argument is sometimes extended still further to moral opposition to "militarism," a somewhat elastic term for what is perceived as too great a presence of the military in American and other societies.

Contributions of the Bishops

In 1983 the American Catholic bishops added another benchmark document to the development of recent Christian just war thought: their pastoral letter, *The Challenge of Peace*. The principal drafter of this document, Fr. J. Bryan Hehir, characterized his efforts as an attempt to stand between the positions of Ramsey and Stein; the result was the rejection of any use of nuclear weapons (nuclear pacifism), strong reservations about any non-nuclear resort to force in the service of national policy (modern-war pacifism), but acceptance of nuclear weapons for the purpose of deterrence until some better way could be found to deter war. Despite the inherent tensions—according to some critics, contradictions—in this position, it has had great influence as a statement of contemporary Christian just war thought.

Where *The Challenge of Peace* most clearly went beyond Ramsey's version of Christian just war thinking was in its effort to relate its argument to the historical Christian just war tradition and in its explicit statement of just war criteria in a form that drew on the classical *jus ad bellum* and not only the *jus in bello*. While the resulting list of criteria does not precisely match the listing that can be derived from earlier sources, it would have represented an important advance in the contemporary Christian use of just war tradition were it not for its underlying pacifist assumption. In addition to rejecting any war involving nuclear weapons and holding strong reservations against even non-nuclear war today, *The Challenge of Peace* erroneously established Christian just war teaching on a presumption against violence. The general effect is to make it so difficult to conceive of a possible use of force justified in Christian terms that the bishops verge on a pacifist rejection of all contemporary war, whatever the reason.

A great deal of the Christian argumentation against American use of military force against Iraq in the Gulf crisis is at least consistent with modern-war pacifism. What the Catholic bishops' version of Christian just war thought does is to skew the moral tradition in favor of making *jus in bello* considerations—or, more accurately, the expectation that *jus in bello* considerations will be violated—do the work for which classic just war tradition developed the *jus ad bellum*. This is a grave error, as I will attempt to show.

DEVELOPMENTS IN INTERNATIONAL LAW

In the medieval period, the developing just war tradition functioned as the "international law" of European societies. Modern international law emerged out of the broader tradition in the sixteenth and seventeenth centuries, paralleling the growth of the modern state system. Throughout the modern period international law has served as one of the major carriers of just war tradition and has developed elements of that tradition in distinctive and significant ways.

Beginning with the Geneva Convention of 1864, gaining momentum with the Brussels Declaration of 1874, and continuing through the two Hague Conferences of 1899 and 1907 and a succession of Geneva Conventions through the Protocols of 1977, positive international law has laid down concrete guidelines and regulations specifying the requirements of the *jus in bello* and imposing sanctions for failure to observe them. "Geneva law" in general defines the requirements of noncombatant immunity or the principle of discrimination in terms of specific forms of treatment to be given to particular classes of persons during a war. "Hague law" in turn treats the means and methods of warfare, addressing in general the requirements of the principle of proportionality.

To the specific rules and categories established here, the Nuremberg Trials at the end of World War II added a more extensive category, that of "crimes against humanity," with both *jus in bello* and *jus ad bellum* implications. Commenting on the state of international law on war twenty-five years after Nuremberg, Tom J. Farer summarized the contents of that law as expressing three fundamental principles: discrimination or noncombatant immunity, proportionality, and "no Carthaginian peace." The first two of these principles, of course, coincide with the broader tradition and parallel Ramsey's *jus in bello* discussed above. In the broader tradition the concept of "no Carthaginian peace"—that is, no destruction during war that would leave the battle area sterile and uninhabitable after the war is over—is generally collapsed into the protection due noncombatants, for after a war is done all are noncombatants. Nonetheless, Farer's way of encapsulating the requirements laid down in the international law version of *jus in bello* has the advantage of emphasizing that what is justifiable in a war must be assessed in terms of its long-term consequences, not just its immediate effects.

Jus in bello v. Jus ad bellum

The implications of the international law *jus in bello* figured importantly in the Gulf crisis in three major ways: (1) judging the actions of the Iraqi occupying forces in Kuwait, (2) determining the parameters within which the coalition forces should operate in employing force against Iraq, and (3) assessing the actions of both sides during the coalition offensive of January 1991, including the intentional destruction undertaken by the retreating Iraqi forces.

In the matter of the *jus ad bellum*, international law generally is somewhat narrower than the just war tradition as a whole. Nonetheless, this relatively narrow focus has the advantage of bringing greater clarity and specificity to the matters involved. The early theorists of international law, beginning with Grotius in the seventeenth century, wrote in the aftermath of a century of terribly destructive and indiscriminate wars of religion, and they sought to block the recurrence of such warfare (what we would call "ideological war") by deemphasizing those portions of the inherited *jus ad bellum* of just war tradition that were capable of being used for ideological purposes.

Their tactic had three components: reducing the allowable means of going to war to those of concrete national interest; emphasizing a formal declaration of war and a public account of the reasons to allow the international community to assess the decision; and stressing the requirement (inherited from the broader just war tradition) that only national sovereigns possess the authority to make war. The revised international law theory of *jus ad bellum* succeeded in dampening resort to ideological warfare, but it opened the way for the development of the idea that any state enjoyed *compétence de guerre* and could decide at any time whether to go to war for its own national interests, as it alone defined them. The result was the period of limited but frequent "sovereigns' wars" in the eighteenth century. Ideological warfare, with its tendency toward totalistic means, again raised its head in the period of the French Revolution and the Napoleonic Wars, and the "sovereigns' war" idea resurfaced at the end of the nineteenth century, culminating in the Great War—World War I.

Efforts of International Organizations

Following the First World War the League of Nations sought to introduce new restrictions into the international law *jus ad bellum* by establishing international arbitration as an intermediary step to be taken before a conflict escalated into armed hostilities. In 1928 a further step was taken in the Pact of Paris, which sought to eliminate recourse to war as a means of settling international disputes. What was condemned was in fact first resort to armed force; defensive second resort was, the Pact's chief proponents made clear, in no way restricted.

These inter-war efforts did not prevent World War II, which combined the worst features of the patterns of ideological warfare and "sovereigns' war." The subsequent war-crimes trials at Nuremberg and Tokyo and the establishment of a new international order in the form of the United Nations sought to restrict still further the existing *jus ad bellum* in international law. This was to be accomplished by strengthening the measures taken in the Covenant of the League of Nations (which set up structures for international arbitration and legal judgment to settle disputes without war) and in enacting the Pact of Paris (which restricted first, i.e., aggressive, resort to military force while permitting second, i.e., defensive, use of such force). The Nuremberg Trials reinforced this effort by extending the concept of "crime against humanity" to initiating aggressive war. Subsequent United Nations debate and international experience of warfare after 1945 clarified the concepts of aggression and defense.

Thus in August 1990, the *jus ad bellum* of international law was authoritatively defined by Articles 2 and 51 of the United Nations Charter: Article 2 prohibited member nations "from the threat or use of force against the territorial integrity or political independence of any state" and empowered the Security Council to preserve peace; Article 51 granted to all nations, acting individually or collectively, the right to resist with force an "armed attack" until the Security Council "takes the necessary measures to restore international peace and security."

MILITARY DOCTRINE AND CAPABILITIES

Historical experience is an important element in the formation of moral consciousness. Two aspects of the experience of military life have been especially important for the development of just war tradition: the growth of a concept of moral identity on the part of people in military life, a concept that translates into standards of how to act in war; and the encounter with war itself, which affects decisions about strategy, tactics, appropriate weapons, and appropriate uses of those weapons. In both these respects the development of just war tradition has been influenced by military factors and, in turn, the broader tradition has shaped the moral identity of military personnel and their way of understanding the moral meaning of war.

In the Middle Ages, for example, the growth of the chivalric code played an important role in forming a consensus on noncombatant immunity, and this knightly code was, in turn, refined and extended by the influence of Christian moral theology and canon law. As for the encounter with war itself, the development of limited war as a norm in the eighteenth century was a direct reflection of the emphasis on *jus in bello* concerns by the moralists and international publicists of the period; in turn, the practice of limited war established empirical standards by which to judge the appropriateness of given means of war and targets in war.

In the contemporary American military context, the concept of moral identity is closely associated with the various service manuals on the law of war and the rules of engagement laid down for a particular situation of the use of military force. The key role played by air power in the war against Iraq and the relevant U.S. Air Force manual, AFP 110–31 [which was the most recently revised service manual on the law or war at the time of the original publication of this chapter], are useful reference points for assessing the military component of the just war debate over American use of force in the recent Gulf crisis. The growing reliance on "smart weapons" and battle by maneuver rather than by mutual attrition also provided a reference point for judging whether the Gulf War would proceed within the framework of the criteria of discrimination and proportionality. I will treat these in turn.

Lessons of the Military Manuals

The U.S. military service manuals on the law of war do not treat the question of resort to war; that is a matter for civilian authority to decide. They focus instead on the *jus in bello*, the limits within which military force may be applied. For AFP 110–31, these limits are defined by the principles of humanity and military necessity.

> Military necessity is the principle which justifies measures of regulated force not forbidden by international law, which are indispensable for securing the prompt submission of the enemy, with the least possible expenditures of economic resources. This concept has four basic elements: (i) that the force used is capable of being and is in fact regulated by the user; (ii) that the use of force is necessary to achieve as quickly as possible the...submission of the adversary; (iii) at the force used is no greater...than needed to achieve his prompt submission (economy of force); and (iv) that the force used is not otherwise prohibited.... Complementing the principle of necessity... is the principle of humanity, which forbids the infliction of suffering, injury, or destruction not actually necessary for the accomplishment of legitimate military purposes [the principle of proportionality of means].... The principle of humanity also confirms the basic immunity of civilian populations and civilians from being objects of attack during armed conflict [the principle of discrimination]. This immunity does not preclude unavoidable incidental civilian casualties which may occur during the course of attacks against military objectives, and which are not excessive in relation to the concrete and direct military advantage anticipated.

Thus the fundamental principles of the *jus in bello* of the just war tradition are stated explicitly in the Air Force's manual as defining the parameters for legitimate acts of war. The role of this manual is not simply to lay out rules for conduct, however; this and the other service manuals on the same topic also provide a reference point for the definition of a professional military ethic and for a moral identity appropriate for a member of the services. As the prospect of armed conflict with Iraq neared, the American military services considered their own role in the conflict in terms such as those in the passage quoted above. Their military planning proceeded in this context. The tradition of just war is evident in authoritative policy statements bearing on who the members of the services are to be and how they are to act in case of armed conflict. However popular the Rambo image may be on the movie screen, it is not the image by which the services seek to define themselves and their mission in peace and war.

Encounters and Associations with War

It is a well-worn cliché that armies and their leaders always prepare to fight the last war, never the next one. In the case of American military preparedness in the Gulf crisis, this was emphatically untrue, though it was taken for granted by a considerable segment of American civilian society. The "last war" for some critics was Vietnam, and the corresponding expectation was a lingering, indecisive presence of American forces in the Gulf region as other coalition members drifted away or became alienated. The "last war" for others was World War II, a conflict that spread to engulf nation after nation and whose prosecution led to strategies, tactics, and eventually weapons of mass destruction.

Influencing both of these "last war" conceptions of what to expect in the Gulf was a new myth, expressed by such authors as Paul Fussell and Michael Herr, that modern war is by its nature grossly and disproportionately destructive, beyond rational control, and inherently at odds with any reasonable political purpose. Preoccupied with the American experience in Vietnam and with the debate over nuclear deterrence, many critics of the U.S. military have used these images to undergird a general opposition to the use of military force by this country—that is, a moral position of modern-war pacifism coupled at times with a more generalized aversion to things military.

Others involved in the moral debates over military policy in the last thirty years have argued, rather, that wars can be waged while avoiding means and methods that are grossly and disproportionately destructive, beyond rational control, and at odds with reasonable political purpose. Those—including myself—who share this view have argued that the Fussell-Herr myth of modern war is simply the wrong way to think about moral responsibility in warfare, and that this responsibility implies developing weapons, strategies, and tactics for war-fighting that allow for use of military force according to the limits given in just war tradition.

Fighting the War at Hand

The influence of this view, combined with two new historical developments, enabled the American military to enter the Gulf crisis prepared to fight the war at hand—not the "last war," however conceived. The two new elements were the all-volunteer army, which necessitated planning that emphasized training and tactics designed to minimize risk to the scarce and costly human resources available under arms; and new technologies that made possible highly mobile, precise weaponry ideally suited to the concepts developed in the historical experience of limited war: limitation by ends, targets, and means.

When Iraq invaded Kuwait in August 1990, American military doctrine and capabilities were in a state of readiness that was clearly not realized by the majority of Americans, many of whom still thought in terms of the images of World War II, the nuclear age, and the experience of Vietnam. They failed to recognize the degree to which their forces were prepared to wage war within the framework of the just war *jus in bello*—relying on moral identity, exemplified by the manuals of the laws of war and the rules of engagement adopted for the crisis, and on military capabilities, exemplified by the incorporation of "smart weapons," enemy intelligence-suppression means and tactics, and a highly mobile force that used its agility to protect the scarce human resources of the American military.

JUSTIFIABLE RESORT TO FORCE

Examining the Gulf War in just war terms requires standing back from the narrowly political, economic, and ideological arguments that were advanced between August 2 and January 16 and concentrating instead on the implications of the criteria for judgment contained in this moral tradition. The conclusions reached by applying these criteria for judgment include concern for the political, the economic, and the ideological, and bear implications for them; yet just war analysis does not reduce to them, singly or together.

The just war tradition is concerned primarily with the questions of when force is justified in the context of statecraft, and what restraints should be observed in this justifiable use of force. Paul Ramsey has called these the questions of permission and limitation, respectively. Classically, the moral criteria developed for guidance on the resort to force are known collectively by the Latin term *jus ad bellum*, while the moral criteria on restraint in war form the *jus in bello*.

The just war tradition has arrived as seven criteria that must be satisfied to justify resort to military force. These include just cause, right authority for the use of such force, right intention, the goal of restoring peace, overall proportionality of good over evil, a reasonable hope of success, and a situation of last resort. I will define each criterion more fully, and then examine each in the context of the decision to use force against Iraq.

The Notion of Just Cause

Just cause classically included one or more of these conditions: defense against an attack, recovery of something wrongly taken, or punishment of evil. These terms derive from Roman law and practice and were incorporated into the developing Christian moral theory of justified war by Saint Augustine in the early fifth century. In the Middle Ages the idea of punishment of evil was stressed by thinkers like Thomas Aquinas, who cited as their warrant Romans 13:4: "For [the prince] does not bear the sword in vain; he is the servant of God to execute his wrath on the evildoer."

In order to avoid defining evil in ideological terms, recent just war theorists have tended to focus on one particular evil, the aggressive use of force by a people or nation against another. There has been a corresponding tendency to emphasize defense against ongoing or imminent attack as the primary or only just cause for resort to force. This is clearly the case in contemporary international law, as provided in Articles 2 and 51 of the United Nations Charter. Yet, it should not be thought that the earlier notions—of recovery of something wrongly taken, and punishment of evil—have evaporated from the tradition; rather, they have been subsumed within a gradually broadened concept of defense that allows retaliation for an attack launched and completed (punishment of evil) and defines wrongful occupation of territory as a state of "continuing" armed attack.

When Iraq invaded Kuwait on August 2, 1990, and declared that the territory that was "formerly Kuwait" was "irrevocably" part of Iraq, a just cause for use of force against Iraq came into being. This was a flagrant case of aggression, one that violated the most fundamental norms of international order, and it was quickly recognized as such by the United States, by the United Nations Security Council, and also by the overwhelming majority of nations of the world. Not only did Iraq's action blatantly violate the letter of Article 2 of the U.N. Charter (prohibiting "use of force against the territorial integrity [and] political independence" of another country), but, more profoundly, it showed utter disregard for the very norm on which the state system, and through it the United Nations itself, stands: a *de facto* acceptance of every state's right to exist.

The presence of just cause alone is not sufficient to justify resort to force; yet this was as clear and unambiguous a case as one could hope to find in the real world, and the brazenness of Iraq's action remained on public display even as the international community tried to expel the Iraqis through a variety of non-military means.

Critics of the use of force against Iraq cited as (at least partial) justification of Iraq's action various forms of "aggression" employed by Kuwait against Iraq: notably, keeping oil prices lower than was advantageous to Iraq and allegedly pumping oil from Iraqi territory by horizontal drilling. Even if these charges were true, such actions clearly fell far short of the magnitude necessary to justify military retaliation. Rather, conflicts of this sort are to be dealt with by negotiation and arbitration; that is what the very idea of a "world order" conveys.

Action by Right Authority

The second criterion for justified use of force is that such action be undertaken by a right authority. In historical terms, this meant a genuinely sovereign prince, that is, one with no political superior. In its early development, the principal function of this criterion was to limit the use of force to those who would rightly employ it, declaring illegitimate any use of force by subordinate nobles, private soldiers, criminals, and even the church. In the modern period the criterion of right authority still seeks to minimize the frequency of resort to force, by limiting it to the political leadership of a sovereign state duly authorized by the legitimate political processes of that state. (The concept of such authority has been extended also to the U.N. Security Council under the conditions specified in the Charter.)

In the case of the Gulf War, right authority for use of force by the coalition of nations cooperating to undo Iraq's aggression was manifest at both the international and national levels. Internationally, such authority was provided by Resolution 678 of the United Nations Security Council. Within the United States, right authority derived first from the president's powers as defined by the Constitution and the War Powers Act, then by the congressional resolutions adopted on January 12 and 13 authorizing use of U.S. military force against Iraq.

Underlying such legal authority is a moral basis for the notion that right authority may use force to serve justice in the international arena. That moral claim is expressed in the same biblical passage, Romans 13:4, that medieval theorists cited to define the idea of justified cause. This passage also embodies an understanding that persons in positions of political authority have a responsibility to uphold the moral of order as such, for without it human community would not be possible, This responsibility is not specifically religious or Western—though it is clearly present both in biblical religion and in the political traditions on which Western societies are founded—but is rather a universal concept, the basis of the idea of "world order" that undergirds international law and the United Nations system. Even if it were exclusively religious or Western, this concept of the responsibilities stemming from legitimate political authority would still impose a moral obligation on the political leadership of the American people and on the American people themselves.

Aspects of Right Intention

Right intention, the third notion bearing on the just war decision to resort to force, was classically defined in two ways: positively, by considering whether the other just war criteria were present; and negatively, by distinguishing itself from wrong intentions such as those enumerated by Augustine: "the love of violence, revengeful cruelty, fierce and implacable enmity, wild resistance and the lust for power, and such like." In the Middle Ages the requirement of right intention was taken especially seriously as a duty for individuals in combat; soldiers were obligated to do penance after battle in case they had fought with forbidden motivations in their hearts. In the modern period the concept of right intention has become a matter of the conduct of states, not the moral attitudes of individuals. It centers, positively, on such goals as protection or restoration of national, civil, and human rights and other values, reestablishment of order and stability, and the promotion of peace. Negatively, right intention today involves avoiding taking another state's territory, violating the rights of individuals or nations, and deliberately depriving a nation of peace and stability.

All these conditions existed when the United States and allied forces decided to take military action against Iraq. While critics sought to portray U.S. involvement in terms of "blood for oil" or as an effort to secure American hegemony in the Gulf region, such charges ignore the naked act of military aggression (and not the first such act on the part of Iraq) that brought the conflict into being. These critics also assumed bad faith on the part of U.S. and coalition leaders who insisted that their goals were simply to restore Kuwait as a nation and to require Iraq to make amends for damage it caused. Clearly, the subsequent military operation by coalition forces kept to these goals. Indeed, so off-base were the critics in depicting larger motives that, looking back on the internal bloodbath and repression that has swept over Iraq after the international cease-fire, one may wonder whether a broader "right intention" might not, in fact, have been justified: deposition of the dictator Saddam Hussein and creation of the conditions for participatory government in Iraq as a way of serving the human and political rights of the Iraqi people.

The Goal of Peace

The existence of a right intention on the part of the coalition in this case also substantially satisfied the requirement that the use of force be aimed at achieving peace. This criterion was understood classically in terms of three values: order, justice, and peace. The first aim of good politics, according to this view, is an order that reflects the natural law, that is, one that establishes things the way they ought to be. This would lead naturally to the existence of justice: a good order is inherently a just one, and maintaining justice protects the right ordering of affairs and relationships within the political community. The establishment of order and justice together produces the third political goal: peace. Peace would flow not only from the right ordering of politics within a society, but from the creation or restoration of a just political order in the relationships within, between, and among nations.

In the case of the Gulf War, the goal of peace was closely tied to the concept of right intention: rolling back Iraqi aggression and restoring Kuwaiti territory and sovereignty (right order and justice), deterring such aggression in the future, restoring the shattered peace of the region, and attempting to set in place safeguards to protect that peace in the future. I will return to this subject later on. What received too little attention, as we can see in retrospect, was the need to establish a just political order internally within Iraq as a key part of securing peace in the Gulf region. Given the focus of international law on affairs between nations, however, and the reluctance of the international community (including the coalition partners) to interfere in the internal affairs of nations, it is understandable that the coalition confined its conception of post-crisis peace to the restoration of order among the affected nations. The broader just war tradition differs from international law on this matter of whether the use of force to achieve peace should extend to efforts to produce the conditions of peace within the offending state; the moral argument imposes a more extensive responsibility than the legal.

(It is worth noting that many of those who insist that modern war is inherently immoral define "peace" as no-resort-to-military-force at all, and make this the first goal of international politics. Though these critics may use just war terminology to argue their case, their argument is fundamentally at odds with the central assumption in just war tradition: that there may be criminal acts against order and justice in the relations among nations and peoples, and that force may be the only way to achieve a stable condition of justice and peacefulness.)

Proportionality of Good Over Evil

The next war concept to be examined is the criterion of proportionality which refers to the effort to calculate the overall balance of good versus evil in deciding whether to use force to right a wrong. One must first assess the evil that has already been done—damage to lives and property, as well as harm to the more intangible values of human rights, self-government, and a peaceful and stable world order. Second, one must calculate the costs of allowing the situation of wrongdoing to continue. Finally, one must evaluate the various means of righting these wrongs in terms of their own costs, as well as the benefits they might produce.

In the debate that took place over U.S. participation in the United Nations–sanctioned use of force against Iraq, the just war criterion of proportionality was widely misapplied. Critics of the use of force vastly overestimated the expected costs of war while paying little attention to the damage already done, and continuing to be done, by Iraq's aggression against Kuwait. For these critics, the moral problem was not Iraq's actions but the American military buildup, which they deemed "disproportionate." The decision whether to take military action requires a much more inclusive and objective weighing of good versus ill.

The calculation of proportionality must take into account the many levels of force that responsible leaders may choose. While there may be occasions in which a buildup would serve as an effective deterrent, there are numerous other ways of engaging in combat, each carrying its own costs and benefits.

Applying the criterion of proportionality is properly an exercise in moral and political judgment, not a mathematical calculation. While it is easy to count military personnel, tanks, airplanes, and munitions, it is more difficult to agree on the value that should be placed on protection of human rights, national territorial and governmental integrity, and other such intangibles. Yet these are among the paramount values the just war tradition seeks to preserve, and their importance is undeniable. Equally undeniable is the fact that different peoples and cultures place different stock in these values. For this reason, governments need to take special care when invoking considerations of proportionality to keep from conceiving the issue in narrowly political or cultural terms.

Reasonable Hope of Success

The decision to resort to force, to be justified, must also rest on a conviction that military action will have a reasonable hope of success. Clearly this, too, is a matter for prudential judgment, since "success" can be interpreted in many ways. While the fundamental goal of just war tradition is the protection and preservation of values—specifically, the establishment of right order, justice, and peace, within this broad context any particular just use of force may have its own specific aims. Indeed, such aims are inherently narrower than the overarching goal of right politics, a goal that is achieved by many instruments, only one of which is the justified use of force.

The use of force may establish the conditions for order, justice, and peace by eliminating the threats posed to them; that is the most realistic definition of "success" in the use of military force. The actual achievement of these goals is the broader work of good statecraft, building on the base of the established conditions. Clausewitz's famous dictum, "War is the continuation of politics by other means," has a corollary: it is the business of politics to build on what a just war makes possible. A justified resort to force will have a "reasonable hope of success" if it lays the groundwork for productive statecraft (or, at the minimum, does not foster a situation that might make such statecraft impossible).

It is inappropriate to demand that a just use of force achieve ends beyond its means. This is why, in both classic and contemporary just war reasoning, the idea of specific and limited war goals is central. It is also why just war tradition developed a *jus in bello*, a set of restraints on what may morally be done when fighting a justified war. The concept of *jus in bello* involves more than insuring that the means of war are justifiable in themselves; it also involves establishing a correct relationship between the belligerents, both during the war and afterwards, since it recognizes that the existence of such a relationship is an important precondition for the creation of a just and lasting peace. "Reasonable hope of success, then, turns on the understanding of just cause and right intention, and includes not only achieving the goals thus established but also observing the limits on means laid out in the *jus in bello*. What is called for, in short, is a reasonable hope of doing what is justified by these moral criteria within the moral limits they define.

War as Last Resort

Finally, before engaging in military action, a government should determine whether the wrongs involved can be redressed by means other than force. It is important to note that the criterion of last resort does not mean that all possible nonmilitary options that may be conceived of must first be tried; rather, a prudential judgment must be made as to whether only a rightly authorized use of force can, in the given circumstances, achieve the goods defined by the ideas of just cause, right intention, and the goal of peace, at a proportionate cost, and with reasonable hope of success. Other methods may be tried first, if time permits and if they also satisfy these moral criteria; yet this is not mandated by the criterion of last resort—and "last resort" certainly does not mean that other methods must be tried indefinitely.

THE CASE OF IRAQ

It is my judgment that all the just war criteria providing guidance on the justified use of force were amply satisfied in the case of the decision to use military force against Iraq. The decision not to continue with negotiations or economic sanctions after January 15, 1991, did not violate the criterion of "last resort." The failure of the Geneva talks, the continued intransigence of Saddam Hussein, the ongoing process of military buildup by Iraqi forces, the continuing systematic rape of Kuwait, the history of Iraq's relations with its own dissident population and its neighbors, and threats of violence by Iraq against those neighbors all provided ample reasons to conclude that non-military means held little possibility of success, and that the continuing atrocities in Kuwait necessitated action.

Indeed, Iraq was an easy case. Most instances are fraught with much more ambiguity. There was no moral equivalence between Iraq and Kuwait, for example, or between Iraq and the coalition nations. Iraq's actions flagrantly violated both international law and the deeper international conscience expressed in the idea of a peaceful and stable world order. Nor were military forces committed by the United States or the other coalition nations behind closed doors; the authorization was public, was worked out in debate, and, when it came, clearly represented the will of the authorizing bodies. The critics' charges of a hidden American agenda were not borne out, either during or after the fact. The use of force was proportionate, given the wrongs that were to be righted. The continual aggression on the part of Saddam Hussein swept away, one by one, other possible means of resolving the crisis short of force. The judgment of a reasonable hope of success was eminently sound. The coalition's military action was motivated by the desire to lay a foundation for peace. While the final establishment of peace in the Gulf region and the Middle East clearly remains to be accomplished, that is the proper task for statecraft, and exceeds the bounds of what military force alone can ever achieve.

MORAL LIMITS ON THE USE OF FORCE

We turn now to the other side of just war tradition, the moral limitations on justified force: the *jus in bello*. Once the decision is made that force is justified, just war tradition sets two conditions on how that force may be employed: noncombatants must be protected from direct, intentional attack (the principle of discrimination), and the specific means of force must be at a level and of a type appropriate to the task at hand (the principle of proportionality of means).

The question of proportionality in combat is similar to the concept of proportionality in deciding whether to resort to force. But in this instance, the calculus of "proportion" hinges more narrowly on the legitimate military goals to be achieved, the forces arrayed on the enemy side, and the least destructive ways to defeat those forces or render them ineffective so as to achieve those legitimate ends. Proportionality is not concerned with the absolute quantities of personnel or weaponry employed, but with their relationship to the existing threat and with their effect. In the case of the Gulf War, the flanking maneuver by which Operation Desert Storm achieved its swift victory displayed a clear case of proportionality of means as opposed to choosing a frontal assault on Iraqi fortifications. Proportionality was evident not only in the low casualties to coalition forces, but also in the relatively low casualties to Iraqi forces, testified to by the large numbers of prisoners of war taken by the coalition.

The principle of discrimination requires that noncombatants should not be directly, intentionally targeted, even in the course of using force that is otherwise proportionate. It is morally meaningful—and empirically possible—to distinguish noncombatants from combatants: the former have no direct material or formal participation in the war, while the latter do. Means of warfare that cannot make this distinction are morally wrong, such as the use of poison gas against civilian populations in an attempt to suppress dissidence, or counter-population bombing in an effort to undermine civilian morale. By contrast, means of warfare that directly, intentionally strike at legitimate military targets—including deployments of troops, munitions depots, weapons-production facilities, and command-and-control centers—are morally and legally permissible, even if noncombatant lives and property are inadvertently put at risk or damaged.

The Challenge of Modern Warfare

Since the 1950s many have argued that contemporary war is inherently indiscriminate and disproportionate. In support of their view, they invoke World War II, the Vietnam War, and, perhaps most prominently, the possibility of a nuclear holocaust. Others have countered that since 1945 warfare has been of a far less deadly variety than World War II, consisting primarily of local conflicts; furthermore these conflicts have, with the exception of the use of chemical weapons in the Iraq-Iran war, relied on conventional weaponry.

The experience of such wars shows that, while individual leaders may wrongly choose to ignore the combatant–noncombatant distinction, it is by no means the case that "modern warfare" has made this distinction any more difficult. Some, including myself, have stressed that the presence or absence of discrimination in war is not a function of the destructive capabilities of the weapons available but a direct product of the intentions of those who employ them. A corollary to this observation is that the destructive capabilities of modern weaponry—conventional as well as nuclear, chemical, or biological—morally require parallel developments designed to limit the collateral damage of weapons, to increase their accuracy, and to create tactical and strategic plans that would ensure that such means of war are used in accordance with the principles of discrimination and proportionality.

The Gulf War clearly showed that contemporary warfare may in fact be conducted within the limits imposed by these two just war principles; at the same time, it showed that doing so—as well as preparing to do so—is still a matter of moral or immoral choice, just as it was in previous ages. "Smart" bombs, highly accurate cruise missiles, even the latest in aiming devices for "dumb" bombs and missiles, as well as intelligence-gathering means that can identify and pinpoint specific buildings as military targets—all these means of war employed by the coalition forces stand in stark distinction to the bombing and shelling practices of World War II and even Vietnam. Critics of the U.S. role in the Gulf War remarked that the great majority of munitions dropped in the air war were not of these high-accuracy types. That charge misses two important points: first, that high-technology weaponry, with its increased ability to satisfy the requirements of discrimination and proportionality, has made possible a very different sort of "contemporary war" than these critics have imagined; second, that even the routine weapons used in the air war did not violate acceptable means of war. The United States did not use such weapons with indiscriminate or murderous intent, and there is evidence that U.S. military leaders deliberately rejected the option of intentional counter-population bombing, as when swift action was taken against Air Force General Michael Dugan in September 1990 when he suggested employing such a tactic against Baghdad.

In contrast, Iraq's conduct of war was in conspicuous violation of the principles of discrimination and proportion. It is important to remember that these principles, like other ideas embodied in just war tradition, are not simply part of the moral heritage of the West; they are present also in Islamic moral tradition, and they are explicitly part of international law. The immoral and illegal warfare tactics employed by Iraq included the conscious use of counter-population targeting of Kuwaiti citizens and others trapped by the invasion, both at the beginning and throughout the occupation; the launching of Scud missiles against Saudi and Israeli cities in direct, intentional counter-population strikes; the loosing of oil into the Persian Gulf in an effort to impede coalition sea and amphibious action; and, at the time of the withdrawal of Iraqi forces, their destruction of Kuwaiti buildings, systematic pillaging of Kuwaiti property, and setting afire Kuwaiti oil wells and facilities. Most of these acts had no military relevance whatsoever, and the damage they created will continue to cause widespread harm for years to come. Such long-term damage is inherently indiscriminate, for, as we have already noted, once a war is over all are noncombatants.

PERSISTENT MISCONCEPTIONS ABOUT WAR

As I have suggested above, thinking about the "last" war (whether World War II or Vietnam) has deeply affected American moral debate over military matters. The World War II countercity bombing of German and Japanese cities furnished models for both sides of the debate over nuclear targeting and deterrence strategy. On the one hand, proponents of strategic nuclear targeting of Soviet cities in the 1950s found their rationale in the countercity bombing that took place during World War II.

On the other hand, opponents of nuclear weapons strategy took their bearings from this same model, viewing modern war as inevitably all-encompassing in scope and indiscriminate in targets. Both sides, then, for very different reasons, found themselves in agreement that "in modern wars there are no noncombatants." Paul Ramsey's effort to assert the just war principle of discrimination, first set out in *War and the Christian Conscience*, was a notable exception in the debate, arguing that, even in modern wars, the distinction between combatants and noncombatants can and must be observed. Unfortunately, the American experience in Vietnam, with its high casualties and the close relation of guerrillas and their civilian supporters, further strengthened the claim that modern wars are inherently indiscriminate and disproportionate. Opponents of the Vietnam War in particular represented it as typical of war in the modern age and used it to argue against use of military force in general.

Imagining War in the Gulf

In the debate over American military involvement in the Gulf crisis much opposition centered on judgments based on this understanding of modern war. Critics feared the war would unleash a holocaust of destruction, and this fear in turn fueled arguments that U.S. deployment of force was disproportionate, that the use in combat of this force would be disproportionate and indiscriminate, and therefore that force should not be employed. The myth of war inherited from the "last" wars thus skewed moral judgments about the rightness of force in this crisis.

The Gulf War, on the contrary, showed that it is possible to fight a contemporary war within the bounds of the just war principles of discrimination and proportionality of means, and that the decision to do so is a moral judgment on the part of the belligerents involved, not a choice forced on them by contemporary weapons. There is, I think, a lesson to be drawn from this: we need to put aside our fears that contemporary war must, by its very nature, be an indiscriminate, disproportionate holocaust, and move on to deliberate the best ways of developing means of force that may be used morally if military action is necessary. In contrast to the destructiveness exemplified in World War II's carpet-bombing of cities and Vietnam's free-fire zones, the Gulf War showed that highly accurate weapons and appropriate plans and policies for their use can limit the overall destructiveness of contemporary war. The Gulf War, in short, is a real-life example of what just war tradition has always held to be true in principle: war is an enterprise capable of being conducted morally or immorally, depending on human decisions.

The Value of Jus ad Bellum

An important implication of the conduct of the Gulf War for the American moral debate on military matters is that we ought now to be able to concentrate on judging the rightness or wrongness of particular possible uses of force in terms of the *jus ad bellum* categories—just cause, right authority, right intention, and so on—instead of falling into the tendency to reason backwards from judgments about whether *jus in bello* should be observed. If war is recognized as subject to human control, and if the means of war are also known to be subject to such control, then the logic of just war tradition is restored: that, first, a decision must be made as to whether a resort to force is justifiable in itself; second, decisions must be made as to how to employ that force in justifiable ways.

These assumptions also carry important implications for the development of American military capabilities. We seem to have moved into a cycle of limited warfare, having passed through a period of world-wide conflicts. Whether this is a genuine cycle or not, or whether total war and limited war are always parallel options, we would do well to note William V. O'Brien's observation that limited war represents the practical application of the just war idea. Whereas the Cold War, as well as the models of the two World Wars, encouraged those engaged in the moral debate to focus on an image of total war, the Gulf War provides a powerful historical example to buttress the moral argument for military preparedness oriented to limited and humanly controllable forms of warfare.

THE GOAL OF PEACE

The earliest modern visions of structures of international cooperation, those of seventeenth- and eighteenth-century theorists like Crucé, Sully, Saint-Pierre, Penn, and Bentham aimed at producing what Saint-Pierre called "perpetual peace" and what Kant similarly termed "eternal peace." Such is the heritage of international organizations like the League of Nations and the United Nations. But this is also the heritage of regional forms of cooperative relationship set up to enable states to settle their differences constructively and to manage their common affairs for mutual benefit. The goal of international order is the goal of a just and enduring peace.

Just war tradition specifies that a justified resort to force in international disputes must aim at producing peace. More broadly, as I have argued above, the tradition understands this peace as one that flows from and accompanies the establishment of a right political order and justice within and among nations.

International law, which is one of the most important carriers of just war tradition in the contemporary world, defines order, justice, and peace in relatively straightforward terms: order is the recognition of the integrity of states; justice is the provision for the recognition of states and formal equality of treatment within a legal community of nations, the United Nations; peace is the state of affairs in which order and justice, thus defined, coexist (or, more narrowly, when no nation or group of nations is threatening another nation or group of nations so as to deny them national rights or political, territorial, or economic integrity). Working from this standard, the U.N. Security Council authorized the use of force to expel Iraq from Kuwait and to restore Kuwaiti territory and national autonomy. The goal was, as much as possible, to restore the *status quo ante bellum*.

A New World Order?

Beyond the scope of international law, however, matters are more complicated. President Bush, in justifying the war, called for a "new world order." Critics of the war argued that it would inflame the entire region, ending whatever stability and limited peace had been achieved there. Thus, both agreed that forcing Iraq out of Kuwait would be only a stepping-stone to peace; the coalition victory, as well as the manner in which it was achieved, would have to set in motion a general reordering of relations among the nations of the region so as to bring about a more general, pervasive, and enduring state of peace. In particular, such a peace would need to include a new mutual security arrangement for the Gulf region itself, replacing the old tripartite balancing of power by Iran, Iraq, and Saudi Arabia, and a settlement of the conflict between Israel and the Arab states.

Obstacles to Peace

Both of these goals will clearly be difficult to achieve and will require intensive efforts well beyond the immediate accomplishments of the Gulf War.

Media attention, meanwhile, has focused on the mix of promise and challenges in the relationship between Israel and its Arab adversaries. There are indeed difficulties aplenty here, and while there is much optimism that they can be overcome, the war against Iraq in fact had little directly to do with the core issues: the right of Israel to exist as a state and the solution of the Palestinian problem. What the war did perhaps create is a new network of relationships that may allow for more productive and trusting interaction among some of the actors in the Israeli-Arab conflict. This will not be easy, given that the Palestinians were on the other side in the war, and that many of them in Jordan long remained captive to the view that Saddam Hussein's forces won. (Indeed, in the summer of 1991, postwar Iraqi Propaganda continued to represent Saddam Hussein as having achieved a great victory by successfully resisting Western and Zionist imperialism.)

The Syrians have their own political goals that may or may not in the long term be compatible with making peace with Israel. The Saudis continue to have their own regional agenda, and are hamstrung as well at crucial points by a religious conservatism that dictates implacable hostility to Israel; while they will no longer dispense great sums of money to the PLO, Jordan, and Iraq, there are no signs that the Saudi government will go beyond a *de facto* neutrality regarding Israel—if they even go that far. As for the Israelis, the war has left them strategically much stronger in the region, and their internal political situation makes them unlikely to accept a compromise involving "land for peace." Again, the chances are not great that the Gulf War will produce a "new world order" in the Israeli-Arab conflict.

A new mutual security arrangement in the Gulf area is more possible, yet still fraught with problems. Fixated by the seemingly intractable problem of an Israeli-Arab peace, Americans have paid far less attention to the broader issues of regional security than those issues deserve. Saddam Hussein's continued grasp on the Iraqi state and use of the machinery of absolute rule against his country's population is a major barrier to progress in settling the larger problem of the future role of Iraq in the region. If there is ever to be a lasting peace in the area, it must be preceded by the rebuilding of Iraq, the creation of some form of democratic self-government there, and the inculcation of values oriented toward peaceful coexistence with its neighbor states. Saddam Hussein's military forces caused great and unwonted destruction to Kuwait and its people; yet Iraq itself—its people, its cities, and its land—has also experienced much destruction, as a result both of the war and of subsequent Iraqi military actions against the Kurds and the Shi'ites. The achievement of a just and enduring peace rests on remedying this situation.

Achieving this goal will be no easy matter, given the vitriolic animosity Saddam Hussein's aggressive actions have aroused in most of his neighbors, including the most powerful ones. Enduring peace will be impossible to achieve if Saddam Hussein remains at the head of the Iraqi state. Equally important, the United States must take the same leadership role in working toward the political reconstruction of Iraq and the region that it took in the fight against Iraq—or, for that matter, in the reconstruction of West Germany and Japan after 1945. This implies a new commitment to the support of human rights in the region and the protection of oppressed minorities, such as the Kurds.

AMERICA AS A MORAL AGENT

The reluctance of the United States to assume a more active role stems largely from its desire to stay within the bounds of what is allowed by international law in rolling back aggression. But the end result may be that the only peace that can be achieved in this region is one limited to that defined by international law, not a "new order" that will be extraordinarily difficult to bring into being.

This is not to minimize some of the accomplishments of the old order. Restoring the territorial integrity and governmental autonomy of Kuwait, reestablishing respect for the anti-aggression rule of international law, restoring credibility to the moral and legal guidelines for resort to force and for fighting justly, restoring to the United Nations the ability to act in the world as its designers intended—these are goals deeply worthy in themselves and fundamental to the preservation of international peace. As always, peace is not something to be set in place and then walked away from; it requires constant tending and reconstruction. The outcome of the Gulf War may not be the ideal peace that everyone longs for. But the war has produced a peace that is surely preferable to the appeasement urged by some in the fall of 1990, and it has strengthened the tools for preserving a minimum of the peace of order among nations.

What should be the role of the United States in the evolving international order? America today stands in a position of unrivaled strength among world powers, and it is clearly the object of much envy on the part of people around the world. While no country can single-handedly deal with all the world's problems, the leadership role of the United States has assumed in the Middle East since August 2, 1990, suggests that Americans might now do a great deal more in the international arena than was conceivable so long as the Cold War lasted. American leadership might be exercised through the United Nations, whose Security

Council functioned in the Gulf crisis as it was designed to function but had not since 1945; American leadership might be exercised through alliances or coalitions of nations dealing with regional problems; or, on rare occasions, America may need to exercise its influence alone.

Using influence does not necessarily mean taking military action, although as Paul Ramsey argued in a passage quoted earlier, the exercise of statecraft inevitably involves the use of national power, and the military represents a component of such power. Thus it is important to keep the just war debate alive in this post-Gulf War era, for its categories may need to be drawn on again in assessing our proper response to crises that may erupt in the future. As the Gulf crisis has shown, it is also important to think of the contemporary means of this moral tradition not simply in terms of the debate over nuclear weapons and deterrence, which preoccupied just war theorists for most of three decades from 1945 until the end of the Cold War, but also in terms of weapons-planning development, strategic and tactical thought, and socialization and training of military personnel. In short, it is time to rethink our moral tradition of statecraft and force it back to its roots, and to reconsider the tradition's implications for present and future policy, anticipating an active American role in the developing world order that lies ahead.

ABSTRACT

In this piece Johnson provides a summary of the just war tradition in the West. He argues that the tradition is rooted in the "customs, attitudes, and practices" that fed it such as the Hebraic world, the classical world, and Germanic culture of the Middle Ages. Informed by Christian thought and natural law philosophy even though more modern and contemporary representations of the tradition have rejected earlier religious dimensions, he shows the tradition to be a middle ground between pacifism and holy war or ideological war.

CHAPTER 3

HISTORICAL ROOTS AND SOURCES OF THE JUST WAR TRADITION

AN OVERVIEW OF THE CULTURAL CONTEXT

The just war tradition of Western culture is a product of the influence of a broad variety of cultural sources over a centuries-long history of development. While strong religious sources and manifestations of this tradition can be identified, it is not a purely or uniquely religious phenomenon. While at times the development and continuity of this tradition have depended heavily on the influence of secular forces, it is not properly reducible to them. Rather, just war tradition is a major moral tradition of Western culture, shaped by both religious and nonreligious forces and taking shape in both religious and nonreligious forms within that culture. Understood as a totality, it encompasses and represents attitudes, beliefs, and patterns of behavior from across the breadth of that culture over time. Identifying its historical roots and sources and sorting out their relationship and their particular contribution to the development of just war tradition is thus a complex task.

Historical and anthropological evidence suggests that every human culture has generated some analogue of just war tradition: consensus of beliefs, attitudes, and behavior that defines the terms of justification for resort to violence and the limits, if any, to be set on the use of violence by members of that culture. Sometimes these have taken the form of elaborate and broadly approved rules for the practice of war, as in China during the period of the warring states, when warfare was carried on as a highly stylized game by the belligerents. Similar gamelike aspects of the justification and limitation of conflict can be observed in medieval chivalry in Western Europe and among the American Plains Indians prior to the coming of white people.

Making armed conflict more gamelike tends to increase its frequency as the price for restraining its destructiveness. The sheer frequency of the resort to armed force for whatever purposes are deemed justified may lead to efforts to impose cultural restraints on such resort, as by controls on who may bear arms, restrictions on who may authorize resort to arms, and more tightly circumscribed circumstances in which use of armed force is held to be justified. When this happens within a culture, the pendulum may swing the other way, and the gamelike aspects of armed conflict may diminish: such conflict becomes no longer a game, but something far more serious. Thus, ironically, restraints on the resort to violence seem historically to have an inverse relationship to restraints on the use of violence within a culture.

The breakdown of a consensus on the proper limits to be observed on the destructiveness of armed conflicts does not come only from a reaction aimed at limiting the frequency of resort to violence. More severe strains on cultural efforts to restrain the destructiveness of such conflicts come from two other factors.

First, the end of war as a game comes when enemies do not play by the same rules. Thus, in practice, cultural restraints on violence are observably difficult to maintain in violent conflicts that cross important cultural boundaries. Then the enemy may be represented as subhuman or otherwise not worthy of the same respect shown adversaries in intracultural combat, or he may be represented as an embodiment of evil forces or values that must be combated at all costs. In either case a more ruthless style of fighting may be justified against him. Even when both belligerents attempt to observe their own conventions of restraint, where these do not match, the conventions are placed under great stress, and their power to mitigate the destructiveness of the conflict in question diminishes. One important expression of this kind of challenge to the effort to restrain the destructiveness of conflicts is the idea of holy war, an armed struggle on behalf of the constellation of values associated with religion and the concept of the divine, or, more broadly, ideological war, armed struggle against threats to the highest values accepted in the culture and against the values represented by the enemy.

Second, the introduction of new technology unanticipated by the older conventions or otherwise not included in them loosens the effect of those conventions on the actual character of combat. Western medieval attempts to outlaw certain weapons correlate with the fact that these were not weapons used by the knightly class; rather, the weapons in question—crossbows, siege weapons, bows and arrows—were those employed by commoners or by mercenary bands. In the American West the introduction of firearms radically disrupted and reshaped the code and practice of the Plains Indians, replacing the custom of counting coup by touching an enemy or stealing something of his as a sign of manhood with the much more deadly practice of using the rifle to wound or kill.

Reciprocally, when restraints are loosened for other reasons, the effect may be to heighten the ideological character of the conflict (as occurred in Iran during the recent war with Iraq) or to encourage the introduction of more destructive means into the conflict (as in Iraq's repeated use of poison gas in the same conflict). In short, cultural restraints on war are universal but somewhat fragile, and they are difficult to extend across cultural boundaries. Thus cross-cultural conflicts tend to undercut the effect of existing traditions of restraint, and such conflicts may also introduce the element of ideological justification for one's own cause and with it the justification of more ruthless, unrestrained forms of conflict.

All these general characteristics of cultural efforts to justify and limit war can be observed, at one point or another, in the just war tradition of Western culture. This tradition has developed around the two foci of justification and limitation, denominated within the tradition by the Latin terms *jus ad bellum*, which defines when it is justified to resort to armed force, and *jus in bello*, which sets the boundaries or limits for the use of justified force. The latter has gamelike aspects, determining who are the proper "players" and who are not (the combatant-noncombatant distinction) and establishing the rules to be observed in the conflict: defining the proper proportionality between means and proximate ends, sometimes attempting to outlaw certain weapons or classes of weapons, and establishing sanctions aimed at protecting from harm in war the rights, persons, and property of noncombatants and individuals rendered *hors de combat*. If the *jus ad bellum* can be said to have gamelike aspects, then its rules have to do with the game of statecraft. In its broadest form it defines what causes justify resort to armed force, who may rightly authorize such resort, what the context must be before it is right for such resort to take place, and what sort of ends may properly be sought by it. In just war tradition taken as a whole, the *jus ad bellum* and *jus in bello* exist as two aspects of the same body of doctrine and practice. Yet between them there are important differences as to source, purpose, and pattern of development, and efforts to draw wisdom from the tradition tend to bring out the tension between them.

Just war tradition represents a middle ground between two more extreme sorts of positions. On the one hand are the various forms of pacifist opposition to war, notably including sectarian pacifist rejection of participation in warfare and utopian pacifist efforts to transform society so as to bring an end to resort to war. At its most restrictive, just war tradition may produce the same practical judgments as such pacifist approaches; yet it differs fundamentally from them in accepting, in principle, that war is sometimes justified for the protection and preservation of important values. At the other end of the spectrum of attitudes regarding war, the highest values of the culture are defined in terms of religion or other transcendent ideology, and unlimited means of war may be justified as appropriate responses to threats to those values. This is the idea of holy war or ideological war. Within Western culture, this idea is historically and thematically a special, extreme conception within just war tradition, arising when religion or ideology transforms the definition of the categories of the *jus ad bellum*. From the beginnings of the modern period, the main line of just war tradition has rejected religion (and implicitly ideology) as a justifying cause for war, and much of the development of this tradition over the last four centuries has focused on restraints that are to be observed in fighting against any enemy for whatever cause. Thus, in general, the just war idea accepts, against pacifism, the possibility that armed conflict may be justified to protect and preserve values and denies, against the idea of holy/ideological war, the justifiability of unlimited means of war in the service of such values.

The deep roots of just war tradition are in the customs, attitudes, and practices of the cultures that have principally fed it: those of the Hebraic world and the world of classical antiquity and, later, those of the Germanic societies of northern Europe. Even after the coalescence of just war ideas and practices into a coherent tradition (a phenomenon of the Middle Ages), much of its development took place insularly within Western culture. Yet more global claims have been made for the ideas of justification and restraint contained within this tradition. Particularly in the modern period major theorists and apologists for these ideas have identified them as grounded in natural law and thus, in principle, knowable by all people everywhere and binding upon them. The Spanish Scholastic Franciscus de Victoria (also, Vitoria) used a form of natural-law argument to extend just war theory into his consideration of relations between the Spanish explorers and settlers and the Indians of the New World. Two generations later Hugo Grotius made the natural-law grounding of just war concepts the basis of the universal law of nations he described in *Of the Laws of War and Peace*. During the nineteenth and twentieth centuries the political and cultural hegemony exercised by Western nations led to the extension of positive international law, expressing just war concepts conceived as grounded in natural law, over much of the globe. Through the vehicle of the international law of war a version of just war tradition exists today far beyond the cultures in which this tradition originally took root and later developed.

THE ORIGINS OF JUST WAR ATTITUDES, CONCEPTS, AND BEHAVIOR

The Hebraic Contribution

The roots of just war tradition in Hebraic culture are to be found principally in the Old Testament stories of the wars of Israel during the Exodus and the wanderings prior to the entry into Palestine (the books of Exodus and Numbers), the era of the conquest and settlement of Palestine (the books of Joshua and Judges), and the period of existence of Israel as a nation with a king, particularly that segment of this latter history having to do with the reigns of Saul and David. Much of what the Old Testament records about war in the earlier periods has to do with war commanded by God, a form of holy war. In such war not only was God conceived as commanding the conflict, but he was understood to be directly involved in the fighting, warring with the divinities of the enemy on the cosmic level even as the soldiers of Israel dealt with their human counterparts on the earthly level. All Israelite males capable of bearing arms were expected to do so. No quarter was to be given; all the enemy, persons and property, were to be "devoted to the Lord for destruction" (Joshua 6:17). Yet such war was not entirely without examples of mitigation. In Joshua 11, which describes the war between Israel and an alliance of cities and peoples, only those cities are destroyed that actively participated in aggressive action toward the Israelites; this is a form of the idea of noncombatant immunity. In Deuteronomy 20:19–20 the fruit trees and vines are explicitly named not to be destroyed, an idea that later appeared as an argument against a scorched-earth policy in warfare, a policy that violates the principle of discrimination.

In a moral tradition whose development extends over centuries, what is most important is the memory and use made of such historical elements by later generations. In normative Jewish thought, as illustrated by the medieval commentator Maimonides, the contribution of the Hebrew Bible to moral tradition on war is summarized in terms of three types of conflict: "religious war" (directly commanded by God), in which participation is mandatory for all males able to bear arms and in which spoils are to be "devoted to the Lord for destruction"; defensive war, in which all males must participate who do not have outstanding religious duties and the prosecution of which involves some mitigation of destruction; and the "optional wars" of kings, offensive wars undertaken at the discretion of kings of Israel, participation in which is excused by a greater range of other obligations and prosecution of which is mitigated by considerations of noncombatancy and proportionality. In Christian thought Ambrose and Augustine both employed the example of the Israelite wars commanded by God as warrant for their own justification of using Roman military force against heterodox forms of Christianity, and the same sources were taken up by later authors in the context of the medieval crusades and the Protestant-Catholic conflicts of the Reformation era. Largely, though, Christian just war thought focused on other issues, and within the broader just war tradition this holy war concept never moved to the center focus of attitudinal, intellectual, and behavioral development. Rather, just war tradition took from Hebraic culture those insights and practices aimed at mitigating the destructiveness of war.

The Roman Contribution

Much of the specific form of the *jus ad bellum* of just war tradition can be traced to late Roman practice. Augustine of Hippo, widely (if somewhat excessively) regarded as the progenitor of the specifically Christian stream of just war thought, drew heavily from what Rome accepted as normative regarding war. This included the very idea of a "just war," a *bellum justum*, the definition of just cause in terms of three conditions (defense, retaking something wrongly taken, punishment of evildoing), the idea that only the highest authorities in the state could authorize violence on behalf of the state, and such other ideas as the requirements of last resort, proportionality of good to evil done, and the goal of peace. More broadly, the Roman concept of justification of war was part of an overall notion of statecraft in which war is an instrumentality of political sovereignty. The concept of divine involvement in justifying war was, in Roman practice, subordinated to the requirement that the fetial priests, officials of the state religion, review every ostensible cause for war by sacrifice and augury and pronounce it justified or unjustified. They could not, in contrast to Hebraic practice, authorize war by themselves on behalf of the gods. Also connected to an overall concept of statecraft is the grounding of the propriety of defensive war in the need to protect the goods provided in Roman society against the inferior goods represented by other societies who made war against Rome. Defensive war was justified, that is, not because of some abstract *raison d'état* but because of the values guaranteed by this particular society and its government. This same concept, inverted, justified war for the purpose of punishment toward societies whose political leadership practiced evil activities against their own members or other persons.

The Early Christian Contribution

Despite some early Christian opposition to participation in war (on grounds that military service involved idolatry, created ritual impurity through involvement in human bloodshed, and represented a context in which moral temptations were pervasive), by the second century there were both Christian participation in war and apologetic acceptance of military service for Christians. In the 170s a significant portion of the soldiers in the so-called Thundering Legion (*Legio Fulminata*) were Christians. Only slightly later the writings of Tertullian of Carthage reveal Christian presence in the military units stationed there. Toward the end of the century the theologian Clement of Alexandria wrote that military service was acceptable for Christian "learners," though not for Christian "gnostics," who were to observe a stricter standard of morality and more detachment from things of the world. For Clement one factor that seems to have argued for Christian participation in military service was the need to protect the values provided by the Roman Empire to its inhabitants. By contrast with the radical eschatological beliefs widespread among first-century Christians, which justified a form of sectarian relationship to the Roman state, Clement lived after hope had waned for the imminent Second Coming of Christ, and for him the Roman state represented an earthly peace and stability necessary to the continued prosperity of Christianity until God's purposes for the world had been achieved.

The majority of commentators on Christian just war tradition do not reach as far back as Clement but trace it to Augustine, bishop of Hippo, in the fourth and fifth centuries. However creative a theologian Augustine was, though, his ideas on just war did not spring fresh from his mind without historical antecedents. Clement and the numbers of Christian soldiers who served in the legions beginning in the second century symbolize and exemplify a shift that was already taking place in their own lifetimes, a change in attitude on the part of Christians toward a positive acceptance of participation in the life of the world, including military service to protect the goods represented by the Roman state. This shift provided the background for Augustine's own treatment of the Roman state in *The City of God* and his justification of military service in protection of the political community represented by that state. The same can be said for Augustine's mentor Ambrose, bishop of Milan, who should at least share Augustine's mantle for making important contributions to the establishment of the theological justification for Christian participation in just wars.

Ambrose, rather than Augustine, was the theorist who first realized that a Christian's obligation to the neighbor in love extends to the obligation to protect him or her from harm being inflicted unjustly. When confronting the case of an evildoer attacking an innocent victim, Ambrose argued, the Christian third party should intervene to protect the victim and is justified in using force against the assailant if necessary to keep harm from the victim. The force that may be used against the assailant is limited, however, by the fact that Christ died for him as well.

This paradigm is basic for the theory of just war in Christian doctrine, because it provides a theological justification for the use of force (the obligation of love for neighbor) that sharply counters arguments for pacifism based on Jesus' own nonviolence, his command to turn the other cheek, and his example of "disarming" Peter at the Garden of Gethsemane. These examples, for Ambrose (and Augustine), were identified as having to do with self-defense, not justified war. Extended to the context of society as a whole, Ambrose's paradigmatic case shows how there are Christian, as well as secular, reasons for fighting, if necessary, to protect that society. At the same time, it implies limits on even the justified use of force and respect for the rights and person of the enemy.

Ambrose's paradigm for justified protection of the neighbor as an obligation of Christian love was implicit in Augustine's major creative contribution to just war tradition, the idea that to be justified, resort to force should be rightly motivated or, as the tradition generally has it, undertaken out of "right intention." The *locus classicus* for this idea is a passage from Augustine that begins by dismissing the idea that "the deaths of some, who would soon die anyway" represent an evil in war. Rather, Augustine went on, what is truly evil is "the love of violence, revengeful cruelty, fierce and implacable enmity, wild resistance and the lust of power, and such like."

This idea that right intention or motivation must be present to justify resort to war on the part of the state—and Christian participation in such war as soldiers—was added, in Augustine's thought and in later systematic accounts of the *jus ad bellum*, to several ideas drawn directly from Roman theory, law, and practice: the general idea of *bellum justum* and, within it, the specific requirements of just cause, right authority, proportionality, last resort, and the goal of peace. Neither Augustine nor Roman doctrine addressed *jus in bello* issues directly, though later theorists (for example, Paul Ramsey) have argued that the principle of discrimination or noncombatant immunity is implicit in Augustine's thought. The later *jus in bello* principles of discrimination and proportionality may also be read, quite straightforwardly, out of Ambrose's paradigmatic case.

The Contribution of Classical Culture

The attitudes and practices of classical culture had their impact on just war tradition both through the idea of the goods represented by a stable political order, to which Christian theologians were gradually converted, and more particularly through the laws and customs of late classical Rome. By Augustine's time an idea of *bellum justum* had coalesced around the requirements that imperial authority alone could rightly authorize force, that there be a just cause (defined as defense, the need to retake something wrongly taken, or the need to punish wrong), and the rest of the *jus ad bellum* ideas previously mentioned. Much later, in the seventeenth century, Hugo Grotius would attribute a form of *jus in bello* restraint to the Romans on the ground that they enslaved their captive enemies instead of killing them, which they were entitled to do by the law of nature. Just cause, in the Roman system, was reinforced by the practice of seeking guidance from the fetial priests, who used sacrifices and auguries to determine their own judgment on the presence or absence of a just cause.

All this has directly to do with formal just war theory as it later developed. Much more in Western attitudes toward justice and restraint in war can, on close scrutiny, be read out of the influence of classical culture. For example, both ancient Greece and republican Rome held it to be an obligation of every male to bear arms in case of emergency, if he was able. Roman culture gradually diminished this requirement, until at the end of the imperial period it was essentially reversed, and citizens were exempted from war, while mercenaries and specialized troops from the fringes of the empire made up the bulk of the armed forces. More broadly, classical culture bequeathed the fundamental concepts of politics and statecraft and of the place of the use of force within the practice of statecraft, which were transmitted to the Middle Ages in legal, philosophical, and theological texts and recovered and elaborated by later theorists. In addition, the concepts of *jus gentium* and *jus naturale* employed by late medieval and early modern thinkers derived directly from Roman culture, as did much of the content placed into these categories.

The Germanic Contribution

Most writers on the idea of just war overlook the influence of Germanic culture on the development of attitudes and practices on war in the Middle Ages. This influence was, however, considerable and was transmitted chiefly through the customs, attitudes, and behavior associated with the knightly class, the direct historical inheritor of the Germanic warrior tradition. It was the knights, more than any other element in medieval culture, who through the code of chivalry shaped the growing tradition on *jus in bello*. The whole idea of a distinction between combatants and noncombatants correlated directly, in the Middle Ages, with the social and functional distinction between knights and nonknights. Observation of the rule of proportionality in combat followed immediately from the recognition that a knight fighting for an enemy was also a member of that larger brotherhood defined by chivalry—as well as from the fact that knights taken prisoner instead of being killed could be redeemed for ransom. Efforts to limit weapons, though formally promulgated by church councils, were aimed at the weapons with which nonknights were typically armed, weapons that killed rather than only injuring and that, in the case of siege weapons, were indiscriminate in their effects.

The traditions of Germanic culture transmitted through medieval chivalry thus contributed to the *jus in bello* of just war tradition, but the major contributions to the *jus ad bellum* are to be found elsewhere, specifically in the inheritance from Roman law and custom and from Christian theology, incorporating elements from Hebraic culture. While Germanic culture certainly had its own conception of when resort to force was justified, who could authorize it, and so on, the direct line of influence in the *jus ad bellum* of just war tradition is from Roman law and custom, transmitted both directly and through Christian theology. Thus the two major aspects of just war tradition, that having to do with just resort to force and that having to do with the proper use and the limits of justified force, derive from essentially distinct cultural heritages that, in the context of medieval Christendom, merged into a single culture. While we have to this point been identifying and examining the sources of just war tradition, the tradition itself, understood as a coherent body of thought and practice including both a *jus ad bellum* and a *jus in bello* and accepted across the breadth of the culture, is a product of the Middle Ages.

THE MEDIEVAL COALESCENCE OF JUST WAR TRADITION

Early Steps

From the breakup of the Roman Empire to the tenth century the just war ideas of the classical world and of late classical Christian theory were ignored in the development of Western culture. At the same time, the Germanic traditions on war had not yet solidified into the attitudes and customs of chivalry. Lack of political unity reinforced the tendency toward general lawlessness on the part of those who bore arms, the descendants of the Germanic warrior class. In the tenth century, as an attempt to put an end to the bullying of landless *milites* (soldiers in the employ of local nobles) and the plundering of peasants and townspeople by armed bands living on the fringes of settled society, several French bishops proclaimed a "peace of God," essentially a declaration that peaceful noncombatants were not to be molested on pain of excommunication for persons who transgressed the peace. The church was immediately supported by the royal officers who bore both political and military authority over the various governmental regions of France, because putting down the bullying *milites* and suppressing bandit bands was clearly in the interest of centralized authority. The idea of the peace of God spread to other regions of Europe but did not become universal. Nonetheless, it represented an important step in the growing cultural consciousness of western Europe, and its provisions for noncombatant protection were picked up in later church doctrine relating to just war tradition.

In the eleventh and twelfth centuries there emerged an idea of a "truce of God," a declaration of certain days as off limits for fighting by Christians. Whereas the peace of God was aimed at ending lawless behavior on the part of miscreants in society—disturbers of the peace, in an apt but later terminology—the truce of God was aimed at restraining people fighting in causes and for authorities that might well be considered just by all affected. The truce of God movement originated in northern Italy, and its effects were strongest there, where it had great popular support. It had no lasting effect, however, on the development of just war tradition.

Nor did the effort to limit specific weapons, already alluded to as one of the approaches made by medieval Western culture to limit the destructiveness of war, work its way into the developing just war tradition as a specific element within the doctrines expressing that tradition. Rather, its long-term effect was to reinforce the broader ideas of discrimination and noncombatant immunity and proportionality, the central concepts of the *jus in bello*. The weapons banned were in fact gradually accepted into the armament of legitimate armies, and eventually the effort to ban them became moot as they were replaced by other weapons. The idea of weapons bans remains seductive, however, and the last century has seen efforts in international law to ban certain types of bullets, air bombardment, certain kinds of naval weapons, gas warfare, and nuclear warfare. Rather than to concentrate on the particular weapons banned, which vary from one historical context to another, it is more instructive to analyze the reasons why they have been banned. These can be traced immediately to the principles of discrimination (such weapons as gas are indiscriminate in their effects) and proportion (dumdum bullets, for example, cause gratuitous harm to their victims). Thus the weapons bans represent a reflection of the consensus on *jus in bello* but are not an independent aspect of it.

The Coalescence of the Tradition

For a tradition to exist, there must be both continuity and convergence of related ideas and associated practices. By such a standard, there is, properly speaking, no just war tradition prior to the Middle Ages, when the various ideas and practices described earlier coalesced into a single, recognizable cultural consensus on the justification and limitation of violence. The benchmark document for the beginnings of this coalescence is the compilation of canon law known as the *Decretum*, written by the monk Gratian in the mid-twelfth century. Gratian's focus was on reducing to essentials and systematizing the Christian tradition as it had been handed down to him, and he knew the influence of the classical and Hebraic cultures only as filtered through the writings of Christian sources. On the subject of war he drew significantly from Augustine, and it was in fact through the *Decretum* that Augustine's importance as a Christian just war theorist was secured. Canonists and theologians writing on war in the next centuries after Gratian depended on his compilation as their window on what was important from earlier writers; Thomas Aquinas, for example, referred only to ideas of Augustine's that had been included by Gratian in the *Decretum*.

The dependence on Gratian was thus at once liberating and constricting. By drawing together and systematizing significant statements on war and Christian morality from acknowledged authorities, he prepared the way for others after him to examine moral issues related to war within the perspective of Christian tradition. The *Decretum* provided a nucleus around which later medieval just war thought formed, as a snowflake crystallizes around a bit of dust. At the same time, though, it was a book of moral definitions and rules, and its perspective on Christian tradition was accordingly restricted to those statements from earlier authorities that matched the purpose of the compilation. Though it provided a base on which later theory could build, this was a narrow base. Gratian's specific concern was to answer the question whether participation in war is ever permitted for Christians. His answer, drawn from Augustine and Isidore of Seville, was that Christians may participate in just wars, defined as those fought to regain something stolen or to repel injury (Isidore) or to revenge injury, punish evil, or restore something wrongly taken (Augustine). Thus the late classical Roman concept of just cause came into the core of the medieval consensus on just war. Other *jus ad bellum* concepts can also be found in the *Decretum*, as well as the germ of a *jus in bello* concept of noncombatant protection. Yet these concepts were sharply truncated and presented without argument or discussion. It remained for later writers to elaborate and build on these ideas that Gratian drew systematically together.

Two successive waves of canonical commentators, known as the Decretists and the Decretalists, followed Gratian in the twelfth and thirteenth centuries. Their major preoccupation was with the juridical definition of right authority, and their collective achievement on this issue was to define and restrict religious authority to wage war and ultimately to reserve authority to make war to secular powers. Their work on authority to make war was paralleled and reinforced by the work of historians and theorists of Roman law, who sought to make this law the model for a new "international law" of Christendom, and by the social, economic, and political pressures that led to the establishment of centralized monarchies as the normative form of government.

These canonical writers also helped to define the growing consensus on noncombatant immunity, though the church's first concerns seem to have been to protect churchly persons (bishops, priests, monks and nuns, pilgrims) and lands from harm during warfare. The broader development of the idea of noncombatant immunity to include all persons not capable of bearing arms (that is, women, children, the aged, the infirm, and the mentally impaired) or not actually involved in bearing arms (peasants on the land, townspeople, merchants, and other "peaceful folk") came out of the code of chivalry and the self-interest of the knightly class. The concept of proportionality as a *jus in bello* restraint also derives from the values and practices of chivalry; aside from the weapons limits, the church did nothing here. It is fittingly symbolic that the earliest expression of a full idea of *jus in bello*, synthesizing the churchly and chivalric contributions, with both an elaborated conception of noncombatant immunity and a requirement of proportional restraint in combat, appears in the work of a fourteenth-century monk, Honoré Bonet, who was a member of the knightly class and wrote for others of this class who remained in the profession of arms.

The theological contribution to the growing definition of the just war idea in the twelfth through fourteenth centuries appears to have been less influential in its own time than that of the other sectors previously mentioned. In any case, its first effect was on the developing theory of just war, not on the practice. Thomas Aquinas's brief discussion provides a useful benchmark, particularly because of the development of his ideas by Neoscholastic just war theorists like Victoria and Suarez in the early modern period. Thomas, who was a contemporary of the Decretalists, defined the concept of just war in terms of three conditions (all part of the *jus ad bellum*): that the war be fought on right authority, have a just cause (which he identified by reference to the role of the prince to punish evil on behalf of God), and be waged with right intention. This rather limited conception implies, but does not say, that just war must always be of a defensive or retributive nature. The concept of right intention (defined by Thomas through the statement of Augustine cited earlier) may be drawn out, though Thomas did not do so, to produce the *jus in bello* ideas of discrimination and proportionality. The *jus ad bellum* mandate that just war aim at the end [aim] of peace was also assimilated by Thomas to the requirement of right intention.

As we examine these developments, we should remember that as we look backwards through history from them, there is quite simply no just war tradition to be discerned earlier than this. Even in these developments, considered singly, the full range of the just war idea did not yet exist. If we think of just war theory in the way that has become normative, including a *jus ad bellum* composed of criteria of just cause, right authority, right intention, proportionality of ends, reasonable hope of success, last resort, and the aim of peace, and a *jus in bello* comprising a broad concept of noncombatant immunity and the requirement of proportionality of means, this cannot be found in any of the medieval sources identified earlier. It cannot even be found explicitly, in full form, in the late medieval writers whose work reveals the existence of a general cultural consensus on just war much like the one just stated, writers like Honoré Bonet and his disciple, Christine de Pisan. Yet such a theory can be read through the ideas of these writers. The weight of evidence, then, shows that by the era of the Hundred Years' War, the late fourteenth and early fifteenth centuries, the core doctrine of just war tradition had coalesced and was functioning as a broad cultural consensus within western European culture on the justification and limitation of war. Major writers on these themes from the sixteenth and seventeenth centuries presupposed this consensus. Yet it was they—or more specifically some of them, including Victoria, Suarez, and Grotius—and not any medieval theorist, who stitched them together into a systematic whole. Just war tradition coalesced into a cultural consensus during the Middle Ages; this consensus was then expressed in systematic theoretical fashion by writers of the early modern period, who also transformed this developing doctrine into the base for modern international law. In its medieval coalescence and in the continuity of ideas and practice from the medieval to the modern periods, just war tradition emerged.

JUST WAR TRADITION IN THE MODERN PERIOD

The Early Modern Development of Just War Tradition

For just war tradition, the beginning of the modern era may be said to have been in Spain in the 1530s, when Franciscus de Victoria, then prime professor of theology at the University of Salamanca, "reread" or summarized his two courses of lectures on the Indians of the New World and the rights of the Spanish toward them. The two *relectiones* ("rereadings") were transcribed by Victoria's students and published under the overall title *Of the Indians Newly Discovered* (*De Indis Noviter Inventis*) in two parts, now normally cited as, respectively, *De Indis* and *De Jure Belli*. Victoria's nominal role as a professor of theology in a Dominican university was to comment on the *Sentences* of Peter Lombard, but he in fact did a great deal more. Earlier he had incorporated the theology of

Thomas Aquinas into his lectures, helping to initiate the intensive study of Thomas that established his thought as a principal theological basis for the Catholic church in the modern period. In the two courses of lectures on the Indians, Victoria took the further step of applying Thomas's conception of the perfection and autonomy of the natural in its own sphere to the Indians and their relationship to the Spanish.

The Indians were not Christians, Victoria granted, but they were humans—rational creatures able to know and understand the law of nature and bound to observe it in their dealings with one another and with the Spanish explorers, missionaries, and settlers. As non-Christians the Indians had invincible ignorance regarding the truths of the Christian faith, including the authoritativeness of the pope both directly and mediated downward through bishops and clergy, and so they could not be held to account for not accepting this authority. Yet they could be held to observance of the truths knowable through natural law and to behavior appropriate to this knowledge. Among the contents of the law of nature, Victoria argued, were the values that generated the requirements of just war. The Indians ought to know, understand, and observe these requirements not because of their promulgation in canon law or other authoritative religious teaching, but simply because the Indians were rational beings capable of knowing the law of nature.

This line of argument represents a major step in the development of just war tradition. While the historical sources of just war ideas and practices include much that is nonreligious, medieval just war tradition was in practical terms a doctrine for Christendom alone. When Christian knights fought against infidels, the rules for intra-Christian warfare did not apply, or applied only in part or so far as possible. Apart from the practical problem, alluded to in the first part of this chapter, of extending one culture's concepts on justification and limitation of force across the boundary with another culture, medieval Christendom was not able to produce a mature theoretical basis for attempting to do this. Victoria, employing Thomas Aquinas's concept of an autonomous and perfect natural sphere with its own law knowable by reason, provided such a theory.

With this fundamental contribution of a normative base for just war tradition in natural law, Victoria brought that tradition into the modern age, and in particular he made possible the extension of just war tradition into modern international law.

The just war theory Victoria set on this natural-law base included a full range of concepts inherited from the medieval consensus. Viewed in relation to the Middle Ages, Victoria's major contribution was to systematize the inherited concepts theoretically and to apply them to his own historical context. Viewed in relation to the modern era, his major contribution was to cast these concepts and their applications in terms of requirements rooted in natural reason, rightly employed. In both respects he was a critical figure, and his work was a crucial step in the development of just war tradition and its transformation into the modern age.

In the *jus ad bellum* Victoria's most creative and far-reaching new idea was what I call "simultaneous ostensible justice"—the recognition that so far as any human observer, however objective, could tell, both sides in a conflict had a just cause for fighting against the other. This idea appears in both *De Indis* and *De Jure Belli* and in contexts applying it to both European and Spanish-Indian conflicts. God, having knowledge superior to humans, can be assumed to know the genuinely just cause in such cases; yet humans alone cannot. Victoria used this reasoning to argue that the belligerents should fight especially scrupulously, not availing themselves of their full rights to injure the enemy—for, after all, one might be mistaken in thinking his own cause just. Grotius, writing in the next century, reiterated essentially the same conception and carried it further: for him, war must be assumed just when duly considered so by the sovereign authority and formally declared by that authority. In Grotius's thought and in the international law tradition after him the *jus ad bellum* thus became closely identified with the existence of sovereign states and their right to exist; the moral concept of just war became a legal concept of duly considered, authorized, and declared war. At the same time, as for Victoria, the implication drawn from this was to strengthen the limitation on violence placed by the *jus in bello*. The great bulk of international law on war accordingly represents elaboration and regularization of the *jus in bello* within the overall framework of just war tradition.

Whereas Gratian, and after him Thomas Aquinas, had focused on the question whether Christians could without sin participate in war, Victoria took this matter as having been settled in the affirmative. Another question that occupied medieval theorists also focused his own attention, however: the question of the relation of religious belief to just war. For the medieval canonists, as we have seen, this was assimilated to the definition of right authority, which was eventually limited to secular sovereigns. For Victoria, writing of the relationship between the Spanish and the Indians, the question was posed differently: might the Indians be converted to Christianity by force of arms? Victoria's answer, consistent with his fundamental position on the natural-law basis of the idea of just war, was a flat no: "Difference of religion is not a cause of just war." Neither is extension of empire nor glory nor advantage to the prince. Just wars may be waged only for causes provided in natural law, for only these bind all men equally.

As in the case of Victoria's position on simultaneous ostensible justice, this denial of religion as affording just cause became consensual among theorists of the following centuries and, in particular, became central to the developing international legal tradition. Before the consensus could form, though, a century of bloody and exhausting wars of religion between Protestants and Catholics in Europe and in the colonial empires of the European states was necessary to give a last practical test to the justification of war by religious reasons.

Victoria's contributions to the development of the tradition's *jus in bello* were essentially those of a systematizer rather than an innovator. He defined a strong position on noncombatant immunity, listing as noncombatants all those classes of people who by reasons of inability to bear arms or peaceful social function do not participate in war. This was where medieval doctrine had left the matter; Victoria drew out the implications to include "those who are able to bear arms, if...they have not shared in the crime nor in the unjust war." Later doctrine on noncombatancy did not improve on this. He employed the rule of double effect, however, to justify the accidental killing of noncombatants in a just war when the normal prosecution of the war could not take place without such killing. Yet he reminded his readers that the right to use any means of war is limited by the principle of proportionality, and that killing even the guilty is allowable only when there is no other way to prosecute a war otherwise just. In all of this Victoria sounds extraordinarily contemporary, for both legal and moral doctrines in the twentieth century have taken essentially the same line.

Though paths of direct influence are difficult to trace, these ideas that surfaced first in Victoria's work became the core of normative moral and legal thought on war in the following centuries. Grotius, as already noted, secured their centrality for the development of international law. In religious thought the Jesuit Suarez and the Puritan William Ames were but two who built essentially similar theories of just war on the newly consensual basis of natural law. Locke and other political theorists of the seventeenth and eighteenth centuries incorporated analogous reasoning into their work. Military codes of conduct, which began to develop in Victoria's own time and became more commonplace in the following two centuries, imposed requirements of military discipline incorporating provisions for noncombatant immunity and restraint by considerations of proportionality that directly paralleled Victoria's.

In the modern period from the seventeenth century to the twentieth the main streams of development of just war tradition have been international law, conceptions of legitimate military practice including military codes of conduct, and political theories that defined and regularized the nature of states and the parameters of their interrelationships. Neither religion nor philosophy had much hand in this. For religion, the conflicts ensuing from the Reformation led to reexamination and efforts to reformulate or reject the inherited tradition, but by the end of the Reformation era the accepted just war doctrine was essentially as Victoria had cast it. Philosophy had no autonomous voice on just war issues but operated within the parameters of international legal theory or political theory. The reawakening of both theology and philosophy as creative streams of just war tradition is a phenomenon of the twentieth century and particularly of the period since World War II.

STREAMS OF DEVELOPMENT OF JUST WAR TRADITION FROM VICTORIA AND GROTIUS TO THE PRESENT

The Law of War in International Law

International legal tradition on the justification and limitation of war moved from theory, exemplified by Grotius in the seventeenth century, to theory coupled with practical experience in statecraft, exemplified by Vattel in the eighteenth, and to the development of positive international law in the form of conventions and general treaties in the nineteenth and twentieth centuries. Georg Schwarzenberger has called this the progress of the requirements of "civilization"; Geoffrey Best has termed it the growth of "humanitarianism" as a brake on national self-interest. However it is described, this stream of development of legal standards for the behavior of states has been a principal historical carrier of just war tradition from the seventeenth century to the present.

The positive law of war of the nineteenth and twentieth centuries represents a crystallization of this stream of development. As it exists today, the international law of war has three aspects: restraints on the behavior of combatants in their treatment of noncombatants of various sorts, including prisoners of war, the wounded on the battlefield, "protected persons" like medical personnel and chaplains (who though in uniform are not combatants), and civilians; restraints on the means of war, including weapons bans (e.g., dumdum bullets) and nonuse treaties directed toward particular weapons (e.g., poison gas) and restrictions on certain kinds of usage of otherwise permissible weapons (e.g, air bombardment of unprotected, noncombatant areas); and restrictions on resort to military force in the settlement of disputes. The first line of approach began with the Geneva Conference of 1864, which produced the first of the Geneva conventions. The second approach traces to the Hague Conferences of 1899 and 1907 but includes later twentieth-century developments relating to means of warfare that produce gratuitous harm, unnecessary destruction, or indiscriminate effect. Together the first and second approaches constitute the *jus in bello* of positive international law. They correlate closely with the *jus in bello* defined by theory and practice in earlier centuries, and they add the advantages of specificity, widespread formal acceptance by states, and the possibility of imposition of sanctions in cases of violations (e.g., the punishments imposed by the war crimes trials following World War II). They have also had a direct influence on national military codes of regulations, though these are the more direct result of another stream of development of just war tradition.

The third approach taken by international law represents an effort, truncated but real, to define a *jus ad bellum* within international law. The major benchmarks in this approach are the Covenant of the League of Nations after World War I, the Pact of Paris of 1928, and the Charter of the United Nations. Two ideas are common to all three of these specific efforts to establish an international-law *jus ad bellum*: the national integrity of sovereign states and the right of self-defense to protect that integrity. Other ideas flow from these: the emphasis on arbitration to settle disputes found in the League of Nations Covenant and perpetuated in the Charter of the International Court of Justice; the renunciation of first resort to force in the settlement of disputes that formed the centerpiece of the Pact of Paris; and the principle of collective self-defense that is joined to the other two in the United Nations Charter.

It will be remembered that medieval and early modern just war theory, following Roman law and practice, recognized three kinds of justifying cause for war: defense, retaking something wrongly taken, and punishment of evil. Positive international law formally recognizes only defense; yet in practice the concept of defense has been stretched to include the other two, as in the Falklands war of 1982 (retaking something wrongly taken) and the justification of "defensive" nuclear retaliation (punishment of evil). The logic of these international law developments is straightforward, however: if there is no higher judge of justice than the nation-state, then its integrity must be paramount, and defense of that integrity against attack must be the only generally acceptable justifying cause for use of military force. Both as an elaboration and regularization of the just war tradition (in the case of the *jus in bello*) and as a truncated statement of it (in the case of the *jus ad bellum*), international law on war remains a major stream of development of just war tradition.

Codes of Military Conduct and the Phenomenon of Limited War

Specifically military traditions represent another stream of development of just war tradition in the modern age. In the sixteenth and seventeenth centuries formal codes of military conduct began to appear, promulgated by monarchs or their generals as a tool of discipline for armies increasingly composed of common men. The significance of this for just war tradition is that these codes put in the form of regulations for the conduct of soldiers elements of restraint that had in an earlier age been part of the socialization of members of the knightly class. The new common soldiers had received no such socialization, and the codes of conduct took their place. These codes were thoroughly practical in orientation; they laid down a floor below which a soldier's behavior could not slip without punishment rather than holding up ideals to which men under arms could aspire. Might soldiers plunder a church in enemy territory? What were the limits to quartering soldiers on civilians or requisitioning supplies from civilian households? What punishment should be exacted for rape? For pillage? What was the appropriate treatment for prisoners? Under what circumstances could prisoners be put to death? In answering these questions the early modern codes of military conduct drew on the *jus in bello* that had coalesced in the centuries before and expressed that *jus in bello* in terms of regulations and sanctions. Though the codes made use of restraints rooted in deeply held moral values, they were first and foremost tools of discipline for unruly men. Maintaining or enhancing the fighting value of armies composed of such men was a major purpose of the codes: soldiers allowed to plunder freely or live like lords in the civilian households where they were quartered could not be brought together into a unified whole on the march or on the field of battle. For this new type of army, discipline had to be unambiguously imposed and in effect at all times. The codes of military conduct, then, represented an externalization into specific rules and sanctions of what had been for the age of chivalry an internal moral sense of how a warrior should behave. Just war tradition was carried forward into the modern age by these new codes, but it was narrowly focused there by the requirements of military discipline. These codes had no *jus ad bellum* at all; that was no matter for a common soldier. Their establishment of the *jus in bello* as a base for military discipline, however, took the earlier consensus squarely into the realm of practical warfare.

The codes of military conduct were severely strained by the century of totalistic wars for religion ensuing upon the Reformation, and indeed they proved unequal to the task of restraining the conduct of these wars. By the end of the Thirty Years' War the concept of religion as providing a justifying cause for war was generally rejected. In the new political arrangements characteristic of Europe for the next century and a half, there developed a type of warfare characterized by minimal *jus ad bellum* limitations and growing *jus in bello* restraints. The former amounted to a consensual acceptance of the position laid down by Grotius: a sovereign of a particular state represented the only "right authority" to make war, the principal justifying reason for war should be the defense of vital interests of this sovereign; difference of religion should be excluded from among the justifying causes; due care should be given to the balance of harm and good a war would do; diplomacy should precede war in the settlement of disputes; and the purpose of war should be the righting of wrongs and the creating of a more just and stable peace. In fact, resting on the sovereign the broad power to judge his own case led to frequent, if limited, armed conflicts; one commentator calls this the era of "sovereigns' wars." But since the sovereigns had to bear the cost of every war in which they engaged, the numbers of men and amounts of resources committed tended to be relatively small. Such war was limited also as to the area of warfare, the targets deemed legitimate, and the impact upon the populations of belligerent states. The structure of such warfare generally provided noncombatant immunity in belligerent countries outside the immediate area of military operations, though noncombatants inside such areas were protected only by the military discipline of the armies.

This phenomenon of limited war was limited chiefly by the segregation of the military sphere from the rest of society. The armies were chiefly composed of professional soldiers, meaning that the bulk of the civilian population of states at war might be left to its own normal business. Tactics and strategy focused on control of strongpoints (including "magazines," fortified storehouses for powder, shot, weapons, food, and transport), not the civilian subjects of the enemy sovereign. Indeed, the civilians might well be one's own subjects at the end of the war, so there was an incentive not to treat them cruelly and to attempt to keep intact the economic base of the society. This was the kind of war reflected in the writings of eighteenth-century jurists like Vattel, who introduced the language of humanitarianism into the rationale for the *jus in bello*.

These restraints on war from within the sphere of military life and the practice of war carried forward and developed only a portion of the inherited just war tradition. Yet what was adapted and reformulated here was connected directly to the practice of war, and this practice shows the results. Equally importantly, the development of restraints on war within the military sphere provides a historical context for the reciprocal flow of ideas with other streams of development of just war tradition. The interpenetration of international law on war and the national codes and practices of war in the late nineteenth and twentieth centuries is one example of this; more recently, the entry by theologians and philosophers into debate over nuclear strategy exemplifies another sort of interaction bringing two streams of development together.

Within American history, the development of the tradition of codes of military conduct reached a high point in the General Orders no. 100

of 1863, promulgated by the general-in-chief of the United States Army for the guidance of forces in the field during the Civil War. This document was prepared largely by an international lawyer, Francis Lieber, who worked with a committee of high army officers. While less developed codes of military regulations had preceded it, this was a much more thorough exploration of what should be allowed in war and what should not. Lieber in effect encapsulated the international law tradition (or at least his interpretation of it) in a code of conduct for a national army. In turn, it had an influence on international legal theory. Within the American military it was the first example of a new type of document whose present representatives are the manuals on the law of war that exist in all the services today.

Limited warfare has been the norm for international armed conflicts since World War II, despite totalistic ideologies that seemed able to justify global holocaust. This period has also brought a development of limited war theory, exemplified in Robert Osgood's work. William V. O'Brien has analyzed several major armed conflicts of the period since World War II as examples of limited war. He argues that the phenomenon of limited war in the contemporary period represents the closest the practice of war can come to the requirements laid down in just war tradition.

Military theory and practice cannot be overlooked either as a source or as a carrier of just war tradition. Through military practice the ideas of justification and limitation of war are put into practical form; both internally within the military sphere of society and in interaction with other streams of just war tradition, military codes of conduct and the phenomenon of limited war have had a lasting effect on the shape of just war tradition.

The Theological Recovery of Just War Tradition

Though isolated examples of reflection on just war tradition and its implications can be found earlier, the principal period of recovery of this tradition and its meaning is the last forty years, and its principal foci are the debates over nuclear strategy and over American involvement in the Vietnam War. Paul Ramsey, whose *War and the Christian Conscience*, published in 1961, did more than any other one book to begin this renewed reflection on just war as a source for Christian moral guidance relative to war, continued to dominate theological just war theory in the Vietnam War period. By the end of this latter era, though, a good many others had actively entered this arena, and debate swirled over the meaning of just war categories for contemporary war—if indeed, as some critics disputed, these categories were meaningful at all in the present age.

What has characterized the theological recovery of just war tradition is a kind of Renaissance mentality, with the motto *ad fontes* ("to the sources") unheralded but vigorously pursued in practice. Ramsey himself went back to Augustine and Thomas Aquinas. Other Protestant ethicists, including Stanley Hauerwas and John Howard Yoder, sought to ground or test just war theory by reference to the Bible, especially the New Testament. America's Roman Catholic bishops, in their 1983 pastoral letter *The Challenge of Peace*, reached back both into Scripture and into church tradition. In general, the mode of recovery followed established theological fashion in Protestant and Catholic circles, with the Protestants tending to ignore the development that had taken place between the early church and the present and the Catholics looking for normative tradition in established church doctrine. Neither sort of theologian has paid much attention to the broader tradition, in which religious development has been through canon law as well as theology, and in which various streams of thought and practice have produced and carried the consensual body of justifications and restraints that make up just war tradition as a whole. To draw these connections has been the thrust of my own work, in distinction from the more properly theological writers.

The recovery of a specifically religious perspective on just war theory is important because of the balance it restores to the tradition as a whole, which had become dominated by the perspective of international law. With religious concerns now being examined directly, it is possible to explore the relation of individual moral behavior to the practice of war in a way not possible when the religious perspective was dormant. It is also possible now to engage in comparative, cross-cultural discussion about justification and limitation of armed violence in terms of religious beliefs and practices. Moreover, this recovery of the theological perspective allows examination and testing of the religious and cultural values that undergird just war tradition. These are as yet mainly items on the agenda for future work by theorists of just war as an element of Western cultural life.

CONCLUSION

The deep historical roots of just war tradition are the roots of Western culture, and the medieval coalescence of this tradition took place as an activity within Western culture. The discovery of the New World opened two routes along which the just war idea might advance: the route of cultural imperialism, according to which western European conceptions of justification and limitation of war would be imposed as requirements of a dominant, and presumably superior, civilization, and the route of universalizing the just war concept, according to which justifications and limitations of war would be read, in principle, out of a common law of nature equally accessible to all of humankind and equally binding on all. The route actually taken was a combination of these two options. The establishment of a natural-law base for the just war consensus inherited from the Middle Ages provided a theory for a culture-blind just war tradition. In fact, though, the Europeans who explored, colonized, and settled other parts of the globe had a strongly culture-conditioned conception of natural law, and the result was that what was universal in theory became a justification for cultural imperialism on the part of the supposedly culturally superior Europeans.

A vignette from Victoria illustrates how this could happen. Confronted with the question whether the Spanish might use military force to coerce the Indians into accepting Christianity, Victoria responded with a strong negative. Yet he pursued the matter by arguing that of course Spanish missionaries had a right to preach Christianity to all who would hear, and that natural law guaranteed not only this right but also the right of free passage for them through Indian lands. If the Indians refused to let the missionaries enter, or if they made captives of the missionaries, then the Spanish were justified in using military force to enforce the missionaries' rights—in effect making war on the Indians. The rights of which Victoria spoke were conceived by him as universal, as "natural"; yet the Indians knew nothing of them. They were in fact historically derived from the customary practices of European societies. In the name of natural law, Victoria was justifying cultural imperialism.

Later theoreticians made no apologies for this: the imposition of international law on the world was justified in the name of requiring civilized behavior from the uncivilized and thus civilizing them. The law of war was presented as imposing requirements of "civilization" as recently as two decades ago. By one means or another, international law on war carried ideas from just war tradition to all parts of the world and imposed practices consistent with that law on cultures greatly removed from the one in which just war tradition had its roots and in which its early systematic development took place. A case can be made, then, that in the form of agreement to the requirements of the international law of war, just war tradition has become global.

The present theoretical task is to reach beyond such de facto acceptance of the international law of war to discover whether it is possible to identify underlying this phenomenon a global consensus as to justice in war. Dominance of other cultures by the West has not entirely run its course, but yet to be explored adequately is the possibility of genuine community of values on matters related to the justification and limitation of force. Identifying exactly where such agreement exists and where it does not is an enterprise that earlier natural law theorists should have engaged in but did not. Doing so in the present context is one way of testing, and perhaps furthering, the development of just war tradition as a global consensus on justification and restraint of war.

BIBLIOGRAPHY

Aho, James A. *Religious Mythology and Art of War*. Westport, Conn.: Greenwood Press, 1981.

Ames, William. *Conscience, with the Power and Cases Thereof.* N.p.: n.n., 1639.

Bainton, Roland H. *Christian Attitudes toward War and Peace*. Nashville, Tenn.: Abingdon Press, 1960.

Barber, Richard. *The Knight and Chivalry*. New York: Charles Scribner's Sons, 1970.

Barkun, Michael. *Law without Sanctions: Order in Primitive Societies and the World Community*. New Haven: Yale University Press, 1968.

Best, Geoffrey. *Humanity in Warfare*. New York: Columbia University Press, 1980.

Bonet, Honoré. *The Trees of Battles of Honoré Bonet*. Cambridge, Mass.: Harvard University Press, 1949.

Born, Lester K. *The Education of a Christian Prince by Desiderius Erasmus*. New York: Octagon Books, 1965.

Cadoux, C. John. *The Early Christian Attitude to War*. New York: Seabury Press, 1982.

Childress, James F. *Moral Responsibility in Conflicts*. Baton Rouge: Louisiana State University Press, 1982.

Contamine, Philippe. *War in the Middle Ages*. Oxford: Basil Blackwell, 1984.

de Pisan, Christine. *The Book of Fayttes of Armes and of Chyvalrye*. London: Oxford University Press, 1932.

de Vattel, Emmerich. *The Law of Nations; or Principles of Natural Law.* Washington, D.C.: Carnegie Institution, 1916.

Delbrück, Hans. *History of the Art of War within the Framework of Political History*, vol. 1, *Antiquity*. Westport, Conn.: Greenwood Press, 1975.

Delbrück, Hans. *History of the Art of War within the Framework of Political History*, vol. 2, *The Germans*. Westport, Conn.: Greenwood Press, 1980.

Delbrück, Hans. *History of the Art of War within the Framework of Political History*, vol. 4, *The Modern Era*. Westport, Conn.: Greenwood Press, 1985.

Ferguson, John. *War and Peace in the World's Religions*. New York: Oxford University Press, 1978.

Ferguson, R. Brian and Leslie E. Farragher. *The Anthropology of War: A Bibliography.* New York: Harry Frank Guggenheim Foundation, 1988.

Fuller, J.F.C. *The Conduct of War, 1789–1961.* New Brunswick, N.J.: Rutgers University Press, 1961.

Gewirth, Alan. *Marsilius of Padua: The Defender of Peace.* New York: Columbia University Press, 1951–56.

Grotius, Hugo. *On the Laws of War and Peace.* Translated by Francis W. Kelsay. Oxford: Clarendon Press, 1925.

Hauerwas, Stanley. *Against the Nations.* Minneapolis: Winston Press, 1985.

Helgeland, John, Robert J. Daly and J. Patout Burns. *Christians and the Military: The Early Experience.* Philadelphia: Fortress Press, 1985.

Johnson, James Turner. *Can Modern War Be Just?* New Haven: Yale University Press, 1984.

Johnson, James Turner. *Ideology, Reason, and the Limitation of War.* Princeton: Princeton University Press, 1975.

Johnson, James Turner. *Just War Tradition and the Restraint of War.* Princeton: Princeton University Press, 1981.

Johnson, James Turner. *The Quest for Peace.* Princeton: Princeton University Press, 1987.

The Laws of Armed Conflicts. Edited by Dietrich Schindler and Jiri Toman. Leiden: A.W. Sijthoff; Geneva: Henry Dunant Institute, 1973.

Locke, John. *Two Treatises of Civil Government.* London: J. M. Dent and Sons; New York: E. P. Dutton and Co., 1924.

National Conference of Catholic Bishops. *The Challenge of Peace.* Washington, D.C.: United States Catholic Conference, 1983.

The Nuclear Dilemma and the Just War Tradition. Edited by William V. O'Brien and John Langan. Lexington, Mass., and Toronto: Lexington Books, 1986.

O'Brien, William V. *The Conduct of Just and Limited War.* New York: Praeger, 1981.

Osgood, Robert E. *Limited War.* Chicago: University of Chicago Press, 1957.

Ramsey, Paul. *The Just War.* New York: Charles Scribner's Sons, 1968.

Ramsey, Paul. *War and the Christian Conscience.* Durham, N.C.: Duke University Press, 1961.

Russell, Frederick H. *The Just War in the Middle Ages*. Cambridge: Cambridge University Press, 1975.

Schwarzenberger, Georg. *A Manual of International Law*, 5th ed. London: Stevens and Sons, 1967.

Scott, James Brown. *The Spanish Origin of International Law*. Oxford: Clarendon Press; London: Humphrey Milford, 1934.

Suarez, Francisco. *Selections from Three Works of Francisco Suarez, S.J.* Oxford: Clarendon Press; London: Humphrey Milton, 1944.

Von Harnack, Adolf. *Militia Christi*. Philadelphia: Fortress Press, 1981.

Walters, LeRoy B. "The Just War and the Crusade: Antitheses or Analogies." *Monist* 57, no. 4 (October 1973): 584–94.

Walzer, Michael. *Just and Unjust Wars*. New York: Basic Books, 1977.

Walzer, Michael. *The Revolution of the Saints*. Cambridge, Mass.: Harvard University Press, 1965.

Wright, Quincy. *A Study of War*. Chicago: Chicago University Press, 1942.

Yoder, John Howard. *When War Is Unjust*. Minneapolis: Augsburg Publishing House, 1984.

Zampaglione, Gerardo. *The Idea of Peace in Antiquity*. Notre Dame, Ind.: University of Notre Dame Press, 1973.

ABSTRACT

This chapter is a lecture originally delivered to the United States Air Force Academy that was subsequently published as a monograph and then as a chapter in *The Leader's Imperative*, J. Carl Ficcarotta, ed., West Lafayette, Ind.: Purdue University, 2001. The essay is a precursor to what would become known as the "responsibility to protect" (R2P). Johnson addresses the increasing concerns regarding intervention across national borders by military. He looks at intervention in the context of statecraft and moral reflection, as well as the use of the just war tradition as a moral source for judging appropriate use of military power to intervene. Finally, he discusses the implications of the just war tradition to protect and support for humanitarian relief efforts.

CHAPTER 4

JUST-WAR IDEA AND THE ETHICS OF INTERVENTION

Intervention across national borders by use of military force has long been a source of controversy and strong opinions. In this essay I address the question of intervention from three perspectives. The first section examines the use of power, including military power, in the context of statecraft and the role of moral debate in shaping policy for such use of power. The second section examines the just-war tradition of Western culture as a source of moral criteria for judging appropriate interventionary use of military power, comparing the classic ethical understanding of the just-war concepts with those contained in international law. Finally, the third section takes up the implications of this ethical tradition for a particularly pressing contemporary question, that of interventionary use of military force to protect and support humanitarian relief efforts.

INTERVENTION: THE USE OF POWER AND THE ROLE OF MORAL DEBATE

As with all uses of power, the question of intervention is not simply a political or military matter or one to be decided by appeal to international or domestic law or to calculations of the proportion between costs and benefits, though it is all of these together. But it is also a question that should be addressed from the perspective of ethical values, principles, and traditions of right action by means of a vigorous and informed moral debate that engages the political, military, legal, prudential, and other aspects of the larger issue, the right use of power. The ethical debate cannot be reduced to making sure that the people involved in these other aspects of the policy- or decision-making process are themselves morally upright people, though this is an important component. It must go beyond this, for what is right or wrong for the individual in terms of his or her own moral responsibilities to family, friends, or nation does not always translate directly into what is right or wrong for the political community, which naturally has a broader and more complicated set of responsibilities.

The ethical debate should proceed by identifying and clarifying relevant ethical wisdom and particular principles to provide ethical guidance and illuminate decision-making throughout the spheres of social responsibility affected. In the case of the use of military power these spheres include the moral life of the individual citizen, the individual in military service, military commanders, contributors to the making of policy, and the head of state and commander-in-chief. To make such guidance concrete, and more generally to make a contribution to living responsibly in a democratic and free society, such ethical debate must engage politics; yet this engagement should take place at the level of application, without the ethical debate itself being driven by political allegiances, ideologies, and commitments. That is, the ethical debate should proceed on its own terms, seeking to rise above the categories through which public argument often takes place: such categories as hawks versus doves, conservatives versus liberals, realists versus idealists. Good ethical reflection on the uses of power may be perceived as now hawkish, now dovish; now politically conservative, now liberal; now realist, now idealist. In itself, though, it is none of these.

The use of power itself, as Paul Ramsey has put it, "is of the *esse* of politics";[1] that is, it is part of the very nature of any political community. The right question is not whether the political community should exercise power but what kind of power it should exercise, when, and for what reasons. Military power is not, of course, the only expression of this characteristic of political communities, but it is an important part of the whole. Rightly used, military force may back up policies or behaviors whose principal expression is not military. Under particular circumstances, direct commitment of military force may be the only means by which a given end may be achieved. So understood, the right use of military force is part of the larger question of the right use of power by the political community and is inseparable from it. Its moral quality in any given case depends in the first place on the answer to this larger question. In this context, military intervention across national boundaries is not an issue to be addressed in isolation but only in the larger forum of the life of the political community, the nation.

To what degree, though, should the ethical debate reach even farther? The nation, after all, does not exist in isolation but interacts with others. Military intervention is one form of such interaction, but so are alliances and efforts at achieving a world order such as the United Nations. Unless one is a thoroughgoing relativist, moreover, ethical values and the principles that express them have a universal claim; they do not stop at the nation's border, or even at the border of one's own culture.

We can see the implications of this vividly in the contemporary context. Traditionally American military interventionary actions have been justified by consideration of our particular national interests or concerns to protect American nationals or in support of American law. The incursions into Grenada and Panama are the most recent cases in which such traditional reasons have been invoked to justify intervention. The case of the Gulf War exemplifies a different kind of reasoning. While U.S. interests were clearly at stake, the Bush administration relied most heavily on two other kinds of justification: first, the violation of Kuwait's sovereignty by Iraq's invasion and the continuing state of "armed attack" resulting from the occupation and annexation of Kuwait, together constituting a threat to international peace; and second, the depredations inflicted by the Iraqi forces against Kuwaiti civilians and the civilian infrastructure, including hospitals, schools, and museums. The former was an argument from the perspective of international law and, in particular, an appeal to the Charter of the United Nations; we may term it an internationalist argument. The latter was an appeal to universal considerations of human rights and common humanity; we may term it a humanitarian argument. The two arguments reinforced each other and together negated the claim of critics of U.S. military action that this was nothing more than an action of naked national interest aimed at protecting the supply of Persian Gulf oil.

The cases of Haiti, Somalia, and Bosnia exemplify a further extension of the internationalist and humanitarian arguments for interventionary use of U.S. military forces. In none of these cases—even that of Haiti, which is within the traditional sphere of interest of the United States and has been the object of American military intervention before—was a sustained national-interest argument advanced as the principal focus of efforts to justify the American military commitment. This is not to say that such an argument could not have been made; indeed, it would have been an important contribution to the ongoing public debate in these cases. The absence of such an argument tends to support the implication that the United States has no interests at stake in such cases as these. Without a national-interest argument, other sorts of justifications, those invoking the global responsibilities of the United States, were put first in the public debate: responsibilities following from membership in the United Nations; responsibilities as a rich, prestigious, and militarily powerful nation; responsibilities as a defender of human rights and a foe of starvation, privation, and the other harms suffered by the civilian populations of the three countries as a result of ongoing strife, which the interventions were intended to ameliorate.

It is important to note the particular moral element in these latter arguments. The internationalist argument appeals to responsibilities incurred as a result of the United States' commitment to maintaining world order and to the United Nations as a framework for multilateral action to respond to localized disasters and threats to international peace. The humanitarian argument appeals to American ideals and values as such, then extends our responsibility to support and protect those values and ideals wherever they are threatened. Both sorts of arguments are altruistic; both play on some of the best in what this nation stands for. Neither is easily subject to the criticisms most commonly directed against national-interest arguments for military intervention these days—that they are racist or militarist or justification for economic exploitation or misguided relics of the Cold War. Indeed, the internationalist and humanitarian justifications for intervention may implicitly challenge justifications based on national interest. Yet the opposite is also true: reasoning based on national interest may challenge that of internationalist and humanitarian arguments and may lead to contradictory judgments on the commitment of U.S. military forces. We have seen internationalist and humanitarian criticism focused against national-interest reasoning for intervention in the cases of Grenada and Panama, and the tables were turned in the debates over intervention in Haiti, Somalia, and Bosnia.

At the same time, it needs to be stated strongly that national-interest arguments, at their best, also are influenced by ethical concerns, concerns that are embodied in the definition of national interest in the first place. This is the meaning of political realism properly understood. The debate among national interest, internationalism, and humanitarianism is not, then, a debate between ethical considerations and concerns that are devoid of ethical content; rather what is at issue with these three perspectives is the nature, source, and relative strength of the ethical values and principles embodied in each.

Ethical analysis, at its best, provides a way to critique such competing justifications and claims and to reach judgments that avoid the particular criticisms each directs at the other; that national interest is inherently selfish; that intentional order is more of an ideal than a reality; that the United Nations structure is ill-suited to be a focus for decisions about military intervention and its nature and scope; that appeals to humanity are often extremely vague and open-ended. At the same time, ethical analysis should be framed in terms inclusive enough so that it can recognize the strengths and potential of each such approach, and particular enough so that it can provide useful guidance for policy and for specific decisions.

Collectively, these criteria constitute a tall order. Yet I will argue, together with other recent theorists of ethics and the use of force, that just-war tradition can meet them. In recent ethical writing on war such a claim has been made from a variety of perspectives. James F. Childress and Michael Walzer have advanced this same argument in a form suited to their own understanding of the nature and role of moral reasoning.[2] For Childress, just-war ideas are *prima facie* categories of ethical judgment, functionally universal within Western culture. That is, these categories represent the way people in our culture naturally think about war and set up a series of tests that any use of force must pass to be morally right. Walzer, in *Just and Unjust Wars*, writes, "I want to recapture the just war for political and moral theory" (p. xiv). Then he undertakes to do so by means of a systematic examination of cases that present the fundamental just-war ideas as having both historical and cross-cultural depth and by a philosophical argument that such standards are universal. Elsewhere, the US. Catholic bishops and such authors as William V. O'Brien[3] have argued for an understanding of just war rooted in natural law and hence universally valid. The prominent Protestant theologian Paul Ramsey, as noted earlier, finds in the idea of just war a general theory of statecraft, a perspective on the use of power in any political community anywhere.

My own approach is to understand the idea of just war as the product of a broad and inclusive historical tradition of experience, thought, and practice whose lasting relevance and power lies precisely in its having been shaped by contributions from many cultural sources and dialogues over time in many different contexts. In the following section I outline this approach to understanding just-war reasoning and to ethical analysis of uses of military force from a just-war perspective.

THE JUST-WAR TRADITION AS A RESOURCE FOR ETHICAL ANALYSIS OF THE USE OF MILITARY FORCE

The just-war tradition in Western culture is best understood as a broad river of ideas and practice moving through history, with specific streams now combining in various ways, now separating and moving along their own paths. This tradition is ethical not in the narrow sense of being a product of philosophical or theological reasoning but in a broader sense of collecting and systematically joining a range of ethical wisdom from many other contexts as well. To be sure, religious and philosophical efforts to define and shape morality have provided major contributions to the tradition as a whole. Yet along with the stream defined by Christian thought and practice and that of philosophical reasoning, there are others, also of major importance: those defined by secular law, both domestic and international; by the traditions of military life and the experience of war; and by the experience and customs of statecraft. Philosophy has helped to shape just-war tradition not only as a distinct stream of thought but as a mode of reasoning attached to religious, legal, military, and political discourse. Dialogue and mutual influence among the various streams have also been important in shaping the tradition as a whole. At times the Christian just-war doctrine developed in interaction with one or more of the other streams of the developing tradition, either influencing or being influenced or both; at other times it developed mainly in dialogue with its own internal concerns.

The development of just-war tradition is accordingly complex. But recognizing this complexity is a way to keep in mind that international law, military guides to conduct in war, and political conceptions of the appropriate use of force are all historically and thematically part of the broad just-war tradition, alongside more specifically moral and religious elements. Just-war reasoning about the use of force is not something alien that is imposed on political judgments or military thinking from outside. By its very nature this approach to the ethics of the use of force is already in dialogue with them. That there are differences of content and emphasis and tensions among these various approaches is, however, also the case, and this points at the necessity of an ongoing and sustained dialogue as the means of spelling out the contemporary implications of just-war tradition. This tradition as a whole reflects the totality of such interaction over history up to our own time.

The purposes of just-war reasoning have been defined by three levels of practical moral concern: the needs of statecraft, of the responsibilities of command, and of the individual moral agent. In the first of these respects it provides, as Paul Ramsey has argued,[4] a theory of statecraft that takes account of the connection between force and politics, establishing criteria for determining when the use of force for social good is justified and when it is not, and setting limits beyond which the justified use of force ought not to go. In the second respect, just-war tradition provides guidance to military commanders, placing their role and responsibilities in a larger context of value to be served by the forces at their command and locating their right to apply such force in relation to the ends rightly sought and the destruction of values to be avoided. Finally, at the level of the individual moral agent, just-war tradition offers moral guidance for conscientiously weighing the question of participation in the use of force and the degree of such participation.

Figure 1. Sources and Development of the Just War Tradition	
Late Classical Era: Deep Roots, Early Expressions	The Bible (Old and New Testaments) Roman law and practice Christian theology: writers such as Clement of Alexandria, Ambrose, Augustine
Medieval Era: Coalescence of a Cultural Consensus	Canon law: Gratian's *Decretum*, writings of the Decretists and Decretalists Scholastic theology The code and customs of chivalry Customary rights and practices of sovereigns The inherited idea of *jus gentium* (law of peoples or nations)

16th to 18th Centuries: Consolidation, Transformation, Differentiation	Transformation to natural-law base: Victoria, Suarez, Grotius, others Theory of international law: Grotius, Pufendorf, Vattel, others Military codes of discipline replacing chivalric code Limited-war theory and practice: "sovereigns' wars"
19th Century: Further Definition within Distinct Streams	Customary international law First Hague Conference Origin of Geneva Conventions Military manuals on the law of war Popular, philosophical, and religious efforts to restrain or end war
20th Century: Elaboration and Growing Interactions	Positive international law *Jus ad bellum*: League of Nations Covenant, Pact of Paris, UN Charter *Jus in bello*: arms limitation treaties and conventions, growth of humanitarian international law Military manuals on law of war, rules of engagement Religious and philosophical recovery of just-war concepts Public debate over war, its meaning and effects

Looked at as a whole, just-war tradition has two major thematic branches, classically denoted by the terms *jus ad bellum* and *jus in bello*. These have to do, respectively, with when it is just to resort to military force and what actions are justified in the use of such force. Historically the *jus ad bellum* has developed around a set of seven principles on how to justify resorting to war: the requirement that a war must have a just cause, be waged by proper authority and with a right intention, be undertaken only if there is reasonable hope of success and if the total good outweighs the total evil expected (overall proportionality), be a last resort, and be waged for the end [aim] of peace. Each of these criteria has a particular meaning as shaped and transmitted by the tradition.

Figure 2. Purposes of the Just War Tradition	
A Guide to Statecraft:	Theory of the use of force by the political community Understanding of the moral qualities of political leadership Protection of fundamental rights and values Relation of ends to means in political life
A Guide to Commanders:	Relation of military command to authority/purposes of political community Understanding of the moral qualities of military leadership Protection of fundamental rights and values in situations of armed conflict Moral limits on means and methods in conflict situations
A Guide to Individuals:	Claims on moral consciousness of individuals at all levels of political and military life Definition of responsibility in relation to the use of force by the political community Definition of the individual's rights and responsibilities in the use of force

Figure 3. The Just War Tradition as a Source of Criteria for Ethical Judgment

The *Jus ad Bellum*: Criteria Defining the Right to Resort to Force

Just Cause: The protection and preservation of value
Classic Statement: Defense of the innocent against armed attack; retaking persons, property, or other values wrongly taken; punishment of evil.

Right Authority: The person or body authorizing the use of force must be the duly authorized representative of a sovereign political entity. The authorization to use force implies the ability to control and cease that use—that is, a well-constituted and efficient chain of command.
Classic Statement: Reservation of the right to employ force to persons or communities with no political superior.

Right Intention: The intent must be in accord with the just cause and not territorial aggrandizement, intimidation, or coercion.
Classic Statement: Evils to be avoided in war, including hatred of the enemy, "implacable animosity," "lust for vengeance," desire to dominate.

Proportionality of Ends: The overall good achieved by the use of force must be greater than the harm done. The levels and means of using force must be appropriate to the just ends sought.

Last Resort: Determination at the time of the decision to employ force that no other means will achieve the justified ends sought. Interacts with other *jus ad bellum* criteria to determine level, type, and duration of force employed.

Reasonable Hope of Success: Prudential calculation of the likelihood that the means used will bring the justified ends sought. Interacts with other *jus ad bellum* criteria to determine level, type, and duration of force employed.

The Aim of Peace: Establishment of international stability, security, and peaceful interaction. May include nation-building, disarmament, other measures to promote peace.

The *Jus in Bello*: Criteria Defining the Employment of Force

Proportionality of Means: Means causing gratuitous or otherwise unnecessary harm are to be avoided. Prohibition of torture, means *mala in se*.

Classic Statement: Attempts to limit weapons, days of fighting, persons who should fight.

Noncombatant Protection/Immunity: Definition of noncombatancy, avoidance of direct, intentional harm to noncombatants, efforts to protect them.

Classic Statement: Lists of classes of persons (clergy, merchants, peasants on the land, other people in activities not related to the prosecution of war) to be spared the harm of war.

I noted earlier, however, that there are differences and tensions among the various component streams of the larger tradition and between each of them and the thrust of the tradition taken as a whole. In the context of considering the justification and limits of the national or international interventionary use of force, it is especially important to consider the tensions between international law, one of the main component streams of just-war tradition, and just-war ideas in their broadest form as classically defined.

The requirement of just cause classically meant one or more of three possibilities: that the use of force in question was for defense against wrongful attack, retaking something wrongly taken, or punishment of evil. Contemporary international law views defense as the only justifying cause for use of force—either defense by one nation or group of nations against an attack from another, or internationally sanctioned defense against a breach of international peace. Yet a closer look suggests that the other two classic ideas have simply been absorbed into a broadened concept of defense. A retaliatory second strike, for example, would classically have been called "punishment of evil": today it is categorized as "defense." The use of force to retake Kuwait from Iraq would have classically been called "retaking something wrongly taken"; in the language of contemporary international law, however, it was "defense" against an "armed attack" that remained in progress so long as Iraq occupied Kuwait. (The Falklands war provides a second recent example of this reasoning.)

So the underlying ideas remain, though the vocabulary has changed to reflect the modern sentiment that the first use of force is morally suspect, while the second use is not. It is not entirely clear whether this contemporary sentiment raises possible problems with the interventionary use of force across national borders for humanitarian reasons; the *prima facie* thrust of classic just-war reasoning is more favorable to such uses of force, not only as properly defending the rights of the innocent but also as "punishment of evil."

The requirement of proper authority limits the right to authorize force to sovereign political entities, that is, those with no superior. Classically this was a way to deny the right to resort to force to local strongmen and to individuals bearing arms. It was not intended to restrain legitimate sovereigns, who, because authorized to use force, could employ it against such local strongmen and marauders. This also has the *prima facie* effect of favoring certain kinds of interventionary uses of force: for example, in combating international terrorism, other forms of international lawlessness such as the traffic in illicit drugs, or systematic and sustained violations of universally recognized human rights. In positive international law, however, the limitation tends to flow the other way: aimed at limiting the right of states to resort to war with other states, it also limits the states' right of intervention. States have nonetheless continued to reserve that right for themselves and to practice it, and so customary international law is somewhat at variance with the black-letter law. Debate over national authority for intervention in the present context, accordingly, is somewhat confused.

Figure 4. The Just War Criteria in Positive International Law

Jus ad Bellum:

Just Cause: National or regional self-defense against armed attack; retaliation for armed attack; international response to threats to international peace.

Right Authority: *Compétence de guerre* possessed by states; some right to authorize force given to UN Security Council; some recognition of insurgency rights.

Right Intention: Not explicitly addressed, implicit in above items.

Proportionality of Ends: In the twentieth century, a tendency to treat the first use of force as the greatest evil, always disproportionate.

Last Resort: Emphasis on international arbitration and/or adjudication; tendency to allow only responsive or "second" use of force after armed attack.

Reasonable Hope of Success: Not explicitly treated.

The Aim of Peace: Greatly stressed. Limits on just causes for going to war, emphasis on *jus in bello* restraints, preference for stability over other values. Currently in process of some reevaluation.

Jus in Bello:

Proportionality of Means: "Hague law," arms limits, bans on means *mala in se*.

Noncombatant Protection/Immunity: Greatly stressed. "Geneva law," various other provisions regarding noncombatants, POWS, "protected persons." Not treated: injury to noncombatants received due to proximity to legitimate targets, longterm damages due to persisting effects of otherwise legitimate means of war.

The requirement of right authority also raises questions about intervention under international auspices. International organizations up to and including the United Nations lack sovereignty in the traditional sense. Lacking sovereignty, does such an organization have any right to authorize force? Classic just-war doctrine would say no, reserving that right for sovereign states. Yet in contemporary debate, international authorization for interventionary use of military force is often claimed, though on the basis of consensus (as in the Security Council resolutions relating to the Gulf War and to the United Nations protective force in Somalia) rather than sovereignty.

Right intention classically referred to the motivation of the individual soldier and meant that he should avoid lust for battle, hatred for the enemy, and other such attitudes. Well into the Middle Ages, for example, soldiers after combat were required to do penance in case, during the heat of battle, they had fought with the wrong intention. In contemporary usage this just-war criterion is closely linked to the idea of the end of peace, where it refers not to the individual soldier but to the purpose of the state in employing military force. In this context it requires that this purpose not serve some aggressive end but establish or reestablish such goals as international order and respect for human rights. International law has no explicitly specified notion of right intention, though arguably one can be deduced from other principles expressed there.

Reasonable hope of success, overall proportionality, and last resort are, for just-war tradition in its classic form, all prudential tests to be applied as additional checks when the above deontological requirements have been met. All are derived historically from Roman practice, and they refer to political prudence at any time and in any culture. International law does not specifically address them, and religious just-war theorists historically have paid little attention to them. Yet they have come to figure prominently in what Paul Ramsey called the *bellum contra bellum justum*[5] in Cold War-era ethical debate: the use of just-war categories to deny the very possibility of a just war. In this reasoning the destructive capabilities of contemporary weapons form the core of an argument that any use of force today must necessarily be disproportionate and hence unjust. It follows that there can be no reasonable hope of success, and that contemporary war can never reasonably be a last resort for serving justice, order, and peace, because it will by its nature create injustice, disorder, and more war. The *bellum contra bellum justum*, then, though sometimes called "just-war pacifism," is really just pacifism. It begins with a presumption against war, and it employs certain dogmatic assumptions about modern weapons to attempt to undercut the possibility of any contemporary just use of force on the grounds of the just-war principle of proportionality.

There are two important problems in this reasoning. First, there is nothing inherently disproportionately destructive in contemporary weaponry. Indeed, sophisticated contemporary guidance mechanisms today allow military targets to be destroyed with far less collateral damage than was the case in earlier conflicts. Second, the concept of proportionality in just-war tradition means the overall balancing of the good (and evil) that a use of force will create against the evil of not resorting to force. It begins with the recognition that a loss of value has already occurred (the just cause) prior to the consideration whether force is justified to restore that value. Rather than implicitly ruling out recourse to force, then the moral requirements of reasonable hope of success, overall proportionality, and last resort continue to be useful tests of the wise use of military power in given contexts.

The moral understanding of justified recourse to the use of force in contemporary American culture takes place in a historical context as reflected in just-war tradition. In general, given a world continuing to be beset by the presence of evil, moral reflection on how best to serve the ends of good statecraft is a perennial need. Yet for much of this century the focus of moral debate has been on a particular form of the use of military force, and sometimes focus has been on war between sovereign states itself as the evil to be countered. During the Cold War, the focus narrowed even further to the possibility of nuclear war between the superpowers. In the present historical context, though, the issues have shifted, and with that shift comes a renewed need to clarify how ethical principles on the use of force apply to military intervention across national borders. In short, what is needed is not only to understand these ethical principles themselves, but to reach an understanding of how they might be translated into the somewhat different language of practical national policy.

THE LANGUAGE OF ETHICS AND THE FORMATION OF POLICY: INTERVENTION FOR HUMANITARIAN REASONS

Where the interventionary use of force is at stake, policy language must be developed to put in practical terms the broader, more theoretical concerns of the just-war principles. For the sake of illustration I draw attention to one recent policy statement on the use of force, interesting in the present context because of its close adherence to just-war categories. This statement, former Secretary of Defense Caspar Weinberger's "six conditions for committing United States military forces" (the "Weinberger doctrine"),[6] emerged in the context of a debate over the interventionary use of military force to combat international terrorism, but the cautions it laid down bore implications for other sorts of potential interventionary uses of U.S. military power as well, up through Operation Desert Storm. It is, in my judgment, an unusually good example of how the tradition of just war may be translated into the language of policy, and in the contexts where it was employed, it served well as a guide to the commitment of U.S. military forces. Yet it has real limitations as well, and in the present historical context, renewed attention needs to be given in policy language to expressing the implications of the moral criteria carried by just-war tradition.

Figure 5. The Just-War Criteria in Policy Language: The "Weinberger Doctrine" of 1984

Jus ad Bellum: "Six Conditions for Committing United States Military Forces"

Just Cause: 1. When it is vital to the defense of national or allied interests.

Reasonable Hope of Success: 2. With the intention of winning.

- Sole object of winning
- Forces and resources sufficient to achieve objectives or not at all

Right Intention: 3. For clearly defined political and military objectives.

- Determine objectives
- Decide strategy

Proportionality of Ends: 4. With correlation between objectives and forces.

- If national interests require us to fight, then we must win.
- Assess and adjust force size and composition as necessary

Right Authority: 5. With public/congressional concurrence.

- Commit American public before American forces

Last Resort: 6. As last resort.

- Only when other means have failed or have no prospect for success
- Military force not a substitute for diplomacy

Aim of Peace: Not explicitly stated but implicit in 1 and 6.

It is important to note first that the context has indeed changed. In the debate over use of military force against international terrorism, against the international traffic in drugs, or even against Iraq after its takeover of Kuwait, a cogent case could be made that national interests were centrally at stake, and the question whether to commit forces or not and how much force to commit hinged on other issues.

Today, though, the interventionary use of military force for humanitarian purposes has moved to center focus, and in such cases national or allied interests may not be directly at stake or of pressing urgency. One is reminded that even in 1984, as his contribution to the debate that produced the Weinberger "six conditions," then Secretary of State George Shultz was framing the issue of just cause much more broadly, in terms of the need "to further the cause of freedom and enhance international security and stability."[7] There is no doubt that many Americans think of this nation's responsibilities abroad in terms of altruism and a high sense of moral purpose for America in the world. As a people we are strong defenders of human rights who are revolted by the abuse of these rights; we believe deeply in freedom and wish its blessings to extend to victims of tyranny; possessed by an optimism that sickness and hunger can be subdued, we are moved by the plight of victims of famine and disease. Theologian H. Richard Niebuhr, commenting on the missionary spread of American culture throughout the globe in the nineteenth century, described it as an effort "to bring light to the gentiles by means of lamps manufactured in America."[8] Where humanitarian impulses arise, such sentiment still surges: We can right the wrongs from which other peoples suffer, it says to us, and thus we ought to do so.

In seeking appropriate policy language for the concept of just cause, then, there is a *prima facie* case that such altruism and idealism should be taken into account. I also believe that such a broader understanding of the possible justifications for use of force better expresses the core moral purpose of the just-cause concept: defense of the innocent, retaking that which has been wrongly taken, punishing evil. What makes the case of intervention by force for humanitarian purposes so hard is that such moral justifications may be greatly compelling, and yet we still, in a given case, should not intervene by military force. There may not be the necessary authority to do so; there may be no reasonable hope of success; military intervention may produce more harm than good; other means of dealing with the crisis at hand may be more effective: and some forms of military intervention may hinder the cause of peace rather than serve it.

I have already suggested that the concept of right authority for the use of force is today confused by the somewhat contradictory implications of the historical ethical tradition, positive international law, and customary conceptions of the rights of sovereignty. As a result almost any imaginable argument for or against intervention that depends on only one of these rationales is open to challenge on the basis of the others, and the strongest authority for intervention comes from adding them together. This was in fact done quite successfully in the case of the Gulf War, where ethical argument, international law, and sovereign decisions by the nations taking part in the coalition against Iraq reinforced one another and established a claim to right authority well beyond what any one of them could have produced alone. Other contemporary cases are not characterized by such strong consensus, and authority for intervention suffers accordingly.

Right authority, though, does not refer simply to the decisions taken at the top; it also requires that the authority over the use of force extend downward through a well-constituted and effective chain of command, so that the forces in the field are genuinely directed by that responsible authority. In the present context, when much argument is being advanced that the United Nations should be regarded as the sole legitimate authority for interventionary projections of force in cases of humanitarian necessity or threats to international peace, it is essential to note that whatever the merits of this argument may be regarding the decisions at the top (a subject of hot debate), the United Nations does not now possess the intermediate structures necessary to project its authority downward to the level of directing the military forces in the field. On my reading of just-war tradition, then, it lacks right authority for commitment of interventionary forces unless this lack is remedied by the provision of a well-constituted and effective command structure by the nations cooperating in the provision of forces. Thus the United States has been correct not only in national-interest terms but also in moral terms to insist on retaining command of its forces when assisting in United Nations interventionary operations. Our national command authority is complete; that of the United Nations as currently constituted is not.

On the subject of right intention, I will simply observe that when the purpose of interventionary action is defined by humanitarian necessity, this goes a long way toward establishing right intent. Such intent is reinforced by a plan for ending the intervention at some future time or under some future conditions and, in the case of internationally sanctioned interventions, by rotation of national contingents over the period of the intervention.

Interventionary uses of military force should also be proportionate to the task at hand. There is a good deal of wrong thinking about this requirement in the moral debate, wrong usage that surfaces in arguments against such-and-such a use of military force as "disproportionate," that is, too large. This was a criticism directed against the U.S. use of force in the Gulf War, for example. It is a version of the *bellum contra bellum justum* identified earlier. But the just-war concept of proportionality does not equate to requiring that low levels of force should always be used. Rather, what proportionality requires is that the level and type of force be appropriate to accomplish the justified task and that the application of that force be such as to bring about more good than harm. This means that overwhelming force, sufficient to blanket hostile activities and snuff them out, may satisfy the criterion of proportionality better than a minimal commitment of force that soon finds itself confined to a fortified enclave and to patrolling and convoying, which may attract attacks and result in more harm than good. Understood this way, the criterion of proportionality reinforces the parallel requirement that uses of military force should be undertaken only when there is reasonable hope of success in achieving the justified mission of intervention.

Confusion also surrounds the way the criterion of last resort is used in recent debate. This criterion does not mean always postponing use of military force until every possible means short of force has been tried. If one comes into a situation late in the day, as is almost by definition the case when a conflict has created urgent humanitarian needs, working this gradualist way might simply postpone what is necessary until still later, perhaps making the situation worse and requiring a more robust, costly, and dangerous intervention when force is finally brought in. Rather, the just-war understanding of last resort is that in every case a determination should be made as to the kind of action that should be taken, with military intervention subordinated to other forms of action if they will work instead. This determination settles whether a situation of last resort exists. Thus it may exist at the initial point of national or international involvement in a crisis. This understanding of last resort also should be understood as serving the parallel requirements of proportionality, reasonable hope of success, and the aim of peace.

The criterion of reasonable hope of success implies, first, suiting the actions taken to the needs confronted, and in this sense it reinforces the conception of proportionality described above. But in the second place making a calculation of reasonable hope of success may serve as a brake on impulses toward a military intervention that is driven by the perception of urgent humanitarian need in the media. Requiring reasonable hope of success, along with last resort, serves as a reminder that military forces should not be seen as a cure-all for ills that other methods have not been able to remedy. The mere fact that nonmilitary forms of humanitarian intervention have been tried and failed in a given case does not mean that military forces should now be committed; in the case at hand they may not work either or may make for a worse situation. The truth is, moreover, that armies, navies, and air forces are not created for this as their primary purpose. The primary purpose of the U.S. military is our national defense, and the services are structured accordingly. These structures may not fit at all well the needs of a situation of humanitarian need, and there may be no reasonable hope of success in a military commitment.

Finally, the aim of peace is closely connected to the other just-war criteria already defined and can be said to be satisfied only when all the other criteria have themselves been met. Additionally, though, it should be noted that to satisfy this last criterion military intervention should be placed in the context of other means of addressing and solving the problem at hand. In some cases, nation-building may be a necessary adjunct to the provision of humanitarian relief or protection of relief efforts or the endangered population. In such cases, the idea of military intervention should include the possibility of not only fighters but engineers, communications teams, military police, and civil affairs units, or of civilian teams that would fulfill these functions and others necessary to the rebuilding of a stable civil order. Unfortunately, this implies a long-term involvement in the society into which intervention is made, and here moral responsibility runs head-on into a lack of political will and, perhaps, resources. I am not sure what this means for given cases of possible military intervention: Are we not to intervene except in those cases where we are willing to make a long-term commitment? I would rather say that our commitment should extend to considering how to restore a peaceful and functioning civil society, and to encouraging and supporting domestic and international efforts in that direction. Such consideration is an essential part of the moral debate about intervention, and it has been mostly lacking in recent American public discourse.

Explaining the aim of peace St. Augustine argued that no one in his right mind makes war in order to create more war; war is too terrible for that. Rather, one makes war in order to create the conditions for peace. We should judge not only war also but intervention by that standard and not lay our military forces on the line without a clear understanding of how their sacrifice will serve the cause of peace in the situation at hand.

NOTES

1. Paul Ramsey, *The Just War: Force and Political Responsibility* (New York: Charles Scribner's Sons, 1968), 5.
2. See James F. Childress, "Just War Theories: The Bases, Interrelations, Priorities, and Functions of Their Criteria," *Theological Studies* 39 (September 1978): 427–45; Michael Walzer, *Just and Unjust Wars.* New York: Basic Books, Inc., 1977.
3. See National Conference of Catholic Bishops, *The Challenge of Peace: God's Promise and Our Response* (Washington, D.C.: United States Catholic Conference, 1983), paragraphs 10, 78–110, and passim; William V. O'Brien, *The Conduct of Just and Limited War* (New York: Praeger Publishers, 1981), 4, 5, 13, 15, 56, 67, and passim.
4. Paul Ramsey, "A Political Ethics Context for Strategic Thinking," in *Strategic Thinking and Its Moral Implications*, edited by Morton A. Kaplan, 101–47 (Chicago: University of Chicago Press, 1973), 124–25.
5. See Paul Ramsey, *The Just War*, "Robert W. Tucker's *Bellum Contra Bellum Justum*," chap. 17 (pp. 391–424).
6. For a statement of the "six conditions," see Caspar W. Weinberger, *Report of Secretary of Defense Caspar W. Weinberger to the Congress*, 5 February 1986 (Washington, D.C.: U.S. Government Printing Office, 1986), 78–79.
7. Cited from George P. Shultz, "The Ethics of Power," *Department of State Bulletin*, February 1984, 1–3. For a comparison of the positions taken by Secretaries Weinberger and Shultz in relation to the just-war criteria, see James Turner Johnson, "The Recourse to War: An Appraisal of the 'Weinberger Doctrine,'" *Small Wars & Insurgencies* 1, no. 2 (August 1999): 160–67.
8. H. Richard Niebuhr, *The Kingdom of God in America* (New York: Harper Torchbooks, 1959), 179.

BIBLIOGRAPHY

Childress, James F. "Just War Theories: The Bases, Interrelations, Priorities, and Functions of Their Criteria," *Theological Studies* 39 (September 1978): 427–45.

National Conference of Catholic Bishops. *The Challenge of Peace: God's Promise and Our Response.* Washington, D.C.: United States Catholic Conference, 1983.

Niebuhr, H. Richard. *The Kingdom of God in America.* New York: Harper Torchbooks, 1959.

O'Brien, William V. *The Conduct of Just and Limited War*. New York: Praeger Publishers, 1981.

Ramsey, Paul. *The Just War: Force and Political Responsibility*. New York: Charles Scribner's Sons, 1968.

Ramsey, Paul. "A Political Ethics Context for Strategic Thinking." *Strategic Thinking and Its Moral Implications*, edited by Morton A. Kaplan, 101–47. Chicago: University of Chicago Press, 1973.

Schultz, George P. "The Ethics of Power." *Department of State Bulletin* (February 1984): 1–3.

Walzer, Michael. *Just and Unjust Wars*. New York: Basic Books, Inc., 1977.

Weinberger, Caspar W. *Report of Secretary of Defense Caspar W. Weinberger to the Congress*. Washington, D.C.: U.S. Government Printing Office, 1986.

ABSTRACT

In this essay, Johnson mines four reasons why the question of preemptive use of force is worthy of consideration. He looks at the question of preemption through the lenses of national security international law, and the idea articulated by recent Roman Catholic thought of a "presumption against war" before presenting an answer in affirmative support of the potential of preemption. He contends that within the just war tradition there are times when preemption is legitimate, enumerating the necessary requirements to justify state use of preemption.

CHAPTER 5

THE QUESTION OF PREEMPTION

Should a nation ever use its military forces preemptively? If so, what conditions are necessary to justify such use of force? There are various ways of approaching this question and seeking to answer it, and they do not all lead to the same answers. At the same time, three considerations suggest that it should be addressed. The first is that reaching a conclusion on preemptive use of military force requires settling the broader question of when it is right to resort to force in the service of national security, in the settling of international disputes, and in the conception of the international order. The second is that pragmatically, preemption must be addressed, because circumstances arise which raise it as a possible policy option. The third consideration is that for many people preemption is always morally wrong, whatever the circumstances, and therefore its place in the spectrum of policy choices should be assessed.

In this paper I examine the question of preemption from four perspectives, concluding with an argument from just war tradition that there is a moral place for preemptive resort to military force. The just war framework bears directly on the question of the place of preemption in national and international politics, for fundamentally just war tradition defines a theory of the right use of force in statecraft. This approach also addresses the circumstances in which preemption may be justified, since the just war approach to the morality of given uses of force takes account of both principles and contexts.

To provide a broader frame for this focal discussion, I examine preemption from three other current perspectives, those of national security, international law, and the "presumption against war" recently argued to be at the base of Christian doctrine on the use of military force.

PREEMPTION IN THE NATIONAL SECURITY CONTEXT

Within the context of thinking about national security, preemption stands alongside deterrence, defense, and retaliation as possible ways by which military force may be employed to protect national interests. These four are interlinked, and preemption is not likely to move to the forefront of policy choice unless there is a serious inadequacy in the others, particularly in deterrence of a threat or the likely efficacy of defense against that threat. A practical reason for caution about preemption follows from the fact that, as first overt resort to force in a conflict, it directly puts lives at risk and may result in war or other forms of retaliation by force, such as terrorist attack. At the same time, the case for preemption in the national security context is that even though it is not without risks or costs, it prevents something worse from happening that otherwise would have taken place. In this context the possibility of preemptive use of military force thus must be taken seriously.

To see how this is so, and to illustrate the interlinked nature of deterrence, defense, retaliation, and preemption, we need only consider the last serious national debate over preemption, which was focused on the particular problem of the nuclear threat posed by the Soviet Union during the Cold War.

This debate was launched by the concern that a nuclear first strike by the Soviet Union might destroy enough of the United States' nuclear forces to remove the possibility of a credible retaliatory strike. If this were so, or were calculated to be so, the deterrent effect of a threatened retaliatory strike would be lost. Indeed, the chances of war might increase, since the nation that launched a nuclear first strike would, on these terms, clearly win. The same reasoning applied, of course, to a first strike by the United States and the possibility that it might remove the ability of the Soviet Union to launch a retaliatory strike. In such an eventuality, there is an incentive to strike first, since the only way to achieve protection against an enemy's first nuclear strike would be to launch a preemptive strike before the enemy did so. While the framework of nuclear deterrence was essentially established by the time of the Eisenhower presidency, a renewed focus on the possibility that deterrence might fail was one element providing the context for the military restructuring undertaken during the Reagan era. Two components of that restructuring aimed specifically at dealing with the logic that pointed toward a preemptive first nuclear strike. The first were efforts to enhance nuclear deterrence, such as reducing the lead time necessary to launch a retaliatory strike and a shift in emphasis away from land-based nuclear forces toward the relatively invulnerable submarine-launched ballistic missiles. The second component was the Strategic Defense Initiative, the effort to develop a workable defense against strategic missiles. So long as no effective defensive shield could be raised against such missiles, security policy against nuclear weapons had to be centered on deterrence alone, which in turn rested on the threat of retaliation. The prospect of even a partially effective defense changed the balance, both militarily and in terms of policy toward nuclear weapons. A credible defense adds to deterrence, since there is no point to an attack that can be blunted so that it does not achieve its goal. Both these features, enhancing the retaliatory capacity so as to increase deterrence and undertaking to develop a strategic missile defense, undercut and diminished the force of the argument for preemption, which accordingly faded as a policy option. This example illustrates how the case for preemption waxes or wanes according to the relative robustness of the other three purposive uses of military force: deterrence, defense, and retaliation. When these latter are strong, there is effectively no case to be made for preemption in national security terms. When one or more are weak, the case for preemption becomes more urgent. Thinking in terms of non-nuclear threats, since World War II the United States has had no serious reason to fear a conventional armed attack of the kind that have traditionally begun wars: actions by the military forces of one state against another across the latter's borders or against vital national interests of the latter. Strictly in military terms, the United States has been protected against such attacks by a military that has had robust capability to mount an effective defense and, no less important, to retaliate with devastating force. The major exceptions to these generalizations were the Korean and Vietnam wars, two cases in which the United States' defensive and retaliatory capacities were blunted by distance, by other obligations, by the overall strategy, and, in the case of Vietnam, by internal questioning of the idea that national interests were in fact at stake. These exceptions, however, reinforce the general rule. The United States during this period has simply been too strong to attack directly with a conventional armed force. For this reason the question of preemption has not arisen in this context.

By contrast, consider Israel's preemptive attacks against the armed forces of the surrounding Arab states at the beginning of the Six-Day War of 1967. This case is perhaps the most widely debated preemptive use of conventional military force in the last fifty years. In many ways it stands as a classic example of preemption rightly understood, and I will have more to say about it later on. For the present, though, my point is only to contrast the position of the United States in the post-World War II period with that of Israel relative to the threat posed by the surrounding Arab states in 1967. Israel had no capability to deter the expected war, and its ability to defend and retaliate after the anticipated attack had been launched were seriously in question. In this context, preemption rose to first place among the four possible uses of military force in the service of national security.

The kind of non-nuclear threat posed against the United States since 1945 has not been conventional war against American territory but various kinds of lower-level threats. The Korean and Vietnamese conflicts, as well as the Gulf War, represent one type of these: attacks on United States interests abroad using conventional military means. Another form of serious threat, experienced mostly but not entirely abroad, has been that of terrorist activity. A further kind of threat during this period has been criminal activity, exemplified by the drug trade. Military doctrine on limited war and low-intensity conflict, as well as corresponding policy, has responded to these forms of threat to national security in various ways. With the end of the Cold War and the collapse of the Soviet Empire the possibility of nuclear war no longer represents the major security threat to the United States and its interests. Instead, these latter dangers have gained in relative importance, and some of these are threats for which there is a deficiency in both deterrence and defense. Indeed, since the context of such threats is no longer bipolar but multipolar, the problem of adequately meeting them is more complicated. It is in this context that the question of preemptive use of United States military force once again arises.

Where deterrence and defense lack effectiveness, retaliation and preemption are left as the only means for military response to threats against national security. In such a circumstance there is little or no reason to prefer the former over the latter. If a threat is certain, why is it better to wait until it is realized to respond to it? Earlier I noted two cautions which apply to preemptive uses of force: they put American lives at risk and escalate a conflict to the shooting stage. But the former also applies to any use of force, including retaliation. Waiting to retaliate after harm has been done does not in itself confer possession of the moral high ground. In national security terms, such waiting in the face of a certain attack is just foolish; in moral terms, as I will argue below, the issue is not who uses force first but whether the use is justified or not. Retaliation has no moral priority over preemption. Indeed, if a threat is such that lives are already at risk, and if an attack is certain; or if the conflict has already begun covertly, through proxies, or at a lower level than open war, then preemptive resort to force may represent the best way to conceive a military response, if a military response is itself the best way to counter the threat at hand.

PREEMPTION IN THE CONTEXT OF INTERNATIONAL LAW

In practice any decision to employ military force preemptively must take account of the fact that there is a substantial body of opinion that international law prohibits first resort to force in the settlement of disputes among nations, whatever justifications for such action may be present. This approach to restraining the incidence of war is relatively new, dating only to the Pact of Paris (or Kellogg-Briand Pact) of 1928. Current positive international law relating to this approach is defined by certain language in the United Nations Charter. Article 2 of the Charter prohibits members "from the threat or use of force against the territorial integrity or political independence of any state," while Article 51 explicitly confers on individual states or groups of states acting collectively the right to use force to resist "armed attack" from another party.

Where one comes down on the status of preemptive resort to force in positive international law depends on how one reads these two passages from the Charter. The debate has centered on exactly what is forbidden and what may be defended against. The language employed in the two critical passages is importantly different. Article 2 forbids "the threat or use of force," while the explicit sanction of self-defense in Article 51 is aimed at "armed attack" (emphasis added in both cases). If the latter is read restrictively, so that the only justified resort to force is in response to "armed attack," and if Article 51 is understood as taking precedence over the language of Article 2 because of its specificity about when force is allowed, then the result is a reading of positive international law that rests on a first-use, second-use distinction. On this reading all first resorts to force constitute "armed attack," while second uses are justified defense against such attack. Applying this to the now-classic case of the Six-Day War, Israel's preemptive strike against the forces of the Arab states was unjustified (as Charles de Gaulle argued at the time), even though the latter were on the verge of attacking Israel themselves, because first use of force is the "armed attack" prohibited in the Charter, while second use is the permitted action of self-defense.[1] An opposite line of argument, however, has also developed on what is forbidden and what permitted by the Charter. Since Article 2 forbids not only the use but also the threat of force, and since customary international law prior to the Charter had always allowed preemptive response to a threat under way, Article 2 has the effect of maintaining this customary allowance of preemption. On this reading the language of Article 51 only specifies one kind of case in which self-defense is clearly permitted. As Morton Kaplan and Nicholas Katzenbach put it, "The wording...does not clearly forbid self-defense prior to armed attack but only sanctions self-defense as permissible in case of armed attack.[2]"

My purpose here is not to marshal the full case for one or the other of these readings of contemporary international law, but only to identify the two sides of the argument and the main line of reasoning attached to each. My own judgment, approaching the issues as a historian, is that the latter reading is the better one. This is borne out by the actual practice of states since 1945, the practice that establishes "customary" international law, that is, the law that states actually believe applies. In state practice during this period there have been numerous explicit references to Article 51 as justifying armed response to a prior use of force (the Coalition action against Iraq in the Gulf War and British action against Argentina in the Falklands War provide two prominent recent examples), but states have implicitly maintained their traditional right to resort to preemptive use of force when an attack is imminent. The United States in particular has held to this customary understanding of international law on the use of force, as in the debate over nuclear preemption discussed above, for example. But the other side of this argument has significant support, and so it must be taken seriously whenever a case of preemption arises.

PREEMPTION IN THE CONTEXT OF A MORAL "PRESUMPTION AGAINST WAR"

In their widely influential 1983 pastoral letter, *The Challenge of Peace*, the National Conference of Catholic Bishops of the United States wrote the following: "The Church's teaching on war and peace establishes a strong presumption against war which is binding on all; it then examines when this presumption may be overridden, precisely in the name of preserving the kind of peace which protects human dignity and human rights."[3] A bit later this was reiterated in a slightly different form: the decision to go to war, "especially today, requires extraordinarily strong reasons for overriding the presumption in favor of peace and against war."[4]

In the context of the pastoral letter this understanding of the basis of Christian moral doctrine on war led to a position not unlike the first-use, second-use reasoning found in contemporary debate over the meaning of international law on war. While recognizing "the principle of legitimate self-defense," however,[5] *The Challenge of Peace* limited even the use of force for this purpose. Self-defense by armed force was allowed only "if necessary as a last resort,"[6] interpreted to mean that "all peaceful alternatives must have been exhausted" in order for resort to armed force to be justified.[7] This was a significant restriction of the right of use of force even in self-defense.

Exactly what the argument of the American Catholic bishops in *The Challenge of Peace* means for actual policy on the use of force has been much debated since even before the final version of this document appeared. Indeed, what it means in terms of moral guidance for Catholics remains controversial. The pastoral letter is not an official teaching of the Catholic magisterium, and no such formal teaching has identified Christian doctrine on war as beginning with a "presumption against war." Yet in the context of American debate over the resort to armed force the pastoral letter has had an undoubted effect. Seeking a broader authority for the position taken by the American bishops, Fr. J. Bryan Hehir has argued that recent papal statements on war are consonant with the idea of a "presumption against war" as defined in *The Challenge of Peace*.[8] In one place Hehir interprets a statement of Pope John Paul II on the Gulf War as follows: the resort to force in this case "is not justified even though a just cause exists."[9] Other religiously based opinion on this conflict, non-Catholic as well as Catholic, accepted the extreme understanding of last resort in *The Challenge of Peace* and argued against a forceful response to Iraq's aggression on the grounds that all possible nonforceful means had not been exhausted.[10]

The "presumption against war" in action appears to imply that even defensive responses to previous armed attacks may not be morally justified. Preemption of a threat by conventional logic of the argument advanced there would seem to leave little if any space for such resort to force. If even after an attack has begun last resort inhibits a military response, is it conceivable that last resort would not prohibit a preemptive strike?

The only specific discussion of first use of military force found in this document is focused on nuclear weapons. The historical context of *The Challenge of Peace* was, after all, the debate over United States policy on the use of nuclear weapons for deterrence and in war. In that context the American Catholic bishops ultimately accepted the possession of such weapons for deterrence while denying the morality of using them in war for whatever reasons.[11] In this discussion they specifically opposed the development and possession of nuclear weapons directed toward a "first-strike" capability, but more broadly, they rejected any "war-fighting" strategy involving nuclear weapons as immoral. So preemption, in the sense of a nuclear first strike, is clearly rejected here, but it seems that retaliation in response to a previous enemy strike is also ruled out. For nuclear weapons, then, the "presumption against war" issues in a prohibition of the use of nuclear weapons whatever the justifying circumstances, whether first (preemptive) or second (retaliatory) strike.

JUST WAR TRADITION AND PREEMPTIVE USE OF FORCE

The previous two sections have identified serious arguments against preemptive use of armed force rooted in an understanding of positive international law and in the recent claim of a "presumption against war" in Christian moral doctrine. My earlier discussion of preemption in the context of national security considerations, by contrast, identified a place for preemption alongside the other forms use of armed force may take (deterrence, the justifying causes for defence, and retaliation). In my discussion of international law I have already argued for a reading of positive and customary law preserving preemption as an element in the right of self-defense. In the present section I want to focus on the moral argument through an examination of the implications of just war tradition for the question of preemption.

The first thing to say is that, counter to the argument of the American Catholic bishops, Christian just war theory does not begin with a "presumption against war." The evil the early theorists who shaped Christian just war thought addressed was not war or violence but injustice. According to Augustine, quoted approvingly by Thomas Aquinas, injustice in the use of force might be manifest in "the passion for inflicting harm, the cruel thirst for vengeance, an unpacific and relentless spirit, the fever of revolt, the lust of power, and such like things."[12] By contrast, rightly directed uses for force aim at good: "True religion looks upon as peaceful those wars which are waged not for motives of aggrandizement, or cruelty, but with the object of securing peace, of punishing evil-doers, and of uplifting the good."[13] The role of the ruler, and more broadly of proper statecraft in general, was accepted as defined by Paul in Romans 13:4: "He beareth not the sword in vain: for he is God's minister to execute wrath upon him that doth evil."[14]

The justifying causes for resort to force accepted in classic Christian just war thought were the same ones that had been accepted by imperial Rome: defense, recovery of something wrongly taken away, and punishment of evil. For the medieval theorists this was set within a concept of politics as defined by three goods or purposes: order, justice, and peace. The goal of good statecraft, following the passage from Romans, is to act in God's stead to ensure an order in accord with justice; this in turn was understood to be the way to the third good, peace. Without order and justice real peace could never exist.

It is noteworthy, in the present context, that the question of preemption was not specifically addressed in just war theory from the time of Augustine, in the fourth century, until Grotius, writing in the 1620s. The order of the use of force, so important in the twentieth century, was simply not an issue for classic just war thought, whether by ecclesiastics or by secular writers. What was important was the reason for resort to force: whether it served justice or not. Indeed, one influential interpreter of the medieval scholastic tradition on just war argues that the purpose of punishing evil constituted the most important justifying reason for resort to force in this tradition.[15] There was clearly no "presumption against war" at work here.

The first direct discussion of preemption by a theorist in the line of just war tradition is that of Grotius in *The Law of War and Peace*, first published in 1625. His argument remains a model of moral clarity and may be taken as establishing the baseline for the implications of just war reasoning on preemption. Following the inherited tradition, Grotius identified defense, recovery of property, and punishment as justifying causes for resort to force. Going beyond earlier writers, though, he continued by explicitly including preemption in his concept of defense: "The first just cause of war…is an injury, which even though not actually committed, threatens our persons or our property."[16] Medieval just war thought had defined the prince's role in using force to be proactive in response to evildoing; Grotius's shift of focus was to recognize that such evildoing extends to preparations for armed attack, not simply the attack itself. He took pains to clarify what he had in mind:

> The danger [to be defended against] must be immediate, and as it were, at the point of happening. If my assailant seizes a weapon with an obvious intent of killing me, I admit too that I have a right to prevent the crime.[17]

In his argument for preemptive use of force under certain clear conditions Grotius was developing an implicit argument from within just war theory, not introducing an innovation. Similarly, James Brown Scott finds a tacit approval of preemptive defense in Grotius's predecessor Vitoria.[18] In both these early modern theorists the acceptance of preemption reflected a common assumption that protection of justice centrally requires protection of the state, an assumption which led to an emphasis on defense as just cause that is thoroughly modern. This focus on defense reflected a different sensibility from that found in the medieval theorists. The latter were perfectly willing to justify many resorts to force which would in twentieth-century context be liable to criticism as cases of "first use" of force. Their rationale was to appeal to the just causes of punishment of evil and recovery of things wrongly taken. Grotius (and implicitly Vitoria) built on this and reshaped it by allowing first use of force also when the just cause is defense of the state.

Grotius's explicit discussion of preemption made it possible for him to distinguish justified preemptive uses of force from unjustified offensive uses—a kind of distinction lost in the first use-second use dichotomy in contemporary positive international law, and in the moral argument based on a "presumption against war." Grotius's distinction demonstrates his conviction, reflecting the fundamental conception of just war tradition as a whole, that the focus must be on the justice of a particular resort to force, not on who first attacks, and not on the presumed evil of force in itself.

No sooner did Grotius declare preemptive resort to force to be allowable in defense than he began to erect safeguards against unwarranted offensive uses of force. "[P]ersons," he wrote, "who regard any sort of fears as a just ground for the precautionary killing of another person are themselves greatly deceived and deceiving to others."[19] Later he limited resort to preemption still further:

> But quite inadmissible is the doctrine proposed by some, that by the law of nations it is right to take up arms in order to weaken a rising power, which, if it grew too strong, might do us harm.... [T]hat the

> bare possibility that violence may be some day turned on us gives us the right to inflict violence on others is a doctrine repugnant to every principle of justice.[20]

In short, to employ preemptive self-defense it is necessary that the enemy's intent to attack be absolutely certain. Even in such cases Grotius counseled caution and other efforts to defuse the crisis (though he did not take the extreme "last resort" position described in the previous section of this essay), reasoning that war is a 'horrible' thing."[21]

The final safeguard Grotius provided to prevent justified preemption from degenerating into unjustified attacks based on "any sort of fears" was the requirement that, when a war is begun, its causes be stated publicly so that "the whole human race, as it were, might weigh the justice of them."[22] Thus the right of states to judge whether they have a just cause to resort to armed force is limited by their being implicitly held accountable in a court of "the whole human race."

In summary, Grotius' development of the idea of just cause for resort to armed force both embodied the established just war tradition and further developed its implications. His argument for preemption followed from his emphasis on defense among the justifications for resort to force he drew from earlier just war thought. Yet he was the first theorist in this tradition to examine preemption explicitly. Doing so allowed him to strengthen the moral argument for defense of the state while also reiterating cautions about using military means for aggression and other self-serving ends.

In both these respects Grotius held to the center of the essential just war idea as defined by Augustine and later medieval just war theory. On this conception the fundamental justification for resort to force is injustice, and what is evil in war is various sorts of self-serving rationales in the place of the service of justice. The horrors of war caution against rash resort to arms, but desire to avoid them does not take precedence over the idea that in some cases resort to arms is the only effective way to deal with a serious violation of justice. In all these respects Grotius, like just war tradition before him, held to a position significantly different from those defined in the first use-second use of force dichotomy in international law and the "presumption against war" argument of the American Catholic bishops. If we follow through the just war argument as focused by Grotius, what implications does it have for the contemporary context? Let me offer three general considerations.

First, the behavior of states since 1945 has not ratified the effort in Article 2 of the UN Charter to disallow cross-border projections of force except after a first military attack. In regard to impending military attacks, the analysis and argument put forward by Grotius correspond closely to the actual state of contemporary customary international law and the standard for what is morally allowable in resort to armed force.

Second, the current scene requires recognition that, at the level of the state, a threat may not take the form of an impending military attack but may nonetheless pose a "clear and present danger" to national security. Such nonmilitary threats include the drug trade, terrorism and nonmilitary forms of hostile acts by the leadership of foreign countries or with their approval and support. Defense against such threats may include preemptive resort to force, including such varied sorts of action as seizing drug-transporting ships at sea, a covert military strike against a training center for terrorists, or an action designed to give notice to a foreign government that it should cease support of activities hostile to the United States. At the same time, Grotius's caution should be kept in mind. Lacking an imminent attack, seeking nonmilitary ways of dealing with such threats should be preferred.

Third, at a level including groups of nations, a major element in the present context is the possibility of uses of military force in response to major violations of universal values which the local government has not sought to remedy (indeed, it may itself be the source of the violations) or is unable to correct. While the term "intervention" is usually applied to such uses of force, this kind of military action may be preemptive, deterrent, defensive, or retaliatory depending on circumstances. Interventionary uses of force are preemptive if the violations in question represent a threat, even if indirect, to national values and interests and/or to international peace and security.

Reflection on preemption in just war terms in the present context requires a prior acceptance of the idea of just cause for resort to military force as defined in terms of the need to protect justice. Just cause may in some cases proceed from concerns of national interest that include but go beyond immediate threat of military attack, and in other instances it may proceed from concern to protect universal values, remedy their violation, and prevent violations from continuing. The use of military force that is justified in these ways is more analogous to police work than to war. It is far from the kind of resort to force envisioned in past international legal efforts to restrict military action to responses to armed attack, where the focus was on preventing the initiation of war between nations—war that might escalate to become total in its means and draw other nations into it so that it became global. While the concept of just cause just described includes this as an extreme possibility, it chiefly has to do with far more restrained and local applications of military force. Where, in this reasoning, do interests end and ideals begin? In the present environment these are not discrete alternatives but mutually supplemental sources for the idea of justice in just cause for resort to armed force. Indeed, I would carry this argument further. If the paradigm is that provided by a narrow reading of Article 51 of the United Nations Charter, so that individual states and regional organizations of states may resort to force only in armed self-defense against attack by other armed force, then the argument from national or regional security interests fits it well. But recent history has produced a different paradigm, one in which the rights reserved in positive law to the United Nations are exercised in a *de facto* manner by regional organizations and individual states, as in the coalition responding to Iraq's aggression in the Gulf War, the intervention in Somalia, and the NATO presence in Bosnia. On this paradigm not only state interests narrowly conceived, but also broadly recognized values must be taken into account.

As compared to the skepticism about all uses of force in recent Catholic teaching, the understanding of the current state of affairs I have sketched is one more obviously akin to the reasoning employed by classic Christian just war theorists to describe both the responsibility to use force in service of the neighbor and the limits of such uses of force. The denials of the right to resort to force even when just cause exists which were put forward in recent papal statements and paralleled in much other recent religious discourse on war do not apply when what is assumed is not a war of nations on the model of the World Wars or a massively destructive nuclear exchange between the superpowers, but a limited application of force which is in accord with internationally accepted values and which takes place with the express or tacit authority of the community of nations, even though national interests may also be served by such action. These considerations apply to preemption as well as to the other forms use of force may take: deterrence, defense, or retaliation.

NOTES

1. For discussion see Henri Meyrowitz, *Le Principe d'egalite des belligerents devant le droit de la guerre* (Paris: A. Pedone, 1970), pp. 144–48.
2. Morton A. Kaplan and Nicholas deB. Katzenbach, "Resort to Force: War and Neutrality," in Richard A. Falk and Saul H. Mendlovitz, eds., *The Strategy of World Order, vol. II, International Law* (New York: World Law Fund, 1966), p. 290 n. 3.
3. National Conference of Catholic Bishops, *The Challenge of Peace: God's Promise and Our Response* (Washington, D.C.: United States Catholic Conference, 1983), p. 22 at par. 70 (emphasis added).
4. Ibid., p. 27 at par. 83 (emphasis in text).
5. Ibid., pp. 22ff.
6. Ibid., p. 24 at par. 75.
7. Ibid., p. 30 at par. 96.
8. J. Bryan Hehir, "Just War Theory in a Post-Cold War World," *The Journal of Religious Ethics*, vol. 20, no. 2 (Fall, 1992), pp. 248–52.
9. Ibid., p. 250.

10. See, for example, "Testimony of Archbishop Roach Before a Senate Committee." pp. 117–29 in James Turner Johnson and George Weigel, *Just War and the Gulf War,* (Washington, D.C.: Ethics and Public Policy Center, 1991), especially pp. 125–26; see also pp. 93.
11. *The Challenge of Peace*, op. cit., pp. 56–62 at pars. 178–99.
12. Thomas Aquinas, *Summa Theologica*, II/II (New York et al., Benziger Brothers, Inc., 1947), p. 1360 at Q. 40, Article 1.
13. Ibid.
14. Quoted ibid.
15. Alfred Vanderpol, *La Doctrine scolastique du droit de guerre* (Paris: A. Pedone, 1919), p. 250.
16. Hugo Grotius, *The Law of War and Peace* (Roslyn, NY: Walter J. Black, Inc.), p. 72 at Book II, Chapter I, section 2.
17. Ibid., p. 73 at Book II, Chapter I, section 4.
18. James Brown Scott, *The Spanish Origin of International Law* (Oxford: The Clarendon Press; London: Humphrey Milford, 1934), pp. 200–207.
19. Grotius, op. cit., p. 73 at Book II, Chapter I, section 4.
20. Ibid., p. 77 at Book II, Chapter I, section 17.
21. Ibid., pp. 74–75 at Book II, Chapter I, section 9.
22. Ibid., p. 267 at Book II, Chapter XXVI, section 4.

ABSTRACT

In this essay from the late 1990s, Johnson traces the fundamental elements of and major changes in just war thinking during the 20th century, with an emphasis on the recent three decades of thought regarding just war and policy implications of those conversations. As a tradition of moral reasoning regarding the use of force, the just war tradition has been a mediating position for centuries and Johnson argues that its relevance remains strong in the present era.

CHAPTER 6

THE BROKEN TRADITION AND QUESTION OF WHETHER FORCE CAN BE USED JUSTLY*

In the ongoing argument between foreign policy realists and idealists, the just-war tradition of moral reasoning about the use of force has played a crucial mediating role for centuries. Rooted in the conviction that all human action—even in the distinctive field of international affairs, and even in the extremity of war—is susceptible to moral scrutiny and judgment, the just-war tradition has insisted that moralists take a realistic account of politics as an arena of conflict in which the quest for justice and peace is inevitably fraught with ambiguity and disagreement. Its mediation has also enabled statesmen to maintain an accepted role for moral judgment in the very domain—that of war—farthest from the regular application of human compassion, law, and comity. Just-war theory has, in short, been a civilized and civilizing agent in the darkest corners of the human social endeavor, and it has kept the church from straying too far from the realm of this world.

The ancient question "How can the use of force serve just ends?" that has been the centerpiece of Christian reflection on just war from the fifth century has lost none of its urgency today. Indeed, post-Cold War international politics offers a fertile field for reflection by moral

* A later and edited version of this manuscript appeared under the title "The Broken Tradition."

philosophers and statesmen alike, as the world stands on the edge of the third millennium of the common era. With the fear of and focus on superpower nuclear tensions now subsided, world politics offers situation after situation in which one can imagine the use of proportionate and discriminate force serving just and prudential ends.

Yet, as in other disciplines and sub-disciplines that treat such matters, just-war theorists often find themselves at sea today. The reason, however, has less to do with the confusions of the post-Cold War world or the classic canons of just-war thinking than with the intellectual deterioration of that theory itself in influential quarters. Precisely when statesmen might well look to just-war theory for guidance on the always-tangled questions of relating appropriate means to desirable ends, many contemporary just-war theorists are engaged in a process of self-marginalization. Pressed by the experience of two world wars and the special circumstances of the nuclear age, and tempted by secular ideological notions, these theorists have altered the very ground on which the theory itself has stood for more than a thousand years. While the core of just-war tradition is based on opposition to injustice, the recent metathesis is based instead on a "presumption against war"—a very different matter indeed.

The burden of this essay is to trace briefly the essential elements and philosophical bedrock of just-war theory, and to show how it has changed over the last century—and especially over the past three decades. I argue that recent changes reflect contingent judgments on the nature of modern war that do not match the character of contemporary armed conflicts. I conclude by suggesting that, in its original form, just-war theory remains relevant to the challenges faced by statesmen today. I illustrate this relevance by identifying several contemporary policy implications that follow from understanding the just-war idea as aimed against injustice rather than against the use of force itself.

THE CLASSIC JUST-WAR IDEA

The just-war tradition addresses two issues regarding the morality of the use of force: when it is right to resort to armed force, and what it is right to do when using force—*jus ad bellum* and *jus in bello,* respectively. While these two issues are related, the question of permissibility has priority, for absent the determination that a use of force is morally justified, even the most strictly delimited means are, in terms of the just-war tradition, unjust.

The requirements of *jus ad bellum* are clear in the theory, especially as developed by Thomas Aquinas in the thirteenth century. Above all, the resort to force must have a just cause. It must also be authorized by a competent authority, and it must be motivated by the right intention. And it must pass four prudential tests: that it be expected to produce a preponderance of good over evil; that it has a reasonable chance of success; that it be a last resort; and that its expected outcome establish peace. Some commentators add that a just war must also be formally declared, but most agree that the first three requirements subsume this one as well.

The requirements of *jus in bello* are also clear. The use of force must be discriminate (it must distinguish the guilty from the innocent), and it must be proportional (it must distinguish necessary force from gratuitous force).

A study of the just-war tradition suggests that, above all, the first requirement of *jus ad bellum*—that it have a just cause as a response to injustice—is the font of the entire tradition. This becomes obvious if we examine several benchmark figures in the evolution of just-war theory.

The origins of a specifically Christian tradition on just war are to be found in the thought of Augustine and his mentor, Ambrose of Milan, in the fourth and fifth centuries. They inherited—and did not challenge—a Christian consensus that the example and teaching of Jesus required that Christians not defend themselves when attacked but should instead turn the other cheek when confronted with violence. But first Ambrose and then Augustine reasoned that the prohibition of self-defense did not imply that a Christian might not defend his neighbor when attacked. On the contrary, they argued, it is a duty of Christian love to defend the innocent in such circumstances. Not providing such defense is itself morally wrong: as Ambrose wrote in first advancing his insight, "He who does not keep harm off a friend, if he can, is as much in fault as he who causes it." Augustine concurred and expanded the point.

Clearly, Ambrose and Augustine began with the duty of love to protect the innocent, not with a presumption against doing harm, even to an enemy. They reasoned that the duty to protect the innocent permitted use of force against the wrongful attacker up to the level needed to prevent the attack from succeeding, though it must not exceed this level, since the evildoer is himself considered to be someone for whom Christ died. Thus, the consideration of restraint in the use of force arises only after the duty to use force is recognized, and restraint follows not from a presumption against harm but from the same duty of love directed toward the evildoer.

The logic of this position was in turn developed by the medieval heirs of these early figures, beginning with Gratian and other canonists in the twelfth and thirteenth centuries. But in retrospect, the position of Thomas Aquinas looms as especially important, both because of his general influence on later Catholic thought and because of his dependence on Augustine himself in the matter of just-war theory.

In order for a war to be just, Thomas Aquinas wrote, three things are necessary, namely: sovereign authority, just cause, and right intention. Since we are particularly interested in the conditions that justify resort to force, it is useful to look first at how Thomas (citing Augustine) defined just cause:

> Just cause is required, namely that those who are attacked, should be attacked because they deserve it on account of some fault. Wherefore Augustine says: A just war is wont to be described as one that avenges wrongs, when a nation or state has to be punished for refusing to make amends for the wrongs inflicted by its subjects, or to restore what has been seized unjustly.

This focus is also clear in Thomas' discussion of the requirement of sovereign authority for a just war. Defining this requirement he cites a text frequently quoted in medieval writing on the ethics of war, Romans 13:4: "The sovereign beareth not the sword in vain: for he is God's minister, an avenger to execute wrath upon him that doth evil." Thomas continues, "so too, it is [a sovereign's] business to have recourse to the sword in defending the common weal against external enemies."

That the resort to force in itself is not the moral problem here is all the more clear when Thomas turns to the requirement of right intention for a just war, again quoting Augustine:

> True religion looks upon as peaceful those wars that are waged not for motives of aggrandizement, or cruelty, but with the object of securing peace, of punishing evil-doers, and of uplifting the good.

What is morally condemnable in war, Thomas continues, is not force itself but the use of force with the wrong intention, namely "[t]he passion for inflicting harm, the cruel thirst for vengeance, an unpacific and relentless spirit, the fever of revolt, the lust of power, and such like things." As for the argument that prudential considerations may overrule the presence of just cause, Thomas leaves judgment to the sovereign; it is not a matter for the Church to determine, and certainly not to determine in advance for all war.

Moving forward from the medieval base into the modern period, two other benchmark figures, Francisco de Vitoria (1492–1546) and Hugo Grotius (1583–1645), illustrate the essential continuity of this conception of just war. They did, however, introduce two changes made necessary by the modern period. In medieval times, the just-war tradition applied only to wars between Christians, not between Christians and non-Christians (notably Muslims), and, theologically speaking, Western Christianity was still monolithic. With the Spanish expansion into the new world there arose the question of the propriety of colonial wars against non-Christian peoples, and then came the dilemmas occasioned by the Protestant Reformation. The first change introduced by Vitoria and solidified by Grotius was to locate the justifying causes for war squarely within natural law and the law of nations, thereby ruling out appeals to religion (or other ideological causes) as justifying resort to war. The second was the recognition that in a given conflict both sides might appear to have just cause.

In the context of the first development, these theorists regarded war as provided for by both nature and the law of nations as a means of settling otherwise intractable disputes. As to the second issue, one might guess, on the face of it, that if both sides in a conflict appear to have just cause, then the tradition would enjoin them not to fight; that is, it would see ambiguity itself as a restriction on *jus ad bellum*, the very right to go to war. Certainly, if there were a presumption against war within the core of the tradition, it would have been most likely to present itself here. But neither Vitoria nor Grotius reasoned this way. Rather, accepting war as a last-resort means of settling disputes, they focused instead on the idea of simultaneous ostensible justice—the perception of justice on both sides at once—as the base for more attention to restraint in war, thus feeding the development of the *jus in bello*, the rules limiting the conduct of war. Also, both of these early modern just-war theorists give explicit attention to the purpose of just use of force to right injustices, as for example Vitoria's contemporary-sounding argument for the use of force to oppose pillage, rape, and indiscriminate killing.

Clearly, the development of Christian just-war tradition follows a line of reasoning focused on the rightness of the resort to force to combat the evil of injustice, and that development did not construe at any point the use of force to be a moral problem in itself. In classic just-war theory the use of force is morally problematic only when it is the source of injustice. But even then, wrong uses of force do not call force itself into question, but instead justify the resort to force to set matters right. What Christian just-war doctrine is about, as classically defined, is the use of the authority and force of the rightly ordered political community (and its sovereign authority as minister of God) to prevent, punish, and rectify injustice. There is, simply put, no presumption against war in it at all.

THE EVOLUTION OF AN IDEA

If the idea of a "presumption against war" cannot be traced to the theorists who gave Christian just-war theory its classical form, then where does it come from? The answer, I suggest, is that it has developed out of a particular response to the phenomenon of modern war, a response that understands the nature of war today necessarily to threaten human values, not to provide a means of protecting them. This understanding depicts war in its contemporary form as inherently suspect. A widely known rendering of this view is in Paul Fussell's *The Great War and Modern Memory:* Modern war is senseless, out of control, massively destructive of human values and life values, leaving behind harmful consequences that linger long after the shooting is done.[1]

Since the idea of a "presumption against war" as informing just-war theory has been explicitly adopted by the American Catholic bishops in their 1983 pastoral, *The Challenge of Peace,* it is instructive to follow the evolution in Catholic thought of the perception of modern war as inherently destructive of value. Here, as in other religious criticism of modern war, we encounter additional themes: negative judgments on the purposes of modern secular states, references to the growth of "militarism," and a conception of modern weapons as inherently too destructive to serve value. It is important to note that this negative perception of war is not simply a reaction to the age of nuclear weapons. It was well established long before the nuclear age. Fussell traces this conception of war to the terrible experience in the trenches of 1914–18, but for Catholic thought it begins at least as early as 1870, when a formal position paper, or *Postulatum,* was presented to Vatican Council I, challenging the justice of the form of war practiced by modern states.

Reflecting the experience of the Franco-Prussian War of that same year, and perhaps also the American Civil War that had ended five years earlier, this *Postulatum* explicitly cited the venal motivations of states and the danger of large standing national armies as a special evil. It argued that such armies fostered a spirit of militarism, tended to foment wars in order to finance themselves through conquest, and led to conflicts so destructive as to be "hideous massacres" that the church could not regard as just. So far as the *jus ad bellum*? was concerned, the argument of the *Postulatum* precluded the possibility of a first use of force being just, no matter what its aim—and after the grotesque slaughter of the First World War some forty-five years later, the argument could only have seemed more self-evident than ever. The document did, however, admit the right of second use of force in defense against attack. Together, this undercutting of the first use of force along with the acceptance of second use (defined as defense) was to become an element not only for later Catholic thought but also for twentieth-century international law.

Following the Great War and reflecting the experience of that conflict, a gathering of prominent theologians at the 1931 Conventus of Fribourg thus distinguished between defense, which they regarded as lawful, and the argument for war from national "necessity," which they declared not lawful. In the context of the provisions for arbitration of disputes established by the League of Nations, and the renunciation of first use of force established for the signatories to the Pact of Paris, the Conventus took the position that it was wrong to initiate any resort to arms to settle a dispute without first recourse to arbitration.

These two documents set the terms for a critique of war that ends as a "presumption against war." Since the Second World War various official and nonofficial statements have called into question whether, given the nature of modern war, even the just cause of defense can legitimize resort to armed force. Statements of the various popes to this effect are especially interesting because of their authoritative force, even though they represent only a fraction of the full range of recent Catholic thought on war.

Pope Pius XII, whose papacy (1939–58) extended through the Second World War and the beginning of the nuclear age, in effect forbade "all wars of aggression, whether just or unjust," as John Courtney

Murray put it.[2] For this pope a "war of aggression," Murray notes, was identified with any offensive use of force, whatever the justifying reason. Defensive war, on the other hand, was acceptable—though Pius hedged this allowance more tightly than earlier just-war writers. His reasoning on first and second resort to force came together in his 1956 Christmas message, which reflected the context of the Hungarian revolution and its repression by Soviet military power. This statement is interesting as an example of the refashioning of traditional just-war concepts into a somewhat different doctrine from that defined by the classic theorists. In a particularly vivid passage Pius wrote:

> There is no further room for doubt about the purposes and methods that lie behind tanks when they crash resoundingly across frontiers.... When all the possible stages of negotiation and mediation are by-passed, and when the threat is made to use atomic arms to obtain concrete demands, whether these are justified or not, it becomes clear that...there may come into existence in a nation a situation in which all hope of averting war becomes vain. In this situation a war of efficacious self-defense against unjust attacks, which is undertaken with hope of success, cannot be considered illicit.

In context, this was a pointed condemnation of the Soviet invasion alongside a somewhat lukewarm acceptance of the Hungarian resistance. Pius used just-war language, but his priorities were importantly different from those of classic just-war theory. There, as we have seen, the classical focus was on three concerns: the justice of the cause for resort to force, the existence of authority to do so, and the intention with which it would be used. Pius, however, focused elsewhere: on the evil of first resort to force itself (tanks crashing "resoundingly across frontiers") and the requirement of last resort (the threat of further force without making use of "negotiation" and "mediation"). While he allowed defensive use of force, he subjected it to further limits: only self-defense against "unjust attacks" is allowed; "reasonable hope of success" (the classic criterion) has been refashioned into "efficacious self-defense...undertaken with hope of success"; and the defensive resort to force is not explicitly just, but only "cannot be considered illicit."

Pius' reasoning here expressed a "presumption against war" without employing the term. While his reference to atomic arms introduced a new element in the context of resort to force, Pius' focus in this passage was clearly not that these particular weapons are especially evil and to be avoided but that the use of force is especially evil and to be avoided. His negative attitude toward resort to force was thus not a particular result of the atomic age; rather it was of a piece with the distrust of arms, armies, and the use of force expressed earlier in Catholic thought, in the denunciation of large standing armies and militarism in 1870, and the emphasis on arbitration in 1931.

Giving his own weight to this new emphasis, Pope John XXIII, in the *Pacem in Terris* encyclical of 1963, called for the banning of nuclear weapons, a general reduction of other arms, and the development of an international regime based on common consent that would resolve disputes short of war. In a widely discussed passage he wrote:

> [I]n this age which boasts of its atomic power, it no longer makes sense to maintain that war is a fit instrument with which to repair the violation of justice.

Catholic pacifists of our day have argued that this statement not only condemned all war in the nuclear age, but rejected just-war theory as well.[3] By contrast, Protestant theologian Paul Ramsey understood John XXIII as working within the just-war framework, but ruling out two of the three classical just causes for resort to force—recovery of something wrongly taken and punishment of evil—while leaving only defense as justified.[4] Even if Ramsey's less radical interpretation is correct, much has been given up in this statement for, after all, to repair the violation of justice was precisely what classic just-war doctrine was about.

As these examples show, twenty years into the nuclear age it was clear that Catholic (and not only Catholic) thought on just war had shifted focus to a concern that the first resort to force under any circumstances held great potential for injustice and that, accordingly, such resort must be avoided. The defensive use of arms remained a moral possibility, although an increasingly questioned one. In Pope Paul VI's 1965 address to the United Nations General Assembly, this evolving line of reasoning about just war reached for a new resolution. While issuing the ringing challenge, "[N]ever again war, war never again!", Paul also admitted that "so long as man remains...weak, changeable, and even wicked...defensive arms will, alas! be necessary." But he stopped short of explicitly saying that it is morally allowable to use such arms. In the context of prevailing Cold War strategies, this statement suggested support for deterrence but not for active defense should deterrence fail. Hence, his point was to draw a double distinction: between the possession of offensive arms, which he regarded as morally evil, and defensive ones, whose possession he permitted; and between the possession of and use of the latter.

It was no great distance from these distinctions to what amounted to a position of nearly unconditional pacifism—the basic rejection of just-war logic altogether with the new understanding that, for Catholics at least, religion mandates a "presumption against war." The logic of the paradigm was spelled out vividly in the 1983 pastoral letter of the American Catholic bishops, *The Challenge of Peace*. Its starting point is not the problem of preventing injustice, but its insistence that:

> Catholic teaching begins in every case with a presumption against war and for peaceful settlement of disputes. In exceptional cases, determined by the moral principles of the just-war tradition, some uses of force are permitted.[5]

The definition of exceptional cases is suggested by two statements that follow the above. The first defines self-defense against aggression as a right and duty of every nation, and the second rejects offensive war as morally unjustifiable whatever the circumstances. Later, in the text of the letter itself, these themes are elaborated and linked to earlier Catholic tradition, as well as to the effort in international law to outlaw wars of aggression and, ultimately, to eliminate war altogether by international common consent. The right to resort to force, however, as defined in the bishops' letter, is more stringent than that understood in international law because it imposes further limitations: that resort to force must be subject to prudential tests, including the requirements of last resort, probability of success, and overall proportionality.

Defined thusly, the implication of the presumption against war is to push just-war theory close to outright rejection of any resort to force. While *The Challenge of Peace* focused specifically on nuclear weapons, it clearly nurtured the more general inclination that, in the present age, the use of any military force is morally questionable because it could escalate into nuclear force. Hence, the words of John XXIII--that in the present age war may no longer be employed to remedy the violation of justice—and hence the trajectory of recent Catholic teaching on war, which seems to leave no doubt that the intent is to avoid all resort to force.

The idea that just-war tradition is rooted in a "presumption against war" is clearly an innovation; the question is whether it is a justified innovation. I think not. Indeed, this sort of thinking should be a cause for concern not only to Catholics, but to anyone who believes that moral reasoning has a place in the affairs of statecraft. This is so for two reasons: first, because "presumption against war" thinking effectively destroys the logic of just-war theory by putting *jus in bello* above *jus ad bellum*, and by putting lesser, prudential considerations within *jus ad bellum* above major ones; and, second, because the assumptions about the nature of war on which it is based are flawed.

THE LOGICAL PROBLEM

From the perspective of pure moral argument, the problem with the "presumption against war" idea is not only that it is radically at odds with the classical idea of just war, but that the nature of the judgment upon which the claim is made is inadequate. Rather than flowing from a deontological moral principle (a "categorical imperative," as Kant put it), the "presumption against war" is a product of prudential judgments about the nature of modern war.

The problem with prudential judgments such as those incorporated into the presumption against war logic is not only that they are prudential, but that they are contingent. In other words, they are not based on an unchangeable moral principle, but on a condition in the world that is not only subject to change but fated to change. Pure moral reasoning about justice and injustice lives in the realm of absolutes, of deontological reasoning: One obeys a moral principle not because of the consequences of obeying it, but because it is right. Moral judgments—applied moral reasoning—obviously must assess contingent conditions, but such judgments must not be guided by them. It is precisely for this reason that medieval and early modern just-war theory placed responsibility for the four lesser prudential concerns included in *jus ad bellum*—that it produce a preponderance of good over evil, have a reasonable chance of success, be a last resort, and that its expected outcome be peace—on the competent authority who determines whether to resort to armed force.

In other words, these lesser but still very important concerns pertain to the function of statecraft, not moral analysis. The role of the moralist is to insist on the application of the three essential, non-contingent elements of *jus ad bellum*—just cause, competent authority, right intention—and to specify that the prudential elements be taken into account. But the moralist is not to usurp the role of statecraft by specifying how they are to apply or what they mean for specific instances or periods of time. The "presumption against war" view, by reversing the weight of essential and contingent considerations, would vitiate statecraft and presume to tell sovereigns how to conduct their affairs—a most worldly and untraditional presumption at that. From the perspective of moral reasoning, too, it gives pride of place to judgments about contingent conditions over obligations inherent in moral duty.

THE PRACTICAL PROBLEM

To the extent that it is taken seriously, "presumption against war" thinking also has clear implications for the shape of public policy on the use of force. For if war is always presumptively wrong, the moral frame for policy debate over the use of force is reduced to the arena of those very limited exceptional circumstances that may override this presumption. What the 1983 pastoral letter meant for policy on nuclear weapons, relating both to deterrence and to possible use, was well-examined at the time the letter appeared: It was, politically, an attempt to advance the campaign for a nuclear freeze, and it was justified largely on the basis of the claim that neither the demands of discrimination nor proportionality could possibly be met in any use of nuclear weapons.

One can still argue such matters today, for the chances of a major nuclear exchange between the United States and Russia (or China) are not completely nil. But in the contemporary environment, policy questions relating to very different forms of the national use of force and occasions for such use are at center stage. The types of forces involved are different, the justifications entered into debate are different, and the authority for employment of force is different. The key issues now relate to conventional, not nuclear arms; they involve low-intensity conflict and various forms of interventionary uses of military force, not superpower deterrence or war; the goals served are often defined by broadly held international values, not national interests narrowly construed; and the question of the rightness of the use of force encompasses not only cases in which unilateral action by the United States is at issue, but also cases in which the United States is a participant in groups of nations ranging from ad hoc coalitions (such as that against Iraq in the Gulf War), to regional alliances (like NATO or the OAS), to the United Nations.

RESTORING JUSTICE TO JUST-WAR REASONING

Despite the existence of such variable circumstances, some modern just-war theorists have marginalized themselves to the point where they can barely speak to such matters. It is hard to see how, from a posture defined by the "presumption against war," uses of force can be justified for reasons of national interest other than resistance to a direct attack in progress (and perhaps not then, if the prudential tests are not met), even in the face of serious threat to national security or for international order purposes. Yet these kinds of cases provide the context for debate over the use of force today: threats to national interest take such forms as terrorist attack and the drug trade; recent international order concerns include rolling back aggression (the Gulf War), promoting human rights and democracy (Haiti), and ending an indiscriminately destructive civil war (Bosnia). Just-war theory, if brought back to its real roots, can be relevant to all these contingencies. The way to do this is to restore the centrality of the idea of justice to reasoning about the use of force.

There is no question that classic just-war theorists were motivated in their thinking about the use of force by the desire to prevent, punish, and remedy injustice, and even to do so at risk to oneself—as per Ambrose and Augustine. The purpose of statecraft followed from this: The role of the sovereign was to act as minister of God to police injustice. So, unless it is granted in advance that the resort to force always produces the greatest injustice, the matter remains open to case by case, or class by class, investigation. If one undertakes such an investigation, it becomes clear that the uses of military force typical of the present day do not justify the judgments underlying "presumption against war" arguments. In those arguments, it will be recalled, two themes stand out: first, that the moral possibility of national purpose has been subverted by the militarism imposed by large military establishments, for which the only cure is disarmament; and second, that the destructiveness of modern weapons, especially nuclear weapons, severely restricts and perhaps removes the possibility of their use as instruments of moral purpose.

Neither of these themes holds up as a general descriptive statement of the nature of contemporary states and statecraft as such, or of the actuality of war once begun. Both are particularly outmoded in the post-Cold War context. In the first place, the wars that have occurred since the end of the Cold War do not exemplify a destructiveness inexorably beyond human control, or aims that far outrun the ends of politics, but rather a reality shaped by human decision-making and expressive of rational political purposes—however wrong we may judge such purposes to be in discrete cases. These conflicts have all been limited in significant ways; none has ushered in a global holocaust or escalated to all-out use of conventional military might. Nor is this only a post-Cold War phenomenon. In truth, the face of armed conflict since the end of the Second World War suggests that modern war is characterized by localized and limited, though sharp, conflicts in which ethnic or religious differences or local political disputes provide the proximate causes, rather than totalistic clashes on the model of the two world wars or the feared global nuclear showdown.

Indeed, while the reality of recent conflicts has been terrible enough, the rape of Kuwait, the starvation of civilians in Somalia, the ethnic massacres of Rwanda and the former Yugoslavia have not shown a destructiveness different in essence from what was known by Vitoria, Grotius, or their predecessors. (Grotius, after all, lived during the Thirty Years' War, still arguably the most devastating conflict Europe has ever experienced.) All these conflicts have been condemned by the international community, and each has, in different ways, occasioned action to relieve suffering and bring the conflict to an end. In these responses the military means of the great powers have been brought to bear in limited rather than totalistic ways and with varying degrees of success. None of these forms of action is consistent with the view of modern war described by the "presumption against war" perspective.

Three general lessons may be deduced from the experience of these recent conflicts. The first is that the perception of the nature of war underlying the "presumption against war" idea is seriously at odds with reality, and that the reality of recent conflicts fits very closely the perception of war found in classic just-war theory. The second is that the recent conflicts cited have helped define the limits of what individual states and groups of states can do to prevent or mitigate war. The United

Nations has had success (and failure) at peacekeeping, but other international coalitions have been necessary where peace does not exist or exists only tenuously, as in the cases of the Gulf War and the current NATO intervention in Bosnia. The third lesson is that the major powers have employed their military forces in these conflicts in ways that have gone substantially beyond a narrow definition of their national interests to include humanitarian and international order concerns. This is just the opposite of what they were expected to do on the model of the state in modern Catholic just-war thinking that emphasizes their militarism, national chauvinism, and venality.

JUST CAUSE AND RIGHT AUTHORITY

These three lessons suggest that the approach to war found in classic just-war reasoning remains relevant to contemporary conflict. At the same time the tradition of such reasoning needs to recognize the particulars of the contemporary international context, especially the specific violations of justice likely to occur, and the variable notion of authority for the use of force that has emerged in responses to recent conflicts. Together these developments point the way to new applications of just-war thought.

The truth is that the classic just-war concept defines the issues in ways that correspond closely to the conditions under which contemporary policy on uses of force must be shaped. There is a place, in just-war terms, for the employment of military force in the contemporary world: not only for defense of national interests—which is, after all, maintained in papal teaching, positive international law, international custom, and realist doctrine—but also for purposes the classic just-war theorists called the punishment of evil and the recovery of something wrongly taken. These latter uses are often, but not always, interventionary in character, and they are often, though not always, undertakings of groups of states operating not only on their own authority but also on that of the United Nations Security Council.

The fundamental policy implication for just-war reasoning, rightly understood, is thus not only that there is a place for the use of force under national authority in resistance to armed attack, but also a place for employment of military means in response to broader kinds of threats to national security, and to the values and structures that define the international order. In the face of such threats force may be the only means likely to produce the desired results: protection of the values at stake (whether this takes the form of preventing starvation, rectifying the criminal looting of civil order, ending indiscriminate warfare against enemy populations, or rolling back interstate aggression). In contemporary context it is well to remember that the conditions of the rightful resort to force to protect these values and end the threat to them is precisely what classic just-war theory aimed to define. Such uses of force for good should not be held hostage to an imagined "presumption against war."

NOTES

1. Paul Fussell, *The Great War and Modern Memory* (New York: Oxford University Press, 1975).
2. John Courtney Murray, *Morality and Modern War* (New York: Council on Religion and International Affairs, 1959), p. 9.
3. Ronald G. Musto, *The Catholic Peace Tradition* (Maryknoll, NY: Orbis Books, 1986), p. 190.
4. Paul Ramsey, *The Just War: Force and Political Responsibility* (New York Scribner's, 1968), pp. 190–210.
5. National Conference of Catholic Bishops, *The Challenge of Peace* (Washington, DC: United States Catholic Conference, 1983), iii; cf. 22.

ABSTRACT

This essay was the annual Kuyper Lecture of the Center for Public Justice, "Can Force Be Used Justly?," given at Gordon College, Wenham, MA, November 2001. Johnson presents Christian components of the early presentation of just war as a foundation of the legitimate use of force. He also presents his perspective of opposition to the 1983 pastoral, *The Challenge of Peace,* written by American Catholic bishops in which they articulate a "presumption against war."

CHAPTER 7

CAN FORCE BE USED JUSTLY?

INTRODUCTION

Is it ever moral to kill another human being? At a less extreme level, is it moral to use force to punish or to coerce another? Christian pacifists answer the question of killing with a strong no, citing the command of Jesus to turn the other cheek when struck on the one and his order to Peter to put away his sword and not defend him when the soldiers came to arrest him. Many Christian pacifists also have reservations about the use of force for punishment or coercion. But there is also a strong Christian tradition of allowing the use of force, up to and including deadly force, at the agency of the political community and subject to stringent moral constraints. This tradition too is biblically grounded, and it has developed within the mainstream of Christian theological reflection from the early church through the Middle Ages to the Reformation and down to the present. This tradition links the moral right to use force to the public good and to God's plan for the government of the world between the fall and the final culmination of his plan at the end of history. Unlike pacifism, it does not identify violence itself as evil but rather distinguishes between the use of force for evil and for good, between that for private ends and that undertaken for the service of justice, good order, and peace.

This tradition is that of the idea of just war, though it is about the moral right to use force as such, not just about war as we understand that term. It is, as Paul Ramsey first argued some forty years ago, fundamentally about permission to use force, up to and including deadly force, along with limitation in the employment of that force. Properly understood, it bears on the state's right to use force for justice, order, and peace against those who do evil both internally to the society and against external enemies. It includes the questions of punishment and coercion as well as the awesome question of taking human life. In my discussion here today I want to examine this perspective on these questions regarding the moral use of force. I will do this in two stages. First, I will undertake to explain what this moral perspective entails by an examination of the origin and coalescence of the just war idea. Second, I will bring this discussion of the moral use of force into the present by connecting it to three pressing contemporary issues: internationally, the question of intervention and the fight against terrorism, and domestically, the use of the death penalty.

I. THE COMING TOGETHER OF A TRADITION ON THE MORAL USE OF FORCE

I want to begin examining the origin and coalescence of the just war idea by reading several quotations from Augustine, one from the early medieval theologian Isidore of Seville, and one from Paul's Epistle to the Romans. First, from Augustine:

> If the Christian religion forbade war altogether, those who sought salutary advice in the Gospel would rather have been counseled to cast aside their arms, and to give up soldiering altogether. On the contrary, they were told: "Do violence to no man;...and be content with your pay." If he commanded them to be content with their pay, he did not forbid soldiering. (*Letter to Marcellus* cxxviii)

Again from Augustine:

> The natural order conducive to peace among mortals demands that the power to declare and counsel war should be in the hands of those who hold the supreme authority. (*Contra Faustum* xxii.75)

And:

> A just war is...one that avenges wrongs, when a nation or state has to be punished, for refusing to make amends for the wrongs inflicted by its subjects, or to restore what it has seized unjustly. (*Questiones in Heptateuchum,* q.v. *super Josue*)

From Isidore of Seville:

> A war is just when...it is waged in order to regain what has been stolen or to repel the attack of enemies. (Gratian, *Decretum,* Second Part, XXIII.II.I)

Returning to Augustine:

> What is evil in war? It is not the deaths of some who will soon die anyway. The desire for harming, the cruelty of avenging, an unruly and implacable animosity, the rage of rebellion, the lust of domination and the like—these are the things which are to be blamed in war. (*Contra Faustum* xxii.74)

And this:

> We do not seek peace in order to be at war, but we go to war that we may have peace. Be peaceful, therefore, in warring, so that you may vanquish those whom you war against, and bring them to the prosperity of peace. (*Letter to Boniface* clxxxix)

Finally, from the book of Romans:

> For rulers are not a terror to good conduct, but to bad. Would you have no fear of him who is in authority? Then do what is good, and you will receive his approval, for he is God's servant for your good. But if you do wrong, be afraid, for he does not bear the sword in vain; he is the servant of God to execute his wrath on the wrongdoer. (Romans 13:3–4)

These few passages constitute the core of the idea of just war as it first came together in Christian moral thought in the Middle Ages and as it should be defined in reflection on the moral use of force today.

The first passage refutes the argument that Christians ought to reject all forms of the use of force, but affirms that they may without sin serve in the armed forces of the state—which in the context of the time also meant in the role of police. The second passage defines and restricts the right to resort to force to the "supreme authority" in the political community, implicitly denying it to everyone else who would employ force on his own behalf, that is, anyone who would, in the language of the first passage, "do violence" to another. The third and fourth passages clarify the limited range of causes that justify resort to force: for Augustine, punishing wrongdoing and restoring what has been unjustly taken away; from Isidore, retaking that which has been stolen and defending against unjust attack.

Other causes that some might wish to include as justifications for resort to force are absent here; these are passages that strictly limit while specifying what the sovereign authority must look for. In the fifth passage I have quoted Augustine defines what becomes the just war requirement of right intention. It is for him a matter of inner attitude or, we might say, mindset toward the use of force itself and toward those against whom it is to be used. One does not use force justly if he is seduced by the power it gives him or if he uses it out of blinding hatred towards the enemy. For Augustine and his medieval successors, this was perhaps the most central requirement of all, for it drew the distinction between acting out of sinful *cupiditas* or self-love—the kind of intentionality from which all the sorts of evil intentions denounced in the passage arise and the kind of love which the presence of grace inspires, *caritas* or charity, love that is directed towards the good of the neighbor, the triumph of the heavenly city, and life in the presence of God. The last passage from Augustine defines the ultimate purpose to which all moral uses of force should aim: the restoration of peace where there has been war, along with a caution that in order to gain peace, one must fight "peacefully," that is, in a way that does not undermine the achievement of peace but supports it.

Romans 13:3–4 stands as a kind of motto for medieval and early modern Christian thinking about the just use of force: it belongs properly to the role of political authority as an element in God's government of the world. In the immediate context of the passages I have quoted, it gives the religious reason why force should morally be restricted to the highest authority in the political community. Among medieval and early modern just war theorists, this is the main use to which this passage from Romans was put. But the passage also had another kind of influence: if the ruler is the servant of God who is to act in the stead of God to punish evil, some reasoned, then this tells us what the ruler himself must be and what ought to be the quality of his rule and of the society he governs. Thus Romans 13:3–4 also became a foundational passage for a tradition of reflection on the good ruler and the good state, a tradition that found its culmination in Erasmus' *The Education of a Christian Prince* and, beyond Erasmus, helped to influence modern political theory on what good government should be and what it should aim at.

Taken all together, then, these sparse passages I have quoted have had a great influence on western thought on the just use of force within the context of life in political community. They first appeared in close, thematic connection together with other passages from the Bible, from Augustine, and from other magisterial Christian theologians in the canonist Gratian's *Decretum* from the middle of the twelfth century. Their purpose there, and the purpose of canon law generally, was to guide Christian moral behavior by specifying right and wrong uses of force by Christians in the context of God's overall government of the world.

The later canonists focused mostly on the question of the use of force by the governing authority and on limiting the number of kinds of people who could claim a right to have recourse to arms. A century and a quarter after Gratian the passages from Augustine and from Romans were used as the backbone of Thomas Aquinas' discussion of just war in the *Summa Theologica*, where they were tied especially to the concept of responsibility in good government as exercised by the just ruler. These two concerns, on the one hand for the moral behavior of individual Christians and on the other hand for the exercise of just rule, remained central to the development of normative Christian thinking about the use of force right through the Middle Ages and into the era of the Reformation and beyond. Luther, Zwingli, and Calvin, like the canonists and the scholastic theologians before them, mainly addressed the question of the just use of force in the context of thinking about the rights and responsibilities of government—Luther more exclusively on governmental authority, the Reformed theologians with more balance between such authority and the moral responsibilities of Christians living under such authority.

In later Reformed thinkers, like the Puritan theologian William Ames, the balance shifted more toward the rights and responsibilities of individual Christians in relation to the use of force and to government in general, and this has been the line of development generally followed by the main line of western thought, secular as well as religious, throughout the modern era.

We see this in different ways, for example, in Hugo Grotius and in international law, where governing authority is understood in a *de facto* way, as morally neutral in character, and the focus is on the limits of the use of force by those who act in the service of the state; and in the development of democratic theory from Locke forward, where the rights of government are tied explicitly to those of citizens, and the use of force accordingly has to be described first of all in terms of the protection of those rights. This is the frame from which we instinctively approach matters of the use of force today, the frame defined by the tradition associated with Grotius on the one hand and that associated with Locke on the other. But in order to remain true to the idea of just war and its implications for government and for individual moral conduct as originally defined in Christian thought, we need to look beyond the modern frame to what the passages I cited above were taken to mean when they were first placed together, and how their meaning was amplified by other ideas.

What of these other ideas? I will say more about them in a moment. First, though, I want to underscore the meaning and importance of the four ideas already identified by means of the passages quoted at the beginning: sovereign authority, just cause, right intention, and the aim of peace. These are fundamental deontological requirements, requirements that limit the use of force to sovereign authority and then impose binding duties on that authority: to ensure that the cause is one of the just causes identified, the mindset is not one of evil intention, and the purpose is the reestablishment of peace. It is important, in the original definition of these requirements, that sovereign authority comes first, for that authority is the only one who properly can determine whether the other three requirements are satisfied. This understanding of the moral priorities disappears at the beginning of the modern period, when sovereignty becomes simply a *de facto* characteristic of commonly recognized states. Yet a moral component to sovereign authority—the idea that there are genuinely good and bad exercises of such authority—is an essential part of the whole Christian theory of justified resort to force, and we need to find a way to talk meaningfully about this again.

Now to the additional ideas that amplified these four core essentials in the medieval and early modern effort to define a systematic Christian way of thinking about just resort to force. First, anyone who knows recent just war thinking must have noted that three moral criteria often emphasized today are not included in these four core deontological requirements. These three are that the use of force contemplated be expected to do more good than harm (the criterion of proportionality), that it have a reasonable hope of success, and that it be a last resort. It is only in recent listings of the just war criteria that these are named separately and often put on a level with, or even ahead of, the requirements of sovereign authority, just cause, right intention, and the purpose of establishing peace.

There is a reason they do not appear with such prominence in earlier thought: they are prudential criteria, and when they appear in earlier just war thought they are concerns that those in sovereign authority must satisfy in judging whether, finally, to resort to force even when the cause is just, the intention is right, and the purpose is to establish peace. When sovereign authority becomes a *de facto* possession of every state and is no longer a quality possessed by right of governing according to the natural moral order of the cosmos or the will of God, then these prudential requirements change their character and become part of the general moral critique of the use of force. Yet, I would stress, they have a secondary, supportive role relative to the four core concerns, and it is a serious distortion of just war thinking to give them the equal or dominant role they often are given today, usually by persons interested in denying that there is ever any justified resort to force.

All the ideas I have been discussing pertain to what came to be called the *jus ad bellum,* the rules for resort to war. The justice of resorting to force was, in fact, the main concern of the twelfth- and thirteenth-century Christian writers who first began to make the idea of just war into a coherent, consistent, consensually binding whole.

As I have already mentioned, the church moralists historically first approached the idea of right conduct in the use of force through the prism of the requirement of right intention or mindset toward force and the enemy. A series of church councils, beginning as early as the ninth century, imposed the requirement of confession and penance on warriors returning from battle in case they had fought with a wrong intention, hatred of the enemy, say, or bloodlust, or pride in their own dominance over an adversary. As a sanction, they were not to be admitted to Mass until the penance was completed. But beginning in the tenth century two other approaches to defining just conduct in war emerged, approaches which continue today to define the idea of *jus in bello,* the rules for conduct in war.

One approach was the introduction of the idea of noncombatant immunity by means of lists of classes of persons—women, children, the aged or infirm, peaceful townspeople, peasants on their land, persons engaged in religious pursuits, and others—who, as the typical rationale put it, took no part in war, and therefore should not have war waged against them. Today we have been taught by Paul Ramsey and others to think of this as the moral principle of discrimination, but the traditional approach, defining classes of people as noncombatants to be protected from the ravages of war, is still followed in the Geneva Conventions.

The second historical approach to defining justified conduct in war was the introduction of the idea that certain means of war, and in particular certain weapons, are so dangerous—indiscriminate in their effects or disproportionately destructive—that they should be banned and those who use them anathematized. This is more than Ramsey's *in bello* principle of proportionality, much used in recent moral debate on war. The traditional approach, once again, is found in the law of armed conflicts, which includes specific limits on certain forms of targeting and outlaws certain particular weapons.

When we assemble all these ideas I have identified, we are face-to-face with the idea of just war as it has been historically defined in Christian tradition. There are also secular versions of this tradition, and at times the main line of development has been carried more by secular thinkers and institutions than by Christian moral reflection. Today we have versions of just war thinking in international law, as I have already suggested, in military codes of conduct, in the thought of political philosophers like Michael Walzer, and even in the language of policy. But there are reasons to maintain a specifically Christian perspective on this issue, not only for informing the behavior of individual Christians who may be involved in the use of force as ordinary police or soldiers or in command roles, up to the highest level of government, but also as a way of contributing to a vigorous public debate aimed at understanding the justifications and limits of the use of force in the nation and the world today.

II. THINKING IN A JUST WAR WAY ABOUT THREE CONTEMPORARY ISSUES

I want now to turn to three contemporary issues involving the use of force by governmental authority: internationally, the question of military intervention for the sake of protecting human rights, and the fight against terrorism in the aftermath of the September 11 attacks; domestically, the question of the use of the death penalty.

I have chosen these first two issues not only because of their immediacy—American military forces today are deployed for both purposes abroad—but because they allow us to confront a very interesting tendency in some American Christian thinking about the use of force in international contexts: that the use of military force to protect American national interests is bad, or at least gravely morally suspect, while use of such force for the protection of the human rights of others, especially if this has no national interest component, is good. Thus we find the following language in a 1998 Resolution of the Presbyterian Church (USA): "[Intervention] must constitute humanitarian rescue and not cloak the pursuit of the economic or narrow security interests of the intervening powers" (PCUSA, "A Just Peacemaking and the Call for International Intervention for Humanitarian Rescue," criterion 3).

While no rationale is provided for this, I suggest something like the following logic for it: that serving one's own economic or security interests is inherently selfish, and thus perhaps, in Augustinian terms, a reflection of sinful *cupiditas,* human self-love infected by pride, while humanitarian rescue in the absence of any economic or security interests is unselfish, and thus an expression appropriate to the self-giving of Christian love for neighbor. But the sentiment expressed here has also taken other forms. It has provided the thrust of much Christian criticism of the American and western involvement in the Gulf War: the "blood for oil" argument. At other times the argument is made in terms of the need for consistency: if the United States is genuinely concerned for international order, or for human rights, or for some other good of similar magnitude, and wishes to use force to protect that good, then it ought to be willing to use force in all cases where such issues are at stake, not just some. If we did not intervene in Rwanda or in Tibet, the consistency argument goes, how can we be trusted to have good motives in the Gulf War or in Bosnia—or perhaps in the fight against terrorism?

The last major version of this argument I will mention is the one advanced by the American Catholic bishops. In their 1983 pastoral, *The Challenge of Peace* (National Conference of Catholic Bishops 1983), they defined Catholic just war tradition as beginning with a "presumption against war" and went on to define a position, admittedly focused on the problem of nuclear weapons, that was severely critical of planning, policies, and actions aimed at the use of armed force for purposes other than deterrence. "War-fighting" to protect national interests thus was rejected. Ten years later, however, in their 1993 statement, *The Harvest of Justice Is Sown in Peace,* while continuing to hold to the "presumption against war" and arguing strongly for building down national military capacity, they warmly embraced the cause of humanitarian intervention, citing Pope John Paul II that "[t]his is a duty for nations and the international community" (National Conference of Catholic Bishops 1993: 15).

Let me briefly say what I think is wrong with these arguments, not from the perspective of realism, but from the perspective of normative Christian tradition on the political community, government, and justified use of force.

First, from this perspective it is precisely the obligation of the state, and of the highest authority in every state, to see to the good of that political community: to protect its people's lives, safety and security, and livelihoods, to safeguard the bonds of commonality and mutuality that bind its people together into a community, and to protect those high values which serve justice, stability and peace both domestically and internationally. The national interest may, of course, be defined more broadly, but it must at least include these factors and others like them, or else the moral reason for the state's very existence is undermined. If one thinks the national interest is being defined too broadly or is being distorted, then that is a proper focus for public debate, but no person in political authority or in military service should fear decisions or actions that serve national interests as such: to serve such interests is what the political community exists for in the first place. Turning the matter around, when those in political authority do not protect their people's good but rather subvert that good for their own benefit, this is exactly the sort of situation which may justify an external intervention on the people's behalf.

Second, the Presbyterian statement and other arguments like it forget the essential difference between public and private morality. It is one thing to insist on an individual morality of unselfish self-giving toward others. But in the case of the political community those others include one's fellow citizens, and their good must be taken into account as well as that of persons in other communities. The individual, as individual, may give himself or herself totally for the sake of the other, but this is not the case for the political community or those who serve it in positions of authority to guide its policies and actions. Their obligations, as public servants, are different, and it is a distortion to hold their decisions for the sake of the whole community to the standards of individual unselfishness.

Third, if we take seriously the prudential requirements that a use of force be expected to do more good than harm, have a reasonable hope of succeeding in its purpose of reestablishing justice and creating peace, and be a last resort among the options available, a raw consistency (e.g., why the Gulf War and not Tibet?) is clearly not part of the moral answer to the question whether to use force in a given case. There are cases in which the use of force might be justified in terms of the four deontological criteria in the just war *jus ad bellum*, but in which the decision to use force would not be morally the right decision because of these prudential considerations. One ought to be morally consistent, but the right kind of consistency is taking account of all the relevant considerations, not gerrymandering them to suit the desired outcome.

Fourth, and particularly against the policy statements of the American Catholic bishops, what we find in Christian just war tradition is not a presumption against war but a presumption against injustice. The use of armed force is not itself the moral issue, but whether the use of force does or does not serve the cause of a just human order and the goal of peace. There are serious moral issues in the use of nuclear weapons, the Catholic bishops' original focus. I myself think their 1983 statement is deeply flawed in its analysis of these issues. But in any case, to extend a critique aimed at eliminating nuclear weapons into a more general negative judgment on national uses of armed force for other purposes that serve the national interest is to go too far, for reasons I have already given.

Still with all this said, intervention to halt and redress gross violations of human rights is a special and very interesting problem for moral uses of armed force. The thrust of moral and legal thinking on war for the last four centuries has been to restrict the right to use force to that of sovereign powers to respond to threats to their territorial borders, or by extension, threats to citizens and national interests outside those borders. From this perspective armed intervention by outsiders across territorial borders looks like aggression in moral terms, and it looks like a violation of sovereignty as defined in international law. What I have just said about armed intervention also applies to international war crimes tribunals. Thus it is no surprise that a central element in Slobodan Milosevic's response to his being brought before the International Criminal Tribunal for the Former Yugoslavia was to claim sovereign rights for himself as a former head of state and to deny any external jurisdiction in the matters for which he had been indicted. More broadly, any government whose territory is the focus of armed intervention has, according to standard provisions of international law, the right to use armed force to protect itself.

This is one side of the issue. The other side is the claim that protection of human rights is a higher value than territorial immunity and the standard definition of sovereign rights. In international law the growth of international human rights law since 1945, coupled with the Genocide Convention and the extension of the law of armed conflicts to apply to all kinds of such conflicts and not only formal wars between states, provides substantive grounds for arguing that the standard protections due sovereignty, including the sanctity of territorial borders, no longer apply in cases of gross violations of human rights, whether these be the result of government action or of inaction. In the moral frame, the argument is as many Christian bodies have framed it: there is a moral responsibility to come to the aid of the victims of such persecution.

Complicating the national debate has been the argument over whether United States military forces should be used for humanitarian interventions like those in Bosnia and Kosovo whether this is their proper mission, whether such use degrades their ability to protect and defend the United States, whether it is right to put at risk people who enlisted for other purposes. Can anything useful be added to this debate from the standpoint of just war reasoning? I think it can, with implications also for thinking about the moral use of force more broadly. Let me make three observations.

First, we need to recall in this connection the close relationship between the exercise of sovereign political authority as defined in Christian tradition and the right—indeed, at times the obligation—to use force. This is what Romans 13:4 historically was understood to be about. First, the ruler is defined as "God's servant for your good," that is the good of the people. This was understood not as an indicative statement, but as a normative one: the ruler who does not act as God's servant for his people's good is no longer rightly a ruler. This understanding of the normative obligations of political authority is what lay behind Calvin's well-known allowance that inferior magistrates might depose rulers who misuse their office. Earlier, though, the right to take such action was understood by Christian thinkers to lie with other rulers. Thus Romans 13:4 continues, "if you do wrong, be afraid; for [the ruler] does not bear the sword in vain; he is the servant of God to execute his wrath on the wrongdoer." This is the source of the idea of punishment of evil which, we recall, is one of three justifying causes for resort to force recognized in just war tradition. For thinkers in this tradition from the twelfth to the sixteenth centuries this allowed what we would today call interventionary uses of force when a ruler failed seriously to carry out the obligations of his office. Thus there is clearly a moral argument in Christian tradition in support for use of force across borders in such cases—not only for humanitarian reasons, but also, for example, when the governing authorities support or do nothing to stop evildoing that reaches beyond borders to harm others.

My second observation is that this moral argument pertains to those in authority in sovereign political communities. It has to do with what they may, and perhaps ought, to do in their own capacities. Some in the debate over intervention have argued that intervention must always be authorized by the United Nations Security Council; others have argued only that intervention must always be multilateral. I do not believe that just war analysis leads inevitably to either conclusion. These are effectively prudential arguments employed to seek to curb aggression in the name of humanitarian intervention. Prudentially, there is certainly good sense in the effort to achieve international agreement that an intervention is justified. Ultimately, though, in moral and political terms, this is a matter for those in authority in each society to determine. International law leaves room for collective and even individual actions without explicit Security Council approval. This allows collective actions like that of NATO over Kosovo or that of surrounding African states after the Rwandan genocide, as well as individual interventions like that of Nigeria in Sierra Leone during one of the worst stages in the conflict there. Prudential concerns imply collective action and even Security Council approval; the moral justification, though, pertains to the responsibility of individual states and those in authority in them.

My third observation is that the right to punish evil in this way must be used only with caution, for it can all too easily be misused. This is why, I think, war for religion has been so decisively rejected in Western moral and legal thought on the use of force from the Reformation era onwards. It is also, I suggest, why present-day justifications for intervention coalesce only around exceptional cases of violations of human rights, despite what this implies for the suffering an oppressed people must endure before they can receive help. That is, the evil that is to be punished, if the use of force across borders is to be just, must be palpable and incontrovertible; it must be associated with the clear failure of a state to do what political communities exist to do: provide a just and peaceful order for their members.

These same considerations apply to the fight against terrorism, except that here the cause of defense comes into play along with that of punishment. As for defense, there is no moral requirement that it be only passive, like imposing tighter security at airports and at borders; what is morally allowed also includes projections of force. This may be unilateral on the part of the society injured directly, but the permission to defend also includes the forming of formal and *ad hoc* alliances and other forms of multilateral cooperation. That which it is justified to defend against is not only acts that are in progress, in the sense of warding off a blow already descending, but also anything that constitutes a real and certain threat to the society as a whole or in any of its parts. The same act may be both defensive and punitive.

If we think about the measures that might rightly be used against those responsible for the September 11 attacks on America, others who may have assisted in those attacks or be involved in planning or preparation for others, and those who support their actions and provide safe haven, there is in my mind no doubt that actions up to and including the use of armed force are justified according to the moral reasoning we find in just war tradition. At the same time the requirement of right intention means that any response ought to be carefully gauged in terms of the wrong done or offered and not be characterized by any of those evils Augustine named: the desire to dominate, a cruel thirst for vengeance, an unruly and implacable animosity towards whole groups of people, or the desire simply to strike back, to give harm indiscriminately because indiscriminate harm has been received. The governing final goal should be, after all, to create peace where now there is animosity and conflict. While means of response up to and including military ones are justified by this moral reasoning, there is no implication that military action should be the only proper response or that it be the preferred form of response. Rather, what is justified by the need to defend and punish is the response, whether it take the form of military force or not. If force is employed, it should be discriminating in its targets and proportionate in its destructiveness, including the possibility of collateral harm. In terms of the morality of the use of force, broadly speaking, there is no difference between what just war thinking implies for the use of force against terrorists and what it implies for the use of force against states. What complicates the matter is the calculus of effectiveness required for the choice to use force in the first place and, in the use of force, the very real problem of identifying the proper targets and striking them in such a way as to minimize the harm to those people among whom terrorists often shelter themselves, but who are not themselves terrorists.

Terrorism as it exists today is evil in its own particular ways. There has been some debate over the years, renewed after the September 11 attacks, over whether terrorism is more like criminal activity or war. If the former, the argument goes, then the way to deal with it is by security measures, police work, and judicial procedures; if the latter, then diplomacy, economic sanctions, and ultimately military force are the means of choice. The truth is that terrorism is like both, and both sorts of measures should be used as appropriate.

In just war terms, terrorism is criminal activity in that it proceeds from leaders who lack right authority and the responsibility that goes with it, or else, in the case of state-sponsored terrorism, those in authority intentionally keep themselves removed from the organizations and agents who carry out the acts of terror. In either case the test of politically responsible authority is not met. Terrorism also lacks just cause, in that its purpose is not to restore justice but to balance a perceived injustice with another injustice. It lacks right intention in that it is motivated by a general hatred and desire to dominate. It lacks concern for the end [aim] of peace because its method is intentionally to cause chaos and strife. In *jus in bello* terms, its peculiar evil is that its trademark is direct, intentional attacks on the innocent as its chosen way of seeking to hurt its chosen enemies. Osama bin Laden's 1998 *fatwa* calling for a *jihad* against "Jews and crusaders" calls on every Muslim to attack every American, wherever he or she may be vulnerable. This is the direct opposite not only of Christian tradition on noncombatancy and the provisions of international law, but also of the clear teaching of normative Islam, where the combatant-noncombatant distinction is as clear as it is in Western moral and legal tradition. If anyone doubts that the September 11 attacks were aimed at innocents, one need only ask, what did the thousands who died there do to deserve that? The answer is nothing. They were merely instruments by which the terrorists sought to attack the nation as a whole. In criminal-law terms, these attacks were murder; in law-of-armed-conflicts terms, they were crimes of war. There should be no escaping this.

What makes terrorism unlike criminal activity as usually conceived is its international and global character, including its necessary dependence on the support and protection of friendly governments. Other contemporary phenomena like the trade in drugs also meet this test, and similarly fall between criminal activity and war. In such cases the term "war" is not an improper one for the national response. Indeed, just war tradition in its origins never distinguished between the use of force by the political community to combat disturbers of justice, order, and peace at home or abroad. The critical distinction made there was between use of force for the public good (*bellum*) and private use of force (*duellum*). We should not worry overmuch about use of the term "war" in the fight against terrorism. It is, in just war terms, a proper *bellum* for the use of all levels of force as appropriate by the national authority to respond to this profound form of evildoing.

Finally, I turn to a specifically domestic issue, the question of capital punishment. Just war thinking can provide moral guidance on this for the reason I have just mentioned: the critical moral issue is not the domestic-international distinction but the difference between use of force by public authority and for the public good and use of force by private persons for their own purposes. From the moral perspective I have been discussing there is no question that the public authority has the right to execute the death penalty on the worst offenders against the public good. This, I think, should not be in question. Indeed, Augustine thought it so unworthy of debate that he used the example of the public hangman to explain why a Christian should not fear to serve the political community as a soldier. The moral problem arises only after the questions of authority and just cause have been settled.

What of right intention? In a recent issue of *First Things* Avery Cardinal Dulles offers the following judgment:

> For better or worse, the state in our secular democratic societies is seen as a creature and instrument of the people, bound to carry out the will of the majority. In a society so governed, it becomes difficult to see the death sentence as representing the divine order of justice. Rather, it is seen as implementing the sovereign will of the people, whose appetite for vengeance grows with what it feeds on. (*First Things* No. 115, September 2001, 15)

On the face of it this observation seems to suggest that use of the death penalty is wrong for structural reasons in democratic societies but might be right in nondemocratic ones, where the death sentence might truly represent "the divine order of justice." One wonders why this same line of argument would not extend to calling in question a democracy's right to use force in defense or retaliation for an armed attack. In any case, I have already shown why I do not accept this line of reasoning either for myself or as a true representation of the Christian moral tradition on the use of force. What I want to focus on in Dulles' statement is something else: his suggestion that the death penalty is inappropriate in American society because it is connected to a popular "appetite for vengeance" that "grows with what it feeds on." This directly concerns whether use of the death penalty satisfies the moral requirement of right intention. My answer is, yes and no.

Augustine's term when defining wrong intention was "the cruelty of avenging" or "a cruel vengeance"; what he was concerned to avoid was cruelty, not vengeance as such, which in the absence of cruelty has a different moral character. In other words, what Augustine had in mind seems to me similar to our ban against "cruel and unusual" punishments.

Dulles' usage seems to assume that the desire for vengeance is in itself an example of wrong motivation and opposed to justice. I think he has a point, but I would not make it so globally as he does. We have recently witnessed the phenomenon of courts allowing persons injured by a crime to make emotional appeals during the sentencing process, appeals designed to lead to harsher sentences for those convicted. One can argue that this serves justice by making more visible the nature of the harm done. Yet one does not have to approach this from the position of a fastidious concern for the isolation of the judicial process to see that this raises real questions about the intentionality of the sentencing process. There is a reason for sequestering juries in cases involving crimes that have raised great public outcry; similarly, I think courts should not allow personal appeals by victims of crimes to attempt to influence the sentencing process. Doing so puts in question the presence of right intention in the judicial process.

Further moral questions are raised by asking whether the death penalty produces more good than harm and whether it is genuinely a last resort. In the case of war these questions always apply to the specific case at hand; new cases require new calculations. Applied to the domestic use of the death penalty, this model would at minimum require the abolition of mandatory death sentences, so that each case would be decided independently, with justice meted out on the merits of the case. Can anything be said more generally? I think that in principle it should not, since prudential judgments by their nature must be revisited again and again as conditions change. The results of one such decision at a given time, under particular conditions, should not be made into a moral absolute. But that may be one of the best reasons for a new consideration of the proportionality of the use of the death penalty—to question the use that has crystallized out of past decisions made under their own circumstances.

As for whether the death penalty constitutes a proper last resort, I would argue that it does not as presently constituted. Last resort, like proportionality, needs to be decided on a case-by-case basis. What this implies is, as in the case of proportionality, doing away with mandatory death sentences but retaining, for certain crimes, the possibility of the death penalty at the end of the moral spectrum of possibilities.

One of the current arguments against the use of the death penalty in the United States is that the judicial processes which lead to its imposition are very often systematically flawed with the result that the careful discrimination called for loses out to conviction of the wrong people. This is the same territory as the just war requirement of discrimination or noncombatant immunity, which requires that the innocent not be directly, intentionally targeted, that efforts be made to identify them correctly (for example, not treating all members of an enemy society as if they were proper objects of attack), and that means be chosen that do not unduly punish them. In other words, when applied to thinking about the use of the death penalty, just war reasoning raises questions as to whether the punishment properly targets the guilty, whether it tends to target racial minorities and the poor as groups, whether it should not give way to other forms of punishment where there is some ambiguity as to these factors. To pursue this line of thinking further, consider that the just war idea of noncombatant immunity has historically identified the mentally incompetent as properly immune from direct, intended attack. This argues against imposing the death penalty on the mentally retarded, and not only those deemed legally insane.

The overall thrust of the moral argument regarding the use of force is the same, I believe, for both the international and domestic cases: resort to deadly force is permitted under specific conditions, but it is also morally limited. Even in an armed conflict justified in terms of the deontological criteria, there are prudential restraints that are to be taken into account, and in using justified force there are limits that should be observed. At the extreme of possibility, it is possible to imagine a conflict in which the enemy is not killed but simply imprisoned or otherwise made incapable of fighting. In the domestic context this is the reality, not a utopian image, for prison provides a real option to death for control of criminals who might otherwise be judged to deserve death for their actions against the society.

These are but a few considerations applying just war reasoning to consideration of the moral issues involved in the death penalty. While I have not explored them in depth, I have attempted to identify a line of argument that comes from such reasoning: that while the option of the death penalty may rightly remain for exceptional cases, the moral argument works against mandatory death sentences for whole classes of crimes, and it implies that the use of the death penalty should otherwise be limited because of the existence of other alternative penalties and because of the problem of violating discrimination, that is, killing people who do not deserve, in justice, to be killed.

CONCLUSION

What I have been arguing is that Christian moral tradition on the political community and the use of force by it for the service of the public good continues to offer relevant moral guidance for contemporary debates over the use of force, whether internationally or domestically. This argument rejects the position that there is never any justification for the use of force, whether by individuals or by governments acting on behalf of their political communities; I believe Christian thought carries a different message. My argument also rejects two other methods in ethical reasoning found in contemporary Christian thought: the pacifist claim that the only place to look for moral guidance is the Bible or the experience of the early church, or some combination of both, and that contemporary issues should be approached principally by an effort to live an individually Christ-like life.

My argument against the first is that while these are properly ultimate reference points for Christian living, there is a kind of arrogance in not being willing to take account of what previous generations of Christians have done in their own moral reasoning to respond to the guidance they find there. We are historical beings, and we live this out most completely when we take into account the normative traditions shaped by the historical effort to live out the meaning of Christian life. This means taking moral traditions seriously.

As for the emphasis on the Christ-like life, this is always properly a goal for individual Christians. But it is not nearly so simple to do so as many seem to assume, and certainly not so simple to do so in every respect and not simply in the one respect of rejecting violence. It is important to avoid being selective in representing what being Christ-like implies: the New Testament record is not single-minded on this in regard to the question of force, and in any case the use of force is but one part of a larger moral package, not all of which advocates of an ethic of Christ-likeness may be prepared to embrace. A further issue is the difference between private and public morality: responsibility for life together in political community introduces many more, and much more complex, moral obligations than we find in the moral life of the single individual. One has to work out what this means, if one is in a position of public responsibility, and just war tradition is effectively the collective moral wisdom produced over a long history of trying to figure this out.

Concern over the morality of the use of force is properly worth addressing at any time and place. In the present context, though, it seems to me utterly necessary to do so. For Christians, this means understanding what Christian tradition yields on the good of the political community and on the use of force in the service of that good.

ABSTRACT

In this essay, Johnson emphasizes the differences between traditional and extremist concepts of jihad. In the pursuit of using force in order to uphold high ideals of values and beliefs, both traditional Islamic and Christian just war thought aspire to protect the common good.

CHAPTER 8

JIHAD AND JUST WAR

In February 1998, long before the September 11 terrorist attacks on America, Osama bin Laden and four other leaders of radical Islamist groups in various countries issued a fatwa, or religious ruling, calling for jihad against "the crusader-Zionist alliance" in the following language:

> In compliance with God's order, we issue the following fatwa to all Muslims: the ruling to kill the Americans and their allies—civilians and military—is an individual duty for every Muslim who can do it in any country in which it is possible to do it, in order to liberate the al-Aqsa Mosque [Jerusalem] and the holy mosque [Mecca] from their grip, and in order for their armies to move out of the lands of Islam.... This is in accordance with the words of Almighty God, "and fight the pagans all together as they fight you all together," and "fight them until there is no more tumult or oppression, and there prevail justice and faith in God."

While more examples of bin Laden's thinking emerged after the September 11 attacks, this fatwa stands as a fundamental statement of his rationale for a campaign of violence against America and the West: an appeal to the Islamic tradition of defensive jihad by which every Muslim is obligated, as an individual duty, to take up arms against invaders. It lays out the justification not only for the attacks of September 11, but also for other terrorist attacks linked to bin Laden's al-Qaida group, notably, the bombings of the two American embassies in East Africa and of the U.S.S. *Cole.* It also provides a warrant for future attacks by "every Muslim who can do it in any country in which it is possible to do it"—in short, for a continuing war by terrorist and other means by Muslims against "Americans and their allies," an ongoing clash of civilizations. How should this call be understood in relation to the Islamic tradition? And how does it compare to the just war tradition of Western culture?

The classical Islamic conception of jihad in the sense of warfare comes not from the Qur'an directly, where the term jihad is used to refer to the believer's inner struggle for righteousness, but from the jurists of the early Abbasid period (the late-eighth and early-ninth centuries AD), who developed it in the context of a general effort to clarify the nature of the Islamic community, the proper leadership of that community, and the community's relations with the non-Islamic world. Central to this conception was a legal division of the world into two realms: the *dar al-Islam* or abode of Islam, and the remainder of the world, defined as the *dar al-harb* or abode of war.

The *dar al-Islam,* as the jurists understood it, had existed since its creation by the Prophet Muhammad himself, who had been its first head. It is a community at once religious and political, and thus its ruler, like the Prophet, was understood to be supreme in both spheres. There could be at any time only one right ruler, understood to be the successor of the Prophet and inheritor of his authority. Because of its character—its essential unity, its rule by a successor of the Prophet, its governance according to divinely given law—the *dar al-Islam* is fundamentally different from the rest of the world, which is torn by perpetual conflict and is a constant threat to the peace of the *dar al-Islam.* A general, lasting, universal peace is impossible until the *dar al-harb* is no more, when the whole world has become the *dar al-Islam,* a place within which submission (*islam*) to God is the law of the land. Until then war between the two realms is the normal state. Yet at the same time extended periods of peace are possible by means of treaties between the *dar al-Islam* and non-Islamic societies.

This conception formed the background for the jurists' conception of the idea of jihad as warfare. As they described it, this warfare could take two forms: that of the *dar al-Islam* as a body under the authority of its legitimate ruler, the caliph for the Sunni tradition, the imam for the Shiite—a conception that encompassed offensive war against the general threat and organized collective defense against attack—and an emergency form of defensive jihad against a direct attack on the *dar al-Islam* by a force from some part of the *dar al-harb*. In the former case the duty to take part in jihad was conceived as a collective one, with some Muslims fighting and others playing other roles, including simply going about their normal lives; in the latter case, though, to fight was an individual duty, incumbent on all Muslims who were able to do so in the immediate area of the aggression.

These were significantly different forms of warfare. The collective jihad was a thoroughly rule-governed activity, from the requirement of the caliph/imam's authority to that of a declaration of hostilities and a call for peace to a form of combatant–noncombatant distinction to extensive discussion of the disposition of spoils by the ruling authority. The jurists clearly understood this as the norm for the warfare of the *dar al-Islam*. This form of jihad drew upon the religious unity of the Islamic community even as it depended on the social and institutional relationships that comprised the Islamic state; the proper exercise of jihad on this model strengthened the *dar al-Islam* and the role of its ruler both religiously and politically.

The jihad of emergency defense was another matter entirely. It assumed an acute emergency in which normal religiously and socially prescribed relationships and structures were erased. The model the jurists had in mind was simple: a direct attack across the border of the *dar al-Islam* by a force from the *dar al-harb* in some particular place remote from the *dar al-Islam*'s center of authority and power. Against this attack Muslims in the area were to rise up in arms, on their own authority, as a kind of *levée en masse*. The individual duty to take up arms crossed and eliminated all the usual divisions: not only healthy men of fighting age but women, children, the aged, and the infirm were to fight to the limit of their ability to do so. Correspondingly, the rules of collective jihad did not apply: the enemy was the invading army, so noncombatants were not present and thus played no part in the conflict. While the jurists admitted this form of jihad in time of dire emergency caused by overt aggression, there was an inherent tension between it and the collective jihad of the *dar al-Islam* under the authority of the caliph/imam. In practical terms, local leaders on the frontiers might (and did) use the excuse of the jihad of emergency to challenge the legitimacy of the central authority. However, this form of jihad was originally meant to be an exceptional response to an exceptional circumstance, not the norm for Muslim warfare.

It is generally agreed within Islam that jihad of the first sort is impossible today, as there is no central caliph or imam. This gives new importance to what was originally considered to be an exceptional case: the idea of jihad as an individual duty in the face of external aggression. In the Islamic mainstream this conception has developed along lines compatible with international law to allow Muslim heads of state to organize and execute defense collectively, though on the juristic model they do so on the basis of the individual responsibility of all their people to respond to aggression. The historical model for such action is the medieval hero Saladin, who though only a regional commander (not the caliph) organized and led a successful defense against the armies of the Second Crusade. In theory, this mainstream conception of defense respects the patterns of relationships within the society as well as the limits to be observed in fighting, the most important of which are understood to come from the Prophet Muhammad himself.

However, the last hundred years or so have seen the development of another line of interpretation of jihad. First appearing in North Africa as an ideology for resistance against colonialism, by 1960 it was being used as a justification for terrorist attacks against Israel, and in the 1970s and 1980s it was adapted to justify armed struggle by terror and assassination in such states as Iran, Egypt, and Algeria against rulers who were nominally Muslim but were judged to be tools of the West. It is out of this tradition that bin Laden's fatwa has emerged.

This radical form of jihad makes several critical assumptions not found in the traditional conception or in the mainstream theory. First, the *dar al-Islam* is conceived as any territory whose population is mainly Muslim and which was once part of the historical *dar al-Islam.* By this reasoning any non-Islamic state existing within the territory of the historical *dar al-Islam,* as well as all non-Islamic presence within that space, must be resisted and subdued or eliminated. Further, the "aggressors" are deemed to be all those who support such states or non-Islamic presence, so that the usual lines of distinction between combatants and noncombatants are erased, with the result that all individuals are considered acceptable targets. Further, because of its origins in an "emergency," there are no limits on means in this struggle. Finally, all Muslims are faced with the duty to take part in this struggle, so that it ultimately becomes one involving individuals rather than politically organized communities; anyone who accepts this duty—men of fighting age, women, children, or the aged or infirm—becomes a combatant in the war.

This extreme interpretation of the idea of defensive jihad implicitly rejects much of the actual history of Muslim societies and the Muslim faith. It leaves scant room for toleration of "people of the book," as prescribed in the Qur'an, because it treats the simple presence of Christians and Jews in dominantly Muslim societies as an act of aggression. It also leaves no room for differences of interpretation as to what Islam requires; its reading of Islamic law is narrow and unyielding on doctrine and behavior alike. Social developments identified with modernity are rejected as un-Islamic, even if large numbers of Muslims have accepted them without losing their faith.

Bin Laden's fatwa reflects all these assumptions. The United States is deemed an aggressor against all Islam because of the presence of U.S. troops in Saudi Arabia, despite the fact that they are there by agreement, and despite the fact that their purpose is to protect Saudi Arabia, not to dominate it. Likewise, the "protracted blockade" against Iraq is viewed as an assault on the Iraqi people, despite the fact that Saddam Hussein's diversion of resources for his own purposes is the real cause of their suffering. The same could be said of bin Laden's hostility to U.S. support for "the Jews' petty state" and "its occupation of Jerusalem and murder of Muslims." In other words, the United States has become the embodiment of the *dar al-harb*, engaged in aggression against Islam, despite the fact that millions of Muslims live and enjoy freedom of religion within its borders. But bin Laden's fatwa takes the radical line of jihad to new extremes when it calls for any and all Muslims to kill any and all Americans—"civilians and military" alike—in any country in which it is possible to do it." No longer a defensive war, this is jihad on the offensive.

Bin Laden and his associates in the fatwa of course lack the religiously mandated authority to wage such war, as they do not bear the mantle of succession to the Prophet. That is why they try to describe the war against America as a defensive one. By painting the entire nation of America as guilty of "aggression," the fatwa can set aside the limits imposed on warfare by normative Islamic tradition, which includes no direct, intended killing of noncombatants and no use of fire, which is prohibited among Muslims because it is the weapon God will use in the last days. Bin Laden's jihad not only pits Islam against America, the West as a whole, and ultimately the rest of the non-Islamic world; it also seeks to overthrow the contemporary Muslim states and mainstream views of Islamic tradition among the great majority of contemporary Muslims.

To be sure, the early Abbasid jurists also thought the relation of the Islamic and non-Islamic worlds to be one of inherent conflict, and their notion of the collective warfare aimed at ensuring the eventual submission of the entire world to God reflected this. Yet they never defined this eschatological goal as one that could be achieved only by war or even primarily by war. And in the absence of any universal Muslim ruler bearing the mantle of authority of the Prophet, Muslim tradition and Muslim life have found ways of pursuing this goal by other, nonmilitary means. The radical ideology of jihad changes this, making the use of violent means, indiscriminately and without principled limits, a binding obligation for all Muslims.

While the idea of just war is deeply rooted in Western culture, it is perhaps more strongly institutionalized today in international law, in American military doctrine and practice, and even in political culture than at any time since the age of Vitoria. Though the just war tradition has important Christian roots, it differs from the Islamic juristic tradition in that it can be employed without explicitly religious premises. Similarly, in Western political thought and theology more generally, the nature of the political community, the role of government, and the use of armed force are conceived in secular rather than religious terms. All these features differentiate just war tradition from the juristic tradition of jihad by the *dar al-Islam* on the authority of the caliph/imam.

Yet there are also significant points of contact, which reveal important common interests. I have already suggested this by noting that mainstream Islamic thought and political practice have developed in a way compatible with international law and orderly, peaceful interaction with non-Muslim nations. More specifically, both traditions link the right to use armed force to the exercise of legitimate governing authority for the protection and common good of the governed community. That common good, moreover, is defined normatively in terms of high ideals of value and behavior, not in terms of repression and intolerance. Both traditions recognize that even the use of force justified in this way is not without limits when it comes to the question of who may be targeted and the means that may be used against aggressors. These are all matters on which there can and should be a pursuit of common cause. The radical doctrine of jihad advanced as the justification for contemporary terrorism is a challenge to both of these traditions, and people of good will from both communities have reason to reject it.

ABSTRACT

In this essay Johnson examines the just war approaches of Thomas Aquinas and Martin Luther for *jus ad bellum* regarding just cause and the use of force. Johnson places responsibility squarely with the sovereign leadership for moral assessment and action and also finds the concept of "regime change" within the just war tradition.

CHAPTER 9

AQUINAS AND LUTHER ON WAR AND PEACE: SOVEREIGN AUTHORITY AND THE USE OF ARMED FORCE

1. "WAR" IN CONTEMPORARY USAGE AND IN AQUINAS AND LUTHER

My subject is Aquinas and Luther on the authority for use of armed force. They would have said "the authority for war," but their use of the word "war" would not have been congruent with our own. In modern international law a state of war is a formal state of relations between two or more states, different from both a state of peace and a *status mixtus*, a mixed state between war and peace. In some contemporary ethical discourse "war" denotes military action engaged in by a state for reasons of national interest, and thus it is different from uses of military force for other reasons, like supporting international peacekeeping operations or humanitarian intervention, which may be undertaken for more altruistic motives.

The restricted meaning of "war" in international law has led to the general adoption of the term "armed conflict" to apply to all such conflicts that do not meet the legal criteria for war—civil conflicts like those in the former Yugoslavia; conflicts in which at least one of the actors is not a state, like that between the United States and Al Qaeda; conflicts between or among states that are wars in every way except for being formally declared and recognized.

Different issues are behind the contemporary ethical usage I have mentioned. I think it is significant that the distinction between "war" and peacekeeping or humanitarian interventionary uses of armed force is a product of the post-Cold War world, in which it has become possible for the United States to use its military in ways that would not risk a nuclear confrontation with the Soviet Union. In particular, pressure grew all through the 1990s for the United States to commit military forces for peacekeeping and conflict management and to address egregious cases of humanitarian need caused by local armed conflicts, including abuses engaged in by governments bent on some version of "ethnic cleansing." But in the ethical debates of the 1960s, 1970s, and 1980s, framed to address the early stages of nuclear deterrence policy, the Vietnam war, and the nuclear policies of the Reagan years, many participants, and especially influential segments of the Catholic and Protestant Christian ethical community, became deeply distrustful of government, of the state as an institution, and of "war" as an activity of government on behalf of the state. Thus when the possibility emerged for uses of military force for purposes defined by goals higher than the state—international peace-keeping, defense of human rights in conflict-torn societies—those ethicists who had committed themselves to a dubious or outright negative position on "war" found themselves in an awkward position. Their opposition to "war" had led them to oppose virtually everything military; now they were in a position of supporting means up to and including military action, and the military resources necessary, to meet the humanitarian needs they felt so deeply.

One approach to this tension was adopted by the General Assembly of the Presbyterian Church (USA) in 1998, which in a resolution concerning the use of military force for humanitarian intervention set the following condition: "[Intervention] must constitute humanitarian rescue and not cloak the pursuit of the economic or narrow security interests of the intervening powers."[1] To my mind there are numerous problems with this criterion as stated, but my point here is simply to note the sharp difference drawn between "humanitarian rescue" and national economic or security interests. The Presbyterian statement insists that these can and should be separated. Why they should be separated is simply assumed. I suggest it is because a long history of similar resolutions had established such a pervasive distrust of uses of the idea of national interest that pursuit of such interest had become by definition immoral. Thus acceptance of military force for humanitarian rescue required a sharp break from uses of such force for national interest purposes.

A more fully developed illustration of this same tension between types of use of armed force is provided by the 1993 statement of the United States Catholic bishops, *The Harvest of Justice Is Sown in Peace.*[2] Written as a "pastoral reflection" to mark the ten-year anniversary of their far more widely known pastoral letter, *The Challenge of Peace*,[3] the 1993 statement early on affirms the position of the earlier pastoral letter that Catholic tradition on war begins with a "presumption against war," a position that had been used over the intervening years to undergird a general opposition to United States use of military forces. A notable example of this understanding of the "presumption against war" is the statements of NCCB officials at the time of the Gulf War,[4] which put so much emphasis on the just war criteria of last resort, reasonable hope of success, and overall proportionality as to effectively rule out or postpone indefinitely any use of military force to expel Iraq from Kuwait. *The Harvest of Justice*, written only two years later, began by embracing this same commitment to the "presumption against war" idea (rendered here more generally as "a strong presumption against the use of force")[5] and argued strongly for building down national military capacity. Yet not many pages later, the bishops warmly embraced the cause of humanitarian intervention, citing Pope John Paul II that it "is a duty for nations and the international community."[6] Given the language of the "strong presumption," this embrace of the use of force for humanitarian intervention is something of a leap, unless such use of force is conceived as something other than "war."

Neither Aquinas nor Luther would have understood the effort to make a distinction between the use of force for purposes of national interest and the altruistic use of force for humanitarian purposes. For them another distinction was paramount, the same one that had been central for Augustine and, overall, stands at the center of the just war tradition: the distinction between the use of force by public authority for the public good and that on private authority for whatever reasons. The former was termed *bellum*, war, while the latter was *duellum*, literally a duel. We have been taught by Paul Ramsey and others to think of Augustine's just war thought as centered on the implications of Christian love (charity or *caritas*) for noncombatant immunity and the protection of the innocent neighbor from unjust harm. Whatever the merits of this argument for justifying Christian participation in war, it is a theological extrapolation. When Augustine himself wrote about war, the subject of *caritas* comes up only indirectly and implicitly, as in the well-known passage from *Contra Faustum* (xxii.74) used by the tradition to define wrong intention: "What is evil in war? It is not the deaths of some who will soon die anyway. The desire for harming, the cruelty of avenging, an unruly and implacable animosity, the rage of rebellion, the lust of domination and the like—these are the things which are to be blamed in war." These are all intentions motivated by wrongly directed love, *cupiditas*, though this term is never used here or in the surrounding context. What *caritas* implies is another sort of intention: "We do not seek peace in order to be at war, but we go to war that we may have peace. Be peaceful, therefore, in warring, so that you may vanquish those whom you war against, and bring them to the prosperity of peace."[7] It is significant that this last passage, with the imperative on how to prosecute war, is addressed to Count Boniface, a Roman official with responsibility for public order in his region and the command of troops to maintain that order. This was in line with Augustine's general position that only the public authority could justly use military force, stated succinctly in this passage: "The natural order conducive to peace among mortals demands that the power to declare and counsel war should be in the hands of those who hold the supreme authority."[8] *Bellum* may be just or not, depending on the circumstances; *duellum* can never be.

It is significant that all these passages I have quoted from Augustine are found in Aquinas's discussion of just war in the *Summa Theologica* III, Q. 40, and I have cited them as they appear there. The point to note is that these passages and a relatively small number of others, first assembled and put together in a cohesive form by the canonist Gratian in the mid-twelfth century, defined Augustine's contribution to just war tradition as it developed in the Middle Ages. Here authority was central to the possibility of justice in the use of force, for this was part of God's government of the world. In the medieval tradition and right on up into the era of the Reformers this idea was axiomatically expressed by an often-quoted biblical passage, Romans 13:3–4: "For rulers are not a terror to good conduct, but to bad. Would you have no fear of him who is in authority? Then do what is good, and you will receive his approval, for he is God's servant for your good. But if you do wrong, be afraid, for he does not bear the sword in vain; he is the servant of God to execute his wrath on the wrongdoer" (RSV).

The majority of recent Christian ethical debate on morality and war, even that framed in just war terms, has lost sight of this element of the Christian tradition regarding political authority and the use of force. Those who follow Paul Ramsey's thought on just war only so far as his rendering of Christian just war thought in terms of the implications of love for noncombatant immunity and protection of the neighbor tend to have a just war theory that ignores the tradition's *jus ad bellum* and tends to make what Ramsey called a *jus contra bellum justum* out of the practical impossibility of entirely avoiding harm to noncombatants in contemporary war. Ramsey himself, by contrast, insisted that the just war idea is part of a general theory of statecraft, and he linked the permission with limitation he derived from Christian love to the requirements of political community, to guide those in authority in those communities.[9] But even among those who have a fuller view of the traditional criteria for just war, listings such as found in the official statements of the United States Catholic bishops,[10] the influential treatment of Michael Walzer in *Just and Unjust Wars*,[11] and, I must confess, my own writings up to about seven or eight years ago, regularly give priority in discussion of the *jus ad bellum* to the idea of just cause, though the traditional listings put sovereign authority first. In the contemporary listings what is variously rendered as "right" or "competent" authority typically follows in second place, where it is typically described in formalistic terms as whatever authority happens to be in place within a state and where it is simply given the role of authorizing what is previously known to be justified in terms of the just cause. I think there are two main reasons for this prioritization and de-emphasizing of the authority criterion. First, this way of thinking about the relation between just cause and authority for use of force follows from the Westphalian conception of the state and of international relations and directly parallels the structure of international law, where the resort to force by any state against another is prohibited unless it is in defense against an armed attack from the other.[12] With the justifying cause thus described, the role of authority is simply to authorize appropriate measures of defense, up to and including the use of force. For some others a second, and perhaps in the end more powerful, reason may be the fundamental mistrust of the state itself which I have already mentioned and thus of its authorizing the use of force on behalf of its own interests. Whatever the reasons, though, in the priority given to just cause and the relative de-emphasizing of the authority requirement recent just war thinking contrasts markedly with what we find in earlier normative just war tradition, and especially for our current theme, with what we find in the thought on war of Thomas Aquinas and Martin Luther. Let me now turn to these, beginning with Aquinas on war.

2. AQUINAS ON SOVEREIGN AUTHORITY

Aquinas's Question 40 "On War" in the Secunda Secundae of the *Summa Theologica* treats four points of inquiry: "(1) Whether some kind of war is lawful? (2) Whether it is lawful for clerics to fight? (3) Whether it is lawful for belligerents to lay ambushes? [and] (4) Whether it is lawful to fight on holy days?" These were all questions hotly and extensively debated during the Middle Ages, though it must be said that by the time Thomas wrote, there was a broad consensus on the answers, a consensus to be found in the canon law developed by Gratian and his two waves of successors, the Decretists and the Decretalists.[13] Thomas's answers here were important for their own time not as breaking new ground but as putting the consensus into a broader systematic theological framework, and they became much more important in the modern period, after Vitoria's lectures on the question "On War" and especially after the place given Aquinas's theology as a whole in and after the Counter-Reformation. To put this another way, his contemporaries would have found no new or strikingly off-beat positions here, and moderns may take him as a reliable window on the main line of just war tradition as it had developed by his time. My focus in the present context is on the First Article, where the discussion of authority for just war is found.

Aquinas's language in this discussion is widely familiar. In his own answer to the question whether war is sinful ("I answer that"), he lays out the conditions for a just war: "In order for a war to be just," he writes, "three things are necessary." He then briefly identifies these conditions: sovereign authority, just cause, and right intention. In terms of the usual contemporary listings of the categories, he really names four conditions as we would understand them today, because right intention as he describes it here has two components, one positive and one negative. The positive side of right intention is the aim of peace, and contemporary just war commentators usually list this as a distinct criterion within the *jus ad bellum*. The negative side is, as noted earlier, the avoidance of wrong intention. Aquinas puts it this way, using language borrowed from the canon law: "True religion looks upon as peaceful those wars that are waged not for motives of aggrandizement, or cruelty, but with the object of securing peace, of punishing evil-doers, and of uplifting the good." As he continues he treats the positive and negative components of right intention further, using language from Augustine to explain both wrong intention[14] and the end [aim] of peace.[15]

But let us for a moment think about the present passage, which describes right intention in this way: "the object of securing peace, of punishing evil-doers, and of uplifting the good." Compare this with his description of just cause using this language from Augustine: "A just war is wont to be described as one that avenges wrongs, when a nation or a state has to be punished, for refusing to make amends for the wrongs inflicted by its subjects, or to restore what it has seized unjustly."[16] Now, the canon law from Gratian onwards included this statement, which renders just cause in terms of punishment of evil and recovery of that which has been wrongly taken, but it also included another statement on just cause from Isidore of Seville: "A war is just when ... it is waged to regain what has been stolen or to repel the attack of enemies."[17] Aquinas surely knew this passage from Isidore; every canonist and theologian did. The standard medieval listing of just causes, both before Aquinas and after him, combined Isidore and Augustine: defense against attack, punishment of evil, recovery of that which had been wrongly taken. Aquinas's usage is more, I think, than an expression of preference of Augustine over Isidore, and Aquinas certainly justified action in self-defense elsewhere.[18] But the language he chooses for himself and borrows from others in his definition of both just cause and right intention is, I think, quite intentionally focused on the prevention of evil, the setting right of wrongs already done, the punishment of evildoers, and overall the promotion of good. These are all precisely what the good ruler is to do. So it is very significant, I think, that Aquinas's list of the requirements for just war begins with the requirement of sovereign authority, and so that we do not miss the significance of this requirement, its first priority in his listing of the three necessities for a just war, he reminds us by the way he casts the requirements of just cause and right intention.

Here is how Aquinas defines the requirement of sovereign authority:

> For it is not the business of the private individual to declare war [*bellum*], because he can seek for redress of his rights from the tribunal of

> his superior. Moreover, it is not the business of a private individual to summon together the people, which has to be done in wartime. And as the care of the common weal is committed to those who are in authority, it is their business to watch over the common weal of the city, kingdom or province subject to them. And just as it is lawful for them to have recourse to the sword in defending that common weal against internal disturbances, when they punish evil-doers, according to the words of the Apostle (Rom. xiii. 4): *He beareth not the sword in vain: for he is God's minister, an avenger to execute wrath upon him that doth evil*; so too, it is their business to have recourse to the sword of war in defending the common weal against external enemies.[19]

Two things stand out here: the sharp distinction between the rights of the sovereign and those of private persons relating to war and the strong connection between the sovereign's right to wage war and his positive responsibilities as the one given charge for the common weal. The former follows from the latter. In this Aquinas is absolutely at one with the main line of medieval tradition. There is a fundamental moral difference between the use of the sword by one in sovereign authority or on his behalf and use of the sword by a private individual. The former may wage *bellum*, which is the use of the sword on behalf of the common good; the latter may not.

Aquinas's treatment of defense as just cause fits hand-in-glove with his interest in distinguishing between the use of the sword on sovereign authority and on that of a private person. He does not appeal to the right of self-defense in discussing the sovereign's right to the sword but rather cites the sovereign's responsibility to defend the common weal. A private person may justly defend himself or others for whom he has responsibility from an attack; that is, in fact, the only justified use of the sword by private individuals which Aquinas appears ready to allow. But, as I suggested earlier, it is significant that Aquinas does not speak when discussing war of "defense against attack" but of "defense of the common weal"; what the sovereign is to defend against is "internal disturbances" and "external enemies." His reasoning is not to generalize from the right of self-defense against harm but to particularize from the sovereign's responsibility to seek the good for the society he governs. This is a very different sort of right to the sword from that allowed to private persons. Nor should one reason backwards to the private individual from other uses allowed only to the sovereign: to punish evil, to restore that which has been wrongly taken, both internally to the society and externally. Private individuals have no right of recourse to the sword for such reasons; they should instead appeal to their superior for justice, and it is the superior's "business," as Aquinas puts it, to seek to give it to them.

In short, Aquinas's understanding is that it is the responsibility of sovereignty to uphold the good and seek to ensure the common weal which give him the right to employ the sword. The right to use armed force to punish evildoers and right wrongs is the other side of the responsibility, in natural law and under God, to govern so as to serve good. Thus perhaps one should not read Aquinas on sovereign authority in the Question "On War" without also reading his short treatise *On Princely Rule* (*De Regimine Principiae*), where the prince's responsibilities are laid out in more detail. This comparatively neglected work in Aquinas's corpus properly belongs to that stream in medieval political literature which culminates in Erasmus's *The Education of a Christian Prince* (Born, 1965);[20] it is a literature focused on defining the exercise of ruling authority in fundamentally moral terms, terms determined by the good of the political community and the ruler's responsibility for seeking that good for his particular community. In the century after Aquinas the ruler's responsibility would be put in the language of the Augustinian trilogy order, justice, and peace by such otherwise different political writers as Marsilius of Padua (*Defensor Pacis*)[21] and Dante;[22] it is the ruler's responsibility to impose an order which embodies justice and thus produces peace. While Aquinas does not use this specific formula or utilize Augustine's phrase "the tranquillity of order" (*tranquillitas ordinis*) in his discussion of princely rule or the sovereign's authority to use the sword, the lines of his thought trend toward the same end. Order alone is not enough, but it is a necessary prerequisite for justice and peace.

The respected European commentator Alfred Vanderpol remarked of the just war theory of Aquinas and scholastic theology in general that it was focused on punishment of evil as a way of serving *la justice vindicatif,* literally "vindicative"—not vindictive but vindicative—justice, the justice of vindication, of setting things right.[23] While this correlates closely with Aquinas's two just causes for war—punishment of evil and restoring what has been wrongly taken—I think there is more to be said; his conception of sovereign authority is put not only in such terms but more broadly as "defense of the common weal." As noted earlier, the antipathies generated by opposition to nuclear weapons and to the Vietnam War have produced a legacy in some Christian ethical writing about war of distrust of the state and its power. The large state in particular has been a target of much suspicion. As a part of this suspicion, the idea of the state and its power as a source of good has been trumped by the idea that the state, in pursuit of its self-interest, tends to use its power for injustice, not justice, for evil, not good. Such an idea is, I think, well exemplified by the Presbyterian statement cited earlier, when military intervention is justified provided it has nothing to do with national interest. But the historic Christian position on ruling authority and its power was motivated by something very different: a fear of the injustice of chaos, the free rein absence of political order gives to individuals to pursue their private selfish ends to the detriment of others. I could cite many examples from the whole range of Christian thinking on politics and just war from Augustine through the Reformers; let me take just one example, the medieval phenomenon known as the Peace of God.

This was a movement which developed and flourished in southern and southwestern France during the late tenth and into the eleventh centuries. These were regions in which a settled, peaceful life was routinely disrupted by violence from three kinds of sources: armed conflicts among local knights and barons over power and land, bullying and extortion by the landless knights and men-at-arms employed by these local lords, and robber bands living on the fringes of organized society who would periodically raid towns, villages, and travelers to take whatever they could for their own use. In short, these regions were the "wild west" of medieval France. The Peace of God movement was an attempt to deal with this chaotic, unjust state of affairs. It originated in the action of regional councils of bishops, like that of the Council of Le Puy in 975 and that of Charroux in 989.[24] The action the bishops took aimed at first at protecting the church's own: churches and their attached lands, clergy, religious, pilgrims on the road and their property; soon it extended to protection also of innocent townspeople, peasants on the land, and the property of both. The bishops' weapon was excommunication and thus the threat of damnation. This essentially religious movement quickly took on a temporal component, as the regional counts (a term which, at this period, designated a royal official with regional authority and the armed forces to enforce that authority) took up the cause so as to extend royal authority and order into the affected regions by putting down the violence and punishing those who were its source. The Peace of God movement—so-called because the bishops' councils typically adopted a statement establishing a "peace of God" around all the persons and properties identified for protection and issued anathemas against those who violated this "peace"—struck a deep chord in medieval thought about politics and just war. It was the immediate, practical source of the idea of noncombatant immunity within Christian just war thought (and parenthetically, the categories of protected persons it named are effectively those protected today by the Geneva Conventions), and it was also an important contributor to the canonical debate over authority to wage war which began with Gratian and developed with his two generations of successors, and whose outcome Aquinas assumed and adopted in his Question "On War."

For medieval thinkers about politics and the use of armed force, to state the matter shortly, the fear was chaos, and to stress the responsibilities of sovereign authority and the goods of political order was the answer; the fear was not of violence as such, as critics of war today would typically have it, but of violence in the service of private, selfish ends—all the things Augustine listed as "wrong intentions"—"the desire for harming, the cruelty of avenging, an unruly and implacable animosity, the lust of domination and the like"—a list the canonists and Aquinas prominently included in their own writings. Perhaps in an age when we have come to know the evil terrorism can do we can understand this medieval concern better than we could earlier. Yet the more general point to draw from the priority Aquinas, along with medieval just war tradition in general, gave to the requirement of sovereign authority for the use of force is to look behind that requirement to its foundation in the conception of the good political community and the responsibility of the sovereign authority to support its common weal and defend it against threats from both within and without. This is a lesson about how we ought to think about politics and about the meaning of sovereignty, one important not only for our own society and its government but also for other societies and the international realm as a whole.

3. LUTHER ON SOVEREIGN AUTHORITY

Let me now turn to Luther. The parameters of Luther's thought on war are defined by four of his writings: *Temporal Authority: To What Extent It Should Be Obeyed* (1523),[25] *Against the Robbing and Murdering Hordes of Peasants* (1525),[26] *Whether Soldiers, Too, Can Be Saved* (1526),[27] and *On War against the Turk* (1529).[28] Perhaps most people who know anything at all about Luther on war know him through his treatise against the peasants, which one standard collection excerpts under the title, "Stab, Smite, Slay."[29] But this is the wrong place to begin. The best beginning-point is the earliest and most fundamental of these writings, the treatise *Temporal Authority*. This work establishes the general framework of Luther's political theory around the concept of the two "kingdoms" (that of God and that of the world) with their respective "governments" (the spiritual and the temporal or secular). This is the proper place to begin examining Luther's thought on war, because like Aquinas, and in the mainstream of the just war tradition Luther inherited and employed, for Luther the question of authority is the most fundamental one for the justice of use of the sword. So it is here that we begin.

The distinction between the spiritual and the temporal was passed on to Luther and his contemporaries as part of their common intellectual heritage from the Middle Ages, though Luther and his papalist adversaries interpreted the meaning of the distinction in sharply different ways. The papalists of the previous century and Luther's own time held that the spiritual authority not only has its own exclusive sphere but also occupies a place of superiority over the secular within the world. On this view the papacy could create and depose rulers or discipline them as needed. Further, the papacy itself (though not subordinate bishops and clergy) possessed authority for use of the sword, both to protect true religion and to punish dissent and heresy, and also to oppose temporal rulers judged guilty of misgovernment, especially if that were manifest in opposition to the true religion of the Catholic church. This was the so-called "two swords" doctrine. Based on an allegorical reading of Luke 22:38, "And they said, Lord, here are two swords. And he said unto them, It is enough" (RSV), this theory justified military coercion on the authority of the church and even the direct command of military forces for this purpose.

Luther, opposing this papalist construct of authority, argued that properly understood, the spiritual and secular or temporal authorities occupy their own realms; that neither has authority over the other outside its own realm, and within each other's realm each was subordinate to the other. In the worldly "kingdom," then, rightful authority belongs to the secular powers, extending even to the external regulation of religious matters. This follows from the divine institution of government in the beginning of time. Likewise, in the kingdom of God spiritual authority is supreme; yet this does not extend to any authority over worldly government. Every Christian, for Luther, is a citizen of both realms but has different responsibilities, and owes different allegiances, in each. The dialectic tension that this conception establishes is intensified by his picture of the world as a disorderly, sinful state of being in which the responsibility of the secular government is to use force and punish those who are evil to protect the righteous. This duty of the worldly authorities gives them the power of the sword. But there is no power corresponding to this in the godly kingdom, where evil is to be combated not by the sword but by the Gospel. Nor, because of the separation between the two realms, do the spiritual authorities have any command over the secular powers in their use of the sword.

Protestant commentary on this dispute, in my experience, has tended to render it as a fundamental difference between Catholic political thought and that of the Reformation. While this interpretation certainly fits the dispute as it played out during the Reformation era, it misses a great deal of the larger picture. In fact the "one sword"—"two swords" argument, using the terminology of the Reformation era, or the dispute over the relative extent of temporal and churchly authority, using the terms of the broader debate, had already been engaged in the early canonical writings of the twelfth and thirteenth centuries, where the terms were remarkably like those reflected in Luther's discussion. The canonists in question, Gratian's two waves of successors, the Decretists and the Decretalists, approached the matter through specific attention to the question of the authority necessary for just war. Did the Pope have it, as vicar of Christ on Earth, and if so, did subordinate archbishops and bishops have it? Their answer as to the latter was explicitly no: the right of the sword is denied to bishops, archbishops, any other clergy and religious, and none of these may bear arms or fight in war either. This is the position reflected in Aquinas's answer to the question whether clergy may take part in war. By the time he wrote it was a settled issue. The case of the Pope was slightly different; over several decades of debate the canonists gradually defined a more and more restricted right to authorize war by the Pope alone: by the end of this development of canon law that right was limited to the case of crusade, and even there it was not connected to actual commitment or command of troops. Even in a crusade the Pope was not to be a general; command of troops was reserved to secular authorities. But giving the Pope authority to initiate crusades had an opposite side: it meant the temporal authorities could not authorize war for religion. So what of authority for use of the sword, for authorizing a just war, in all cases other than the crusade? The canonists agreed on this fairly early, in their effort to deny *duellum* while allowing *bellum* to serve the good: only those temporal authorities with no temporal superior have such a right. This meant in practice only kings, the emperor, and princes of traditionally independent states could justly authorize use of armed force. Anyone who had a superior to whom he could turn for the adjudication of disputes does not, the canonists agreed, possess the necessary authority for use of armed force. Again, this was a settled matter by the time of Aquinas, and it is reflected in his position. In short, using the language of the Reformation era, the canonists' answer was essentially the "one sword" position, but with the single exception of the Pope's right to authorize crusades—which would then be fought by the secular authorities with the forces under their commands.

The thirteenth-century resolution of the question of authority necessary to wage just war effectively reserved that authority to temporal sovereigns, but left one small crack in the door for the supreme spiritual authority, the Pope, to authorize resort to the sword: the case of crusades. In the fifteenth century, in the context of the struggle for power between the popes and the Holy Roman emperors, supporters of the papacy in this struggle widened the crack to give the popes the necessary authority to use arms against the emperors. The device was to use excommunication or other form of ecclesiastical discipline against the emperors and their supporters; then the Pope could authorize use of force against them. It is here that the "two swords" idea first gained strength. I think it is safe to say that the canonists of the twelfth and thirteenth centuries did not anticipate such a manipulation of their conclusions. But in any case, the papalist arguments put forward in the context of the struggle between the papacy and the empire, once established there, were easily turned against the Reformers and their supporters in the next century. Luther's advocacy of the "one sword" position was in fact in line with the conclusion reached in the thirteenth century and reflected in Aquinas's understanding of authority for just war. The "two swords" position, while strong enough in theory and in political power to inflame the wars of religion, was never in fact deeply rooted in Christian doctrine or law, and after the end of these wars it disappeared. In the secular sphere, by the end of the Thirty Years' War warfare for religion was utterly repudiated. In the religious sphere, no Pope for more than three centuries has claimed the right to authorize force of arms in the name of religion. So Luther's position on the nature of authority for the sword, though the focus of controversy at the time, was in fact the more orthodox, in terms of both its antecedents and the subsequent history of Catholic doctrine.

Let me put this a different way: the "one sword" doctrine reveals Luther's acceptance of the main line of just war thinking, according to which the temporal government alone possesses the sovereign authority to employ military force in terms of Romans 13:3–4. For medieval writers and for Luther *bellum* meant the prince's use of force against both external and internal enemies. Government has the dual obligation to ensure justice and peace for its citizens and to ensure their protection against injustice and violence imposed by others. While Aquinas derived the right to authorize war and to use force in a just cause from the natural order as well as from Romans 13, Luther, with his reliance on "scripture alone," focused on Paul and interpreted the allowance of force in terms of the broader theological standard of Christian love, as in this observation from *On War against the Turk*: "it is...a work of Christian love to protect and defend a whole community with the sword and not let the people be abused."[30] In this way he, like Aquinas, connected just cause to the authority necessary for war. Again like Aquinas, he also linked authority for war to the aim of peace, as in this passage from *Whether Soldiers, Too, Can Be Saved?* where Luther employs language very much like that of Augustine which Aquinas quoted in explaining the end of peace: Luther writes, "What else is war but the punishment of wrong and evil? Why does anyone go to war except because he desires peace and obedience?"[31] In this treatise Luther is specifically addressing the question whether Christians should accept military service. His answer is that not only should the Christian not avoid military service; it is a duty for him, as a way of contributing to order, peace, and justice in the kingdom of this world. For the private Christian individual, this is part of his good citizenship: "Christians...do not fight as individuals or for their own benefit, but as obedient servants of the authorities under whom they live."[32] As for the rulers themselves, "[E]very lord and prince is bound to protect his people and to preserve the peace for them. That is his office; that is why he has the sword, Romans 13 [:4]. This should be a matter of conscience for him. And he should on this basis be certain that the work is right in the eyes of God and commanded by him."[33]

"Bound to protect his people and to preserve the peace for them." It is the prince's "office," but it should also be "a matter of conscience for him." This is similar language to that which Luther used the previous year in *Against the Robbing and Murdering Hordes of Peasants*:[34] "If [the ruler] does not fulfill the duties of his office by punishing some and protecting others, he commits as great a sin before God as when someone who has not been given the sword commits murder" (the latter the case of the peasants). "If he is able to punish and does not do it... he becomes guilty of all the murder and evil these people commit." And a bit later, "The rulers have a good conscience and a just cause; they can, therefore, say to God with all confidence of heart, 'Behold, my God, ... you have given me the sword to use against evildoers' (Romans 13 [:4])." By contrast, the peasants have no such right of the sword; their killing is murder, their collective action in arms not just war but rebellion and revolution; "a bad conscience and an unjust cause." But what can Luther have meant by this last judgment? After all, we know from his *Admonition to Peace*[35] that he was in sympathy with many of the peasants' grievances. How, then, can they have an "unjust cause"? This points us back to the importance of the requirement of sovereign authority as understood in normative just war tradition: the sovereign, as the one responsible for an order which serves justice and peace, is the one who is able to judge whether a just cause exists or not in a given case, just as he is the one who must, if he decides to use armed force, do so with right intention (or as Luther puts it, a "good conscience"). No one not in the sovereign's position, finally, is able to do this. Advice from others should be solicited, but in the end the sovereign's right to use force comes from his responsibility for order, justice, and peace. The peasants are not in that situation; their resort to arms can only be unjust, disorderly, destructive of peace, an act of wrong intention ("bad conscience," as Luther puts it). So the question of authority is the central one where use of the sword is concerned; only from its perspective can the justice of the cause be determined and the right intention be maintained.

But what if the ruler is manifestly a bad ruler? What if he has neglected or flouted his responsibilities for the common good or used his power to do manifest evil? The answer cannot be armed resistance, because persons not in sovereign authority cannot justly take the sword on their own authority. Private individuals may disobey and accept punishment, flee to another political community, or, if uncertain as to the justice of the ruler's government, "obey without peril to their souls."[36] The ruler's fate is in God's hands. But it is also, under the proper circumstances, in the hands of other rulers, whose obligation to punish evil and support good may extend to war against this evildoer, his punishment, and his deposition. "Regime change" is not a new idea, but one we find in the just war conception of sovereign authority for just war, rooted in the notion of sovereign responsibility for promoting the good and punishing evildoers.[37]

4. CONCLUSION

To sum up: The requirement of sovereign authority for the justified use of armed force in the service of the political community—what historically was known as *justum bellum*, which we render as "just war," is at the center of Christian just war tradition, as we see exemplified in the thought of Aquinas and Luther. It is also, though I have not argued this here, at the center of secular streams of thought which have contributed to just war tradition in the broader, cultural sense, and to the development of that tradition as a whole. Recent Christian just war thinking has wrongly neglected this moral requirement. Paying it once again the attention it should have places the right to use force where it properly belongs, within the responsibility of government to support the common good, to defend against evil, and to punish evildoers. That is, examination of the positions and reasoning of Aquinas and Luther on sovereign authority for the use of armed force leads us once again to consider the moral dimensions of the idea of sovereignty as an element in a theory of domestic and international politics. For medieval and Reformation thinkers political order was necessary for justice and peace; the corollary was that those in positions of sovereign authority have the obligation to construct an order which serves justice and peace. The problem with private use of force was that, however just the causes claimed, they can never be truly just, because they arise from people who do not have the right to use force. I suggest that this too is a matter which needs serious consideration in contemporary moral thought about war.

NOTES

1. Presbyterian Church, "Just Peacemaking and the Call for International Intervention for Humanitarian Rescue" (resolution adopted by the 1998 General Assembly, 1998), criterion 3.
2. National Conference of Catholic Bishops, *The Harvest of Justice Is Sown in Peace* (Washington, D.C.: United States Catholic Conference, 1993).
3. National Conference of Catholic Bishops, *The Challenge of Peace: God's Promise and Our Response* (Washington, D.C.: United States Catholic Conference, 1983).
4. See James Turner Johnson and George Weigel, *Just War and the Gulf War* (Washington, D.C.: Ethics and Public Policy Center, 1991), 99–103, 117–129.
5. National Conference of Catholic Bishops, *The Harvest of Justice*, 5.
6. Ibid.,15.
7. Saint Augustine of Hippo, *Letter* clxxxix *To Boniface*, cited in Thomas Aquinas, *Summa Theologica*, II/II, Q. 40, A. 1 (New York: Benziger Brothers, 1947).
8. Saint Augustine of Hippo, *Contra Faustrum*, 400–404, in *Corpus ecclesiasticorum latinorum*, vol. 25, edited by Josephus Zycha (Prague and Vindobonae: F. Tempsky; Lipsia: G. Freytag, 1891), xxii. 75.

9. See further Paul Ramsey, *The Just War: Force and Political Responsibility* (New York: Charles Scribner's Sons, 1968), 19–41; and *Speak Up for Just War or Pacifism* (University Park, PA, and London: Pennsylvania State University Press, 1988), 183–212.
10. National Conference of Catholic Bishops, *The Challenge of Peace* and *The Harvest of Justice*.
11. Michael Walzer, *Just and Unjust Wars* (New York: Basic Books, 1977), 51–124.
12. Cf. Walzer's "legalist paradigm"; Walzer, *Just and Unjust Wars*, 61–62.
13. See further Frederick H. Russell, *The Just War in the Middle Ages* (Cambridge: Cambridge University Press, 1975), 55–212.
14. The passage from *Contra Faustum* xxii. 74 cited earlier.
15. The passage from the letter to Boniface cited earlier, *Letter* clxxxix.
16. Saint Augustine of Hippo, *Quaestiones in Heptateuchum*, q. x, *super Josue*.
17. Gratian, *Decretum*, Second Part, XXIII–III, in *The Ethics of War*, ed. Gregory Reichberg, Henrik Syse, and Endre Begby (Malden, MA; Oxford; and Carlton, Victoria, Australia: Blackwell Publishing, 2006), 104–23.
18. Notably in Aquinas, ST II/II, Q. 64, A. 7.
19. Aquinas, ST IT/I, Q. 40, A. 1.
20. Lester Born, *The Education of a Christian Prince by Desiderius Erasmus* (New York: Octagon Books, 1973).
21. See Alan Gewirth, *Marsilius of Padua: The Defender of Peace*, vol. II, *The Defensor Pacis* (New York: Columbia University Press, 1956).
22. Dante Alighieri, *De Monarchia* (Oxford: The Clarendon Press, 1916).
23. Alfred Vanderpol, *La doctrine scholastique du droit de guerre* (Paris: A. Pedone, 1919), 250.
24. See further Philippe Contamine, *War in the Middle Ages* (Oxford: Basil Blackwell, 1984), 271ff.
25. In Martin Luther, *Luther's Works*, vol. 45 (Philadelphia: Muhlenberg Press, 1962).
26. In Martin Luther, *Luther's Works*, vol. 46 (Philadelphia: Fortress Press, 1967).
27. Ibid.
28. Ibid.
29. Clyde L. Manschreck, *A History of Christianity* (Englewood Cliffs, NJ: Prentice Hall, Inc., 1964), 37–88.

30. Luther, *Luther's Works* vol. 46, 121.
31. Luther, *Luther's Works* vol. 46, 95; cf. Aquinas, ST IL/II Q. 40, A. 1.
32. Luther, *Luther's Works* vol. 46, 99.
33. Ibid., 121.
34. Ibid., 53.
35. Ibid., 3–43.
36. Luther, *Luther's Works* vol. 45, 126.
37. Two large issues related to this observation should be noted, but this paper is not the place for discussing them fully. First, the medieval and early modern idea of sovereignty differs significantly from that developed in the system that developed out of the Peace of Westphalia that ended the Thirty Years' War. The moral definition of sovereign authority employed by Aquinas and Luther alike hinges on the sovereign's responsibility to serve the common good of the political community over which the person in authority is sovereign. The idea of sovereignty in the Westphalian system, by contrast, is defined by a particular territory and by the exercise of rule over that territory. Thus on the Westphalian system the principal (and ultimately the only) recognized just cause for war is self-defense against an attack that threatens the territorial integrity of the political community that is attacked, while on the normative conception of sovereignty found in medieval and early modern political thought the sovereign's duty to ensure the good by punishing evildoers holds a prominent place among the recognized just causes for resort to *bellum*. Similarly, under the Westphalian system a ruler may claim the protection of sovereignty for whatever he may do internal to his own society while in the position of rule; thus Slobodan Milosevic, on his first appearance before the International Criminal Tribunal for the Former Yugoslavia after his indictment, refused to recognize the court's authority because he was head of state when he committed the actions for which he was indicted. By contrast, for medieval and early modern thinkers a ruler who abuses the people under his charge the way Milosevic has been charged with doing is not properly a sovereign but a tyrant, an unjust ruler. Such a person enjoys no protections of sovereignty and not only may but ought to be deposed.

    The second issue is who may depose such a ruler. As I have argued above, in medieval and early modern just war tradition the sovereign's right to resort to *bellum* to punish evildoers is not limited to evildoers within that sovereign's own political community but includes evildoers wherever they may be found. That right includes removal and punishment of tyrants in other political communities. But at the same time medieval and early modern political thought allowed for such removal and punishment by others within the tyrant's own political community.

Often this idea is traced to Calvin's allowance that "lesser magistrates" may depose a ruler who rules unjustly (Calvin 1957: Institutes, Book IV, Chapter XX.). But Aquinas already allowed subjects to depose a tyrannical ruler in his discussion of sedition (Summa Theologica IVI, Q. 42, A. 2), an allowance that was well known in late medieval and early modern thought.

Both lines of thought, that from just war tradition and that from the tradition on the right of subjects to depose unjust rulers, conceive of the grounds for action against such a ruler in exactly the same way: he has not served the common good but has used the authority of rule to serve his own interests, and thus has done not good but evil. The preference today would be for internal action to remove such an unjust ruler, in line with the Westphalian conception that what matters in sovereignty is territorial integrity over against all other states. The preference in medieval and early modern tradition, I would argue, was for action by another ruler, one properly engaged in discharging the obligations of sovereign authority. We know this mainly negatively, by such evidence as Luther's rejection of the German peasants' authority to resort to force against their rulers and by other published arguments against rebels. Even in the case of tyranny, the division between *bellum* and *duellum* was hard for medieval and early modern theorists to overcome; thus removal of a tyrant—"regime change" in contemporary parlance—was first the responsibility of proper sovereigns, who (by contrast with private persons of whatever social rank) had the right of using the sword for the public good.

BIBLIOGRAPHY

Alighieri, Dante. *De Monarchia*. Oxford: The Clarendon Press, 1916.

Aquinas, Thomas. *Summa Theologica*. Vol. II. New York: Benziger Brothers, Inc., 1947.

Augustine, of Hippo, Saint. *Contra Faustrum*, esp. 400–404. In *Corpus ecclesiasticorum latinorum*, vol. 25, edited by Josephus Zycha, 249–797. Prague and Vindobonae: F. Tempsky; Lipsia: G. Freytag, 1891.

Born, Lester K. *The Education of a Christian Prince by Desiderius Erasmus*. New York: Octagon Books, 1973.

Calvin, John. *Institutes of the Christian Religion*. 2 vols. Grand Rapids, Michigan: Wm. B. Eerdmans Publishing Company, 1957.

Contamine, Philippe. *War in the Middle Ages*. Oxford: Basil Blackwell, 1984.

Gewirth, Alan. *Marsilius of Padua: The Defender of Peace*. Volume II, *The Defensor Pacis*. New York: Columbia University Press, 1956.

Gratian. *Decretum*, Second Part, XXIII-III. In *The Ethics of War*, edited by Gregory Reichberg, Henrik Syse, and Endre Begby. Malden, MA; Oxford; and Carlton, Victoria, Australia: Blackwell Publishing, 2006. 104–23.

Johnson, James Turner, and George Weigel. *Just War and the Gulf War*. Washington, D.C.: Ethics and Public Policy Center, 1991.

Luther, Martin. *Luther's Works*. Vol. 45. Philadelphia: Muhlenberg Press, 1962.

Luther, Martin. *Luther's Works*. Vol. 46. Philadelphia: Fortress Press, 1967.

Manschreck, Clyde L. *A History of Christianity*. Englewood Cliffs, New Jersey: Prentice Hall, Inc. 20 Journal of Religious Ethics, 1964.

National Conference of Catholic Bishops. *The Challenge of Peace: God's Promise and Our Response*. Washington, D.C.: United States Catholic Conference, 1983.

National Conference of Catholic Bishops. *The Harvest of Justice Is Sown in Peace*. Washington, D.C.: United States Catholic Conference, 1993.

Presbyterian Church (USA). "Just Peacemaking and the Call for International Intervention for Humanitarian Rescue." Resolution adopted by the 1998 General Assembly, 1998.

Ramsey, Paul. *The Just War: Force and Political Responsibility*. New York: Charles Scribner's Sons, 1968.

Ramsey, Paul. *Speak Up for Just War or Pacifism*. University Park, Pennsylvania, and London: Pennsylvania State University Press, 1988.

Russell, Frederick H. *The Just War in the Middle Ages*. Cambridge: Cambridge University Press, 1975.

Vanderpol, Alfred. *La doctrine scholastique du droit de guerre*. Paris: A. Pedone, 1919.

Walzer, Michael. *Just and Unjust Wars*. New York: Basic Books, 1977.

ABSTRACT

This chapter from a 2003 book on terrorism presents a strong moral argument against terrorism. Illustrating his argument using the September 11, 2001 attack, Johnson contends that terrorism is never morally or legally acceptable. A proper response to terrorism entails moral reflection and discourse as well as other means. He believes that the U.S. response to the attacks of September 11, 2001 met just war criteria and indicates a rethinking of political responsibilities and moral response to global terrorism.

CHAPTER 10

JUST WAR THEORY: RESPONDING MORALLY TO GLOBAL TERRORISM

On September 11, 2001, almost 3,000 people died when three hijacked airliners loaded with jet fuel crashed into the World Trade Center towers and the Pentagon and a fourth plane crashed in western Pennsylvania after passengers attempted to overcome the hijackers. In all four cases the deliberate intent was to take American lives on American soil—in the words of a *fatwa*, or religious ruling, authored by Osama bin Laden and four associates in 1998 that may be taken as the manifesto for these attacks, "to kill the Americans and their allies…in any country in which it is possible to do it."[1] It is important to note that the effort by Osama bin Laden and his associates to ground such attacks in Islamic tradition has since been condemned by mainstream Muslim authorities. Part of their purpose was to protect Islamic tradition from distortion and co-optation for private purposes, but part reflects a deep truth shared by the moral traditions of both Islam and the West—that it is wrong directly and intentionally to attack the innocent.

TERRORISM IN MORAL PERSPECTIVE

What was centrally wrong, in moral terms, about the attacks of September 11 may be put this way: The people who died and were wounded there, the people who died and were wounded by their efforts at rescue, all the other people who have suffered harm as a result of the attacks had done nothing to deserve what happened to them. This is the essential moral difference between unjustified killing and killing that can be morally justified (or more broadly, between unjustified and justified uses of force). It is essential to emphasize that the combatant-noncombatant distinction is not the same as the military-civilian distinction. In peacetime both military and civilians are, in moral terms, noncombatants. Likewise, in war some civilians may perform as combatants, while some people in the military (e.g., chaplains, medical personnel) are noncombatants because of their function.

What justifies the killing of soldiers in wartime is that killing someone who directly and intentionally threatens another human life by his or her own actions is fundamentally different, in moral terms, from killing someone who does not pose such a threat. While pacifists may reject all killing for whatever reason as unjustified, nonpacifist moral tradition accepts the possibility of war as justified because of the threat posed to the innocent. The difference between acting as an agent of this threat and not doing so is the root of the distinction made in moral thinking about war and in international law between combatants and noncombatants. However regrettable it may be, it is morally justified and lawful to kill combatants in wartime; it is never morally justified or legal to kill noncombatants in wartime or to kill anyone in a political dispute outside of war, because when there is no state of war, all are by definition noncombatants.

What was wrong, then, at the most fundamental level in the attacks of September 11 was that in a time of peace these attacks aimed directly at the deaths of people who were simply going about their ordinary lives, who were not themselves engaged in a threat against the lives of others. This was as true of the uniformed military personnel targeted in the attack on the Pentagon as well as the civilians there, in the World Trade Center towers, and on all four hijacked planes. What was morally wrong in the September 11 attacks is also a characteristic of the phenomenon of terrorism in general—it deliberately chooses noncombatants as its targets.

Related to this is a second basic problem with the September 11 attacks and much terrorism in general—a generalized animosity toward a whole group of people and their way of life that is taken as justifying violence. While Osama bin Laden and his associates identified several specific United States policies as the basis for violent response, they moved seamlessly to hold responsible all Americans and American culture generally for those specific policies. In their 1998 *fatwa* and in statements made after the September 11 attacks they represented America and the West as engaged in a war of humiliation and annihilation against Muslims, justifying a similar war of annihilation by them and all Muslims back toward all Americans, allies of America, and Western culture generally. Thinking in this way is morally wrong for two reasons. First, it deliberately denies the essential moral difference between combatants and noncombatants in a military struggle, which was just discussed; second, it exhibits what Augustine called an "implacable animosity" toward an entire culture—an unreasoned hatred that cannot be satisfied except by the annihilation of the designated enemy.

Taken together, these two characteristics of the September 11 attacks and of the phenomenon of terrorism more broadly show why noncombatants are intentionally the targets of choice. First, they are defined as guilty simply by being members of the hated society; second, they are "soft" targets, easier to attack with the limited means available to terrorists; third, a successful deadly attack on ordinary people in a society, people going about their everyday lives, implicitly reveals the impotence of their government, which failed to protect them, and undermines the assumptions that make everyday life in that society what it is. So for terrorism it is not simply that the combatant-noncombatant distinction is erased; perversely, it is kept in a certain way, as the most innocent, ordinary people are made the targets of choice. Thus terrorism reverses the moral priorities of killing in war: It deliberately chooses to kill the innocent rather than seeking to avoid harm to them.

A third deep-rooted moral problem with the September 11 attacks was their source. There is a fundamental moral difference between uses of violence to protect a political community by those responsible for the well-being of that community and the use of violence by any individual or group for other reasons. The September 11 attacks were launched by members of Al Qaeda, an organization constituted for the purpose of terror, with planning, direction, and support from the leaders of the organization itself. In moral and legal terms, such an organization has no standing to use violence in pursuit of its ends. It is essentially a criminal organization, a mafia—self-constituted, responsible to no political community, acting on behalf of its own ends. Whatever the high moral goods claimed as justifying their actions, the people who planned, directed, supported, and carried out those actions had no moral right to do so.

Terrorism, in short, is deeply evil. The threat it poses touches values essential to private life and life in community, including not just our own national community but the order of international society as a whole. The response to it, accordingly, must be correspondingly deeply rooted in the reaffirmation of those values it threatens and in the commitment to protect them and their embodiment in the institutions of personal and common life. That is, the response has to be one that includes not only military, diplomatic, economic, intelligence, and police efforts; it also has to include a moral analysis aimed at reaffirming the values threatened and criticizing and rejecting the terrorist rationales. Accordingly, it has to be cross-cultural, since the threat posed by the new global terrorism touches every major culture on the globe. In the context of American society this moral analysis has to begin with a reorientation of U.S. public moral discourse on the rights and wrongs of the use of force.

TERRORISM AND AMERICAN MORAL DISCOURSE: THE NEED TO RETHINK THE MORAL STATUS OF THE USE OF FORCE

Prior to the September 11 attacks, very little attention was given to the problem of terrorism in American moral discourse on the use of armed force and the problem of war. Rather, the moral debate tracked and responded to the kinds of conflicts in which the United States was involved or was perceived as likely to be involved. Thus in the context of the 1960s, when Paul Ramsey's work (*War and the Christian Conscience* and *The Just War*)[2] revived interest in the idea of just war as a focus for moral reflection on war, the central concern was with nuclear weapons, deterrence, and the possibility of nuclear war. That same concern dominated the debates of the 1980s, when books like Jonathan Schell's *The Fate of the Earth* held up a vision of the aftermath of nuclear war as a "republic of insects and grasses"[3] and the United States Catholic bishops' 1983 pastoral letter *The Challenge of Peace* laid down a "presumption against war" as the first step in a moral argument that rejected all use of nuclear weapons and only temporarily accepted possession of such weapons as a deterrent.[4] In between these two periods of focus on nuclear weapons lay, of course, the Vietnam War, which provided the central focus of moral discourse related to war in the 1970s. Part of the enduring value of Michael Walzer's *Just and Unjust Wars* was that it had a broader compass, advancing its moral analysis and argument by means of historical examples ranging from classical Athens to World War 1I—though it also had significant focus on the Vietnam War and the problems of nuclear weapons[5]

As thc cxamplcs of Ramsey, Walzer, and the U.S. Catholic bishops demonstrate, this period from the early 1960s to the end of the 1980s and the end of the era of the Cold War was marked in moral debate by the introduction, consolidation, and increasing use of the idea of just war as the focus for analysis and argument. There was also, however, running through this same period a strong stream of pacifist opposition to war. Three broad forms of this opposition can be distinguished. First there was the pacifism of total rejection of all war, based either in religious conviction or in personal philosophical rationales. Second was a form of rejection of war based on the judgment that contemporary war is inherently indiscriminate and disproportionate in its destructiveness. This kind of argument—sometimes focused only on the destructive potential of nuclear weapons but at other times made more broadly in terms of the destructiveness of the wars of the twentieth century—has been variously called modern-war pacifism, nuclear pacifism, and just war pacifism; it used the just war categories of discrimination and proportionality to carry on what Ramsey in various places termed a *bellum contra bellum justum*, a "war against just war" in favor of a pacifist rejection of all contemporary warfare as immoral. Finally, there was the form of opposition to war that focused on the perceived immorality of the state and its policies. First coalescing as a form of moral opposition to the American involvement in Vietnam, this kind of pacifism nurtured a suspicion of government, of the military, and of the idea of national interest as a justification for the use of armed force.

What one finds on examining the moral debates of this roughly thirty-year period is that even as the language of the just war categories has become more dominant in these debates, the assumptions of the latter two forms of pacifism have persisted and shaped a significant moral opposition to the use of armed force by the state for reasons based in the national interest. The case of the moral debate over the Gulf War provides a striking example of both these tendencies. On the one hand, in justifying the American use of armed force in that conflict, the first President Bush used language that closely tracked the traditional just war categories; and the actual application of that force, first in Operation Desert Shield and then in Desert Storm, fit the requirements of those categories perhaps as well as any military operation could do so in real terms. It also was a casebook application of the requirements of international law for the resort to armed force, and conduct in the use of that force (see James Johnson and George Weigel, *Just War and the Gulf War*).[6] The use of precision-guided munitions for the first time in combat made possible a level of discrimination in attacks against military targets never before reached; this also lowered the level of collateral damage significantly and changed the calculus of proportionality relative to results achieved versus total damage done. When the ground war began, it took place in areas where there was effectively no noncombatant population, either because of the nature of the terrain or because, as in the case of Kuwait City and its environs, the Iraqis had driven the noncombatants out.

Yet the moral discourse from this conflict reveals much opposition to the American resort to armed force in the first place and to the manner of use of that force in the conflict.[7] Arguments against the resort to force called in question the United States motives (the "no blood for oil" argument), accused the United States of having contributed to the crisis by its earlier support of Iraq (the "dirty hands" argument), held out the specter of an escalating conflict that would engulf the region and perhaps the world and would involve the use of weapons of mass destruction (the disproportionality argument), and favored an extended search for nonviolent options (the last resort argument). Once the air war began, criticism was directed against the bombing of dual-use (military-civilian) facilities like the electric power network and bridges; late in Desert Storm the attacks on retreating Iraqi Republican Guard elements on the Basra Road were castigated as indiscriminate (because these elements were no longer organized as a fighting force) and disproportionate (because the air attacks were unopposed); after the war the total destruction caused, including the deliberate torching of the Kuwaiti oil fields by the retreating Iraqis, was laid at the feet of the American decision to use armed force. We see here the marks of all the broad forms of opposition to armed force identified earlier—refusal to acknowledge that resort to force is ever justified; the expectation that any use of force will inevitably escalate to all-out war; the ready identification of all uses of force as indiscriminate and disproportionate; a deep-rooted suspicion of motives of national interest as inherently tainting any possible just cause; a suspicion of government rationales as deceptive and immoral.

In all of this the growing phenomenon of terror was generally ignored in civilian moral discourse, though in military contexts there was a significant effort to stimulate moral discussion in the 1980s, first in response to the truck bombing of the Marine barracks at Beirut airport and later in connection with the larger phenomenon of low-intensity conflict. But aside from the work of the people involved in this effort there was another line of moral discourse critical not of terrorist activity itself, nor of the people behind it, but of the U.S. policy that had led to the Marine presence in Lebanon and of U.S. uses of military force in response to low-intensity threats in Latin America and elsewhere. This was, indeed, a pattern throughout this period—if terrorism did not affect the United States directly, it was ignored in the moral literature on war; if it did do so in any way, such as in the case of the Marine barracks bombing, the United States support of the Contras in Nicaragua, or the use of military forces in the war on the drug trade, the fact of terror became an occasion for moral criticism of United States policy, the administration, and the U.S. military.

During the 1990s after the Gulf War and up to the September 11 attacks, something of a sea change began to appear in American moral discourse on war as erstwhile opponents of use of military force joined with others closer to the just war mainstream to argue for the interventionary use of military force in response to human rights abuses and complex humanitarian emergencies caused by civil war. Some of the old suspicion over the use of force remained, however. Two examples will illustrate the persistence of such suspicion. In 1993 the U.S. Catholic bishops issued a new statement on the use of armed force; though it represented intervention as a "duty" in the face of egregious violations of human rights, it distinguished between such uses of military force and "war" for purposes of national interest, about which the bishops continued to have serious reservations. In 1998 the General Assembly of the United Presbyterian Church formally adopted a resolution, titled "Just Peacemaking and the Call for International Intervention for Humanitarian Rescue," in which it strongly supported the idea of using military force for humanitarian intervention, yet cautioned that in no case should humanitarian purpose "cloak" the pursuit of national interest.

I suggest that the terror attacks of September 11 have decisively changed the balance in American moral discourse about the use of military force and, at a deeper level, about the purpose of government in relation to the public good. While a small amount of moral criticism was advanced early after the attacks, sounding the old themes that the attacks somehow resulted from flawed U.S. policies toward Israel and the Arab world, the presence of U.S. military forces in the Middle East, and American dependence on oil, this line of moral discourse never became the mainstream. Rather, a near unanimity quickly emerged and has persisted on the justifiedness of an American military response, on the moral obligation of the Bush Administration to undertake such a response and on its competence to do so, and on the general obligation of the government to undertake measures aimed at increasing homeland security, apprehending potential terrorist actors, and interdicting terrorist activity throughout the world. There has been no criticism of the place of national interest in justifying these measures as they have developed, and no second-guessing of the use of military force in the campaign in Afghanistan (in sharp contrast to the cases of Somalia, Bosnia, and Kosovo). In the September 11 attacks terrorism came home to America, and one result has been a significant refocusing of moral attitudes toward the government, its purposes, and the role of military force in the pursuit of those purposes.

RESPONDING MORALLY TO A TERRORIST ATTACK

How to think morally about the response to acts of terror? The answer is not, in principle, different for this and for other forms of attacks against the public good and the order that supports it. The essentials of the answer were put succinctly over seven centuries ago by Thomas Aquinas in his "On War."[8] What is necessary for a war to be just, he argued, are sovereign authority, a just cause, and a right intention, including both avoidance of wrong intentions and the aim of achieving peace. At the time he was writing, Aquinas was not yet the authority that he has since become, but his pithy treatment of the question of war in moral terms serves in his own historical context as a window on a cultural consensus that already had coalesced around its central elements, the moral requirements he cited. This consensus drew heavily on the work of Augustine some eight hundred years earlier, and through him, on the Hebraic and the classical Roman and Greek traditions—the deepest roots of Western civilization. In short, Aquinas's formulation reflects a fundamental and deep-seated moral valuation of the use of armed force in relation to the ideals of public life. The just war tradition, which is the term we use today to refer to the concrete expression of that valuation by means of definite moral requirements for the just use of armed force, thus tells us important things about who we are as moral beings and what we should—indeed, must—do in the face of injustice.

Much recent just war reasoning differs from that of Aquinas—and I think wrongly—in two important ways. First, it has typically placed the requirement of just cause first, over that of sovereign authority (usually rendered in recent terms as "right" or "competent" authority); second, it has tended to focus on the prudential requirements of last resort, that the use of force be expected to cause more good than harm, and that it have a reasonable hope of success. These three prudential requirements did not appear in Aquinas's listing of the necessities for a just war. What is to be made of these differences? How do they bear on the question of a moral response to the terror attacks of September 11 and the general phenomenon of terrorism?

Aquinas, following Augustine, began by requiring sovereign authority for two basic reasons. First, this concept made a moral distinction between use of force by public authority for the public good and uses by private persons for private ends. In medieval terms, this distinction was put as that between *bellum* and *duellum*. This was an important distinction in a cultural context in which every knight could claim to have the right to use the sword on his own judgment and in which banditry was widespread. What Aquinas said reflected the work of more than a century of canonical thought and political efforts to deal with such endemic violence—similar in important ways to contemporary terrorism—by restricting the right of resort to armed force to the highest temporal authorities, those with no superior able to adjudicate their differences. At the same time, this work emphasized the responsibility of those in sovereign authority to ensure justice, both in their domains and in their relations with other sovereigns. This was a concern deeply rooted in classical political thought, and it has continued at the center of Western political theory: The reason for the existence of the political community is to serve the good of those within it and to serve the general order within which all political communities exist and on which they depend—those in political authority have as their fundamental responsibility to ensure these goods against harm. Understood within this frame, Aquinas's placing the requirement of sovereign authority first in his listing of the requirements for a just war was not simply accidental; it followed from an understanding of the nature of the political order in itself.

Thinking of the requirement of sovereign authority first emphasizes that protecting the political community and the order within which it exists is what government is ultimately for. The sovereign authority thus has responsibility to weigh and make judgment on the presence of just cause and to initiate action not marked by a wrong intention and aimed at the achievement of peace. Much recent just war thinking, typified by the two statements of the U.S. Catholic bishops cited earlier, has placed the question of just cause first, as if it can be determined in the abstract, so that response by a "competent" authority simply follows this determination. Yet who can rightly determine the existence of a just cause for the use of armed force on behalf of the political community? Should it be moralists, who by their profession focus on problems of moral analysis and judgment? This seems to be the implication of subordinating the authority to use force to the determination of just cause. Yet there is a basic problem with this line of reasoning: Moralists—indeed, anyone other than the person or persons in the position of sovereign authority—do not have responsibility for the common welfare or, indeed, for the institutional system of order in which the values they seek to determine are preserved. Nor do they have the wherewithal to act to serve these goods. They have a role in the moral determination whether to resort to force, but it is a supportive, advisory one. The ultimate determination belongs to the sovereign authority, who bears the responsibility for the common good and has command of the resources able to serve it.

The idea of just cause itself, in classic just war terms, requires one or more of three purposes—defense against an attack already made or in progress, recovery of something wrongly taken, and punishment of evil. By the terms of the United Nations Charter, only self-defense—by an individual state or a collectivity of states—against "armed attack" is allowed. Though the international law requirement seems on the face of it more restrictive, in practice the idea of defense has expanded to include the ideas found in the just war formulation as well as the idea of retaliation even when it can serve no defensive purpose, as in a nuclear second strike. The British use of military force in the Falklands War was justified in international law as a defensive reaction to an ongoing "armed attack" by Argentine forces; yet since Argentina had already occupied and claimed the islands, the British use of military force was clearly also an effort to retake them for Britain. Similarly, in the case of the Gulf War, the international law justification for use of force against Iraq was collective defense against an ongoing "armed attack," the occupation of Kuwait. Yet since Iraq had announced its annexation of Kuwait, this military response was clearly also an effort to retake it and restore the Kuwaiti government. At the same time, the direction of the force used also clearly sought to punish Iraqi leader Saddam Hussein for initiating the aggression and his elite forces, the Republican Guards, for their role in the takeover. So the older moral formulation of the idea of just cause still has force, though in international law this formulation is buried in an expanded notion of what counts as defense.

A terrorist attack initiated and carried out by a non-state actor is not the same as an "armed attack" initiated and carried out by a state, but in just war terms this is a distinction without a difference, because in either case the common welfare of the political community that has been attacked is under assault, and the governing authority of that community has the responsibility to act to defend it, to recover anything wrongly taken in the attack, and to punish those responsible and their supporters.

So in just war terms there is no doubt that the attacks of September 11 constitute just cause for a response up to and including the use of United States military force.

Yet there are still other moral tests, tests that the sovereign authority has the responsibility to apply and satisfy. Of those identified in Aquinas's listing, two remain: the avoidance of wrong intention in the sense of those motivations first rejected by Augustine—the desire to dominate, a lust for power, an implacable animosity, cruelty in seeking vengeance, and so on—and the aim of achieving peace. If it were true, as Osama bin Laden in 1998 claimed, that the United States is engaged in a war against Islam, "occupying the lands of Islam in the holiest of places, the Arabian Peninsula, plundering its riches, dictating to its rulers, humiliating its people, terrorizing its neighbors, and turning its bases in the Peninsula into a spearhead through which to fight the neighboring Muslim peoples,"[9] in short, if the United States were in fact engaged in a war of imperial domination based in an implacable animosity toward Muslims and toward Islam, then this would constitute wrong intention, and action motivated in this way would be unjust. Yet the reverse is in fact true: The United States presence in Saudi Arabia and the Gulf states is defensive, not offensive; this presence, as well as the continuing economic and military pressure on Iraq, is the direct result of responding to Iraq's aggression in 1990–1991; the use of military force and other measures since the September 11 attacks have been clearly purposed as a response to those attacks and the threat of others, not an attack on Islam.

Is any credence at all to be given to the argument of bin Laden and his supporters? One must grant that there is a fundamental cultural gap between his perspective and that of the United States and of Western culture generally. Bin Laden has repeatedly characterized America and the West as "crusaders" supporting "Zionists," while (as noted) appealing to the Islamic tradition of defensive *jihad* to justify killing "the Americans and their allies—civilian and military" as "an individual duty for every Muslim who can do it in any country in which it is possible to do it."[10] This is an explicitly religious way of casting the conflict and the motivations on each side. The roots of bin Laden's argument lie in a view of the world first defined by Muslim jurists in the period from the late eighth through early tenth centuries, according to which the world is divided into two spheres, the territory of Islam (*dar al-islam*) and the territory of war (*dar al-harb*). All conflict comes from the territory of war; all peace is found in the territory of Islam. This latter territory is at peace because it is ruled in accordance with God's law by a ruler who has inherited the dual mantle of political and religious leadership from the Prophet Mohammad. Thus any attack on the territory of Islam is, by definition, aimed against it not just as a political entity but also against the religion of Islam. This conception of the inherent relation between religion and politics is also turned outward to describe the territory of war. Bin Laden's characterization of the West in terms of religiously defined animosity—"crusaders" supporting "Zionists" —reflects this worldview. On it there simply is no possibility of a state founded on secular values taken to be universal, no possibility of a state acting out of concern for the welfare of its own citizens as defined in the terms of constitutionally granted rights and a deeper respect for human rights, a state in which religious freedom guarantees the existence of a pluralistic religious culture. By contrast with this worldview, however, war for religion has been explicitly ruled out in Western conceptions of politics since the Peace of Westphalia, and the idea of a separation between the sphere of faith and that of temporal order goes back much earlier; it is found, as I suggest earlier, in the basic just war understanding of the rights and responsibilities of sovereignty, including the right and responsibility to use force on behalf of the common welfare. By this latter measure it is bin Laden and his supporters who manifest implacable animosity toward America and the West, who desire to dominate it, who seek to inflict harm against it simply because it is there.

Thinking of these competing worldviews suggests why the achievement of peace in the war against terrorism will require much more than success in the use of coercive force. To suppress terror and establish an order of life in which innocent people do not become the targets of violence aimed at some larger goal is a necessary priority, but there also needs to be another kind of struggle, a multifaceted one aimed at establishing a world-view in which difference does not translate to hostility. Here a major part of the problem is to be found in the world of Islam itself, where religious reflection and political theory need to reopen understanding of the experience and thought of the Muslim past so as to enunciate an understanding of the world on such terms as just described as authentically Islamic. For the simple fact is that Muslim states have never constituted a single politico-religious *dar al-islam*; such states have lived in peace with non-Muslim neighbors for extended periods; and today Muslims live with religious and cultural freedom in all kinds of states (indeed, with more room for the diversity inherent in Islam than has been allowed in states like Afghanistan under the Taliban, theocratic Iran, or Wahhabi-dominated Saudi Arabia). The United States and other Western societies can take the lead in establishing and enforcing a world order in which terrorism is unambiguously criminalized and rooted out, but the problem of the use of Islamic tradition to rationalize and justify terrorism is a problem that needs to be addressed and resolved by Muslims themselves.

Three prudential concerns—that use of force be a last resort, that it be expected not to create more harm than good, and that it have a reasonable prospect of success—have figured prominently in some recent just war thinking, again notably that of the United States Catholic bishops. The bishops have taken the position that their tradition includes a primal "presumption against war," which the various *jus ad bellum* tests must overcome for a use of force to be justified. Neither the idea of such a "presumption" nor the three prudential tests were part of the listing of what is necessary for a just war found in Aquinas and other formative just war thought. There the moral conception of the use of force is strikingly different: Force may be used for good as well as ill, and the just war idea spells out what is necessary for it to be used as a tool for good.

It may, of course, be understood that, while the three prudential criteria just mentioned were not among the necessities for a just war as recognized in formative just war theory, they may be counted among the considerations one in sovereign authority must take into account after deciding, on the basis of the criteria of just cause, right intention, and the aim of peace, that use of force in a given case is morally justified. That is, the prudential criteria have a secondary role—given that a use of force in the case at hand is justified, is it prudent to use such force at the moment. I take it that the Catholic bishops and others who have followed their line of thinking—including some who are not interested in the full range of just war reasoning at all but use the just war criteria to oppose use of force—are saying something different—that resort to force is not morally justified unless these prudential criteria are unambiguously satisfied. The problem is that the prudential tests are interpreted in such a way that unambiguous satisfaction is essentially impossible to achieve. The criterion of last resort is understood as meaning that all measures short of force must have been tried and found to fail before force is justified, when as a prudential criterion for moral decision it properly means that the moral agent considers whether nonforceful means are likely to reach the justified end or not; and if not, then only force remains. The criterion of no greater harm than good has been habitually interpreted by reference to a view of modern warfare that represents it as inherently so destructive that, in the terms of Pope John XXIII in *Pacem in Terris*, it can no longer serve justice, when in fact the face of warfare has decisively changed as a result of precision-guided weaponry, able to strike an intended target without great collateral damage. The criterion of reasonable hope of success has been interpreted eschatologically, so that the peace sought is the ultimate peace with justice of the City of God, not the relative peace possible in the actual world. So there is a place for use of these prudential criteria in the decision whether to use force, but they need to be used properly, in a way that reflects their secondary role in the moral decision whether to resort to force and accepts the possibility for using force in the service of good—not in a leading role and not as a way to bolster a presumption that the use of force is always *prima facie* wrong.

In the response to terrorism, a strong case can be made for a wide range of types of action, of which the use of military force is only one. The reason is that terrorism is a multifaceted phenomenon, and terrorist acts cross many of the lines we habitually draw in contemporary life. It makes sense most of the time to draw distinctions between police work and military action, between domestic surveillance and espionage, between uses of force (whether domestic or foreign) and other measures including economic and diplomatic ones. But the phenomenon of terrorism runs across these ordinary distinctions, so that in some ways it is a police problem and in others a military one; in some ways a domestic problem and others a foreign one; in some ways a problem to be addressed by economic means, in others by diplomatic means, in others by military means. Accordingly, the usual just war calculations of proportionality, last resort, and reasonable hope of success are made more complex, but by no means impossible. The moral agent simply has to think in a multivariate way, seeking to maximize the good and minimize the harm of chosen paths of action overall, while using different means to address different aspects of the problem. This is in no way inconsistent with the basic moral perspective of just war thinking—that the sovereign authority has the responsibility to act on behalf of the political community to protect it from danger and remove threats to its common life and the individuals who make it up, including threats to the values that define the community and knit it together.

In my judgment, a moral response to the terrorist attacks of September 11 and the continuing threat posed by the authors of those attacks justifies a robust but finely tuned military response like the one directed against Al Qaeda and the Taliban in Afghanistan, and more broadly they justify use of military force against other targets as appropriate in the future. Yet the actual use of military force in the future needs to be determined morally through a review of the full range of concerns laid out in the *jus ad bellum*. There is also no doubt in my mind that those attacks and the continuing threat justify the range of nonmilitary responses we have seen. But in it all, the aim of those in political authority must remain the protection and defense of the American political community, the values on which it is based, and the larger framework of values and institutions that constitute the international order. The responsibility to do this at once confers the authority to act and sets limits on what may be done, for a just response must finally respect who we are as a people and the values we hold, both those specific to our own political community and those shared with others within the international order.

Once the decision has been made that the use of force is morally the right choice, the focus shifts to how that force is in fact used. In recent just war thinking this matter, traditionally called the *jus in bello*, is typically treated, following the example of Paul Ramsey, in terms of two moral principles—discrimination and proportionality of means. Discrimination means avoidance of direct, intentional harm to noncombatants. It may be derived deontologically, as it was for Ramsey, or teleologically, as it is for utilitarian philosophers who use this term, but in either case the result is the moral obligation not directly and intentionally to harm noncombatants. Proportionality of means, by contrast, is an inherently teleological idea, following from a prudential calculation of the least destructive means available to carry out an attack on a justified target.

Both these principles are problematic in practice. The problem with the use of the principle of discrimination is that even if one postulates that it is never morally right to attack noncombatants directly and intentionally, it is still necessary to say who the noncombatants are; the idea of discrimination in itself does not do this. Thus the contemporary use of the principle of discrimination opens itself to fuzziness, disagreement, and confusion as to just who counts as a noncombatant. Is everyone in a modern society in some sense a combatant because of the integrated nature of modern societies? Are all citizens in a democracy combatants if they concur in their government's use of force? Are soldiers who are not actively fighting but have not laid down their weapons and surrendered to be counted as noncombatants, as some moralists argued about the Iraqi Republican Guards on the Basra Road in the last stages of the Gulf War? All these kinds of reasoning can be found in the literature. The principle of discrimination turns out to be not so distinct after all, and to have importantly variant meanings.

The principle of proportionality of means has different, but equally bothersome, problems. Most important, there is widespread variation in how to apply it. Sometimes the measure seems to focus on outputs, at other times on inputs. Sometimes it seems simply to refer to a high level of destructiveness, not measured against the ends achieved but against the moralist's personal idea of what counts as disproportionate force. This can lead to an utterly wrong judgment as to appropriate level of force, as when the use of overwhelming force is decried as disproportionate even if, as is usually the case, using such a level of force is the best way to lower the level of casualties. Sometimes proportionality of means is conflated with the *jus ad bellum* idea of overall proportionality of the choice to use force, a conflation that leads to serious confusion when applied to the decision what to do in a given case. Sometimes this principle is used to argue that the risk to both sides in combat should be relatively equal, as in the criticism of the bombing campaign against Serbia over Kosovo for being carried out from a height that made the pilots unreachable by anti-aircraft fire and missiles. All these are, to my mind, wrong ways of using the idea of proportionality of means. There is a proper use of this principle, a use in accord with its fundamental meaning that requires measuring the means used against the results to be achieved, so that the most moral form of force is that which achieves the justified object at the cost of the least destruction. But even here there is disagreement among moralists as to whether to count only harm to the enemy or also harm to one's own forces. In sum, the principle of proportionality is even more problematical, in practice, than the principle of discrimination.

Fortunately there are alternatives to the use of these two principles, and these alternatives are in fact truer reflections of just war tradition than are these principles. The ideas of discrimination and proportionality of means do not appear anywhere in just war thought prior to Ramsey; they are his invention. What one finds running through earlier just war tradition is something much more closely mirrored in the positive international law on armed conflicts—definition of noncombatant immunity by the identification of classes of people who normally, because of personal characteristics or social function, take no part in war and thus should not have war directed at them, and efforts to ban certain specific kinds of weapons as contributing to indiscriminate or more destructive warfare. Similar ideas are also found in other cultural traditions; thus to focus on them provides a link with those traditions that is less direct if one seeks to work from the principles of discrimination and proportionality.

So far as protection of noncombatant immunity is concerned, beginning with the classes of persons who deserve such protection because their personal condition (age, physical or mental illness, gender) or social function (essentially all persons in civilian occupations who do the same job whether their nation is at war or not) is to start where the principle of discrimination must go if it is to be anything more than an abstract idea. However one gets to this point, the important thing is the principle of justice: The people in these classes do nothing to deserve to be attacked, and thus they should not be. They are simply going about their normal lives as best they can, and even if their society is at war, this should not make them targets. Understanding this reveals what is most heinous about terrorism. It inverts the places of combatants and noncombatants relative to the use of force, so that it is noncombatants who are explicitly targeted by terrorist acts. Moral conduct in the use of force, by contrast, requires respecting the natural immunity of such persons, except when in individual cases they engage in activities that make them combatants—like women who serve in combat roles in the military, for example, or like child soldiers in some contemporary civil wars. Such people are not noncombatants despite belonging to traditionally defined classes of noncombatants, but recognizing them as combatants because of their activity in carrying on war does not destroy the immunity of other women and children who do not do so. These exceptions do not diminish the general rule; because they are exceptions, they make the general rule more important to observe.

As for means in combat, working from limits or bans on the use of particular weapons does not lead to the confusions and differences of interpretation encountered in moralists' efforts to apply the principle of proportionality. Arguably, the restraints imposed by limits or bans on particular weapons may not be restrictive enough for some readings of the requirements of the moral principle of proportionality. The reason is that not all weapons that are often criticized as causing disproportionate damage are limited or banned in international agreements or in national policy or law. Examples of such weapons include antipersonnel mines and cluster bombs, which have also been criticized as indiscriminate. Yet used with care, targeted directly on combatants who could not be reached otherwise except by more destructive means, such weapons as these may actually be morally the weapons of choice. From all accounts, this is how such weapons have been used by American forces in Afghanistan.

As I suggested earlier on, a significant current in American moral discourse on war continues to be driven by assumptions about war shaped by the images of high-altitude carpet bombing and the possibility of the use of nuclear weapons in contemporary warfare. Some early criticism of the American military buildup directed against Al Qaeda and the Taliban incorporated such assumptions. But it is time for just war thinkers to recognize that American military capabilities today are very different from those of World War II and the strategic nuclear debates. The difference is at root technological, but dramatically improved technology has been reflected in new tactics. Precision-guided munitions directed to their targets by laser illumination or by GPS units incorporated into them have dramatically changed targeting expectations. One of the reasons in the past for developing targeting strategies aimed at large areas was that smaller targets could not be hit with any accuracy. This was also one important reason for increasing the yield of nuclear warheads to the multi-megaton range. If one could expect no more than to hit within several hundred yards of a hardened target, then the weapon's destructive power had to be increased so as to deal with that fact. PGM capabilities have altered these expectations—these can hit within tens, not hundreds, of yards of the center of their targets, which for practical purposes means bullseye capability. Use of such munitions more exclusively, made possible by inexpensive retrofitting of formerly "dumb" bombs, has been a feature of the Afghanistan campaign. This leads to two important tactical changes. First, the number and size of warheads necessary for a decisive strike against a particular target has sharply diminished. With this has come also a radical diminution in collateral damage, the sort of harm that in traditional just war thinking had to be dealt with by reference to the rule of double effect as unintended but undesired. The second tactical change is that close combat support of ground forces is possible even from high-flying, relatively invulnerable platforms, including B-52s, bombers that were previously known best for their carpet-bombing capability.

Moral reflection and discourse on war needs to take account of these dramatic changes. The simple truth is that the new technologies of warfare make honoring the moral requirements of the just war *jus in bello* much easier and more straightforward, and the new tactics reflecting these technologies carry this possibility into practice. The war on terrorism should make maximum use of these new technologies and tactics.

CONCLUSION

The gist of what I have been arguing can be put simply, in terms of several propositions. First, terrorism is a distinctive phenomenon that disregards or inverts fundamental moral values, and thus challenges not only the persons and societies directly targeted by terrorist activity, but also those fundamental moral values themselves, and thus through them all personal and social life. Accordingly, terrorism is deeply evil. Second, as a result the response to terrorism must include moral reflection and discourse as well as other means. While this response should take place in every culture, in the American context this requires close attention to the idea of just war and its context in a moral conception of the political community. This in turn means rethinking and backing away from certain tendencies in American moral thought on war, tendencies rooted in a misreading of the purposes of the political community, the right to use force in pursuit of those purposes, and the nature of modern warfare. Whatever one may say about the justifiability of those tendencies in the historical contexts where they first appeared, they have wrongly skewed moral thinking about the use of force by the political community, and they need to be left behind. Third, in military terms the American response to the attacks of September 11 has thus far satisfied the moral criteria of just war tradition. Indeed, I have argued that reasoning from those criteria obligated such a response. The means used have shown that we are in a new day as regards conduct in the use of armed force, so that the moral distinction between the justified use of such force and terrorist acts is drawn the more sharply. At this point we do not know where the struggle against terrorism may lead, but the moral direction laid out in just war tradition, including the conception of the responsibilities of the political community assumed there, provide lasting guidance for this struggle.

NOTES

1. Osama bin Laden, et al., "Jihad Against Jews and Crusaders: World Islamic Front Statement," 23 February 1998. Available at http://www.library.cornell.edu/ colldev/mideast/wif.htm.
2. Paul Ramsey, *War and the Christian Conscience* (Durham, NC: Duke University Press, 1961); and *The Just War* (New York: Scribners, 1968).
3. Jonathan Schell, *The Fate of the Earth* (New York: Alfred Knopf, 1982).
4. National Conference of Catholic Bishops, *The Challenge of Peace* (Washington, D.C.: United States Catholic Conference, 1983).
5. Michael Walzer, *Just and Unjust Wars* (New York: Basic Books, 1977).
6. James Turner Johnson, and George Weigel, *Just War and the Gulf War* (Washington, D.C.: Ethics and Public Policy Center, 1991), 7.
7. Johnson and Weigel, *Just War*, Part Three.
8. *Summa Theologica* I/II, Q. 40, Al.
9. Bin Laden, "Jihad."
10. Osama bin Laden, "Jihad." John F. Burns, "Bin Laden Stirs Struggle on Meaning of Jihad," *The New York Times* (2002), 1,15.

BIBLIOGRAPHY

Johnson, James Turner and George Weigel. *Just War and the Gulf War*. Washington, D.C.: Ethics and Public Policy Center, 1991.

National Conference of Catholic Bishops. *The Challenge of Peace*. Washington, D.C.: United States Catholic Conference, 1983.

Ramsey, Paul. *The Just War*. New York: Scribners, 1968.

Ramsey, Paul. *War and the Christian Conscience*. Durham, NC: Duke University Press, 1961.

Schell, Jonathan. *The Fate of the Earth*. New York: Alfred Knopf, 1982.

Walzer, Michael. *Just and Unjust Wars*. New York: Basic Books, 1977.

ABSTRACT

This essay was an unpublished lecture, "Catholic Just War Thought: The State of the Question," given at The Gregorian University, Rome, Italy, 2004; and later appeared as an abbreviated article, "Just War As It Was and Is," *First Things*, 2005. Johnson provides a historical overview of the just war tradition in Catholic canon law and theology and notes the lack of a contemporary single Roman Catholic perspective. It is his contention that "Catholic moral theology needs robustly to reestablish a connection with the broader and deeper just war tradition, and especially with the form given that tradition in the classic period of its development."

CHAPTER 11

CATHOLIC JUST WAR THINKING: THE STATE OF THE QUESTION

INTRODUCTION AND OVERVIEW

The just war tradition came into being in the crucible of western culture during the Middle Ages as a way of thinking about the right use of force in the context of responsible government of the political community. With deep roots in both ancient Israel and classical Greek and Roman political thought and practice, the origins of a specifically Christian just war concept first appeared in the thought of the great late classical theologian Augustine. A systematic, developed just war theory, though, came only some time later, beginning with Gratian's *Decretum* in the middle of the twelfth century, maturing through the work of his two generations of successors, the Decretists and the Decretalists, and taking theological form in the work of Thomas Aquinas and others in the latter part of the thirteenth century. Later in the Middle Ages, and particularly during the era of the Hundred Years' War, this canonical and theological conception of just war was further elaborated by incorporation of ideas, customs, and practices from the chivalric code and the experience of war, from renewed attention to Roman law, especially the *jus gentium*, and from the developing experience of government.

All this took place within a maturing theory of politics first lined out by Augustine in *The City of God*, which conceived the good society as one characterized by a just order and thus one at peace both within itself and with other polities similarly justly ordered. Within this conception of politics the ruler's right to rule was defined by his responsibility to secure and protect the order and justice, and thus the peace, of his own particular political community and also to contribute to orderly, just, and peaceful interactions with other such communities.

The place of the justified resort to force within this overall conception was, for medieval and early modern thinkers alike, encapsulated in a verse from the Apostle Paul, Romans 13:4: "For [the ruler] is God's minister to you for good. But if you do evil, be afraid; for he does not bear the sword in vain. He is God's minister, an avenger to execute wrath on him that does evil." The use of armed force in this conception was thus both strictly justified and strictly limited: it might be undertaken only on public authority and for the public good. As Aquinas summed it up in Question 40 of the Secunda Secundae of the *Summa Theologica,* for a resort to the sword to be justified, it must be on the authority of a sovereign, for a just cause tightly defined, and for a right intention, which included both avoidance of evil intentions and the positive aim of securing peace—peace understood, after Augustine, as *tranquillitas ordinis,* the tranquillity of a just political order. Elsewhere in the developing tradition, limits were set on how such justified force might be used: lists of classes of persons normally to be treated as noncombatants, not to be harmed directly and intentionally in their persons or property, and lists of weapons not to be used because of their indiscriminate or especially deadly effect.

This was the tradition of just war in its classic form. Taking explicit shape in Christian theology and canon law, it was also a Christian tradition in a broader sense: the collected consensus of the Christian culture of the West on the justified use of force, set squarely within a normative consensus on the purpose of political order. This conception of just war was passed to the early modern age and known and used by such theorists as the Neoscholastics Vitoria, Soto, Molina, and Suarez, by the Protestant Reformer Martin Luther, the Puritan theologian William Ames, the theologically trained jurist Hugo Grotius, and others at the dawn of the modern era. For them all it constituted the consensual normative wisdom.

Because of the cultural changes of modernity, however, during the modern period just war tradition has been carried, developed, and applied not as a single cultural consensus but as distinct streams in Catholic canon law and theology, Protestant religious thought, secular philosophy, international law, military theory and practice, and the experience of statecraft. Thus we find a presence of just war tradition in the theorists of the law of nations and in positive international law; we have a form of this tradition in modern military codes, rules of engagement, and praxis; and two of the most important theorists of just war over the last forty years have been the Protestant theologian Paul Ramsey and the political philosopher Michael Walzer. All these streams of thought have also produced other normative conceptions of the political community, of the roots and responsibilities of government, and of the relations among such communities. In the modern context the just war teachings of the Catholic Church lie alongside these contributions to the developing tradition from other spheres.

Yet it is one of the great losses of just war thinking—and of modern societies—that from the middle of the seventeenth century through the middle of the twentieth creative religious efforts to think through the meaning and implications of this tradition have ranged from occasional to notably lacking. In Catholic thought the idea of just war remained as an element in the canon law and moral theology, but largely without substantive development, almost as a historical artifact. Perhaps more important in the larger picture, the concept of just war found here became increasingly disconnected from the ongoing developments in Catholic thinking about the proper purpose of political order and the proper institutions to embody that purpose. The Catholic theory of international relations, which had originally been framed in terms of the Augustinian understanding of political order, justice, and peace in individual political communities and their interrelations, became increasingly tied to developments in secular international law, as we see in such works as John Eppstein's *The Catholic Tradition of the Law of Nations.*[1] Protestant thought, meanwhile, influenced by the moral idealism and historical optimism of the eighteenth and nineteenth centuries, followed a similar course but moved closer and closer to a form of utopian pacifism in which war would be eliminated because of the increasing perfection of human social institutions.

The last forty years have brought a recovery of the idea of just war in Christian ethical discourse, and this has invigorated a larger engagement with the just war idea in policy debate, in the military sphere, in philosophical thought, and in engagement between moral reflection and international law. As a result of these developments just war debate is more robust and widespread than in any period since the age from Vitoria to Suarez and Grotius. But important elements of the connection with the earlier tradition, the idea of just war in its classic form, have been lost in much of this debate, including in recent Catholic thought. On one hand, confusion has emerged between the Church's commitment to its teaching on just war and what has come to be called "the Catholic peace tradition," a tradition of avoidance or renunciation of participation in armed force historically associated with the religious life but, since the Second Vatican Council, made over into a case for pacifism for Catholic laity as well. On the other hand, a line of interpretation of the just war idea has developed which has been influenced by the secular philosophical concept of prima facie duties, from prudential (and contingent) judgments about the inherent immorality of contemporary war, and from well-intentioned but rather too utopian investment in the United Nations system.

I will return to these themes below, but for now my point is a simple one: Catholic moral theology needs robustly to reestablish a connection with the broader and deeper just war tradition, especially with the form given that tradition in the classic period of its development. This is both important and necessary, in my view, for three fundamental reasons. First and most basic is the substantive reason: looking to the tradition in its classic form will bring Catholic thought on just war back into engagement with the conception of the use of force as a tool to be employed in the proper exercise of government to combat evil and other forms of injustice in the service of the public good: justice, order, and peace in the political community and in the relations among political communities. Second, robust reflective engagement with the tradition of the church is an essential element in the Catholic way to theological and moral clarity. Other elements are, of course, important as well: engagement with Scripture, philosophical reasoning, and reflection on the empirical nature of the world. Protestant ethical reflection does all these as well, in different ways and with different emphases. But Catholic moral thought is distinctive because it holds that wisdom resides in the record of the Holy Spirit's interactions with the faithful through the history of the church. For this reason, one cannot be truly Catholic without respecting and seeking to understand the record of the tradition, and one cannot have a genuinely Catholic contemporary understanding of just war without a robust engagement with the church's normative tradition on just war and its place in the theory of statecraft and international order. Third, it is important for the broader contemporary just war debate for Catholic moral and political thought to reconnect with this normative tradition and to use that connection to advance and enrich that debate. Such enrichment is sorely needed. The conception of sovereignty as moral responsibility in classic just war tradition contrasts importantly with the morally sterile concept of sovereignty in the Westphalian system, which has protected tyrants while they rob, oppress, torture, and kill their citizens. The conception of justice in a good social order as rooted in the nature of things and expressed through human moral responsibility for one another contrasts sharply with contemporary conceptions of justice, especially in international relations, as merely procedural, without substantive normative content. The conception of peace as an ordered tranquility, which must continually be worked for throughout history, contrasts markedly with the utopian ideal of peace found in some religious and other thinking about the possibilities of international order, not to mention with the empirical reality of conflict within states and the often conflictual relation of states and nonstate actors in the contemporary world.

In the following section I will look more closely at these concepts, central to the classic just war *jus ad bellum*, through the window of the formulation given them by Thomas Aquinas. Then, in the next section, I will examine some of the ways recent Catholic just war thinking has, in my judgment, gone astray from this model. Finally, in the last section of this paper I will suggest what Catholic just war thinking, reengaged with the classic just war tradition, would have to offer the contemporary world.

CLASSIC JUST WAR THEORY: AQUINAS'S FORMULATION

For a number of reasons, Aquinas's formulation of the idea of just war provides a useful place to begin reengaging the classic just war tradition in its specifically Christian form. Let me identify three of the most important of these reasons. First, his formulation reflects and summarizes the debates of the previous century and a quarter in which the canonists and previous theologians collected, thought through, and systematically organized earlier normative Christian thought on the use of armed force. In particular, it exemplifies pithily and powerfully how Augustine's thought on Christian moral and political responsibility lies at the center of this developing tradition. Second, Aquinas's conception of just war was the reference point for later theorists at the beginning of the modern era, including both Catholic theorists like Vitoria, Molina, Soto, and Suarez and Protestants like Luther, Ames, and Grotius. Understanding Aquinas's conception of just war is essential for understanding critical figures like these. Third, Aquinas's conception of just war places the resort to armed force squarely in the frame of the sovereign's responsibility for the good of the public order. His three conditions necessary for a just resort to force—sovereign authority, just cause, and right intention—correspond directly to the three goods of the political community as defined in Augustinian political theory: order, justice, and peace. This conception thus provides a measuring rod for how contemporary just war thought should be set within a moral theory of good politics, both within and among societies. There is, of course, a great deal more to the recovery of the full scope of just war tradition than to recover Aquinas on just war. But he is a good place to begin.

"For a war (*bellum*) to be just," Aquinas writes, "three things are necessary"; then he enumerates these as sovereign authority, just cause, and right intention.[2] The first thing we should note here is the concept of *bellum*, usually translated "war." In contemporary usage "war" has certain particular meanings which we may wrongly read back into his. In positive international law it refers to a specific relationship of conflict between or among states, and more broadly, to "armed conflict" that may involve nonstate actors within states or across national borders. In the debates over humanitarian intervention in the 1990s, some moralists made a distinction between "war," which they understood as having to do with state uses of armed force for their own interests, and intervention by military force for humanitarian purposes, which they regarded as altruistic and not "war"; thus the United Presbyterian Church in the United States in 1998 adopted a resolution that accepted uses of military force for humanitarian intervention only so long as there were no national interests being served; use of force for those interests was opposed. In some quarters "war" refers only to aggression by military force, to be opposed not by "war" but by "legitimate self-defense." In the post-9/11 American debate, critics have assailed the term "war on terrorism" as wrongly emphasizing military force and deemphasizing reliance on law-enforcement methods—and so on.

Bellum in medieval usage referred to any use of armed force by a sovereign ruler, whether this force was applied internally to that ruler's society or externally. Its opposite was *duellum,* the use of force by private authority and thus presumptively for private purposes. *Bellum*, on the terms of just war theory, might be just or unjust, depending on circumstances; *duellum* could only be unjust. The roots of this distinction lie in Augustine's thought: the service of private ends by private persons manifests *cupiditas,* wrongly directed, self-centered love or motivation, while the effort by those at the head of communities to serve the good of those communities, though imperfect, shows the effect of a concern for justice informed by *caritas,* rightly directed love. (It is for this reason, I suggest, that Aquinas places his discussion of just war in the context of his treatment of the virtue of *caritas.)* Only a person in a position of responsibility for the good of the entire community might rightly authorize the use of the sword. Anyone not in such a position who resorts to the sword, for reasons however lofty, is guilty of disturbing the public good. The only exception to this is the use of arms in response to an attack underway or immediately offered, but even this allowance disappears when public authority is at hand to combat this evil.

So the authority of a sovereign is necessary for a just war because we are here talking about *bellum,* the only kind of resort to the sword that may be just. That Aquinas puts this requirement first is not accidental but follows from the logic of the concept of just war being set out: only uses of force of sovereign authority have the potential to be justified; thus this is the primary criterion. Moreover, it is an element in the sovereign's responsibility for the public good that he (or she or they, depending on the particular case) must weigh the cause offered and determine whether it is just or not and must use force so as to manifest right intention. The Neoscholastics usefully elaborated on this responsibility, including within the sovereign's responsibility to weigh the cause, the responsibility to get advice from knowledgeable persons; yet ultimately, responsibility for the decision whether to use force rests with the sovereign alone. As a sign on Harry Truman's desk put it while he was President, "The buck stops here."

In listing the just causes for war Aquinas named two, citing them by means of a quotation from Augustine: recovery of that which has been wrongly taken and punishment of evil. Not explicitly named here is the single just cause for a state's resort to force on its own authority clearly allowed in contemporary positive international law: self-defense against an attack underway or clearly imminent. The canon law from Gratian onward had included such defense in its listing of just causes for resort to arms, citing Isidore of Seville as the source.[3] Aquinas surely knew the canonists on just war; so his omission of one of the three just causes recognized by the canon law needs some explanation. Keeping in mind the importance of Romans 13:4, Alfred Vanderpol argued that for Thomas and scholastic just war theory in general, punishment of evil was the overweening just cause for resort to armed force so that defense against attack was included within this category.[4] This is, I think, on the right track, but I suggest that what is included in what needs to be reversed. Within the logic of Aquinas's just war theory, defense of the common good, protecting just order and therefore peace, is the central rationale for just war as a whole. Punishment of evil and retaking that which has been wrongly taken are thus two specific justifying causes within this larger conception of defense of the common good. That Aquinas does not follow the canonists in explicitly naming defense against attack as a just cause for resort to force follows, I suggest, from his commitment to this larger conception of defense. Of course, the sovereign had the right to authorize resort to the sword in defense against attack underway or immediately offered; even private persons had such a right. But Aquinas does not build up a conception of defense as just cause on the basis of the private right of self-defense; rather, he builds down from his overall conception of the sovereign's responsibility for the good of the political community. So far as the need of defense provides just cause for public use of the sword, then, it comes from the responsibility of government to protect order, justice, and peace, not simply from the right to respond to an attacker in kind. For a variety of reasons, including most importantly, the change in the idea of sovereignty to the Westphalian model, the development of international law on the state's right to use force has proceeded just oppositely, focusing on the right of self-defense. Recovery of that which has been wrongly taken and punishment of evildoing are not explicitly named as justifications for the use of armed force by states in international law, but arguably they have been subsumed into the concept of self-defense: the former being recast as defense against an armed attack still in progress, as in the recovery of Kuwait from Iraq in 1992, the latter being recast as the right of retaliation. In any case, we see that there are some significant differences between the idea of just cause in classic just war tradition and in contemporary international law. It may be that here moral reflection on the former may provide a useful critical perspective on the latter.

The third necessity Aquinas names for there to be a just resort to arms is right intention. If one reads recent Catholic just war thinking, one regularly finds the idea of right intention collapsed into just cause or used to reinforce that moral requirement, as in this formulation from the United States bishops: "Force may be used only for a truly just cause and solely for that purpose."[5] For Aquinas the requirement of right intention is much more than this. He treats this requirement two ways, negatively and positively. Negatively, he rules out evil intentions, exemplified in Augustine's list from *Contra Faustum:* "What is evil in war? It is not the deaths of some who will soon die anyway. The desire for harming, the cruelty of avenging, an unruly and implacable animosity, the rage of rebellion, the lust of domination and the like—these are the things which are to be blamed in war."[6] Positively, right intention is the purpose of establishing or restoring a disordered peace. Again quoting Augustine: "We do not seek peace in order to be at war, but we go to war that we may have peace."[7] Both the positive and the negative aspects of right intention are included in this third quotation, which Aquinas draws from the canon law (but wrongly ascribes to Augustine): "True religion looks upon as peaceful those wars that are waged not for aggrandizement, or cruelty, but with the object of securing peace, of punishing evildoers, and of uplifting the good."[8] Right intention, then, as defined by Aquinas, includes both the avoidance of wrong intention and the positive aim of securing peace. It does not simply reduce to a restatement or reinforcement of the requirement of just cause. Rather, it focuses on two other things: the state of mind of the one who authorizes the war and those who fight under that authorization, and the fundamental moral purpose for all uses of force, to achieve the peace that comes only with a justly ordered community. So once again, his conception of just war takes us back to the conception of politics within which—and *only* within which—the resort to armed force may be both justified and necessary. This is the full meaning of just war on his understanding.

RECENT CATHOLIC THOUGHT ON WAR

Recent Catholic thought on war has, as I suggested earlier, diverged in important respects from the classic understanding of just war. The differences can be seen across a variety of official and nonofficial statements of the Catholic perspective in recent debates over uses of military force. Let me identify three important expressions of this divergence. First, in a phrase invented and popularized by the United States Catholic bishops, Catholic just war thought is represented as beginning with a "presumption against war," so that the function of the just war criteria is redefined as only to overturn this "presumption" in special cases. Second, the logic of the classic just war tradition is reversed, so that within the *jus ad bellum* several recently-invented prudential criteria are employed as if they were the most important, with correspondingly diminished attention to the fundamental deontological criteria, those described as "necessary" by Aquinas. Third, the context has shifted: by contrast to the traditional Catholic conception of the political community, and politics within such communities, as the means of achieving real if limited justice for human life in the world, and a corresponding theory of international relations, recent Catholic thought on war often treats the state as a locus of injustice and the goals of particular states as inherently at odds with the achievement of common human goals, while an internationalism defined in terms of the United Nations system is defined as the best means to those common goals. Let me address each of these in turn.

The question of the "presumption against war"

The idea that Catholic just war teaching begins with a "presumption against war," more recently phrased as "a strong presumption against the use of force," first appears in the United States bishops' widely read

1983 pastoral letter, *The Challenge of Peace*.[9] In the context of its original adoption, this conception had three important roots. First, it reflected a judgment about modern warfare as inherently grossly destructive, so much so that it could never be conducted morally or be an instrument of moral purpose. In the immediate context of *The Challenge of Peace*, this conviction was focused specifically on the question of nuclear weapons and whether they might ever be morally used; the United States bishops' answer was no, and in this they reflected a far wider judgment of opponents of nuclear weapons over the world. Though in certain ways this pastoral letter drew on the thought of Paul Ramsey, the statement (without mentioning him by name) explicitly rejected Ramsey's conception that even in the case of nuclear weapons the key issue is human moral control:[10] by contrast to his argument for a rational, politically purposive possible use of nuclear weapons—namely, counter-forces warfare—the U.S. bishops rejected any and all possible "war-fighting" uses and plans for use of such weapons. Their conclusions about the likely result of any war involving nuclear weapons mirrored Jonathan Schell's contemporaneous image of global nuclear destruction and the end of human life: a "republic of insects and grasses," as he famously put it in *The Fate of the Earth*.[11]

While the United States bishops focused on nuclear war, a more general judgment about modern war as inherently unjust had been present in Catholic thought since at least 1870, the year when a group of bishops, in a *Postulata* addressed to Pope Pius XI and the First Vatican Council, excoriated the expense of "huge standing and conscript armies" and the prospect of "illegal and unjust wars, or rather hideous massacres spreading far and wide."[12] The subsequent experience of the two World Wars reinforced, for many, this judgment on modern warfare. The generic term for this form of opposition to war as such is "modern-war pacifism," with "nuclear pacifism" being one of its specific forms. One root of the idea of a "presumption against war" was thus this kind of judgment against modern war as such. The widespread nature of this judgment is likely one of the reasons this "presumption against war" concept, original to the United States Catholic bishops, has since 1983 become more broadly accepted as descriptive of the just war idea.

The problem with this conception of gross destructiveness as inherent in modern warfare, though, is that it is a contingent judgment being made to do service as a permanent truth. By contrast to the model of the two World Wars or imagined models of a global nuclear holocaust, the actual face of warfare since 1945 has been that of civil wars and regional armed conflicts. Such armed conflict has indeed been bloody, sometimes genocidal, sometimes terroristic, and always characterized by violence directed toward noncombatants; yet there has been no "World War III," or rather, given the ubiquity of this kind of conflict, this is in fact the face of "World War III." The destructiveness of these recent wars has everything to do with the choices made by those who fight them and nothing to do with any alleged inherent destructiveness of modern weaponry. In other words, the modern-war pacifists got it wrong: their contingent judgment does not describe a permanent truth about warfare in the modern age. Modern war, like all war before it, is moral or not, depending on the moral choices made by those who fight it. It is not the choice to fight which is inherently wrong, as the "presumption against war" has it; it is the choice to fight for immoral reasons and/or by immoral means.

In its original context the second important root of thc "presumption against war" idea was a formulation of this concept of just war set out in the Jesuit journal *Theological Studies* in 1978 by James F. Childress, an American academic ethicist of Quaker background.[13] In this article Childress formulated just war theory in terms of the logic of *prima facie* duties as defined by the philosopher W. D. Ross. Childress argued that war is fundamentally morally problematic, as the killing in war goes against the *prima facie* duty of benevolence, which rules out, *prima facie*, killing or inflicting harm on other persons: "[B]ecause it is *prima facie* wrong to injure or kill others, such acts demand justification."[14] In just war theory the function of the various criteria is to provide this justification or, as Childress also puts it, to "overrule" the *prima facie* obligation.[15] *The Challenge of Peace,* without reference to the logic of *prima facie* duties, replicates the structure of Childress's argument exactly: just war theory begins with a presumption against war, and the just war criteria function to override this presumption (or to show that it should not be overridden) in particular cases.

The problem with reconstructing a just war theory based on the logic of an ethic of *prima facie* duties is that it has nothing to do with Catholic just war tradition, the logic of that tradition, or the ethic on which that tradition is based and which it expresses. Childress's argument is an interesting thought experiment, useful if there were no tradition of just war from which contemporary debate on war and morality might take its bearings, but his argument takes no account whatever of that tradition: though it borrows the tradition's terminology (terms like "just war" and "right intention"), it redefines the content of those terms to fit the *prima facie* duty paradigm. The result is something quite different from the Catholic concept of just war, whatever the United States bishops may have thought when they made Childress's conception of just war their own.

The third root of the U.S. bishops' recasting of the Catholic conception of just war as beginning with a "presumption against war" was the pragmatic need to find a compromise between proponents of traditional Catholic just war theory and those Catholics who, under a variety of influences, had come to regard their faith as opposing war altogether. This opposition was distinctly different from the "modern-war pacifist" position, though adherents of both found they could make common cause in opposing contemporary warfare. That Catholicism could be regarded as pacifist is in many ways an odd notion, but the adherents of this position argued that the Second Vatican Council, in calling for the spirituality of the religious life to be expanded among the laity, implicitly extended the traditional non-involvement in war of the religious to all faithful Catholics. A "Catholic peace tradition" was described which blurred or erased the historical (and doctrinal) distinction between the "higher" morality of the religious and the "lower" morality of those in temporal life.[16] There is, to be sure, a Catholic peace tradition, in the sense that there is a strong tradition denying the right of the sword to clergy and religious and assigning to the latter the obligation to pray for the realization of God's peace. But there is also a tradition, that of just war, which describes the moral obligations of those in secular life, including those with the responsibilities (under God) of temporal rule, and the possibilities of peace in this world before the triumph of the City of God. This latter tradition is the tradition that includes the Augustinian conception of good politics as a just, and thus peaceful, social order; an associated conception of international relations; and the idea of just war defining the instrumentality of the just use of force in the service of both. The contemporary *Catechism* gets it exactly right:

> Respect for and development of human life requires peace. Peace is not merely the absence of war, and it is not limited to maintaining a balance of powers between adversaries. Peace cannot be attained on earth without safeguarding the goods of persons, free communication among men, respect for the dignity of persons and peoples, and the assiduous practice of fraternity. Peace is "the tranquility of order." Peace is the work of justice and the effect of charity.[17]

There is no "presumption against war" here. Nor do I find one in Pope John Paul II's strong words about the obligation of humanitarian intervention: that "humanitarian intervention be necessary where the survival of populations and entire ethnic groups is seriously compromised."[18] On the Catholic conception of just war, the use of force may be necessary to right wrongs and to establish peace. Forgetting this, or reworking the just war idea so that it is nothing more than a set of rules for overriding a general judgment that force is morally suspect in itself, is to change the substance of the tradition.

What is wrong with attempting to forge a compromise between these two fundamentally different conceptions of Catholic ethics regarding war, the "peace tradition" of the religious life and the just war tradition of secular life, is precisely that they are so fundamentally different. Historically and conceptually these two ethics were distinct: they applied to people in two distinct walks of life; one had to do with ultimates, the other with historical realities. In Catholic understanding there should be no conflict between them, because they operate on different planes. Casting Catholic just war teaching as beginning with a "presumption against war" and defining criteria whose function is to say when, if ever, that presumption can be overridden is being faithful to neither of these Catholic traditions, that of the religious life or that of just war.

The problem of the prudential jus ad bellum *criteria*

As we have seen, Thomas Aquinas's *jus ad bellum* consists of three deontological requirements: sovereign authority, just cause, and right intention, including the end [aim] of peace, often listed as a separate requirement in recent just war thought. These are also the requirements recognized by the Neoscholastics and by early Protestant thinkers on just war. In recent writing on just war, however, it has become the norm for three prudential criteria to be added: last resort, the expectation that the good done by the resort to force will outweigh the evil (the criterion of overall proportionality, to be distinguished from the *jus in bello* requirement of proportionality), and a reasonable hope of success. Exactly when and under what circumstances these began to be used is unclear. John Eppstein, writing in *The Catholic Tradition of the Law of Nations* while still under a strong influence from World War I, argues that proportionality and last resort are to be found in the arguments of the Neoscholastics,[19] but the texts he cites do not clearly make the case. It is likely, I suggest, that these prudential criteria reflect the same uneasiness with modern war that gave rise to modern-war pacifism. Arguably they are elements in the prudent exercise of statecraft, but including them as specific requirements of the *jus ad bellum* is a comparatively recent development.

Once they are there, though, the question is how they are to be used. My own judgment is that they should be understood as supportive criteria, secondary to the primary deontological requirements. This understanding retains the fundamental logic and the priority of the classic just war criteria while providing a structured role for prudential exercise of statecraft. On this model resort to force is justified only when it is undertaken by sovereign authority, for a just cause, and with a right intention, including the purpose of establishing or restoring peace. By consideration of the prudential criteria, then, the sovereign authority determines whether the use of force already determined to be justified is in fact wise to undertake. It may not be. Not everything that is morally justified is in fact prudent to do. But to determine that a particular use of force is imprudent is not the same as determining that it would be unjust.

Recent just war thought, though, has included many examples of using the prudential criteria as if they were the primary components of the just war decision of whether force is morally just. Consider this from former United States President Jimmy Carter, writing in the context of the winter 2003 debate over whether the United States should use force to end the Saddam Hussein regime in Iraq: representing himself as "thoroughly familiar with the principles of a just war, " Carter goes on to list those principles as he understands them: last resort, "with all nonviolent options exhausted"; discrimination, proportionality "to the injury we have suffered"; legitimate authority, and a peace superior to what exists.[20] The two classic just war requisites listed, legitimate authority and the end of peace, are listed last here, behind last resort, proportionality, and the *jus in bello* principle of discrimination, which here does duty as a *jus ad bellum* requirement.

The problem is not just with non-Catholics or secular policy types. Consider this from the *Catechism*: after reducing the just causes for resort to force to one, self-defense, this is further limited in paragraph 2309 by four prudential conditions, all of which must be satisfied: "the damage inflicted by the aggressor on the nation or the community of nations must be lasting, grave, and certain; all other means of putting an end to it must have been shown to be impractical or ineffective [last resort]; there must be serious prospects of success; the use of arms must not produce evils and disorders graver than the evil to be eliminated. *The power of modern means of destruction weighs very heavily in evaluating this condition*" (emphasis added). The section concludes, "These are the traditional elements enumerated in what is called the 'just war' doctrine." Now, it is possible to read these requirements in the way I suggested earlier is the right way: as supplemental to the fundamental requirements of classic just war tradition, as enumerated by Aquinas and others. But somehow right intention, including the end of peace, has been forgotten here, and these prudential requirements are represented as themselves being "the traditional elements in what is called the 'just war' doctrine." Moreover, how is it possible to read the reference to "the power of modern means of destruction" without recalling the place of this judgment in leading to the "presumption against war" idea? And what can be meant by the reference to "what is called the 'just war' doctrine," if not to suggest that the idea of just war is problematic? In this section I believe the contemporary Catechism has importantly lost sight of just war tradition.

As these examples show, one problem with the use of the prudential criteria is their being used in such a way that they displace the deontological requirements of classic just war tradition. Another problem arises when they are used as a springboard to a functional pacifism, when the bar is set so high as to be, in practice, unlikely or unable to be cleared by any reasonable statecraft. Consider again the case of the United States Catholic bishops, this time in their official opposition to the use of armed force to eject Iraq from Kuwait after Saddam Hussein's army had aggressively annexed that country in 1990. Testifying before the Senate Foreign Relations Committee Archbishop John R. Roach, speaking on behalf of the United States Catholic Conference, held out the prospect of an indiscriminate air war, a conflagration that would spread to the entire Middle East, and a result that might leave "the people of Kuwait, the Middle East and the world" worse off than if force were not used.[21] Since the people of Kuwait had already had their country taken from them and were being systematically robbed and horribly brutalized, it is hard to imagine how, realistically, they could have been made worse off by a use of force to eject the occupiers. And Roach's references to the

Middle East carry the message that he assumed that use of force against Saddam Hussein's forces would produce a regional conflagration. As to the people of the world, Roach did not mention the international law argument against aggression or anticipate the Security Council's finding Iraq guilty of aggression and threat to international peace and security. In short, I do not see how Archbishop Roach's use of the prudential criteria here can be read in any other way than as to seek to prevent the use of force in the face of the most obvious case of international aggression since World War II. Of course, there were others at the same time making similar claims, just as President Carter made them a decade later in the context of another debate over the justness of the United States using force against Saddam Hussein's Iraq; but that underscores my main point: that the contemporary use of the prudential criteria of last resort, proportionality, and reasonable hope of success is to treat them as if they were the main themes in the just war idea, to interpret them so as to magnify the evils to be expected from a resort to force, regardless of any arguments for the justice of the cause, and thus to transform the "presumption against war" into a functional pacifism. Once more, just war tradition deserves better.

The state as the problem

It is no secret that the state system has been under attack by various kinds of critics for some time. Among the variety of arguments offered, the one most relevant to our present theme is that the rise of international institutions under the umbrella of the United Nations system represents the leading edge of a new global system of government that has superseded the state in important respects, including the right to judge when it may justly resort to armed force.

If we examine this argument, then it is quickly apparent that the debates over humanitarian intervention by military force in the last decade, over the creation of international criminal tribunals in a number of cases, over the idea of a state's "universal jurisdiction" in cases of violations of the Genocide Convention or other "crimes against humanity," over how far the global war on terror may proceed without violating the rights of states, and most recently, over the United-States-led use of force against the Saddam Hussein regime in Iraq have raised important points of positive and customary international law, and in every one of these cases the outcome remains unsettled.

The current international system has its ideological roots in the Enlightenment and is closely tied to the advocacy of such a system as a way of achieving what Kant called "perpetual peace." In the context of Enlightenment-inspired optimism about the possibility of perfecting human institutions in history, this became a utopian form of pacifism in which the right kind of international institution would mean the end to all war.[22] But the United Nations system itself expresses this ideal. Formed in the immediate aftermath of World War II, the United Nations in its Charter embraced the goal of ending war and sought to implement this by the method already tried in the 1928 Pact of Paris (Kellogg-Briand Pact), despite its inability to prevent the German and Japanese aggression that initiated the war whose shadow lay over the Charter. But though Article 2 of the Charter sought to outlaw any use of armed force between or among states except in defense against aggression, it did not clearly define what counted as aggression—a matter that remains unsettled, as the recent debate over what counts as legitimate preemption testifies. Moreover, the Charter in Article 51 explicitly permitted individual and collective resort to force in self-defense, thus reaffirming the customary law sanctity of the idea of self-defense, but without doing anything to limit the rights of states to decide when they were threatened and thus able to resort to force in defense. Finally, in Chapter VII the Charter gave the Security Council the authority to authorize force in cases of threats to international peace and security, without clearly defining what such threats might look like and without taking account of the fact that the states who are members of the Security Council at any given time might have different views on this matter because of their own perception of their national interests. The United Nations is far from a world government. Its efforts to limit and restrain the use of force default importantly to the decisions taken by individual states. Its management of world crises has proven so inept as to raise the question of whether, in its institutional incarnation, the United Nations is at all able to achieve the goals of the Charter.

The relentlessly negative portrayal of the state as an institution rooted in the kinds of thought mentioned earlier has both disregarded the positive attributes and accomplishments of the state system and ignored specific differences in how particular states are constituted and how they have behaved. In the internationalist realm such criticism of states often comes with an equally uncritical positive attitude toward the possibilities of international order as expressed in the United Nations. The United Nations has indeed been the focus of much success in establishing an international order based on high moral value. Yet it has also had conspicuous failures. In the arena of its responsibilities regarding the use of armed force, I suggest its failures are the results of fundamental limitations imbedded in its character as an international organization: it is not, in the language of an earlier generation of political thought, a perfect political community. It lacks in itself the attributes necessary to make it capable of effectively acting out its role as stipulated in the Charter. It lacks cohesion, so that its policies and decisions have led to inconsistency in the conflicts it has addressed. It lacks sovereignty but depends on agreements among its sovereign member states. It lacks accountability to the people whose rights and dignities it professes to represent. It lacks an effective chain of command for military forces it may place in a conflict, so they cannot be an effective arm of international statecraft. In terms of just war tradition regarding the just use of force, its most important defects are those stemming from the lack of sovereign authority. Since without such authority there is no entity competent to determine just cause, exercise right intention, aim at the establishment of peace, and control armed forces in accord with the moral limits of the *jus in bello*, this lack of sovereignty means that the United Nations as an institution cannot have a *jus ad bellum* in the fundamental just war sense. Legally, the lack of these characteristics undermines the positive-law definition of just cause whereby certain rights are reserved to the Security Council while being denied to individual states or other organizations or groupings of states.

All this is not to say that states themselves as a category or as individuals always conduct themselves according to the highest standards. Many states fail one or more of the standards just mentioned, often also failing in the most elemental way their obligations to secure the good of their people. States too must be held to these standards. But international organization has not superseded the state; its best functioning in the end depends on the best functioning of states.

Traditional Catholic thinking about international relations was based in an older understanding of and appreciation for individual political communities as the loci within which a social order embodying justice in all its aspects might be established and maintained, thereby securing peace as the tranquillity of that just order. No other human community, on this conception, has this character. Because of the responsibilities of the political community, its leadership possessed certain powers and rights, including those of the use of force. As George Weigel observes in his paper for this conference, some recent comments by officials of the Holy See have expressed the position that today only the Security Council "can legally authorize and morally legitimate the use of armed force in the pursuit of peace, security, and order."[23] As I noted above, this is not clear in contemporary debate over the meaning of positive and customary international law, and the case for this position must be argued, not merely asserted. Weigel makes the same point with specific respect to the position of the Catholic Church. I suggest that within the Catholic context, the proper frame for such an argument is to recover the classic tradition of just war in its placement within a normative understanding of good statecraft in the service of the goods the political community exists to secure.

SOME PARTICULAR CHALLENGES

I want to conclude by identifying four particular challenges to be met in recovering classic just war tradition for moral reflection, policy, and action regarding the use of armed force today. These have been implicit in what I have said thus far, but my point now is to highlight them as a way of bringing this discussion to a close. The first three correspond to the three requisites found in classic just war tradition for a *jus ad bellum,* a just resort to armed force, requisites we have seen through the lens of Aquinas's just war theory. The fourth challenge arises from how war is conceived, for this is fundamental both for the question of a just resort to force and for right conduct in the use of such force.

The first challenge is to recover the moral element in the classic just war conception of sovereign authority: a conception of sovereignty as responsibility for the common good. This conception contrasts importantly with the Westphalian conception of sovereignty as rule over a particular territory and the people it contains, a conception embodied in the United Nations system of international order. This latter understanding embodies real benefits, but it also has glaring faults. As far too many historical examples have shown, it provides no limits but rather gives cover to individuals and parties who use the powers of rule to menace and oppress their own people and others while seeing to no higher end than their own aggrandizement. Something is very deeply flawed in a conception that casts the mantle of sovereign protection over demonstrably evil rulers as diverse as Mobutu, Milosevic, Saddam Hussein, and Kim Jong Il. The classic just war conception of sovereignty as moral responsibility provides a frame within which good rule can be distinguished from bad, for encouraging the best and critically addressing the worst, with promise for a more morally robust understanding of the international order.

The second challenge is to examine in depth what should count as just cause for use of force in the contemporary context. The classic just war tradition gives us three benchmarks: recovery of that which has been wrongly taken, punishment of evil, and overall defense of the common good. How can and should these benchmarks provide guidance in the present confused debate, with rival claims being made on behalf of the limits on just cause provided in the United Nations Charter, a well-developed sense that resort to force by individual states is not only proper but obligatory to end and remedy egregious abuses of basic human rights, and a newly invigorated conception of states' right to defend themselves in the face of the evils of terrorism and the proliferation of nuclear, chemical, and biological weapons? I have my own ideas on this, but my point here is that this question needs to be seriously engaged. All these claims are worth taking seriously, and all have their often passionate partisans. It is not enough simply to endorse or dismiss one or another of these disparate conceptions of the right use of force unexamined. Reengaging classic just war tradition provides a principled avenue to creative moral reflection on these various claims and the debate among them.

Third, the question of right intention deserves to be examined closely and weighed carefully in any use of armed force. The classic tradition rightly held that not all uses of armed force are morally equivalent: some are wrongly motivated, while others aim at right. The two aspects of the concept of right intention address these two opposite possibilities. Such intention in classic just war tradition, as we have seen, includes the avoidance of wrong intentions, which easily translate from Augustine's list into familiar contemporary evils: aggressive war for the aggressor's sole benefit; wars for reasons based in religious, ethnic, or ideological difference; use of force aimed at terrorizing or oppressing those on whom it falls for the benefit of the wielder of power. At the same time, right intention means that the resort to force should be aimed at restoring peace where it has been disordered or establishing it where it has never been. I suggest that this means that for any use of force to be justified, it should not only respond to the disordering or absence of peace but also include concrete plans, including the provision of resources, for creating a peaceful society in the aftermath of conflict. Thinking in this way requires giving up on the idea that all uses of force are morally equivalent because all force is evil. It also carries important implications not only for individual states which employ force for just cause but also for the responsibilities of other states in the international order and for that order as a whole.

The fourth challenge is to confront realistically the face of contemporary war. Earlier I identified, in order to fault it, the conception that all modern war is inherently indiscriminate and disproportionate in its destruction, so that modern war as such must be opposed. Such a conception of modern war is the root of the idea that just war theory, at least today, must begin with a "presumption against war." The sort of war envisioned has as its models the carnage of the trenches in World War I, the bombing of cities in World War II, and the imagined global catastrophe that would result from a superpower nuclear war. This conception of war also has as its villains the states who engage in it, so that states, instead of being potential sources of human good, become recast as the agents of massive evil. The influence of this understanding of war can be easily identified in recent debates over particular uses of force. But as I have noted, the actual face of recent warfare differs markedly from this: civil wars, uses of force initiated by non-state actors, massive harm to the innocent not because of the use of horrific weapons but because they are made the direct targets of weapons ranging from knives to automatic rifles to suicide bombs. The actual villains here are not states as such but regional warlords, rulers who oppress their people to maintain or expand their power, individuals and groups who use religious or ethnic difference as a justification for oppression, torture, and genocide. This is, as I suggested earlier, the real "World War III," not a repeated and more horrible update of the bombing of Dresden or Hiroshima. The opponents of "modern war" as inherently unjust seem to me to have missed all this. But they also seem to me to have missed something else that is very important. As progressively shown in the Gulf War of 1990–91, the bombing campaign of Serbia over the oppression of the Albanian Kosovars, the campaign in Afghanistan aimed at Al Qaeda and the Taliban, and most recently (and most fully) in the recent use of armed force to remove the Saddam Hussein regime in Iraq, the United States, and to an important degree also the British, have channeled high technology in ways that allow war to be fought according to the actual principles of the just war *jus in bello*: avoidance of direct, intended harm to noncombatants and avoidance of disproportionate harm in the use of otherwise justified means of war. The results, for those who care to look at them, are simply astonishing, especially by contrast to the level of destruction and the harm to noncombatant lives and property found, say, in carpet bombing. This too is the face of modern war. So taking seriously the actual face of warfare today requires not reference back to the destruction of the World Wars or an all-out superpower nuclear exchange but two essentially opposed actualities: on the one hand, non-state actors and rapacious warlords and heads of state who use relatively unsophisticated means to gain their ends through directly, intentionally targeting, terrorizing, and killing noncombatants and, as in the case of the destruction of the World Trade Center towers or the bombing of the Madrid trains, intentionally causing lasting property damage proportional only to their outsized judgment of their own cause; on the other hand, a state, one of the two greatest nuclear powers, which instead of veering toward nuclear holocaust has used its intellectual and economic capital to develop weapons, tactics, strategies, and training directed toward maximizing discrimination and proportionality in the use of armed force. Both these developments in the actual face of war need to be taken seriously and integrated into a contemporary moral assessment of war based on a recovery of the classic meaning of the just war tradition.

NOTES

1. John Eppstein, *The Catholic Tradition of the Law of Nations* (London: Burns Oates & Washbourne Ltd., 1935).
2. Thomas Aquinas, *Summa Theologica,* II/II, Q. 40, A. 1.
3. *Corpus Juris Canonici,* Pars Prior, *Decretum Magistri Gratiani,* Pars Secunda, Causa XXIII, Q. II, can. 1.
4. Alfred Vanderpol, *La Doctrine scholastique du droit de guerre* (Paris: A. Pedone, 1919), p. 250.
5. National Conference of Catholic Bishops, *The Harvest of Justice Is Sown in Peace* (Washington, D.C.: United States Catholic Conference, 1993), p. 5.
6. Aquinas, *op. cit.,* quoting from Augustine, *Contra Faustum* xxii.74.

7. Aquinas, *ibid.,* quoting from Augustine, *Letter to Boniface* clxxxix.
8. Aquinas, *ibid.,* quoting from Canon *Apud.,* Casa xxiii., Q. 1.
9. National Conference of Catholic Bishops, *The Challenge of Peace* (Washington, D.C.: United States Catholic Conference, 1983), p. 72; cf. *The Harvest of Justice Is Sown in Peace,* p. 5, and United States Conference of Catholic Bishops, *Statement on Iraq* (http://www.usccb.org/bishops/iraq.htm).
10. *The Challenge of Peace,* pp. 47–49, 58; cf. Paul Ramsey, *War and the Christian Conscience* (Durham, North Carolina: Duke University Press, 1961), Chapter 12 and *passim.*
11. Jonathan Schell, *The Fate of the Earth* (New York: Alfred Knopf, 1982).
12. Cited in Eppstein, *op. cit.,* p. 132.
13. This essay also appears as Chapter Three of James F. Childress, *Moral Responsibility in Conflicts* (Baton Rouge and London: Louisiana State University Press, 1982), pp. 63–94. In the following I cite from this source.
14. *Ibid.,* p. 71.
15. *Ibid.,* pp. 73–74.
16. See, for example, Ronald G. Musto, *The Catholic Peace Tradition* (Maryknoll, New York: Orbis Books, 1986).
17. *Catechism of the Catholic Church,* # 2304.
18. Pope John Paul II, "Address to the International Conference on Nutrition," *Origins* 22:28 (December 24, 1992), p. 475.
19. Eppstein, *op. cit.,* p. 122.
20. Jimmy Carter, "Just War–Or a Just War?" *The New York Times,* March 9, 2003, Section 4, p. 13.
21. "Testimony of Archbishop Roach Before a Senate Committee," in James Turner Johnson and George Weigel, *Just War and the Gulf War* (Washington, D.C.: Ethics and Public Policy Center, 1991), p. 127.
22. On this "world order" form of pacifism see further my discussion in James Turner Johnson, *The Quest for Peace: Three Moral Traditions in Western Cultural History* (Princeton and Guildford, Surrey: Princeton University Press, 1987), Chapters IV and V.
23. George Weigel, "Catholic International Relations Theory in the 21st Century," presented at the Pontifical Gregorian University, Rome, April, 2004; typescript, p. 15.

ABSTRACT

This essay examines the concept of just war in both classical and contemporary contexts. The first half of the article applies the classical form in a post-World War II context to contemporary conflict from an American perspective; the second half critiques contemporary just war themes as tested against classical just war tradition.

CHAPTER 12

THE JUST WAR IDEA: THE STATE OF THE QUESTION

I. SETTING THE CONTEXT

One of the most striking and most important developments in American moral discourse on uses of military force over the past forty-odd years has been the recovery and practical use of the idea of just war to guide moral analysis and judgment. As a result, various forms of just war discourse can be found today in religious, philosophical, military, political, and legal contexts, and while there is an important common substratum uniting these, there are also notable differences and even tensions. What should be said about this? How should these contemporary forms of just war reasoning be tested against historical just war reasoning (which has also taken diverse forms), or indeed, should it be tested in this way at all? In particular, what is to be said about new themes that have appeared in recent just war discourse and have in some versions of the contemporary just war idea become the principal moral criteria for whether a resort to force is justified or not? In short, what should be the parameters within which contemporary just war reasoning develops?

This essay examines the idea of just war in two ways. Section I is historical and thematic, identifying major benchmarks in the recent recovery of just war thinking, exploring characteristic elements in each, and setting them against the deeper just war tradition which first came together in the Middle Ages and has continued to develop in the modern period. Section II identifies and analyzes several major themes that have been put forward in contemporary just war discourse, judging them by reference to the deeper tradition of just war. Throughout the essay, I argue for a contemporary conception of just war that is solidly grounded in this deeper moral tradition. This leads me to be critical of certain elements in the recent recovery and restatement of just war thinking. My aim, in short, is to answer not only the question of what the contemporary just war idea is, but also what it ideally should try to be.

In the United States, before the contemporary recovery of just war thinking began, moral discourse on war was largely polarized between various forms of pacifist rejection of all war as inherently evil and an embrace of total war, expressed sometimes in terms of political realism and at other times in the language of crusade, as the necessary means of combating and wiping out evil when thrust upon us. Indeed, these two poles tended to converge in practical terms, since the pacifist's rejection of war in any form, for whatever reason, as inherently evil left nothing to say about possible moral limits to war once it had begun, while the idea of total war ruled out such limits in principle. Thus, the carnage in the trenches of World War I, the destruction of entire cities by strategic bombing in World War II, and even the introduction of atomic weapons could be looked at, from the pacifist's perspective, as evidence of the inherently evil nature of war, while from the opposite end of the spectrum they could be justified as what was necessary to defeat the aggressors who had started the war. What was missing in these two extreme approaches to moral discourse about war was a conception of the use of force that accepted it as a sometimes necessary tool of good statecraft, but at the same time set strict yet meaningful moral restraints on the resort to force and the practical application of such force.

A. The shaping of the classical just war tradition

There was, of course, an old and deeply embedded tradition in Western culture that understood war in a very different way from either of the polar opposites I have mentioned. This was the just war tradition. On the terms of this tradition, the use of armed force might serve good or evil depending on whether it was undertaken on the authority of a sovereign, that is, a person or persons responsible for the common good of his/her/their political community, whether it was undertaken to protect that common good, or the broader fabric of relations on which all political communities depended, against injury or the threat of injury, and whether it was undertaken out of a right intention—not to do an injustice to another but to seek to preserve or establish peace. The deepest roots of this tradition reach back into the history of biblical Israel and into the thought and practice of classical Greece and Rome. A specifically Christian version of it traces at least to Augustine in the fourth and early fifth centuries. A coherent and systematic form of this tradition came together in the Middle Ages, over roughly the three centuries from the canonist Gratian's magisterial collection, the *Decretum*, in the mid-twelfth century to the end of the Hundred Years' War in the mid-fifteenth century. At the beginning of the modern period, seminal thinkers from Francisco de Vitoria (1492–1546) to Hugo Grotius (1583–1645) assumed the terms of this tradition and applied them to the political conditions of their own times.

The tradition these thinkers inherited had taken shape as a broad cultural consensus, one whose content had been shaped by inputs from a wide variety of sectors of medieval culture: church law and theology; secular law, including the recovery of the Roman legal concepts of *jus gentium* and *jus naturale;* the code of knighthood (the chivalric code); works of political theory, especially the literary tradition defining the responsibilities of the good ruler; and the practical experience of government and of warfare.

In its classic form as it had come together by the end of the Middle Ages, the just war idea consisted of two parts: one defining when resort to armed force is justified (later called the *jus ad bellum*), the other defining right conduct in the use of armed force (the *jus in bello*). The *jus ad bellum* included three requirements: that only someone in sovereign authority, and thus responsible for the common good of the political community, could justly authorize resort to armed force; that there must be a just cause, specifically defense of the common good against serious injury, recovery of something wrongly taken, or punishment of wrong-doing; and that resort to armed force must manifest right intention—not aggression, domination, implacable enmity, just plain cruelty or the like, but the intention to protect, restore, or establish peace. These three requirements corresponded directly with the three ends of good politics in the Augustinian tradition of political thought: order, justice, and peace. Thus defined, the justified use of armed force was understood to be a tool for aiding the achievement of these ends and protecting them when established. All other uses of force were by definition unjust, notably including all uses of armed force by private persons on their own authority and all uses of force manifesting tyrannical intent. The *jus in bello* included two major elements: a listing of classes of persons who normally, by reason of their personal characteristics (age, gender, degree of mental or physical competence) or social function, were to be regarded as noncombatants and not to be directly, intentionally attacked during a just war; and some rather moribund efforts to define certain means of war as impermissible because of their inherently indiscriminate or disproportionate effects.

B. Development of the just war idea in the modern period

Beginning in the sixteenth and early seventeenth centuries, this unified common tradition broke apart and subsequently developed in separate streams of thought and practice. Grotius effectively began one of these separate streams in his *De Jure Belli ac Pacis* (1625), where he took the inherited tradition of just war, reinterpreted it in terms of natural law and the common practices of nations, and refashioned it into a theory of the law of nations or international law. Another distinct stream developed within the military sphere, with such writers as Pierino Belli (1502–75) focusing on that portion of the just war tradition having to do with conduct in war and, at the same time, with the emergence of codes of military discipline that remade just war ideas from a system of morality into a set of rules for disciplined conduct under arms. A third stream led into the realm of secular philosophy, eventuating in the "perpetual peace" movement of the Enlightenment era and effectively losing contact with the just war idea as reflecting perennial necessities of statecraft. In the religious sphere, Protestant theology gradually lost conscious sight of just war tradition, while Catholic thought maintained it as a doctrine but generally paid no attention to it.

With the rise of the absolutist state beginning in the seventeenth century, the just war *jus ad bellum* decayed into the idea of a *liberum jus ad bellum*, the right of the absolute sovereign to initiate war for reasons of state. At the same time, the requirement of a public declaration of war came to be stressed, so that others could judge the decision to go to war and react as they might. The moral restraints of the just war *jus ad bellum* thus effectively disappeared, being replaced by calculations of interests and the relative likelihood that other states might respond to a declaration of war by making war against the initiator. At the same time, and perhaps in some sort of compensation for the greater freedom to initiate war implied by the *liberum jus ad bellum*, greater attention was given to the elements of the *jus in bello*: protection of noncombatants and limits on the means of war, including both weapons and tactics. The practice of limited war (or "sovereigns' war," as it has sometimes been called) during the eighteenth century illustrates both these developments. The emergence of both the theory and practice of total war in the early nineteenth century temporarily eclipsed this emphasis on limiting the conduct of war, but by the time of the American Civil War it was once again possible for writers on international law to speak of "the laws and customs of war," by which they meant effectively the content of the just war *jus in bello*: avoidance of harm to noncombatants and a sense that the means of war should not be unlimited. The political theorist Francis Lieber's *Guerilla Parties* (1862) and *Code* (1863), as well as the U.S. Army's *General Orders No. 100* (1863), based on Lieber's *Code*, put all this into the form of military law and rules of engagement. At about the same time, the first Geneva Convention (1864) put one kind of noncombatant protection—amelioration of the condition of the wounded in armies fighting each other in the field—into the form of an international agreement. The subsequent development of a positive law of armed conflict in international law reflects both Lieber and the first Geneva Convention. In the United States military, *General Orders No. 100* (1863) initiated a way of thinking about the government of military forces in combat that has eventuated in the present-day Code of Military Discipline, specific codes of conduct in all the service branches, and increasingly detailed rules of engagement for specific military contexts.

As this illustrates, the military and legal spheres have continued to develop their distinctive approaches to regulating the conduct of war; yet this history also illustrates a substantive dialogue between these two spheres. It also shows the significant continuing presence of just war tradition in both. James Brown Scott in the 1930s, and more broadly the Carnegie Institution's series *Classics of International Law*, demonstrated the historical linkage between just war tradition and international law at the beginning of the modern period.[1] For anyone who knows just war tradition, however, the thematic and structural content of the positive law of armed conflicts demonstrates the connection in its own way: in both just war tradition and the law of armed conflicts, there are lists of classes of persons defined as noncombatants, together with prohibitions on harming them directly and intentionally; in both, there are limits on the means of war, including bans on weapons and restrictions on how acceptable weapons are to be used. The same linkage is also visible in the military code and in the rules of engagement for recent conflicts involving United States forces.

As regards the resort to war, the picture is somewhat different. Here the convergence has been between international law and the philosophically based version of just war thought that produced the "perpetual peace" literature of the Enlightenment era. That literature sought to limit resort to force by individual states through creating a new super-state structure for international relations, so that only under the authority of the super-state institutions could armed force be rightly used. At the same time, the "perpetual peace" tradition aimed toward abolishing war, seeking instead to settle all international disputes through arbitration. It was but a small step conceptually to the League of Nations (1920), the Kellogg-Briand Pact (1928), and the United Nations (1945). What is lost here is the just war tradition's realistic focus on the possibility of genuine order, justice, and peace only in the context of particular political communities and the tradition's effort to define the use of armed force in terms of the responsibility of the sovereign to protect the common good. The line of development in both this philosophical tradition and in positive international law has responded to the excesses of the absolutist state, which rests on assumptions about sovereignty and international order that can be traced to the Peace of Westphalia in 1648.[2] These assumptions are inherently problematical from the standpoint of just war tradition. But together they establish a context in which just war discourse about the resort to armed force is difficult, because it goes against the assumptions about the state and international order that are embodied in the effort to abolish war and to create an international institution superior to individual states.

To return more explicitly to the matter of why just war discourse disappeared from moral reflection on war and armed force during the modern period, the developments I have just sketched show how philosophical thought on these matters moved in the direction of an internationalist pacifism. At the same time, there was also a movement in exactly the opposite direction, toward justifying the absolutist state and its totalistic quest for power by whatever means, a movement that produced both Nazism and Stalinism. Taken along with the development of internationalist pacifism, this shows exactly the kind of polarization I identified earlier, between rejection of war as such as inherently evil and an embrace of total war. In the United States, internationalist pacifism became an important element in the pacifistic rejection of all war, while the reaction to Nazi and Stalinist totalitarianism fueled the idea that war against such enemies—and by extension, all war—should be prosecuted without limits.

Religious moral thought, as I indicated earlier, effectively forgot its just war heritage over the course of the period from the seventeenth century through the middle of the twentieth, following along the same lines as sketched out above for internationalist philosophy and international law. At the same time, other forms of pacifism unique to the religious context also grew. Christianity has a long tradition of sectarian, or world-rejecting, pacifism. In not entirely self-consistent but psychologically persuasive ways, sectarianism's critique of the state could recognize common cause with the critique of the state in internationalist utopianism. British historian Martin Ceadel has studied this closely for Christian pacifism in England in the context of the two World Wars; what he found was convergence of very unlike forms of pacifism prior to the wars, followed by a falling apart of the convergence during the wars themselves, and then a coming together again after the wars ended.[3] The American pattern seems to have been the same.

C. The contemporary recovery of the just war idea

It is possible to identify three important benchmarks in the contemporary recovery of the just war idea. The first is the work of Paul Ramsey in the 1960s. In two books, *War and the Christian Conscience*[4] and *The Just War: Force and Political Responsibility*,[5] Ramsey developed and used a version of just war thinking to challenge both liberal Christian pacifism and the political realism of the policy community in the context of the debates over nuclear weapons and, to a much lesser degree, the war in Vietnam.[6] He based his reconstruction of just war theory fundamentally on the theology of Augustine. To the liberal Christian pacifists, he made an argument based on the obligations of Christian love, as he read this through Augustine and through the New Testament story of the good Samaritan. Love of neighbor, Ramsey argued, does not imply that Christians should stand aside when others are being threatened or harmed. Rather, such love implies what Ramsey called a "twin-born" attitude toward the use of force: first, permission to use force to protect the innocent neighbor from such harm; second, limitation on the force used, because the assailant is also a neighbor whom Christians are commanded to love. The concept of love as permitting, and even requiring, the use of force to protect the neighbor set the use of armed force once again on the table of moral possibilities for Christian ethics; fundamentally, it was the basis for a *jus ad bellum*. Similarly, the theme of limitation served as the basis for Ramsey's *jus in bello*, which he developed in terms of two moral principles, discrimination and proportionality. Discrimination, or not directly and intentionally harming noncombatants, he defined as an exceptionless moral rule deriving directly from the obligation of love. Proportionality, by contrast, required the operation of moral prudence, since it implied a calculation of the likely effects of a particular use of force.

In entering the secular policy debate, Ramsey shifted his language somewhat. There he argued that both the permission to use force and the limitation on such force follow from the nature of politics itself: as he put it, force "is inseparable from politics' *proper* act of being politics, inseparable from the well-being of politics, inseparable from the human pursuit of the national or the international common good by political means."[7] The principles of discrimination and proportionality equally follow from consideration of the orientation of good politics toward the common good. Now, these two arguments seem quite different, but for Ramsey they were connected: though the latter argument does not explicitly recognize the moral demands of love, he understood love as embedded in the order of things after the manner of Augustine's argument in *The City of God,* so that the goals of good politics are the same as those of an individual ethic of love of neighbor.

Ramsey only relatively infrequently drew out elements of his *jus ad bellum* and never developed it systematically, arguing that the choice to resort to force is a matter for good statecraft, not for a moral theoretician. Yet he had no inhibition about developing at length the implications of his *jus in bello*, which he regarded as bearing not only on the policy sphere but also on the sphere of personal morality. The result was a somewhat one-sided just war theory that spoke powerfully and directly about the obligation not to harm noncombatants and to limit overall destruction but only treated the question of moral resort to force in general terms.

Ramsey also did not seek to engage the historical just war tradition in his effort to recover the just war idea. He wrote as a theologian interpreting a fundamental Christian theological ideal and as a political philosopher interpreting classical understandings of politics. This is evident, I suggest, in his definition of the limits to be observed in using force by means of two moral principles, whereas the classical tradition had defined its limits in terms of concrete listings of categories of persons not normally to be targeted in war and concrete efforts to ban or restrict specific means of war. Military and legal usage, as I have shown above, held on to the language and method of the classical just war tradition on the *jus in bello*, but Ramsey, reaching back over the historical tradition to the theology of Augustine, produced a more generalized and simultaneously more abstract conception of the *jus in bello*.

While Ramsey's work initiated the recovery of just war thinking in American moral discourse on war, the particular form and focus of his work also left a legacy of problems for that discourse as it has subsequently developed. Two problems in particular should be noted. The first follows from Ramsey's reliance on the idea of moral principles rather than the concrete restrictions found in the historical tradition. While the principle of discrimination translates fairly directly into identifying classes of noncombatants who should never be directly, intentionally targeted, its lack of specificity left the door open for arguments that in modern war there are no noncombatants. The difficulty for the principle of proportionality has been that the concept is harder to keep focused. As a result, in subsequent usage the concept of proportionality has been made to mean essentially whatever one might want it to mean in a given argument. The second problem follows from Ramsey's emphasis on the *jus in bello* and relative lack of focus on the *jus ad bellum*. This has opened the door to a widespread phenomenon in recent just war discourse, making the *jus in bello* categories do *jus ad bellum* duty. Specifically, some have argued, if discrimination and proportionality are moral obligations in the use of force, then if they are not observed or cannot be expected to be observed, there can be no just resort to force. Ramsey himself opposed this line of argument, calling it a *bellum contra bellum justum*, that is, a "war against just war." Nonetheless, it has provided a powerful tool in the hands of opponents of nuclear weapons and of all modern war as inherently indiscriminate and disproportionate, and thus never able to be just.

The second major benchmark in the recovery of just war thinking for American moral discourse on war is Michael Walzer's 1977 book *Just and Unjust Wars*.[8] In the preface, Walzer explicitly embraces the goal of such a recovery: "I want to recapture the just war for political and moral theory."[9] Like Ramsey, Walzer's analysis did not engage historical just war tradition. Unlike Ramsey, however, Walzer was not interested in making connections with either the requirements of love of neighbor or with classical political theory as the basis of his analysis. Rather, he proceeded through a series of close looks at specific historical cases, first to establish war as a moral reality, then to treat in order the questions of justified resort to war, conduct in war, and individual responsibility in war. The result was a conception of just war that treated the justification of force as a response to an unambiguously recognizable evil (aggression, harm to the innocent) and the limits on force as avoidance of evils similarly easily recognized (rape, war against civilians, torture, terrorism). Walzer's book placed discussion of the just war idea squarely in the frame of philosophical and political-theoretical debate. Its effort to ground just war in universally recognizable moral reactions gave it broad appeal, and the sensitivity with which Walzer drew out the implications of specific historical cases brought readers into his argument at a very basic level. That *Just and Unjust Wars* is now [2006] in its third edition and has been for some years a central text used at the United States Military Academy testifies to its importance and its continuing influence.

The publication in 1983 of the United States Catholic bishops' pastoral letter *The Challenge of Peace* provides the third major benchmark in the recovery of just war thinking in American moral discourse about the use of armed force.[10] Unlike the case of Ramsey and Walzer, this document explicitly engaged historical just war tradition, though it did so somewhat spottily, and its overall position was also significantly shaped by nuclear pacifism and by the broader sectarian pacifism associated historically with the monastic movement within Catholicism. Like the historical just war tradition, *The Challenge of Peace* defined a distinct *jus ad bellum* and *jus in bello*, describing each by a listing of concrete criteria for moral deliberation. But its reading of contemporary war reflected two factors that loomed large in the historical context out of which this document came: concern over the destructive potential of nuclear weapons and, more broadly, of modern warfare as such, as well as an increasingly influential argument that what was beginning to be called "the Catholic peace tradition" defined pacifism as an ideal for all Catholics, not only those in the life of the religious orders. The result was an understanding of just war that significantly diverged from that found in the classical tradition.

The bishops began with what has become a trademark idea for them: that Catholic teaching "establishes a strong presumption against war."[11] On this formulation, the just war criteria exist only to provide the possibility for exceptions, in particular cases, to this general rule. This understanding differs significantly from how the use of force is regarded in the classical just war tradition, where it is morally neutral in itself but may be good or evil depending on circumstances. When used by someone in a position of sovereign authority to protect the common good by restoring or establishing justice with the end of creating peace, armed force was understood as an instrument of positive good; when it was understood as evil, it was because one or more of these necessary factors was lacking. The idea that just war tradition begins with a "presumption against war" first appeared in *The Challenge of Peace*. Where did it come from? Briefly, I regard it as expressing three different influences, two of which

I have already mentioned: first, concern over the destructive potential of nuclear weapons and, more generally, of modern warfare as such; second, the growing influence of faith-based pacifism. The first of these tapped into a century-old effort to reject modern war as inherently too destructive to serve any value, a position generically known as "modern-war pacifism," of which nuclear pacifism was a particular expression. The second depended on an idea coming out of the Second Vatican Council (1962–65), that all Catholics should seek to realize in their own lives elements of the spirituality of those in the religious life, including their rejection of participation in war. The drafting committee that produced *The Challenge of Peace* included persons who wanted the entire document to reject war for both these reasons; and as a result, treating the just war criteria as having to do with individual exceptions to a general "presumption against war" was in fact a compromise position between this Catholic and modern-war pacifist position and the inherited doctrine on just war as found in earlier tradition. The third influence that led to this formulation had to do specifically with the language and structure of thought expressing it. This influence was a 1978 article, "Just War Theories," published in the influential Jesuit journal *Theological Studies*.[12] The author of this article, James F. Childress, was an academic ethicist of Quaker background; though published in a Catholic journal, this was in no way an attempt to analyze Catholic thinking on the just war criteria but rather undertook to understand the idea of just war in terms of philosopher W. D. Ross's concept of an ethic of *prima facie* duties. Childress argued that war is fundamentally morally problematic, as the killing and other harm that takes place in war goes against the *prima facie* duty of nonmaleficence: "Because it is *prima facie* wrong to injure or kill others, such acts demand justification."[13] In just war theory, he went on, the function of the various criteria is to provide this justification or, as he also put it, to "overrule" the *prima facie* obligation. *The Challenge of Peace*, though without reference to Childress's article or to the logic of an ethic of *prima facie* duties, replicates the structure of this argument exactly: just war theory begins with a presumption against war, and the just war criteria function to override this presumption (or to show that it should not be overridden) in particular cases.

The specific list of *jus ad bellum* criteria provided in *The Challenge of Peace* differs in important ways from the traditional listing. As I have noted, the classical *jus ad bellum* included three requirements: sovereign authority, just cause, and right intention (the end of promoting peace), a formulation already settled by the time of Aquinas. These three requirements correlated directly with the ends of good politics as conceived in Augustinian political theory: order, justice, and peace. It was important for classical just war tradition to put the *jus ad bellum* requirements in this order, because doing so expressed a priority: only one in sovereign authority could justly employ force, and he could do so only in pursuit of justice and for the end of peace. *The Challenge of Peace*, by contrast, lists the *jus ad bellum* criteria as follows: "just cause, competent authority, comparative justice, right intention, last resort, probability of success, and proportionality."[14] These last three had been explicitly named also by Childress. While they are arguably prudential concerns that ought to be taken into account in the decisions of statecraft, they never appeared as distinct, formal requirements of the just war idea before this. Their use, both in *The Challenge of Peace* and subsequently, has largely been to reinforce the "presumption against war," that is, to deny the possibility of a just war today. Placing just cause before what the bishops called "competent authority" makes the determination of just cause for the use of force something that takes place prior to the exercise of that authority, suggesting that people other than those in such authority make the call as to whether there is just cause for the use of force. The addition of the category of comparative justice, described as "designed to relativize absolute claims" in a dispute, is also described as "designed to emphasize the presumption against war."[15] Its historical context centered on arguments in the public sector that placed the American democratic system morally higher than the "evil empire" of Soviet Communism: the requirement of comparative justice denied that such claims provided a justification for resort to armed force.

As for the bishops' treatment of the *jus in bello*, I have already discussed how, in the classical just war tradition, the matter of moral limitation on conduct in war was approached in two ways: by defining specific classes of people normally to be regarded as noncombatants because of personal characteristics or social function, and thus not made the object of direct, intended harm in war; and by setting restrictions on the means of war. As I have also already noted, international law and military tradition have taken shape around the same two approaches. *The Challenge of Peace*, however, adopted the language of Ramsey, defining its *jus in bello* through two principles, which it listed in reverse order from Ramsey's: proportionality and discrimination. The context of the discussion makes clear why the bishops placed proportionality first: "the destructive capability of modern technological warfare" and the expectation that any war, "however initially limited in intention and in the destructive power of weapons employed," would escalate to "the use of weapons of horrendous destructive potential." As a result, the bishops judged, "today it becomes increasingly difficult to make a decision to use any kind of armed force."[16] On this reasoning, then, the bishops' *jus in bello* in effect took on a *jus ad bellum* role: having given up on the possibility that uses of armed force might remain limited once begun, the bishops used their *jus in bello* principles to question the possibility of a just resort to armed force in the first place.

Whereas Ramsey's and Walzer's influence had up to this point been largely limited to relatively narrow religious, intellectual, and policy circles, *The Challenge of Peace* had a far broader impact. The drafting committee held public hearings and heard testimony from a wide variety of types of people, including representatives of the Reagan administration. The second draft of the pastoral letter made the front pages of both the *Washington Post* and the *New York Times*, where its text was printed in its entirety. Numerous colleges and universities held conferences and hosted talks relating to the developing pastoral letter and the larger topic it dealt with. The U.S. Army's annual conference of its major command chaplains—the colonel-level chaplains assigned to the Army's various major command regions throughout the world—included a focus on this developing statement and what its implications might be for a military whose membership was very heavily Catholic. After the final version of *The Challenge of Peace* was adopted, the United States Military Academy included presentations and a discussion of the letter in its annual Senior Conference, whose audience is senior military and civilian defense officials. *The Challenge of Peace* has also had a longer-term effect in that its way of presenting the idea of just war has been adopted by others, both Catholic and non-Catholic, as what this idea means.

In any case, by the time *The Challenge of Peace* was published, the recovery of the idea of just war as a focus and resource for moral reflection and debate on the use of armed force was an accomplished fact. The just war idea is now part of the curriculum at all the United States service academies and at the war colleges; in the civilian academic world, it not only has entered the curriculum in such diverse fields as philosophy, political science, and religion but has continued to be treated in academic conferences and in campus lectures; and it has been an element in public debate over the use of armed force in every conflict since the 1980s.

My own place in this recovery of the just war idea has been dual: to seek to identify and recover the historical tradition in its setting and fundamental purpose, and to apply an understanding of just war based in knowledge of that tradition to contemporary issues. These dual aims have produced two different kinds of books: three historical studies, *Ideology, Reason, and the Limitation of War*,[17] *Just War Tradition and the Restraint of War*,[18] and *The Quest for Peace: Three Moral Traditions in Western Cultural History*;[19] and two books of moral analysis and argument focused on contemporary issues in armed force and its use, *Can Modern War Be Just?*[20] and *Morality and Contemporary Warfare*.[21] Over the last decade or so, I have also engaged in comparative historical and thematic study of the tradition of jihad in Islamic religion and culture, expressed in two jointly edited books, *Cross, Crescent, and Sword*[22] and *Just War and Jihad*[23] and in my own *The Holy War Idea in Western and Islamic Traditions*.[24] I understand just war tradition as expressing fundamental values in Western culture, expressed in different ways in different cultural and historical contexts. Just war is not a theory but a tradition, in which a variety of theories can be found; it is not simply a product of religion or theological reflection, but a way of thinking about statecraft and the use of force within the context of statecraft that has implications for law, international order, military affairs, and other aspects of individual and common life. One of my goals has been to restore, at least in part, the dialogue across now-distinct disciplines and social sectors that shaped just war tradition in its classical form. More substantively, however, I am convinced that it is necessary to attend to both the form and the content of the classical just war tradition and to the underlying values it expresses. I agree with the classical just war tradition, as well as with Ramsey and Walzer, that the use of power, including the use of armed force, is a necessary element in the good exercise of statecraft. I also agree with these contemporary theorists that it remains possible to make moral distinctions today, as ever in the past, about when it is justified to have recourse to armed force, that it is possible to formulate policies and make decisions based on those judgments, and that it is possible to act in morally informed and discriminating ways to carry out those policies and decisions. In short, I believe the absolute pacifists are utterly wrong about the shape of human communal life in history, and I believe the modern-war and nuclear pacifists are fundamentally mistaken in arguing that the advance of weapons technology (and also, perhaps, the nature of the contemporary state) makes war immoral as such. This conditions both my contribution to recent debates on matters having to do with armed force and its use and my reaction to the arguments put forward by some others in these debates, including certain theorists who profess to lay out what the idea of just war requires. Let me now turn to some specific ideas that have been prominent in recent just war discourse, examining them from my own perspective tutored by the just war tradition in its classical form.

II. IMPORTANT THEMES IN CURRENT JUST WAR DISCOURSE

A. Is there a presumption against war or against the use of military force?

That there is such a presumption is, as we have seen, the position taken by the U.S. Catholic bishops in *The Challenge of Peace*. There it was framed as a "presumption against war" to be found in Catholic teaching but held to be universally binding. In the bishops' 1993 statement *The Harvest of Justice Is Sown in Peace*, the phrasing was slightly different: "The just-war tradition begins with a strong presumption against the use of force."[25] A third phrasing appeared in the bishops' November 2003 "Statement on Iraq": "the strong presumption against the use of military force."[26] These changes, I think, were adopted to fit better the context of uses of military force short of formal war between states, and I do not read in them any important change in meaning. The critical question, however, is whether such a presumption actually is to be found in the tradition. My answer is no. I have argued this in other connections, including my 1999 book *Morality and Contemporary Warfare*.[27] Briefly stated, my argument against the claim that just war tradition begins with a "presumption against war" is that such a presumption is nowhere to be found in the classical tradition as it took shape in the Middle Ages and developed through much of the modern period. What one finds there is a "presumption against injustice," as in the standard medieval formulation that a resort to force is just if it seeks to repel an injury, to restore something wrongly taken, or to punish evil. Augustine's emphasis, as Ramsey saw clearly, was to defend the neighbor against unjust attack; the emphasis of Aquinas and scholastic just war thinking after him was, as the French scholar Alfred Vanderpol put it, "vindicative justice," that is, an action to reestablish justice by vindicating those who had received injustice.[28] Similarly, in the transition to the modern period, the increasing emphasis on self-defense followed from the concern that force should be used to maintain or reestablish justice in international relations. On my reading, the beginnings of the idea of a "presumption against war" are to be found in moral outrage against the destructiveness of modern war, specifically as read through the examples of the Franco-Prussian War and World Wars I and II. The idea's near relation is modern-war pacifism and its particular expression, nuclear pacifism.

Now, who is right about the place of this "presumption against war" in relation to just war thinking? Fr. J. Bryan Hehir, who was the principal drafter of the 1983 pastoral letter of the U.S. bishops, writes in a review of my *Morality and Contemporary Warfare*:

> Johnson has often stated his view that such a construct [that of the presumption against war] is detrimental to the use of just war tradition and cannot be found in the classical authors. I think all would concede the last point and contest the first.... [T]he substantive reason for placing a presumptive restraint on war as an instrument of politics is, in my view, entirely necessary. Both the instruments of modern war and the devastation of civilian society which has accompanied most contemporary conflicts provide good reasons to pause (analytically) before legitimating force as an instrument of justice.[29]

I am happy that Hehir has conceded my point about the primacy of justice, and the absence of a presumption against war, in the authors who classically defined the idea of just war and thus gave a coherent shape to the tradition. For them it was not force as such that was wrong; for force, they believed, could be an instrument of good as well as of evil, depending on how it was used. Hehir's challenge is now directed to this last point, the idea that force can be anything other than an instrument of evil, and his argument is that "the instruments of modern war and the devastation...which has accompanied most contemporary conflicts" provide the reasons for maintaining a presumption against war. That is, war today is inherently too horrible to be a neutral instrument of good or evil. I note that this is the modern-war pacifist argument in a nutshell. It is, however, problematic in several fundamental ways. First, it tars all uses of force with one brush. I do not see the equivalence between the devastation caused by Iraq's 1990 invasion of Kuwait—including its destruction of much of Kuwait City and its intentional setting on fire of Kuwait's oil fields when its forces were forced out—and the destruction caused by the allied forces against Iraq in response to this aggression, up to and including the air strikes against structures in Baghdad and dual-use targets such as communications nodes and the power grid. Nor do I see the equivalence between the ethnic cleansing of Bosnia (and more recently, Kosovo) and the air strikes used with the aim of bringing such warfare against noncombatants to an end. Moreover, the doctrine, training, technology, and actual employment of force by the United States military in both Afghanistan in 2002 and Iraq in 2003 provide a strong indication that the weapons of contemporary warfare are not all inherently grossly destructive, as Hehir wrongly assumes, and that they do not lead necessarily to "the devastation of civilian society." His description of "the instruments of modern war and the devastation...which has accompanied most contemporary conflicts" fits the model of World War II very well, and it also reflects the concerns about the level of destruction that would arise from superpower nuclear war, the focus of the 1983 pastoral letter. However, it has little to do with the actual face of contemporary war, whether the low-technology warfare of Somalia or Rwanda (or of contemporary terrorism) or the high-technology warfare the United States military now practices. Nor does Hehir's argument make any distinction as to how, by whom, and to what ends armed force is used. Contrary to Hehir's argument and the idea of the "presumption against war," for just war tradition as a whole the mere existence of military power does not itself stand as an evil, for it remains within the compass of moral decision whether and how to use the power available. That is where the focus of just war thinking traditionally has been, and in my view it is where it should properly remain.

I confess to some puzzlement as to what the "presumption against war" means in practical terms when, as in much recent religiously based language, it stands alongside a vigorous argument in favor of armed intervention in defense of human rights when these are being egregiously violated. To take an example, the U.S. Catholic bishops' 1993 statement *The Harvest of Justice Is Sown in Peace* includes a citation from Pope John Paul II that "humanitarian intervention [is] obligatory where the survival of populations and entire ethnic groups is seriously compromised" and follows it with the judgment that "military intervention may...be justified to ensure that starving children can be fed or that whole populations will not be slaughtered."[30] If intervention in such circumstances is an "obligation," and if the obligation may include military means when they are all that will suffice, then where is the presumption against such means? Further, what does it add to the moral analysis to include such a presumption, when the analysis itself already takes account of concerns of last resort, reasonable hope of success, and the requirement that the means used not cause more harm than good? May not, in some circumstances, a preference for a nonmilitary response to egregious violations of human rights lead to a worse disaster than the quick use of military force? (I think of the case of Rwanda in 1994. Many who observed the beginnings of that massacre, including the Canadian general commanding the United Nations peacekeeping force, believed that a limited use of professionally trained and equipped military force early on against the marauding Hutu gangs could have prevented the genocidal killing of Tutsis that ensued.)

B. What constitutes "last resort" in the use of military force?

Disagreement over the meaning of the just war criterion of "last resort" is closely related to the idea of the "presumption against war." Let me take as an example the debate during 1990–91 on whether to use force against Iraq to expel it from Kuwait and punish its aggression. At that time, much religious opinion, Catholic and mainline Protestant alike, opposed the use of force against Iraq for a variety of reasons, arguing instead for other measures, including economic and diplomatic sanctions, to compel Iraq to withdraw and to set things right. Use of military force against Iraq, it was argued, should not be undertaken until it was clear that all these other measures, including economic and diplomatic sanctions, had had time to work. Opposition to the use of force, accordingly, was put (in part) in terms of the just war requirement that resort to force be a last resort, understood by those opposing the use of force to require that all other measures conceivably available be used and found to fail first. A decade later, by contrast, one no longer heard about how the sanctions should have been given time to work; rather, moral concerns were being loudly voiced over the effects of the existing sanctions on the civilian population of Iraq. If this was a problem a decade later, it was surely a problem in 1991.

In the debate of 2002–03 over whether to use armed force to remove the Saddam Hussein regime, the U.S. Catholic bishops did not appeal to the "last resort" criterion in their formal statement arguing against the use of such force. Others, however, did so, interpreting this criterion as meaning that every other alternative should first have been tried and proven ineffective. A prominent example of such reasoning was that of former president Jimmy Carter in a *New York Times* op-ed piece that appeared on March 9, 2003.[31] Carter here explicitly appealed to the idea of just war, placing the criterion of last resort first among the just war principles as he listed them (last resort, discrimination, violence "proportional to the injury we have suffered," legitimate authority, and establishing a peace that is "a clear improvement over what exists"). Last resort, he argued, means that "all nonviolent options [must be] exhausted."

But the just war criterion of last resort does not mean that everything except military force must first be tried and have failed. Rather, this criterion, like the resort to force itself, has to be interpreted via a judgment as to the proportionality of proposed nonmilitary means—whether they will cause more good than harm—and as to whether they have any reasonable hope of success. That is, last resort is a criterion to be used in analyzing whether force is the most reasonable and proportionate choice, among all the choices available, to bring about the justified end. It is wrong to use the criterion of last resort as a means of postponing indefinitely any resort to military force.

C. What should we say about sovereign authority today?

At the beginning of his question "On War" (*Summa Theologica* II-II, q. 40, a. 1), Thomas Aquinas (1225–74) lays down that for a war to be just, three things are necessary: sovereign authority, just cause, and a right intention, which for him included both the aim of peace and avoidance of wrong intention, such as the desire to dominate, "implacable animosity," or lust for personal gain or power. (He drew all of these requisites from Augustine, whom he cited in explaining them. They had been introduced into the canon law tradition in the twelfth century via Gratian, who also drew them from Augustine.) It is very interesting and important that Aquinas began by requiring sovereign authority, and it is especially notable since nearly all present-day accounts of the *jus ad bellum* begin with the requirement of just cause. There are two fundamental reasons why Aquinas began here. First, for him as for Augustine and Gratian before him (and the whole thrust of classical just war tradition after him), only the person in sovereign authority, and not any private person, has the right to resort to force. Thus, the sovereign has the ultimate responsibility to weigh whether a just cause exists and decide whether to use force to correct any violation of justice that may appear. Second, the sovereign is responsible for the common weal—immediately, the good of the society over which he is sovereign, and less immediately, the good of the larger order of societies. (Aquinas developed more fully the sovereign's responsibilities in his treatise *On Princely Government*, and to understand more broadly what sovereignty was understood to entail in medieval and early modern thought, one should consult the body of literature on the good ruler right down through Erasmus.) So authority to resort to armed force, for Aquinas, had to be sovereign authority, because of the sovereign's particular responsibility for the common weal of his society and the order of nations as a whole. This is what lay behind Aquinas's use in this connection of Romans 13:4, a biblical passage much cited in medieval just war discourse: "For rulers are not a terror to good conduct, but to bad.... [The ruler] does not bear the sword in vain; he is the servant of God to execute his wrath on the wrongdoer." What might this imply today?

The first thing to ask is where "sovereign authority" to use force, one of the principal requirements of the just war tradition, lies today. There are three contenders: the United Nations, and in particular the Security Council; regional security alliances; and individual states. In positive international law, individual states, and by extension alliances of states, have the right and authority to resort to force in defense against an armed attack, whether credibly threatened or in progress. Most armed interventions historically have fitted under this rule; this was the international-law justification for the armed response to Iraq after its takeover of Kuwait. Beyond uses of armed force in defense, the United Nations Charter gives the Security Council the responsibility to authorize such force to deal with threats to international peace and security. This allows for Security Council-authorized military actions, including armed interventions, when the Council has determined that a threat to international peace and security exists.[32]

Positive international law derives from the Westphalian system of international order, in which the bedrock assumption is the right of territorial sovereignty. On this assumption the ruling authorities of any state were long held to have the right to do whatever they might wish in dealing with their own population, whatever its shape or consequences. It was only in the wake of World War II and the Holocaust that this conception began to be modified and limited by the growth of a new body of positive international law defining human rights and establishing protections based on them. This new level of recognition and protection of human rights provides much of the impetus for humanitarian intervention in the contemporary context. What is not settled either in positive or in customary international law is exactly what authorities have the right to undertake armed interventions for protection of human rights. Is this to be understood by extension of the right of individual states and alliances of states to use force in defense of themselves or of others who ask for help? Or is it to be understood by extension of the Security Council's right to authorize force in cases of threats to international peace and security? Recent history provides examples of all three sorts of actors and both kinds of rationales for humanitarian interventions.

In traditional just war terms, the state is inherently most capable of meeting the moral requirements of the idea of sovereign authority. The United Nations lacks several important attributes of such authority: it is not in fact sovereign, taking its power from the agreement of its constituent states; it is not responsible or accountable to the people of the world, but only to these states; and it lacks command and control mechanisms, so that it cannot direct the use of force responsibly. Regional security alliances such as NATO have a level of authority, in just war terms, somewhere between that of sovereign states and the United Nations. Concern to maintain the moral meaning of authority to use force leads me to caution internationalists that there remains an important place for individual action by properly governed and rightly motivated states. I am dubious of efforts to restrict the authorization of humanitarian interventions or other uses of force to the United Nations alone. Besides the problems with understanding the United Nations as possessing sovereign authority in the just war sense, it is a sad fact that the United Nations (and in particular the Security Council, which according to the Charter is the body that may authorize the use of armed force in response to threats to international peace) is often prevented from taking action by internal politics. Recent examples include the cases of Rwanda and Kosovo, not to mention Iraq in 2002–03. As for uses of armed force by regional alliances, such as the NATO intervention over the conflict in Kosovo (undertaken in the absence of a Security Council mandate, though the Council's approval was given after the action), I think we should regard these essentially as the consensual joining together of individual states in support of a purpose widely recognized in international humanitarian law. Indeed, such consensus is important as a check on the motivation of any such intervention; on this I agree with J. Bryan Hehir and others.[33] The more robust the consensus the better; yet I would insist that the just war understanding of authority means that individual states may also act alone in cases of pressing need.

The moral understanding of the concept of sovereign authority is also what gives states, groups of states, and the Security Council the right to override territorially defined sovereignty when the latter is being abused. When do the rights and protections of sovereignty disappear, on this moral analysis? Under either of two conditions: first, when the governing authorities violate the basic human rights of some or all of their people (since the sovereign's authority to rule follows from service to the common weal, sovereignty is lost, in the moral sense, when state power is used to oppress some or all of the people who live under its rule); and second, in the case of rogue states, states that employ their power to menace others (this, I take it, is the moral meaning of the international-law concept of threats to international peace and security). On this understanding, humanitarian intervention and other uses of force against a state or government that has engaged in massive human rights abuses or that threatens other states or the international order as a whole do not violate the sovereign rights of the state or government that is the object of the intervention, because it has already forfeited those rights by its wrongdoing.

Thus far, I have been discussing issues in the current debate that have to do with the justified resort to force: that is, issues relating to the question of the *jus ad bellum*. Now let me turn briefly to the current state of thinking related to the question of *jus in bello*, right conduct in employing justified force.

D. The question of discrimination

First, what is the current thinking about what discrimination requires? The baseline of most recent just war thought on this subject has been the formulation of Paul Ramsey: discrimination requires that there be no direct, intentional attacks upon noncombatants, though the rule of double effect allows indirect, unintentional collateral harm to noncombatants from attacks against combatant targets. Michael Walzer, in *Just and Unjust Wars*, added a further qualification to the meaning of the double effect rule: that the attacker, "aware of the evil [collateral harm], ... seeks to minimize it, accepting costs to himself."[34] With this background, there are two fundamental questions having to do with what discrimination requires in the current debate. The first is a perennial one: Exactly what is the distinction between a combatant and a noncombatant in contemporary armed conflicts? The second comes from the difference between Ramsey's and Walzer's interpretations of what double effect requires.

As to the first of these questions, recent debate has reintroduced the idea that in contemporary war the combatant-noncombatant distinction collapses. I have never found this argument convincing, and I do not think we need to go beyond Ramsey's and Walzer's response to it: that the argument is overblown, and that there are in every conflict some people who would be noncombatants by any reasonable reckoning. There is good historical reason to hold that the problem with modern warfare is not that the combatant-noncombatant distinction blurs or disappears, but that such warfare has often involved the conscious decision to target noncombatants. An example from World War I is provided by the German Navy's deliberate choice to bombard undefended English channel towns in violation of Hague Convention IX of 1907.[35] Between the two World Wars, the theory of strategic bombardment developed as an explicit rationale for attacking noncombatants as a way of undermining the enemy's civilian morale and hurting its ability to wage war. During the Cold War, though the rule of double effect was often invoked (beginning with Ramsey) as a way by which at least some use of nuclear weapons might be morally justified, the fact remains that the destructiveness of an actual nuclear attack would cause extraordinarily high levels of harm to noncombatants—whether they were directly, intentionally targeted or not.

It helps the cause of the combatant-noncombatant distinction that one of the most evil features of many contemporary armed conflicts, as of contemporary terrorism, is that this distinction has in fact been turned on its head, so that it is not just ignored, but noncombatants have been preferentially targeted as a way of prosecuting war. (Think of the Rwanda genocide, the ethnic cleansing in former Yugoslavia, the terrorism in Northern Ireland, Israel, and Sri Lanka, the amputations of limbs of noncombatants in the conflict in Sierra Leone, the deliberate targeting of the World Trade Center towers in the 9/11 attacks, the deliberate endangering of noncombatants as a tactic used by the Fedayeen Saddam in Iraq in 2003, and the similar targeting of civilians by the Iraqi insurgents today.) But it does not help the idea of this distinction that the air war against Serbia over Kosovo trended in its final days toward something increasingly like strategic bombing, which by definition is bombing aimed at the civilian noncombatant society of the enemy, not at his armed forces or his government. The drift toward justifying such targeting is insidious when it occurs, and it needs to be headed off by planners and target selectors before it develops. At the same time, I think it needs to be said clearly that from the perspective of just war tradition (and, indeed, from both Ramsey and Walzer) there is a real moral difference between (1) hitting a legitimate target with collateral noncombatant harm and (2) directly, intentionally hitting the noncombatants. The mere fact that noncombatants suffer from a bombardment, for example, does not mean that the bombardment was unjust, though it may become unjust if disproportionate. Appreciation for this distinction was not always present in the moral debate over nuclear weapons, and it is not always present now.

The second question, though, is how far the attacker must go, morally speaking, in seeking to avoid collateral harm to noncombatants. What degree of risk or cost should the attacker shoulder? Walzer's argument, or something like it, seems to me to lie behind the moral disquiet some critics expressed over the way the Kosovo intervention was carried out: by planes flying high above the range of Serb air defenses, so that the pilots bore essentially no risk. A similar argument might be made regarding the air war over Afghanistan in 2002 or Iraq in 2003, where in both cases the defense against such attack was minimal. What can one say about this argument? I am sympathetic with the thrust of Walzer's argument, but I think it is wrongly used when it is applied in such cases as these. There is no moral responsibility to take risks and incur costs to oneself when it makes no difference in the outcome, or when the difference made would be negative. Whether a contemporary precision-guided missile (PGM) hits the intended target is not affected by how high the pilot is flying, so long as he remains within the required range. Indeed, for some PGMs (for example, JDAM-equipped bombs) it is necessary for the pilot to fly high so that the aiming device has time to acquire the necessary satellite signal. A further, and different, kind of consideration is that bombing with PGMs may be more accurate when there is no threat from air defense, since such damage-limiting factors as time of day, angle of attack, and choice of weapons-delivery platform then become more important. Indeed, in some cases, higher collateral damage may result from a low-flying plane than from a high-flying one. Walzer makes an important moral point, but it must be applied intelligently, taking into account the realities of the kind of warfare in question. The important moral questions, in any case, are the selection of the target and the means used to attack it.

The principle of discrimination imposes a moral requirement to develop and employ weapons capable of close accuracy and thus able to be less destructive in their effect. Contemporary precision-guided munitions are thus a morally important development, since they are inherently more capable of being used discriminately (and their lower yields make them more proportionate in their effects as well). Some critics have charged that the nature of these weapons—their ability to discriminately hit a given target and cause little or no damage beyond it—may lead to their being used more frequently, perhaps capriciously. Certainly in the recent context, where there have been many pressures for humanitarian intervention and for action against rogue states, the availability of cruise missiles, laser-guided bombs, and other precision-guided munitions may suggest a relatively cost-free line of action that circumvents the moral consideration that should be undertaken before any use of force. If this is the case, then the problem is a possible misuse of the *jus ad bellum* decision, not of the *jus in bello* discrimination and proportionality of these weapons themselves.

The weapons themselves, of course, are only part of the story: also needed is the will to use them discriminately and the embodiment of this will in the training given to those who use them, the development of strategies and tactics for their use focused on avoiding harm to noncombatants, and the monitoring of targeting decisions by a team including experts in the application of the requirements of the law and morality regarding noncombatant immunity. In all these respects, the United States military is currently far out front in development of the capacity to fight so as to minimize harm to noncombatants. The role of the moralist in regard to the conduct of war should be to hold that conduct to the standards that these capabilities have made possible.

E. What constitutes disproportionate force?

I have already referred, in the *jus ad bellum* discussion above, to the argument of modern-war pacifists, also called just-war pacifists, that modern war is inherently disproportionate in the destruction it causes. I have never found this argument convincing. One problem is: disproportionate to what? It is clear that modern warfare as exemplified by the two World Wars was very destructive; but that modern warfare is inherently so remains to be proven. In any case, the only way to measure moral proportionality in the use of force is to compare the destruction caused with the good produced (which also includes the evil averted). In the *jus in bello* sense, some just war thinkers have in the past interpreted the requirement of proportionality as meaning opposing force with similar force and no more. This seems to have been one reason for moral criticism of the massive force deployed against the Iraqis in Operation Desert Storm and, in the Kosovo intervention, criticism of the air campaign. But opposing force with similar force can lead to more destruction, not less, as each force is bloodied similarly by the other, additional forces are drawn in on both sides, and the conflict drags on and escalates. There is a proportionality argument for the use of overwhelming force, though this is seldom admitted by persons who regard force itself as the central problem. Again, the proper measure of proportionality in just war terms is harm done against good done;

calculation of whether a given amount of force is proportionate or disproportionate follows from that.

But this calculation of proportionality also requires us to ask whether a particular means is the best way to a desired end. The air campaign against Serbia did nothing directly to protect the ethnic Albanian Kosovars, and it may, as some have argued, have triggered worse violence against them by the Serb troops and paramilitaries in Kosovo. Admittedly, the air strikes were expected to cause the Serb forces to cease their violence against the Kosovars, and it was bad calculation that this did not happen. It is also the case that ground-force options were very limited. Yet this discrepancy between ends sought and means employed is the sort of thing one should look at when thinking in terms of the just war requirement of proportionality during an armed conflict, rather than the matter of how much destruction, in raw terms, has been created.

The particular problem of attacks against dual-use targets (those which have both civilian and military uses) raises questions of both discrimination and proportionality. Discrimination does not mean that such targets cannot be morally attacked; rather, the rule of double effect implies just the opposite. Nevertheless, considerations of proportionality may limit such targeting or argue against it entirely. Dual-use targets include power grids, communications nodes, critical highways, railroads, bridges, and the like. These can be legitimate military targets in terms of the criterion of discrimination as defined via the rule of double effect. But military forces typically have a range of backups for all these that noncombatant society lacks. Thus, the collateral damage to noncombatants from an attack on a dual-use target may be disproportionately greater than the damage to the combatants. Again, proportionality requires measuring the damage caused against the justified end. Attacks on dual-use targets may sometimes satisfy this calculation, but sometimes they may not. The decision to attack such targets is thus not just a matter of whether discrimination is satisfied; proportionality must be satisfied as well. For whatever reason, the decision was made in Operation Iraqi Freedom, before the use of armed force began, not to target dual-use facilities. I regard this decision as morally very significant. This was a general rule that might be (and was) overruled in specific, limited instances, when the military value of a facility was judged to be sufficient to warrant its destruction. This illustrates the right way, in my judgment, to approach the targeting of dual-use facilities: saying no to such targeting in general, but with the possibility of overriding this general rule if considerations of military value warrant it and if the requirements of discrimination and proportionality can be satisfied.

F. What about the end of peace?

I find it deeply ironic that the U.S. Catholic bishops' 1983 pastoral letter *The Challenge of Peace* did not include the end of peace in its listing of the just war criteria. It is the more tragic that most recent just war debate has paid little attention to this, and that, as events have shown, planning for Operation Iraqi Freedom included disproportionately little on the peaceful rebuilding of Iraqi society, compared to the attention given to the military campaign itself. Nor did the U.S. Catholic bishops address this issue in their "Statement on Iraq"—a fact not excused by the context of their being opposed to the use of force in the first place.

Surely the just war tradition regards the purpose of achieving a genuine peace as a necessary element in the decision on whether the resort to force is justified or not. But having such a purpose implies having the will to achieve it and taking the necessary steps, including planning and commitment of resources, to achieve it. Moreover, the just war tradition includes significant resources for helping to understand what such peace means in fact. In the first place, this peace is the result of creating a justly constituted social and political order. Second, the responsibility of establishing such an order and providing for its continuation and protection is among the obligations of sovereign authority—the same sovereign authority that must make the decision to use force in the first place. The rightness or wrongness of the decision to use force is not simply about the use of force itself, so long as it lasts, but a commitment to the purpose of peace at which the use of force should aim. It is an immoral choice simply to declare military victory and depart.

I suggest that we have, in practical terms, learned a great deal about what is needed for the actual establishment of the conditions for social and political peace in societies ravaged by war (and by previous egregious abuses of human rights) through the experiences of Bosnia and Kosovo. These show both how difficult it is, and how long it is likely to take, to create the conditions for genuine peace. Fundamental institutions have to be rebuilt, often from scratch; the infrastructure of civilian life needs to be repaired or rebuilt; and not least the people who have good reason to mistrust one another must be brought to learn how to live cooperatively with one another. It may well be that doing all this is beyond the physical resources of any single nation—even one as wealthy and powerful as the United States—and the cases of Bosnia and Kosovo argue that, in any case, there is much to be said for a genuinely international participation in the effort to rebuild. Diversity in participation in such an effort may lead to a certain level of inefficiency and even chaos, but it also provides a richness that goes beyond what any one nation may be able to provide. Moreover, the cooperation of diverse nations around the achievement of common goals, motivated by common values, provides a powerful model for societies whose populations have been divided by war. Such cooperation also reduces the likelihood that efforts to establish a just social and political order—and therefore a society at peace within itself and with others—will be regarded as "victor's justice."

What is notably lacking in recent just war debate is a serious commitment to explore what the end of peace may require, both negatively—that is, in terms of the effort to oppose a regime that systematically violates the core meaning of peace, a just social and political order for its people—and positively—that is, in terms of the commitment implied by the decision to use force to correct the first kind of evil.

Let me conclude this discussion of the end of peace with a few remarks on a special topic, that of war crimes. The commission of war crimes is directly a war-conduct (or *jus in bello*) issue; but the question of war crimes investigations, prosecutions, and punishment has to do with the end of peace, one of the premier *jus ad bellum* concerns. For a society to punish its own citizens who are guilty of war crimes is an important ideal, an indication of that society's commitment to a just order. Yet in cases in which such national action is unlikely or impossible, international judicial processes offer an alternative. Almost forty years passed between the Nuremberg and Tokyo trials and the present, ongoing war crimes tribunals for Rwanda and former Yugoslavia, but a standing international war crimes court (the International Criminal Court) now exists and the question of war crimes is much in discussion in various contexts today. It has taken a while for this discussion to develop, and it is still developing. For a time, many in the conflict-resolution debate looked approvingly on the Chilean solution for dealing with atrocities during conflict: "lustration," or identification of the atrocities and perhaps the perpetrators, but the extension of amnesty toward them. The South African Truth and Reconciliation Commission leaned heavily on this model, but the commission's work was paralleled by more traditional legal investigations, prosecutions, and punishment of those who did not participate in the lustration process and receive amnesty. The atrocities of Rwanda and the former Yugoslavia were so severe and widespread that the international community united around the creation of war crimes tribunals to deal with the perpetrators. This may have implicitly dealt a death blow to the idea of lustration, as the effort to bring former Chilean head of state Augusto Pinochet to trial suggests. One argument against war crimes prosecutions, favored by some in the diplomatic and conflict-resolution communities, was that the most important thing in armed conflicts is to achieve a cease-fire, and the threat of war crimes prosecutions tended to prevent this. Think, for example, of the very different treatment given to Yugoslav head of state Slobodan Milosevic at the time of the Dayton Accords[36] and now, in the wake of the Kosovo atrocities.

My own judgment is, as I have suggested before, that the aim of a just war is not simply to end the fighting, for peace without justice is no real peace at all. Rather, just war tradition requires a peace with justice, a peace in which the rule of law is established or restored, one in which civil society does not need to cope with the ongoing fear of powerful figures who perpetrated evil acts during the conflict and remain free to engage in similar acts again. The end of peace, thoroughly understood, requires a commitment to achieving such a society, so that the moral work is not done when the decision to resort to force is taken, or when the force is itself being used, but only when a real peace is established in the end. Exactly what this implies, together with how to provide the resources necessary for it, needs to become a much more central part of moral debate on the justified use of armed force.

III. CONCLUSION

Exactly what to make of the just war idea in the contemporary context has been the subject of this essay. While there has been a robust growth and establishment of just war thinking in American moral discourse on the use of armed force over the last four decades, this has sprung from somewhat different conceptions of just war (as illustrated by the three benchmarks I discussed in Section I), has either not engaged the deeper historical just war tradition at all or has done so only spottily, and in some cases has introduced new moral assumptions and criteria which, both in principle and in practice, have reshaped the thrust of just war argument in a way that is at odds with its historical purpose. At the same time, new concerns, such as the meaning of the requirement of sovereign authority in the era of the United Nations and the problem of how to understand the requirement of discrimination in contemporary warfare, have opened the door to a variety of arguments and a corresponding diversity of conclusions.

It is certainly clear that if it is to be a meaningful source for moral wisdom regarding the use of armed force in any historical context, the just war idea must be relevant to that context. The internal development of the just war tradition is in fact a story of its interpretation and adaptation to changing contexts over history, and the contemporary use of just war reasoning should correspondingly be expected to engage the world as it is. But this does not mean attempting to invent the idea of just war anew, treating its categories as shells without content to be filled with contemporary meanings, or modifying it in ways that are at odds with its historical content and intention. Accordingly I have argued that contemporary just war discourse needs to be tested and disciplined by reference to historical just war tradition, especially by reference to the normative content and purpose of that tradition in its classical form as reached by the end of the Middle Ages and the beginning of the modern period. In the previous section of this essay, I have shown how I think such testing ought to be done, using the classical form of just war tradition as a critical tool for dealing with several prominent themes in recent just war discourse. It is simply not the case, I think, that "the making of the moral world" can be divorced from "its present character," as Michael Walzer suggests in *Just and Unjust Wars*;[37] rather, the moral world as it was made in the past continues to be with us in the present, and responsible moral discourse must have a significant dialogue with that past and the processes which made it. A recovered conception of just war thus holds promise on several fronts. Not only does it provide a way of thinking morally about the resort to force, and right conduct in the use of force, as an element in seeking the goods that political community can offer. It also puts us in touch with the moral theory of politics in which the idea of just war took root and out of which it developed. And if we seek to understand, interpret, and apply the idea of just war in the way I have argued for, by engaging the developing just war tradition of the past, then undertaking to think about war in the idiom of just war discourse opens a window into understanding and appreciating the history that has made us who we are, thus informing and deepening how we think about the moral values relating to political community and the use of armed force in the service of such community.

NOTES

1. See particularly James Brown Scott, *The Spanish Origin of International Law* (Oxford: Clarendon Press; London: Humphrey Milford, 1934). Scott (1866–1943), one of the most prominent international lawyers of his generation, was a professor of law at Columbia University, George Washington University, and the University of Chicago, a United States delegate to the second Hague Conference (1907), and a trustee and secretary of the Carnegie Endowment for International Peace (1910–40), where he oversaw the creation of the series, *Classics of International Law.*
2. The Peace of Westphalia ended the Thirty Years' War, the last, longest, and most destructive of the wars of religion following the Protestant Reformation. It is generally regarded as establishing the pattern for international relations in the modern period, based on formally equal territorial states, with difference of religion repudiated as a just cause for war. Its conception of sovereignty, defined by recognized rule over a particular territory and the people living in it, provides the basis for the international system centered on the United Nations.
3. Martin Ceadel, "Christian Pacifism in the Era of Two World Wars," in W. J. Sheils, ed., *The Church and War* (Oxford: Basil Blackwell for the Ecclesiastical History Society, 1983), 391–408.
4. Paul Ramsey, *War and the Christian Conscience: How Shall Modern War Be Conducted Justly?* (Durham, NC: Duke University Press, 1961). The context into which this book appeared was the debate over nuclear weapons, deterrence strategy, and the possibility of use of nuclear weapons in war.
5. Paul Ramsey, *The Just War: Force and Political Responsibility* (New York: Charles Scribner's Sons, 1968). This book ranged more widely than its predecessor, still treating the questions of nuclear deterrence and possible use of nuclear weapons in war, but also including sections on political ethics, on the implications of the Second Vatican Council's treatment of war, and on insurgency warfare and the war in Vietnam. All in all, it is a fuller presentation of Ramsey's thought on war in the frame of Christian theology and political ethics than Ramsey's 1961 book.
6. Ramsey (1924–94), one of the leading Christian ethicists of the twentieth century and longtime professor of religion at Princeton University, over a career that began in the 1940s and ended five decades later, did seminal work on a variety of topics, including the central place of love in Christian ethics, the relationship of love and justice in human communities, and the ethics of medical care, as well as the ethics of the political use of force, the frame within which he developed his conception of just war.
7. Ramsey, *The Just War*, 5.

8. Michael Walzer, *Just and Unjust Wars: A Moral Argument with Historical Illustrations* (New York: Basic Books, 1977). Walzer (1935-), who formerly taught at Princeton University and at Harvard University, is a professor at the Institute for Advanced Study. A prominent and widely cited political philosopher, he has written on a wide variety of topics, including political obligation, nationalism, ethnicity, and economic justice, as well as just war.
9. Ibid., xiv.
10. National Conference of Catholic Bishops, *The Challenge of Peace: God's Promise and Our Response* (Washington, DC: United States Catholic Conference, 1983).
11. Ibid., 22 and elsewhere.
12. James F. Childress, "Just War Theories: The Bases, Interrelations, Priorities, and Functions of Their Criteria," *Theological Studies* 39 (September 1978): 427–45; the citation below is from the version of this paper that appeared as "Just War Criteria," chapter 3 in James F. Childress, *Moral Responsibility in Conflicts: Essays on Nonviolence, War, and Conscience* (Baton Rouge and London: Louisiana State University Press, 1982), 63–94.
13. Ibid. ("Just War Criteria"), 71.
14. National Conference of Catholic Bishops, *The Challenge of Peace*, 28–31.
15. Ibid., 29.
16. Ibid., 31.
17. James Turner Johnson, *Ideology, Reason, and the Limitation of War: Religious and Secular Concepts*, 1200–1740 (Princeton, NJ, and London: Princeton University Press, 1975).
18. James Turner Johnson, *Just War Tradition and the Restraint of War: A Moral and Historical Inquiry* (Princeton, NJ, and Guildford, Surrey: Princeton University Press, 1981).
19. James Turner Johnson, *The Quest for Peace: Three Moral Traditions in Western Cultural History* (Princeton, NJ, and Guildford, Surrey: Princeton University Press, 1987).
20. James Turner Johnson, *Can Modern War Be Just?* (New Haven, CT, and London: Yale University Press, 1984).
21. James Turner Johnson, *Morality and Contemporary Warfare* (New Haven, CT, and London: Yale University Press, 1999).
22. James Turner Johnson and John Kelsay, eds., *Cross, Crescent, and Sword: The Justification and Limitation of War in Western and Islamic Tradition* (New York, Westport, CT, and London: Greenwood Press, 1990).

23. John Kelsay and James Turner Johnson, eds., *Just War and Jihad: Historical and Theoretical Perspectives on War and Peace in Western and Islamic Traditions* (New York, Westport, CT, and London: Greenwood Press, 1991).
24. James Turner Johnson, *The Holy War Idea in Western and Islamic Traditions* (University Park: Pennsylvania State University Press, 1997).
25. National Conference of Catholic Bishops, *The Harvest of Justice Is Sown in Peace* (Washington, DC: United States Catholic Conference, 1993), 454.
26. United States Conference of Catholic Bishops, "Statement on Iraq," available online at: https://www.usccb.org/resources/statement-iraq-2002 [current URL accessed 23 December 2022].
27. See note 21 above.
28. Alfred Vanderpol, *La doctrine scholastique du droit de guerre* (Paris: A. Pedone, 1919), 250.
29. J. Bryan Hehir, "In Defense of Justice," *Commonweal* 127, no. 5 (March 10, 2000): 32–33.
30. National Conference of Catholic Bishops, *The Harvest of Justice Is Sown in Peace*, 15.
31. Jimmy Carter, "Just War—or a Just War?" *New York Times*, March 9, 2003, section 4, 13.
32. Though my discussion here is not directed to the problem of nonstate actors who use armed force, there is no doubt that over most of the historical development of just war tradition, the requirement of sovereign authority was understood to forbid anyone not in a position of sovereign responsibility from having resort to armed force. An example encapsulating this attitude is Martin Luther's position on the German peasants' rebellion of 1525. Though he sympathized with the peasants' grievances, he admonished them to seek peaceful redress. When they instead took up arms, he called on the German princes to put down their rebellion by force, calling it a duty to do so. See Robert C. Schultz, ed., *Luther's Works*, vol. 46 (Philadelphia: Fortress Press, 1967), 3–56. As for contemporary just war thinkers, Ramsey treated the issue only in the context of a discussion of intervention, parrying the Communist claim that "national liberation" movements have a right to use armed force by responding that in fact such movements are proxy wars supported from abroad, not indigenous rebellions. See Ramsey, *The Just War*, 23–24. Walzer, at various places in *Just and Unjust Wars* (see chapters 6, 11, and 18), seems to require that movements which take arms in rebellion against the established authorities must have the purpose of serving the general good of their people. Such was explicitly the position taken by Richard John Neuhaus in Peter L. Berger and Richard John Neuhaus, *Movement and Revolution* (Garden City, NY: Doubleday and Company, 1970); Neuhaus in fact laid down the more stringent

requirement that a revolutionary resort to arms is justified only if it meets all the just war requirements. This is my own position as well.

33. J. Bryan Hehir, "Intervention: From Theories to Cases," *Ethics and International Affairs* 9 (1995), 1–13.

34. Walzer, *Just and Unjust Wars*, 155.

35. For a description of this decision and its context, see Robert K. Massie, *Castles of Steel: Britain, Germany, and the Winning of the Great War at Sea* (New York: Random House, 2003), 319–27.

36. The Dayton Peace Accords, initialed at Wright-Patterson Air Force Base, Dayton, Ohio, on November 21, 1995, and signed in Paris on December 14, 1995, established the framework for peace in Bosnia-Herzegovina, ending its war for independence.

37. Walzer, *Just and Unjust Wars*, xiv.

BIBLIOGRAPHY

Berger, Peter L. and Richard John Neuhaus. *Movement and Revolution*. Garden City, NY: Doubleday and Company, 1970.

Ceadel, Martin. "Christian Pacifism in the Era of Two World Wars." In *The Church and War*, edited by W.J. Sheils, 391–408. Oxford: Basil Blackwell for the Ecclesiastical History Society, 1983.

Childress, James F. "Just War Theories: The Bases, Interrelations, Priorities, and Functions of Their Criteria." *Theological Studies* 39 (September 1978): 427–45.

Childress, James F. *Moral Responsibility in Conflicts: Essays on Nonviolence, War, and Conscience*. Baton Rouge and London: Louisiana State University Press, 1982.

Cross, Crescent, and Sword: The Justification and Limitation of War in Western and Islamic Tradition, edited by James Turner Johnson and John Kelsay. New York, Westport, CT, and London: Greenwood Press, 1990.

Hehir, J. Bryan. "In Defense of Justice." *Commonweal* 127, no. 5 (March 10, 2000): 32–33.

Hehir, J. Bryan. "Intervention: From Theories to Cases." *Ethics and International Affairs* 9 (1995): 1–13.

Johnson, James Turner. *Can Modern War Be Just?* New Haven, CT, and London: Yale University Press, 1984.

Johnson, James Turner. *The Holy War Idea in Western and Islamic Traditions*. University Park: Pennsylvania State University Press, 1997.

Johnson, James Turner. *Ideology, Reason, and the Limitation of War: Religious and Secular Concepts*. Princeton, NJ, and London: Princeton University Press, 1975.

Johnson, James Turner. *Just War Tradition and the Restraint of War: A Moral and Historical Inquiry*. Princeton, NJ, and Guildford, Surrey: Princeton University Press, 1981.

Johnson, James Turner. *Morality and Contemporary Warfare*. New Haven, CT, and London: Yale University Press, 1999.

Johnson, James Turner. *The Quest for Peace: Three Moral Traditions in Western Cultural History*. Princeton, NJ, and Guildford, Surrey: Princeton University Press, 1987.

Kelsay, John and James Turner Johnson, ed. *Just War and Jihad: Historical and Theoretical Perspectives on War and Peace in Western and Islamic Traditions*. New York, Westport, CT, and London: Greenwood Press, 1991.

Massie, Robert K. *Castles of Steel: Britain, Germany, and the Winning of the Great War at Sea*. New York: Random House, 2003.

National Conference of Catholic Bishops. *The Challenge of Peace: God's Promise and Our Response*. Washington, DC: United States Catholic Conference, 1983.

National Conference of Catholic Bishops. *The Harvest of Justice Is Sown in Peace*. Washington, DC: United States Catholic Conference, 1993.

Ramsey, Paul. *The Just War: Force and Political Responsibility*. New York: Charles Scribner's Sons, 1968.

Ramsey, Paul. *War and the Christian Conscience: How Shall Modern War Be Conducted Justly?* Durham, NC: Duke University Press, 1961.

Scott, James Brown. *The Spanish Origin of International Law*. Oxford: Clarendon Press; London: Humphrey Milford, 1934.

Vanderpol, Alfred. *La doctrine scholastique du droit de guerre*. Paris: A. Pedone, 1919.

Walzer, Michael. *Just and Unjust Wars: A Moral Argument with Historical Illustrations*. New York: Basic Books, 1977.

ABSTRACT

In this essay Johnson applies three classic just war elements to the case of torture and argues against it. Three elements of just war apply to torture: what the tradition says on wrong intention, what it says on those not to be directly and intentionally attacked, and the limits it places on morally permissible means. Johnson acknowledges that none of the major classical theorists or jurists of the just war tradition discussed torture, but he contends that the absence does not preclude or prevent subsequent thinkers from building on the thought of the earlier proponents to establish a case against torture or to address other issues that have arisen since the era of the classical just war thinkers.

CHAPTER 13

TORTURE: A JUST WAR PERSPECTIVE

I have been asked to bring a just war perspective to the contemporary debate over torture. I do not believe I have seen any effort to do this in the various sorts of discussions of the problem of torture I have read over the past several years. Rather, the discourse has been framed largely in terms of the "war on terrorism"—arguments over how to combat terrorism, how to protect the lives of those threatened by terrorist attacks, how to preserve United States national security in the face of the threat posed by terrorism, and so on. More specifically, what I have seen—in abundance—is various forms of consequentialist argumentation, including the balancing of lesser and greater evils and debates over whether torture actually works or not to produce useful intelligence.

By contrast, the classic just war tradition is not, *pace* so many contemporary philosophers and ethicists, rooted in consequentialist reasoning. *Pace* also the United States Conference of Catholic Bishops, whose spokesmen since the bishops' adoption of a revised, untraditional form of just war theory in *The Challenge of Peace* in 1983, have regularly given priority to the consequentialist criteria of last resort, proportionality, and reasonable hope of success. These have figured prominently in all their public statements against the use of armed force by the United States.

The classic form of just war reasoning found in the historical tradition is something quite different. All the consequentialist criteria just mentioned have been added to just war reasoning quite recently, dating back no more than about forty years. This is not to say that they do not have their uses in moral argument, only that they are not part of the idea of just war found in the classic just war tradition, as this took shape from the twelfth- and thirteenth-century canonists through Aquinas, theorists of the Chivalric Code, and later theologians like Vitoria, Suarez, Grotius, and the English Puritan William Ames. This classic conception remained intact in the moral tradition until recently and, in a development tracing to Grotius, also provides the moral base for the law of armed conflict in international law. Properly to bring a just war perspective to the problem of torture means looking back into the formal provisions of the classic idea of just war and the moral logic underlying it, then asking what moral wisdom can be drawn from this for thinking about torture.

Formally, the just war idea by the beginning of the modern period included requirements defining both when resort to force is just and imposing limits on how force might be used—the two aspects of just war reasoning later called the *jus ad bellum* and the *jus in bello*. The former included the requirements that use of force be undertaken only on sovereign authority (that is, by a person or persons with final responsibility for the common good of a political community); that it be undertaken only for a just cause (punishing evildoing, retaking things wrongly taken by others, or in other ways defending the common good of the community in question); and that it be undertaken only with a right intention (understood negatively as avoidance of certain specified wrong intentions, positively—as the intention of establishing or reestablishing peace). The limits on how force might be used were defined in two ways: by lists of classes of persons (and their property) not to be made the object of direct, intended attack, and by prohibitions against certain types of weapons and uses of weapons deemed *mala in se*. These formal provisions were conceived deontologically; that is, they established binding moral duties on those involved in the decisions about whether to use force and how to use it, if the former decision were that force is justified in the case at issue.

But underlying this deontological structure of the formal just war rules lay a conception of the moral agent in terms of a virtue theory of ethics. The sovereign, for example, was not conceived simply as whoever happened to be head of a political community, but as one who needed to possess the virtues necessary to exercise political leadership and serve the common good. Similarly, the soldier was not simply anyone who happened to carry arms but one who had had the virtues of the profession of arms inculcated in him. These two forms of moral logic supported each other: a ruler who misused the armed power at his command was understood as a tyrant, not a sovereign, and a soldier was reminded of what his professional virtue required by the just war lists of wrong intentions, illicit targets, and wrongful means. To my knowledge none of the major theorists and jurists who gave shape to just war tradition in its classic form ever discussed torture. But they never discussed counter-city bombing or the use of poison gas, or many other specific matters, either. One may work forward from what they did say, and the moral logics behind that, to issues before us today. What we know as terrorism can never be just, by classic just war standards, because the people who authorize terrorist attacks do not have the moral right to do so and because the direct, intended objects of those attacks are noncombatants. Similarly, a response to a terrorist attack, even if undertaken in the name of sovereign responsibility for the common good, can never morally involve an attack on whole populations of persons among whom terrorists live and take shelter. Such judgments follow straightforwardly and simply from understanding the meaning embodied in classic just war thinking.

For the case of torture two elements of the classic idea of just war apply, and perhaps three: what the tradition says on wrong intention, what it says on those not to be directly and intentionally attacked, and perhaps also the limits on morally permissible means.

First to the matter of wrong intention. For classic just war thinkers this was defined by a passage from Augustine they often quoted:

> What is evil in war? It is not the deaths of some who will soon die anyway. The passion for inflicting harm, the cruel thirst for vengeance, an unpacific and relentless spirit, the fever of revolt, the lust of power, and such like things; all these are rightly condemned in war. (Augustine, *Contra Faustum* xxii.74)

For an extended period in the eleventh and twelfth centuries a series of church councils in western Europe imposed penances on warriors who had taken part in battle, assuming that in the heat of combat they might likely have been motivated by one or more of these wrong intentions and giving them the opportunity to repent and seek to atone for this. For the case of torture, this concept of wrong intention bears directly on any person or persons who inflict it: can they do so without one or more of the wrong intentions Augustine listed, or other similarly wrong intentions? Unless such persons have no moral sense at all (in criminal cases they are understood as psychopathic personalities), I think not, for torture not only harms the person who is its object, but it corrupts and damages the person who does it as well. In itself this is a strong reason why we should not, as a society, endorse torture.

Second, what about the matter of doing no direct, intended harm to noncombatants? Traditional just war thought, as well as the law of armed conflict in international law, approaches this matter by listing classes of persons who normally do not take a direct part in the fighting or in close support of those who do, and prohibiting direct, intended harm to them. The earliest lists include classes of people who normally did not bear arms: women, children, the aged and infirm, clergy and monks, peasants working their land, merchants and pilgrims on the road, ordinary townspeople. In the latter part of the Middle Ages this list expanded to include warriors who had been captured or rendered incapable of fighting by wounds. The most recent formulation in the law of armed conflicts renders all the former and more—under the term "civilians," while specifically naming prisoners of war and the wounded as not to be made the object of further attack. This limitation applies to all persons involved in armed conflict of any kind, including those involving terrorism.

As to the matter of means, the classic prohibition of certain means as *mala in se* serves as a reminder that some means simply ought not to be used in war. The lists that could be compiled of weapons bans and limits in both the moral and international legal traditions quite obviously do not include every single means that ought not to be used. Sometimes the moral repugnance of a given means is itself reason not to have to name it explicitly as wrong to employ. I suggest the distinctive means of torture are of this sort: they are so morally repugnant no second thought should be needed to know that they ought not to be used.

In sum, reflecting on just war tradition yields two very basic and important pieces of moral wisdom, corresponding to the deontological and virtue-ethics aspects of the tradition, respectively. First, there are some things that are never to be done; the rules prohibiting direct, intended attacks on those not taking part in the use of force extend to the prohibition of torture of prisoners. Second, there are some things that a good person may never do; torturing involves intentions that are directly contrary to what it means to be a good human person. Torture is wrong in both these ways. In addition, the means distinctive to torture violate both these concerns. Together, these implications of just war tradition tell us that torture should never be morally allowed.

ABSTRACT

In this chapter, Johnson responds to six essays published in a special edition honoring his thought and work and published in the *Journal of Military Ethics.* He gives a historical overview of the development of the just war tradition in its classical form. Johnson shows how deeply rooted the tradition is in Western thought and theology. He also discusses the recent understanding of the tradition in international law as evidenced in codes of military conduct and international law. In part, his goal is to further develop the just war tradition, seeking "global consensus on justification and restraint of war."

CHAPTER 14

THINKING HISTORICALLY ABOUT JUST WAR

Let me begin by acknowledging the honor these essays pay me. I deeply appreciate the attention the authors have given to my work, and I am especially grateful to Cian O'Driscoll for conceiving this symposium of ideas, organizing it, and seeing it through to publication. That the publication of these essays appears in a special issue of the *Journal of Military Ethics*, and indeed marks my retirement as Co-Editor of *JME*, a position in which I have served since its founding, is another source of pleasure to me, and I thank the Editor of *JME*, my colleague Bård Mæland, for his support to Cian in making this special issue possible.

This contribution of mine is the result of my having been asked to provide a response to these six papers. I want to use the opportunity not chiefly to critique what they say but to build on, clarify, nuance, and in a few rare instances offer a bit of correction building on what these six authors have said, but also to offer something of my own perspective on what I have been doing all these years.

There is a great deal of use of the term "just war" in contemporary literature on the ethics of war, but sadly, much of what appears under that heading is consciously or unconsciously unconnected to the broad cultural and moral tradition that historically has defined just war as a conception and body of practice. My work, by contrast, has been focused on the tradition that has developed and carried this idea historically and the implications to be drawn from this tradition of just war for present-day reflection and, maybe, practical decision-making. The six papers above [in the *JME* issue] also engage this historical tradition, though (as is to be expected from any group of individuals) from different angles and in different ways. Broadly, these papers define a kind of conversation about the meaning of just war both as shaped and transmitted in a historically defined tradition and as having worth for present-day thinking about the ethics of war. This response of mine aims to continue and extend that conversation.

While each of these papers has its own distinctive character, I think of them as belonging to two groups. The first three papers, those by O'Driscoll, Kelsay, and Zehr, bear on the question of how to use history in ethical reflection; that is, their main focus is methodological. The second group of three, those by Lang, Sharma, and Bellamy, all deal with specific problems in applying just war thinking to contemporary uses of armed force. Both concerns, of course, are found in my work, and the distinction I draw between these two groups of papers broadly mirrors that between my three books focused on the Western normative tradition on war[1] and those explicitly seeking to apply the conception of the ethics of war identified there to contemporary issues in the use of armed force.[2] The two books I co-edited with John Kelsay on relating the traditions of just war and *jihad* of the sword[3] fall into the first camp, and so does my own book on the idea of holy war in the Western and Islamic traditions.[4] But a close look at all these books will reveal that the difference is hardly absolute. Indeed, in my thinking both sorts of concerns are always present right alongside one another, since my historical investigations are about moral traditions and their implications in particular historical situations, and my efforts at applied ethics proceed by extrapolating from how just war tradition was applied in such historical situations to how its meaning should be understood in present contexts.

Not everyone has been able to make sense of the results of this admittedly complicated way of "doing" ethics. John Kelsay, mentioned above comments on Terry Nardin's bewilderment at it; I have given papers at societies of academic historians when clearly some in the audience wondered why I did not simply trace the historical facts and not spend so much time on how those facts define an ethical tradition; and there are certainly numbers of contemporary philosophers (and religious ethicists as well) who simply do not see that history has anything at all to do with ethical reasoning. To my mind, of course, this last attitude has led to what is wrong with large parts of recent thinking put forward under the rubric of "just war," but this is not the occasion to go further into that.

Two of the discussed papers above, O'Driscoll's and Lang's, point to the similarity between my way of thinking and that of Alasdair MacIntyre on historical tradition and meaning. Whatever commonality there is probably traces to the interest both of us have in medieval thought and the use of Aristotle there. MacIntyre's *After Virtue* appeared the same year[5] as my second book on just war tradition, *Just War Tradition and the Restraint of War*, and in that book I was already deeply engaged in giving voice to my understanding of the importance of history for ethical reflection and particularly for the ethics of war. I didn't read MacIntyre's work till somewhat later and was delighted to find that we seemed to be speaking different dialects of a common language. In subsequent work I have tried to use his thinking to sharpen my own on certain points, but whatever methodological faults lie in my work are my own, not MacIntyre's.

The case of Edmund Burke is rather different. I read some in Burke thirty-odd years ago in the process of educating myself to teach a course I was woefully unprepared for, but I have never consciously thought of my work as Burkean. It was not an unpleasant surprise, though, to have O'Driscoll point to the likeness. In O'Driscoll's words, Burke's view was that "historical experience, embodied in tradition, provides the best tutor for political practice."[6] I not only agree, but would add "and ethical reflection and practice."

To what conscious influences would I trace my approach to the ethics of war? There were three particular individuals whose work on just war led me into my focus on this topic as the major theme of my scholarship: Paul Ramsey, Michael Walzer, and William V. O'Brien. Ramsey was my doctoral mentor at Princeton, and while I wrote my dissertation on an entirely different topic, his two seminal books from the 1960s[7] introduced me to the idea of just war as a conception of Christian ethics. But along with many positive influences, there was an important negative one: Ramsey wrote as a theologian, developing his particular understanding of just war as an extrapolation of the Christian norm of love of neighbor; he did not engage the historical tradition of just war in its own particulars but lifted out themes from thinkers like Augustine and Aquinas as they fitted his theological purposes. My first just war book[8] was quite consciously an effort to engage the historical tradition, to uncover and follow how Augustine, Aquinas, and others were actually used there. Walzer's *Just and Unjust Wars*[9] appeared between my first and second just war books; I found his use of history engaging and provocative and discussed it in a chapter in my 1981 book; but again, he was not interested in engaging or drawing out the historical tradition, and I was. O'Brien, who drew me closely into the debates (theological, military, and academic) surrounding the writing of the United States Catholic bishops' pastoral letter, *The Challenge of Peace*,[10] in important ways incorporated the idea of just war in his personal life: a retired Army colonel, a professor of government deeply involved in understanding the meaning of international law and its implications for international relations and the use of military force, a deeply committed Catholic convinced of the importance of tradition, and a serious and substantive scholar of ethics, law, and war.[11] He brought a real-world experience and a level of common sense to thinking about the ethics of war that remains rare among academics writing on just war. My long-time engagement with military thinkers, particularly in the war colleges and the service academies, as well as my long-running debate with Catholic thinkers on war (I'm not myself Catholic) is a result of O'Brien's influence and example.

For my convictions about the importance of historical tradition as the basis for finding meaning and guiding that meaning the most important influence was definitely my coursework in the history of Christian thought while I was a divinity student in my early twenties. This experience is also the ultimate root of my impatience with contemporary Christian thought on the ethics of war that misunderstands, misuses, or sometimes completely ignores the historical Christian tradition on just war and its placement in theology, moral teaching, and the interrelation between religion and its social context. Just war tradition is not simply a tradition of Christian thought and practice, but within the broader tradition there is a specifically Christian one, and I believe contemporary Christian moral reflection on the ethics of war is not keeping faith with those who went before when their work and its implications are disregarded, misunderstood, or misused. At the same time, like Burke and MacIntyre, I think it essential to take account of historical experience and traditions encapsulating that experience in politics and ethics.

Let me now turn more explicitly to the papers. Both O'Driscoll and Zehr note my emphasis on what I call the "classic" expression of the just war idea, and both find a tension between this emphasis and my earlier argument for viewing just war tradition as a "rolling story that reflects the sum of its own historical development."[12] Zehr[13] is troubled by this, arguing as follows in her conclusion:

> Johnson's "classic" just war category suggests an essentialist account of just war thinking. However, such a position is difficult to maintain, as moral communities are always engaged in the task of giving reasons for their values. With changing historical circumstances, these reasons, and consequently these values, are likely to change.

O'Driscoll, by contrast, reads the tension between the two themes in my writing more positively, arguing that this is where the distinction between reading me as a hedgehog and reading me as a fox breaks down and judging the result to be "not a failing but a strength."[14] It is perhaps merely human that I prefer O'Driscoll to Zehr on this matter.

O'Driscoll very engagingly and usefully employs the hedgehog–fox categories, as well as his own slightly expanded categories of conservatism, progressivism, and reflectivism, as lenses through which to view my work. These are specially ground lenses, to be sure, as each one brings different details into focus. Or maybe "perspectives" would be a better word for these five categories, as this word suggests looking at the subjects I have treated from different vantage points, seeing different elements of the whole as more or less prominent from each perspective. I confess O'Driscoll's fine-grained and nuanced analysis has led me to thinking about my own thought in ways that had not occurred to me before (e.g., my similarity to Burke noted earlier). But more often his categories serve to raise to light elements in my thinking which I recognize and acknowledge and which are important, though I have not always stressed them. A case in point is O'Driscoll's[15] argument that my "historical hermeneutics reflects a project that is driven by a desire to learn from the past, not just for its own sake, but so that we might build a better future." Hear, hear! It is because of this that I regard it as so utterly and sinfully wrong to forget—as far too much that passes for just war reasoning in contemporary debate does by accident, emphasis, or design—that just war is about seeking to achieve the end [aim] of peace.

But perhaps O'Driscoll's approach does not entirely satisfy Zehr's concern. Accordingly, I would add that I admit to having stressed particular matters in different contexts. We speak, after all, of discussion of the ethics of war as a "debate," and in a debate one needs to identify, meet, and refute the shortcomings of one's opponent's position. Especially in my earlier writings, I was heavily concerned to make the case for historically based reasoning in ethics as opposed to various other prominent forms of ethical reasoning. This debate is still going on, of course; recently I had to argue the importance of a broader account of history in the development of just war thinking about noncombatant immunity against another writer on ethics who argues that the development of noncombatant immunity is simply a logical working out of ideas already found in Aquinas. Different readers will gravitate to one or the other of these positions, but my point here is that the nature of the question being debated shapes how one argues, and it has shaped what I have stressed at different times with regard to the idea of just war. My emphasis on the classic form of the conception of just war, the form given it by the medieval canonist Gratian and his successors and stated pithily in Aquinas's *Summa Theologica* II/II, Q. 40, has developed as a quite conscious response to what I see as a grievously wrong conception of just war, its purpose and its use put forward by the United States Catholic bishops in their 1983 pastoral letter[16] and since advanced by spokespeople of the bishops and taken over as the normative statement on just war by others. I have elsewhere given my reasons for this negative judgment on the Catholic bishops' version of just war,[17] but my point here is simply to note that I began to stress the classic form of the just war idea as a way of reminding the bishops and their supporters that the deep tradition of just war shows us a conception fundamentally different from theirs. I have also made much the same point in arguing against the unhistorical conception of just war put forward in recent Anglo-American philosophy. This is not a "golden age" conception but a way to insist that just war tradition provides both a content and a form, so that if one wants to describe one's position by use of the term "just war" one should pay attention to what this term actually was understood to be and to be about when it was first coherently pulled together.

In this connection I should acknowledge that Zehr is accurate to observe that my own listing of the just war categories has shifted as I have given more emphasis to the classic idea of just war. In my early work I wasn't particularly interested in describing just war in terms of categories; this was because ethical reasoning from categories, as practiced then, was very different from the historically based method I wished to emphasize. When I did decide to describe just war in terms of categories, I simply adopted what was at the time a widespread consensus as to what these were. I used this listing for some time and continue to refer to it from time to time, in various contexts. It has real advantages for linking just war thinking to international law, a major running concern of mine. But reflecting on the elements of the classic idea of just war has led me to see matters somewhat differently, especially in two particular ways: to recognize the systematic links between Aquinas's formulation of the three necessities for just war (sovereign authority, just cause, and right intention including the end of peace) and the three goals of politics assumed in the Augustinian tradition (order, justice, and peace), and to acknowledge more forthrightly a lesson I had learned from Ramsey: that the decision whether to resort to use of armed force is properly the responsibility and right of those in positions of supreme political authority in a society, not that of moralists—or even bishops! In Chapters 1 and 2 of *Morality and Contemporary Warfare*[18] I employ both ways of describing the content of the just war idea and develop each way to its particular purposes; those interested in more on the subject should look there.

Let me now turn to John Kelsay's paper, which I have postponed because of the common issues raised by O'Driscoll and Zehr. Kelsay and I have been friends and sometime collaborators for almost 30 years, and I owe to him my introduction to the tradition of Islamic thought on war. This essay of his, though, treats a different matter. I like the way he begins, by outlining the difference between my way of thinking and the different versions of ethical reasoning as proceeding from principles exemplified in the thought of James Childress and Paul Ramsey. As Kelsay makes very clear, I was engaged in thinking about the meaning of history for ethical reflection from the first. But I especially like his placing my approach over against Childress's method because it applies so well to my ongoing argument with the official position of the U.S. Catholic bishops and their supporters in the academic debates over the use of armed force. For the bishops' foundational statement, their 1983 pastoral letter, directly employs Childress's mode of describing just war and adopts it as the bishops' position, asserting that this is what Catholic just war thinking is and has been. My argument with this position has sought to identify the real and substantial differences between the bishops' idea of just war and that of the actual tradition as found in what I call "benchmark" thinkers—especially people like Gratian in the twelfth century, Aquinas in the thirteenth, and the Spanish Neo-Scholastics in the sixteenth and early seventeenth. Here is where we find what I call the "classic" concept of just war, and that is very different from the "presumption against war" doctrine of the U.S. bishops, which is a barely disguised version of Childress's argument that the just war idea proceeds from the principle of non-maleficence.[19]

I think it is fair to say that my efforts at defining ethical reflection about war through definition and engagement with historical tradition have largely failed in my own home field of religious ethics (Kelsay and a few others notable, and much appreciated, exceptions). This field is and has long been dominated by people who because of their own inclinations or because of the influence of their teachers seek to reduce it to reasoning from principles, whether the principle of love of neighbor (as in Ramsey) or versions of philosophical principles (as in Childress and his teacher James Gustafson).

I know from my publishers that more political scientists have bought my books than people from other academic fields. For political scientists, and especially perhaps those in international relations, the matter is different: here historical patterns and modes of thinking matter, and the ability to draw practical results either for the purpose of analysis or for that of policy is valued. Similarly, for military professionals, reflection on history as well as consideration of how it matters for practical decision-making lies at the core of how they think about who they are and what they do. Increasingly I have come to feel a kinship with both.

Much of my argumentation aimed at showing that just war tradition is not narrowly Christian, especially not narrowly a strand in Christian theology, has been quite explicitly aimed at showing its relevance for policy-making and specific decisions in secular contexts, including the exercise of government and military service. I like to describe just war tradition as a stream that moves through history like a river, remaining the same yet putting down some elements and picking up others as it flows, from time to time dividing into different channels and then, perhaps, recombining. As I have conceived my task, it is to describe this flow and try to make sense of it, while trying to keep the various sub-streams in contact with one another and with the mother stream.

I think Kelsay is absolutely on target to find resonance between how I have thought about just war tradition and its implications both for uses of force and also, more broadly, for responsible exercise of governance, and the model of practical reasoning found in Islamic jurisprudence or reasoning about *shari'a*. Both aim at a continuing dialogue with the community's historical experience and reflection, and both aim to, in Kelsay's[20] words, "articulate a 'fit' between precedent and current circumstance." But there are also important differences: most notably, *shari'a* considers itself based in an inherently immutable law handed down directly from God, while just war tradition, even insofar as it relies on the idea of an underlying natural law, depends on human experience, on discovering the right as one goes along. My model of moral reasoning conceives moral reflection as a continuing dialogue with historical experience and prior moral reflection. The tradition of *shari'a* reasoning proceeds differently.

Yet some of the same practical problems arise both in contemporary *shari'a* reasoning and in contemporary just war reasoning, notably the tendencies to reductionism found in both. For radical Islamists this takes the form of a narrow and doctrinaire reading of the *shari'a* tradition often termed "fundamentalist," after the model of a biblical fundamentalist. One of its results is to use the idea of the *jihad* of individual duty to argue for a kind of Hobbesian war of all against all, except that it is the war of every Muslim against everyone else. In contemporary just war tradition, by contrast, the reductionism has moved the opposite way: to define the use of force as inherently morally wrong, as in the Catholic bishops' notion of a "presumption against war" and arguments drawn from this. The remedy I have offered for these different forms of reductionism is fundamentally the same: to show what the historical tradition actually says and to draw out what it implies. Just as one gets a very different picture of the just war idea from reading Aquinas, say, than from reading *The Challenge of Peace*,[21] one gets a very different picture of the idea of the *jihad* of individual duty when one moves beyond the radicals' own statements and those of their favorite authority, Ibn Taymiyya, to people like the twelfth-century Syrian author Al-Sulami, treated by Kelsay[22] in his book *Arguing the Just War in Islam*, or earlier authorities including Ibn Rushd (Averroes) or the thinkers who originally defined the juristic idea of *jihad*, al-Shaybani and al-Shafi'i. It is important for people who want to be faithful to their moral traditions to know what those traditions actually contain, in fullness and complexity.

As I read Lang's paper I had the sense that to an important extent he describes a conflict that isn't there, or at least one I don't want to be there. His distinction between someone who is "in authority" and someone who is "an authority" is useful, and I agree with him that I belong in the latter category, not the former. But I reject Lang's categorizing my work as describing just war tradition only in its political role. I think rather that I have worked out of all the roles he identifies at various times, in various contexts. The criticism that appears in Bellamy's paper is, after all, aimed at aspects of my work that are "prophetic" according to Lang's categories, and I would argue that my argument with the position enunciated in *The Challenge of Peace*[23] is also an example of such "prophetic" use of just war tradition. As for what he calls the "pastoral" role, as he notes himself, I have had a significant amount of interaction, both personal and through things I have written, with professional military people. Perhaps my interaction with people in the civilian policy community fits this category as well, though perhaps it also bleeds into the category of the "political"; I'll leave it to others to sort that out. As for the "philosophical" role of my approach to just war tradition, I think John Kelsay's paper answers for me. As I read through Lang's paper, I found myself writing in the margin comments like "this is my view" and "right" and "good." So I'm not sure he and I have much of an argument in the end.

This extends in principle to what seems to be Lang's major concern: that those "in authority" in various Christian churches have the right to define their own understanding of the ethics of war. So far so good, though I think we have considerable differences over the actual scope of this authority and the way it is employed in particular Christian bodies. It is not just, as Lang suggests, that my background is in a "free church," one without hierarchy. Clearly even in churches in which there are bishops, their ecclesiological role differs from church to church; not all are understood as having the teaching authority claimed for its bishops by the Roman Catholic Church. And there are more issues persons interested in ecclesiology would need to debate; Ramsey's book cited by Lang offers a good place to begin identifying the relevant questions.

But we do have a real difference over what bishops exercising their teaching authority owe to the tradition out of which that authority comes. Lang would give them far more latitude in defining their own position of just war than I would. Thus he writes, "Rather than seeing them as leaving the stream of just war, the Christian churches as a whole have turned the tradition in a new direction."[24] I'm not at all sure about the category of "the Christian churches as a whole." In the United States the churches of the old Protestant mainline in recent years have turned to language other than that of just war to advance their arguments about ethics and warfare, speaking of the need to "move beyond just war tradition" or to substitute a "just peace" theology for one of "just war." The case of Catholicism is more varied, but the real issue is the position of the U.S. Catholic bishops. They have clearly turned the idea of just war in a "new direction, but Lang and I differ as to whether this is legitimate or not, or a good thing or not.

I think that anyone—church hierarch or not, one "in authority" or only "an authority"—who sets out to use the idea of just war has a debt to the tradition and a responsibility to understand what that tradition actually is and how it came to be what it is, and to use the tradition in ways that fit with this. Specifically, since the tradition of just war is quite broad and includes diverse elements, this implies an engagement with those elements of the tradition closest to what one does oneself, as well as seeking to understand the relation between those particular elements of the tradition and the larger body of tradition of which it is a part. I have understood my work as an effort to provide both examples of doing this and raw material for others to do it. In carrying this through, ideally people taking up this task will refine the method and add to the raw material. If the obligation to engage the tradition in such a way is denied, either by defining and using the just war idea in a way fundamentally inconsistent with the tradition or by explicitly walling that tradition off as not mattering, then I question whether what is going on ought to be called just war reasoning at all. I consider it my obligation to try to talk across such divides, but in the end that effort may be rejected.

Two final points. First, toward the end of his paper Lang characterizes the role of the U.S. Catholic bishops' pastoral letter in and around the year it was adopted, 1983, as "much more of a prophetic one than a policy advocacy one."[25] I know from experience, though, that this was not at all how the process of producing the letter, or the letter itself, was understood in military and public policy circles in the United States. Rather, it was viewed as having clear and immediate policy implications. That the second draft of the letter was published in both *The New York Times* and *The Washington Post*, with front-page lead stories in both, testifies to its being understood as bearing seriously on policy. The letter also frequently takes the tone of a policy document. Lang is correct to insist that those with teaching authority in a church have the right to state that church's views; yet when they enter the field of debate over public policy, then that authority gives them no particular precedence over those who are "an authority" but not "in authority." Second, I confess I think Lang oversteps when he accuses me of "contesting the authority of scripture" by "claiming that [Jesus] did not understand how his teaching related to a wider political context," an idea that he traces to Augustine.[26] This wasn't at all Augustine's point in developing the idea that love of neighbor may require violence; nor was it Ramsey's, whose whole idea of just war is based on the idea of love of neighbor; nor was it mine in taking note of this.

I turn now to Serena Sharma's paper,[27] which is exactly on target in finding "echoes of pacifism in contemporary just war thought" and drawing attention to my efforts to combat this. In fact, one of the reasons I am so unhappy with much that has been placed under the rubric of "just war" in recent years is that it really is a functional pacifism. Sharma makes use of a term that has appeared in the literature for this pacifist presence under the guise of just war thinking: *jus contra bellum*. She traces it to the conception of just war advanced by Paul Ramsey, particularly his overwhelming stress on the *jus in bello* and his comparative neglect of the questions of *jus ad bellum*. A result not intended by Ramsey was to open the door for opponents of any use of armed force at all to argue that in the age of total war and of nuclear weapons, no war can ever be just because the *jus in bello* standards cannot be met. Elements of this argument appear in the United States Catholic bishops' 1983 pastoral and subsequent statements, as Sharma shows. As for my own argument, I have numerous times pointed out that the "presumption against war" idea on which the Catholic bishops founded their idea of just war is not only at odds with classic just war thinking, but it in fact smuggles a pacifist prescription into just war thinking: for just war tradition, the evil is injustice and the use of force is a possible remedy, whereas for the U.S. Catholic bishops, the evil is the use of military force itself. But more radical versions of the pacifist takeover of just war thinking can be found than the example of the U.S. Catholic bishops. And indeed, Ramsey himself, rather early on, wrote decidedly strong refutations of this reading of the implications of his thought, perhaps the strongest of which he entitled "Can a Pacifist Tell a Just War?"[28] His answer was, in present-day language, NO WAY!

Sharma doesn't think I have gone far enough in opposing this creeping takeover of the just war idea by pacifism. Maybe she is right; I don't know. After all, just as contemporary functional pacifists insist that the just war criterion of last resort means that resort to force cannot be justified because there is always something else that could be done instead, perhaps there is in fact something more I might do. But I think my opposition to making just war over into a form of pacifism has been consistent and clear. I never accepted Ramsey's understanding of the primacy of the *jus in bello*; indeed (and this is perhaps a rejection of Sharma's argument about my own use of the *jus ad bellum*/*jus in bello* distinction near the end of her paper), I know that the *jus ad bellum* (though not the term) came first, and I definitely regard it as addressing the issues that are morally prior. The fact that pacifists who want to use the *jus in bello* to undermine it is also wrong, though, because they have dirty hands: there are no conditions ever under which they could accept the justified use of force, and what they want is to find whatever language is convenient to advance their own opposition to the use of armed force for whatever reason. In any case, the creeping influence of pacifism in contemporary just war thinking is a real problem, and Sharma's essay casts important light on it.

Finally, I turn to Alex Bellamy's paper.[29] When I began to read it I was almost immediately reminded of the problem of having a scholarly career that extends over several decades: what you say early on may come back to haunt you many years later. Bellamy is deeply unhappy with an argument I first laid out in the Epilogue to my 1975 book and which I briefly repeated in my 1981 book, where I criticized the "aggressor-defender" conception of the right to resort to force in international law, argued for its modification so as to restore justice to the *jus ad bellum*, and also criticized the United Nations for its role in enforcing the aggressor-defender model. These were early themes in my work, but as stated there they were not major ones; in the 1975 book the pages in question amount to no more than about 5% of the whole book, and the discussion in the 1981 book is an even briefer segment of a longer work. After this I did not discuss the issues involved until almost two decades later, in my 1999 book, and subsequently in some other places, including my 2005 book and several articles. One of these articles[30] appeared in a special issue of *JME* on humanitarian intervention. That Bellamy doesn't take note of it is a bit odd, since he served as guest editor of that issue and solicited the piece from me. But in any case, the discussions in 1981 and before reflect a different context from the more recent one, and context matters.

The reason I focused so heavily in my earlier work on the aggressor-defender concept as defining the right of resort to military force in international law is that this was central to the international discussion of right to use force in that period. I make this plain in the 1975 book, showing how the aggressor-defender trope was used in United Nations debates regarding the definition of aggression and the international arguments over the legality of Israel's preemptive use of force at the start of the 1967 war. So I reject Bellamy's claim that this is not what the international law *jus ad bellum* is about. In the context in which I was writing, it most certainly was, as any review of the debates I have mentioned will show. I stand by my position that this takes justice out of the *jus ad bellum*, because it made everything hinge on first vs. second resort to force, allowing broad latitude in the use of means other than cross-border military force for subversion of a state, but denying effective response if the only such response needed to be cross-border projection of force.

By the time I wrote my 1999 book the context had decisively changed. The Soviet Union had collapsed, and with it the model of conflict that nourished the attention given to outlawing any cross-border uses of armed force. In the mid-1990s this made possible a serious debate over humanitarian intervention to respond to gross violations of fundamental human rights—cross-border uses of force not justified by the aggressor-defender model, and in fact directly opposed to its assumptions. This shift in thinking was nourished by the vigorous growth of international human rights law. In 2001 *The Responsibility To Protect*[31] appeared, using (without identifying it) a just war framework to justify actions that override state sovereignty in the name of fundamental justice. In this context, as I saw the matter, the question had shifted: justice was again on the agenda in thinking about resort to armed force, and the pressing questions had to do with who might act in cases of gross violations of fundamental rights, what means might be allowed, and what degree of international approval would be needed. By this time too the United Nations had amassed a woeful history of management of armed force in peacekeeping operations (including the debacle of the "sanctuary" cities in Bosnia and the abdication of the peacekeeping force in Rwanda at the time of the genocide), and still (contrary to Bellamy) the Security Council was hamstrung in applying Chapter VII rules by the politics of member states.

Bellamy and I see the world, and the United Nations, very differently. But I think I have been right to raise the question of the responsibility and rights of individual states as opposed to those represented by the United Nations. The reasons are in my books and articles, and I will not rehearse them here, but readers are invited to look at them and reflect on the reasoning I offer there—and the view of international affairs I offer there—by contrast to the one Bellamy sets out in his paper.

Incidentally, I would observe that in the effort to show the UN is not as bad as he thinks I make it, at one point Bellamy provides a list of Security Council authorizations of force that, he argues, didn't simply police the aggressor-defender distinction: Korea, Iraq–Kuwait, Somalia, Rwanda, Haiti, and on down to East Timor and Afghanistan. Historically minded people may observe that only the case of Korea antedates my 1975 and 1981 books and that the Security Council authorization of the use of force there was possible only because of the temporary absence of the Soviet Union; and as I have pointed out above, the ground had shifted significantly by the time of the other cases mentioned. My problem with the UN as a vehicle for protection of international justice is that it has not proven able to do what its most enthusiastically positive supporters (and Bellamy seems to be one of these) want to reserve to it alone. The presence of the UN does not negate that the responsibility of individual states is still another matter in its own right, one deserving serious consideration.

A final point: I am genuinely concerned at the "mutual antipathy" Bellamy argues to exist between moral thinkers using just war arguments and international lawyers. Perhaps it is the circles I have moved in, including conferences involving both ethicists and international lawyers from various countries, but I have not found anything like a pervasive "mutual antipathy" in our discussions and relations. Moreover, in my own work I have throughout my professional life sought to emphasize the commonalities and connections between these two modes of discourse, which are both historical and thematic. There are clearly sharp differences between my position and that of those (not only international lawyers) who understand international law as a form of universally binding positive law. Thinking of this, I recalled the Hart–Fuller debates of not many decades ago. My own thinking on the relation of moral valuations and law has been influenced by Lon Fuller and, in the specific arena of international law, Michael Reisman. This leads me to emphasize a conception of international law based in a common-law conception of customary international law. Legal positivists and political realists, each for their own reasons, want there to be a wall between what they do and what those of us engaged in moral discourse do. But I believe I have consistently worked to show that this wall ought not to exist. Happily, I have found that there are many in both law and ethics who agree.

Again, my thanks to all who have given their energy, time, and intellectual efforts to this special issue [*Journal of Military Ethics* 8:3 (2009)]. I hope this discussion continues and spreads.

NOTES

1. James Turner Johnson, *Ideology, Reason, and the Limitation of War* (Princeton and London: Princeton University Press, 1975); James Turner Johnson, *Just War Tradition and the Restraint of War* (Princeton and Guildford: Princeton University Press, 1981); and James Turner Johnson, *The Quest for Peace* (Princeton and Guildford: Princeton University Press, 1987).

2. James Turner Johnson, *Can Modern War be Just?* (New Haven and London: Yale University Press, 1984); James Turner Johnson, *The Just War Idea and the Ethics of Intervention* (United States Air Force Academy, CO: USAF, 1993); James Turner Johnson, *Morality and Contemporary Warfare* (New Haven and London: Yale University Press, 1999); James Turner Johnson, "Just War, as It Was and Is," *First Things* 149: 14–24; James Turner Johnson and George Weigel, *Just War and the Gulf War* (Washington D.C.: Ethics and Public Policy Center, 1991).

3. James Turner Johnson and John Kelsay, *Cross, Crescent, and Sword* (Wesport, CT: Greenwood Press, 1990); John Kelsay and James Turner Johnson, *Just War and Jihad* (Westport, CT: Greenwood Press, 1991).

4. James Turner Johnson, *The Holy War Idea in Western and Islamic Traditions* (University Park, PA, and London: Pennsylvania State University Press, 1997).

5. Alasdair MacIntyre, *After Virtue* (London: Duckworth, 1981).

6. Cian O'Driscoll, "Hedgehog or Fox? An Essay on James Turner Johnson's View of History," *Journal of Military Ethics* 8, no. 3 (2009): 171, doi: 10.1080/15027570903230182.

7. Paul Ramsey, *War and the Christian Conscience* (Durham, NC: Duke University Press, 1961); Paul Ramsey, *The Just War* (New York: Scribners, 1968).
8. Johnson, *Ideology*.
9. Michael Walzer, *Just and Unjust Wars* (New York: Basic Books, 1977).
10. National Conference of Catholic Bishops, *The Challenge of Peace* (Washington, D.C.: United States Catholic Conference, 1983).
11. See William V. O'Brien, *The Conduct of Just and Limited War* (New York: Praeger Publishers, 1981); and William V. O'Brien, *Law and Morality in Israel's War with the PLO* (New York: Routledge, Chapman, and Hall, 1991).
12. O'Driscoll, 171.
13. Nahed Artoul Zehr, "James Turner Johnson and the 'Classic' Just War Tradition," *Journal of Military Ethics* 8, no. 3 (2009): 200, doi: 10.1080/15027570903230216.
14. O'Driscoll, 176.
15. O'Driscoll, 172.
16. National Conference of Catholic Bishops, *The Challenge of Peace*.
17. Most fully in Johnson, "Just War, as It Was and Is."
18. Johnson, *Morality*.
19. See further James F. Childress, *Moral Responsibility in Conflicts* (Baton Rouge, LA, and London: Louisiana State University Press, 1982), Chapter 3.
20. John Kelsay, "James Turner Johnson, Just War Tradition, and Forms of Practical Reasoning," *Journal of Military Ethics* 8, no. 3 (2009): 186, doi: 10.1080/15027570903230208.
21. National Conference of Catholic Bishops, *The Challenge of Peace*.
22. John Kelsay, *Arguing the Just War in Islam* (Cambridge, MA, and London: Harvard University Press, 2006).
23. National Conference of Catholic Bishops, *The Challenge of Peace*.
24. Anthony F. Lang, "The Just War Tradition and the Question of Authority," *Journal of Military Ethics* 8, no. 3 (2009): 209, doi: 10.1080/15027570903230273.
25. Lang, "The Just War Tradition," 212.
26. Lang, "The Just War Tradition."
27. Serena K. Sharma, "The Legacy of *Jus Contra Bellum*: Echoes of Pacifism in Contemporary Just War Thought," *Journal of Military Ethics* 8, no. 3 (2009), doi: 10.1080/15027570903230281.
28. Ramsey, *The Just War*, Chapter 12.

29. A.J. Bellamy, "When is it Right to Fight? International Law and *Jus ad Bellum*," *Journal of Military Ethics* 8, no. 3 (2009): 231–245, doi: 10.1080/15027570903230299.
30. James Turner Johnson, "Humanitarian Intervention after Iraq," *Journal of Military Ethics* 5, no. 2 (2006), doi: 10.1080/15027570600707706.
31. International Commission on Intervention and State Sovereignty, *The Responsibility to Protect* (Ottava, Canada: International Development Research Centre, 2001).

BIBLIOGRAPHY

Bellamy, A. J. "When is it Right to Fight? International Law and *Jus ad Bellum*." *Journal of Military Ethics* 8, no. 3 (2009): 231–45.

Childress, J. F. *Moral Responsibility in Conflicts*. Baton Rouge, LA, and London: Louisiana State University Press, 1982.

International Commission on Intervention and State Sovereignty. *The Responsibility to Protect*. Ottawa, Canada : International Development Research Centre, 2001.

Johnson, J. T. *Ideology, Reason, and the Limitation of War*. Princeton and London: Princeton University Press, 1975.

Johnson, J. T. *Just War Tradition and the Restraint of War*. Princeton and Guildford: Princeton University Press, 1981.

Johnson, J. T. *Can Modern War be Just?* New Haven and London: Yale University Press, 1984.

Johnson, J. T. *The Quest for Peace*. Princeton and Guildford: Princeton University Press, 1987.

Johnson, J. T. *The Just War Idea and the Ethics of Intervention*. United States Air Force Academy, CO: USAF, 1993.

Johnson, J. T. *The Holy War Idea in Western and Islamic Traditions*. University Park, PA, and London: Pennsylvania State University Press, 1997.

Johnson, J. T. *Morality and Contemporary Warfare*. New Haven and London: Yale University Press, 1999.

Johnson, J. T. "Just War, as It Was and Is." *First Things* 149 (2005): 14–24.

Johnson, J. T. "Humanitarian Intervention after Iraq." *Journal of Military Ethics* 5, no. 2 (2006): 114–27.

Johnson, J. T. and Kelsay, J. *Cross, Crescent, and Sword.* Westport, CT: Greenwood Press, 1990.

Johnson, J. T. and Weigel, G. *Just War and the Gulf War.* Washington, D.C.: Ethics and Public Policy Center, 1991.

Kelsay, J. *Arguing the Just War in Islam.* Cambridge, MA, and London: Harvard University Press, 2006.

Kelsay, J. "James Turner Johnson, Just War Tradition, and Forms of Practical Reasoning." *Journal of Military Ethics* 8, no. 3 (2009): 179–89.

Kelsay, J. and Johnson, J. T. *Just War and Jihad.* Westport, CT: Greenwood Press, 1991.

Lang, A. F. Jr. "The Just War Tradition and the Question of Authority." *Journal of Military Ethics* 8, no. 3 (2009): 202–26.

MacIntyre, A. *After Virtue.* London: Duckworth, 1981.

National Conference of Catholic Bishops. *The Challenge of Peace.* Washington, D.C.: United States Catholic Conference, 1983.

O'Brien, W. V. *The Conduct of Just and Limited War.* New York: Praeger Publishers, 1981.

O'Brien, W. V. *Law and Morality in Israel's War with the PLO.* New York: Routledge, Chapman, and Hall, 1991.

O'Driscoll, C. "Hedgehog or Fox? An Essay on James Turner Johnson's View of History." *Journal of Military Ethics* 8, no. 3 (2009): 165–78.

Ramsey, P. *War and the Christian Conscience.* Durham, NC: Duke University Press, 1961.

Ramsey, P. *The Just War.* New York: Scribners, 1968.

Sharma, S. K. "The Legacy of *Jus Contra Bellum*: Echoes of Pacifism in Contemporary Just War Thought." *Journal of Military Ethics* 8, no. 3 (2009): 217–30.

Walzer, M. *Just and Unjust Wars.* New York: Basic Books, 1977.

Zehr, N. A. "James Turner Johnson and the 'Classic' Just War Tradition." *Journal of Military Ethics* 8, no. 3 (2009): 190–201.

ABSTRACT

Johnson addresses the tradition of just war and of jihad, providing historical summaries of each within their cultural contexts. He then shows the similarities and dissimilarities of the traditions and presents the perspective of each tradition with respect to right authority for use of armed force, justification necessary for the use of force, and conduct in the midst of the use of force.

CHAPTER 15

JUST WAR AND JIHAD: TWO TRADITIONS ON THE USE OF FORCE

The cultures of the West and of Islam have produced two distinct moral traditions on the right use of force, that of just war and that of jihad of the sword. Tonight I'll discuss these two traditions. I will identify the main features of each one, sketch their origin and development in their respective cultural contexts, note the different relation of each to the spheres of religion and political life. Then I will briefly compare them on three elements central to both these traditions: the requirement of right authority for use of armed force, that of justification necessary for use of such force, and right conduct in the use of such force. I will give special attention to a common feature of both: that a core requirement for both envisions the justified use of force as a public enterprise to be undertaken by the highest public authority according to established rules in response to wrong. This is especially important to note because, in recent just war thinking, it has been generally downplayed as a moral concern, while in recent radical jihadist thinking it is systematically sidestepped in favor of the idea that jihad of the sword is an individual obligation of every faithful Muslim.

Let us begin by looking at the tradition of just war, beginning at the beginning and examining how the concept of just war was originally defined. A mass of recent philosophical writing on just war traces it no farther back than Michael Walzer's influential book *Just and Unjust Wars*, first published in 1977. The idea of just war is in fact considerably older than that. Much recent religiously oriented discussion of the just war idea traces it to Augustine in the fourth and fifth centuries, and Augustine borrowed the idea from Roman political thought and practice. But Augustine never wrote systematically about just war. By contrast to the subject of sexuality, to which he devoted no fewer than five complete treatises plus portions of others, what Augustine wrote on just war was never more than a few sentences scattered through a variety of types of works on various subjects. A coherent, systematic conception of just war did not exist until some centuries later. It first began to take shape as a section of the canonist Gratian's magisterial compilation of canon law, the *Decretum,* in the mid-twelfth century. It was clarified, developed, and expanded by two generations of canonical thinkers after Gratian, known respectively as the Decretists and the Decretalists. These were all churchly thinkers, priests or monks, but such was the structure of Medieval life that they were in close contact with members of the knightly class involved in government and with war, as well as with other intellectuals engaged in recovering Roman law and those beginning to define human rights. Indeed, some of the same people were involved in all three of these intellectual efforts: defining just war, human rights, and how to think about law itself. The systematic, comprehensive conception of just war, in Latin *bellum iustum*, which came together in this period reflected the influences of all these intellectual efforts as well as the actual practice of governance and warfare. This was the classic statement of the just war idea. It lasted in substantially the same form until the early modern period. Even after that it has endured as a historical tradition, sometimes being carried and further defined in thought on the law of nations, sometimes in political theory, sometimes in the consensually recognized "laws and customs of war" out of which positive international law has come. Its fundamental moral referent was the content of the natural law, assumed to be knowable by everyone through reason.

Three-quarters of the way through the thirteenth century the theologian Thomas Aquinas wrote his massive *Summa Theologiae*, which included a section devoted to just war (ST II/II, Q. 40, "On War"). His discussion concisely summarized the consensus reached by the canonists from Gratian through the Decretalists, and it provided the benchmark for the structure and content of the just war idea for the next several centuries. Present-day theologians who trace the just war idea to Aquinas generally look no further: they are theologians, after all: they have no particular interest in history or in canon law, and they tend to regard Aquinas as inventing the just war idea as a theological concept, with a bit of help from Augustine before him. But this is wrong. Aquinas was summarizing a consensus that has been forged by canon lawyers but reflected the influence of the other streams of thinking and practice I have mentioned earlier.

What we find in this important benchmark figure, is then, a summary statement of the classic conception of the just war idea, but one that needs to be understood through its historical context. Aquinas is good to focus on not only or mainly because of his later central place in Catholic theology after the Counter-Reformation, but, for the developing just war tradition, because he provides a window into the early conception of the just war idea as it coalesced and because he shows how Augustine's scattered writings on just war became central in the coherent tradition.

For a war to be just, Aquinas asserts early in his discussion, three things are necessary: sovereign authority, just cause, and right intention. We ought to note in passing that this list corresponds directly to the list of the three goods or ends of political life as they were then understood, drawing from late classical thought: order, justice, and peace. The authority requirement corresponds to order, the just war requirement to justice, and the right intention requirement to the end [aim] of peace. The end result is a definition of just war so as to satisfy the proper ends of political life as such. This is significant and important, and it is unfortunate that it is generally overlooked in recent just war writing.

As Aquinas develops each requirement it becomes clear that his three would be four in present-day listings, because his right intention has two aspects: avoidance of wrong intentions ("motives of aggrandizement or cruelty") and pursuit of right intentions, which may be grouped together as the goal of achieving peace. My focus here, though, is on the first two necessities Aquinas identifies: in order, sovereign authority and just cause.

Aquinas wrote in Latin, and his first condition for a *bellum iustum*, a just war, was *auctoritas principis*, the "authority of a prince" or "princely authority." The Latin *princeps*, prince, was being rendered by this time in French and English as *souverain*, sovereign. So what Aquinas places as the first requirement for a just use of armed force is that it be authorized by the person holding sovereign responsibility. What exactly did this mean? Staying first with Aquinas himself, what he said about sovereign authority for war needs to be understood from what he said about the responsibilities of sovereignty in his treatise *On Princely Rule (De Regimine Principiae)* and on tyranny, which is not sovereign rule at all but self-serving misrule (ST II/II, Q. 42, A. 2). But looking more deeply to the conception he was working from, the canonical discussions and debates of the previous century had defined sovereignty and its responsibility with some precision. First, the canonists had made use of the Gelasian principle, named for the late sixth-century Pope Gelasius, who in a letter to the Roman Emperor of the time had distinguished between two kinds of authority, the temporal and the spiritual. His aim had been to assert the spiritual authority of his own office, but the medieval canonists used the division he identified to assert the autonomy of temporal rulers relative to that of the Church. Temporal rulers with no superiors—sovereigns—were thus understood to be the judges of last resort in their own domains as to what is required by law, including the natural law. In this role they, and only they, have final authority to interpret what justice requires in the case of any disputes or violations, and in exercising their responsibility for the common good of their political communities—a responsibility placed on them by the natural law—only they might choose to resort to armed force to repair violations of justice and punish wrongdoing. Aquinas's placing the requirement of sovereign authority first was by no means accidental or random: it was because the sovereign ruler has the unique responsibility to determine, for the good of the community governed, where there has been a violation of justice and to seek to repair it and punish the wrongdoer.

We see the importance of this prioritization of the requirement of sovereign authority by looking at what counts, for Aquinas, as just cause for resort to armed force. Citing Augustine, he identifies two just causes—recovery of that which has been wrongly taken and punishment of evil. Self-defense, which is often the only justifying cause recognized in recent just war thinking, is not mentioned here. The reason is that, according to the consensus he was reflecting, any and every person has the right of self-defense against an imminent threat or attack. That is not a matter of *bellum iustum*, just war. Just war comes into the picture only after the initial threat or attack, when only public authority can determine whether there was an injustice in this and if so, whether and how to rectify it. There were two critical distinctions in medieval and early modern just war thought: first, between action to repel a threat or an attack and later action to rectify and punish such a threat or attack, and second, not that between violence and non-violence, as it has become in much recent religious discourse, but between use of armed force on public authority, called *bellum,* war, which might be just or unjust according to circumstances, and *duellum,* duel, which was the word used for any private resort to arms to satisfy a dispute, a resort that never could be just by its very nature. There was no "presumption against war," an idea popularized by the U.S. Catholic bishops and widely used since, and there is properly not any in the broader just war tradition.

All persons in sovereign authority have the responsibility of securing a just and peaceful order within society. In the discharge of this responsibility they may have resort to force, in accord with Romans 13:4, the standard text classically used in just war tradition to describe the sovereign's right in regard to use of armed force, and quoted in this connection by Aquinas: The sovereign "does not bear the sword in vain, for he is the servant of God to execute his wrath on the wrongdoer." But the sovereign may use armed force only on a just cause and only with right intention—not to bully or dominate, but to serve the common good by achieving a just and peaceful order.

Just war was and is about the justified use of force by temporal sovereign authorities for temporal violations of justice—the common good, the peace of the political community and the community formed by such communities in their interrelations. Though religious thought and church law have historically fed just war tradition and carried a portion of it, the just war idea is not about religiously justified or authorized warfare.

What I have been describing is the idea of just war as it came together in the medieval period and developed through the early modern era. With the thought of Hugo Grotius, which had an enormous impact on the modern development of the idea of international law, and empirically with the creation of what has come to be called "the Westphalian system" of international order, conceptions and priorities shifted from those in the inherited just war tradition. Grotius, and after him the Peace of Westphalia, defined sovereignty differently: not in terms of moral responsibility of the sovereign ruler for the common good but in terms of the territory of a political community, the inhabitants of that territory, and their collectively vesting their natural authority of self-rule in a person charged with protecting them, their ancient rights and privileges" (Grotius's term), and their territory from violation. Accordingly, the emphasis placed on the requirement of sovereign authority in earlier thought declined and eventually became nothing more than *competence de guerre,* a right possessed by all independent political entities and thus by those in authority in them. This is reflected in the language used by some recent just war thinkers: not "sovereign authority" as in Aquinas, Luther, and other medieval and early modern thinkers but "competent authority," that is, one who has the right to exercise the 'competence" of making war.

In the idea of just cause the Grotian-Westphalian conception pushes toward ruling out all uses of armed force except in defense, an idea deeply embedded in positive international law as it developed during the twentieth century. If sovereignty is essentially a concept that has first of all to do with territory, then what matters most of all in the use of armed force is whether it is projected beyond the borders of a particular territory and across the borders of another one. The older idea of defense as protection of the common good becomes defense of the territory and its inhabitants from "armed attack," as Chapter 2 of the United Nations Charter puts it. "Armed attack" is forbidden, and the state's right to use force is limited to response to such attack.

Now, while much recent just war thinking incorporates this conception of the justified use of armed force, there are a number of problems with it. I will identify three. First, from the standpoint of just war tradition in its pre-Westphalian form, it allows both too much and too little. There may be times when a use of military force across borders is exactly what is needed to serve order, justice, and peace. This is also implicit, second, in international humanitarian law, on which the right of armed intervention to secure urgent humanitarian needs is based. Third, the effort to limit the right of resort to force has resulted in distortions of the idea of defense, which has been made to include the other two earlier just causes of recovery of that which has been wrongly taken and punishment of evil (e.g., the description of the military effort to remove Iraqi forces from Kuwait in 1991 as "defense" against an "armed attack in progress," that is, the military occupation of Kuwait), and in connection especially with nuclear arms has been made to encompass deterrence and retaliation.

My own judgment—contrary to the legacy of the Westphalian system in the UN Charter—is that we need to seek to recover the core of the earlier idea of sovereignty as a moral concept, implying real responsibilities of government not only within the political community but in the relations among such communities. Not only is this implied by the clear shape of just war tradition before the seventeenth century, but it follows from the growing consensus on the importance of human rights in national and international contexts. In just war thought this means returning to its origins, giving first priority among the requirements for a moral resort to armed force to sovereign authority conceived as responsibility for the common good, as expressed in a just and peaceful social order.

I have been speaking of sovereign authority and just cause in the framework of just war tradition; let me now turn to the matter of right conduct in the justified use of armed force.

The late Paul Ramsey, in his recovery and redefinition of the Christian idea of just war, defined it centrally in terms of two principles having to do with right conduct in the use of armed force: first the principle of discrimination, by which noncombatants may not be directly, intentionally targeted, a principle Ramsey argued comes directly from the requirements of Christian love of neighbor as well as from the proper practice of politics, and a supporting principle of proportionality, which is an application of prudential reason to the context of armed conflict. Ramsey's conception of just war had very little in the way of a formal *jus ad bellum*, fundamentally arguing that the requirement of love of neighbor provides both permission to use force in the neighbor's behalf and limitation of the force used, since the enemy is also my neighbor. One result of his way of thinking about justified uses of armed force, a way he repeatedly sought to counter but could never stamp out, was the argument that if the conduct of war cannot be genuinely discriminating and proportionate, then there can be no just war. This was a line of reasoning that produced the phenomena of "nuclear pacifism" and "modern-war pacifism," or what Ramsey termed a *bellum contra bellum justum,* a war against the very idea of just war. Ramsey regarded such reasoning as forgetting the more basic obligation in love of the neighbor to protect him or her from wrongful harm.

The principles of discrimination and proportionality, and the lines of reasoning built upon them, appear nowhere in just war tradition before Ramsey used them. The traditional way of specifying right conduct in the use of armed force was instead much more concrete. On the one hand, it identified and named classes of persons who, by reason of their personal condition, status in society, or occupation did not normally take part in war and therefore should not have war made against them. On the other hand, it sought to identify means of war that are *mala in se* and forbid their use. Both these approaches have been picked up and developed further in the law of armed conflict, where the Geneva Conventions provide the fundamental statement of noncombatant immunity in terms of classes of people and "Hague law," plus a series of individual agreements outlawing specific weapons and uses of otherwise permitted weapons carry forward the latter approach. The secular shape of these law-of-armed-conflict provisions demonstrates once again how just war tradition is not exclusively or even mainly the product of religious thought or practice but reflects a broad cultural moral consensus. Ramsey's conception of the principle of discrimination may be centrally a Christian theological concept, but the historical definition of noncombatancy and noncombatant immunity by lists of classes of persons was a result of reflection on the meaning of natural justice.

Let me turn now to the concept of jihad of the sword.

The classical Islamic conception of jihad in the sense of warfare is rooted in the Qur'an and in traditions concerning the life of the Prophet Muhammad, but its actual definition came somewhat later, in the work of the jurists of the early Abbasid period (the late eighth and early ninth centuries CE, second and third centuries AH). These thinkers developed it in the context of a more general undertaking to define the nature of Islamic law and, from this basis, to describe the nature of the Islamic community, right leadership of that community, and relations with the non-Islamic world. In doing this they took the idea of jihad, striving or effort in the path of God, which is an essentially moral conception in the Qur'an itself but one whose use had been extended to involve the Muslim community's use of the sword, and defined it to include the use of armed force to protect the Islamic community and to serve the end of bringing the entire world into adherence to the law of God. Providing the background to this conception was a legal division of the world into two realms: the *dar al-Islam* or abode of Islam and the remainder of the world, defined as the *dar al-harb* or abode of war. The *dar al-Islam,* as the early jurists described it, had existed since its creation by the Prophet Muhammad himself, who had been its first head. It is a community at once religious and political, and thus its ruler, like the Prophet, was understood to be supreme in both these spheres. There could be at any time only one right ruler, the caliph or successor of the Prophet and the inheritor of his authority. Because of its character—its essential unity, its rule by a successor of the Prophet, its governance according to divinely given law—the jurists held that the *dar al-Islam* is fundamentally unlike the rest of the world, which is different in all these respects and as a result is torn by perpetual conflict and represents a perpetual threat to the peace of the *dar al-Islam.* A general, lasting, universal peace in the world is impossible until the *dar al-harb* is no more, when the whole world has become the *dar al-Islam,* a place within which submission (*islam*) to God is the law of the land. Until then war between the two realms is the normal state. Yet at the same time extended periods of truce are possible by means of treaties between the *dar al-Islam* and non-Islamic societies.

This is an essentially eschatological conception, but it also resembles Hobbes's conception of the state of nature—and the state of international relations—as "a war of all against all." Expansion-minded Muslim authorities could take this description as a rationale for wars of conquest against the non-Islamic world, but an equally reasonable interpretation would be to understand jihad by armed force as justified only to defend the *dar al-Islam* against threats and attacks from elements of the *dar al-harb* which, for their own reasons, decline to live in a condition of truce.

This conception of the world as divided into two fundamentally different kinds of societies thus formed the background for the jurists' conception of the idea of jihad as warfare. As they described it, such warfare should take the form of striving in the path of God through use of the sword by the *dar al-Islam* as a body under the authority of its legitimate ruler, the heir of the authority of the Prophet Muhammad. (This meant the caliph for the Sunni tradition, the Imam for the Shi'a.) This was a conception that encompassed offensive war against the general threat and organized collective defense against attack). The term used by the jurists for this normative conception of jihad of the sword was the "jihad of collective duty," a duty of the *dar al-Islam* as a whole, with some Muslims fighting and others playing other roles, including simply going about their normal lives. Such jihad might be tactically defensive or offensive, depending on the judgment of the caliph/Imam. Given the overall strategic conception of threat from the *dar al-harb* toward the *dar al-Islam,* all jihad of the sword was strategically defensive. Supporting this conception was the idea of jihad as an "individual duty," which an early jurist defined succinctly as the duty of any able-bodied male of military age to present himself for military service at the caliph's call, with his own horse, military equipment, and food and fodder enough to last for the duration of the campaign. Individuals might provide these necessities out of their personal or family resources, or they might be provided by their tribes or the local communities from which the warrior came.

But there was also another conception of the jihad of individual duty which developed in popular usage along the frontier of the *dar al-Islam* at about the same time: that of an emergency form of defensive jihad against a direct attack across the frontier by a force from some part of the *dar al-harb.* In such cases, the idea of jihad as an individual duty was understood to mean that fighting to resist the attack was incumbent on all Muslims who were able to do so—male or female, of whatever age and physical condition—in the immediate area of the aggression.

These two kinds of jihad were significantly different forms of warfare. The collective jihad was a thoroughly rule-governed activity, requiring the authorization of the caliph/Imam, a declaration of hostilities and a call for peace before the fighting began, and a form of combatant-noncombatant distinction, along with careful attention to the disposition of spoils by the ruling authority. The jurists clearly understood this kind of jihad as the norm for the warfare of the *dar al-Islam,* with the individual duty of participating in jihad understood as supporting the collective effort. This form of jihad drew upon the religious unity of the Islamic community even as it depended on the social and institutional relationships that comprised the Islamic state. The proper exercise of jihad on this model reinforced familial and group relationships and obligations, strengthened the *dar al-Islam* as the institutional expression of the unity of Islam, and enhanced the role of its ruler both religiously and politically.

The jihad of emergency defense was another matter entirely. It assumed an acute emergency in which normal religiously and socially prescribed relationships and structures were erased. The model for such an emergency was simple: a direct attack across the border of the *dar al-Islam* by a force from the *dar al-harb* in some particular place remote from the *dar al-Islam*'s center of authority and power. Against this attack Muslims in the area were to rise up in arms, on their own authority, as a kind of levée en masse. Understood this way, the individual duty to take arms crossed and eliminated all the usual distinctions: not only were healthy men of fighting age to fight to the limit of their ability to do so, but also women, children, and the aged and infirm. Further, the rules of collective jihad did not apply in such a struggle: the enemy to be fought against were the invading army, so that by definition no noncombatants were present, and they had broken the peace by their aggression, obviating the need for an initial offer of peace by the Muslims. While the jurists recognized this form of jihad of individual duty in time of dire emergency caused by overt aggression, there was an inherent tension between it and the collective jihad of the *dar al-Islam* under the authority of the caliph/Imam. In practical terms, local leaders on the frontiers might (and did) use the excuse of the jihad of emergency defense to challenge the legitimacy of the central authority. So this form of jihad was clearly meant as an exceptional response to an exceptional circumstance, not the norm for Muslim warfare.

The historical development of the tradition on jihad of the sword largely took place between these two early conceptions of jihad. Islamic society was never in fact the unified *dar al-Islam* set up as the norm by the early jurists. The geographical spread of Islam was simply too great for actual government by any single ruling authority, and so local government was provided by other authorities bearing different titles: sheikhs, emirs, sultans, even rival caliphs. The Sunni-Shi'a division contributed importantly to this trend as well. Under such historical circumstances the collective understanding of jihad remained the ideal, with the local authority taking the role the early jurists had assigned to the caliph, but more room developed for lower-level authorities to assume this role in their own frames, and juristic thinking developed justifying this by reference to the idea of the jihad of individual duty. This was, for example, the justification for Saladin's raising an army to oppose the European knights of the second crusade, and centuries later it was the justification for the Maghrebi tribal sheikh Abd-al-Kadir to lead an army in revolt against the occupying French. Another direction of thinking used the idea of the jihad of individual duty to refer to the obligation of local rulers to support one another when they were threatened. In short, the jihad of individual duty has historically been understood in various ways, justifying jihad of the sword whenever there is no possibility of meeting the requirements of the jihad of collective duty.

This has become especially important with the rise of radical Islamism as a religious, political, and military movement. It is generally agreed within Islam that no jihad of collective duty is possible anymore, as there is no caliph (for the Sunnis) and no Imam (for the Shi'as). This opens the door to giving increased importance to what was originally the theory of the exceptional case: the idea of defensive jihad understood as the individual duty to respond to external aggression. In the Islamic mainstream this conception has developed along lines compatible with international law, to allow Muslim heads of state to organize and execute defense along collective lines in their own political communities, though on the juristic model they do so on the basis of the individual responsibility of all their people to respond to aggression. Like the model of jihad on the authority of the caliph/Imam, the mainstream conception of defense on the authority of a local ruler respects the patterns of relationships within the society as well as the limits to be observed in fighting, the most important of which are understood to come from the Prophet Muhammad himself.

However, the last hundred years have seen the development of another line of interpretation of the idea of jihad as individual duty. First appearing in North Africa as an ideology for resistance against colonialism, by 1960 this was being used as a justification for terrorist attacks against the new State of Israel, and in the 1970s and 1980s it was adapted to justify armed struggle by terror and assassination in such states as Iran, Egypt, and Algeria, against rulers who were nominally Muslim but were judged to govern as tools of the West. This is the line of development out of which the ideologies of Hamas, al Qaeda, and the Islamic State have come. The conception of jihad in this line of thinking makes several critical assumptions not found in the traditional understanding of jihad or in contemporary mainstream theory. First, the *dar al-Islam* is conceived as any territory whose population is mainly Muslim and which was once part of the historical *dar al-Islam.* By this reasoning any non-Islamic state existing within the territory of the historical *dar al-Islam,* as well as all non-Islamic presence within that space, must be resisted and subdued or eliminated. Further, the struggle to do so is one in which the enemy includes everyone who supports such states or non-Islamic presence, so that the usual lines of distinction between combatants and non-combatants are taken away, and every person from among these enemies may be attacked equally. We have seen the results graphically again and again in attacks by radical Islamist jihadi groups. Nor are there any limits on means in this struggle, because of its emergency nature. Finally, the radical position holds that all Muslims are faced with the individual duty to take part in this struggle, so that doing so or not becomes the decisive measure of whether one is a genuine Muslim or not—and if not, one becomes a potential target.

This interpretation of the idea of jihad as an individual duty is a harsh one, one that implicitly rejects the majority of the actual history of Muslim societies and of Muslim faith. It leaves scant room for toleration of "people of the book" as prescribed in the Qur'an, because it assimilates the simple presence of Christians and Jews in dominantly Muslim societies to aggression. It also leaves no room for difference of interpretation as to what Islam requires; its reading of Islamic law is narrow and unyielding on doctrine and behavior alike. Social developments identified with modernity are rejected as un-Islamic, despite the fact that large numbers of Muslims have accepted them without losing their faith.

This is, ultimately, a conception of jihad of the sword as a necessary clash of civilizations, pitting the radical understanding of Islam against America, the West as a whole, and ultimately other cultures too. But it also has set itself against the rest of the non-Islamic world, putting its own narrow and distorted understanding of Islam against mainstream understandings of the requirements of Islamic history and tradition, against contemporary Muslim states, and against the lives of the great majority of contemporary Muslims. The radicals present themselves as followers of the only true understanding of Islam, and in their ideological frame all Shi'as and all Sufis, as well as all Sunnis who do not accept their conception of true Islam, are worthy of death. So radical jihadism also sets up a clash within Islam itself, one every bit as bloody as that with non-Islamic cultures of the world. Its conception of jihad of the sword makes use of key ideas from the classical conception of such striving, but by picking and choosing its own preferred elements from the jihad tradition it truncates, distorts, and in the end reinvents the idea of jihad of the sword in a way very different from what the tradition as a whole describes.

What, then, are we to make of all this? How are we to understand the relation between these two ways of thinking in religious and moral terms about warfare, that of jihad of the sword and that of just war? In trying to answer this question it is helpful to start with the classic traditional expressions of these two ideas. What we find there include some significant parallels but also some significant differences.

As to the former, both traditions in their classic forms define the justified use of armed force as an undertaking on behalf of the community as a whole, for its protection and good, and requiring the authority of that person understood to be responsible for that good in itself and in relation to other communities. The community is rightly ordered when its government is led by one who respects this obligation and seeks to discharge it, following the dictates of justice and thus serving the peace of the community as a whole. In just war terms, these are the requirements of sovereign authority, just cause, and the end of peace. Though the formal language of the classic description of jihad of the sword is different, these same three requirements may be easily seen there. So both traditions in their classic forms share a common structure. Both also understand the justified use of armed force as involving particular limits on violence: in particular, both reject direct, intended use of such force against classes of people who are not normally involved in the fighting: women, children, the aged, the physically and mentally impaired, and people whose main occupation is with religious duties. Again, this is an important structural element in both traditions in their classic form.

Once we move to the present day, though, this commonality quickly disappears. While I have spoken only generally about how recent just war thinking has developed, there are several ways in which this thinking is different from the classic idea of just war: sovereignty understood as the responsibility of rulers for the good of their societies has been replaced by a conception of sovereignty focused on protection of national territory and interests; just cause has been redefined as self-defense against attack, not the responsibility to serve justice more generally; peace is understood as the absence of any use of armed force, not the end of securing a just order through use of such force; and overarching it all is a broad sentiment, underwritten in international law, that individual states may resort to armed force only when under direct attack. As to limits on conduct in the use of armed force, various trends in recent just war thinking have sought to stress the limits so as to prevent resort to armed force at all.

The radical Islamist conception of jihad of the sword, as we have seen, has moved in the opposite direction. The classical conception of jihad was one focused centrally on the war of collective duty undertaken out of the resources of the Islamic community as a whole on the authority of the leader recognized as the heir of the Prophet Muhammad's authority. With no such leader and no such community as a whole, radical Islamism has instead developed a doctrine of jihad as the individual duty of every Muslim of true faith, and the measure of such true faith is the willingness to engage in such jihad. It has defined the justifying cause for jihad by presenting the very existence of Western culture as an existential threat constituting an emergency requiring a military response. It has rejected the limits found in the classic understanding of jihad of the sword, so that those judged worthy of death are all people who do not accept their radical creed and its implications. The measure of leadership is adherence to this ideology, whatever its costs in life and suffering. Not only is this strikingly different from the direction taken in recent just war thinking, but it stands in stark contrast to the classical conception of jihad of the sword.

The lesson I would draw from this is that there is a possibility of mutual dialogue and learning when we consider the conceptions of just war and jihad of the sword in their classic forms. Their fundamental structural similarities make this possible. That opens the door to a civil interaction in which the differences can be mutually analyzed and possibly overcome, or at least accepted as competing understandings existing alongside one another. There is no intractable clash of civilizations here. Such an intractable clash is, of course, at the center of radical Islamist jihadism. Intellectually and religiously this needs to be countered robustly within the frame of Islamic religion and culture. But while this movement continues to have strength, a military response is also needed, to protect the values of both Western and Islamic societies. In this connection the tradition of just war holds real value because of the fundamental values it embodies: order, justice, and peace.

The idea of just war has followed its own historical trajectory of development. While this idea is deeply rooted in western religion, it is perhaps more strongly institutionalized today in international law, in American military doctrine and practice, and even in political culture than at any time since the dawn of the modern age. Despite the important Christian roots of just war tradition, it differs from the Islamic juristic tradition in that it was never entirely religious in theory or form, and today it is carried at least as powerfully in the legal and military spheres as in specifically Christian form. Similarly, in this tradition as well as in western political thought and theology more generally, the nature of the political community, the role of government, and the place of the use of armed force are conceived in secular rather than religious terms. I have a very low opinion of much recent thinking about the idea of just war, because it has lost sight of the moral and political purposiveness of the just war idea as classically conceived and defined. That needs to be recovered, because in the end it tells us much about who we in the West are in fundamental human terms, but also because the values found there can serve as a reminder of an Islam that the radical jihadists have forgotten.

Almost twenty-one years ago, in the summer, 1993, issue of *Foreign Affairs*, Samuel P. Huntington published an article, "The Clash of Civilizations?", that occasioned much debate at the time, and the debate has continued since, with additional fuel provided by a later book by Huntington on the same topic. Some opposed the very idea that conflict around the globe might in any way be caused by the differing values and their institutionalization in various major civilizations. Others misread Huntington as endorsing the idea of a clash of civilizations in itself—"the West against the rest," as one section head put it. But the title of the article was not declarative; it ended with a question mark, signaling Huntington's underlying purpose. Against the arguments that would be offered by his critics, Huntington was indeed arguing that values, including religious ones, and their institutional expressions matter, and it is a mistake not to take them into account. Twenty-one years later it is hard not to credit this basic argument: the Islamic State and al Qaeda, for their part, forthrightly present their struggle as one against "America and the West," though in the West any effort to recognize their use of religion as justifying their jihad is opposed by some as "Islamophobia." Here, though, is how Huntington ended his 1993 article: after affirming the need for the West to "maintain the economic and military power necessary to protect its interests" in relation to the rise of competition from other civilizations, he continued that doing so:

> ...will also...require the West to develop a more profound understanding of the basic religious and philosophical assumptions underlying other civilizations and the ways in which people in those civilizations see their interests. It will require an effort to identify elements of commonality between Western and other civilizations.

This also is the point I wish to leave with you, but with my focus more specifically on the cross-civilizational conflict with radical Islamist jihadism: meeting and overcoming this challenge will require more than military responses, though these will continue to be needed. Beyond that, though, there is a need for better understanding of the religious and ideological roots of this ideology, its relation to the historical tradition of jihad, and the relation of that tradition to the Western tradition of just war. This effort is already ongoing, but it needs to be broadened and strengthened. It is in all our interests to participate in it.

ABSTRACT

In this work, Johnson traces the idea of holy war from medieval times to the present day. He then contrasts medieval concepts with contemporary Roman Catholic social teaching. With respect to early Christianity, war, and peace, he addresses the thought of Roland Bainton and Leroy B. Walters and also looks at the diverse meanings of "holy war" in biblical studies, theology, and history.

CHAPTER 16

HOLY WAR

I. GETTING AT THE MEANING OF A DIFFICULT CONCEPT

It is hard to get a firm grip on the idea of holy war. The meaning intended by the term "holy war" is enormously varied, depending on context, who is using it, the purpose of the use, what ideas are brought in to define it, and the way those constituent ideas are mixed together. In recent popular, journalistic, and even much scholarly usage the phrase "holy war" has often been employed as if it were synonymous, or nearly synonymous, with both "crusade" and *jihad*, though this distorts and obscures the historical meanings associated with both the latter concepts while adding its own flavors to them.

Calling a conflict, or a kind of conflict, "holy war" has the power to put fire in the heart or to make the blood run cold, depending on whether one is on the side of the holy war in question or is threatened by it. James A. Aho provides a sympathetic scholarly description of how the first of these two senses of "holy war" works:

> Holy war is a teaching technique. It resubstantiates a person's beliefs, "re-nomizing" human existence. It preserves the cosmic world from nothingness or it eradicates absurdity by bringing justice into historical reality. In either case, the holy war is an armed confrontation with Evil.[1]

But from a perspective within post-Enlightenment rationalism, for which the world does not need to be "re-nomized," holy war threatens the rational ordering of the world itself by appealing to norms and powers outside the realm of reason. Similarly, from a perspective within the Westphalian system of world order and its associated understanding of the right to make war and the rules for conduct in war, any invocation of holy war represents a fundamental challenge, setting out its own standards for going to war and for how to make war. From both of these perspectives, holy war can appear an atavistic throwback to primitive, uncivilized times and a call to unrestrained violence for its own sake.

This critical, even pejorative, conception of holy war figures centrally in the well-known typology laid out by Roland Bainton in his *Christian Attitudes Toward War and Peace*.[2] Bainton describes three fundamental Christian attitudes toward war as spaced along a spectrum, with pacifism at one extreme, the crusade or holy war at the other extreme, and the just war idea between them, participating in certain ways in both but distinct from either. On his typology, the key is how the use of force is dealt with in each of these three positions: pacifism utterly rejects the use of force, while just war accepts but limits it, and the crusade or holy war admits unlimited force in the service of its transcendent cause. Here is Bainton's language on this last "attitude":

> The crusading idea requires that the cause be holy (and no cause is more holy than religion), that the war be fought under God and with his help, that the crusaders shall be godly and their enemies ungodly, and that the war shall be prosecuted unsparingly.[3]

There are problems with each of Bainton's three ways of characterizing such war. Leroy B. Walters, taking specific aim at Bainton's description of the crusade idea as antithetical to that of just war,[4] argues that medieval doctrine on the crusades developed by analogy with the simultaneously developing doctrine on just war.[5] He advances this argument in terms of the categories which came to provide the definitive terms of classic just war thought: right authority, just cause, and right intention.[6] Bainton employs the first two in his typology, with his third category being that of the conduct allowed. A close reading of Frederick Russell's fine-grained study of the twelfth- and thirteenth-century canonists[7] yields similar results: when the canonists (and later, the theologians) were thinking morally about the question of war, these were the categories they used. They are in fact quite generally useful categories, even in comparative studies across cultures; I employ them in my own book comparing the holy war idea in Western Christianity and Islam.[8] But everything depends, in context, on the content packed into the categories; by themselves, the empty categories do not lead far. Walters's critique of Bainton, which amounts to a construction of Walters's own conception of holy war, depends on unpacking the meanings of the categories as actually used by the medieval writers: war fought on the authority of a temporal ruler vs. war fought on the authority of the pope, not Bainton's "war…fought under God and with his help"; war fought for the protection of the temporal order vs. war fought for the protection of Christian religion or the Church, not Bainton's "holy" cause. As to the matter of the third category that Bainton cited, "that the war shall be prosecuted unsparingly," Walters noted that he had not found any evidence of a distinction "in the theorists' prescriptions for the conduct of justifiable political and religious wars" and went on to argue that therefore, the developing *jus in bello* rules, as they existed at that time, must have been understood to apply to both.[9] In my own judgment on the matter of unsparing prosecution, two other factors are central: first, some holy war advocates from the Reformation era emphasized that the godliness of the cause imposed the obligation of godly conduct, that is, conduct closely restrained by both internal and external discipline; second, in both the medieval and Reformation-era contexts, there was general agreement that in responding to rebellion (including religious rebellion, that is, heresy or even serious nonconformity), extreme means were justified.[10]

In any case, the kinds of characterizations in play here do not exhaust the diverse meanings that have attached to the idea of holy war. There is a purely descriptive use of the term in Old Testament scholarship, prominently exemplified by Gerhard von Rad's classic study, *Der Heilige Krieg im alten Israel*;[11] the term is also used descriptively in Albrecht Noth's later comparative study, *Heiliger Krieg und Heiliger Kampf in Islam und Christentum*[12] and in my own *The Holy War Idea in Western and Islamic Traditions.*[13]

The earliest use of the term "holy war" I have encountered in print is Francis Bacon's *An Advertisement Touching an Holy Warre*, begun in 1622 and left unfinished but published along with other works by Bacon on various topics seven years later.[14] The *Advertisement* was in the form of a dialogue, with each of several characters presenting a perspective on the question of a possible war between England and Spain. Bacon himself did not make clear his own position on the matter of holy war in this work. He returned to this topic in 1624 in a finished study written by royal request, *Considerations Touching a Warre with Spaine*, where his own understanding of the idea of holy war is set out more clearly: it has to do with establishing the right of the English Monarch to defend Protestant religion in England against an offensive war by Spain to restore Catholicism by force of arms.[15] He makes no claim that war justified in this way may be unlimited.

Bacon's way of using the term "holy war" signals that it was a familiar term in England already when he wrote. This is also clear in a book from the following decade, Thomas Fuller's *The Historie of the Holy Warre*,[16] which applies the term "holy war" to both the medieval Crusades and the Protestant-Catholic conflicts on the European continent during the century after the beginning of the Reformation, up through what we now call the Thirty Years' War, which was ongoing when Fuller wrote. This last war, as well as the French religious wars of the previous century, was marked by unrestrained, even wanton cruelty and violence, but Fuller does not regard this as an inherent characteristic of war fought for religious purposes. Rather he connects this form of conduct in war to a specific criticism directed against Catholic prosecution of war in the name of religion, which he depicts as rooted in papal arrogance, greed, and ambition. He leaves open the possibility of legitimate warfare for religion in the future (perhaps by Protestants?), provided it is conducted properly.[17]

I have previously discussed the matter of holy war in some detail in two contexts already introduced: first, that of English discourse on war from the late sixteenth century through the mid-seventeenth;[18] second, that of an extended comparison between the major Western Christian and Islamic traditions on war.[19] My comments on Bacon and Fuller above, and my earlier comment on Bainton, draw from the former (*Ideology, Reason, and the Limitation of War*), but I also would refer readers to the full discussion there and in the 1997 book (*The Holy War Idea*). In the context of the comparative study of Western and Islamic thought on the idea of holy war I began, as I have begun here, with an examination of what I called there "the many faces of holy war," identifying ten distinct if related meanings associated with holy war.[20] Different ones of these meanings, and different combinations of meanings, appear in various contexts. So the term "holy war" has various meanings, and a major part of the problem of addressing the central question of this chapter is sorting out the component ideas and how they interact with each other in the context at hand.

The just war categories of right authority, just cause, right intention, and right conduct, with various sorts of meanings attaching to them in different contexts, weave in and out of Western Christian discourse that can be described in some way as having to do with "holy war." Some are more central in Catholic thinkers and Catholic teaching; others are more central in Protestant thought. But the historical ground shifts importantly at the beginning of the modern period, and it is reasonable to ask how the earlier debates bear on thinking about war and religion after that shift. I make no claim to comprehensiveness in this present discussion; the aim rather is to identify and explore the most important issues and how they came to bear on the idea of holy war.

II. POSING THE QUESTION: ASSESSING MEDIEVAL AND EARLY MODERN THINKING

Is there a Catholic doctrine of holy war? Certainly a major component of this question has to do with teaching on religious difference and whether religious conformity can and should be enforced by the power of arms. As far as current Catholic teaching is concerned, Gregory Reichberg is directly on target in this summary observation:

> It is now recognized in the official Church teaching that no state, even one where there is a majority of Catholics, can require a profession of faith on the part of its citizens. Religious plurality and religious freedom are now deemed fully acceptable conditions within the modern state.[21]

But what of earlier times? Catholic teaching has not always held the position Reichberg summarizes here, and indeed the contrary position has been the norm, both legally and socially, in most Western societies right up into the twentieth century. (The United States is the most notable exception, but even here, while the First Amendment to the Constitution forbids Congress to establish a national religion, the right of individual states to do so persisted after the adoption of the Bill of Rights.) In the era of the Reformation the formula *cuius regio, eius religio* did not establish religious freedom (except for rulers) but recognized the right of individual rulers to establish a single form of religious conformity within their domains. Protestant as well as Catholic rulers continued to guard this right jealously, and even after European societies finally stopped fighting one another over the right to impose religious conformity on one another, they continued to seek to impose such conformity in their own domains, often by use of arms. So if religious freedom, or to put it another way, tolerance of religious plurality, is central to the phenomenon of war in the name of religion—what has come to be called holy war—it is only part of the story: the larger issue is the conception of society and the role of religion in relation to it.

A particular conception of the interlocked relationship between religion and society is central to the definition of the Islamic idea of *jihad*, which provides a ready comparative frame of reference for thinking about holy war. Some scholars of Islam, like Bruce Lawrence, have explicitly rendered the term *jihad* as "holy war?"[22] Other commentators, like Robin Wright in her 1985 book on the Islamic revolution in Iran, have described jihad as a kind of "crusade."[23] Others before and since have used similar language. Yet "holy war" is not a term used in Islamic thought. In normative Islamic tradition the definition of the good society, the *dar al-islam* or abode of Islam, is intentionally one that joins religion to temporal life. The society itself is defined as the territory ("abode") where God's law, *sharia*, holds sway; its governance is lodged in a ruler recognized to have inherited both the religious and the political authority of the Prophet Muhammad (in Sunni tradition, the caliph; in Shiite tradition, the Imam). While certain forms of non-Muslim religious belief and practice are tolerated, others are not, and even those tolerated must defer to Islamic law in cases of difference or be disciplined or punished if they do not. Religious conformity within the society, then, is understood not in terms of an enforced common faith—indeed, Islamic tradition explicitly repudiates the idea of enforced faith—but common behavior according to Islamic law, ideally flowing from the heart in the case of Muslim believers but subject to enforcement from outside in the case of non-Muslims. Similarly, relations with societies not part of the *dar al-islam* are understood in terms of conformity or non-conformity to Islamic law. These societies, as defined in the classical works of Islamic jurisprudence, collectively make up the *dar al-harb*, the abode of war, so called because, without rule according to God's law, human societies descend into conflict, both internally and in their relations with other societies. *Jihad* of the sword aims at bringing peace to them by causing them to submit to divinely given law. Is such *jihad* "holy war"? Muslims insist that it is not. Yet certainly religion is closely associated with warfare here. This normative Islamic conception clearly overlaps the way Western Christian thinking came, in the twelfth and thirteenth centuries in particular, to treat the relationship between religion and the use of armed force, though there are also telling differences.[24]

On the matter of the conception of society, Charles Cardinal Journet, who treats the subject of holy war extensively in his chapter on the relation between the canonical and political powers,[25] argues that the central issue is that medieval western Europe was a "consecrational society." This might at first blush appear to be the same sort of conception as that of the *dar al-islam* in Islamic thinking, but the actual organization of Western societies, their interrelationship, and the relation between the political and spiritual spheres was conceived differently. Journet summarizes what he means for the relation between religion and war in this way: "by reason of the spiritual values invested in the temporal common good in a consecrational regime, it was this temporal common good itself which the Church required to be defended, by temporal means used in accordance with their own laws."[26] Even in the "consecrational" society, and in contrast to the case of Islamic religion and culture, a distinction is made between the spiritual and the temporal. This turns out to be the key to the difference between the Western way of thinking about the relation between religion and war and that found in normative Islam.

This Western way of thinking, in which a difference is recognized to exist between the religious and temporal spheres, first explicitly appears in a letter of Pope Gelasius I to the Roman Emperor Anastasius in 494:

> There are two powers, august Emperor, by which this world is chiefly ruled, namely, the sacred authority of the priests and the royal power. Of these that of the priests is the more weighty, since they have to render an account for even the kings of men in the divine judgment. You are also aware, dear son, that while you are permitted honorably to rule over human kind, yet in things divine you bow your head humbly before the leaders of the clergy....[27]

This distinction, which never developed in the eastern part of the Empire or in Orthodox Christian doctrine, became critical for Western culture. While Gelasius's specific language asserts the primacy of the spiritual powers over the temporal, the idea that there are two distinct powers turned out to be more fundamental, and the question of the extent of these powers and their relation to each other continued to be argued all through the Middle Ages and into the modern period.

But regarding the specific relation of religion to war, a particular interpretation of the spiritual-temporal distinction became central. In 1144, as part of his preaching of a new crusade after Muslim advances in the Holy Land, Bernard of Clairvaux developed this idea of two distinct powers into that of the "two swords," posing this argument to the pope:

> Since the Saviour suffers anew where He once died for us, both the swords must be drawn which he allowed on the first occasion [Luke xxii.38]. And who should draw them but you? Both swords of Peter must be unsheathed as often as need be, the one at his command, the other at his hand.[28]

This concept was fundamental to subsequent medieval argument about the relation of religion to war. Journet regards the matter as closely tied to his conception of medieval society as "consecrational," writing, "It will...appear that 'holy wars' are bound up with the existence or survival of a consecrational type of Christendom."[29] With the end of this type of society, on this conception, comes the end of the possibility of "holy wars." It would, I think, be better to say that the debate over the relation of religion to war shifts with the conception of society, but that the focus remains on the question of authority. Later, in the Reformation era, the "two swords" idea was opposed by the development in Protestant thought of a contrary idea, that of "one sword"—that only the civil power, and never the spiritual, has the right of the sword. This latter doctrine sat easily alongside the formula *cuius regio, eius religio*, which gave the power of decision regarding the practice of religion to rulers. Whether armed force may rightly be used for certain purposes defined by religion was not in play here, as both sides agreed that force could be used for such purpose; the "two-swords"-"one sword" debate was really about whether the pope, as the possessor of the spiritual power, possessed the right to authorize the use of armed force for these purposes, or whether that right belongs only to temporal rulers in their own domains—the position adopted normatively throughout the Reformation. Interestingly, as we have seen in both Bacon and Fuller, the term "holy war" first appears in the context of this debate.

So identifying medieval society as "consecrational" does not, I think, get to the heart of the matter of the relation between religion and the use of armed force, whether the latter can usefully be described as "holy war" or not, since the idea that religious values are part of the societal common good persists well after the end of the specific society Journet has in mind, that of medieval Christendom. What changes is the answer to the question of who has the authority, and the responsibility, to authorize armed force for the protection of such values. Journet elsewhere, citing the doctrine of the two swords, notes where medieval Christian thinking came out on this: the pope, as head of the Church and possessor of the authority of St. Peter, has the right to authorize war for the defense of the faith (cf. the discussion of Walters above), but since the Church may not itself be directly involved in bloodshed, if the pope does "draw" the sword in this way, he immediately passes it to the temporal prince to use it; alternatively, "in certain grave circumstances," even if the pope himself does not authorize the use of force, he has the power to command the prince to do so.[30] Russell's study of the medieval canonical debates leads readers through the details of the debates over papal authority regarding the sword, showing how the resolution, which Journet's language well describes, was reached in canon law by the middle of the thirteenth century.[31] This conception became settled doctrine in subsequent canon law and theology, and it was the basis for Catholic thinking about religious authorization and justification of war during the conflicts of the Reformation era. What happens in the Protestant doctrine of "one sword" directly rejects this way of thinking: the "one sword" doctrine denies both kinds of authority regarding use of armed force that was given to the pope in medieval doctrine. At the same time, the Protestant doctrine maintained the right to use the sword for the protection of religious values, and even the protection of specific religious institutions, but the doctrine passed that right to the temporal rulers.

Recalling what I have said above about the usefulness of the categories of right authority, just cause, right intention, and right conduct for thinking about the relation of religion to war, I would stress that their specific content in each given context is what makes each form of such thinking distinctive. In the effort to make sense of the concept of holy war, examining each category means coming to terms with both what the developing thought allowed and what it prohibited. As I have been arguing, the "two swords"-"'one sword" debate had to do with identifying who could rightly authorize resort to force: whether the pope could do so, or only temporal rulers. As to the justifying cause, there was no dispute that force could—indeed, should—be used to protect Christian religion, though not to seek to propagate it. In the Reformation era, of course, Catholics and Protestants disagreed fundamentally on which form of Christian religion deserved to be protected, as well as by whom. On the particular matter of conduct, a key factor is that, for both just war and holy war thinkers in the Middle Ages and well into the modern period, involvement in rebellion against established authority trumped any and all restrictions on the conduct of war. This idea, which is in effect the mirror image of the effort to restrain war by limiting the right to authorize it, crystallized in medieval thought during the same period—the late twelfth and early thirteenth centuries—in which the idea of right authority became definitive for the right to resort to armed force. Within the frame of a "consecrational" society, where heresy was understood as a form of rebellion against order (Journet, for example, calls heresy in a consecrational society a crime like theft or murder),[32] it allowed the extreme means used, for example, in the punishment and suppression of the Albigensians. At the same time, though, other forms of rebellion could be put down equally harshly; use of extreme means was not reserved for responses to heresy and religious nonconformity. In the era of the Reformation, while this way of thinking justified the pope's authorization of war by Catholic princes against Protestant ones, it also justified the use of armed force within Protestant as well as Catholic lands against those who professed the contrary religion. Nor was it only a matter of religious conformity: consider Luther's exhortation to the German nobility to "smite and punish," to "smite, slay, and stab" all who were involved in the peasants' rebellion of 1524–25. Rebellion, Luther wrote, "is not just simple murder; it is like a great fire, which attacks and devastates a whole land." It "brings with it a land filled with murder and bloodshed; it makes widows and orphans, and turns everything upside down."[33]

In assessing whether holy war inherently permits unlimited uses of force, then, it is necessary to come to terms with the fact that it was generally accepted that unlimited means could rightly be used against rebels. In the Middle Ages this puts the focus on dissident religious groups and in particular on the rebellion of heresy. In the Reformation era both Protestants and Catholics continued to regard heresy as punishable by death and the use of coercive force as a proper response to all forms of religious nonconformity. The new element here was the more complicated face of rebellion. For a Protestant ruler who had installed a Protestant form of Christianity as the established religion in his or her domain, the effort to re-establish Catholicism, or even to carve out a place in society where Catholics might openly practice their faith, constituted rebellion. At the same time, from the standpoint of the Catholic authorities, the affirmation of Protestant faith by a ruler itself constituted rebellion against papal authority, justifying punishment by force of arms.

We see this phenomenon clearly in the debate between the exiled English Catholic Primate, William Cardinal Allen, and the Anglican Bishop of Winchester, Thomas Bilson, during the 1580s, in the context of the pope's support of the Irish Catholics in their rising in arms against the Protestant English Queen Elizabeth. Allen, writing first, puts the matter straightforwardly: "[N]o crime in the world deserveth more sharpe and zealous pursuite of extreme revenge, than revoulting from the faith to strange religions." All the unfaithful are to be slain "without exception."[34] Temporal rulers who oppose the pope, Allen continued, are by definition rebels, as are all their subjects who follow their lead, since temporal power derives from the spiritual. By contrast, Catholics who rise up against their ruler in the cause of their faith are not rebels, for they are acting in obedience to a law higher than that of their earthly prince. Bilson, writing in direct response to Allen, insists the pope has no temporal authority whatever and thus cannot command in war, so that subjects who oppose their ruler, in matters of religion as in other matters, are in fact rebels, and extreme measures may be used against them.[35] In this dispute the issue is clearly that of the right to rule, and of the authority to employ armed force that comes from this right. Unlimited means are understood as permitted in the punishment and suppression of rebellion against such authority. Both sides in the dispute accept that refusal to follow the ordained religion constitutes such rebellion; their difference is in defining who has the supreme authority. Allen and Bilson are but two voices from the larger debate, which continued till nearly the middle of the seventeenth century; yet their way of framing the issues remained characteristic of this larger debate all the way through.

III. HOLY WAR: A SHIFT IN THINKING

Contemporary thinking about religion in relation to war focuses much more centrally on the question of violence in itself than was the case for medieval and early modern writers treating this subject. We find this, as I have noted, in Bainton's typology, which sorts "Christian attitudes toward war and peace" by ranging them along a spectrum from pacifism, which denies all resort to violence, through just war, which allows violence under some conditions but puts restraints on it, to the holy war or crusade, which Bainton understands as permitting unlimited violence. Recent Catholic thought provides the example of Jacques Maritain's excoriation of the violence and destruction on both sides in the Spanish Civil War, during his discussion, written in 1937, rejecting the claim some were making that the Royalists were fighting a "holy war."[36] For Maritain the use of extreme means is directly opposed to the Christian message, which in one place he renders by citing Luke 9:56: "The Son of Man is not come to destroy the lives of men, but to save them."[37] Or consider the United States Catholic bishops' rendering of the just war idea as defining limited exceptions to a general "presumption against war," a conception first put forward in their 1983 pastoral letter, *The Challenge of Peace*,[38] and made the focus of various later statements on the use of armed force by the United States. Medieval and early modern theorists writing on the subject of just war and holy war simply did not think this way. They rather focused on the question of authorization and justification, holding that the use of armed force could be authorized by either the ruler or the pope for the purpose of Catholic religion and punishing deviation from it. The question of means arose, for them, because such deviation constituted rebellion against the established order, so that extreme means were justified, including death for all the guilty.

Maritain's discussion focuses on the questions of justification for war and conduct in war. The position Maritain rejects, that the Spanish Civil War is actually a holy war, had been argued by a Spanish Dominican, Ignacio G. Menendez-Reigada: "The Spanish national war is a holy war, and the holiest registered in history." Maritain elaborates: "Father Menendez-Reigada justifies this assertion by saying that in the war as it exists what is in play is the very existence of all religion, natural or positive, and that of the natural foundations of society."[39]

The issue here is posed as protection of religion. But for Maritain this does not mean the war should be thought of as a holy war. Rather, he argues, Menendez-Reigada's reasoning "tends to show that the question is that of a just war." So Maritain's first response is to take the matter of holy war off the table as emphatically as the Spanish theologian had it put it there.[40] He goes on to elaborate on this point, arguing that contemporary forms of civilization distinguish more fully between the temporal and the spiritual than was the case earlier, and that in such secular forms of civilization, "the notion of holy war loses all signification."[41] This is the same kind of argument seen in Journet above. But Maritain goes a step further: "there is no longer a place for holy war, but the question of just war remains. The effort to defend sacred values in itself does not make a war holy; this is a matter of justice. Maritain's argument here accepts the use of force as a possible means to protect religious values, but he depicts this as a just war issue, not one having to do with holy war.

Then he shifts to the conduct of the war: the horrible means being used in fighting the Spanish Civil War themselves obviate the idea that the war is in any way holy. In the face of the resulting human misery, calling the war a "holy war" can only multiply the sacrilege caused by the conduct that has caused such misery.[42] To claim holiness in such a context is to risk blasphemy against that which is holy.

Maritain's discussion could be analyzed in much more depth. For the purposes of the present discussion, though, what is most interesting is the shift in the terms of argument exemplified in this discussion. Neither Menendez-Reigada nor Maritain is interested in arguing the right of the spiritual authority, the pope, to authorize war. As for justification, what is at stake, even for Menendez-Reigada, is not punishment of irreligion but protection of religion, and the religion to be protected is not just Catholicism but "all religion, natural or positive, and...the natural foundations of society." For Maritain, though, this is simply a just war justification. And as for conduct, Maritain's most impassioned language is directed to the indiscriminate and extreme destruction employed on both sides.

Maritain clearly wants this to be the end of the line for the idea of holy war, and his language presages that of later Catholic thinking. I mentioned above the U.S. Catholic bishops' *The Challenge of Peace*; consider this language on "religious violence" from their statement marking the tenth anniversary of that pastoral letter:

> Every child murdered, every woman raped, every town "cleansed," every hatred uttered in the name of religion is a crime against God and a scandal for religious believers. Religious violence and nationalism deny what we profess in faith: We are all created in the image of the same God and destined for the same eternal salvation.[43]

This passage is followed by a supporting quotation from Pope John Paul II: "[N]o Christian can knowingly foster or support structures and attitudes that unjustly divide individuals or groups."

The teaching defined here by the bishops is a hundred and eighty degrees from medieval and early modern conceptions. Not only is religious difference not a justification for the use of armed force, but the use of force for religious purpose is described as manifested in forms of violence—murder of children, rape of women, intentional driving of people from their homes—that are inherently immoral.

This document also exemplifies another shift in Catholic thinking: that protection of religion remains a moral imperative, not because of the inherent truth of any particular religion but as a matter of fundamental human rights. This position is developed most fully in the section on humanitarian intervention, where the U.S. bishops, quoting Pope John Paul II and summarizing the concerns he raised, write as follows: "[H]uman life, human rights, and the welfare of the human community are at the center of Catholic moral reflection on the social and political order."[44]

Contemporary normative Catholic teaching has no place for holy war. It is not only that the institutional relationship between the Catholic Church and society has shifted; it is that the theological conception of the proper relationship between them has changed. It is not only that religious plurality and religious freedom are now accepted in Catholic thinking and teaching; it is that the rationale for that acceptance is understood within the frame of protecting a fundamental human right. When papal authority is cited in support of the need to protect religion, it is not to claim the right of the pope to command the secular authorities to protect Catholic religion but rather to use the pope's moral authority to remind secular governments that they should protect the right of religious belief and practice as a fundamental human right, and while they may—if need be—employ force to do so, extreme forms of violence in the name of religion are rejected as intrinsically immoral. Some, like the U.S. bishops, would add that there is a general presumption against violence which requires grave reasons to be overturned. Contemporary normative Catholic teaching has no place for a doctrine of holy war.

NOTES

1. James A. Aho, *Religious Mythology and the Art of War* (Westport, CT: Greenwood Press, 1981), 128.
2. Roland Bainton, *Christian Attitudes toward War and Peace* (Nashville, TN: Abingdon Press, 1960).
3. Bainton, *Christian Attitudes*, 148.
4. Ibid., 14.
5. LeRoy Walters, "The Just War and the Crusade: Antitheses or Analogies?" *The Monist* 57, no. 4 (October 1973): 584–94.
6. Walters, "The Just War and the Crusade," 590.
7. Frederick H. Russell, *The Just War in the Middle Ages* (Cambridge: Cambridge University Press, 1985), 86–212.
8. James Turner Johnson, *The Holy War Idea in Western and Islamic Traditions* (University Park, PA: The Pennsylvania State University Press, 1997).
9. Walters, "The Just War and the Crusade," 591.
10. As to the former reason, see James Turner Johnson, *Ideology, Reason, and the Limitation of War* (Princeton, NJ: Princeton University Press, 1975), 134–46; as to the latter, see further below.
11. Gerhard von Rad, *Der Heilige Krieg im alten Israel* (Göttingen: Vandenhoek & Ruprecht, 1958), published in English as *Holy War in Ancient Israel* (Grand Rapids, MI: William B. Eerdmans, 1991).
12. Albrecht Noth, *Heiliger Krieg und Heiliger Kampf in Islam und Christentum* (Bonn: Ludwig Röhrscheid Verlag, 1966).
13. See n. 8 above.
14. Francis Bacon, *Certaine miscellany works of the Right Honorable, Francis Lo[rd] Verulam, Viscount S. Alban* (London: I. Haviland for Humphrey Robinson, 1629).
15. Bacon, *Certaine miscellany works*, 31–32.
16. Thomas Fuller, *The Historie of the holy warre* (Cambridge: Thomas Buck, Printer to the University, 1639).
17. Fuller, *Historie*, Book I, chaps. 9, 10; Book V, chap. 9.
18. Johnson, *Ideology*, 87–149.
19. Johnson, *The Holy War Idea.*
20. Ibid., 37–42.

21. Gregory M. Reichberg, "Norms of War in Roman Catholic Christianity," in *World Religions and Norms of War*, ed. Vesselin Popovski, Gregory M. Reichberg, and Nicholas Turner (New York: United Nations University Press, 2009): 142–65, at 155.
22. Bruce Lawrence, "Holy War (*Jihad*) in Islamic Religion and Nation-state Ideologies," in *Just War and Jihad*, ed. John Kelsay and James Turner Johnson (Westport, CT: Greenwood Press, 1991), 141–60.
23. Robin Wright, *Sacred Rage: The Crusade of Modern Islam* (New York: Linden Press/ Simon & Schuster, 1985).
24. For fuller discussion of the classical Islamic juristic idea of *jihad* see Johnson, *The Holy War Idea*, chapters 3–5, *passim*; see also John Kelsay, *Arguing the Just War in Islam* (Cambridge: Harvard University Press, 2007), 97–124.
25. Charles Cardinal Journet, *The Church of the Incarnate Word* (London: Sheed and Ward, 1955), chapter VI.
26. Journet, *Church*, 37.
27. Cited from www.newworldencyclopedia.org/entry/Gelasius_I, accessed January 29, 2009.
28. Cited from Journet, *Church*, 81.
29. Ibid., 70.
30. Ibid., 80.
31. See n. 7 above.
32. Journet, *Church*, 72.
33. Martin Luther, *Luther's Works*, vol. 46 (Philadelphia: Fortress Press, 1967), 50; see further 49–55.
34. William Cardinal Allen, *A True, sincere, and modest defence of English catholiques that suffer for their faith both at home and abrode* (London: William Cecil, 1585), 103.
35. Thomas Bilson, *The True difference betweene Christian subjection and unchristian rebellion* (Oxford: Joseph Barnes, Printer to the University, 1585), 379–81.
36. Jacques Maritain, *Préface au livre d'Alfred Mendizabal,Aux origines d'une tragédie: La politique espagnole de 1923 à 1936*, 1215–55, in *Jacques et Raïssa Maritain, Oeuvres Complètes*, vol.VI (Fribourg: Éditions Universitaires/Paris: Éditions Saint-Paul, 1984), 1237–43.
37. Maritain, *Préface*, 1243, my translation.
38. National Conference of Catholic Bishops, *The Challenge of Peace* (Washington, DC: United States Catholic Conference, 1983).

39. Maritain, *Préface*, 1238, n. 18.
40. Ibid.
41. Ibid., 1239–41.
42. Ibid., 1244.
43. National Conference of Catholic Bishops, "The Harvest of Justice Is Sown in Peace," *Origins* 23, no. 26 (December 9, 1993), 450–64, at 458.
44. National Conference of Catholic Bishops, "The Harvest of Justice," 461.

BIBLIOGRAPHY

Aho, James A. *Religious Mythology and the Art of War*. Westport, CT: Greenwood Press, 1981.

Bainton, Roland. *Christian Attitudes toward War and Peace*. Nashville, TN: Abingdon Press, 1960.

Johnson, James Turner. *The Holy War Idea in Western and Islamic Traditions*. University Park, PA: The Pennsylvania State University Press, 1997.

Johnson, James Turner. *Ideology, Reason, and the Limitation of War*. Princeton, NJ: Princeton University Press, 1975.

Journet, Charles Cardinal. *The Church of the Incarnate Word*. London: Sheed and Ward, 1955.

Kelsay, John. *Arguing the Just War in Islam*. Cambridge: Harvard University Press, 2007.

Lawrence, Bruce. "Holy War (*Jihad*) in Islamic Religion and Nation-state Ideologies." In *Just War and Jihad*, edited by John Kelsay and James Turner Johnson. Westport, CT: Greenwood Press, 1991.

National Conference of Catholic Bishops. *The Challenge of Peace*. Washington, DC: United States Catholic Conference, 1983.

National Conference of Catholic Bishops. "The Harvest of Justice Is Sown in Peace." *Origins* 23, no. 26 (December 9, 1993): 450–64.

Noth, Albrecht. *Heiliger Krieg und heiliger Kampf in Islam und Christentum*. Bonn: Ludwig Röhrscheid Verlag, 1966.

Reichberg, Gregory M. "Norms of War in Roman Catholic Christianity." In *World Religions and Norms of War*, edited by Vesselin Popovski, Gregory M. Reichberg, and Nicholas Turner. New York: United Nations University Press, 2009.

Russell, Frederick H. *The Just War in the Middle Ages*. Cambridge: Cambridge University Press, 1985.

von Rad, Gerhard. *Holy War in Ancient Israel*, translated and edited by M. J. Dawn. Grand Rapids, MI: William B. Eerdmans, 1991.

Walters, LeRoy. "The Just War and the Crusade: Antitheses or Analogies?" *The Monist* 57, no. 4 (October 1973): 584–94.

Wright, Robin. *Sacred Rage: The Crusade of Modern Islam*. Cambridge: Harvard University Press, 2007.

ABSTRACT

This essay considers the tension between traditional moral use of force by rulers—and right of rebellion and natural law for the ruled. Johnson views the thought of Luther, Aquinas, and Augustine before looking at the modern period of the mid-sixteenth century forward with respect to the idea of rebellion. He then looks at the contemporary environment and modern Islamic moral tradition.

CHAPTER 17

AD FONTES: THE QUESTION OF REBELLION AND MORAL TRADITION ON THE USE OF FORCE

"Stab, smite, slay!" These are not the words of Bashar al-Assad telling his forces how they should deal with the Syrian rebel movement, or indeed those of any other contemporary political leader, but rather the words of Martin Luther exhorting the German nobility to a harsh response to the Peasants' Rebellion of 1524–1525.[1] His writings show that he sympathized with many of the peasants' grievances so long as these did not issue in rebellion, but when they turned to force of arms, he responded sternly. This was not a peculiarity of Luther. Consider the following from an English courtier, Thomas Churchyard, writing admiringly of the treatment of Irish rebels in 1579 by Sir Humphrey Gilbert, commander of the English army sent to put down the rebellion:

> He further tooke this order infringeable, that when soever he made any ostyng [military campaign], or inrode, into the enemies Countrey, he killed manne, woman, and child, and spoiled, wasted, and burned, by the grounde all that he might, leavyng nothing of the enemies in saffetie, whiche he could possiblie waste, or consume.[2]

Nor was this way of thinking about how to deal with rebellion limited to the sixteenth century. Consider these passages from Thomas Aquinas's *Summa Theologiae*—the first from "On Strife":

> Strife seems to be a kind of private war. [As such,] strife is always sinful.... For if an officer of a prince or judge, in virtue of their public authority, should attack certain men and these defend themselves, it is not the former who is said to be guilty of strife, but those who resist the public power.[3]

And this from "On Sedition":

> Sedition is contrary to the unity of the multitude, viz., the people of a city or kingdom.... It is evident that the unity to which sedition is opposed is the unity of law and common good, whence it follows manifestly that sedition is opposed to justice and the common good.... It is a mortal sin.[4]

The only exception Aquinas made was for the case of tyrannical rule, where he argued that subjects are not bound to obey tyrannical orders from the ruler.[5] Still, Aquinas argued that subjects should simply withhold obedience to wrongful orders, not rise in armed rebellion. While in extreme cases it is not a sin to overthrow a tyrant, it is subordinate rulers who should take the lead in this task (here Aquinas anticipated Calvin on the overthrow of an unjust ruler by "lesser magistrates"), not the people at large. The underlying reason is the responsibility the subordinate rulers have to use their ordering power in the service of justice and peace; other people may have the individual right of self-defense, but they do not have this larger responsibility for the common good, given that the overthrow of a tyrannical government by popular uprising may lead to social and political chaos and even worse injustice than that under the tyrant. Thus, Aquinas argues, the situation must be extreme to justify the overthrowing of a tyrant: "If there be not an excess of tyranny it is more expedient to tolerate for a while the milder tyranny than, by acting against the tyrant, to be involved in many perils which are more grievous than the tyranny itself."[6] The reasoning here is not simply a defense of political order as such, but an acknowledgment of the centrifugal forces always present in communal life and the danger they may pose to justice and peace.

Continuing our probe backward in time, we may also recall Augustine's counsel to the Roman authorities that they should use armed force to put down the rebellious Donatists, not because they were heretical Christians, but because they were engaged in acts constituting rebellion.[7] More fundamentally, Augustine argued that a just use of armed force was possible only on the authority of government; private persons had no right to resort to force.[8] This became one of the core requirements for a just war (*bellum justum*) among the canonists of the twelfth and thirteenth centuries and in Thomas Aquinas's summary of the three requisites for a just war: sovereign authority, a just cause defined by the obligation to vindicate justice, and a right intention that included both the avoidance of wrong dispositions and the overall end [aim] of peace. These three requisites corresponded directly to the three defining goods of politics—order, justice, and peace—which Augustine had drawn from classical political thought, and which medieval theorists, working from Augustine, made the center of their conception of politics.

On this conception, while the three goods were all understood as interrelated—a peaceful society had to be one that is justly ordered, a just society had to be one manifested in a peaceful order, and so on—order was in a real sense *primus inter pares*, first among equals, because only through order could justice and peace be established. Without it there was no possibility of achieving justice, and thus no prospect for peace. This is the conception that lies behind Augustine's discussion of the peace that may be established by just war in the City of Earth: not *pax*, which is the final peace of the City of God, that is, the full manifestation of justice in the form of the saints together with God in the heavenly realm outside of time, but rather a more limited but real kind of peace, the "tranquility of order" (*tranquillitas ordinis*). The lack of complete justice in the City of Earth was accepted because of the value of the degree of real justice and peace it achieved, manifested in social and political "tranquility." The medieval thinkers who gave the idea of just war a systematic, coherent shape in treating the requisites for a justified use of armed force prioritized the authority of a sovereign ruler—a ruler above whom no one else had authority—because they understood such a ruler as having the responsibility of responding to violations of justice (some "fault" that manifested injustice) that undercut domestic peace. Together, these three goods defined the common good of a community, as medieval political thought understood it, and this common good was understood to rest above all on the sovereign's maintenance of a just and peaceful order.

Martin Luther and Thomas Churchyard, early in the modern period, were heirs to this way of thinking about government and the good of political communities. While their language on how rebels should be treated rings more harshly than that of Augustine or Thomas Aquinas, and while in Churchyard's case it reads more as a defense of order as such than of the effort to achieve or maintain justice that legitimates order, it is consistent with the earlier conception of the limits on the right to use armed force and the importance of order in securing the common good of society. Moreover, we should not forget that for Aquinas, sedition, which includes incitement to rebellion and rebellion itself, is a mortal sin. For him that was saying enough.

But from roughly the middle of the sixteenth century through the first third of the seventeenth, or, more specifically, from the Spanish Neo-Scholastic Francisco de Vitoria through Hugo Grotius, a succession of writers on politics and war moved to reconceptualize the location of the authority to undertake war, and in doing so reshaped the understanding of the relative roles of the governing authorities and the populace as a whole within a political community. This reconceptualization, which focused on the justifying cause for resort to war, is clearest in the writings of Grotius. Aquinas had listed two justifying causes for war—recovery of that which has been wrongly taken and punishment of wrongdoing—both of which referred directly to the conception of the sovereign's responsibility to set right violations of justice so as to ensure the common good. The meaning of justice, and thus both of these ends, was understood as defined by natural law. Aquinas did not mention defense as a just cause, because earlier canonical thought had established that every individual has the right of self-defense. What *bellum iustum* was about was the need to use armed force after the fact of a violation, because the right of self-defense did not extend to the recovery of things wrongly taken or punishment of the violator; this right belonged to the public authority, not to individuals. This conception stood well into the modern period and is visible in both Luther and Churchyard.

However, with other early modern thinkers, including Vitoria and Grotius, this idea was rethought as the concept of natural law was tested—first by the encounter with the Indians of the New World and then, even more seriously, by the breakup of the unity of the Christian society of Europe due to the Reformation. In this new context, justice could seem to be in the eye of the beholder, as both Catholic and Protestant princes claimed to be enforcing justice in using force against religious dissenters. What remained was the idea that each individual, by natural law, has the right of self-defense against attack. The prince's right to use armed force was accordingly reframed as being delegated to him by the people of his political community to act on their behalf for their defense. This is the origin of the distinctively modern idea that defense against aggression is the basic justifying cause for a state's resort to war.

What of the matter of rebellion? On the older conception, the sovereign could use force against behavior that he understood as endangering the order, justice, and peace of his political community. But the division of Europe into Protestant and Catholic polities changed that, since now the use of force could be directed by the authorities against religious dissent in the name of maintaining public order. The redefinition of the right to use armed force came in reaction to this division. It is instructive that Grotius began to write on the laws of war in support of the "ancient rights and privileges" of the (Protestant) Dutch against the overlordship of the (Catholic) king of Spain in the Netherlands. For him, the Catholic king did not have the right to employ armed force to impose the Catholic religion on the Protestant Dutch, but rather the Dutch had the right to defend themselves against such force. That is, his focus on defense as the only justifying cause for war, and on the right of the prince to use force as delegated to him from his people to act on their behalf, was set out in the context of an ongoing rebellion against the ruling authority—a rebellion that Grotius believed justified.

Let us scroll ahead to the present day. When we think about the justification for armed intervention provided by the concept of the "responsibility to protect," it necessarily implies the right of the affected populations to resist such maltreatment by their government by means up to and including armed rebellion. Such is the present-day legacy of the kind of thinking employed by Grotius. Here the protection of the basic rights of the people is understood as a bedrock principle of public order (and justice and peace), justifying international actions including the use of armed force across state borders for the protection of a threatened populace, even though such action would under other circumstances be understood as a violation of state sovereignty. This reasoning was explicit in the case of the Libyan revolution.

Present-day moral thinking, too, has significantly tilted toward favoring the right of rebellion. This appears in various ways. Most, if not necessarily the best, contemporary moralists writing about just war list the just war criteria as beginning with "just cause" (rendered in terms of the international-law limit to self-defense against aggression); and they subordinate "competent" or "legitimate" authority (rendered as a *pro forma* requirement) to second or third place. Since many such moralists want to use this way of thinking about the just war criteria to limit or forbid states to resort to arms, the idea that a government should have the right to use force to vindicate justice is effectively off the table for them. Preference for the disadvantaged and for human rights in general translates into a positive attitude toward popular rebellions, even when the likely outcome may include the overthrow of one kind of authoritarian government by another kind. Support for the victims of oppression, in some circles, even trumps the reluctance to grant the state any right to use armed force except in response to armed attack, as in the 1997 resolution of the General Convention of the United Presbyterian Church to support humanitarian intervention by armed force, but only in cases when no national interest is being served.

In moral thought there has been only a limited effort to defend the importance of order as necessary for justice and peace. In just war thinking a major example remains the 1970 book *Movement and Revolution* by Peter Berger and Richard John Neuhaus. Berger and Neuhaus argued that the leadership of a just revolution must enforce a just order among those participating in the revolution, and must offer a reasonable prospect of a just order in the society as a whole if the revolution succeeds. Such reasoning is true to the classical model shaped by the medieval canonists and summarized by Aquinas, where the role of sovereign government is prioritized as necessary for a just and peaceful society, but it sets a far higher bar for the justification of revolutionary activities than that set by the aim of protecting fundamental human rights, as in the responsibility to protect idea. Moreover, where the very idea of justice is contentious, as in the case of the Taliban in Afghanistan or the radical Islamist rebels in northern Mali, surely more needs to be said about what, exactly, the standard of "a reasonable prospect of a just order in the society as a whole" means. By contrast, the Arab Spring revolutions in Tunisia, Egypt, and Libya were all undertaken by disparate groups of people with somewhat different identities who were united only in the purpose of removing the existing regime. In such cases, the only way to apply the standard of "a reasonable prospect of a just order in the society as a whole" is not prospective but retrospective. That is, the rebels in these cases were first of all aiming at the overthrow of unjust rulers, and thus an unjust order; yet it may not be clear while the fighting is going on that the rebels are acting to create a just order to replace the overthrown unjust one. That can only be determined in hindsight once a new order has been established. The same is the case with the ongoing revolution in Syria. While this standard holds up an important moral end, it gives no clear guidance for judging a particular resistance or revolutionary effort while it is under way. It remains to be seen where moral thinking on this matter will come out.

ASSESSING ISLAMIC MORAL TRADITION

At the beginning of this essay I briefly alluded to President Bashar al-Assad's harsh treatment of Syrian opponents of his regime. Given how Western thinking on order versus the right of rebellion has developed, what can be said about the normative Islamic moral tradition on politics?

First, classic Islamic law on the *dar al-Islam* defines a society that is religio-political in nature, in which the rule of Islamic law defines the proper order of the society for all its members, and in which the role of the ruling authority, defined as a ruler who has succeeded to the religious and political authority of the prophet Muhammad, is to ensure that all members of that society behave according to the divinely given law. Moreover, the ruler has the responsibility both to defend that law and the society it defines against external threats, and to spread the rule of that law throughout the rest of the world, characterized as the *dar al-harb*, the realm of conflict or war, which is defined as such because it lacks the proper order given in Islamic law. Clearly, the good of order has first priority here, and justice within society depends on this order.

But what if there is injustice? One finds three answers. First, if the injustice takes the form of rebellion against the rule of the Prophet's successor and the law of Islam, the rebels are to be treated as part of the *dar al-harb*, and they may be the object of *jihad* of the sword. Second, if the injustice takes the form of rebellion against some interpretation of Islamic law by the ruler or authorities serving him, then this presents a different matter, that of the *akham al-bughat*, or "rulings concerning rebellion." If the rebels form a coherent group and follow a different but defensible understanding of Islamic law from that being imposed on them, and their overall aim is reconciliation within the community as a whole, then the authorities must treat them with moderation, negotiate with them, and seek reconciliation themselves. The third answer is that adopted by the sizeable Shia minority within the majority Sunni, and Sunni-ruled, Caliphate. In Shia doctrine the caliphs are unjust rulers who do not deserve to be obeyed because they do not genuinely stand in succession to the authority of the Prophet. In the failure of reconciliation, Shia

Muslims should follow "protective dissimulation," appearing to obey the unjust ruler but at the same time withholding genuine assent.

This is the basic shape of classical Islamic jurisprudence regarding government and rebellion. For reasons internal to Islamic law the law itself has not changed, even though circumstances have changed. Thus, there is considerable tension between the classical conception of government and rebellion and present-day Muslim practices and thinking. Most majority-Muslim states today are governed by rulers who do not stand as successors to the Prophet (the notable exception is Iran, whose clerical leaders profess to be acting on behalf of the absent Twelfth Imam, who is in "occlusion" until the end of the world comes near).

Criticism of secular rulers, who do not rule in service to Sharia law, has been one of the principal features of radical Islamism, as notably given expression in the pamphlet *The Neglected Duty* by Muhammad Abd al-Salam Faraj. This so-called "creed of Sadat's assassins" cites various elements of the Islamic tradition to justify armed rebellion against such rule, with the goal being to establish government strictly in accordance with Sharia as the radicals understand it. Radical Islamists have formed a part of all the rebellions of the Arab Spring, with the establishment of the radical understanding of Sharia among their goals, but other groups contributing to these revolutions have had other goals, as Nigel Biggar's contribution to this roundtable exemplifies for the case of Syria. More generally, Muslims are enjoined, as a requirement of their faith, to uphold justice and to work for justice where there is injustice. Exactly what this may mean in a revolutionary context remains contended.

Reflection on moral traditions of the past is valuable as a reminder both of important moral principles, some of which at least may have receded from view over time despite their perennial importance, and also of how differing perspectives and perceptions of needs at given times (including our own) may shape moral priorities and decision-making. Robust moral judgment is still needed to determine what to draw from such reflection and how to deal with the consequences of different conclusions. Being a moral person is not easy. Being a person charged with the responsibilities of government, in which one has responsibilities for the well-being of one's own society and for contributing to the welfare of societies as a whole, is harder yet. Reflection aimed at understanding historical moral traditions is a tool that can contribute importantly to this process.

NOTES

1. Martin Luther, "Against the Robbing and Murdering Hordes of Peasants," in Helmut T. Lehmann and Robert Schultz, eds., *Luther's Works, vol. 46: Christian in Society III* (Philadelphia: Fortress Press, 1967), p. 54.
2. Thomas Churchyard, *A Generall Rehearsall of Warres* (London: Edward White, 1579), Sig. Q. ii.
3. Cited from Gregory Reichberg, Henrik Syse, and Endre Begby, eds., *The Ethics of War* (Malden, Mass.: Blackwell Publishing, 2006), pp. 182–83.
4. Ibid., p. 185.
5. Ibid., p. 195.
6. Ibid.
7. Augustine in various places; see Ibid., pp. 81, 86–89.
8. Ibid., pp. 81–82.

ABSTRACT

This 2013 article traces and breaks down various iterations of the just war concept, from its origins in the late twelfth century to modern reinventions. Influential thinkers appraised include contemporary philosophers Jean Bethke Elshstain, Jeff McMahan, David Rodin, and Brian Orend.

CHAPTER 18

CONTEMPORARY JUST WAR THINKING: WHICH IS WORSE, TO HAVE FRIENDS OR CRITICS?

The increasingly widespread and energetic engagement with the idea of just war over the last fifty years of thinking on morality and armed conflict—especially in English-speaking countries—presents a striking contrast to the previous several centuries, going back to the early 1600s, in which thinkers addressing moral issues related to war did so without reference to the just war idea.

From the late twelfth century to the early seventeenth century a well-defined tradition on just war enjoyed broad cultural acceptance in the West. This framed the resort to force in terms of the responsibilities of sovereign political rule and the political ends of order, justice, and peace, and established limits on conduct in the use of justified force. This tradition had been shaped by philosophical, theological, and political thinking on natural law, by military thought and practice, by legal traditions reaching back into Roman law, and by accumulated experience in the government of political communities. In the cultural context of the Middle Ages, all these overlapped and interpenetrated one another to an important degree.[1]

But under the conditions of the Modern Age this cultural consensus broke down, and the various fields of influence that had shaped the earlier tradition on just war became increasingly distinct from one another and so tended to lose contact with one another.[2] In some arenas creative efforts to engage the idea of just war disappeared altogether: for example, the Spanish Jesuit Francisco Suarez (1548–1617) and the English Puritan William Ames (1576–1633) were the last important theological writers to do so until the twentieth century. In other arenas the ideas defined and set in relationship with one another within the historical just war tradition were redefined and rearranged into new frames of thinking, in which these ideas remained, but their links to earlier just war tradition were downplayed and gradually forgotten.

This was the case with modern thinking on international law, which is heavily indebted to Grotius's reframing of the inherited tradition of just war into his conception of the law of nations in his influential *De Jure Belli ac Pacis* (*On the Laws of War and Peace*), first published in 1625.[3] In regard to this latter line of development, I have argued that in this way the just war tradition was effectively transformed into a tradition of law, and basic concepts from the earlier tradition on just war were thus maintained as legal ideas right up to the present.[4] A forceful presentation and documentation of this historical relationship is provided by *Classics of International Law*, a Carnegie Institution series mostly published between the two world wars.[5] But most contemporary international lawyers ignore this historical connection between the law and the idea of just war, treating the law simply as a product of positive agreements among states.

In any case, by the beginning of the early seventeenth century the connection to the idea of just war as defined in the historical tradition had been transformed and effectively lost as a basis for creative, systematic moral reflection on war. While the Carnegie Institution series did valuable service in making available the writings of a broad variety of thinkers who worked with the just war tradition that they had inherited and who laid the groundwork for the transformation associated with Grotius, it did not lead to new systematic thinking around the idea of just war. Indeed, while its last volumes were still fresh from the press,

Reinhold Niebuhr, in his important theological work *The Nature and Destiny of Man* (1941), derided and rejected what he called "the Catholic theory of a 'just war'" (despite the broad use of the inherited just war tradition by Protestant thinkers in the Reformation era) in the process of an extended criticism of the Catholic conception of natural law (which he identified with the theology of Thomas Aquinas). Niebuhr here showed no knowledge of the broader historical tradition of just war or the rich tradition of moral and political theoretical reflection associated with it, but to recognize this is part of my point about the general loss of consciousness of this tradition: in this he exemplified his generation and those before him. For his conception of just war, Niebuhr provided only a brief quote from Suarez's *Tractatus de Legibus*—including the following, which he made the focus of his criticism: "First, it must be waged by a legitimate power. Secondly, its cause must be just and right. Thirdly, just methods must be used." Niebuhr then went on to dismiss the concept as assuming "obvious distinctions" between "justice" and "injustice" and between "defense" and "aggression," despite the fact that judgments on these matters are "influenced by passions and interests."[6] Niebuhr did not know Suarez's longer, focused, and detailed treatment of just war in the work devoted fully to it, *De Bello*, which provides an extended discussion that presents the matter of justice in war not in terms of absolute certainty (as Niebuhr wrongly argues), but in careful and nuanced language about making judgments among relative claims.[7] The broader just war tradition is full of such discussion. But what Niebuhr read from the short passage of Suarez allowed him to make the point that he desired (which had been forged in his rejection of pacifism in the 1930s): that the use of armed force may sometimes be necessary, but that it is never without injustice and is always tragic. Thus, just war thinking, as Niebuhr depicted it, is accordingly irrelevant, introduced simply for the purpose of being rejected.[8]

THE TWO MAIN AVENUES OF CRITICISM OF JUST WAR THINKING: POLITICAL REALISM AND PACIFISM

Up through World War II and the beginnings of the nuclear age, Niebuhr's position represented one of the major options for mainstream American Protestantism; the other was a form of pacifism based on the ideal of abolishing war through the creation of a world order by international law. In broad terms, these two options have remained as the twin avenues of criticism of the idea of just war: realism and pacifism.

While Niebuhr is generally recognized as being one of the architects of political realism (the other being Hans Morgenthau), present-day political realism has evolved into a rather more simplistic position than Niebuhr's, having become identified with the rejection of any place for moral values in the sphere of practical politics and the insistence that political decision-making should instead be based on interests alone. This is a conception that traces to neither Niebuhr nor Morgenthau but to Robert Osgood's *Ideals and Self-Interest in America's Foreign Relations* (1953).[9] From this latter perspective, what is wrong with just war reasoning is that it injects value considerations into policy and practical decisions about the use of military force by states and nonstate groups, and attempts to set limits on the use of such force even at the expense of national interests. This conception of realism is problematic on its own terms, as the interests of a state or nonstate group inherently reflect that entity's defining values; the interests would be worth nothing if they did not. More precisely, then, the realist criticism of just war thinking should be understood as proceeding from a clash of values between those expressed in the realist conception of national interest and those expressed in the just war idea. Understood this way, the criticism deserves attention, though it is hardly devastating to the just war idea.

The nature and effects of pacifist criticism of just war thinking are more complex and harder to evaluate. To think about pacifism more precisely, there are two main kinds that can be identified: one rooted in the moral rejection of all use of violence and another rooted in an abhorrence of the destructiveness of war, an association of war with the system of rival states, and the ideal of abolishing war by bringing into being a universal government replacing the state system.[10] Each has taken a variety of historical forms, and in some circumstances they have made common cause. Pacifist criticism of just war thinking has varied accordingly. Historically, pacifism of the first sort has produced sectarian movements advocating withdrawal from society, but this is not how contemporary pacifists have operated. Rather—as we can see, for example, from the activities of the Peace Churches—they have sought to establish mechanisms for resolution of conflicts and reconciliation, both of which can be viewed as challenges to the just war-based idea that at least some conflicts require the use of force to resolve and correct injustices. A second example is that of the Pax Christi movement in American Catholicism, to whose influence the signature idea in the 1983 U.S. Catholic bishops' pastoral letter on war and peace, *The Challenge of Peace*, can be traced: the notion that Catholic just war thinking always begins with a "presumption against war" as something inherently sinful and to be avoided.[11] This is a pacifist idea; just war tradition in fact treated the use of armed force under the conditions of just war as serving a moral good by combating threats to justice, good order, and peace. As for world-order pacifism, historically this was manifested in support for the League of Nations and the United Nations, and in general it shows up in opposition to any use of force that might serve national interests. Another example is provided by David Rodin's argument (discussed below), whereby the idea of just war can be realized only in the case of a universal government that uses force to police injustice.

In my judgment, pacifist criticism has been more effective than that of political realism, in that it has pressed the idea of just war to be more in line with pacifist ideals, and has thus undermined and displaced the core conceptions of the just war idea. This shows up in various ways in contemporary just war thinking—not only in the cases just mentioned, but in others as well. Compared to criticism from these two main enemies of the just war tradition, political realism and pacifism, though, the nature of much contemporary just war thinking poses a more serious threat to the tradition. Contemporary treatments of just war offer diverse accounts of its core values, structure, and purpose; the methodology for its understanding and use; and its relationship to political and moral life. Which one is to be believed? What lessons are to be learned for thinking about morality and the use of armed force? The answers offered are controverted, sometimes mutually contradictory, and sometimes at odds with the conception of just war as defined in the historical tradition, thus weakening the idea of just war even as it has become more widely discussed.

THE RECOVERY (AND REINVENTION) OF THE JUST WAR IDEA

From the early 1600s until the appearance of the Protestant theologian Paul Ramsey's two books *War and the Christian Conscience: How Shall Modern War Be Conducted Justly?* (1961) and *The Just War: Force and Political Responsibility* (1968), there was no serious book-length study that attempted to establish the just war idea as a proper center for either religious or secular reflection on morality and war.[12] Ramsey's method was that of a theologian, but the story is similar for political philosophy, where intellectual reflection on war had turned to world-order pacifist efforts to abolish war through the creation of some form of world order superior to the state system. In this way of thinking, the idea of war as a use of force that individual political communities might use to serve the proper purposes of political order was denied. This intellectual trend toward a form of pacifism was reinforced by the growing destructiveness of war as experienced and anticipated during the nineteenth and much of the twentieth centuries. Not until Michael Walzer characterized his purpose in *Just and Unjust Wars* (1977) with the words "I want to recapture the just war for political and moral theory"[13] did the possibility of using the just war idea in serious political philosophical thought emerge. Ramsey's and Walzer's respective works constitute two of three pillars of the recovery of the just war idea in contemporary moral thought about war; the third is the U.S. Catholic bishops' *The Challenge of Peace*, which, besides its influence in Catholic circles, spurred a public policy debate in the United States and parts of Western Europe that has been ongoing.

None of these three pillars built their understandings of just war on the earlier just war tradition, though the traditional conception had existed in a remarkably coherent and consistent form from the high Middle Ages until early in the modern period. That traditional conception, as noted earlier, had placed the justification of the use of armed force in the context of the responsibility of the sovereign ruler to ensure the good of the governed political community. A series of thinkers working within the inherited tradition of just war, culminating in Grotius, reshaped this original conception so as to emphasize the right of individual self-defense as the most fundamental element of natural law and defined government as the agent of a civil community that is responsible for its general defense against aggression. This idea stuck and became the bedrock of the developing conception of the law of nations and international order. It is, of course, central in the present-day conception of the state's right to resort to armed force in self-defense.

Ramsey, Walzer, and the U.S. Catholic bishops offered three different conceptions of just war to respond to their perception of the issues at the time they wrote; and these three approaches produced conceptions of just war that not only did not connect to the earlier normative tradition but also presaged the subsequent thinking about just war.

For Ramsey, the issues to be addressed had to do principally with the nuclear debates of the 1950s and 1960s; for Walzer, the Vietnam War; and for the Catholic bishops, the nuclear debates of the early 1980s and the nuclear strategy of the Reagan administration. Ramsey's main normative source, typical of American Protestant Christian ethicists of his generation and before, was the Christian ethic of love for neighbor, which Ramsey understood especially as manifested in Augustine's conception of the idea of *caritas* in the historical movement from the City of Earth to the City of God. He used this reading of the ethic of love to set out a position that differed from the two poles of mainstream

American Protestant Christian thinking about war at the time that he wrote, which were the Niebuhrian characterization of war as sometimes necessary but always tragic and sinful, and forms of pacifism based in the ideal of a new world order and the moral rejection of war. Ramsey argued that the Christian obligation of love of neighbor both justifies the use of armed force—to protect the neighbor against unjust attack—and limits it, because one may never rightly attack anyone not involved in the use of armed force against one's neighbor.[14]

Walzer, for his part, built his conception of just war principally on a normative base in human rights, though he developed his exposition via a creative use of historical examples aimed at showing a common understanding of just and unjust uses of force.[15] The positive content of international law relating to war, which he calls "the legalist paradigm,"[16] looms large in Walzer's presentation of the just war idea, especially in regard to certain issues—and in particular those he develops under the rubric "the theory of aggression." And it is fair to say that he seems to regard this paradigm as providing a kind of baseline, moral as well as legal, to which just war reasoning must refer.

As for the U.S. Catholic bishops, while *The Challenge of Peace* argued that the conception of just war defined therein came out of the Catholic just war tradition, in fact it restated a conception of just war based on a philosophical conception of an ethic of *prima facie* duties as earlier described by James F. Childress, a religious ethicist of Quaker background, in the Jesuit journal *Theological Studies*.[17] On this conception the idea of just war was made to begin with a "presumption against war," with the various just war criteria functioning not positively, to provide guidance as to when the use of force might be a moral obligation, but negatively, to define those rare cases in which the "presumption against war" might be overturned.[18] Here the primary criterion for such a possibility was that the use of force be in self-defense against attack—a conception directly reflecting international law but not historical just war tradition. This was further restricted by limits on the authority to resort to armed force and a requirement that, even in the face of manifest injustice, there must be a comparative preponderance of justice on one's own side. The shadow of modern-war pacifism (a version of pacifism rooted in world-order pacifism and one that was likewise committed to the abolition of war), and particularly of nuclear pacifism (where opposition to war stemmed from the magnitude of destruction to be expected from the use of nuclear weapons), lay over both Ramsey's and the Catholic bishops' work. While Ramsey expressly offered his understanding of just war in opposition to widespread Christian pacifism, the Catholic bishops, in embracing the "presumption against war," effectively accepted a basic pacifist premise about the inherent evil of war as such.

THE SUBSEQUENT DEBATE: JUST WAR REINVENTED AGAIN AND AGAIN

Against this background, the stage was well set for a proliferation of conceptions of just war, and that is in fact what we find in recent just war literature. I have nearly forty books on my shelves (more, if collections of essays are counted) that treat the topic of just war, including Ramsey's, Walzer's, and those of the U.S. Catholic bishops, in addition to my own work—and this is by no means a complete list of what has been published on the subject in recent decades. In the books I own, most of the authors treat just war as a positive resource for moral assessment of the use of armed force, though some treat it critically and dismissively. Yet each one understands and represents the idea of just war somewhat differently, depending on the moral perspective and method of the author; how just war is defined and its components; its purpose and proper use; the relative emphasis given to the decision to use armed force (*jus ad bellum*) and conduct in the use of such force (*jus in bello*); the moral criteria named, the order in which they are named, and the priorities among them; and the contemporary implications drawn from individual criteria and from the overall conception of just war. These differences may be taken, from one perspective, as signs of a healthy moral debate, but from another perspective they reveal a serious lack of common agreement as to exactly what "just war" means in itself and what it implies for moral reflection on the use of armed force in the contemporary context. Some examples will illustrate this.

Sometimes the difference is over what counts as defining the idea of just war itself: to take a sample from my shelf, recent books by Alex Bellamy, Davis Brown, J. Daryl Charles, Robert L. Phillips, Mark Totten, Albert L. Weeks, and Craig M. White all define just war in terms of a list of criteria for the decision to go to war (*jus ad bellum*) and for conduct during war (*jus in bello*).[19] The listings of Brown and Totten are essentially the same as what I would myself give, beginning with the classic criteria of sovereign authority, just cause, and right intention, including the end [aim] of peace; then adding the prudential criteria widely applied today—reasonable hope of success, proportionality of ends, and lack of reasonable alternatives (last resort); and finally defining right conduct in war in terms of discrimination and proportionality of means. White offers a list with the same headings. All the others named, though, shift the order and priority of the criteria or combine some of them or simply do not mention certain criteria: for example, Charles and Weeks begin with just cause; Phillips starts with last resort; Bellamy begins with right intention. Where they begin telegraphs the position of these authors on what is more important or most fundamental. Several authors do not mention the end of peace (a fault also of the U.S. Catholic bishops' listing of just war criteria), perhaps reflecting the widespread contemporary view that war and peace are mutually exclusive. All include right authority as a requirement for a just war, though differing somewhat as to its priority. With the exception of White and Weeks, all define war-conduct in terms of the two moral criteria of discrimination and proportionality, which has become commonplace in contemporary moral writing on just war. (The tradition had instead proceeded by concrete lists of categories of persons not to be the object of direct intended attack and by lists of means of war deemed *mala in se*; the law of armed conflict follows this approach, which benefits from its concreteness.) White's book is focused only on the rightness of the war decision in the case of the 2003 invasion of Iraq and does not discuss war conduct, while Weeks's discussion of conduct in war is based not on moral argument but on the extent it complies with the law of armed conflict.

Do these differences matter? Yes, indeed. According to the historical tradition, which among these authors Totten renders best, the requirement of sovereign authority holds first priority, since the sovereign, as the one ultimately responsible for the common good of the political community, has the responsibility for dealing with wrongdoing in such a way (including the possible use of armed force) as to maintain the justice and peace of that community. On this conception, the use of armed force is just only if the one responsible for the good of the political community uses it to serve that good: this is the classic conception of *bellum iustum*. But as I have noted earlier, during the early modern period the focus shifted to one particular kind of injustice—armed aggression across a state's border—and the role of the ruler was redefined as the agent of the political community. As the moral tradition of just war was reshaped into international law, just cause, defined narrowly as self-defense against attack, became the primary criterion for the right to use armed force, and the authority criterion became "proper" or "legitimate" authority, referring to whatever person or body in a given community was charged with organizing a response to such aggression. In this way the broader concerns of justice were effectively bracketed out of consideration, and peace was understood simply as the status quo before an aggressive attack was launched or as the state of affairs between states not at war. As the nature of war itself became increasingly totalistic and more destructive, the growth of various forms of opposition to war hardened the perceived divide between war and peace, so that they were conceived as opposites: here the idea of a just war as a way to peace became an oxymoron, whereas in classic just war thinking the just use of force was conceived as a necessary tool in the service of peace.

The effects of such influences appear in the shifts in content and priorities within the various lists of the criteria used to define the just war idea by contemporary authors, including those I have singled out above.

But these authors also disagree on how just war thinking should be used and to what purpose. For example, Charles and Phillips are mostly concerned with influencing the moral judgment of individuals relative to particular possible uses of armed force, while White and Weeks employ their versions of the just war criteria in a checklist fashion to demonstrate the wrongness of the decision to invade Iraq in 2003. Others, including the philosopher Jeff McMahan, have used utilitarian reasoning to define the *jus in bello* criteria so that it is all but impossible to satisfy them, and thus almost no use of force can be just. In contrast, Jean Bethke Elshtain defines her version of the just war idea within a broad discourse on politics based heavily on an interpretation of Augustine's moral and political thought to argue for the justified use of armed force to respond to serious injustice, aiming specifically at justifying the war against terrorism.

A closer look at Elshtain and McMahan as well as two other contemporary philosophers will illustrate how the perspective and ethical methodology employed in recent just war thinking vary widely, as well as how they differ from the historical just war tradition. First, let us consider Elshtain, whose moral perspective and method are broadly reminiscent of Ramsey's.[20] Elshtain anchors her understanding of just war in an interpretation of Augustine's moral and political thought, focused notably on *The City of God.* What matters for her are certain ideas—chiefly, justice, peace, and love—as defining the morality of the use of armed force. Armed attack is a major violation of justice and peace, thus justifying an armed response; but other violations, including uses of armed forces to repress segments of a state's own population, may also, for her, justify the use of force. Similarly, love of neighbor may justify resort to armed force when a neighbor is threatened or harmed out of malice. The classic conception of just war defined in the historical tradition, by contrast, also used Augustine as a major source, but worked from a very different set of passages, first collected by the twelfth-century canonist Gratian. These passages provided the basis for Aquinas's discussion of just war a bit more than a century later, and the conception of just war defined there was still normative for Martin Luther early in the sixteenth century. The emphasis in the historical tradition on sovereign authority (understood as responsibility for the good of the political community) derives from this set of passages; so do the definitions of just cause (in terms of reparative and punitive justice but not self-defense) and right intention (including the end of peace, but also including avoidance of malicious intentions). All in all, this is a somewhat different conception of just war, and a significantly different use of Augustine in relation to it, from that found in Elshtain (or, for that matter, Ramsey). But this historical tradition as it came together after Augustine's time does not interest her, as it did not interest Ramsey; she believes Augustine offers the core, and her method is to reach back over the intervening history to what she considers relevant from his works. By contrast, other recent writers, including Bellamy and Totten, make a point of examining how the moral ideas have been shaped by history; their conception of the nature, purpose, and proper use of the just war idea varies from Elshtain's accordingly.

McMahan, like contemporary philosophers in general who have written on just war, treats Walzer's conception of just war as the contemporary standard, though he does so in part to criticize major elements of it. But he also shows some awareness of the historical tradition on just war and regards it as superior in important ways. In his 2005 article "Just Cause for War," published in this journal, he begins by observing that "until quite recently, contemporary just war theory and international law recognized only one cause for war: self- or other-defense against aggression."[21] This characterization, of course, fits Walzer's treatment of the question of justification for resort to war under the rubric of "aggression" and his use of international law as defining "the legalist paradigm." McMahan argues, to the contrary, that "there can be various just causes for war other than defense against aggression, that both sides in a war can have just cause, and so on," and that this conception of just cause "has roots in an older tradition of thought." Later in the article he cites Aquinas and several early modern thinkers (including Grotius, Vattel, Vitoria, Suarez, and Pufendorf) as representatives of the "older tradition" he has in mind. While he engages these historical thinkers as partners in dialogue, McMahan does not seek to develop the positions of any of them in detail, but rather uses what they said on specific issues in which he is interested to provide a springboard for his own thought. In this connection, it is interesting that he does not note the irony that the reduction of just cause for use of force to defense against attack traces to Grotius and was advanced by Vattel and Pufendorf, later thinkers on the law of nations.

In his 2009 book, *Killing in War*, McMahan parts ways significantly with both the "older tradition" and with Walzer, arguing that the justifications for killing during war are no different from what they are in other contexts, including individual self-defense.[22] Here he returns to certain themes treated in the 2005 article, including the question of whether both sides in a war can be fighting justly (the phenomenon I have called "simultaneous ostensible justice," first suggested by Vitoria and later taken up by Grotius). Historically, this referred to the complexity of justifications for many, perhaps most, armed conflicts, and the possibility that both sides might, as far as even an objective observer could tell, have right on their side. From it derived the idea that Walzer later called "the moral equality of soldiers and the development of rules for conduct in war (the laws of armed conflict) that began with the assumption of such equality. In short, this line of thinking, which began with reflection on the moral complexity of war, shifted away from emphasizing the justification of resort to war to emphasizing efforts to mitigate harm done during war. McMahan, relying on the tools of analytic philosophy, places the stress back on the problem of justification, rejecting the idea of simultaneous ostensible justice, so that the cause of belligerents has to be either just or unjust (or neither). Soldiers, then, are not morally equal, since their liability to be attacked varies according to the cause in which they are fighting. Of course, McMahan provides a far more nuanced analysis of this matter than this summary characterization conveys. But we can nonetheless see from this brief look at his argument that it is in considerable tension with the historical tradition. However, the point I want to make is a deeper one: that, as I have argued extensively in my own work, the historical just war tradition reflects a complex mixture of influences, and the idea of just war developed there is not at all well rendered by a discrete methodology like that of analytic philosophy. Indeed, there is some irony in that to the degree the use of such a discrete methodology succeeds on its own terms, it distances itself from the broader idea of just war as defined in the historical tradition and the complex realities that produced it and that it seeks to engage.

The conceptions of just war—its sources, what is important in it, and what it should be understood to imply—are so different between Elshtain and McMahan as to suggest that they are not in fact talking about the same thing at all. Still other lines of variation appear when other recent philosophical writing on just war is brought into focus. Three general observations will help to set this work in context. First, philosophical attention to the just war idea is relatively recent, with the most important work appearing only within the last decade or a bit earlier. Second, in accord with what I observed at the beginning of this article, this writing on just war has come from philosophers in English-speaking countries. And third, the philosophical work as a whole rests heavily on the conception of just war put forward by Michael Walzer in *Just and Unjust Wars*, though different scholars have used Walzer in different ways (frequently, as we have just seen in McMahan, to criticize and correct some element in his thinking, meanwhile accepting his overall treatment of just war as normative). As further examples of recent philosophical thought on just war, I will look briefly at two other philosophers recognized as having written importantly on this subject: David Rodin and Brian Orend.

Rodin's work dealing with just war includes articles and edited books as well as a major authored book, *War and Self-Defense*, published in 2002.[23] Like Walzer, he begins from a base in human rights; also like Walzer, he regards the question of self-defense as critical for the justification of the use of armed force. But unlike Walzer, who generally follows contemporary international law in its limiting a state's right to resort to force in self-defense, Rodin takes a different approach. Rodin begins with the assumption that the requirement that a state may use force only in defense is based on an analogy with the individual's right to self-defense when attacked. Then, after close examination, he argues that this analogy does not hold up, so the requirement of *jus ad bellum* is not satisfied. But if this is so, he concludes, then soldiers are not justified in fighting. As an alternative to this conception of just war, which Rodin argues is morally wrong, he sketches a normative understanding that depends on the creation of a universal state with "a world monopoly of military force together with a minimal judicial mechanism for the resolution of international and internal disputes."[24] Only such a state would be justified in resorting to the use of military means to enforce international law.

Rodin's conclusion, if not his analysis, turns out to share important features with the conception of just war in the historical tradition, though he makes no effort to examine the possible connections (and there are also important differences). In the historical tradition the idea of just war does not rest on self-defense, but rather is described as repairing injustice and punishing wrongdoing. But the reason self-defense is not included among the named just causes in the traditional conception of just war is that, while it assumes that everyone possesses by nature the right of self-defense against attack, just war was about something else: that is, action to set things right after such an attack and to seek to prevent future wrongdoing. As with Rodin's view, the historical conception of just war made a strong distinction between public and private use of force, but unlike Rodin it located the right of public use of force in reparative and punitive action—arguing that the right of self-defense held by private individuals does not extend that far, and describing the justification of use of force for these purposes as rooted in the responsibility of government for the common good of the community. The requirement of sovereign authority, which held first priority in the historical tradition, had this priority precisely because sovereignty was understood to include responsibility for the good of the community as a whole. This seems essentially what Rodin wants to claim about his universal state. But of course no universal state exists; rather, there are multiple independent states. On Rodin's analysis, these may not wage just war; only the universal state may do so. Rodin does not take up the matter central to the traditional conception of just war: the responsibility of government in each state for the common good and for maintaining relations among independent states to the same end. In contrast, Rodin provides a contemporary example of the way others before him used the just war idea to reason to world-order pacifism, in which "war" (understood as conflicts between and among states) is abolished and all use of force has the character of policing. One wonders whether, in the world as it is, the historical model, with its stress on the responsibility of individual governing authorities to uphold justice and punish injustice, does not offer a path to more serious engagement with the realities of contemporary armed conflict.

The third contemporary philosopher I want to single out is Brian Orend. (A good summary of his understanding of the ethics of war appears in the *Stanford Encyclopedia of Philosophy*, available online at plato.stanford.edu/entries/war.) He has written two books explicitly on the ethics of war: one on Walzer's understanding of war and justice, and one on human rights. He is a Kantian, and as such he frames the subject of his work *The Morality of War* (2006) in terms of current international law and just war theory defined as "a set of moral rules which societies should follow during the beginning, middle, and end of war."[25] Such a framing may lead the reader to expect a narrowly legalistic discussion, a form of the "checklist" use of just war categories I faulted earlier. But Orend does not fall into this trap, producing a discussion that is more careful and nuanced. He begins with a survey of the historical evolution of just war thinking and then explores its application in the context of a wide range of recent major military conflicts and the ongoing effort to deal with terrorism. Yet there is still the matter of thinking of this whole moral enterprise in terms of rules to be used as a checklist, as opposed to the classical just war concern of moral wisdom.

Orend's historical survey of the development of just war thinking is much too brief and, frankly, unfocused to explain how and why the normative categories defining just war—as he understands the process—came into being and developed as they did. His aim seems to be to show that the rules in which he is interested are grounded in a deep historical moral consciousness. As a result, he traces the origins of just war thinking back through Augustine to Cicero and Aristotle, but then moves rapidly to the early modern period, largely skipping over the medieval thinkers who actually gave the idea of just war coherent form. This gets the priorities all wrong: there may have been an idea of just war in Aristotle, but there was no systematic just war theory in him or in Cicero or, for that matter, in Augustine. And when modern thinkers such as Vitoria and Grotius came along (both rightly highlighted by Orend for their contributions), the conception of just war they received and worked with was one deeply shaped by the historical context in which it had taken its normative shape. Thus, the work of the medieval thinkers needs to be looked at closely. The changed historical context of the sixteenth and seventeenth centuries was a major reason why both Vitoria and Grotius (along with others who wrote on war and morality during this period) added new ideas, reconceived others, and generally contributed to the reshaping of the just war concept. Orend's method presents the outcomes (the rules defining just war as he understands them), but it does not investigate or explain how and why they came to be.

The work of each of the contemporary philosophers I have briefly commented on here has merit in its own frame, yet in each case the frame is limited, and the resulting conceptions of just war and their implications turn out to be different from one another and from the idea of just war as found in the historical tradition. In the end, these contemporary philosophical examples are three more cases of reinventions of the idea of just war.

RECOVERING THE JUST WAR IDEA (FOR REAL)

As the above discussion shows, I regard contemporary just war thinking as plagued by a number of problems. The late John Howard Yoder, a Mennonite pacifist, once privately complained to me that he found efforts to debate with just war thinkers frustrating, because it seemed to him that everyone seemed to have a different idea of just war. I am not entirely sure what to make of Yoder's complaint, since he was the author of a book that identified numerous distinct varieties of religious pacifism, finding problems with most of them.[26] (How should a just war thinker, then, debate with a religious pacifist?) Nor am I prepared to say that the situation in just war thinking is quite as bad as Yoder represented it; I think there is at least a family resemblance present amid all the diversity of different accounts. Nor is diversity itself a bad thing: it provides openings for new ideas and new developments of old ones. This is why, when speaking of just war, it is better to describe it as a tradition of thought rather than as a theory. There have been many particular just war theories, but insofar as they hang together with sufficient commonalty, they all belong to just war tradition. At the same time, though, a tradition needs sufficient commonalty, a coherence of basic conceptions and agreements as to meaning and purpose. In this, a moral tradition like that of just war is like language: speakers may differ broadly as to vocabulary, pronunciation, syntax, intonation, and all the other features that make it possible to speak, say, of British English and American English while recognizing both as English. Yet at some point a local version of a language may become so different, so unintelligible to persons from different localities that it has to be recognized as a different language, as in the evolution of distinct Romance languages from a common Latin source. I suggest the same is the case with just war tradition: at some point a new direction in just war thinking needs to be recognized as no longer a form of just war thinking but as something else. Take the case of the international law on armed conflicts. As I have frequently argued (including in the discussion above), this historically developed out of the earlier just war tradition and, during most of the modern period, carried major elements of that tradition, even while recasting them in the form of law rather than that of moral discourse, refocusing them, and to some degree truncating them.

But the widespread contemporary way of thinking of this law as the positivistic product of international agreements intentionally cuts the relationship to the moral tradition: the law thus conceived is simply whatever is possible for nations to agree upon. This is not a new version of the just war tradition any longer; it is a new way of thinking entirely, a new "language."

In the case of contemporary moral discussion about just war, the danger of something like this happening—that the common features among the various discussions are submerged by the differences—is twofold. One is the separation of just war discourse among different academic or professional contexts and disciplines. This already happened in the definition of just war in different ways during the efforts to recover the just war idea in the period from the 1960s through the 1980s. The modes of discourse of Ramsey and Walzer, for example, had little in common, and this continues to be the case for their successors. The case of the U.S. Catholic bishops illustrates a further kind of danger for just war reasoning: that of reconceiving the idea of just war itself in an effort to find reconciliation with pacifist critics.

As I have made clear, contemporary just war thought would benefit from giving more attention to the historical tradition. Having the historical tradition in mind as a point of reference would have a welcome disciplining effect, frequently lacking in contemporary understandings of just war, helping to ensure that everyone who claims to be arguing from a position in just war reasoning is, at least on major matters, speaking a common language. This would also tend to insulate contemporary just war thinking from being defined as something different: anti-war pacifism, as in the case of the U.S. Catholic bishops; world-order pacifism, as in the case of Rodin; or an uncritical acceptance of the content of positive international law as providing the moral parameters for judging the morality of the use of armed force. And it would remind friends and critics of just war alike that there is a core substance to the idea of just war, so that just war is not whatever one wants to say it is for his or her own particular purposes.

The classic conception of just war was focused on the problems of good government, not on individual morality. It developed within a set of assumptions about such government expressed as the three ends of politics: order, justice, and peace, with justice understood by reference to historical precedents, context, and natural law, and peace defined as what Augustine had called the "tranquility" of an order ruled by the doing of justice. The three ends of politics were conceived as interrelated and mutually dependent, though the good of order had a lexical priority as necessary to ensure the other two. The requisites for a just war, or more precisely a justified use of armed force in the service of these ends, corresponded directly to them: the necessary authority to the end of order, the requirement of just cause to the end of justice, the requirement of right intention to the end of peace. As noted, this conception of just war gave first priority to restricting the authority for just war to sovereign rulers (rulers with no temporal superiors), because only persons in such positions had final responsibility for the common good of the community. It defined just cause for resort to armed force in terms not of self-defense against attack (assumed to be a right possessed by everyone in the moment of an attack), but rather in terms of repairing wrongs done and punishing wrongdoing. And it defined the purpose of such resort to force both in terms of the avoidance of wrongdoing itself and in terms of the end of restoring or establishing peace. All this is summarized by Aquinas, but these basic terms, and this overall understanding, reflected both the specific work of the century of canonical thought before him and, more broadly, the influence of secular law and military and political practice on which the canonists drew. This conception, moreover, remained essentially intact for the next three and a half centuries. For the canonists and Aquinas, the matter of conduct in just war was understood to be regulated by the requirement of right intention, but the canon law already by their time included a definition of noncombatancy in the form of lists of classes of persons normally not to be attacked in person or property during war and a listing of means of war not to be used. In the period of the

Hundred Years' War this was added to by drawing from the chivalric code or *loi d'armes*, which rendered in Latin became *jus in bello*, a term subsequently used for the whole part of just war tradition defining right conduct during war.

The world in which this classic conception of just war came together and endured was, of course, very different from our own. Yet the moral values expressed in this conception, while revealed in that historical context, are not limited to it. Taking this conception of just war seriously implies, first, that the use of armed force be understood in the larger frame of a theory of good politics. If we do not agree on such a theory, then the need to find a coherent frame for talking about the use of armed force should spur efforts to find one. These concerns bear serious implications for how sovereign responsibility, justice, and peace should be thought of, both within individual political communities and in the relations between and among such communities in the world as a whole. That is, reflection on the idea of just war is not simply about the uses and limits of use of armed force, and present-day conceptions of just war that cast it in this mold are mistaking what just war is about: it is about the entire frame of life in a political community, which just war exists to serve. Second, taking the classic conception of just war seriously puts the focus on this service itself, that is, on the moral goods the justified use of armed force seeks to secure. This is very different from a conception of just war principally understood as defining limits on the use of armed force, which is itself thought of as morally tainted—a focus all too frequent in recent just war thinking. Third, taking the classic conception of just war seriously implies that present-day just war thinking should not so easily define the terms of just war as identical to those of individual morality regarding the use of armed force. These are different realms for the classic just war idea. The responsibilities of government and of private individuals are different; their rights, accordingly, are different, and their moral imperatives are different. And, fourth, though not by any means least, reflection on the classic idea of just war as a conception formed so as to reflect wisdom garnered from various spheres of life and thought—including theology and philosophy, church and secular law, professional military life, and the practice of government—should push any contemporary just war thinker toward probing for interaction and dialogue across the normally differentiated spheres of contemporary life. I have sought to do this in my own work, and the best of contemporary just war thought does so as well. These examples show that there is no single right way to do it, but there are great differences in the degree to which such dialogue is pursued and in the end that is sought.

Finally, I want to demur once more from the idea found in much recent just war thinking that one should think of just war in terms of rules that can be applied to any and every use of armed force to tell us whether that use was just or not. Frequently this conception is underscored by the insistence that every one of the criteria must be satisfied for the use of armed force to be just, a requirement that, if taken seriously, would make unjust wars of the American Revolution, the Civil War, and American involvement in World War II. I do not deny that there may be some exceptionless moral rules regarding the use of armed force, but the problem is knowing what these are and what they imply in any given case. *That* requires moral judgment, and once one is in the sphere of moral judgment, the clarity offered by the idea of an exceptionless rule quickly becomes lost. Moreover, not all the criteria generally recognized today as part of the just war idea have the same character or the same priority. As traditionally understood, the ethics of just war is a practical art, not a science; the responsible party makes a decision, following the guidelines laid out but also attempting to discharge the responsibility given him or her to pursue justice and peace and thus serve the common good. This is a conception that corresponds to the Greek notion of ethics as having to do with *arête*, excellence achieved through practice (which includes the possibility of making mistakes and learning from them). Rules are important for this *praxis*, but they do not themselves yield the right and the wrong.

NOTES

1. The conception of just war here was substantially defined by the canonist Gratian in his *Decretum* and the work of his two generations of successors, the Decretists and the Decretalists, and summarized and placed in a theological framework by Thomas Aquinas. This conception reflected and incorporated the influence of Western churchly thought; the recovery and development of Roman law, including the ideas of natural law and *jus gentium*; and the practical experience of government and warfare. The classical conception of politics as directed toward the common good defined by three goods or ends (order, justice, and peace) was directly reflected in the major requirements of *bellum justum*, just war: the good of order in the requirement that such uses of force be authorized by a temporal ruler with no temporal superior, the good of justice in the requirement that such uses of force be for regaining that which had been wrongly taken and punishing evildoing (not self-defense against attack, which was taken to be guaranteed to all individuals and communities directly by natural law), and the good of peace in the requirement that all just uses of force aim at reestablishing and protecting peace as the result of a just order within the political community. In these just war requirements, sovereign authority was given priority because of the sovereign ruler's personal responsibility, given in the natural law, to maintain order, justice, and peace; the ability to initiate the use of armed force followed from this responsibility. The conception thus defined endured well into the modern period and was only finally reshaped into an importantly different idea in the mid-seventeenth century. For detailed examinations of this historical development, see my early books, *Ideology, Reason, and the Limitation of War* (Princeton, N.J.: Princeton University Press, 1975) and *Just War Tradition and the Restraint of War* (Princeton, N.J.: Princeton University Press, 1981). For more recent summary treatments of the framing of the idea of just war in this historical tradition, see my *Morality and Contemporary Warfare* (New Haven, Conn.: Yale University Press, 1999), pp. 44–51; and *Ethics and the Use of Force* (Farnham, U.K.: Ashgate Publishing, 2011), pp. 16–20 .
2. For a detailed discussion of this transition, see my *Ideology* and *Just War Tradition*, cited above; for more recent summary discussion, see my *Morality and Contemporary Warfare*, pp. 51–57.
3. Of the many translations and edited publications of this work, I prefer Hugo Grotius, *De Jure ac Pacis Libri Tres*, vol. II, in James Brown Scott, ed., *Classics of International Law* (Oxford: Clarendon Press, 1925).
4. Johnson, *Ethics and the Use of Force*, pp. 75–100.
5. Carnegie Institution of Washington, *Classics of International Law* (Oxford: Clarendon Press, 1911-ongoing).

6. Reinhold Niebuhr, *The Nature and Destiny of Man* (New York: Charles Scribner's Sons, 1964), vol. II, p. 283.
7. For important excerpts, see Gregory Reichberg, Henrik Syse, and Endre Begby, eds., *The Ethics of War* (Malden, Mass.: Blackwell Publishing, 2006), pp. 357–59. The entire work is included in the Carnegie Institution series cited above.
8. Niebuhr later returned a bit more positively to the idea of just war in an article coauthored with the Episcopal bishop and theologian Angus Dun, which made use of several of the categories drawn from just war thinking (but without systematically engaging the historical tradition as a whole) to argue against a pacifist interpretation of the meaning of Christianity. Niebuhr never again returned to this argument in later writing. See Angus Dun and Reinhold Niebuhr, "God Wills Both Justice and Peace," *Christianity and Crisis* 10 (June 13, 1955), pp. 75–78.
9. Robert E. Osgood, *Ideals and Self-Interest in America's Foreign Relations* (Chicago: The University of Chicago Press, 1953).
10. The historical development of these two kinds of pacifism is examined in my *The Quest for Peace* (Princeton, N.J.: Princeton University Press, 1987).
11. National Conference of Catholic Bishops, *The Challenge of Peace* (Washington, D.C.: United States Catholic Conference, 1983), pp. iii, 22 and 26.
12. Paul Ramsey, *War and the Christian Conscience* (Durham, N.C.: Duke University Press, 1961); and Paul Ramsey, *The Just War* (New York: Charles Scribner's Sons, 1968).
13. Michael Walzer, *Just and Unjust Wars* (New York: Basic Books, 1977), p. xiv.
14. Ramsey makes this point numerous times, in various ways, but the most concise and focused statement of it is in *The Just War*, pp. 142–147.
15. Walzer, *Just and Unjust Wars*, p. xiv and elsewhere.
16. Ibid., pp. 61–62.
17. James F. Childress, "Just War Theories: The Bases, Interrelations, Priorities, and Functions of Their Criteria," *Theological Studies* 39, no. 3 (1978), pp. 427–45.
18. *The Challenge of Peace*, pp. 27–28, par. 83–84.
19. Alex Bellamy, *Just Wars: From Cicero to Iraq* (Cambridge: Polity Press, 2006); Davis Brown, *The Cross, the Sword, and the Eagle* (Lanham, Md.: Rowman & Littlefield Publishers, 2008); J. Daryl Charles, *Between Pacifism and Jihad* Downers Grove, Ill.: InterVarsity Press, 2005); Robert L. Phillips, *War and Justice* (Norman, Okla.: Oklahoma University Press, 1984); Mark Totten, *First Strike* (New Haven, Conn.: Yale University Press, 2010); Albert L. Weeks, *The Choice of War* (Santa Barbara, Calif.: Praeger Security International, 2010); and Craig M. White, *Iraq: The Moral Reckoning* (Lanham, Md.: Lexington Books, 2010).

20. Jean Bethke Elshtain, *Just War Against Terror* (New York: Basic Books, 2003).
21. Jeff McMahan, "Just Cause for War," *Ethics & International Affairs* 19, no. 3 (Fall 2005), pp. 1–21.
22. Jeff McMahan, *Killing in War* (Oxford: Oxford University Press, 2009).
23. David Rodin, *War and Self-Defense* (Oxford: Oxford University Press, 2003).
24. Ibid., p. 187.
25. Brian Orend, *The Morality of War* (Peterborough, ON: Broadview Press, 2006), p. 4.
26. John Howard Yoder, *Nevertheless: The Varieties and Shortcomings of Religious Pacifism* (Scottdale, Pa.: Herald Press, 1971).

BIBLIOGRAPHY

Bellamy, Alex. *Just Wars: From Cicero to Iraq*. Cambridge: Polity Press, 2006.

Brown, Davis. *The Cross, the Sword, and the Eagle*. Lanham, Md.: Rowman & Littlefield Publishers, 2008.

Carnegie Institution of Washington. *Classics of International Law*. Oxford: Clarendon Press, 1911-ongoing.

Charles, J. Daryl. *Between Pacifism and Jihad*. Downers Grove, Ill.: InterVarsity Press, 2005.

Childress, James F. "Just War Theories: The Bases, Interrelations, Priorities, and Functions of Their Criteria." *Theological Studies* 39, no. 3 (1978): 427–45.

Dun, Angus and Reinhold Niebuhr. "God Wills Both Justice and Peace." *Christianity and Crisis* 10 (June 13, 1955): 75–78.

Grotius, Hugo. *De Jure ac Pacis Libri*, vol. II. In *Classics of International Law*. Edited by James Brown Scott. Oxford: Clarendon Press, 1925.

Johnson, James Turner. *Ethics and the Use of Force*. Farnham, U.K.: Ashgate Publishing, 2011.

Johnson, James Turner. *Ideology, Reason, and the Limitation of War*. Princeton, NJ: Princeton University Press, 1975.

Johnson, James Turner. *Just War Tradition and the Restraint of War*. Princeton, NJ: Princeton University Press, 1981.

Johnson, James Turner. *Morality and Contemporary Warfare*. New Haven, Conn.: Yale University Press, 1999.

Johnson, James Turner. *The Quest for Peace*. Princeton, NJ: Princeton University Press, 1987.

National Conference of Catholic Bishops. *The Challenge of Peace*. Washington, D.C.: United States Catholic Conference, 1983.

Niebuhr, Reinhold. *The Nature and Destiny of Man*. New York: Charles Scribner's Sons, 1964.

Osgood, Robert E. *Ideals and Self-Interest in America's Foreign Relations*. Chicago: The University of Chicago Press, 1953.

Phillips, Robert L. *War and Justice*. Norman, Okla: Oklahoma University Press, 1984.

Ramsey, Paul. *The Just War*. New York: Charles Scribner's Sons, 1968.

Ramsey, Paul. *War and the Christian Conscience*. Durham, NC: Duke University Press, 1961.

Reichberg, Gregory, Henrik Syse, and Endre Begby, eds.. *The Ethics of War*. Malden, Mass.: Blackwell Publishing, 2006.

Totten, Mark. *First Strike*. New Haven, Conn.: Yale University Press, 2010.

Walzer, Michael. *Just and Unjust Wars*. New York: Basic Books, 1977.

Weeks, Albert L. *The Choice of War*. Santa Barbara, Calif.: Praeger Security International, 2010.

White, Craig M. *Iraq: The Moral Reckoning*. Lanham, Md.: Lexington Books, 2010.

ABSTRACT

Johnson explores international human rights law and the use of force through two different lenses: 1) the Westphalian concept of sovereignty; and 2) the "Responsibility to Protect" (R2P) doctrine for the protection of citizens' human rights from violations by their own state governments.

CHAPTER 19

RELIGION, VIOLENCE, AND HUMAN RIGHTS: PROTECTION OF HUMAN RIGHTS AS JUSTIFICATION FOR THE USE OF ARMED FORCE

The connections among human rights, religion, and the use of armed force are quite complex and always developing. So far as positions associated with American religious bodies are concerned, these three themes came together significantly during the 1990s, when, in the wake of the end of the Cold War, it became possible to think positively about the possibility of employing military force, without risking a third world war, to seek to stop major violations of human rights in the various local conflicts, fueled by ethnic, religious, and other cultural differences, that were proliferating around the globe. Let me note one prominent example that explicitly linked the justification of the use of military force to the protection of basic human rights: that of the United States Conference of Catholic Bishops in their 1993 statement *The Harvest of Justice Is Sown in Peace*, which devoted a significant discussion to humanitarian intervention, citing Pope John Paul II as "outspoken in urging that 'humanitarian intervention be obligatory where the survival of populations and entire ethnic groups is severely compromised'" and continuing by observing that the Pope judged this "a duty for nations and the international community." While the statement continued by cautioning that "nonmilitary forms of intervention should take priority over those requiring the use of force," it also allowed that "military intervention may sometimes be justified to ensure that starving children can be fed or that whole populations will not be slaughtered."[1] Major American Protestant bodies also supported such intervention during this period.

The development of international law was gradually moving toward a similar conclusion, though it should be noted that the idea of human rights has not always been central in this movement: for example, in the major documents in the development of positive international law on armed conflict, one does not find "human rights" as a category.[2] Though these documents have defined and progressively expanded the protections to be given to various classes of people, from persons wounded in combat and their caregivers to prisoners of war to civilians as a general category, the most general rationale for the developing law is typified by the reference to "the interests of humanity and the ever progressive needs of civilization" in the Preamble to the 1907 Hague Convention IV, and the latest formal positive-law addition to the law of armed conflict, the 1977 Protocols to the 1949 Geneva Conventions, makes the protections provided simply a matter of agreement by the signatories to the terms of the rules themselves.[3]

But while the law of armed conflict was developing along its particular trajectory, international human rights law was coming into being and developing along a separate route, beginning with the Universal Declaration of Human Rights and the Genocide Convention (both from 1948) and growing to include two Covenants adopted by the United Nations in 1966 (the International Covenant on Civil and Political Rights and the International Covenant on Economic, Social, and Cultural Rights, each with optional protocols; together with the Universal Declaration these make up the International Bill of Human Rights), as well as a number of other conventions, covenants, and protocols with various levels of authority treating additional particular rights-related issues, including racial discrimination, discrimination against women, the status of refugees, the rights of children, religious discrimination, the rights of migrants, the rights of indigenous peoples, and torture.[4] As a result of this line of development, human rights has become a major category in contemporary positive international law.

At the same time, there remain differences, some not insubstantial, among the various international statements as to the nature of the rights defined, their sources, the protections to be given them, and the sanctions, if any, to be imposed on violators. Some of these differences are rooted in culture, including religious belief and practice; some trace to particular political aims of the states and blocs of states in connection to particular agreements. Not all the rights identified in the various international legal instruments have the same priority. When one compares the protections explicitly given or implied in international human rights law to those in the international law on armed conflict, the latter are clearly more specific and focused as operational guides, though human rights law has increasingly come to be used to provide a broader frame and rationale for the particular protections and restraints set out in the law of armed conflict.[5]

The law of armed conflict has to do with what is allowable in the use of military force when it is underway, not with the decision to use such force in the first place. By the terms of the main line of thinking in positive international law, the fundamental justification for resort to armed force has been defined not as protection of human rights but as defense against armed attack across a state's territorial borders.[6] The language in the United Nations Charter explicitly prohibits the first use of force for the settlement of disputes among states, but this has customarily been understood as implying the principle of non-interference in the affairs of any state within its own borders. Sovereignty understood on this way of thinking thus is defined first and foremost in terms of the sanctity of territorial borders relative to other sovereign entities. Cross-border projections of force by other states, for whatever reason, are thus defined as aggression, justifying a reactive use of force in defense.

By contrast, from the high Middle Ages until this new conception took root in the so-called "Westphalian system," sovereignty was understood to have to do with the responsibility of government to protect and serve the common good of the people governed. This older conception disappeared with the redefinition of sovereignty in terms of territorial sanctity.

An unintended but quite real result of this evolution in international law has been to leave governments free to treat their own populations, or selected portions of those populations, any way they please. The Genocide Convention of 1948 was framed in specific reaction to one egregious example of systematic maltreatment of a particular group of people, that of the Nazis toward the Jews in Germany and the territories Germany held during World War II.[7] More broadly, the development of human rights law has aimed at prohibiting certain forms of maltreatment by defining particular rights that should be honored and not violated. Yet where such violations, even flagrant ones, might occur, the use of military force to stop them and seek to remedy them remained, according to the positive law, a breach of territorial sovereignty that could be construed as an "armed attack" against the state in question.

Such was the state of affairs during the wars of the breakup of Yugoslavia, during the Rwandan massacre of 1994, and during the other conflicts cited earlier. Such was the state of affairs when the United States Conference of Catholic Bishops wrote in 1993 that "military intervention may sometimes be justified to ensure that starving children can be fed or that whole populations will not be slaughtered." I doubt that the members of the Conference of Catholic Bishops or other American religious bodies adopting statements favoring the use of armed force for humanitarian purposes—that is to say, for the protection of basic human rights—during this period realized that they were advocating what, in terms of Article 51 of the United Nations Charter, might be construed as an "armed attack" on a sovereign state, against which that state had the right to defend itself by armed force.

I would pause here to emphasize two particular points: first, despite the growth of human rights law, by the time of the crises of the 1990s it was possible only to single out the most basic rights—the right to life and to food to sustain life—as possibly justifying the use of military force to protect them; and second, that such use of military force could be construed as illegal according to the language of the United Nations Charter.

The crises of the 1990s, though, also produced a reaction directly bearing on international law: that of the ad hoc International Commission on Intervention and State Sovereignty (ICISS), which in 2001 published its conclusions in the form of a report with the title *The Responsibility to Protect*.[8] This report began with a list of "principles for military intervention," organized as an interpretation of the categories of just war (but without mentioning the just war idea as such). First among these principles it cited "the just cause threshold," defined as existing under either of two circumstances:

> A. large scale loss of life, actual or apprehended, with genocidal intent or not, which is the product either of deliberate state action, or state neglect and inability to act, or a failed state situation; or
>
> B. large scale "ethnic cleansing," actual or apprehended, whether carried out by killing, forced expulsion, acts of terror or rape.[9]

The principles continued by specifying that the intention of such intervention "must be to halt or avert human suffering," that the intervention is justified only when every non-military option to resolving the crisis has been explored, that the intervention "should be the minimum necessary to secure the defined human protection objective," and that it must offer "a reasonable chance of success" in securing the justifying objective.[10]

The ideas put forward in *The Responsibility to Protect,* (R2P) have since been examined and analyzed in significant detail in numerous articles and in books by international lawyers and international relations specialists.[11] Though ICISS was neither a governmental body nor one operating under the agency of the United Nations, R2P (or "RtoP," as in the articles cited above), as its report quickly became known in shorthand, was subsequently adopted into United Nations usage, being affirmed unanimously at the 2005 World Summit conference and reaffirmed by Security Council resolutions, though exactly what it implies, authorizes, and requires remains to be debated and decided in the context of every crisis in which it is invoked. To understand the current status of the still ongoing debate over humanitarian intervention by military force, which also extends to the ethical implications of religious reflection on such possible uses of force, it is necessary to acknowledge the presence of R2P, even if in present status its meaning is more limited than in original form, still somewhat unclear in detail, and interpreted differently by different states as applying to their rights, responsibilities, and obligations in the international sphere, when faced with serious behavior of the sort identified with R2P's "just cause threshold." What is defined by R2P as to be protected reflects what is clearly considered a broad consensus as to fundamental rights possessed by all persons. In this sense R2P denies a tension between the development of human rights law and the prohibition of "armed attack" across a national border. Under the specific circumstances defined by R2P, military action to stop and seek to remedy the particular kinds of serious violations of rights named is not to be construed as constituting "armed attack," that is, military aggression that may be defended against.

The ICISS Report thus seeks to reconcile the Westphalian-system-based conception of sovereignty, with its included norm of non-intervention, with its own conception of sovereignty as responsibility by arguing that the latter is the result of each state's voluntarily joining the United Nations "as a responsible member of the community of nations."[12] The Report argues that this does not do away with the Westphalian norm "but is a way of saying that the more traditional notion of state sovereignty should be able to embrace the goal of greater self-empowerment and freedom for people, both individually and collectively."[13] The result is not a "transfer or dilution of state sovereignty" but rather "a necessary re-characterization."[14]

Well, perhaps. This "re-characterization" of state sovereignty is a noble statement of *lex ferenda* (what should be the law) but hardly an accurate description of the reality of the world as it is. States, whether well-governed or ruled by predators, have a real interest in being secure inside their own borders, and the core element in the Westphalian definition of sovereignty, namely the sanctity of territorial borders, establishes a powerful protection of that security. To speak of this simply as "the norm of non-intervention" refers only to one implication of that conception, namely the matter of how the government of a state actually rules. The ICISS Report seeks to find a way to justify abrogating the norm of non-intervention for specific sorts of cases of bad rule: when the ruling authorities engage in acts that directly produce "large scale loss of life," or "ethnic cleansing," or fail to prevent such acts by others, either by inaction or by inability to do so. But the justifying language employed by ICISS speaks of a more general shift in the relationship of state sovereignty to international order, and this may be a bridge too far in the framing of international law. Well-governed states have no real reason to delegate to the Security Council decisions about their actions that might provide a pretext for some loss of national security. In the case of the badly governed states that the ICISS Report aims specifically to target, the motivation is even less: why should the rulers of such states, whose own actions proceed from their effort to favor one portion of their population at the expense of others, or to absolutize their power over the whole society, or to accumulate personal riches at the expense of national welfare, regard UN membership as in any way opening the door to interference by other states in what they do? The result, after all, at the minimum may be the loss of some of their power and its benefits, and beyond this they and their close associates may be taken into custody and tried for violating international law.

The implications of this can be seen in the case of the only clearly R2P-related military intervention thus far: the Security Council's authorization to NATO to use force to protect civilians during the armed uprising against the Qaddafi government in Libya. The end of regime change was not part of the formal authorization, but the NATO air attacks developed rather quickly as *de facto* air support for the rebellion's aim of ousting Qaddafi and his regime. Indeed, how could the intervention have succeeded in its authorized aim without the end of removing the regime responsible for the intended harm of civilians? And how could the regime have allowed itself to change its behavior, since doing so would have left the rulers without authority and power at least, dead at worst, and subject to international war crimes proceedings if still alive? All the incentives for a predator regime are for it to resist intervention and seek by any means to stay in power; all the incentives for intervention point toward regime change. At this writing these same problems are being played out on a larger scale in Syria.

The ICISS Report specifically links its new (or "re-characterized") conception of sovereignty to the conception of human rights laid out in the 1948 Declaration and the 1966 Covenants on human rights. I want to say two things about this, the first rather summarily, and the second in somewhat more detail. The first point is one I have already made earlier: the conception of human rights offered here is by no means the comprehensive, seamless garment the ICISS Report represents it as being. Serious differences of perspective and understanding of purpose lay behind each of the agreements cited, as well as the other international statements on human rights that make up the whole body of international efforts to define human rights. Within the United Nations structure such differences tend to come out in the form of political differences within the UN Commission on Human Rights and in the Security Council. In these contexts consistent agreement and adherence to a common ideal is a chimera; decisions and actions in particular cases are ruled instead by political considerations. This provides a shaky foundation for weakening the rule of non-intervention in the internal affairs of states.

My second point has to do with whether the nature of rights language itself makes it the best base for restoring an idea of sovereignty as responsibility. To explore this concern I want to return us to the historical context out of which both the premodern idea of sovereignty as responsibility took shape as an element in the coalescence of the classic idea of just war, and the Western idea of human rights first appeared. That historical context was the canonical, juridical, and theological reflections of the late twelfth and early thirteenth centuries.

As to just war, though it has earlier roots, to pull together and shape a coherent conception of just war as a guide for moral behavior and statecraft was the accomplishment of canonical thinkers during the last half of the twelfth century and the first half of the thirteenth, beginning with the canonist Gratian's compendious work, the *Decretum*, and including the contributions of his two generations of canonical successors, the Decretists and the Decretalists. Aquinas's well-known discussion of just war in the *Summa Theologiae* summarizes the canonical conception developed over the previous century and places it in his own theological framework.[15]

This coalescence and definition of the idea of just war took place in an especially rich intellectual environment that included influence from Christian sources, the rediscovery of Roman law, Germanic traditions, and coalescing patterns of political life. Much of what the canonists did aimed to achieve a synthesis among these disparate influences. Roman law offered a persuasive model of such a synthesis, defining a normative relationship linking the positive law by which Rome governed to the laws and customs of particular peoples in the Empire (the *jus gentium*) and the underlying, or overarching, structure of the law of nature (*jus naturale*).

Of particular importance for thinking about both the use of arms and individual rights was the term *jus*. This Latin word, as employed in this period and beyond, carried several meanings which we normally distinguish from one another in English usage today: 1) right, in the sense of proper or correct; 2) right, in the sense of a claim one individual has in relation to another or to others; and 3) law, not in the sense of *lex*, or man-made positive law, but in the sense of the law that is "in one's members" or in nature, or the law that is expressed through expected customary behavior. As regards the use of arms, every member of the knightly class in this period was understood to possess the right of arms, *jus armae*. This was a carryover from Germanic custom; people not of the knightly class had no such right. Nor, by canon law and church custom, did clerics and religious, whatever their social rank. For those to whom it applied, this was understood as an individual right: it was at once "right and proper," in the sense of being accepted as correct, and a reflection of the natural and customary order of things. But the right to carry and employ arms in support of one's individual claims over others (*jus armae*) was not the same as the right of war (*jus bellare*), which referred to the right landed knights or higher nobles had to use arms for the good of the whole society encompassed by their landholdings. The right to war, *bellum*, referred specifically to the rights and responsibilities of a landed member of the knightly class to govern his lands and the people living on them, maintaining their personal security both relative to one another (and to the landowner himself) and to others from outside. Government on this conception was essentially judicial in function, having the right of collective use of armed force (*bellum*) to maintain justice in the face of some fault.[16] Other uses of arms were not *bellum* but *duellum*, the settlement of private quarrels.

But the right to undertake *bellum* was not yet just war, *bellum justum*. On this the canonists made an especially valuable distinction. When they defined the concept of just war, *bellum justum*, they reserved this specific term for the use of armed force by a temporal ruler with no temporal superior to correct and punish an injustice already accomplished with the aim of vindicating justice (*justitia*, the right order of things) and thus ensuring the peace of the common order. The settled concept of *bellum justum* thus depended on the idea of the right of arms, the *jus armae*, but limited and channeled it to define the place of the use of armed force in the exercise of governing responsibility.

The Latin term employed for a temporal ruler with no temporal superior, one who alone had the right to wage *bellum justum*, was *princeps*, prince. In contemporaneous French and English the word *princeps* was replaced by *souverain*, sovereign. Thus the just war idea, as it came together in the late twelfth and early thirteenth centuries, centered on a conception of sovereignty as responsibility—the same phrase employed in the ICISS Report to define "the responsibility to protect," but with a significantly different derivation and meaning. In classic just war thinking sovereign responsibility is for the common good of the society, to be exercised to vindicate justice after some injustice has occurred and gone unrectified and/or unpunished. It is fundamentally a responsibility to and for the moral order itself, understood as an order in accord with the natural law, itself understood as a manifestation of the divine will as embedded in the natural order. This is a very different conception of sovereignty as responsibility from that of *The Responsibility to Protect*, where the responsibility is owed to groups of people by virtue of rights they are understood to possess as individuals simply by virtue of their humanity. This is a conception of rights that did not exist before the modern age, or indeed, before the work of such thinkers as Hobbes, Locke, and Rousseau.

The medieval and early modern conception of the rights possessed by individuals did assume that these rights were grounded in custom and/or nature, but different individuals were understood as having rights depending on status, condition, age, and gender. Moreover, these rights were conceived as claims that particular individuals might make in relationship to others. People of higher social status were understood as having greater rights (that is, claims) over their social inferiors than the other way around. But some rights, those understood to be deeply rooted in nature or custom, entitled persons of socially inferior status to make a claim against a social superior. Consider the original rationale for what we today call noncombatant immunity (a recent term). Both church teaching and the chivalric code laid down that classes of persons who do not normally participate in war should not be directly, intentionally attacked in *bellum*.[17] The rationale in each case proceeded from the moral order itself "downward" to this protection of the classes of noncombatants named in the various lists: for the churchly rules, these had committed no fault and thus it would be unjust to harm them; for the chivalric writers, harming people who did not bear arms would bring dishonor on the knight who did so. Of course, people in the protected classes were understood to have a "right" to be left alone, but in the frame of thinking at the time this was a claim against those who might attack them, a claim that justified immediate self-defense against such attack or a subsequent claim for justice against the perpetrators. This is very different from saying that such a claim to be left alone defined their immunity from being attacked.

In the interest of space I will mention only one more point about the medieval understanding of the right, and justice, involved in using armed force. A present-day reader who does not know the historical context cannot help wondering why Aquinas does not list self-defense as one of his just causes for *bellum justum*, given the dominant place of the idea of self-defense in present-day international law and just war thinking about justified resort to armed force. But in Aquinas's context, the reason is simple. In 1245, Pope Innocent IV, whose ecclesiastical specialty was canon law, addressed and provided the final ruling on a matter that earlier canonists had left in some dispute. He wrote:

> It is permissible for anyone to wage war in self-defense or to protect property. Nor is this properly called "war" (*bellum*) but rather "defense" (*defensio*). And when someone has been [wronged], he may lawfully fight back on the spot (*incontinenti*), that is, before he has turned his attention to other matters.[18]

But this right of self-defense, Innocent made clear, does not extend to righting the wrong done by the attacker/thief after the moment of wrongdoing has passed; then it becomes a matter of justice to be executed only by one in the position, and with the responsibility, of punishing wrongdoing and vindicating justice. This is the specific province of *bellum justum*, and Aquinas's listing of what counts as just cause reflects this. Self-defense, as understood from this perspective, is not at issue; that time is past. Of course, the temporal ruler with no temporal superior may react "on the spot" to an armed attack, but in this his rights are not different from those of anyone else. So in terms of the classic conception of just war which came together in the twelfth and thirteenth centuries and endured essentially intact until the modern age, just war is not fundamentally about self-defense against attack but about the vindication of justice after that justice has somehow been disordered, whether by armed force or by other means.

Aquinas and his contemporaries also had a specific word for the oppression of people by their rulers: tyranny. Against tyranny, which manifests injustice, there is a right of defense possessed by all those who are the objects of the wrong done. But, if we consider Aquinas's discussion, this right does not extend to neighboring temporal rulers to end the tyranny and punish the tyrant, for such rulers have no authority over the tyrannical ruler. The neighboring rulers may assist those directly affected by the injustice of tyrants, but they must be asked. This was not "humanitarian intervention" in the present-day sense but "intervention by invitation," another category in present-day law.

How did things change so as to get to the understandings embodied in the Westphalian system? I will give a very compressed answer. Over a bit less than a century from Vitoria to Grotius (that is, the last part of the sixteenth century and the first part of the seventeenth) a series of thinkers, including these two, recast the understanding of natural law relative to the right to use armed force so that it referred no longer to the responsibility of the temporal ruler with no temporal superior to maintain justice, and thus a peaceful order, but instead referred to the right of each individual member of a society to self-defense against attack. This was understood by these thinkers as the fundamental right guaranteed by natural law, with other rights depending on it. On their conception ruling authorities in each society possessed the right to use armed force only as delegated to them from the individual members of their societies, and they had this right, as did the individuals, only for defense against attack. As given specific form by Grotius, this conception became the bedrock of the Westphalian system of international order and of the new science of the law of nations, developed by Grotius's intellectual successors. On this new way of thinking sovereignty ceased to be defined in terms of the moral responsibility of the ruler for the common good of the political community governed, for that good was now understood as contingent on the right of self-defense belonging to each member of that community. Sovereignty, accordingly, was redefined in territorial terms, with a violation of sovereignty being an attack across the frontiers of a political community threatening the members of that community. The underlying rationale based on the natural right of everyone to self-defense against an attack in process quickly was forgotten, so that the new norm became simply the sanctity of the political community's borders. This is the conception that endures in positive international law. Ironically, then, the shift in the history of political ideas towards emphasizing the right of self-defense as the fundamental natural right made the delegated ruler responsible only for protecting the individual members of the political community against attack from outside. It did nothing to shield those members against attacks from those holding power inside the political community. The older idea that the ruler is responsible to the moral order for serving the broader common good of the community disappears here, and indeed the very idea of the common good disappears from the discussion of political order as the idea of individual rights moves to center stage.

We can see this as an example of the working of the law of unintended consequences. Once the unintended results are in place, it is not entirely clear how to remove them without a change in the whole system of assumptions that opened the door to these negative results. This is, I think, the problem that *The Responsibility to Protect* tries hard to solve but does not quite succeed in solving, because it leaves all the assumptions in place. If political communities are understood as protected against threats from one another by the rights of their citizens to protect themselves individually and communally against outside interference, the responsibility to protect themselves against threats from inside the community also rests upon them.[19] Of course they may fail at this; they may not be able to effectively protect themselves and their rights against one another or against ruling authorities who may oppress them. The political theorists of the eighteenth century thus came to speak of the "virtue" needed in a populace for it to be able to exercise self-rule. We find the same idea in the present day among those who argue that civil wars need to be allowed to run their course, whatever the cost in suffering, until one side prevails and is able to establish rule. On this view, humanitarian intervention by a third party interferes with the natural process needed to establish a viable self-governing political community. I do not endorse this view but wish only to remind us all that it fits very well the assumptions built into the Westphalian system and into positive law regarding the use of armed force. If we want the triumph of an international order in which protection of human rights justifies the interventionary use of armed force by third parties, then we need to be aware that it is also the protection of human rights that lies behind the system of international order that has produced a conception of sovereignty as territorial integrity, so that any armed intervention is by definition aggression that may be fought against. The argument as currently stated does not lead to a conclusion but to a dilemma. It may be that the emphasis on human rights here needs to be fundamentally rethought in order to resolve this dilemma.

This leads me to a final observation about the relation of religious values and reflection to all this. Though there are good reasons why secular political thought in the West has developed to emphasize human rights, and while such an emphasis also fits well with certain approaches to religious ethics, it does not fit well with others, and there are also additional resources available to religious ethical thought about the political order, its good, and the place of the use of armed force in relation to it. The line of medieval thinking I have described above represents the use of one such resource: the idea of natural law as a form of moral order understood to be inherent in the nature of things yet also understood to be ultimately rooted in the divine mind and will. Another resource is the stress on the Christian obligation of love for neighbor rooted in response to the grace given in Christ which, for example, is central to Paul Ramsey's conception of good politics. Still another is the tradition of divine command ethics, which conceives the Christian's responsibilities in the political sphere according to obedience to the will of God known to the Christian by virtue of his or her relationship with God. Another is an ethic shaped around the guidance for human life provided by the scriptures, as in fundamentalist Christian use of the Bible, the Jewish rabbinical tradition's reliance on Torah, and Islam's central focus on Shari'a. Non-Western religious traditions offer still other resources for ethics. All these approaches yield understandings of ethics that are in some tension with one another and with the secular ethic of human rights; yet there is also the possibility of finding common ground among them. Comparative study of religious traditions offers important possibilities for finding overlaps and new insights, including possibilities connected with the idea of human rights and the responsibilities of governing. In any case, resolving the dilemma identified earlier—that a focus on individual human rights underlies both the principle of non-intervention and the idea that there is a responsibility for humanitarian intervention—remains a challenge, one to which religious ethics may well be able to provide a creative response. And where better to publish such efforts than in the *Journal of Religious Ethics*?

NOTES

1. National Council of Catholic Bishops, *The Harvest of Justice Is Sown in Peace* (Washington, D.C.: United States Catholic Conference, 1993), 15–16; sec. II.E.4.
2. These documents are collected in *Documents on the Laws of War*, 2nd ed., eds. Adam Roberts and Richard Guelff (Oxford: Clarendon Press, 1989) and *Documents on the Laws of War*, 3rd ed., eds. Adam Roberts and Richard Guelff (Oxford: Clarendon Press, 2000).
3. See, for example, Protocol II, Part I, Articles 1 and 2 in *Documents on the Laws of War*, 2nd ed., eds. Adam Roberts and Richard Guelff (Oxford: Clarendon Press, 1989), 449–50.
4. For more, see http://www.un.org/en/rights.
5. For example, the offenses listed as "crimes against humanity" in Article 7 of the Rome Statute of the International Criminal Court include protections given in the various international human rights agreements referred to above, while in Article 8, "war crimes" are first defined in terms of specific violations of the law of armed conflicts but then additionally defined by reference to the same offenses that appear in Article 7 (see International Criminal Court 1998).
6. The roots of such thinking in fact lie in a very narrow conception of natural right, but international law focuses on the fact of a state's territorial borders. I return to this matter later in this essay.

7. Leo Kuper, *Genocide* (New Haven, Conn.: Yale University Press, 1981), 20.
8. International Commission on Intervention and State Sovereignty (ICISS), "The Responsibility to Protect," co-chaired by Gareth Evans and Mohamed Sahnoun (Ottawa, Canada: International Development Research Centre, 2001).
9. Ibid., XII.
10. Ibid., XII.
11. Of particular interest for ethicists is the series of articles published beginning in 2005 in the journal *Ethics and International Affairs*: see Alex J. Bellamy, "What Will Become of the 'Responsibility to Protect?'", *Ethics and International Affairs* 20, no. 2 (2006): 143–69 and "The Responsibility to Protect–Five Years On," *Ethics and International Affairs* 24, no. 2 (2010): 143–69; Alex J. Bellamy, Simon Chesterman, James Pattison, Thomas G. Weiss, and Jennifer Walsh, "Libya, RtoP, and Humanitarian Intervention," *Ethics and International Affairs* 25, no. 3 (2011): 251–92; Alan Buchanan and Robert O. Keohane, "Precommitment Regimes for Intervention: Supplementing the Security Council," *Ethics and International Affairs* 25, no. 1 (2011): 41–63; Edward C. Luck, "RtoP: Growing Pains or Early Promise?", *Ethics and International Affairs* 24, no. 4 (2010): 349–65; and Jennifer W. Welsh, "Implementing RtoP: Where Expectations Meet Reality," *Ethics and International Affairs* 24, no. 4 (2010): 415–30.
12. ICISS, par. 2.14.
13. Ibid., par. 2.13.
14. Ibid., par. 2.14.
15. I have argued for this conception for many years; for its most recent iteration see James Turner Johnson, *Ethics and the Use of Force* (Farnham, Surrey: Ashgate Press, 2011), chap. 2. For the documentary evidence see *The Ethics of War: Classic and Contemporary Readings*, eds. Gregory M. Reichberg, Henrik Syse, and Endre Begby (Malden, Mass.: Blackwell Publishing, 2006), 104–24, 169–82.
16. See, for example, Gratian's citation of Isidore of Seville linking just war to the function of a judge in *Decretum*, Part II, *Causa 23*, Question II, Canon 1 (Reichberg, Syse, and Begby 2006, 113).
17. For fuller discussion of these conceptions of noncombatant immunity and their relationship see James Turner Johnson, *Just War Tradition and the Restraint of War* (Princeton, NJ: Princeton University Press, 1981), 131–50.
18. *The Ethics of War*, 150.
19. This logic also leads to the acceptance of the right of rebellion, but that is another story.

BIBLIOGRAPHY

Bellamy, Alex J. "What Will Become of the 'Responsibility to Protect?'" *Ethics and International Affairs* 20, no. 2 (2006): 143–69.

Bellamy, Alex J. "The Responsibility to Protect–Five Years On." *Ethics and International Affairs* 24, no. 2 (2010): 143–69.

Bellamy, Alex J., Simon Chesterman, James Pattison, Thomas G. Weiss, and Jennifer Walsh. "Libya, RtoP, and Humanitarian Intervention." *Ethics and International Affairs* 25, no. 3 (2011): 251–92.

Buchanan, Alan, and Robert O. Keohane. "Precommitment Regimes for Intervention: Supplementing the Security Council." *Ethics and International Affairs* 25, no. 1 (2011): 41–63.

Documents on the Laws of War, 2nd ed., edited by Adam Roberts and Richard Guelff. Oxford: Clarendon Press, 1989.

Documents on the Laws of War, 3rd ed., edited by Adam Roberts and Richard Guelff. Oxford: Clarendon Press, 2000.

International Commission on Intervention and State Sovereignty (ICISS). "The Responsibility to Protect." Co-chaired by Gareth Evans and Mohamed Sahnoun. Ottawa, Canada: International Development Research Centre, 2001.

International Criminal Court. *Rome Statute*. 1998. Available at: https://www.icc-cpi.int/sites/default/files/Publications/Rome-Statute.pdf.

Johnson, James Turner. *Just War Tradition and the Restraint of War*. Princeton, NJ: Princeton University Press, 1981.

Johnson, James Turner. *Ethics and the Use of Force*. Farnham, Surrey: Ashgate Press, 2011.

Kuper, Leo. *Genocide*. New Haven, Conn.: Yale University Press, 1981.

Luck, Edward C. "RtoP: Growing Pains or Early Promise?" *Ethics and International Affairs* 24, no. 4 (2010): 349–65.

National Conference of Catholic Bishops. *The Harvest of Justice Is Sown in Peace*. Washington, D.C.: United States Catholic Conference, 1993.

Reichberg, Gregory, Henrik Syse, and Endre Begby, eds.. *The Ethics of War*. Malden, Mass.: Blackwell Publishing, 2006.

Welsh, Jennifer W. "Implementing RtoP: Where Expectations Meet Reality." *Ethics and International Affairs* 24, no. 4 (2010): 415–30.

ABSTRACT

This 2015 essay argues that law and moral discourse must adapt and protect noncombatant immunity in the cases of asymmetric and irregular warfare. Johnson looks at the historical background of the idea of noncombatant immunity as well as the idea in international law and recent moral discussion. Even though there are particular challenges for noncombatant immunity where there is asymmetric and irregular warfare, the doctrine must be upheld and continuously monitored.

CHAPTER 20

THE EROSION OF NONCOMBATANT IMMUNITY IN ASYMMETRIC WAR

The protection of noncombatants from direct, intended harm during armed conflicts is recognized as being of major importance in both the law of armed conflict and moral thinking about war. Indeed, it has been a particularly distinctive feature of both the law and moral discourse on war since World War II, occupying a place of major importance in both. Asymmetric warfare, though, poses significant challenges to the effort to protect noncombatants in the way of war. In such warfare, recognizing noncombatants is not always clear, and each party to the conflict may have a different conception, up to and including denial that the enemy has any noncombatants. Moreover, the very definition of asymmetric warfare indicates that the means available and employed by each party in the conflict are different in character, so different standards may apply to the weapons used by each and to their targets. Another issue is accountability. Violations of noncombatant immunity may be punished as a war crime, but the irregular nature of the forces on one side in asymmetric warfare makes investigation and prosecution of suspected crimes extremely difficult. Consequently, soldiers in the regular force may be held to a higher standard than those in the force opposing them. This article explores issues posed by asymmetric war and irregular warfare more generally to the protection of noncombatant immunity, arguing that both the law and moral discourse need to adapt to meet these problems.

HISTORICAL BACKGROUND

War is inherently destructive of lives, property, and the fabric of ordinary life. For some people, this fact is ample reason to abolish war. A considerable body of literature making this argument reaches from Erasmus's *Dulce bellum inexpertis* (War is sweet to them that know it not) through literary and historical works reacting to the loss of life in World War I to antinuclear books like Jonathan Schell's *The Fate of the Earth*.[1] For other people, however, like the various kinds of advocates for total war throughout history, this inherent destructiveness is a virtue to be amplified in the entire subjugation or even elimination of the enemy. In contrast to both of these positions, all the major cultures of the world have produced moral and legal traditions as well as other institutional structures that undertake to restrain the destructiveness of war.

In the just war tradition as it developed in the medieval West, canon law between the late tenth and thirteenth centuries identified certain classes of people who should not have war made against them (i.e., not subject to direct, intentional attack): the clergy, members of religious orders, pilgrims on the road, women, children, the aged, the physically and mentally infirm, peasants on the land, townspeople, and innocent travelers, as well as their property. The reasoning here was straightforward. These classes of people do not normally take part in war and so should not have war made against them. If any individuals from any of these classes should engage in the war or give direct support to it in any way, then they forfeit their immunity.[2] In the period of the Hundred Years' War (mid-fourteenth through mid-fifteenth centuries), the chivalric code was absorbed into the developing tradition on just war, naming the same categories of people as noncombatants but adding provisions specifically concerning combatants. Knights taken prisoner in combat should not be killed but might be held as prisoners for ransom or released on parole (if they promised not to engage in the fighting for the duration of the war). Any non-knights serving in the enemy army, though, might be killed. This latter provision was actually an effort aimed at mitigation of war by limiting it to men of the knightly class, those properly socialized in how to fight and in whom they should properly fight.

In the modern period, the restraints on war defined in just war tradition provided the basis for the development of codes of military discipline and for a conception of customary rules for warfare—"the laws and customs of war." These in turn laid the foundation on which positive international law on war began to develop in the latter part of the nineteenth and early twentieth centuries.[3] Although the law of armed conflict in contemporary international law is defined by the agreement of states to be bound by the rules it specifies, this background in Western moral tradition remains visible in how the law is structured and what it contains.

The "regular"—that is, rule-defined—warfare established in this way fundamentally depends on the agreement of states. In the early development of positive international law regulating the conduct of war, the states signatory to the formal agreements were bound by the law. Those states, in turn, agreed to regulate their armies accordingly. The context assumed was a formally declared war involving parties to the agreement described as "belligerents" (i.e., states engaged in war).[4]

Other kinds of armed conflict were not addressed in the law at this early stage for major reasons. First, the deep historical precedent was to regard all such armed conflicts as unjust. The underlying just war tradition in Western culture had originated in an effort to limit the right to use armed force in a violence-prone society by restricting that right to a temporal ruler with no temporal superior. Others who resorted to force were understood as acting unjustly and harming the peace of the society in question, whether they were persons internal to that society or external to it, projecting armed force across its borders.[5] As this moral tradition developed, it continued to regard any form of "private" use of armed force as inherently unjust, whatever the reason for it. One finds a particularly striking historical example in Luther's explosive reaction to the German peasants' rebellion of 1624, when he exhorted the German nobility to "stab, smite, slay" the peasants in arms without mercy—though earlier he had shown sympathy with the peasants' grievances.[6]

A decisive turning point in the historical tradition came in the American Civil War, when the Union decided—but only after spirited debate—to treat the Confederates as legitimate belligerents, not as rebels whose rights were not guaranteed by the "laws and customs of war" as understood at the time.[7] But the older way of thinking remained in the use of armed force against indigenous rebellions in the colonial wars of the later nineteenth century. This mind-set produced an unhappy legacy: the sowing of the seed of unlimited war in the collective memories of the peoples of former colonies, a seed that has borne repeated fruit and is exemplified today in the ongoing wars of Central and West Africa and in the attacks on civilians justified in the ideology of al-Qaeda and the behavior of those it has inspired.

PROTECTION OF NONCOMBATANTS IN RECENT LAW AND MORAL DISCOURSE

As noted earlier, in its early development, positive international law on war held states responsible for any violations. A decisive shift in the law as to who is accountable, from states to individuals, begins with the war crimes tribunals after World War II. The first unequivocal language marking this shift appears in Article IV of the 1948 Genocide Convention: "Persons committing genocide or any of the other acts enumerated in Article III shall be punished, whether they are constitutionally responsible rulers, public officials or private individuals." Articles V and VI continue by spelling out the procedures for punishment of such persons.[8] The 1949 Geneva Conventions similarly identify individual persons to be held finally accountable for violations of any of the conventions, though they make the contracting states responsible for their punishment.[9] The 1949 Conventions also took two other important steps away from previous assumptions about the international law regulating armed conflict, extending its requirements to parties in conflict even when they are not signatories of the conventions and to certain noninternational armed conflicts.[10] Finally, the 1949 Conventions offered the most fully developed legal regulations up to that time for treatment of the whole spectrum of persons who might be victims of war: not only combatants rendered *hors de combat* by sickness, wounds, shipwreck (at sea), or being taken prisoner but also civilians as a class (to which the whole of 1949 Convention IV is devoted).

The 1977 Protocols to the 1949 Conventions continue along the same trajectory, aiming to "reaffirm and develop the provisions protecting the victims of armed conflicts and to supplement measures intended to reinforce their application," addressing both international armed conflicts (Protocol I) and certain forms of noninternational armed conflicts (Protocol II).[11] The protection of civilians in the way of war is particularly fully developed, with parties to an armed conflict required to "distinguish between the civilian population and combatants and between civilian objects and military objectives and accordingly shall direct their operations only against military objectives."[12] As this language suggests and the later definition of civilians clarifies, the term civilians here refers to those classes of people who in the moral literature are normally referred to as "noncombatants."[13] Thus with the 1949 Conventions and the 1977 Protocols, the positive law of armed conflict has importantly converged with the concerns of the deeper moral tradition to mark off such classes of people and avoid direct, intended harm to them. This convergence is also signaled in another way. The requirement that civilians be distinguished from combatants has given rise to the idea of a "principle of distinction" between these two types of people, corresponding directly to the "principle of discrimination" generally used in recent moral discourse.

Although the first responsibility for enforcing the requirements specified here and punishing violations is placed on the parties to the conflict, the establishment of war crimes tribunals for specific conflicts and, ultimately, creation of the International Criminal Court have provided a legal framework beyond the level of the states for punishing persons who have violated the rules thus established. The Rome Statute of the International Criminal Court gives it jurisdiction over four categories of offenses: genocide, crimes against humanity, war crimes, and aggression.[14] Since, in practice, not all states can be relied on to enforce the rules against these kinds of actions, in a fundamental sense this is a logical next step following on the definition of such behavior in armed conflict as criminal and assigning responsibility for such behavior to the individual persons who have committed it. Creation of such tribunals also puts pressure on states to punish the sorts of violations listed.

Recent moral discourse relating to protection of noncombatants has by no means been so broadly gauged or so finely grained. That portion of moral discourse which is pacifist includes all that is done in war within its overall critique and condemnation of war as such as inherently evil. If we think of the three pillars of the recovery of the just war idea—Paul Ramsey's two books from the 1960s, Michael Walzer's *Just and Unjust Wars* a decade later, and the United States Catholic bishops' pastoral letter *The Challenge of Peace*—both Ramsey and the Catholic bishops essentially left the matter of noncombatant immunity at the level of nuclear strategy.[15] For both, the focus was United States military policy and actions. They simply did not address how to transfer this reasoning in some way to limitation of the behavior of others in irregular warfare of the recent sort. Walzer's development of his analysis by use of historical examples from various wars led him into more fine-grained considerations of whether someone is a noncombatant or not and exactly what protections are owed to noncombatants in various kinds of circumstances. In this vein, he extended requirements of the rule of double effect beyond where Ramsey had left the matter, introducing a third stipulation that the military act in question positively seek to avoid or minimize harm to noncombatants. However, this element was only one in a large study undertaking a more general exploration of the requirements of just war for modern war as a whole, illustrated by the historical examples provided. These illustrations were valuable for anchoring Walzer's reflections, but they look back in time. Further, in his discussion of noncombatant immunity, Walzer did not anticipate the ways irregular warfare has come to be fought.

If we think of more recent moral discussions of contemporary warfare, we find similar trajectories. Consider, for example, talks about the moral implications for noncombatants of dual-use targeting or drone strikes. Frequently such moral discourse has concentrated on showing the immorality of such practices, with the result that they effectively become an attack on how the United States makes war. So far as similar practices are adopted by other highly developed countries, they too become a target for the same criticism. Every war, though, has two sides (at least), and the protection of noncombatants is a matter of the policies and practices of all parties to a conflict. This includes the terrain of contemporary irregular warfare, which recent moral discourse has largely failed to engage. Although it is right to raise moral concerns about drone strikes that mistakenly or disproportionately kill civilians, the direct and intended targeting of civilians has become a common feature of irregular warfare of all sorts, and moral discourse has neither engaged this directly nor considered how to weigh it in calculations of proportionality when criticizing actions used against forces employing such means. The moralists here might well look to the example of the lawyers regarding the full range of discourse needed. Moreover, they might well do more to take into account the moral difference between directly and intentionally attacking civilians and harming them collaterally or by mistake when the direct and intended purpose of an action is an attack against a combatant target.

A significant influence on both moral reflection (particularly that growing out of the work of Walzer) and law in recent decades has been the growth in attention to human rights since World War II.[16] As statements of an ideal, the body of material defining various kinds of human rights is impressive, and protection of the rights identified transfers easily to parameters for the protection of noncombatants in the law of armed conflict and moral discourse on war. Yet, the ideal is not the same as the reality. There remain differences, some substantial, among the various international statements as to the nature of the rights defined; their sources; the protections given them; and the sanctions, if any, to be imposed on violators. Some of the disparities are grounded in cultural differences, including religious belief and practice as well as long-standing cultural mores. Some trace to particular political aims of individual states and blocs of states; others reflect the influence of nongovernmental organizations and private voluntary organizations on the shaping of given agreements. Not all the rights identified in the various international instruments have the same priority, and, indeed, it is difficult to know exactly how to chart the relative priority of all the kinds of rights identified. When one compares the protections explicitly given or implied in international human rights law to those in the international law on armed conflict, the latter are clearly more specific and focused as operational guides. Increasingly, however, human rights law has come to be used as providing a broader frame and rationale for the protections and restraints set out in the law of armed conflict. For example, the offenses listed as "crimes against humanity" in Article 7 of the Rome Statute of the International Criminal Court include protections based in the various human rights agreements. In Article 8, though, "war crimes" are defined first in terms of specific violations of the law of armed conflict but then additionally defined by reference to the same offenses named in Article 7.[17] Yet, the fact remains that the differences referred to above make this much less a precise listing of rights-based offenses than it is intended to be.

The law of armed conflict has proceeded by establishing rules for the conduct of warfare, including the protection of noncombatants: the goal is "regular" or rule-governed warfare. At least thus far it has not entirely succeeded in this objective, but the framework it has defined is an impressive one. Fundamentally, even though for more than half a century the law has sought to hold individuals accountable for violations of the established rules, the law depends ultimately on the cooperation of states. The content of the law is itself understood to be the product of agreements among states, including the assent to be bound by the rules agreed to. In reality, of course, some elements of this framework of rules enjoy less general support than others, and states often disagree on the meaning of matters to which they have formally acceded. Further, states are not equal in their ability to enforce the established laws during circumstances of armed conflict. The rule-governed warfare the law seeks to create thus remains a goal rather than a completed achievement.

PARTICULAR CHALLENGES TO NONCOMBATANT PROTECTION IN IRREGULAR AND ASYMMETRIC WARFARE

The discrepancy between goal and reality is aggravated when one or more of the parties to an armed conflict ignores, denies, or overrides the rules—that is, in irregular warfare in all its forms, including asymmetric conflicts. The nature of irregular warfare presents serious challenges to the effort to limit the destructiveness of warfare by regularizing it. Four particular kinds of issues are especially problematic.

Cultural Differences

First, recent irregular warfare has frequently been defined in terms of significant cultural differences, particularly ethnic or religious dissimilarities or both, between the warring parties. When a conflict is framed in this way, from the perspective of each side all members of the enemy group—not just those persons who function as combatants—are perceived as equally enemies and may be deemed liable to be killed, driven out, or subjected to other damage. Examples abound, including the wars of the breakup of Yugoslavia; the Rwandan genocide of 1994; the Tamil-Sinhala conflict in Sri Lanka; the frequent, recent, and ongoing wars in Central Africa; the simmering Pakistani-Indian conflict; and the terrorist activity of such groups as the Irish Republican Army and al-Qaeda. As a particular example, realist analysts have often tended to dismiss the religious element in al Qaeda's actions, but doing so ignores the plain language of statements from its leaders, which describes an ongoing struggle on behalf of Islam itself against Western aggression.[18] The cause for war is depicted as religious, and all Americans and their allies are equally subject to being killed, with no distinction between combatant or noncombatant. The appeal to norms that transcend anything in common between the parties to the conflict effectively makes everyone identified with the enemy worthy of being attacked and killed: all Americans are guilty of attacking "Allah, his messenger, and Muslims." Al-Qaeda rejects efforts to provide for noncombatant protection defined not only in just war tradition and in international law but also in Islamic tradition.

What can be said against this? In the West, the horrors of religiously motivated warfare experienced in the Thirty Years' War led to the denial of religion as a justifying cause of war, beginning with the Peace of Westphalia. That denial carries over into international law, in which the only legitimating cause for a state to go to war is defense against "armed attack" or assisting another state in its own defense against such attack. So what is at stake in the claim that religion justifies attacks against civilians and military alike is both a denial of the combatant-noncombatant distinction and a denial of the effort to exclude religious difference from among the justifying causes for war. The same can be said for the claim that ethnic difference justifies war—indeed, justifies indiscriminate war—as exemplified, for example, by the Hutu massacre of Rwandans of Tutsi and mixed ethnicity in 1994. Quincy Wright observed several decades ago in his pioneering book *A Study of War* that war across major cultural boundaries is especially hard to moderate, and here we see this manifest in the denial that internationally recognized norms in fact matter in such warfare.[19] Reaffirming and enforcing these norms present a problem to the entire international community.

Exactly how best to do so, though, remains largely unaddressed and uncertain, as enforcement in particular would likely require more aggressive use of military measures against violators. But who is to do this? At this writing, French troops are in the Central African Republic assisting the government against insurgents who have routinely attacked civilians. Recently, French troops also intervened in Mali to repel advances by fighters from al-Qaeda in the Islamic Maghreb who, as they took over population centers, routinely attacked ordinary civilians. At the same time, though, the United States and Britain have withdrawn all troops from Iraq, and the Iraqi government has proven unable to offer secure protection to its population from al-Qaeda-affiliated insurgents; further, NATO nations have withdrawn their forces from Afghanistan, and United States forces are scheduled to withdraw in 2014 [withdrew in 2021]. Except for France's willingness to intervene militarily as needed in former French colonies, no Western country today shows much interest in such military action, even in cases of serious humanitarian need. Nor do they have much room to do so in terms of international law. The iteration of the Responsibility to Protect doctrine that came out of the 2005 World Summit has restricted authority to intervene for such purposes (except in cases of intervention by invitation, as exemplified by the French in the Central African Republic and Mali) to the Security Council. The council has authorized such action only once—in the case of the Libyan revolution—and has a much more general record of not acting. Nor does the institutional structure of United Nations peacekeeping operations provide much hope for the kind of robust military action that would be needed in cases of serious danger to a civilian population caught in the midst of irregular war, as memorably exemplified by the failure of peacekeeping forces in Rwanda at the time of the 1994 massacre to stop it or protect the victims.

Distinction between Noncombatants and Combatants

Even if all members of the enemy group are not regarded as equally subject to targeting, the question of exactly who is a noncombatant and who a combatant in irregular warfare may be unclear and, in practice, difficult or impossible to discern. In such warfare, combatants are typically attired in the clothes they would normally wear in their civilian lives; they may continue to live at home with their families or be sheltered and fed in friendly neighborhoods; they may move into and out of combatant functions frequently and seamlessly. Paul Ramsey once acidly commented that no just war thinker ever assumed noncombatants would be separated from combatants by roping them off "like ladies at a medieval tournament."[20] In fact, though, medieval just war thinking proceeded by identifying classes of persons—including women as a class, not just "ladies at a...tournament"—normally to be treated as noncombatants. Ramsey's observation may have been useful in the context in which he offered it (an argument for counterforce nuclear targeting and against counter-population targeting). Irregular warfare, though, is conducted by individuals and small groups of fighters in contexts where noncombatants are typically among and around the combatants on one or both sides. Thus, it is of the utmost importance to recognize the noncombatants—not only to permit the targeting of combatants but also, and very importantly, to let the fighters on both sides know who among the enemy poses a threat.

In this respect, one particular element in the development of international law on armed conflict has in fact contributed to creating ambiguity regarding who is a combatant and who a noncombatant. Francis Lieber's rules concerning members of irregular groups involved in warfare, originally set out in the context of the American Civil War but subsequently adopted into international law at the 1907 Hague Conference and carried forward intact in the 1949 Geneva Conventions, required that the following conditions be satisfied:

> (a) that of being commanded by a person responsible for his subordinates;
>
> (b) that of having a fixed distinctive sign recognizable at a distance;
>
> (c) that of carrying arms openly;
>
> (d) that of conducting their operations in accordance with the laws and customs of war.[21]

Consider, by contrast, this language from the 1977 Geneva Protocol I, Article 44, paragraph 3, which modifies conditions (b) and (c) above:

> Recognizing...that there are situations in armed conflicts where, owing to the nature of the hostilities an armed combatant cannot so distinguish himself, he shall retain his status as a combatant, provided that, in such situations, he carries his arms openly:
>
> (a) during each military engagement, and
>
> (b) during such time as he is visible to the adversary while he is engaged in a military deployment preceding the launching of an attack in which he is to participate.[22]

What does this mean in practice? An example will help to answer this question. During the invasion of Iraq by American forces in 2003, according to news stories at the time, members of the Fedayeen Saddam (a paramilitary group) approached an advancing American unit dressed as ordinary Iraqi Bedouin.[23] When they got close enough to attack, they opened their robes, took out weapons, and opened fire. Since Iraq had not ratified the 1977 protocols, one may argue that the Fedayeen were governed by the rules of 1949 Geneva Convention III, by which this was clearly a violation of the law of armed conflict. (The same holds from the perspective of the United States, which has signed but never ratified the 1977 protocols.) Nonetheless, from the perspective of the 1977 protocols, the matter is more ambiguous. More to my present point is that such behavior (other similar incidents occurred) led the American troops to mistrust all civilians, treating them as combatants until proven otherwise. This mind-set led to a number of events in which civilians were fired on as they approached checkpoints in vehicles while attempting to flee combat areas. In other words, the behavior of the Fedayeen, which might be read as permitted by the modified Lieber rules found in 1977 Protocol I, undermined the protection of noncombatants by creating ambiguity as to who is a noncombatant and endangered genuine noncombatants who were behaving in a way that seemed to pose a threat.

The 1977 Protocol I, of course, pertains to international armed conflicts, and so it applies to the 2003 Iraq war (though neither the United States nor Iraq have ratified the protocols). But the sort of behavior found in the above example, as well as the same sort of effect, is endemic to noninternational conflicts in which the combatants very often dress the same way as civilian noncombatants and use this fact to gain military advantage. That the Lieber rules as modified by 1977 Protocol I may have a tendency to import this erosion of noncombatant protection into noninternational conflicts suggests that some new attention to this version of the Lieber rules may be in order. At the very least, moralists might take critical note of the effect of the change in these rules on eroding the combatant-noncombatant distinction as it has to be made in the heat of combat.

Decisions Regarding Weapons and Targets

Insofar as the armed conflict in question is asymmetric, widely different means are available by each party to the conflict, and each has equally dissimilar structures for command and control. This fact returns us to an issue already broached in the above discussion of the first challenge posed by irregular warfare to noncombatant protection. As a result of the asymmetry between the parties to the conflict, different standards may apply to the types of weapons used by each party and the decisions made concerning their targets. Although almost any weapon can be used discriminatingly or indiscriminately, a fundamental difference exists between the direct, intended targeting of noncombatants or intentionally disregarding of noncombatants present in a targeted area and the effort to target only combatants while accepting the possibility of harm to noncombatants and seeking to minimize it. That is, the issue is not centrally the weapons themselves (e.g., missile strikes from remotely piloted aircraft [drones] versus the explosion of a car bomb by a suicide bomber) but the nature of the decision behind a given strike and its intention. The actual nature of a particular strike and the trail of decisions leading to it are relatively straightforward to investigate for a sophisticated, well-organized military force. By contrast, irregular forces have every incentive to promote ambiguity in the results of their actions and to keep hidden their decision trail, the motives for the particular decision, and the person or persons responsible for it. These persons are also typically kept hidden, so bringing them to accountability is difficult and may be impossible, at least in the limited time frame in which it would easily be tied to the harm to civilians in question. The moral critics of contemporary asymmetric war have tended to go after the low-hanging fruit represented by the actions of the more highly organized and technically able party to the conflict, and the law is more easily applied to the military actions of well-organized and well-armed forces. Reaching inside the command and decision structure of irregular groups, however, is often impossible, and the perpetrators of specific actions deemed wrong are often beyond the reach of sanctions or even (in the case of suicide bombers) dead.

One way to think about this matter is that perhaps it would be good to return to the older standard whereby irregular warfare itself was regarded as wrong so that persons engaged in it could be proceeded against as persons without combatant rights. The difficulty with this approach is that it may slide into extreme measures involving the disregarding of all rights for persons identified with such warfare. To approach the matter this way is hard in any case for democracies (as the controversy over the "enemy combatants" detained at Guantanamo exemplifies), though relatively easier for autocratic or despotic governments. At the same time, though, moral warrant for it can be found in both the Western and Islamic traditions—to name only two of the major cultural and moral traditions involved in asymmetric conflicts today.

Accountability

There remains the problem of adjudicating accountability. Violations of noncombatant immunity may justify punishment as a war crime, but in irregular warfare the nature of the forces and their actions makes the gathering of evidence, the identification of responsible individuals, and the capture of those to be tried difficult or even impossible, undercutting the legal process. When the conflict in question is also asymmetric, with regular forces on one side and irregular ones on the other, the potential for enforcement of the rules for right conduct is also asymmetric. For regular forces the functioning of command and control, including the keeping of records for each operation, provides a chain of evidence that is, in principle, straightforward to access. Consequently, one can identify the persons involved in the violation in question and, at least in principle, determine responsibility for the violation. As a result, soldiers in the regular force can be held to a higher disciplinary and judicial standard for their conduct than those in the irregular force opposing them. Their relative vulnerability on this count also opens the door for political motivations in singling out cases to investigate and/or prosecute. This prospect puts the fairness of the law in question and thus further undermines its protections as to be trusted. Thus, not only is noncombatant protection undermined, but also military personnel on the side that is held to the rules are disadvantaged relative to those on the other side, who may fight unrestrainedly with no substantial fear of being judicially held to account for their actions.

CONCLUSION

This article has been a pessimistic review of the matter of noncombatant protection in contemporary asymmetric warfare. Although the protection of noncombatants has developed as a major theme in both moral reflection on warfare and the international law of armed conflict, efforts to offer such protection remain fragile. This protection is especially endangered in irregular warfare, in which irregular forces may not share the underlying moral values and purposes defining such protection but may offer different justifications that define everyone as an enemy worthy of death and other harm. These same forces, typically nonstate actors, ignore or deny the restraints laid out in international law and in any case cannot easily be reached by sanctions the law provides. We need to pay more attention to the negative implications of this situation by all who are or may be in a position to affect future policy and action.

NOTES

1. Desiderius Erasmus, *Bellum Erasmi* (London: Thomas Berthelet, 1533); and Jonathan Schell, *The Fate of the Earth* (New York: Knopf, 1982).
2. James Turner Johnson, *Ideology, Reason, and the Limitation of War: Religious and Secular Concepts, 1200–1740* (Princeton, NJ: Princeton University Press, [1975]), 43–46.
3. See, for example, 1907 Hague Convention IV, Preamble, in Adam Roberts and Richard Guelff, *Documents on the Laws of War*, 3rd ed. (Oxford, UK: Oxford University Press, 2000), 69–70.
4. Ibid., Arts. 1 and 2.
5. James Turner Johnson, *Sovereignty: Moral and Historical Perspectives* (Washington, DC: Georgetown University Press, 2014), 28–32. Cf. Johnson, *Just War Tradition and the Restraint of War: A Moral and Historical Inquiry* (Princeton, NJ: Princeton University Press, 1981), 127, 162–65.
6. Clyde L. Manschrek, *A History of Christianity*, vol. 2 (Englewood Cliffs, NJ: Prentice-Hall, 1964), 36–38.
7. Johnson, *Just War Tradition*, 306–22.
8. Roberts and Guelff, *Documents*, 181–82.
9. See, for example, 1949 Geneva Convention I, Art. 49, in Roberts and Guelff, *Documents*, 198.
10. Ibid., Art. 2; and 1949 Geneva Conventions, Common Art. 3, in Roberts and Guelff, *Documents*, 198–99.
11. 1977 Protocol I, Hague Convention IV, Preamble; cf. Protocol II, preamble, in Roberts and Guelff, *Documents*, 422–23, 483–84.
12. 1977 Protocol I, Art. 48, in Roberts and Guelff, *Documents*, 447.
13. Ibid., Art. 50, 448–49.
14. See Art. 5, par. 1, in "Rome Statute of the International Court," accessed 11 December 2014, https://www.icc-cpi.int/sites/default/files/Publications/Rome-Statute.pdf.
15. Paul Ramsey, *War and the Christian Conscience: How Shall Modern War Be Conducted Justly?* (Durham, NC: Duke University Press, 1961), and *The Just War: Force and Political Responsibility* (New York: Charles Scribner's Sons, 1968); Michael Walzer, *Just and Unjust Wars: A Moral Argument with Historical Illustrations* (New York: Basic Books, 1977); and National Conference of Catholic Bishops, *The Challenge of Peace: God's Promise and Our Response* (Washington, DC: United States Catholic

Conference, 3 May 1983), http://www.usccb.org/upload/challenge-peace-gods-promise-our-response-1983.pdf.

16. See, for example, David Rodin, *War and Self-Defense* (Oxford, UK: Oxford University Press, 2003). For international statements on human rights, see "Human Rights," United Nations, accessed 13 December 2013, https://www.un.org/en/global-issues/human-rights.
17. See "Rome Statute."
18. See, for example, the declaration of "Jihad against Jews and Crusaders: World Islamic Front Statement," Federation of American Scientists, 23 February 1998, http://www.fas.org/irp/world/para/docs/980223-fatwa.htm.
19. Quincy Wright, *A Study of War*, 2nd. ed. (Chicago: University of Chicago Press, [1965]), 1344–54.
20. Ramsey, *Just War*, 145.
21. 1907 Hague Convention IV, Annex, Art. 1, in Roberts and Guelff, *Documents*, 73. The language here is that found in 1949 Geneva Convention III, Art. 4 (2), in ibid., 246. The provisions are the same as in the earlier contexts.
22. Roberts and Guelff, *Documents*, 444–45.
23. *New York Times*, 24 March 2003, B6; and "Iraqis Fake Surrender and Put Prisoners on TV," *Star Ledger* [Newark, NJ], 24 March 2003, 1.

BIBLIOGRAPHY

Erasmus, Desiderius. *Bellum Erasmi*. London: Thomas Berthelet, 1533.

Johnson, James Turner. *Ideology, Reason, and the Limitation of War: Religious and Secular Concepts, 1200–1740*. Princeton, NJ: Princeton University Press, 1975.

Johnson, James Turner. *Just War Tradition and the Restraint of War: A Moral and Historical Inquiry*. Princeton, NJ: Princeton University Press, 1981.

Johnson, James Turner. *Sovereignty: Moral and Historical Perspectives*. Washington, D.C.: Georgetown University Press, 2014.

National Conference of Catholic Bishops. *The Challenge of Peace: God's Promise and Our Response*. Washington, D.C.: United States Catholic Conference, 3 May 1983. http://www.usccb.org/upload/challenge-peace-gods-promise-our-response-1983.pdf.

Ramsey, Paul. *The Just War: Force and Political Responsibility*. New York: Charles Scribner's Sons, 1968.

Ramsey, Paul. *War and the Christian Conscience: How Shall Modern War Be Conducted Justly?* Durham, NC: Duke University Press, 1961.

Roberts, Adam and Richard Guelff. *Documents on the Laws of War*, 3rd ed. Oxford, UK: Oxford University Press, 2000.

Rodin, David. *War and Self-Defense*. Oxford, UK: Oxford University Press, 2003.

Schell, Jonathan. *The Fate of the Earth*. New York: Knopf, 1982.

Walzer, Michael. *Just and Unjust Wars: A Moral Argument with Historical Illustrations*. New York: Basic Books, 1977.

Wright, Quincy. *A Study of War*, 2nd ed. Chicago: University of Chicago Press, 1965.

ABSTRACT

In this previously unpublished 2015 presentation Johnson considers the revitalization of the just war tradition in the aftermath of World War II. He notes that the greatest catalyst was Paul Ramsey, who in the 1960s published *War and the Christian Conscience* (1961) and *The Just War* (1968). These writings from a Christian perspective were followed by Michael Walzer's philosophical and political perspective in *Just and Unjust Wars* (1977). Johnson shows continuity with earlier just war thought and its influence on the "law of nations" but also acknowledges that the classic expression of the just war tradition "did not make it unscathed into the modern age."

CHAPTER 21

THE JUST WAR IDEA AND THE CONTEMPORARY SECURITY ENVIRONMENT

Good evening. I have been asked to talk about the just war idea and the contemporary security environment in the context of the ongoing series on religion and national security. The more I thought about how to address these issues, the more I realized that it is necessary first to clarify exactly how we should best think about all of them: the just war idea, national security, and the role of religion in relation to both. So that is where I want to begin.

Over the last fifty years the idea of just war has become an important focus for moral reflection about the use of military force in response to harm and threats of harm to our society, our people, our values, and our interests—and not only our society, but that of the West as a whole and even the international order itself. Just war is addressed in courses at all the U.S. military service academies and the war colleges, as well as in their counterparts in such NATO allies as the U.K., Norway, and The Netherlands. Among civilian academics it has become a hot topic among philosophers and regularly is treated in one or more sessions of the annual meeting of the International Studies Association, as well as being the subject of a steady stream of books.

All these examples are from the secular sphere of American life, though religious themes and influences appear in the contexts I have mentioned. Specifically in the sphere of religion, the most outstanding and consistent advocates of a version of just war thinking have been the

United States Catholic bishops. Their 1983 pastoral letter, *The Challenge of Peace*, played an important role in bringing the just war idea into American public consciousness, and since then spokesmen for the bishops, as well as others they have influenced, have made use of the conception of just war described there on a number of occasions. Liberal Protestant institutions and individuals, for their part, have largely avoided just war reasoning; thus the Council of Bishops of the United Methodist Church, in their own 1996 pastoral letter, *In Defense of Creation*, explicitly stated the wish to "move beyond" just war thinking. Nor has just war language and thinking developed importantly among Evangelical Protestant Christians, though a notable contrast is provided by the letter sent to President George W. Bush in the fall of 2002 over the signatures of several well-known Evangelicals, led by Richard D. Land, President of the Ethics and Religious Liberty Commission of the Southern Baptist Convention. The occasion for this letter was the debate that culminated in the invasion of Iraq the following year and the overthrow of the Saddam Hussein regime. The letter took the form of a careful just-war analysis of the decision whether to invade or not, leaving the decision itself to President Bush.

The growth and spread of just war reasoning in recent decades is all the more striking because, prior to the 1960s, there was none at all to be found in moral discourse, whether here or in other Western countries. A deep and rich tradition of just war had held sway, representing a general cultural consensus in the West from the middle of the twelfth century until well into the modern period, but the Protestant Reformation brought an end to important assumptions in that consensus and introduced new ideas about individual and political life. Hugo Grotius's work during the Thirty Years' War, the last and arguably the worst of the century of religious wars that marked the era of the Reformation and Counter-Reformation, significantly reshaped the inherited tradition on just war within his conception of the law of nations, and in this form the just war idea was carried into the Westphalian era and beyond. In this new legal form the tradition of just war became "the laws and customs of war," and as positive international law on war began to develop the older moral tradition was referred to by reference to the "interests of humanity," as in 1907 Hague Convention IV and elsewhere. As positive international law was gradually reconceived to be simply the result of agreements among states, the idea of an underlying moral component receded and disappeared, though as late as the early 1960s respected figures like Myres McDougal and Georg Schwarzenberger could speak, respectively, of the dictates of "humanity" and "civilization." But the just war tradition itself, when it was acknowledged at all, was treated as an artifact of the past, as Reinhold Niebuhr had done in his work *The Nature and Destiny of Man* in the early 1940s.

Though the just war idea remained an element in the canon law of the Catholic Church and some Protestant denominations, the last serious theological attention to it for nearly three and a half centuries was given by the Spanish Jesuit Francisco Suarez and the English Puritan William Ames, both writing in the early 1600s. When philosophy began to develop as an independent field of inquiry during the Enlightenment, it moved in a different way when thinking about war: toward various conceptions of a new form of international order in which war would be abolished. Toward the end of the nineteenth century religious thinkers also took up this line of thought, and the idea of abolishing war was also fueled by the increasing destructiveness of war in the nineteenth and early twentieth centuries. As a result varieties of pacifism and internationalism became increasingly prominent in religious thought and sentiment during this period, and they have remained so ever since. In the 1930s and 1940s Reinhold Niebuhr staked out his Christian realism as a counter to this, but could only come up with the idea that war is a "necessary evil," not a means to protecting or establishing value but only one for averting worse evil. For practical purposes the just war idea was dead.

All this began to change in the 1960s, when the Christian ethicist Paul Ramsey published two books seeking to recover the idea of just war and apply it to thinking about nuclear weapons and deterrence. The first of these books, *War and the Christian Conscience* (1961), explicitly presented the Christian idea of just war as more faithful to the ethic of Jesus—specifically, the obligation of Christian love of neighbor—than pacifism. Where use of force is concerned, love issues in two principles: permission and limitation. The Christian is obligated in love to protect an innocent neighbor from harm, and permitted to use force to do so; yet at the same time, the force that can be used is limited, because the wrongdoer is also a neighbor for whom Christ died. As he developed this line of thinking Ramsey had little to say about the resort to armed force, which is referred to in the tradition as *jus ad bellum*; his conception of just war centered on two principles defining the moral limits to how such force may be used: discrimination or noncombatant immunity, which he regarded as implied directly by love of neighbor, and proportionality, which meant a moral calculus as to how much force may be used against the wrongdoer. In the latter part of the 1961 book and in a number of essays gathered together in a 1968 book, *The Just War*, Ramsey developed this conception of just war further and applied it, first, to the debate over nuclear weapons and their use for deterrence and possibly in war. Though he repeatedly insisted that the just war idea is part of a larger theory of political order, he never explicitly developed this connection.

Ramsey's two books from the 1960s began the recovery of just war thinking that I have referred to earlier. The second pillar of this recovery was Michael Walzer's *Just and Unjust Wars*, first published in 1977. "I want to recapture the just war for political and moral theory," Walzer wrote in the preface to that work. He went on to define a conception of just war that included both a *jus ad bellum* (which he called "the theory of aggression") and a *jus in bello* (which he called "the war convention"). It was based importantly in international law, which he called "the legalist paradigm," but methodologically it also depended heavily on analysis of particular cases used by him to provide a window into a basic common moral sense related to the issues discussed. Whereas Ramsey's work was known and discussed only within the relatively limited fields of Christian ethics and the scholars he engaged who were deep into the debates over nuclear deterrence, its specifically Christian orientation limited the attention given it. Walzer's work, by contrast, was an exercise in secular political philosophical thought, and it drew a much broader audience, though initially this audience remained largely academic. His thinking, though, like Ramsey's, was known and respected in policy debates. But though Walzer also wrote about justice and political life, he never integrated his thinking on just war into this broader inquiry.

Opening the just war idea to a wider public was the achievement of the United States Catholic bishops in their effort during 1982 to draft a pastoral letter on nuclear weapons and in the letter itself, published under the title *The Challenge of Peace* in 1983.

Though the drafting process occasioned a significant number of conferences, symposia, and academic lectures, what really brought the whole matter to the broader public was the second draft of the pastoral letter. Reflecting the influence of a significant nuclear pacifist group of bishops, backed up by a broad coalition of laity and members of religious orders opposing war altogether and nuclear weapons in particular, this draft identified nuclear weapons as immoral in themselves and called for the United States to renounce their use and abolish them entirely. The draft was published in full by both *The Washington Post* and *The New York Times*, along with interpretive stories in each paper. Some of you here tonight may remember this and the hullabaloo that followed. If the bishops said nuclear weapons are immoral, then what would this mean for the large number of Catholics in military service, particularly those with direct responsibilities for the nuclear weapons in place as a deterrent and for possible use in war against the Soviet Union—which had no equivalent of the Catholic anti-nuclear party with which to contend? Responding to a widespread negative reaction to the second draft of the pastoral, the bishops retrenched, and the result was the third and final draft, which with a few minor changes became the final version of the pastoral letter. By this time the idea of just war was firmly on the table for public discussion and use across the broad variety of contexts I mentioned earlier.

But what was this idea of just war that had been recovered and inserted into American moral debates over war? Ramsey's and Walzer's ways of thinking about just war and developing it as a base for moral reasoning were quite different and appealed to largely different groups. The Catholic bishops, in their quest for a resolution of the divide among themselves and in the American Catholic church more generally, produced a third conception of just war: one that begins with a general "presumption against war" and then provides, through various moral criteria, tests for when this general presumption may be overridden. In theory this provides a place for the use of armed force to serve certain political ends, for example, the bishops' definition of just cause in 1983: "to confront 'a real and certain danger,' to protect innocent life, to preserve conditions necessary for decent human existence, and to secure basic human rights." In their 1993 statement marking the tenth anniversary of the pastoral letter they rephrased this somewhat: "Force may be used only to correct a grave, public evil, i.e., aggression or massive violation of the basic rights of whole populations." Either of these ways of describing just cause for the use of force opens the door to broader consideration of the possibility of positive uses of force as a proper instrument of national purpose. But in practice the bishops have never moved in this direction. Despite the language in these two statements on just cause for the use of force, the bishops' conception of just war is focused on the evil of the use of force and on avoiding such use, not on the possible goods the use of force might serve in specific instances.

Subsequent just war thinking bears the marks of the significant diversity that appears in the effort to recover the idea of just war for thinking about morality and war. Ramsey's idea of just war as rooted in the Christian ethic of love of neighbor has been taken up in books on war by two Oxford theologians, Oliver O'Donovan and Nigel Biggar, and in other works by Protestant Christian ethicists. His use of Augustine is reflected in Jean Bethke Elshtain's understanding of just war. Philosophers writing on the ethics of war generally trace their thinking to Walzer, and much philosophical writing on war is devoted to analysis and criticism of one or another idea lifted out of *Just and Unjust Wars*. The Conference of Catholic Bishops itself and spokesmen for it have been perhaps the most notable adopters of the conception of just war as ultimately proceeding out of a "presumption against war," though various academic writers have accepted the bishops' conception of just war as normative in their own work.

To be sure, though, antedating the contemporary recovery (or reinvention) of the just war idea there is a deep and rich historical tradition of just war thinking in Western culture, and it will be useful to describe this briefly before returning to the current state of affairs. The deep roots of just war tradition reach back into Roman and Greek thought and practice and into Hebrew religion and culture as described in the Old Testament, and the late classical theologian Augustine, who took these influences into his own work, is often described as the first Christian just war theologian. Augustine, though, never provided a coherent, systematic statement of the just war idea (this by contrast to the subject of sexuality, to which he devoted several distinct treatises): what he said about just war took the form of brief statements on different aspects of the just war idea found in a broad variety of works on different subjects, from a theological refutation of Manichaean thought to a commentary on the Pentateuch. Yet these scattered statements were identified and included in a series of collections of canons (rules to guide Christian life) which began to appear in the sixth century, then taken over and arranged into a consistent, systematic conception of just war seven centuries after Augustine's death by the canonical writer Gratian in a collection called the *Decretum* (completed in 1148), which quickly became the standard compilation of Christian canonical thinking. As for the conception of just war found there, various matters needed further exploration and filling out, and this was provided by the two generations of Gratian's canonist successors, generally known as the Decretists and the Decretalists. Their work was completed by the middle of the thirteenth century: an important reference point is the ruling on just causes for war and the authority necessary for just war, and thus more broadly on the definition of just war, by Pope Innocent IV in or around 1250. Innocent had been a canonist before becoming Pope, and he was a prominent member of the second generation of commentators building on Gratian's *Decretum*. On self-defense Innocent ruled that the natural law gives everyone the right of defense against an attack immediately threatened or in progress. This is Innocent's language: "It is permissible for anyone to wage war in self-defense or to protect property. Nor is this properly called 'war' (*bellum*) but 'defense' (*defensio*)." Once the attack is over, repairing any violation of justice and punishing any wrongdoer is no longer a right of the individual but the responsibility of the prince, that is, the sovereign temporal ruler. This was a responsibility understood to be given in natural law, but medieval and early modern writers on just war frequently added divine sanction by referring to Romans 13:4b, in which the ruler is defined as "an avenger" who acts in the name of God and his justice to "execute wrath on the evildoer." Just war (*bellum iustum*), then, is the use of force if necessary for these purposes. Innocent's brief ruling effectively brings to a close the canonists' development of a systematic, coherent definition of just war.

Roughly a quarter of a century later Thomas Aquinas summarized the canonical consensus in addressing just war in his *Summa theologiae* (II.II, Q.40): a just war requires "the authority of a prince," a just cause defined as "recovering that which has been wrongly taken and punishing the wrongdoer," and a right intention, which Aquinas defined negatively in terms of avoiding several explicitly bad intentions that had been listed by Augustine and positively in terms of the end [aim] of peace. It is important to emphasize that Aquinas here was following the carefully won consensus of the canonical commentators from Gratian to Innocent and his contemporaries: his achievement was not to invent this conception of just war but to place it in a theological context, complementing the canonical context in which it had been originally formed. This is often missed, to their detriment, by present-day commentators seeking to work from Aquinas's conception of just war to whatever conclusion they wish to reach from it.

For the canonists, in working towards a systematic, comprehensive consensus on just war, were closely involved in medieval political and legal life as well as with Christian tradition and the life of the church, and their conception of just war reflected the influences of all these spheres of life. They were working during the era of the early crusades, and it is striking that they defined the concept of just war as pertaining entirely to the sphere of temporal government. They did this by citing a late fifth-century pope, Gelasius, who wrote to the Roman Emperor of the time defining the temporal and the spiritual as two distinct spheres of authority. His aim was to defend his own spiritual authority against usurpation by the temporal emperor, but the medieval canonists turned this around, defending the authority of temporal rulers against claims of overlordship by the spiritual authorities—the bishops and the pope. Just war, as they described it using the Gelasian principle, can be authorized only by a temporal ruler with no temporal superior (a conception which at about this time began to be described in French and English as *souverain*, sovereign). Its justification was provided by the responsibility of such a ruler to defend and secure justice in his or her political community, to the end of the common good of that society, its peace. Let us note two things about this understanding of just war. First, it was in no sense a conception of holy war, for it made no room for war to be authorized by religious authority or for religious purposes. Though it was specifically defined and maintained by scholars working for the Church, it had to do with temporal government and its responsibility, which the canonists identified with the office of the ruler of each independent political community. This should be suggestive to us as we think about whether the just war idea is in any sense a specifically "religious" one as we today conceive this term. Second, the definition of just war as requiring sovereign authority, just cause, and the end of peace corresponded directly to the three ends of politics passed on to medieval political thinkers from the classical age: order, justice, and peace. The parallels are direct: the responsibility exercised in sovereign authority corresponds to the end of order; the conception of just cause corresponds to the end of justice; and the end of peace is the same in both conceptions. What we find in what I like to call this "classic" conception of just war was, then, in fact an expression of a general understanding of the role of force in securing the ends at which political life properly aims. This was the conception of just war inherited by Aquinas, summarized by him, and placed into a theological framework heavily influenced by Aristotelian thought, including thought on ethics and politics. When we think today of the relation of the just war idea to national security, I suggest we might learn from this: the proper understanding of the use of armed force always has to be placed within a considered and consensual understanding of the nature and ends of the life of the political community. I will return to this point later on, but for now let me just say that most recent just war thinking fails this test.

The classic conception of just war, defined by the canonists and summarized and adapted by Aquinas, became the focus of a tradition of just war that remained the norm well into the modern period. It withstood the division of Western Christianity into Catholic and Protestant. The just war idea has been frequently described as "Catholic": Reinhold Niebuhr described it this way in order to dismiss it in his work *The Nature and Destiny of Man*, and it has been a favorite theme of political realists wishing to reject its relevancy for contemporary thinking about political life. But in fact the classic conception of just war appears clearly in Luther's writings on war and the use of armed force; the English Puritan theologian William Ames worked directly from Aquinas in his widely influential book *Conscience, With the Power and Cases Thereof*; and a whole string of Protestant thinkers who contributed to the transition of just war tradition into the idea of the law of nations—importantly including Gentili, Grotius, and Pufendorf—were all proud Protestants.

In any case, the classic conception of just war did not make it unscathed into the modern age. The answer to why this was the case is that the story is quite mixed. First, attention to the just war idea has been episodic and limited to a segment of the American religious spectrum. Statements from the United States Catholic bishops have been frequent, consistently focused on their own understanding of the just war idea, and arguably more influential for the larger public debate. The

Catholic bishops' entry into this debate came in 1982–83, during the drafting and eventual publication of their pastoral letter, *The Challenge of Peace*, in 1983. This received a good deal of debate in various spheres and occasioned the issuing of statements on war by several major Protestant denominations, the last and most substantial of which was a book-length study, *In Defense of Creation*, on behalf of the United Methodist Church Council of Bishops in 1986. The debate during 1990–91 over use of military force to expel Iraqi troops from Kuwait after Iraq's invasion and absorption of that country included significant interventions by spokesmen for the U.S. Catholic bishops, who argued from the understanding of just war laid out in *The Challenge of Peace.* Other major religious interventions in this debate did not make use of the just war idea at all. Later in the 1990s religious bodies entered the debate over humanitarian intervention occasioned by the atrocities of the Bosnian war and the Rwandan genocide. Notable uses of the just war idea in this debate came, once again, from the U.S. Catholic bishops, this time in a new major statement, *The Harvest of Justice is Sown in Peace*, in 1993, but Protestant denominations also addressed the question of humanitarian intervention, with a version of just war invoked by the United Presbyterians in a 1996 statement approving such intervention by military force only if there is no national interest involved.

The last time the idea of just war was used as a major focus for specifically religious statements on the use of armed force was in the debate prior to the invasion of Iraq to overthrow the Saddam Hussein regime in 2003. There were three such statements: a letter to President Bush from Bishop Wilton D. Gregory, president of the United States Conference of Catholic Bishops, a one-sentence statement signed by one hundred Christian ethicists associated with the Society of Christian Ethics, and another letter to President Bush, this one initiated by Richard D. Land, President of the Ethics and Religious Liberty Commission of the Southern Baptist Convention and signed by a number of other well-known Evangelical Christians. The Gregory letter and the Christian ethicists' statement both focused closely on the question of preemptive use of force, and both squarely rejected preemption. The Land letter was more broad-gauged, providing a list of just war criteria and testing the prospective use of force against them. Unlike the Gregory letter and the Christian ethicists' statement, the conclusion of this analysis was that the tests had been met, leaving the choice whether to use military force up to the President.

Again, the picture here is a mixed one. In the first place, the religious statements have all come as entries to debates over specific questions regarding the use of military force: that in the 1980s over nuclear weapons, deterrence, and the possible use of such weapons in war; that in 1990–91 over use of force against Iraq after its invasion and takeover of Kuwait; that later in the 1990s over humanitarian intervention occasioned by the atrocities in the Bosnian war and in Rwanda; and that in 2002–03 over the invasion of Iraq to overthrow the Saddam Hussein regime. Second, so far as the just war idea was invoked by the religious participants in these debates, it was generally used to the purpose of opposing military force. A notable example is the definition of just war provided and employed by the U.S. Catholic bishops: the just war idea is presented as existing in the context of a general "presumption against war and military force," which can be overridden only if all the listed criteria are fully satisfied. In practice spokesmen for the bishops have focused on the prudential criteria of last resort, reasonable hope of success, and proportionality, judging them all not satisfied, with the result what one critic has called a "functional pacifism." The United Methodist bishops, for their part, made a point of expressing their aim as to go beyond just war thinking, and they too ended up taking a negative position against military force. The United Presbyterians, as already noted, opposed use of military force in response to humanitarian harm unless it were not in the U.S. national interest to use such force, a position which in effect ruled out humanitarian intervention involving military force. Against the background of these examples, the Land letter stands out as the exception, employing just war analysis but offering it only as advice, leaving the decision about use of military force to the U.S. President.

None of these interventions addressed the matter of national security in any comprehensive way. Except for the Land letter, all focused on the evil of violence, seeking to avoid the use of military force altogether.

ABSTRACT

In this previously unpublished 2015 presentation Johnson discusses changes in the just war tradition since the 1960s showing the continuity and discontinuity with the classic just war tradition. He argues that the "classic conception of just war got the fundamentals right in its moral definition of sovereign authority, just cause, and right intention, and … contemporary just war reasoning ought to pay a great deal more attention to that classic statement of the idea of just war."

CHAPTER 22

GETTING IT RIGHT: CHANGES IN JUST WAR THOUGHT ON SOVEREIGNTY, JUST CAUSE, AND RIGHT INTENTION FROM THE CLASSIC JUST WAR IDEA TILL TODAY

If one surveys the field of contemporary writing on just war, one might easily be confused as to exactly what constitutes the idea of just war, or might wonder if just war means anything other than what individual authors want it to mean. To take simply a sample from my own shelf, recent books on just war by Alex Bellamy, Davis Brown, J. Daryl Charles, Robert L. Phillips, Mark Totten, Albert L. Weeks, and Craig M. White all define just war by a listing of criteria for the decision to go to war (*jus ad bellum*) and for conduct during war (*jus in bello*). Brown's and Totten's listings are essentially what I would myself give if asked for such a list, beginning with the classic requirements of sovereign authority, just cause, and right intention, including the end [aim] of peace; then adding several prudential criteria widely applied today—reasonable hope of success, proportionality of ends, and lack of reasonable alternatives (last resort); and finally defining right conduct in war in terms of the principles of discrimination and proportionality of means. Though I myself prefer to think of right war-conduct as it was done in the historical just war tradition and also in positive law on war, defining noncombatancy by specific categories of types of people and seeking to restrict the means of war by specific limits on certain kinds of weapons. White offers a list with the same headings and in the same order, limited to the war-decision categories only, but the way he describes his categories is defined by his purpose of arguing the injustice of the U.S. invasion of Iraq in 2003, and he uses them as a backwards-looking checklist to criticize that war, not as a forward-looking basis for moral reflection on whether to employ military force in a particular crisis and how to use it if employed. This latter approach, not the backwards-looking checklist employed to bolster political argument, is what the idea of just war is about, as I understand it.

Moving on down the listings of criteria given by the other authors I have mentioned, all these other authors shift the order and priority of the criteria named or combine some of them or simply do not mention some. For example, Charles and Weeks begin with just cause; Phillips starts with last resort; Bellamy begins with right intention. Just cause is also the first criterion given in the definition of just war given by the United States Catholic bishops in their widely influential 1983 pastoral letter, *The Challenge of Peace*, and subsequent statements. Where each of these listings begins telegraphs the author's position on what is most important or most fundamental. Seven of the recent authors, as well as the Catholic bishops, do not mention the end of peace as a moral criterion in the decision to use military force, reflecting a widespread contemporary view that war and peace are not interrelated but mutually exclusive. All include right authority as a requirement for just war, though they put it below just cause in priority and sometimes describe it in legal or political terms as "legitimate" or "competent" authority.

Describing right conduct in the use of military force by reference to the principles of discrimination and proportionality is universal among these examples and also familiar in the wider discussion of just war, and it has also migrated into the law of war or international humanitarian law, where "discrimination" is rendered as the principle of "distinction" and is derived from the positive requirement to distinguish combatants from civilians (whom the writers on ethics would prefer to call "noncombatants"). Both the ethicists and the lawyers use the term proportionality, though there is wide variation among the sources as to how to calculate it. Thinking about right conduct in the use of military force in terms of the two moral principles of discrimination and proportionality is a particular feature of just war discourse from the last fifty or so years, having originated in the work of Paul Ramsey on just war in the 1960s.

If one looks for a bit more order in recent work on just war than the disparate examples I have just cited suggest, then it is useful to think further about Ramsey and his influence, that of Michael Walzer roughly a decade later, and that of the U.S. Catholic bishops a few years after Walzer. Though the just war idea is centuries old and can be argued to represent, as one author has put it, "the way we in the West think ethically about war," it effectively disappeared from ethical reflection on war from roughly the middle of the seventeenth century until the last fifty years. The works on just war of Ramsey, Walzer, and the Catholic bishops stand as important benchmarks in the recovery of just war thinking that has taken place in the last fifty years. Yet none of them tried to recover the earlier historical idea of just war, either how it was defined, the impact it had, or how it was used. Rather, each of the three invented the just war idea anew, giving a particular stamp to it. Their successors have largely followed suit.

The differences among subsequent writers on just war trace back, in different ways, to the influence of these different benchmark reinventions of the idea of just war. Ramsey, a Christian ethicist, has had a particular impact on just war writers seeking to explore the ethics of war and military force from a Christian normative standpoint. The recent book by Nigel Biggar, *In Defence of War*, stands importantly in this tradition of ethical reflection. Ramsey's influence can also be seen in *The Challenge of Peace* and in later authors like Charles, though how his influence is put to use in these sources is rather different from how Ramsey developed his own thinking, and sometimes completely at odds with it—for example, the argument of the Catholic bishops that contemporary warfare is almost always unjust (nuclear war is always so)—because the criteria of discrimination and proportionality can't be met.

The same disconnects can be noted in the influence of Walzer. When Anglo-American philosophers discovered the idea of just war, they presented it as in Walzer's work: they have not looked further. But philosophers writing on just war have not sought to draw out Walzer's thinking as a whole; rather they have picked up one or another theme or specific idea from it and developed their own discourse centered on analyzing that theme or idea and drawing its meaning out to their own ends. A prominent example is David Rodin's use of the human rights idea, prominent in Walzer's thought on war, to argue for the injustice of any contemporary war except one authorized by a universal state with "a world monopoly of military force together with a minimal judicial mechanism for the resolution of international and internal disputes." Another example is Jeff McMahan's critique of what Walzer calls the moral equality of soldiers, with McMahan arguing that there is no such moral equality: for him only soldiers in a just war have the moral right to fight, and without a just cause soldiers are, in effect, war criminals. These authors work to conclusions very different from anything Walzer himself has ever said. Walzer himself has commented that the philosophers' discussions of just war have become less about war and more about philosophy. Self-referentialism is typical of academic disciplines, and it has its value, but the big picture tends to get lost, and the subject tends to become just a case to be argued about.

The just war conception of the U.S. Catholic bishops has a special place in the evolution of recent thinking on just war, because far more than the work of the two academics, Ramsey and Walzer, and that of other academic writers also working on the just war idea from a perspective more shaped by history, including William V. O'Brien and me, the debate centered on the production and publication of *The Challenge of Peace* succeeded in drawing significant attention in military and political circles and among a broader public. It has also had significant long-term effect, so that it deserves a closer look. Fundamentally this effect has been to shift the meaning of the just war idea to make it about limiting the possibility of resort to war, whatever the cause.

The impulse that led to this pastoral letter came initially from Catholic opponents to war generally and to nuclear weapons and the possibility of nuclear war in particular. In the context of the buildup of U.S. nuclear capacity under the Reagan Administration in response to a perceived "missile gap" between U.S. and Soviet nuclear capabilities, members of the U.S. National Conference of Catholic Bishops who were personally anti-war and anti-nuclear wanted the Conference of Bishops to issue a statement condemning nuclear weapons and nuclear war. Their influence reached a high-water mark in the language of the second draft of the pastoral letter, which took an unyielding position against nuclear weapons and war generally. This draft, when it appeared, received unprecedented publicity for such a statement, appearing in full in both *The New York Times* and *The Washington Post* with extensive accompanying stories. Many in government and the military were deeply worried about the position taken in this draft statement, fearing that if the Catholic bishops adopted such a position as a matter of collective policy, Catholics serving in government and the military who had responsibilities within the system of nuclear deterrence could not be trusted to carry out those responsibilities.

The second draft of the pastoral letter did not survive, because of criticism from within the Conference of Bishops as well as from outside, and *The Challenge of Peace* as it finally was issued was based on a third, quite different, draft that presented Catholic moral teaching on war as including two traditions, a pacifist rejection of all war and the tradition of just war, which were described as linked and ultimately expressing different perspectives on a single basic idea: a moral "presumption against war." In fact such an idea never appeared in classic just war thought, the conception that appeared in Catholic canon law until 1918: there the aim is to prevent and remedy injustice, and the use of armed force may be justified for this purpose. In any case, within the moral frame established by this anti-war "presumption," the bishops defined the idea of just war as being "an effort to prevent war" by "establishing a set of rigorous conditions"—seven *jus ad bellum* criteria and two for the *jus in bello*—all of which must be unambiguously met for a war to be "morally permissible." The criteria named by the bishops included classic ones—just cause, what was here called "competent" authority, and right intention, though these were defined in new ways—but also several new ones: comparative justice, last resort, probability of success, and overall proportionality. Though a theoretical resort to war is possible here, in practice spokesmen for the bishops have, through arguments favoring the new prudential criteria, repeatedly argued against resort to war—even in the debate over use of force to undo Iraq's invasion and takeover of Kuwait in 1990–91. One critic has called the position taken in *The Challenge of Peace* and subsequent statements a "functional pacifism," and it is important to keep in mind that this conception of just war was described as being "an effort to prevent war."

I have dwelt in some detail on the U.S. Catholic bishops' conception of just war not only because it defines the third major stream in recent just war thinking, alongside those coming out of Ramsey's and Walzer's ideas of just war, but because for many the very idea of just war is a Catholic idea, so that what the U.S. bishops say it is must be right. Their list of the just war criteria has spread broadly in secular just war thinking, and so has the interpretation of the criteria in ways aimed at limiting sharply any justified right to use armed force or to deny it entirely. Thus to recall the list of recent authors of books on just war I mentioned earlier, Charles, Weeks, Phillips, and White all present lists of just war criteria that closely match the list given by the bishops, and Charles and White go out of their way to stress, like the bishops, that each and every one of the listed criteria must be unambiguously satisfied for a just resort to armed force. The result is a conception of just war that is fundamentally oriented toward preventing resort to war whatever the circumstances. In line with this aim, the Vatican now has an office of *jus contra bellum*, a recently constructed Latin term for moral reasons against war in all cases.

I have a good deal of respect for both Ramsey's and Walzer's lines of reasoning, though they each have their own limits and are very different from the classic conception of just war that I believe should be kept in central focus, but I regard the conception of just war put forward and defended by the U.S. Catholic bishops as fundamentally mistaken. The major good it did was to bring the just war idea into a broader debate, including within policy and military circles; yet its conception of the just war idea itself and how it is to be used has been entirely bad.

So how should we act to try to get the matter of just war right as a source for ethical reflection and action looking forward to the possibility of war and trying to find ways by which a justified use of force can serve our own security and that of the world, seeking to rectify injustices and create the conditions for peace? My answer is that these aims are best served by thoroughly understanding the idea of just war as it came together in its classic form and endured as a cultural consensus for several centuries. That conception focused not on avoiding violence as such but on the responsibility of good government to fight injustice by seeking to rectify it and to punish wrongdoing, all to the good of each political community and the collective good of all political communities, understood as inseparably linked so that harm to the good of one becomes harm to the good of all.

That classic conception was a reflection of Western culture in a broad sense: it incorporated engaged reflection on law, religion, human rights, the natural order of things, and both political and military experience. It began to come together in the work of a canon lawyer, a scholar named Gratian, in the middle of the twelfth century, was developed and refined by two generations of successors over a bit more than a century after that, and is best known through the summary account given by a theologian, Thomas Aquinas, in his major work the *Summa theologiae*, three-quarters of the way through the thirteenth century. In that account, which focuses on the decision whether to use force to rectify injustice and serve general peace, three requisites for a just war, a *bellum iustum*, are defined: sovereign authority—the authority of a temporal ruler with no temporal superior over the political community for which he has responsibility; just cause—setting right injustice and punishing those responsible for the injustice; and right intention—defined negatively as the avoidance of specific wrong intentions and positively as the intention to reestablish peace by restoring a just order. This conception of just war stands as the classic statement of the just war idea. Though described in the work of a theologian, it reflected a broad cultural consensus, and it held as a norm for over three hundred more years—an impressive track record. Again, this conception of just war focused on the decision to use armed force—what would today be called the *jus ad bellum*, though that term did not appear till several centuries later, when it was a legal term, not a moral one, and referred narrowly to the formal obligations of a state when moving to the legal status of being at war.

Aquinas's account did not specifically treat the matter of right conduct in the use of armed force, but the canon law by his time already included statements on this: a definition of noncombatant immunity by means of listing certain categories of people who normally were not directly engaged in war and thus should not have war directed at them, and a list of certain weapons not to be used in war because their effects were inherently indiscriminate and disproportionate. Separately the code of chivalry was also developing its own rules for right conduct in war, the *loi d'armes* or, in Latin, *jus in bello*. Later on, in the period of the Hundred Years' War, these two approaches to defining right conduct in the use of armed force were brought together and added to the conception of just war succinctly defined by Aquinas. This consolidated conception of just war was the one carried into the modern period, where it was gradually reshaped into a theory of the law of nations. Within this latter frame the essentially moral idea of "just" war fell out of fashion, being replaced by the idea of legal or "regular" war—war according to the rules or "laws and customs of war" accepted consensually by nations in their interactions.

We need to look a bit more closely at the meaning of the classic statement of just war as summarized by Aquinas's three conditions. First, just war had to do with *bellum*, a term we translate as "war" but which, in the medieval context, referred to the organized collective use of armed force on behalf of the political community for the good of that community as a whole under the authority of a person with governing responsibility. Any other use of armed force was *duellum*, which gives us our word "duel." In context this term referred to uses of force, whether by individuals or groups, that were not for the public good but for private gains or to settle private quarrels. While *duellum* was common for members of the knightly class through much of the Middle Ages, one reason for the emergence of the idea of *bellum iustum*, just war, was to attempt to root it out as destructive of public peace, order, and justice. Aquinas's terminology reflects this. His first necessity for a just war was "the authority of a prince," which meant the authority of a temporal ruler with no temporal superior. A ruler of this sort was also being referred to by the late twelfth century in French as *souverain*, in English "sovereign." So Aquinas's *acutoritas principis*, "the authority of a prince," could also be rendered as "sovereign authority." Such a person, a sovereign ruler, was, within his (or sometimes her, or even their) own political community, the person with final responsibility for the good of that community—its order, justice, and peace, in the language of the time. Everyone else within that community could in principle, and should in practice, refer any disputes upwards to his or her superiors, and any disputes not resolved at a lower level were the responsibility of the prince, the sovereign, to resolve. This way of thinking delegitimized *duellum* as a means of settling disputes, restricting the right of the use of armed force to the sovereign. But the sovereign's responsibility for the good of the whole community meant that he or she was responsible for rectifying any violation of justice within that community, for any violation of justice affected the community's overall order and its internal peace.

It was not just random, then, that Aquinas listed "the authority of a prince," sovereign authority, first among his three necessary conditions for a *bellum iustum*, a "just war." For the sovereign was the one person having the responsibility, understood as given him or her in the natural law, to rectify any injustice that might threaten the good of the community, to determine whether doing so would require armed force or not, and to reestablish a just order, all to the end of the community's peace. The other two conditions Aquinas named as necessary for a *bellum iustum*, just cause and right intention, were further specifications of the sovereign's moral responsibility. Just cause was defined as to restore that which had been wrongly taken, that is, to rectify the injustice at issue, and to punish the wrongdoer—for unlike much present-day thinking according to which punishment of any sort is inherently vindictive, punishment in the Middle Ages was understood as necessary to restore the balance of justice. Right intention, in turn, Aquinas defined two ways. First, he cited a well-known passage from Augustine listing wrongful personal intentions that had no place in the use of force to correct a wrong: "the desire for harming, the cruelty of avenging, an unruly and implacable animosity, the rage of rebellion, the lust of domination and the like." These bore specifically on the internal moral disposition of the ruler and those who fought under his authority. Response to a threat to the community was a *moral* responsibility, after all, and it could not be undertaken by persons with immoral dispositions. So this was one dimension of the requirement of "right intention." But a few paragraphs later Aquinas listed a broader aim, the end of peace, distinguishing uses of armed force in the service of this end from uses of force motivated by other intentions. The latter might technically be cases of *bellum*—collective uses of armed force on public authority—but they could not be *bellum iustum*—just uses of armed force—unless they were intended to serve the end of peace.

The outcome of all this was to define the idea of just war in a form that remained normative through the rest of the Middle Ages and into the Modern period and which still remains as the classic statement of just war, setting a standard for any subsequent effort to draw out the meaning of just war.

There are subtle interrelationships of ideas in this classic statement, and it is perhaps not surprising—though no less inexcusable—that most recent writing that claims to be about "just war" has missed them entirely. First, the responsibility for authorizing use of armed force is recognized here as belonging to the person or persons at the top of the pyramid of political authority in a given political community, because only he, she, or they have final responsibility for the good of that community. This is why Aquinas, in agreement with the canonical tradition before him, put "the authority of a prince" first among his requirements for a just war, and its importance is entirely missed in those present-day lists of the just war criteria that put just cause first and demote what is termed "competent" or "legitimate" authority to some subordinate position. This is perhaps understandable, though Augustine, with his sharp eye for the effects of sin in self-interest, would have certainly raised an eyebrow: putting just cause first, over the authority criterion, puts the right to determine just cause in the hands of the moralist—the individual writer on just war, or the U.S. Catholic bishops—despite the fact that such people do not bear the awesome responsibility of seeking to ensure the public good of the political community. The classic conception of just war, I think, got it right.

Second, the classic conception of just cause, as summarized in Aquinas's list of the necessities for a just use of armed force, is defined in terms of restoring justice where there has been injustice and punishing those responsible for the injustice. Restricting a political community's right to resort to force to cases of self-defense, as provided in the UN Charter and in much recent just war theorizing, was not part of the classic statement of just war, because at the time the right of self-defense against an attack immediately threatened or in progress was understood as given by natural law to anyone and everyone, and it needed no further authorization. But once the moment of the attack had passed, rectifying the injustice it had left in its wake was no longer a matter for private judgment: this became a responsibility for the sovereign. So it is not that the classic understanding of just war did not provide for defense of the community in the face of a threat or an actual attack; it was just that this obligation was assumed. The focus then shifted to how to restore the justice that had been violated by the threat or attack, and that is what classic just war thought specifically sought to address. I think we should be deeply concerned, for moral reasons, about contemporary versions of just war thinking that have as their aim avoiding any resort to violence. For then injustice stands, and those responsible are left with the power to go on unopposed. The classic conception of just war, I think, got it right.

Finally, what of right intention, the third classic requirement for a just war? The wrong intentions identified by Augustine and preserved in the classic account of just war remind us that political leaders are charged with rising above their own personal motivations when considering whether to use armed force in the service of the good of the community as a whole. Applied to warriors, it also serves as a reminder that individual soldiers, however much they may feel the loss of a comrade and have come to hate the enemy, have the responsibility to rise above that, for they are not given the right to kill and to destroy because of their own personal hurts but to protect, defend, and uphold the good of the community they serve.

The reality, of course, is that these dimensions of hurt are part of the experience of every person who has been in combat, and they are not to be denied. My point is that the classic idea of just war reminds us that revenge for these hurts don't represent the final moral purpose of taking part in combat. In the very different moral and religious climate of the Middle Ages, for about a century there was a canonical requirement that soldiers returning from combat confess any wrongful intentions they had had, do penance for them, and only then receive absolution and be readmitted to the life of the church. This was, we might reasonably say, a way of seeking to deal with the reality of combat and PTSD. In the just war frame, it served to remind returning warriors that what they did in combat they did on the authority of others and in the service of the good of the community as a whole. This problem has generally been neglected in recent writing on just war. It would be good, I think, if we sought to do more.

But the second dimension of right intention is the end of peace. This is all too often omitted in recent lists of just war criteria. It is not there in Ramsey or in Walzer. The Catholic bishops reduce it to an element of the *jus in bello*, removing it entirely from the moral intentionality that should be present in the decision to use armed force in a particular context. This fits the way the states of war and peace are handled by the bishops and in international law: war and peace are separate and distinct; peace ceases to exist when war begins, and it comes back into being when war ends. In the frame of moral argument that begins with opposition to war as evil in itself, there is no place for peace in the conception of war. But again, I think the classic conception of just war got it right: peace means much more than the absence of war, and we need to have a way of thinking morally about war that recognizes when it is essential to the service of peace.

Overall, I have been arguing that the classic conception of just war got the fundamentals right in its moral definition of sovereign authority, just cause, and right intention, and I think contemporary just war reasoning ought to pay a great deal more attention to that classic statement of the idea of just war. I myself have been particularly drawn to it in recent years because of what it says on how to think about political responsibility and service to the public good. But the theorists who worked to define and interpret the classic conception of just war worked within very different historical frames from one another and from us, and so the point should always be how to understand what and how those thinkers were about, and how we today might best, in the context of our own historical frame, think of the responsibilities of political leaders and the communities they serve in seeking to ensure the good of their neighbors in their own political community and in the world at large. Getting it right is a perennial challenge that we should all seek to meet, and enrolling the witness of history helps toward meeting that challenge successfully.

ABSTRACT

This article from *Providence* magazine discusses the relationship between Christian ethics and statecraft. Johnson believes that Christian thought should engage political realism but must do so acknowledging the complexities of the political landscape and international arena as well as the fact of American pluralism. However, he believes that cross-cultural studies and interaction such as found in his work on just war and *jihad* may provide a way forward.

CHAPTER 23

CHRISTIAN ETHICS & THE REALM OF STATECRAFT: DIVISIONS, CROSS-CURRENTS, & THE SEARCH FOR CONNECTIONS

Providence magazine seeks engagement between Christianity and American foreign policy, an effort that necessarily must proceed not upon a smooth playing-field but rather on a landscape strewn with numerous obstacles. In the United States, religious engagement on matters of public policy is as old as American society itself, and its possibility is in no way vitiated by the doctrine of separation of church and state. Such engagement does not have to do with replacing religious judgments and decisions with those of the political process; rather it proceeds as a form of citizen engagement in that process, seeking to inform it and to help it better operate—my own aim throughout my work is on how to understand the ethical traditions of just war and *jihad* of the sword. The task of such engagement is well worthwhile, but to be effectively carried out the obstacles must be recognized, understood, and negotiated. In what follows I will first lay out some of the most important obstacles, the challenges they pose, their respective weaknesses, and some thoughts on opportunities they offer; then I will offer some thoughts on how best to bring Christianity into engagement with American foreign policy.

An especially difficult obstacle to such engagement is that political realism as it exists today seeks to deny any place whatever for ethical or other value concerns, religious or not, in the policy arena, reserving that arena for considerations of interests alone. On this conception ethical values and arguments are expressions of idealism and assimilated to utopianism, as in Robert Osgood's benchmark study *Ideals and Self-Interest in America's Foreign Relations*. The realist, Osgood wrote,

> is skeptical of attempts to mitigate international conflict with appeals to sentiment or principle or with written pledges and institutional devices unless they express the existing configuration of national interests or register the relative power among nations. He believes that if power conflicts can be mitigated at all, they can be mitigated only by balancing power against power and by cultivating a circumspect diplomacy that knows the use of force and the threat of force as indispensable elements of national policy. (9)

This position is not without its own serious problems. The acknowledged founders of realism, Hans Morgenthau and Reinhold Niebuhr, had conceived it somewhat differently, leaving room for the working of ethical values and arguments, and the conception of realism as summarized by Osgood does not acknowledge its own dependence on ideals and values at the core of the conception of what counts as "American national interests" and the priorities among them. Nonetheless, realism in its current form wants nothing to do with ethical values or arguments based on them when they are presented as bearing on policy, unless they are transformed into the language of interests. This resistance is a formidable obstacle to efforts to engage Christianity with the formulation and administration of foreign policy, but it is best met by a robust challenge to the assumptions of realism itself, making way for an embrace of ideals and values as essential elements in conceiving national interests and policies.

At the same time, the challenge posed by realism is a reminder that Christian and other religious efforts—indeed, any efforts motivated by deep ethical concerns—to enter policy debates must take with utmost seriousness the complexities of the empirical landscape and the possibilities offered there. This was ultimately what Reinhold Niebuhr's conception of Christian realism sought to do (see, for example, his early books, *Christ and Culture* (1932) and *An Interpretation of Christian Ethics* (1935), where he was first working out this position). Niebuhr avoided the attractions of believing that Christian ethical effort could transform American society into the Kingdom of God on earth but nonetheless championed such an effort in a chastened spirit of recognition of human sinfulness and finitude. Such a position is not utopian; it is realistic on its own terms.

A second and very different kind of obstacle to Christian ethical engagement in the sphere of public policy is that the United States today has become more religiously pluralistic, with the changing contours of American Christianity itself and these various forms of Christianity coexisting alongside varieties of the other major world religions as well as various forms of indigenous religious expression, including some that are radically individual. But such change is not inherently negative, and indeed the respect for religious freedom that makes it possible is a core American value. The American religious landscape has never been static, and the diversity of religion in America has historically fed a constant renewal that has been a major contributor to the strength of religion in America and its contribution to the national character. So the current multivalent religious landscape in the United States presents a challenge best met with new focus on how to understand and live out the basic meaning of Christianity and how to engage creatively and with nuance debates over public policy, including foreign policy.

There is also another way that the challenge of religious diversity in American society may prove a benefit rather than an obstacle. Encountering diverse religions opens doors to better cross-cultural understanding, and this carries obvious positive implications for engagement in the sphere of foreign affairs. I will return to this below with specific reference to my own work on the Islamic tradition of *jihad* of the sword.

A third kind of obstacle is that religiously-based ethical values and arguments coexist with, and compete with, other sorts of conceptions of ethics and support for policies in accord with such conceptions. Domestic examples abound, many of them having to do with sexuality and sexual behavior, but in the arena of foreign policy this competition is illustrated by the rise of a revisionist version of just war theory within the frame of analytic philosophy. So far as its ethics is concerned, this revision is utilitarian, and while some revisionist just war thinkers appeal to a basis in human rights, the conception of rights is an abstract one divorced from its historical and thematic Christian connections.

Now, the tradition of just war that the revisionists seek to replace incorporates important Christian influences, but these are not acknowledged in the revisionist accounts. When such different positions as represented by the revisionists arise, it is important to be able to recognize them for what they are, that is, positions that have only some terminology in common with the historical tradition of just war; a Christian conception of the morality of the use of armed force does not distill into a utilitarian argument, even one based in an abstracted philosophical conception of human rights. This is just one example, but whenever the same issues arise across the whole arena of debates over policy, the same argument applies.

Finally, I would mention the obstacle posed by the fact that there is no single Christian position on the sphere of political life and the relationship between it on the one hand and the sphere of Christian life on the other. We can describe the differences in various ways, but what is by now a classic catalogue of them was provided by H. Richard Niebuhr in *Christ and Culture*. Niebuhr identified five major approaches, analyzing each one and connecting it to the thought of particular theologians.

In his first approach, Christ against culture, he identified with the first-century church as well as later approaches like Tolstoy's; his second, the Christ of culture, he described as the position of liberal Protestantism, connected historically with the "culture-Protestantism" of the nineteenth-century German theologian Albrecht Ritschl among others; his third, Christ above culture, he developed as the approach historically associated with Catholic theology and especially Thomas Aquinas, with his conception of the theological and natural virtues and their interrelation;

his fourth, Christ and culture in paradox, he associated with the Apostle Paul, Martin Luther, and others; while the last approach he treated, Christ transforming culture, he connected particularly to the thought of Augustine and described as exemplified in the twentieth century in the theology of F. D. Maurice. Niebuhr did his best to treat these various positions evenhandedly, but the ideal of "freedom in dependence" he developed in his concluding chapter seems particularly close to his positive characterization of the "Christ transforming culture" or "conversionist" position he characterized as "the present encounter with God in Christ" and as an "awareness of the power of the Lord to transform all things by lifting them up to himself" (195).

This inventory remains useful, not least because of the theological connections Niebuhr made and the fact that every one of these positions can be found in present-day American Christianity. The first and fourth of these positions separate Christian life from life in political community, while the second effectively collapses the two, seriously diminishing or even removing the possibility of a critical engagement based on a difference between them. These positions thus do not offer a fruitful frame for engagement between Christianity and foreign affairs. The two remaining positions, by contrast, provide different frames for such engagement, both connected to important theological positions and also expressed in historical manifestations. Examining these in more detail thus takes us into constructive possibilities for the kind of engagement being sought in the present and future contexts.

In considering these two possible frames, I would note the need to go beyond Niebuhr's analysis in *Christ and Culture*, for he missed some important things and, I think, did not rightly understand others.

An important example of both limitations is that, like his older brother Reinhold, he did not have an appreciation for the distinct and independent authority of the idea of natural law in medieval thought apart from Aquinas's theological synthesis. This affected his understanding of the position he associated with Aquinas's theology, which for him epitomized the "Christ above culture" perspective.

Medieval thought recognized a distinction between what it called the realms of the "spiritual" and the "temporal." A fuller and more accurate account of how these were understood in the medieval frame would require closer and more appreciative understanding than provided in *Christ and Culture* of the canonical thought that preceded Aquinas, for it was the canonists of the late twelfth and early thirteenth centuries who recovered the idea of natural law from Roman law and political thought and placed their understanding of it within their thinking on just war and political order. In their understanding of this concept and its application to human moral choice, natural law was by no means a fixed framework, as both Niebuhrs and much of Protestant thought more generally have treated it, defined finally by the authority of the revealed law of God as interpreted by and through the authority of the church. Rather, on the medieval conception, this law was built into nature itself and served to give temporal life its own autonomous place. The idea of natural law thus heightened the importance of human moral judgments and decisions in the operation of the temporal order. Natural law referred to a rationally accessible reference point for guiding moral decision-making, but the final judgment as to the meaning of this law in a given case was a matter for moral choice.

How this understanding worked was epitomized in the canonists' conception of temporal sovereignty. This conception was based in the Gelasian principle (named after the late sixth-century Pope Gelasius) of a distinction between spiritual and temporal authority. On this distinction, while the former kind of authority belongs to the Church, it does not extend to temporal rule, and authority and responsibility for temporal affairs belongs to temporal rulers, with those having no temporal superiors—sovereign rulers—exercising supreme authority in their own political communities. While individual judgments as to the natural law might differ and lead to conflicts, resolving such conflicts was the power and responsibility of temporal sovereigns in their function of judges of last resort as to right and wrong within their domains, in their making and enforcing their own judgments as to the requirements of natural law in the specific contexts at hand.

A ruler's judgments might be self-serving or otherwise flawed, and thus the ultimate test of their rightness or wrongness in terms of their conformity to the natural law was whether these judgments contributed to the common good of the community ruled—its overall order, justice, and peace. A ruler might be a tyrant, and this could be measured both by that ruler's own people and by neighboring sovereigns using their own judgments as to the requirement of the natural law that the common good is to be served. Of course, that good can be served in various ways, and responsible efforts to act according to the natural law might thus take many forms. On this conception the temporal sovereign, and in no way the spiritual authorities, was responsible for judging what the natural law required so as best to serve the community governed. Nor did this conception of sovereignty mean that might makes right, for the sovereign's judgments were themselves subject to judgment by others within the temporal sphere. The point is the moral autonomy of temporal judgments. Temporal authority, on this conception, has its own autonomy relative to the spiritual authority of the Church, but it is bound by fundamental responsibility for the good of the society governed, and by extension for the good of neighboring societies.

There is, of course, a good deal more to say about this than these brief sentences provide, and further discussion can be found in the first chapter of my *Sovereignty: Moral and Historical Perspectives*. Sufficient for now is to sum up by noting that on this conception more generally the idea of natural law functioned as a guide to practical moral reasoning by persons operating within the context of worldly life. Moral decision-making, on this model, had to do with making a responsible effort to understand and apply the natural law. It took the form of practical moral reasoning in the context of life in community within the temporal order. In laying on each individual the obligation to take this responsibility seriously, this notion also laid a special responsibility on those individuals with sovereign political authority, those charged with exercising this responsibility for the good of the entire community.

I suggest this way of thinking about political decision-making as itself a moral enterprise aimed at the common good of the political community—and of the interactions among such communities worldwide—can be a fruitful element in an engagement between Christianity and foreign affairs. It entails respect for the political order and the persons involved in its working, but it also serves as a reminder that this order must be oriented to the common good, both of our own political community specifically and of the larger interconnected reality of all political communities more generally, and that those responsible for the working of political order and relationships can be held to account for their judgments and decisions. That the political sphere itself, including the justified use of force in the service of the goods of political community, exists for the purpose of human flourishing is deeply rooted in Christian doctrine and should not be forgotten. (Consider the pithy statement provided in Romans 13:1–4; Romans 13:4 was frequently cited in connection with the classic idea of just war.) An important reason for Christian engagement with the public sphere is to remind those involved in the making of policy and in political decision-making that such human flourishing should always be their goal.

In the historical context I have been describing, natural law referred to a widespread consensus as to the nature of the common good and the ends of politics. Pursuing this method in the effort to relate Christianity to foreign affairs today requires identifying and pursuing agreements on core values that transcend the borders of states and cultures. This returns me to a point I raised earlier in relation to the encounter of diverse religious beliefs in the context of American society. In my own work on moral traditions on war, I have sought to identify agreement across differing religions and cultural frames by bringing just war tradition into comparative dialogue with the *jihad* tradition and, more recently, with the varied moral traditions on war found in Chinese history. I have also argued that international law and international agreements short of formal law show where such agreement across cultures exists and what are the limits of such agreement. Thus, of particular relevance to my work on the contemporary implications of just war thinking, I have taken pains to treat the law of armed conflict, today widely called international humanitarian law, as expressing shared moral consensus. The language of natural law was appropriate to the context of the twelfth and thirteenth centuries. Whether or not the term is used today, the functions it referred to remain, if under different names, and therefore finding the best contemporary language for natural law is critical to religious ethical engagement with the sphere of foreign affairs. This is not in any way to compromise Christian ethical values and concerns in the process of seeking such engagement, but rather a way to frame such values and concerns so that they respect the different role and responsibility of government from those of the religious sphere and can be recognized as relevant in the political sphere.

Let me turn now in a different direction, to Richard Niebuhr's reading of Augustine and the idea of Christ transforming culture. The transformationist or (Richard Niebuhr's preferred term) conversionist understanding of the Christ-culture relationship fitted well the assumptions of mainline American Protestantism that had taken shape earlier in the twentieth century—defined first by Walter Rauschenbusch and the Social Gospel movement, then chastened and redefined by Richard's older brother Reinhold in his thinking on Christian love as related to natural justice—and Richard Niebuhr's own theology belonged to this distinctively American theological tradition. The influence of his thinking in this way about the relation of Christianity to political life shows up in the work of Paul Ramsey, who did his doctoral work under Richard Niebuhr at Yale and who adopted and developed a version of this way of thinking as a way of describing the working of divine love within history progressively to shape politics toward its own ideal end.

This conception, in Ramsey's work, depended centrally on a particular way of reading Augustine's understanding of divine love or *caritas*, charity, as a theology describing how this love is operating within history to transform the world toward the City of God. For "bookends" to this way of thinking, see the second chapter of Ramsey's *War and the Christian Conscience* (1961) and his essay "A Political Ethics Context for Strategic Thinking" in the edited volume *Strategic Thinking and Its Moral Implications* (1973). Augustine's thought thus described provided a powerful basis for a Christian politics aimed at Christian participation in this transformation. Even when its possibilities were limited, as in Reinhold Niebuhr's characterization of love as an "impossible possibility" for human striving marked by sin and finitude, the ideal variously called the "City" or "Kingdom" of God still provided the ultimate pattern for the kind of world Christians ought to seek to create.

But Augustine's theology was in fact a good deal more complex than this reading on its own allows, and taking this into account, I suggest, leads to a different but still positive mandate for engagement between Christianity and the sphere of political life. As the medieval historian R. A. Markus observed in his essay in *The Church and War*, Augustine went through three periods in his thinking about the relation of Christianity to politics, including war, and only in the second of these, marked by the rule of a Christian emperor and Christian officials open to advice from Church leaders, did he seem to have an idea that the City of Earth (City of Man) might itself, through identification with the Church, be capable of reform towards the City of God. In the third period of Augustine's life, Markus notes, which included imperial and other efforts to suppress the influence of Christianity and restore that of the old Roman religion and was also marked by the rising strength of Arian Christianity in the form of the power of the Germanic societies that were increasingly carving the Empire up into distinct kingdoms, Augustine moved away from whatever optimism he may have had about the possibility of transforming earthly society and focused on the City of God as referring to the life of the saints in heaven with God and the angels.

Within this latter conception, Christians were pilgrims in an alien land, but they nonetheless had an obligation to act so as to maintain the best of the Roman order so as to provide a basis for the life of the Church as it moved towards its own realization as the City of God. To argue for maintaining a society for the goods it offers despite its flaws is far from arguing that divine love, *caritas*, can in history remake earthly society so as to diminish and ultimately remove those flaws, but the former still provides a mandate for Christian engagement with the affairs of the political order. Acting so as to contribute to the goods society offers is itself morally good.

The transformationist conception of Christian possibility was also found in another important place: the idea of America's destiny as the Kingdom of God on Earth, a topic to which Richard Niebuhr had devoted his earlier book *The Kingdom of God in America*. Niebuhr there criticized how this idea had developed, at one point referring caustically to the coming together of missionary and commercial activity in foreign lands during the nineteenth century as "bring[ing] light to the Gentiles by means of lamps manufactured in America" (179), but he never rejected the idea in itself or the ideal it set for American society in history. This, one might say, is the transformationist theme in a nutshell. I think Reinhold Niebuhr was right to point out that, because of human sin and finitude, our best attempts toward a love-informed justice nonetheless carry with them seeds of future injustice, so that the Kingdom of God can only be an ideal to aim at, not one ever to be achieved by human efforts in history. But even if the ideal cannot be realized in history, the existence of that ideal constitutes a moral charge, so that the good life is one that seeks to strive toward it. This way of thinking corresponds well with Augustine's insight that preservation of the best that political community can produce also presents a moral charge. This, in the end, is the value of the transformationist understanding of Christianity's proper relationship to the world.

What I have been describing, beginning with two of the perspectives Richard Niebuhr described in *Christ and Culture* but building on this to take account of elements in Christian thought Niebuhr did not treat, is effectively how I think about my own work in the sphere of the ethics of war. I think of the idea of just war tradition, the focal core of my work, as itself the result of a process of engagement among different sources of influence: Christian thought and ethics, to be sure, but also the theory and practice of politics, the theory and practice of military life, and other influences. When the classic conception of just war came together in the twelfth and thirteenth centuries it manifested a broad cultural consensus on the place the use of armed force should have in the effort to serve the ends of political life. Though it was principally, in the first place, a product of canonical reasoning, debate, and decision, and though the particular summary account of this consensus given by Aquinas in the frame of his theology provided the standard statement of the just war idea that endured well into the modern age, this was by no means a narrowly Christian idea imposed on Western society by the Church. Rather its force and endurance came from its being a product of dialogue between the spiritual and the temporal in which both were respected and the conclusions reached respected the goods of temporal life in political community. How to replicate such dialogue and to produce such a fruitful and enduring end should be the aim of any effort at engaging Christianity with American foreign affairs.

REFERENCES

Johnson, James Turner. *Sovereignty: Moral and Historical Perspectives.* Washington, D.C.: Georgetown University Press, 2014.

Markus, R.A. "Saint Augustine's Views on the 'Just War.'" In W. J. Sheils, *The Church and War.* Oxford: Basil Blackwell for The Ecclesiastical History Society, 1–13, 1983.

Niebuhr, H. Richard. *The Kingdom of God in America.* New York, Evanston, and London: Harper and Row, 1937, reprint ed., 1951.

_______. *Christ and Culture.* New York: Harper & Brothers.

Niebuhr, Reinhold. *Moral Man and Immoral Society.* New York: Charles Scribner's Sons, 1932.

_______. *An Interpretation of Christian Ethics.* New York: Meridian Books, 1935.

Osgood, Robert E. *Ideals and Self-Interest in America's Foreign Relations.* Chicago: The University of Chicago Press, 1953.

Ramsey, Paul. *War and the Christian Conscience.* Durham, North Carolina: Duke University Press, 1961.

________. "A Political Ethics Context for Strategic Thinking." In Morton A. Kaplan, ed., *Strategic Thinking and Its Moral Implications,* 101–47, Chicago: University of Chicago Press, 1973.

ABSTRACT

This essay looks at recent interpretations of Augustine by just war proponents Paul Ramsey and Jean Bethke Elshtain. Johnson then considers Augustine's thought in its historical context and Ramsey's understanding of Augustine and war with respect to the idea of Christian love. He then views Aquinas's reading of Augustine as inherited through Gratian's *Decretum* (1148).

CHAPTER 24

READING AUGUSTINE

Augustine's influence runs deep and broad through Western Christian doctrine and ethics. This paper focuses on two particular examples of this influence: his thinking on political order and on just war. Augustine's conception of political order and the Christian's proper relation to it, developed most fully in his last and arguably most comprehensive theological work, *The City of God,* is central in both Catholic and mainline Protestant thinking on the political community and the proper exercise of government. Especially important in recent debate, the origins of the Christian idea of just war trace to Augustine. Exactly how Augustine has been read and understood on these topics, as well as others, has varied considerably depending on context, so the question in each and every context is how to read and understand Augustine.

Paul Ramsey was right to insist, in the process of developing his own understanding of just war, that in Christian thinking the idea of just war does not stand alone but is part of a comprehensive conception of good politics. This also describes Augustine's thinking. Those writers on just war who separate it from the larger context of good politics—and in recent debate there have been a good many of these—omit something essential to both: for the just war idea, its direct connection to political order, justice, and peace, the three goods classically defining the nature and purpose of politics; and for the sphere of government and statecraft, the necessity of a just but limited role for the use of coercive force. To treat each of these topics properly requires treating them as connected. When they are separated, one or another kind of distortion is the result.

It is, of course, possible to approach either or both of these topics without taking account of Augustine's thinking or its influence, or indeed any form of Christian perspective at all. My focus on Augustine here reflects my judgment as to the impossibility of doing full justice to either without attending to his influence, so deeply embedded is he on these topics in Western experience and ways of thinking. But to take account of his influence also requires recognizing and coming to terms with the different ways Augustine's thinking has been used in different contexts. How to make useful sense of these differences? This is the fundamental problem for any reading of Augustine on these subjects.

My discussion begins by examining the use of Augustine by two prominent recent thinkers on just war, Paul Ramsey and Jean Bethke Elshtain, in the process of beginning to look more closely at Augustine's thinking in his own context. Then I turn to a very different way of reading Augustine and examine the way his thought was carried (and in the process, transformed) during the Middle Ages up to the coalescence of a systematic understanding of just war in the twelfth and thirteenth centuries, again setting this over against Augustine's thought in its own context. Each of these historical contexts yields a different picture of Augustine's thinking, and so I conclude this discussion by suggesting how to use these varied perspectives to shape a reading of Augustine and his influence for the present context.

PAUL RAMSEY'S READING OF AUGUSTINE

Among recent thinkers on just war, Ramsey has a seminal role. Not only did his two books from the 1960s, *War and the Christian Conscience* and *The Just War: Force and Political Responsibility*,[1] take the first major step in recovering and redefining the just war idea for the context of contemporary warfare, but his use of Augustine, especially in the first of these books, set a pattern for later thinkers to build on. In chapter two of this book, titled "The Just War According to St. Augustine," Ramsey undertakes a theological exegesis of Augustine on Christian love (which

Ramsey here calls "charity," following the King James Version and reflecting Augustine's term *caritas*). From this he develops his own distinctive conception of just war built on the Christian's obligation to love the neighbor, employing Augustine's discussion of love in *On the Morals of the Catholic Church* XV, a passing reference to *City of God* V, and then, in numerous citations and at more length, *The City of God* XIX.[2]

Ramsey is not deterred by the fact that the first of these works says nothing at all about just war or the use of force as an instrument of neighbor-love. His argument is rather that the conception of love defined there serves as the theological basis for Augustine's entire ethic. After establishing the foundations of Augustine's theology in this way, Ramsey then devotes the rest of his chapter to an extended discussion focused on *City of God* XIX, developing Augustine's concept of just war as an element in his understanding of political ethics and particularly his conception of justice. This choice is interesting because Augustine says relatively little directly about war here, and he does not make the connection to divine charity that Ramsey regards as central. So one must follow Ramsey's reasoning, not simply Augustine's words, to find this connection.

How Ramsey understands and draws out the connection to Augustine's theology of charity is especially well illustrated by his use of *City of God* XIX, chapter vii. Here Augustine directly discusses war, but his purpose is to show how war contributes to the misery of human life in sin. In this passage, which Ramsey quotes at length, Augustine writes, "For it is the wrongdoing of the opposing party which compels the wise man to wage just wars." Here the problem is sin, and Augustine links the justification of opposing it to prudence, not charity. Yet Ramsey argues that charity is present nonetheless in that wisdom. His thinking here reflects the description of Augustine's overall methodology given by Ramsey's doctoral mentor H. Richard Niebuhr in his book *Christ and Culture*,[3] where Augustine's theology is characterized as an example of "Christ the transformer of culture." Ramsey puts his own version of the idea this way: "[S]ince the nature of that city in which men together attain their final end is divine charity, as a consequence even earthly cities began to be elevated and their justice was infused and transformed by new perspectives, limits, and principles."[4] That is, charity draws human justice towards it; its effect is present even when unacknowledged. This understanding permeates Ramsey's discussion throughout his chapter on Augustine on just war, and he carries it forward into his own conception of just war as centered on the Christian responsibility of love for the neighbor threatened or harmed by injustice. Ramsey's reading of Augustine is that of a theologian seeking to draw out the meaning of Augustine's theology for the idea of just war.

Yet Ramsey the theologian was also working out of his own theological context, which was one in which the centrality of love for Christian ethics was defined in terms shaped by late-nineteenth-century Protestant liberalism, the Social Gospel movement of the early twentieth century with its drive to transform society toward the Kingdom of God on Earth, and the influence of Reinhold Niebuhr, with his emphasis on love transforming justice. In this context Augustine's own focus on love was especially attractive.

But Ramsey's reading of *City of God* XIX as an expression of a theology of love as one in which divine charity is drawing human justice towards it reflects Ramsey's own theological context rather than Augustine's position. As R. A. Markus has observed,[5] Augustine did in fact hold a view something like this for a time during the middle period of his life, when the imperial establishment of Christianity as Rome's official religion promised reforms that would gradually change the nature of society towards the good. This changed in the last period of his life, when his duties as a bishop, his struggle against the Donatists, a shift in the imperial religious climate back toward paganism, and finally the combined military-political-religious threat posed by the Arian Vandals all fed a darkening of his attitude toward the possibilities of history. Peter Brown calls this change in Augustine "the lost future."[6] By the time he wrote the last books of *City of God*, including Book XIX, Augustine was thinking in terms of this darker conception of human history, not his earlier optimism. Markus describes the change in these words: "In the

City of God, and especially in its last books, Augustine turned his back on the mirage of the 'Christian Empire' of the Theodosian dynasty, and on the assumptions about God's hand in human affairs which had sustained it."[7] His conception of the justification for Christian participation in a just war accordingly shifted to a more modest one: to help maintain the order of the world, however fatally marred by sin, until God's purposes for it had finally been realized. Again to cite Markus: "[W]ar now became for him one of the tragic necessities to which Christians must at times resort in order to check the savagery which is liable to break out between, as well as within, political societies."[8] This is a somewhat different understanding of the nature of the Christian moral justification for participating in just war than that read out of Augustine by Ramsey.

JEAN BETHKE ELSHTAIN'S READING OF AUGUSTINE

I turn now to a briefer look at Jean Bethke Elshtain's reading of Augustine. Unlike Ramsey, Elshtain was not a theologian but a political scientist, though she made significant use of Christian ideas in her work. This is especially true for her thinking about just war, most fully given voice in *Just War Against Terror*, chapters three and seven.[9] As she shows here, her understanding of just war is fundamentally shaped by Augustine, and two comments she makes—"The origins of this tradition are usually traced from St. Augustine's fourth-century masterwork, *The City of God*" (actually completed in 425) and "For Augustine, a resort to force may be an obligation of loving one's neighbor, a central feature of Christian ethics"[10]—correspond to the two features highlighted in Ramsey's reading of Augustine on just war.

But a fuller look at her references to just war and its use shows a close fit to the references to Augustine provided in Aquinas' question "On War." The parallels include her characterization of just war on just cause, right authority, and limits on means;[11] the citation of Romans 13 as providing the scriptural basis for Christian authorities to use force;

the rejection of certain motivations for resort to war;[12] the aim of resisting evil;[13] and Augustine's connection of just war to the end—aim—of peace.[14] She makes these references without citations to Augustine, suggesting that this understanding of just war has become so embedded in her mind as not to need such justification, though a look at Aquinas' corresponding citations from Augustine shows that they come from a variety of works (Letter 138 to Marcellinus, *Contra Faustum*, his commentaries on the Heptateuch and on the Sermon on the Mount, and Letter 189 to Boniface). Moreover, none of these references directly links just war to the idea of Christian love of neighbor. The one citation of Augustine Elshtain does provide, supporting one of her comments on the relation of just war to peace, is to *City of God* XIX.[15] Aquinas cites Letter 189 to Boniface on this topic. The diversity of Aquinas' citations of Augustine on just war reflects the way the historical tradition from which he drew recalled Augustine's teachings on just war, while Elshtain's readiness to root Augustine's just war thought in the *City of God* mirrors the influence of Ramsey in American Christian just war thinking.

MODERN READINGS VS. MEDIEVAL READINGS

Neither Elshtain nor Ramsey refers to the way the historical tradition between Augustine and Aquinas defined and carried what Augustine said about just war and how it manifested the diversity in Augustine's thought on this topic. How Augustine was read here differed in major ways from the readings offered by these recent interpreters. The development of this medieval tradition of interpretation reflected important facts about its historical context and the changing nature of Christian religion.

First, there was an enormous difference between that age and our own in literacy and in the availability of published material. Today one can affordably access online all the major works of Augustine, other Fathers of the Church, Aquinas' *Summa*, and other resources, either in the original Latin, English, or other major languages. Most of these were already in print before the advent of the internet: Ramsey's reading of Augustine depended on the availability of a somewhat excerpted version of *City of God* and *On the Morals of the Catholic Church* in a Random House two-volume collection published near the beginning of his academic career.[16]

By contrast, during Augustine's lifetime and increasingly as the Middle Ages developed, only a narrow range of people could read and write: the educated elite, a range of clergy, and some among the monks in monasteries. This situation was aggravated as the Roman Empire in the West came apart by the emergence of regional vernaculars and the decline in general knowledge of Latin, the language in which the Christian authorities had written. Moreover, during this period books were extremely expensive, a consequence mostly of the hours required to produce each copy but also to a lesser degree the materials composing them. Peter Brown comments that in the fourth century (that is, during most of Augustine's life) "each copy of the Gospels cost as much as a marble sarcophagus,"[17] and this relative cost carried through the following centuries. When even individual volumes were so expensive, only the wealthy and, increasingly as the Middle Ages developed, monastic houses and major bishoprics could afford to own and maintain libraries. At the same time, these were the places where knowledge of Latin could be maintained. Augustine's writings themselves made up an extensive library, and even in his own time not all his works were generally available. After his death this became a more acute problem—not only for his writings but also for the works of other important Christian authorities.

The character of Christian religion in Europe also changed in this period. During Augustine's lifetime the Christian ideal, strongly influenced by Platonism, was the life of seclusion and contemplation. Augustine sought to follow this pattern in his early life as a Christian and never gave it up as an ideal even after accepting the office of bishop, with its necessary involvement in worldly affairs and the lives of his priests and congregation. This ideal remained for the medieval Church, but it was increasingly channeled by a distinction between those who had received the particular vocation to the "religious" life—monks and nuns—and those who had not, the majority of people of all social ranks. The religion of the latter had to be defined in some other way than by worldly renunciation, seclusion, and contemplation.

These three needs—the great expense of books, widespread popular illiteracy, and a simplified form of religious and moral guidance for the majority of the population who had not received the calling to monastic life but still wanted to live as Christians—were met by the emergence of a new kind of Christian literature: collections of selections from the teachings of Christian authorities gathered and laid out as *canones*, canons or ritual and ethical rules for Christian living. The resulting volumes could be relatively inexpensively reproduced and circulated among bishops and clergy to use in their guidance of the faithful.

AQUINAS' SREADING OF AUGUSTINE, THROUGH GRATIAN

Collections of canons began to be circulated, according to Peter Brown, coincident with the collapse of the Western Empire, which provided a vacuum of unity and leadership the Church sought to fill. There were numerous such collections, building on one another as older volumes disintegrated from use and time, and most of them have been lost. In the twelfth century, their legacy was preserved and represented in two major collections, those of Ivo of Chartres and Anselm of Lucca, which provided the basis for the first systematic compilation of canon law, Gratian's *Decretum*, completed in 1148. The discipline of canon law effectively began with this work, and so does a comprehensive, systematic conception of just war.

Among the topics specifically treated by Gratian was the topic of just war,[18] which earlier had been defined only in a scattered, non-cohesive way in the collections of canons by selections from various works by various authors. The *Decretum* brought the canons together and organized them to address particular issues with the use of armed force. After two generations of canonists, Gratian clarified what was meant in particular cases and added content where there were gaps.

Aquinas' question "On War" came at the end of this process and directly reflected and summarized it with its definition of just war by three requisites (princely or sovereign authority, just cause, and right intention, which included avoidance of evil purposes and the aim of producing peace) and his heavy reliance on references to Augustine to provide authority for the main elements of the just war idea. All of Aquinas' references to Augustine came from Gratian. These references were, as noted earlier, from works of a wide variety of sorts: polemical treatises, biblical commentaries, and certain of Augustine's letters. In addition to these, all of which Aquinas took over, Gratian's references included selected biblical passages as well as various other works of Augustine: additional commentaries and sermons, Book I (but not Book XIX) of *City of God*, additional use of the *Contra Faustum*, and *On Free Will*. All these he placed alongside selections (that is, canons) from other early authorities, notably including Isidore of Seville and Pope Gregory the Great.

None of the passages Gratian included in this first systematic compilation on just war mentioned love of neighbor, and indeed there was no effort to give them a theological context. Rather, these passages were taken simply for their own content, and their authority as rules for Christian life was assumed because of their authors. Contrary to Ramsey, Elshtain, and a good deal of recent Christian thought on the just war idea, when this idea first coalesced into a systematic form, it was not presented as deriving from love of neighbor, and it was based on citations from a broad variety of Augustine's works, not Book XIX of *City of God*.

Two major concerns were reflected in this medieval conception of just war, in the canons chosen to define it, and in how they were interpreted. These concerns were the disorder and violence endemic to the society of the time and the nature of the relation between the Church and the temporal authorities in governing society. The canonists' definition of just war addressed both these concerns by giving lexical priority to the responsibility of sovereign temporal authority in the just use of armed force, then hedging this by defining this use as requiring a just cause and direction to the end of social peace. The result was a conception of just war that, as noted earlier, mirrored the understanding of the goods or final purposes of politics as inherited from the classical world. This first systematic understanding of just war was thus placed inseparably within an overall normative conception of politics and its purposes.

The immediate implication of this way of thinking about just war was to limit the right to use armed force to the sovereign authority in each political community—a major step in a society in which every male member of the knightly class claimed the right to use the sword on his own choosing, and particularly to settle disputes. Gratian set aside this claim by using canons from Augustine and Isidore to define the sovereign in every political community as the judge of last resort in all cases of disputes, and to place the right to use armed force in the hands of this ultimate authority alone to enforce his judgments. Any and all uses of arms by persons not in sovereign authority here became a disordering of the justice and peace of the political community, and Gratian here cited Augustine on the need for just war to respond to injustice and restore justice and peace—a topic addressed in several of the Augustinian canons he cited.

The canonists after Gratian reached outside Augustine and other Church fathers to Roman law, recently rediscovered and being examined by some of the same canonical thinkers who were working on the just war idea first shaped by Gratian. From Roman law they drew the idea of natural law, defining the sovereign's responsibility in terms of being guided by the natural law in determining justice in particular disputes and in establishing and enforcing justice in the political community as a whole. Any political authority who flouted the natural law was not properly a sovereign but rather a tyrant, subject to removal and replacement by others within the community or, under special conditions, by other sovereigns.

Underlying the canonists' thinking on all these matters was their handling of the relation between the churchly and temporal authorities regarding the government of society. Some of Augustine's writings, including his correspondence with two high Roman authorities in Africa, Marcellinus and Donatus, could be read to place the authority of the Church over that of the temporal authorities. The canonists of the twelfth and thirteenth centuries instead distinguished sharply between these two kinds of authority, giving the temporal realm autonomy in its own affairs and reserving Church authority to the spiritual realm. To do this they drew on a letter from a late fifth-century pope, Gelasius, to the Eastern Roman emperor of the time, in which Gelasius made exactly this distinction. His purpose, in context, was to assert his authority in spiritual matters while granting that the emperor had all authority in temporal matters. But the medieval canonists' theory of politics and conception of just war turned the emphasis around, using this "Gelasian principle" to assert the autonomy of temporal sovereigns within the sphere of temporal government and reserving the authority of the Church to spiritual matters. The effect was to further strengthen their idea of sovereign authority and the responsibilities it entailed.

When one reads Gratian's *Decretum* on just war, one finds a conception of just war built mainly on passages drawn from a number of Augustine's works, with selections from other Church authorities playing supportive roles, all drawn together in a systematic frame determined by Gratian. His immediate successors, while honoring the pride of place given to Augustine, drew from additional sources—most importantly the idea of natural law and the Gelasian principle—to interpret the implications of this canonical collection and to reinforce it. There is no indication they were seeking to replace the authority of Augustine, but rather to draw it out, place it in a larger context, and thus apply it to the context of life as they knew it.

WHAT'S LOVE GOT TO DO WITH IT?

Theirs was a very different reading from that which has been commonplace in Christian understandings of just war since the work of Ramsey, which begins with Augustine's theology of love and defines just war as proceeding from the idea that Christian love of neighbor ought to be manifest even in the use of armed force toward another. In the work of the medieval canonists, the idea of just war is embedded in the goods of politics as defined by the law of nature. In Ramsey and much other recent Christian just war thought, just war results from the Christian obligation to love one's neighbor. In the former, just war does not stand over and against the practice of politics but embodies and serves the goods of politics. In the latter, by contrast, it is necessary to find some mediating connection between the ethic of Christian love and the secular arena of politics: hence the idea that love has entered history and is inexorably transforming history towards God's ends for it. There is much power in the idea that Christians ought to seek to express love of neighbor in their dealings with others, but this is not itself a guide for the use of armed force in the service of politics in an unchristian world.

Both the readings of Augustine found in these different conceptions of just war extend and transform what Augustine himself did with the idea of just war, though they do so in very different ways. Augustine himself never wrote a systematic treatise on just war (by contrast, for example, with his numerous distinct treatises on aspects of sexuality). Rather, his thoughts on just war were occasional, scattered through works of various sorts, and conditioned by context. In most of these cases, Augustine's observations about war are functionally secondary, illustrating whatever larger point he is aiming to make. So what he says about killing in war in *De Libero Arbitrio* I serves to illustrate his larger point about the presence of *libido* (lust, or self-centered love) in acts of self-defense by contrast with its absence in the action of a soldier acting on orders from a superior; his enumeration of wrongful motivations in war in *Contra Faustum* 22 is part of a larger argument against Faustus over whether the Old Testament deserves to be a guide for Christians; and the comment about the necessity to wage just wars to oppose evildoing that appears in *City of God* XIX provides an illustration of his larger point about the violence, chaos, and injustice in the world as he knows it. In his commentaries on various books of the Old Testament, what he says about war comes from that period of his life in which he believed Roman imperial policy was doing the work of God in this world. And in other cases, notably his Letter 93 to Vincentius, Letters 133 and 138 to Marcellinus, and Letters 185 and 189 to Boniface, his references to the idea of just war reflect the context of the ongoing struggle with the Donatists and his effort to enlist imperial Roman military help in this. Pulling these together to produce a systematic view of just war requires a reading that imposes a common purpose and order on them, and that is what both the modern readings I have been discussing provide.

Each of these readings' strength is also the source of problems. For Christians, Ramsey's reading of Augustine on just war has the important strength of the central place it gives to the idea of love of neighbor and the connection of this moral obligation, through Augustine, to the New Testament, and particularly to the parable of the Good Samaritan. It also, as indicated above, fits squarely within a century and more of Protestant thought about the ethical nature of Christian life. But its special Christian character makes it appear sectarian and irrelevant to non-Christians, and it is difficult to extend it to the needs of secular politics.

The conception of just war read out of Augustine by the medieval canonists has the strength of placing just war squarely within the sphere of temporal political life and its responsibilities, but its intentional sundering of this conception from the sphere of the Church and its reliance on natural law rather than an ethic drawn from the Bible opens it to the criticism that it is non-Christian and paves the way for alternative ways of thinking about Christian responsibility in the face of violence and injustice. As to the centrality of natural law in this conception of just war, Protestants have long been uncomfortable with the idea of natural law, and Reinhold Niebuhr's explicit rejection of the just war idea in *The Nature and Destiny of Man*[19] came in the course of an extended criticism and rejection of the Catholic conception of natural law as he understood it.

In my own work on just war, I have focused on its development and transmission as a tradition within Western culture as a whole, with the specific Christian contribution as one element alongside others in the overall tradition. On this conception there have been multiple kinds of inputs into the overall tradition, and in the modern period this has resulted in somewhat different ways of carrying the tradition in the arenas of Christian theology, academic philosophy, military theory and praxis, and international law. The problem here is taking pains to bring these different streams into mutual communication, which I have tried to do not only by identifying present-day commonalities among them but by showing how they are connected to the unitary pre-modern conception. This approach makes use of a reading of Augustine, but my reading has sought to show how Augustine in himself and as seen through his interpreters fits within the tradition of just war as a whole. It is not an approach that produces a privileged Christian conception of just war, but it seeks to understand the Christian element in the tradition as a whole and to bring contemporary, specifically Christian, conceptions of just war into conversation with the disparate other streams of just war tradition and with the moral traditions on politics and war developed in other cultures.

This work seeks commonality not only in the particular outcomes of these various streams of moral reasoning but also in the moral bases for such reasoning. Providing a moral base was the function natural law played for the medieval canonists who produced the classic systematization of the idea of just war and, *pace* Niebuhr, something that functions like this is needed in contemporary reasoning about just war. I have argued that positive international law on war serves in somewhat this way for contemporary discourse on war and political order, but the commonality expressed there remains relatively thin, and it is an intellectual reach to assume that a particular state's agreement on a specific point of the positive law genuinely or fully expresses that state's underlying values.

For these reasons I have increasingly argued for an effort to develop a thick dialogue across cultures on fundamental moral values and their implications for politics and war. I believe any such effort must take special pains to explore the thinking of important historical figures in the moral traditions of each culture. For the West, this must include Augustine and not only the variant readings discussed above but also the influence of other ideas potentially relevant to the subjects of war and politics. That is, much remains to be done in exploring how to read Augustine.

ABSTRACT

This article looks at the influence of Christian ethicist Paul Ramsey on the revitalization of the just war tradition in the 1960s. Ramsey's *The Just War: Force and Political Responsibility* (1968) and its predecessor *War and the Christian Conscience* (1961) reinvigorated just war discussion in ethical, policy, and military thought and debate. Written in the context of the 1960s, the Cold War, and the debate over nuclear weapons, Ramsey's work had an immense influence. Coupled with Michael Walzer's 1977 book *Just and Unjust Wars,* these thinkers and their books served as pillars that stand on the earlier classic expression of the tradition enabling contemporary discussions of the tradition and its ongoing relevance.

CHAPTER 25

PAUL RAMSEY AND THE RECOVERY OF THE JUST WAR IDEA

The year 2018 marked the fiftieth anniversary of the publication of Paul Ramsey's *The Just War: Force and Political Responsibility.*[1] It takes far less than fifty years to forget most books, but there are three important reasons why *The Just War* should be remembered and read by those who haven't yet encountered it, or reread by those who have. The first reason is that this book, together with its older sibling *War and the Christian Conscience,*[2] began the contemporary recovery of the just war idea for ethical, policy, and military thought and debate. The second reason is that Ramsey's theological methodology in these books, centering on the Christian idea of love of neighbor, remains a provocative model for focused Christian ethical thinking about these matters. And third, in addition to developing a love-based conception of just war, Ramsey also undertook a robust engagement with the then ongoing secular policy debate about nuclear weapons, their possible use in war, and deterrence. By the time *The Just War* was published he had also entered the policy debate over issues connected to the war in Vietnam. His engagement in both these debates was well grounded, knowledgeable, and substantive, with much that remains relevant for present-day debates over nuclear weapons, uses of armed force, and the role of power in international politics. Each of these reasons deserves a close look.

First, Ramsey's two books from the 1960s began the recovery of the just war idea that has proceeded vigorously for the last half-century. When Ramsey wrote these books no one had produced a scholarly, theologically-based volume on just war for over three and a half centuries, since the publication of Francisco Suarez's lecture *De Bello*, first delivered in the academic year 1583–84. Gentili and Grotius, younger contemporaries of Suarez, treated just war in their writings, but used the tradition not as a focus in itself but as a basis for their more substantive interest in the law of nations. In Grotius and his scholarly successors Pufendorf, Wolff, and Vattel, just war tradition was in fact transformed into a law of nations founded on common agreement among the nations of Western Europe. During the American Civil War, Francis Lieber and others referred to this body of common agreement on war as "the laws and customs of war." As positive international law began to come together late in the nineteenth century it was on this customary-law basis. As international positive law on war continued to develop during the two world wars and afterward, though, the link to the moral tradition of just war disappeared altogether, and even the connection to the earlier "laws and customs of war" disappeared from the positive law, which in the twentieth century came to be entirely regarded as based on positive international agreements.

By the time Ramsey wrote in the 1960s, not only had the moral idea of just war long faded from the scene, but also the specifically religious stake in this moral idea. One important result was the drift of the churches and Christian individuals either towards acceptance of the international order as an expression of moral imperative or, as regards war, to a pacifist rejection of all war in international relations. Ramsey took note of the latter in the Introduction to *War and the Christian Conscience* (pp. xvii-xxiii) while arguing that the implications of the Christian ethical ideal of love pointed to very different outcomes. He never left behind his argument against pacifism as he further developed his thought on just war: Chapter 12 of *The Just War* laid out a response to the Catholic pacifist James Douglass, who had attacked the just war idea as defined by Ramsey in *War and the Christian Conscience* as inadequate to the Christian ethic of love, and his final book on the subject, a critique of the United Methodist Bishops' pastoral letter "In Defense of Creation" was titled *Speak Up for*

Just War or Pacifism.[3] Pacifist opposition to war of any kind for any purposes remained an important current in Christian thought, feeding into both opposition to nuclear weapons and to the war in Vietnam—the two contexts in which Ramsey developed and argued his just war position in the 1960s. In international political relations and in military affairs there was simply no conception of the idea of just war. Both Christian and secular internationalist forms of pacifism grew to fill the space left for moral reasoning in both arenas. Ramsey's effort to recover the just war idea thus was importantly an effort to counter this development.

Pacifist opposition to war was, in Ramsey's view, ultimately inadequate as a moral stance on war: when wars nonetheless took place, pacifism, with its leveling of all forms of violence and all reasons for it as equally evil, had nothing left to say except "stop." Ramsey's effort to restore just war reasoning to thinking about war and its conduct aimed to ensure that morality had something more to say: hence his subtitle to *War and the Christian Conscience: How Shall Modern War Be Conducted Justly?* His reflections led him inexorably to consideration of the morality of power and its use in the practice of responsible politics and to thinking about the use of force in relation to the moral use of power: hence the subtitle to *The Just War: Force and Political Responsibility.* Though he defined just war as rooted in the obligations imposed by Christian love of neighbor, which many Christians regarded as entirely bearing on person-to-person relationships, for Ramsey this love also imposed obligations on the responsible use of political power, up to and including the use of armed force. Before him Reinhold Niebuhr had argued much the same about the necessity of a morally informed politics, though for him Christian love could not reach so far, and the relevant moral criterion was justice. Niebuhr too sought to address and answer questions pacifism could never treat adequately, but he had no use for the idea of just war, which he dismissed (using a reference to Suarez on another matter) as an expression tied to Catholic theology on natural law, which he entirely rejected.[4]

For Ramsey, when he wrote his two books on just war in the 1960s, the development of nuclear weapons and the policy debates about deterrence and the possible use of these weapons in war made the need for a new, substantive Christian approach to thinking about the ethics of war all the more pressing. His turn to the just war idea provided a new way to think morally about nuclear weapons and about the ethics of war more generally, and it set in train a current of moral reflection that still flows strongly. I have in other contexts described the recovery of the just war idea in the latter part of the twentieth century as resting on three major legs: Ramsey's two just war books from the 1960s together make up the first leg; Michael Walzer's *Just and Unjust Wars*,[5] which appeared nine years after Ramsey's *The Just War*, and the United States National Conference of Catholic Bishops' pastoral letter, *The Challenge of Peace*,[6] which appeared six years after that, define the second and third legs. Both of the latter made reference to Ramsey. Walzer to disagree with him on matters concerned with nuclear deterrence. The bishops both invited Ramsey to present his thinking on just war to the drafting committee of bishops charged to prepare the pastoral letter and in the letter itself as one of the earlier figures acknowledged in a note on "representative surveys of the history and theology of the just-war tradition." Both Walzer and the bishops developed their own distinctive conceptions of just war. Walzer did this on the basis of human rights and positive law on war, which he called "the legalist paradigm" but nevertheless took quite seriously. The bishops adopted a conception of just war first developed on the basis of the philosopher W. D. Ross's ethics of *prima facie* obligation. Walzer's book drew political philosophers into the arena of debate on just war, which today has eventuated in the "revisionist" just war thought best known in the work of Jeff McMahon and Cecile Fabre. The Catholic bishops, because of the attention by national media to the work of the drafting committee, proved the vehicle by which the idea of just war would enter a broad public consciousness and, because of their assumed influence over Catholics in military service, brought discussion of just war firmly into the arena of military thought and teaching on the ethics of war. Both these books, then and since, have made important contributions to the recovery of just war thought. Without the two books by

Ramsey that first drew attention to the just war idea, though, one may reasonably ask whether the recovery of the just war idea would have in fact begun, and Ramsey's influence continues to run deep in moral reflection on just war.

Neither Ramsey, Walzer, nor the Catholic bishops, though they all sought to recover the just war idea and its use, sought to recover just war tradition in itself. Others motivated to write about just war beginning in this same period did look back to the earlier tradition, which had a long history and substantial impact. An important figure among these others was William V. O'Brien, professor of government at Georgetown, whose *The Conduct of Just and Limited War*[7] employed the understanding of just war in Thomas Aquinas's *quaestio* "On War" (*Summa theologiae* II/II, Q. 40), exploring it for the contemporary context by connecting it to the theory and practice of limited war, then itself the subject of much discussion in scholarly and policy circles. O'Brien in fact did more with Aquinas on just war than it occurred to the bishops to do, and his book stands as a fuller link to the earlier Catholic tradition than the bishops' pastoral letter provided. This was also the period in which I began my own work on the just war idea, but for me this meant to recover this idea as defined and carried in the historical tradition from the high Middle Ages into the Modern Period. What struck me about this tradition was how it came into being and developed as a result of both religious and secular influences, so that the idea of just war that resulted defined a broad cultural consensus as to the purpose of armed force (broadly, response to injustice that could be countered no other way), the necessary authority for use of such force (that of the sovereign ruler, who bore final responsibility for a just and peaceful order in the political community and in relations among such communities), and right conduct in the use of armed force thus defined and mandated.

While I continue to think there is value to be gained from attending to this historical tradition and the idea of just war found there, there is also value in the effort of Ramsey, Walzer, and the Catholic bishops to understand just war in terms of contemporary forms of moral reasoning.

This leads us to the second reason for returning attention to Ramsey's *The Just War* and *War and the Christian Conscience*: his use of the Christian ethical ideal of love of neighbor as the basis for his conception of the just war idea. When Ramsey began his scholarly career and when he wrote his two just war books from the 1960s, the love ideal had been central in Protestant Christian individual and social ethics for more than a half-century. But the way this ideal had been understood and applied left a somewhat mixed legacy, and Ramsey, for his part, took a somewhat different tack.

One part of this legacy reached back to prominent late nineteenth-century preachers like Henry Drummond, who understood the dimensions of such love as providing a moral pattern by which each individual Christian could live a Christ-like life. This remains a theme in some sectors of American Protestantism today. More particularly, though, in the early twentieth century this way of thinking, which was essentially that Christian life should be one of individual perfection, fed into the development of Christian pacifism, and thus it was a perspective that Ramsey opposed in his own understanding of love and his thinking on just war.

Another part of the love legacy developed most strongly in the early decades of the twentieth century: Walter Rauschenbusch's transformation of the love ideal into a social ethic whereby American society as a whole could be developed through love into the Kingdom of God on Earth. The movement that came out of this theology was the Social Gospel Movement. Like the Christian individualistic moralism that traces back to Drummond and his contemporaries, this movement continues to have influence in certain aspects of contemporary American Protestantism.

Reinhold Niebuhr, though, early in his career wrote two books opposing Christian individual and social idealism and the conception of love it assumed: *Moral Man and Immoral Society*[8] (first published 1932) and *An Interpretation of Christian Ethics*[9] (first published 1935). Niebuhr, the most influential Christian ethicist in the generation before Ramsey's, rejected both Drummond's and Rauschenbusch's ways of thinking and indeed all those streams in Christian ethics rooted in the optimistic idealism of the late nineteenth century, which presented Christ-like love as able to be realized both in individual relations and in social life. Rather, he argued, such love is always an "impossible possibility." In individual relations such love was impossible because only Christ has the power to love in this way, while in societies such love is impossible because of conflicting claims not all of which can be realized due to human finitude. While he granted that a Christian individual might succeed in self-giving love to another individual when granted grace by Christ to do so, this is Christ at work, not the Christian individual's moral power. Nor does what is possible in any Christian as an individual extend to social relations, both within the political order and in relations among nations: here the best that could be achieved was a form of justice that approximated love. Understood this way, the moral use of force had to do with serving justice, which among other things aimed at combating evils. But this reasoning did not lead him to the concept of just war; just the contrary. In his next major work, *The Nature and Destiny of Man*,[10] in the context of an extended criticism and rejection of Catholic natural law theory, he dismissed "the Catholic theory of a 'just war' as a case in point" (Niebuhr 1964: 283 and n. 1). As Niebuhr's theological method was so heavily weighted toward laying bare the conflicts of power and interests within and among nations, conflicts rooted in human finitude and sinfulness, he never in fact developed a positive theologically-oriented way of talking about the ethics of war—either the resort to war or the conduct of war. This was the realist side of his Christian realism, which opened the door to extreme measures of war in the effort to combat evil that stood in the way of a just order that might approximate the possibilities of love.

Ramsey's working from the moral ideal of love of neighbor to his concept of just war sought to fill the empty middle ground between pacifist rejection of all war, indeed any use of military force, and the limits of Niebuhr's Christian realism, which opened the door to all-out methods of war. The pacifists, Ramsey argued, were wrong to regard the use of armed force in itself as evil; rather, when the neighbor is threatened or harmed by the actions of another, the obligation to love that neighbor becomes the obligation to protect him or her from the offered threat or action, and this may justify the use of armed force. At the same time, the offender is himself a neighbor whom the Christian must love, and this means that in such a situation only such means may be used that are sufficient to protect the neighbor-victim. Thus, argued Ramsey, the Christian mandate to love the neighbor generates two different moral directives in the case of war: on the one hand, permission—even obligation—to use armed force to protect the neighbor who is being menaced or attacked, and on the other a restraint on the force that may be used against the enemy, who is after all also a neighbor the Christian is commanded to love. This was a very different way of thinking about war from that of Niebuhr, an aspect of whose Christian realism was to present war as fundamentally participation in evil, justified only in a consequential way by the need to prevent a greater evil. Ramsey's conception of just war was fundamentally different from Niebuhr's Christian realism; Ramsey's centered on his understanding of the meaning of the unconditional obligation of all Christians to love the neighbor, which he focused in two moral principles: permission and limitation/restraint. In traditional just war terms, the former established the *jus ad bellum*, the moral rationale for resorting to war, while the two together established the *jus in bello*, the moral limits for fighting in war.

Unpacking the latter, Ramsey turned to the rule of double effect, which he developed out of Thomas Aquinas's reasoning on the question whether it is lawful to kill a man in self-defense.[11] For Ramsey, this rule is not derived from natural moral reasoning but is rather an expression of love, a moral rule of procedure that expresses how the Christian should exercise love of neighbor. Exploring this for the case of war, and in the context of the moral dyad permission and limitation, love allows using force against an enemy because of the threat the enemy poses to harm one's near neighbors, the noncombatants on one's own side; yet it never allows direct and intended use of force against noncombatants on the enemy's side, because they too are functionally innocent of prosecuting the war. This reasoning allows indirect and unintended harm to enemy noncombatants as a secondary, unwilled result of the permitted harm to enemy combatants.

Thinking in this way, Ramsey rejected Niebuhr's position that in social contexts an ethic of love can only be approximated, becoming an ethic of justice. Ramsey's argument was that love is present all the way through, and double effect shows the way to moral action in accord with what love requires.

While Ramsey used Aquinas and later thinkers to explore the rule of double effect, his core understanding of the ethic of neighbor-love depended directly on the Scriptures. Ramsey's first book, *Basic Christian Ethics*,[12] provides his most thorough and systematic exploration and analysis of the ideal of love, and this is the basis on which he argues in his just war books of the following decade. Whereas Niebuhr had grounded his rejection of the Social Gospel ideal of the Kingdom of God as a human possibility in a barbed critique focused on human weakness and sin, Ramsey simply dismissed the idea of the Kingdom of God as human possibility in history as something "few Christians" in fact accept.[13] What remains, though, from Jesus's own eschatological expectations is the idea that God may break into history at any time, and to be ready one must follow Jesus's ideal of love of every neighbor as a manifestation of perfect obedience to God.[14] Ramsey's derivation of the ethic of neighbor-love was thus deeply and intentionally scriptural, originating directly in the teachings of Jesus as recorded in the New Testament.

Ramsey laid all this out in the first third of *Basic Christian Ethics*. In the remainder of that book he built from this basis to his own conception of a Christian ethic for the full range of human life: how the ethic of love relates to other kinds of value, to human virtue, to the obligation to protect the neighbor in times of need, to the valuing of human personality for its own sake, to necessity of love for the creation and preservation of community, and ultimately to provide a foundation for social policy and life in community. The direct antecedents of his thinking on just war can be found in his discussion of "A Preferential

Ethics of Protection and the Teachings of Jesus" and "A Christian Ethic of Resistance"[15] and particularly his analysis of the implications of the Gospel parable of the Good Samaritan there. In his discussion of Christian love there is nothing remotely resembling the self-centered focus on personal moral perfection found in Drummond. There is a positive judgment on human moral possibility that falls somewhere between Rauschenbusch's untrammeled idealism and Niebuhr's deep pessimism. Ultimately the result is a conception of neighbor-love which, though Christians encounter it in the teachings of Jesus, in fact is a necessary ingredient for human social and community life the world over. Love, for Ramsey, does not make a moral claim only on Christians; its implications claim everyone. In an echo of earlier Christian ethical and political thought he concluded *Basic Christian Ethics* by arguing for the importance of the Christian conception of humanity and human relations as necessary for the fullness of life in community. Thus he anticipated the kind of argument he also made in his conception of just war: the idea of just war begins specifically with the Christian moral obligation of love of neighbor, but it extends inexorably to apply across the whole range of human experience.

As Ramsey developed his understanding of just war he largely, if not entirely, left the matter of just resort to war to the arena of statecraft, arguing that as a moralist he had neither the expertise nor the status required to lead a political community into war—a caution other moralists and theologians have not often heeded. His position on this mirrored the thought preserved in classical just war tradition, where the necessary authority for resort to just war lies not in the spiritual realm but is specifically temporal: the classical just war requirement of sovereign authority as necessary for just resort to force correlated directly with the responsibility such a sovereign authority has for the good of the political community as a whole.

Ramsey's major concern was with how war is fought, the arena of the just war *jus in bello*, and specifically the moral limits love of neighbor places on war-fighting. He developed these limits with particular reference to the possible use of nuclear weapons. Ramsey's entry into the debate over nuclear weapons and their use provides the third major reason for attention to *The Just War* and its earlier sibling, *War and the Christian Conscience.*

Given the centrality of love of neighbor in Ramsey's understanding of just war and its implications, it is striking that in the phase of his career that began after *The Just War*, when he shifted his focus powerfully to medical ethics, he chose a different biblical norm, covenant, as the center of his position. It is not as if covenant had no place in his earlier ethics: it ties closely to his strong emphasis on community in *Basic Christian Ethics*, though there he had connected community to the norm of love. He never explained why he made this shift, but doing so opened new possibilities for his reflections on ethics. Nor is there any inherent tension between these two norms: rather, neighbor-love for Ramsey creates and preserves community, and community is marked by covenantal relationships among its members. The idea of covenant was also central in the theology of Jonathan Edwards, to whose thought Ramsey shifted his focus in the final stage of his career as he engaged in editing some of Edwards' *Works*. Nor did Ramsey entirely abandon writing on love in the later years of his career and life: among the examples of this, Edwards' own emphasis on love stands out.

But Ramsey's shift in focal ethical norms leaves behind an interesting question: What should Christian ethics today do when seeking to enter debates over political ethics, specifically with reference to the idea of just war as a component in debates over policy and practice regarding war? There is no longer the broad interest in the norm of love that Ramsey drew on in his early books on just war. This interest was, for better or worse, tied to liberal Protestantism, and it did not successfully cross over into today's dominant Evangelicalism. So maybe a Christian political ethic based on the norm of covenant offers new possibilities, though this takes us beyond the immediate context of Ramsey's two just war books of the 1960s.

The third reason for carefully recalling Ramsey's *The Just War* and its earlier just war sibling has to do with the rich substance of his engagement, in these books, with the energetic theoretical and policy debates that were then going on in the secular policy community. These debates centered on nuclear weapons, their possible use in war, and deterrence, and a bit later on, issues raised by the war in Vietnam. Ramsey read deeply and widely within this secular policy debate, and the people he cited in his extended and probing analyses—Oskar Morgenstern, Herman Kahn, Thomas Murray, Kenneth Boulding, Thomas Schelling, Albert Wohlstetter, Peter Green, and others—were major figures in that debate. Ramsey was no dilettante in his scholarship: he always immersed himself deeply in any subject he treated, and so his engagement in the secular policy debates of the 1960s was that of one with a right to be there—a peer of the partners he engaged in dialogue, not a pretender.

An important lesson to be learned from attention to Ramsey's analytical and argumentative entry into these secular debates is that the serious ethicist must become well-grounded in the subject he or she would treat. A second lesson has to do with the enduring substance of Ramsey's discussions then: while the topics he engaged were just being thought through for the first time, they were not unique to that era but continue to arise in policy debates up through the present. The answers given then, as well as the complications uncovered, thus continue as relevant in the present context. An important value in Ramsey's careful, detailed entry into the debates of that earlier time is their drawing attention to issues that continue to demand to be dealt with, as well as answers that continue to have force.

An example of this is the present-day debate, which so far has mostly been carried on in policy circles, over how United States' nuclear weapons should be upgraded. Existing nuclear weapons systems, both warheads and delivery vehicles, are aging, and much of their technology reflects what was possible decades ago. An element in the current debate is whether to move to downsized nuclear weapons with lower yield than the ones they would replace, both because downsizing technology is more advanced today and because the accuracy of delivery systems today is much greater than that of the systems being replaced. Much of Ramsey's reasoning about counter-forces nuclear targeting bears directly on the issues in the current debate over downsizing. The same can be said about other ideas advanced in Ramsey's *The Just War* and its earlier sibling.

RAMSEY AND REINHOLD NIEBUHR: A CLOSER LOOK

Earlier I briefly discussed the thought of Reinhold Niebuhr and Ramsey's critical relationship to it. For a variety of reasons it is hard to think about Paul Ramsey's thinking on just war and its relation to the sphere of political life without thinking also of the work of Niebuhr, and I want to return to that earlier discussion in a more focused way. Ramsey's *The Just War* bore the subtitle *Force and Political Responsibility*; these two themes were also major subjects in the work of Reinhold Niebuhr. The central ethical norm in Ramsey's conception of just war and his development of that conception as a guide for policy and political decisionmaking was Christian love; this same moral focus runs through Niebuhr's work from its beginnings in the 1930s to his final work in the 1950s. Yet on close look not only did Ramsey's way of conceiving and working with the norm of Christian love differ importantly from Niebuhr's, but also Ramsey's thinking about political responsibility and the use of armed force through the idea of just war differed significantly from Niebuhr's outright rejection of the just war idea and his particular effort to define a moral place for the use of armed force in international relations. The latter was closely tied to Niebuhr's conception of Christian realism, and so we return to the question, what is the relation of Ramsey's just war thinking to Niebuhr's Christian realism?

Niebuhr's Christian realism was a development and expression of a particular theological perspective Niebuhr had developed early in his career and expressed in two books from the 1930s referred to above, *Moral Man and Immoral Society* (1932) and *An Interpretation of Christian Ethics*

(1935). In the first book he described two forms of Christianity: "orthodox" and "prophetic," the former referring to the established churches that stressed doctrine and rules for behavior which, in Niebuhr's view, misrepresented Christianity and locked it into patterns of the past, and the latter referring to a form of Christianity which worked from a focus on love to continual criticism and reformation of these patterns and also of social and political injustices. In *An Interpretation of Christian Ethics* he covered similar ground through the conception of love as an "impossible possibility"—impossible for human action alone because of human imperfection and sinfulness, but possible for God working in history. Part of Niebuhr's conception of Christian realism was tied to this judgment on the possibilities and limits of politics relative to the ideal of love: politics inherently requires the use of power, which must be accepted as "a necessary evil. But it must know that it is an evil and that injustice inevitably flows from its unchecked expression." It was a short step from this both to Niebuhr's argument for the struggle against Hitlerism (a clear moral evil requiring coercive opposition) and his rejection of the just war idea as he understood it.

Niebuhr had only a very limited idea of just war, tied to a brief passage from the seventeenth-century Spanish Jesuit Francisco Suarez. For Niebuhr the just war idea was an expression of "orthodox Christianity," based in the idea of natural law, which for Niebuhr overstated the possibilities of human reason and action for good in the world and belonged to a past age. This dismissal of the just war idea appeared in volume 1 of *The Nature and Destiny of Man* in the context of a critical rejection of natural law; just war, as an example of an idea based in natural law, Niebuhr used to exemplify what was wrong with natural law, and his rejection of the just war idea was collateral damage. But Niebuhr's discussion there showed how thin was his understanding of just war and what Suarez wrote on it. The passage Niebuhr quoted from Suarez was from the latter's *De Legibus*, where just war is treated only briefly and in a limited way, and Niebuhr showed no knowledge whatsoever of Suarez's longer treatise *De Bello*, which laid out his full understanding of just war.

On war, Niebuhr's position was that evil must be opposed, but the realities of the imperfection and sinfulness of the world mean that the opposition necessarily also will involve the use of evil means. This was fundamentally a utilitarian ethical position of maximizing the good while minimizing the evil, though Niebuhr advanced it in the name of the divinely-assisted possibility of a prophetic understanding of Christian love to oppose evil in the world.

The two poles of Niebuhr's Christian realism are thus his conception of human sinfulness and imperfection which require reformation and his idea of Christian love as able to call this out "prophetically" and to seek to remedy it, while necessarily introducing new forms of injustice in the process.

Ramsey's understanding of the power of Christian love to shape individual lives and social forms was deeply different. The son of a Methodist minister who served churches in northern Mississippi, Ramsey was taught that Christian love could indeed change individuals toward moral perfection, and through them society, though no one should ever expect that this changing could be completed in this life, and "backsliding" was always a real possibility. His preferred part of the Bible was the New Testament (for him the Bible should be read backwards, first the New and then the Old Testament), rather than the Hebrew prophets who provided the model for Reinhold Niebuhr's "prophetic" Christianity. In his divinity school and doctoral studies Ramsey chose to work not with Reinhold but with his brother H. Richard Niebuhr, who had a much deeper theological education, a nuanced historical and theological understanding of American Christianity, and a particular affinity for the thought of Augustine. Ramsey's clearest and most succinct explanation of how Christian love bears on political reality in history comes not in either of his just war books from the 1960s but from an essay he contributed to an edited volume published five years after *The Just War*.[16] There Ramsey drew directly from Richard Niebuhr's characterization of Augustine's theology as "transformationist" in his book *Christ and Culture*.[17] Richard Niebuhr had argued there that Augustine understood divine grace to have entered history once and for all with Christ and subsequently is working within history to transform it toward the City of God at the end of time. Ramsey similarly argued that Christian love is now a force working within history to shape and transform politics, and thus the effects of love should properly be taken into account in the pursuit of good politics. As he put the matter then, "Ethics are not logically, externally related to politics. These two distinguishable elements are together in the first place, internally related."[18] Or as he wrote more pithily later in this article, "the just war theory [is] an ethics intrinsic to the nature of politics and to a purposeful use of force."[19] This is a way of thinking very different from Reinhold Niebuhr's.

What does this tell us about Ramsey's relation to Christian realism? Earlier I wrote that Ramsey's conception of just war was fundamentally different from Niebuhr's Christian realism. Ramsey never used the term "Christian realist" of himself, and he was certainly not a Christian realist in the way Reinhold Niebuhr defined this term. But Christian realism can also be understood more generally as referring to a position that takes account of both the limits and the possibilities of historical life in its individual, social, institutional, and political forms. Augustine certainly did this, and so did Ramsey. It might be more revealing to refer to Ramsey as an Augustinian realist, but both Augustine and Ramsey were Christian realists in the more general sense I have defined. The difference from Reinhold Niebuhr is that both Augustine and Ramsey held that there are positive norms that Christians should follow in their historical lives, that their efforts should embody the possibilities placed in them by love, and that these efforts should be directed at two ends: preservation of the world despite the presence of sin as long as history lasts, and preparation of the world for its final transformation at the end of history, when the City of Earth will give way to the City of God. This is the sense in which Ramsey's understanding of just war and its place in relation to policy and political decisionmaking can be described as a Christian realist position, though it is quite different from Reinhold Niebuhr's conception of Christian realism.

CONCLUSION

The recent fiftieth anniversary of the publication of Paul Ramsey's *The Just War* provides the occasion for this piece, but thinking about this book necessarily leads to reflection on the shape of his earlier thought and ideas developed there. While the centrality of Christian love of neighbor was Ramsey's moral focus in both *The Just War* and its earlier sibling on the same topic, *War and the Christian Conscience*, more broadly Ramsey's Christian ethics reflected the influence of the New Testament on his thinking. His emphasis on love of neighbor came directly out of this. As I noted above, in fundamental ways his multifaceted development of the implications of Christian love of neighbor in his first book, *Basic Christian Ethics*, provided the foundation for the structure of moral argument he erected in writing on the idea of just war. Specifically for his subsequent writing on just war as based in an ethic of Christian love, Ramsey's discussion of the biblical story of the Good Samaritan in Chapter V on Christian Vocation provides a preview of the position he later took on the idea of just war. Here he approvingly quoted an earlier writer, L. A. Garrard,

> When I try to imagine what would have happened had Jesus come upon the scene a little earlier than the Good Samaritan, I find it more natural to suppose that he would have helped the traveler in his struggle with the thieves than that he would have waited until the man was injured and the thieves departed before coming to his aid.[20]

Ramsey returned to the Good Samaritan story in *The Just War*, picking up where he had left off in *Basic Christian Ethics*:

> It was a work of charity for the Good Samaritan to give help to the man who fell among thieves. But one step more, it may have been a work of charity for the inn-keeper to hold himself ready to receive beaten and wounded men, and for him to conduct his business so that he was solvent enough to extend credit to the Good Samaritan.

> By another step it would have been a work of charity, and not of justice alone, to maintain and serve in a police patrol on the Jericho road to prevent such things from happening. By yet another step, it might well be work of charity to resist, by force of arms, any external aggression against the social order that maintains the police patrol along the road to Jericho.... [W]hat do you think Jesus would have made the Samaritan do if he had come upon the scene while the robbers were still at their fell work?[21]

Ramsey here describes the moral motivation as "charity" (Christian love), but by his reasoning in "A Political Ethics Context" it is also the proper work of politics to do all these things: what is required by love is not distinguishable from what is required by politics properly understood and practiced.

In both his fundamental thinking about Christian love and its relation to other ethical norms and his application of this thinking to the idea of just war, Ramsey separated himself from the thinking of Reinhold Niebuhr. Just war is a positive implication of Christian love, not a necessary evil to combat a greater evil. So far as it is based in natural law, Ramsey's discussion of natural law and other forms of philosophical ethics in *Basic Christian Ethics* presents them as not in opposition to love but as pointers toward what love requires. A realistic appraisal of the world is a necessary element in Ramsey's ethical thinking in general and his work on just war as a part of this; yet his Christian realism was not that of Reinhold Niebuhr, and it provides much that is worth considering for a Christian engagement with the arena of international affairs.

NOTES

1. Paul Ramsey, *The Just War: Force and Political Responsibility* (New York: Charles Scribner's Sons, 1968).
2. Paul Ramsey, *War and the Christian Conscience: How Shall Modern War Be Conducted Justly?* (Durham, North Carolina: Duke University Press, 1961).

3. Paul Ramsey, *Speak Up for Just War or Pacifism* (University Park, Pennsylvania, and London: The Pennsylvania State University Press, 1988).
4. Reinhold Niebuhr, *The Nature and Destiny of Man* (New York: Charles Scribner's Sons, 1964), 283. Originally published in two volumes, vol. 1, 1941, vol. 2, 1943.
5. Michael Walzer, *Just and Unjust Wars* (New York: Basic Books, 1977).
6. National Conference of Catholic Bishops, *The Challenge of Peace: God's Promise and Our Response* (Washington, D.C.: United States Catholic Conference, 1983).
7. William V. O'Brien, *The Conduct of Just and Limited War* (New York: Praeger Publishing, 1981).
8. Reinhold Niebuhr, *Moral Man and Immoral Society* (New York: Charles Scribner's Sons, 1932).
9. Reinhold Niebuhr, *An Interpretation of Christian Ethics* (New York: Harper & Brothers, 1935).
10. Niebuhr 1964, 283 and n. 1.
11. Thomas Aquinas, *Summa theologiae* II/II. Q. 64, Art. 7; Ramsey 1961, 39–59.
12. Paul Ramsey, *Basic Christian Ethics* (New York: Charles Scribner's Sons, 1950).
13. Ibid., 35.
14. Ibid., 39.
15. Ibid., 166–84.
16. Paul Ramsey, "A Political Ethics Context for Strategic Thinking," in Morton A. Kaplan, *Strategic Thinking and Its Moral Implications* (Chicago: The University of Chicago Center for Policy Study, 1973), 101–46.
17. H. Richard Niebuhr, *Christ and Culture* (New York: Harper & Brothers, 1951), chapter 6.
18. Kaplan 1973, 125.
19. Ibid., 144.
20. Ramsey 1950, 170 n. 3.
21. Ramsey 1968, 142–43.

APPENDICES

APPENDIX A

CHARTS ON THE JUST WAR TRADITION

Figure 1. Sources and Development of the Just War Tradition	
Late Classical Era: Deep Roots, Early Expressions	The Bible (Old and New Testaments) Roman law and practice Christian theology: writers such as Clement of Alexandria, Ambrose, Augustine
Medieval Era: Coalescence of a Cultural Consensus	Canon law: Gratian's *Decretum*, writings of the Decretists and Decretalists Scholastic theology The code and customs of chivalry Customary rights and practices of sovereigns The inherited idea of *jus gentium* (law of peoples or nations)
16th to 18th Centuries: Consolidation, Transformation, Differentiation	Transformation to natural-law base: Victoria, Suarez, Grotius, others Theory of international law: Grotius, Pufendorf, Vattel, others Military codes of discipline replacing chivalric code Limited-war theory and practice: "sovereigns' wars"

19th Century: Further Definition within Distinct Streams	Customary international law First Hague Conference Origin of Geneva Conventions Military manuals on the law of war Popular, philosophical, and religious efforts to restrain or end war
20th Century: Elaboration and Growing Interactions	Positive international law *Jus ad bellum*: League of Nations Covenant, Pact of Paris, UN Charter *Jus in bello*: arms limitation treaties and conventions, growth of humanitarian international law Military manuals on law of war, rules of engagement Religious and philosophical recovery of just-war concepts Public debate over war, its meaning and effects

Figure 2. Purposes of the Just War Tradition	
A Guide to Statecraft:	Theory of the use of force by the political community Understanding of the moral qualities of political leadership Protection of fundamental rights and values Relation of ends to means in political life
A Guide to Commanders:	Relation of military command to authority/purposes of political community Understanding of the moral qualities of military leadership Protection of fundamental rights and values in situations of armed conflict Moral limits on means and methods in conflict situations
A Guide to Individuals:	Claims on moral consciousness of individuals at all levels of political and military life Definition of responsibility in relation to the use of force by the political community Definition of the individual's rights and responsibilities in the use of force

Figure 3. The Just War Tradition as a Source of Criteria for Ethical Judgment

The *Jus ad Bellum*: Criteria Defining the Right to Resort to Force

Just Cause: The protection and preservation of value

Classic Statement: Defense of the innocent against armed attack; retaking persons, property, or other values wrongly taken; punishment of evil.

Right Authority: The person or body authorizing the use of force must be the duly authorized representative of a sovereign political entity. The authorization to use force implies the ability to control and cease that use—that is, a well-constituted and efficient chain of command.

Classic Statement: Reservation of the right to employ force to persons or communities with no political superior.

Right Intention: The intent must be in accord with the just cause and not territorial aggrandizement, intimidation, or coercion.

Classic Statement: Evils to be avoided in war, including hatred of the enemy, "implacable animosity," "lust for vengeance," desire to dominate.

Proportionality of Ends: The overall good achieved by the use of force must be greater than the harm done. The levels and means of using force must be appropriate to the just ends sought.

Last Resort: Determination at the time of the decision to employ force that no other means will achieve the justified ends sought. Interacts with other *jus ad bellum* criteria to determine level, type, and duration of force employed.

Reasonable Hope of Success: Prudential calculation of the likelihood that the means used will bring the justified ends sought. Interacts with other *jus ad bellum* criteria to determine level, type, and duration of force employed.

The Aim of Peace: Establishment of international stability, security, and peaceful interaction. May include nation-building, disarmament, other measures to promote peace.

The *Jus in Bello*: Criteria Defining the Employment of Force

Proportionality of Means: Means causing gratuitous or otherwise unnecessary harm are to be avoided. Prohibition of torture, means *mala in se.*

Classic Statement: Attempts to limit weapons, days of fighting, persons who should fight.

Noncombatant Protection/Immunity: Definition of noncombatancy, avoidance of direct, intentional harm to noncombatants, efforts to protect them.

Classic Statement: Lists of classes of persons (clergy, merchants, peasants on the land, other people in activities not related to the prosecution of war) to be spared the harm of war.

Figure 4. The Just War Criteria in Positive International Law

Jus ad Bellum:

Just Cause: National or regional self-defense against armed attack; retaliation for armed attack; international response to threats to international peace.

Right Authority: *Compétence de guerre* possessed by states; some right to authorize force given to UN Security Council; some recognition of insurgency rights.

Right Intention: Not explicitly addressed, implicit in above items.

Proportionality of Ends: In the twentieth century, a tendency to treat the first use of force as the greatest evil, always disproportionate.

Last Resort: Emphasis on international arbitration and/or adjudication; tendency to allow only responsive or "second" use of force after armed attack.

Reasonable Hope of Success: Not explicitly treated.

The Aim of Peace: Greatly stressed. Limits on just causes for going to war, emphasis on *jus in bello* restraints, preference for stability over other values. Currently in process of some reevaluation.

Jus in Bello:

Proportionality of Means: "Hague law," arms limits, bans on means *mala in se*.

Noncombatant Protection/Immunity: Greatly stressed. "Geneva law," various other provisions regarding noncombatants, POWS, "protected persons." Not treated injury to noncombatants received due to proximity to legitimate targets, long-term damages due to persisting effects of otherwise legitimate means of war.

Figure 5. The Just War Criteria in Policy Language: The "Weinberger Doctrine" of 1984

Jus ad Bellum: "Six Conditions for Committing United States Military Forces"

Just Cause: 1. When it is vital to the defense of national or allied interests.

Reasonable Hope of Success: 2. With the intention of winning.

- Sole object of winning
- Forces and resources sufficient to achieve objectives or not at all

Right Intention: 3. For clearly defined political and military objectives.

- Determine objectives
- Decide strategy

Proportionality of Ends: 4. With correlation between objectives and forces.

- If national interests require us to fight, then we must win.
- Assess and adjust force size and composition as necessary

Right Authority: 5. With public/congressional concurrence.

- Commit American public before American forces

Last Resort: 6. As last resort.

- Only when other means have failed or have no prospect for success
- Military force not a substitute for diplomacy

Aim of Peace: Not explicitly stated but implicit in 1 and 6.

APPENDIX B

JAMES TURNER JOHNSON AND THE DISSEMINATION OF THE JUST WAR TRADITION: AN ANNOTATED BIBLIOGRAPHY

Timothy J. Demy and Gina G. Palmer

Ideas, like people, are complex. Not unlike people, ideas also have genealogies—ones that can be traced through the decades and centuries. Such lineages will note key individuals, writings, events, and other concepts that influenced and shaped the idea under consideration. The just war tradition is such an idea. As a moral and ethical framework for thinking about the complexities of war, few scholars in the last fifty years have provided a more cogent and consistent voice on the just war tradition—in the broadest sense of the word—than has James Turner Johnson.

The following pages provide an extensive, though not exhaustive, bibliography of Johnson's writings on the topics of war and peace. In reviewing and reading the writings, one is struck by the depth and breadth to which Johnson analyzed and applied the just war tradition. Several things regarding the corpus of Johnson's work are worth noting.

First, readers will appreciate the magnitude of his writings, reflecting a commitment to scholarship and communication beyond academic and professional obligation and demonstrating his belief in the importance and relevance of just war tradition in a world beset with conflict. His many works include books, monographs, chapters, journal articles, magazine articles, opinion pieces, book reviews, and review essays.

Second, one finds in Johnson's writings consistency. He has a consistent methodology and style. This is not to say that the writings are repetitive. They deal with the same subject, but they are nuanced and varied. One finds central themes such as the protection of noncombatants or comparative religious views of warfare, but also a host of other topics—all stemming from a belief that ongoing moral analysis of warfare through the lens of the just war tradition remains viable and critical in the present age. Moreover, Johnson has spent the last half-century not just as a professor but also as a student embedding in the work an intellectual curiosity and a systematic approach, as one concept and historical era builds on another in his books and articles.

Third, Johnson's work is foundational but also current. It is foundational in that he provides history and context for the subject of the just war tradition. It is current in that the writings frequently apply the tradition to contemporary events and issues. A reader studying his writings from the 1970s and 1980s will readily find that he is applying the just war tradition to the realities and concerns of the Cold War era. One finds in the 1990s the application of the tradition to the events of a post-Cold War world: from the American experience in the Middle East and Operations Desert Shield and Desert Storm to the closing years of the decade with the fragmentation and conflict in the Balkans, his writings were part of the renewed scholarly and public interest in the applied just war tradition. With the dawn of the twenty-first century, Johnson's work addressed the just war tradition's understanding of terrorism and non-state actors. As the decade and century progressed, he looked at the wars in Afghanistan and Iraq, bringing to bear the principles of the tradition and tying them to wider issues, notably those of political sovereignty. In the last decade, he has continued to articulate the relevance of the just war tradition to present and future military operations, in part by mentoring and encouraging the next generation of just war scholars.

Fourth, Johnson's writings are informed by a commitment to the just war tradition as developed within Christianity in the West. He reminds readers that ideas do not arise in a vacuum. Yet, he also does not limit his work solely to the religious domain. In part, the tradition has specific religious roots in Christianity, but it also has developed and functions in an international regime that does not share the religious commitments of some proponents of the tradition. His work is also unique due to a decades-long interaction with non-Christian religious traditions in the West and East looking at shared, similar, and exclusive aspects of the just war tradition. Within the Christian dialogue and development of the tradition, Johnson has addressed contemporary Protestant and Roman Catholic understandings and nuances and been critical of each when he thought they misunderstood or misrepresented the historical foundations of the just war idea.

Fifth, there is diversity in the audiences to whom he writes. He does not write solely for an academic audience, or ecclesiastical audience, or military audience, or legal audience, or popular audience. He writes for readers in each of these groups (and others), and across these groups. He writes for individuals seeking an understanding and application of moral analysis to war—past, present, and future.

The items presented below are listed chronologically with three groups—books, chapters published in books, and articles. Items such as book reviews and review essays are not annotated or listed. Nor are writings from websites included in the entries below. It is hoped that this will provide readers and researchers a helpful tool for understanding the influence of James Turner Johnson and the value of the just war tradition.

BOOKS (IN CHRONOLOGICAL ORDER)

Love and Society: Essays in the Ethics of Paul Ramsey. Edited with David H. Smith. Missoula, MT: Scholars Press, 1974.

> Johnson studies Paul Ramsey's thought on war in relation to classic just war doctrine and shows how it differs. The keys to Ramsey's thought are his understanding of *charity* from Augustine and moral military *strategy* from Aquinas. On the former, he contends that Ramsey uses these thinkers not because of their connection to the historical development of the just war tradition, but because of their theology. He attributes Ramsey's interest in strategy to the rise of nuclear weapons technology.

Ideology, Reason, and the Limitation of War: Religious and Secular Concepts 1200–1740. Princeton and London: Princeton University Press, 1975.

This is Johnson's first just war book and one of his earliest writings on the subject. It draws heavily on materials Johnson found at the Huntington Library while researching the topic during a fellowship he received in 1970. Using the Library's large volume of work printed in the era of the Continental Wars of Religion and the English Puritan Revolution, Johnson explores the interaction between religion and secular society with respect to just war doctrine. He shows how the doctrine emerged, arguing that there is a similarity between the doctrine of the late Middle Ages and the doctrine in the century after the Reformation. He also demonstrates the relationship between the secularized writings of Grotius, Locke, and Vattel, and 20th-century problems of war.

Unique in the work is an appendix, "The Puritan Revolution as Crusade," in which he evaluates ideas of Roland Bainton and Michael Walzer, who argue the Civil War should be viewed as a crusade (Bainton) and a revolution (Walzer).

Just War Tradition and the Restraint of War: A Moral and Historical Inquiry. Princeton and Guildford, Surrey: Princeton University Press, 1981, reprinted 2016.

Johnson's second book, foundational to his subsequent thought and writings, was grounded in new research and written in the context of developing interest in the U.S. and U.K. of the just war tradition. It continues the line of inquiry in *Ideology, Reason, and the Limitation of War* but also includes ideas that were largely unexplored at that point. He follows the expansion of the tradition in the post-Reformation centuries to the closing decades of the 20th century.

Of particular note in the work is the first section wherein he views the relationship between the just war tradition and moral reflection. In part, this entails a chapter on two books that had recently been published and which continue to be standard titles on war, morality, and the restraint of war—Michael Walzer's *Just and Unjust Wars: A Moral Argument with Historical Illustrations* (1977) and Paul Fussell's *The Great War and Modern Memory* (1975). A second chapter focused on how cultural traditions affect the problem of regulating violence. A third chapter looked at the idea of natural law as a central component of historical just war thinking. Each of these continued to be significant themes in Johnson's future writings.

The second section views the medieval coalescence of the just war idea and follows its transition to the modern era. The third and final section views modern war and attempts to restrain it. It contains a chapter on the thought of Henry W. Halleck and Francis Lieber and their shaping of the moral and legal tradition during the American Civil War and a chapter on recapturing the just war tradition as a moral and theological tradition in the 20th century.

Can Modern War Be Just? New Haven and London: Yale University Press, 1984.

The eight chapters of this book originated as lectures and essays Johnson gave during the several years prior to the book's publication. The book's purpose was to bring to bear just war perspectives on the problems posed by contemporary warfare and ways of thinking about it. The work reflects the cycle of debate over nuclear strategy and national defense during the last years of the Carter administration and the first years of the Reagan administration. Whereas Johnson's earlier works viewed the just war tradition primarily through its historical development, this volume looks at the tradition as a guide to practical moral decisions about current weapons and how the role of force is understood in political life. Examples of contemporary 1980's concerns that he addresses include the cruise missile and the neutron warhead.

The Quest for Peace: Three Moral Traditions in Western Cultural History. Princeton and Guildford, Surrey: Princeton University Press, 1987.

In this work, Johnson argues that a central idea of the just war tradition, dating to Augustine, is that just war should aim toward peace and reconciliation. Johnson looks at the political theory inherited from Cicero and Roman thought and practice that was assumed when just war tradition first came together in the 12th and 13th centuries. In it, politics is defined by three goods or ends—order, justice, and peace. These are each inseparable from one another: good order is the sum of justice and peace in the community; justice is the sum of order and peace; peace is the sum of order and justice. The three requirements for a just resort to force put in place by the 12th- and 13th-century canonists and summarized by Aquinas in his Question 40 from the *Summa Theologiae*, "On War," were sovereign authority, just cause, and right intention. These corresponded directly to the three ends of politics itself. Thus, the classic idea of just war reinterpreted and rephrased the goods of politics as requirements for the use of armed force in the context of the responsibilities for the government of a political community—a *res publica.* Articulating and demonstrating such linkage is the fundamental purpose of the book.

Cross, Crescent, and Sword: The Justification and Limitation of War in Western and Islamic Tradition. Edited with John Kelsay. Westport, CT: Greenwood Press, 1990.

As one of the two editors, Johnson wrote the Introduction for this work. The book was part of the outgrowth of four conferences held at Rutgers University during 1988–89. Their focus was on the relationship between Western and Islamic religious and cultural traditions on war, peace, and statecraft. As an endeavor to bridge the gap of knowledge and understanding between the study of the West and the study of Islam, the contributors sought to address broad topics in the histories of the two traditions in a cooperative dialogue.

Just War and Jihad: Historical and Theoretical Perspectives on War and Peace in Western and Islamic Traditions. Edited with John Kelsay. Westport, CT: Greenwood Press, 1991.

A companion volume to *Cross, Crescent, and Sword,* this book looks at the Western and Islamic backgrounds that influenced statecraft, international law, and the aims and limits of warfare and peace. The first chapter, "Historical Roots and Sources of the Just War Tradition in Western Culture" by Johnson, provides a historical summary review of the tradition. Such a review early in the book is something that became an intentional part of Johnson's subsequent books. In doing this, he has been able to consistently present the tradition to new readers and widening audiences.

Just War and the Gulf War. With George Weigel. Washington, D.C.: Ethics and Public Policy Center, 1991.

In this co-authored book, Johnson and Weigel evaluate the then-recent Operations Desert Shield and Desert Storm from the perspective of the just war tradition. Specifically addressed are the decision to use military force against Iraq, the conduct of the war, and the intensive moral debate regarding the war. In the opening chapter, "The Just War Tradition and the American Military," Johnson addresses the war in light of the just war tradition. He argues that with respect to *jus ad bellum,* military intervention was justified. So too, with respect to *jus in bello,* was the war justified—especially in light of the use of then-new "smart weapons." Co-author George Weigel views the religious debate regarding the war in American religion, especially Roman Catholicism and mainline Protestantism. The third section provides ten key documents about the war from religious bodies, religious leaders, and President George H. W. Bush.

The Just War Idea and the Ethics of Intervention. (Monograph.) The Joseph A. Reich, Sr., Distinguished Lecture on War, Morality and the Military Profession. United States Air Force Academy, CO: USAF, 1993.

> This lecture addresses the increasing concerns regarding intervention across national borders by military force. Johnson looks at intervention in the context of statecraft and moral reflection, the use of the just war tradition as a moral source for judging appropriate use of military power to intervene, and the implications of the just war tradition in the protection of and support for humanitarian relief efforts. It also contains five very useful charts.

Beyond Confrontation: Learning Conflict Resolution in the Post-Cold War Era. Edited with John A. Vasquez, Sanford M. Jaffe, and Linda Stamato. Ann Arbor, MI: The University of Michigan Press, 1996.

> Johnson and co-editor John A. Vasquez penned the brief "Introduction: A Time for Resolution" pages to this ten-chapter book. Johnson also wrote the chapter "International Law and the Peaceful Resolution of Interstate Conflicts," in which he shows the distinct connection between the just war tradition and international law. Written in the middle of a decade rife with global conflicts and much concern about reconciliation, the work seeks to provide an interdisciplinary approach to the politics of peace and techniques for international conflict resolution. The work illustrates Johnson's concern for peace within the just war tradition.

The Holy War Idea in Western and Islamic Tradition. University Park, PA: Pennsylvania State University Press, 1997.

> In this work, Johnson draws upon an extensive array of historical scholarship to present the historical development of the idea of holy war in the Christian West and Islam. In the West, the separation of church and state in secular society is widely accepted as a norm for political life. In Islam, the conception of religion is integral to the political order. Each of these views affects how holy war is

understood by the respective culture. The work offers a comparative study of how the cultures historically have defined the interrelationship of religion, statecraft, and war.

Morality and Contemporary Warfare. New Haven and London: Yale University Press, 1999.

As he did in his 1984 book *Can Modern War Be Just?,* Johnson focuses his writing in this book on the moral tradition of just war with respect to contemporary warfare. He contends that the legacies of the Vietnam War and fear of nuclear war created a need for renewed moral debate. The years of the 1990s featured civil wars, regional power conflict, and international criminal activities that used organized violent force. Such things require response from just war tradition proponents. Johnson presents a moral basis for when armed force can be justified and addresses issues such as military intervention, warfare against noncombatants, and cultural and religious differences that enhance conflict.

The War To Oust Saddam Hussein: Just War and the New Face of Conflict. New York: Rowman & Littlefield, 2005.

This work is Johnson's first book-length treatment of post-9/11 events and 21st-century conflict from the just war perspective. He explicitly addresses Operation Iraqi Freedom and looks at the broader context of ongoing conflict between the West and radical Islam. Significant details include a discussion of Samuel Huntington's "Clash of Civilizations" thesis, a moral response to terrorism from a just war perspective, and brief analyses and responses to Paul Ramsey's ideas of just war and to the U.S. Catholic bishops 1983 pastoral letter *The Challenge of Peace.* With respect to the moral use of armed force to oust Saddam Hussein, Johnson addresses six specific questions pertaining to Operation Iraqi Freedom and what he also believed to be the course of future conflict.

Ethics and the Use of Force: Just War in Historical Perspective. Farnham, Surrey: Ashgate Press, 2011.

In this volume, Johnson provides a detailed historical overview of the just war tradition, addressing some of the primary practical and theoretical challenges. He also looks at and corrects some of the contemporary misuses of the tradition. The work addresses topics such as just war vs. realism, interdisciplinary ethical concerns in war, and debates related to the international law of armed conflict. The eleven chapters of the volume demonstrate the breadth of contributions to the just war tradition. Notable in the book and relevant to a resurgence of interest is the chapter "Reinhold Niebuhr's Christian Realism and the Idea of Just War."

Sovereignty: Moral and Historical Perspectives. Washington, D.C.: Georgetown University Press, 2014.

Readers find in this work an in-depth moral and historical analysis of the concept of sovereignty in the classical just war framework (including Aquinas, Luther, and Grotius) and the Westphalian and post-Westphalian understandings of the idea. Notable in the work is his presentation in the final chapter on the relationship between the conceptions of sovereignty and "Responsibility to Protect" (R2P).

The Ashgate Research Companion to Military Ethics. Edited with Eric D. Patterson. Farnham, Surrey: Ashgate Publishing, 2015.

This is a large volume with 31 chapters by a wide array of authors. The editors provide a general introduction framing the issues and section introductions. Additionally, Johnson writes a chapter on "Enforcing and Strengthening Noncombatant Immunity." In his chapter, he argues that post-World War II conflict has eroded both the idea of noncombatant immunity and efforts to protect noncombatants. He reviews contemporary challenges of protecting noncombatants and reflects on how noncombatant immunity might be strengthened.

Just War Tradition and the Restraint of War: A Moral and Historical Inquiry. Princeton, NJ: Princeton University Press, 2016.

Reprint of his 1981 book. (See above.)

Ethics and the Use of Force: Just War in Historical Perspective. New York: Routledge, 2016.

Johnson views the contemporary debates of the just war tradition and the developments in the tradition during the last fifty years. The extensive introduction frames the book with a discussion regarding the role of present-day just war thought in the debates about the use of armed force and the uses and abuses of history in thinking about the just war tradition. Johnson divides the book into four sections: two moral traditions on the use of armed force, just war and international law, just war and political realism, and pressing contemporary problems.

CHAPTERS IN BOOKS (IN CHRONOLOGICAL ORDER)

"Morality and Force in Statecraft: Paul Ramsey and the Just War Tradition," in *Love and Society: Essays in the Ethics of Paul Ramsey.* James Turner Johnson and David H. Smith, eds., Missoula, MT: Scholars Press, 1974.

See above under books by date.

"Just War, the Nixon Doctrine, and the Future Shape of American Military Policy," in *1975 Year Book of World Affairs.* George W. Keeton and Georg Schwarzenberger, eds. London: Stevens & Sons Ltd., 1975.

This essay surveys what were then recent studies of post-World War II strategy by writers such as Sir Robert Thompson, Russell F. Weigley, Robert W. Tucker, Ralph B. Potter, and others. Some argued that there was a definite military policy, yet others argued that none existed. Johnson contends that the military policy and strategy of various administrations were complex and, in the case of the war in Vietnam, imprecise and poorly persuasive. He looks to history, specifically holy war doctrine in post-Reformation England, to understand the intellectual roots of American attitudes towards war and then compares aspects of the Nixon Doctrine with the classical just war tradition.

"Weapons Limits and the Restraint of War: A Just War Critique," in *Society of Christian Ethics Selected Papers, 1980.* Waterloo, Ontario: Council on the Study of Religion, 1980.

Johnson's paper looks at how the just war tradition might be used when considering nuclear arms control. He contends that nuclear deterrence is permissible ethically, politically, and militarily as long as war remains a reality or potential in the present age.

"Applying Just-War Doctrine to Nuclear Deterrence," in *The Nuclear Arms Debate: Ethical and Political Implications.* Robert C. Johansen, ed., Princeton, NJ: Center of International Studies, Princeton University, 1984.

This work arose from a 1983 conference at Princeton University. Johnson contends that the 1983 U.S. Catholic bishops' letter, *The Challenge of Peace*, focuses on the extremes of the nuclear debate and does not advance the debate beyond where it was twenty years previously. He also argues that the bishops' letter in some critical areas does not fit within the larger just war tradition.

"Crusade," "Deterrence," "Just War," "Nuclear Warfare," "Peace," "Puritan Ethics," and "War," in *Dictionary of Christian Ethics*, 2nd ed., James F. Childress, ed., Philadelphia: Fortress Press, 1985.

Written in the midst of the Cold War, these entries are in a standard reference work on Christian ethics. They offer a succinct overview of each of the topics.

"Threats, Values, and Defense," in *The Nuclear Dilemma and the Just War Tradition.* William V. O'Brien and John Langan, S.J., eds., Lexington, MA, and Toronto: Lexington Books, 1986.

> This volume arose from a 1984 conference at Georgetown University entitled "Justice and War in the Nuclear Age" and in the immediate aftermath of the publication of the U.S. Catholic bishops' pastoral letter, "The Challenge of Peace: God's Promise and Our Response." Johnson argues that nuclear weapons have not made the just war tradition obsolete. On the contrary, the tradition has much to offer in discussions of nuclear warfare. He also addresses the topic of "supreme emergency."

"Deterrence, Defense, or War-Fighting? A Just-War Analysis of Recent Strategic Developments," in *Ethics in the Nuclear Age.* Todd Whitmore, ed., Dallas, TX: Southern Methodist University Press, 1989.

> The chapter and the book arose from a two-year workshop seminar at the Divinity School of the University of Chicago. The purpose was to create a forum to discuss the 1983 U.S. Catholic bishops' letter, *The Challenge of Peace.* His chapter provides moral analysis from the just war perspective of what were then recent strategic developments in East-West power relations. He provides a critique of nuclear deterrence strategy looking specifically at the Strategic Defense Initiative (SDI) and improvements in nuclear weapons.

"The Moral Significance of the Weinberger Doctrine," in *The Recourse to War: An Appraisal of the Weinberger Doctrine.* Alan Ned Sabrosky and Robert L. Sloane, eds., Carlisle Barracks, PA: U.S. Army War College, 1988.

> This chapter argues that the Weinberger Doctrine of former Secretary of Defense Caspar Weinberger (1981–1987), provides a "clear and persuasive contemporary example of just war thinking." Noting that the doctrine is almost entirely a statement of *jus ad bellum,* it reviews Weinberger's six conditions for committing military

forces and finds that they are consistent with the major categories of historical just war thought.

This work was also published as "Just War Thinking and Its Contemporary Application: The Moral Significance of the Weinberger Doctrine," *Small Wars and Insurgencies* 1:2 (1990) 146–70.

"Does Defense of Values by Force Remain a Moral Possibility?" in *The Parameters of Military Ethics.* Lloyd J. Matthews and Dale E. Brown, eds., Washington, D.C.: Pergamon-Brassey's International Defense Publishers, 1989.

See below under articles. The article title is slightly different: "Threats, Values, and Defense: Does Defense of Values by Force Remain Morally Possible?"

"The Muddle of American Pacifism," in *Peace Betrayed? Essays on Pacifism and Politics.* Michael Cromartie, ed., Washington, D.C.: Ethics and Public Policy Center, 1990.

Using Guenter Lewy's then-recent book *Peace and Revolution: The Moral Crisis of American Pacifism* (1988), Johnson looks at the complexity of American pacifism, especially in the Vietnam and post-Vietnam War eras. He argues that within American pacifist circles, there is a blurring of objection to all war in the pursuit of a world without war and conscientious objection. Also, within the conscientious objection realm, he finds there to be inconsistencies. He argues that American pacifism has internal ethical and political challenges that do not serve its public voices and goals.

"International Norms and the Regulation of War," in *The Long Postwar Peace: Contending Explanations and Projections.* Charles W. Kegley, ed., New York: Harper Collins, 1990.

Johnson addresses the difficulties and complexities of regulating war. He contends that such is especially true in the post-World War II realist perspective of international relations with intellectual roots that date to the "perpetual peace" theory of earlier centuries. He shows differences between the international law approach of avoiding war and that of deterrence theory. He focuses on the production of norms and the underlying values that produce them.

"Can Contemporary War Be Just? Elements in the Moral Debate," in *After the Cold War: Questioning the Morality of Nuclear Deterrence.* Charles W. Kegley, Jr. and Kenneth L. Schwab, eds., Boulder, CO: Westview Press, 1991.

Johnson discusses three major phases in a cyclical pattern of debate regarding ethics and the military, focusing on nuclear weapons in the United States since World War II. He presents the role of the just war tradition in what were then recent debates on nuclear weapons and provides some critical reflection on the thought of Paul Ramsey and the U.S. Catholic bishops' Pastoral Letter. He concludes with three observations regarding strategic deterrence.

"Introduction," in *Cross, Crescent, and Sword: The Justification and Limitation of War in Western and Islamic Tradition.* James Turner Johnson and John Kelsay, eds., Westport, CT: Greenwood Press, 1990.

See above under books by date.

"Historical Roots and Sources of the Just War Tradition," in *Just War and Jihad: Historical and Theoretical Perspectives on War and Peace in Western and Islamic Traditions.* James Turner Johnson and John Kelsay, eds., Westport, CT: Greenwood Press, 1991.

See above under books by date.

"Introduction," in *Just War and Jihad: Historical and Theoretical Perspectives on War and Peace in Western and Islamic Traditions.* James Turner Johnson and John Kelsay, eds., Westport, CT: Greenwood Press, 1991.

See above under books by date.

"The Just War Idea and the American Search for Peace," in *The American Search for Peace: Moral Reasoning, Religious Hope, and National Security.* George Weigel and John R. Langan, S.J., eds., Washington, D.C.: Georgetown University Press, 1991.

Johnson presents a case arguing that the just war tradition is profoundly about peace, though not solely about peace. He then asks to what extent the moral tradition is embodied in the actions and thoughts of Americans regarding war. Next, he asks whether Americans should be guided by it, and if so, how that is best accomplished. To do so, he provides an overview of the just war tradition with respect to secular political philosophy, international law, military ethics, military policy, and theology.

"The Just War Tradition and the American Military," in *Just War and the Gulf War.* With James Turner Johnson and George Weigel. Washington, D.C.: Ethics and Public Policy Center, 1991.

See above under books by date.

"Religion, Conflict, and Ethnic Identity in the Sri Lankan Conflict," in Manus I. Midlarsky, ed., *The Internationalization of Communal Strife.* London and New York: Routledge, 1992.

Johnson provides a case study of Sri Lanka in the volume that emanates from a 1991 conference at Rutgers University.

"Just-War Tradition and the War in the Gulf," in *War in the Twentieth Century.* Richard B. Miller, ed., Louisville, KY: Westminster/John Knox Press, 1992.

Johnson's writing is one of four items in a section on the war in the Persian Gulf. In a five-page essay written during Operation Desert Storm, he argues for the continued use of just war principles in the conflict.

"Does Democracy Travel? Some Thoughts on Democracy and Its Cultural Context," in *Ethics & International Affairs: A Reader.* Joel H. Rosenthal, ed., Washington, D.C.: Georgetown University Press, 1995.

This chapter looks at political ideas beyond the just war tradition in considering the viability in other parts of the world of liberal democratic self-government as it has arisen in the West.

"Introduction: A Time for Resolution," in *Beyond Confrontation: Learning Conflict Resolution in the Post-Cold War Era.* John A. Vasquez, James Turner Johnson, Sanford M. Jaffe, and Linda Stamato, eds., Ann Arbor, MI: The University of Michigan Press, 1995.

See above under books by date.

"International Law and the Peaceful Resolution of Interstate Conflicts," in *Beyond Confrontation: Learning Conflict Resolution in the Post-Cold War Era.* John A. Vasquez, James Turner Johnson, Sanford M. Jaffe, and Linda Stamato, eds., Ann Arbor, MI: The University of Michigan Press, 1995.

See above under books by date.

"Just War Tradition and Low-Intensity Conflict," in *Legal and Moral Restraints on Low-Intensity Conflict.* Alberto R. Coll, James S. Ord, and Stephen A. Rose, eds., Newport, RI: Naval War College, 1995.

This chapter is from a book in an international law studies series initiated by the Naval War College in 1901 that continues to the present. Johnson provides an overview of the just war tradition in American moral and legal thought and then applies the tradition to low-intensity conflict. He argues that the tradition is well-suited to clarifying ethical concerns in such conflicts.

"War for Cities and Noncombatant Immunity in the Bosnian Conflict," in *Religion and Justice in the War over Bosnia.* G. Scott Davis, ed., New York and London: Routledge, 1996.

> Written during the period of conflict in the Balkans, Johnson argues that the armed conflict in the aftermath of the breakup of the former Yugoslavia significantly and tragically affected noncombatants. Frequently this was an intentional and integral part of the conflict. Though often heralded as "postmodern" or "future" war, Johnson contends that it is not a new form of warfare. Rather, it is one that was unexpected for this era and this geography. The conduct of the war in Bosnia and Herzegovina, especially the siege warfare of the Bosnian Serbs against the Bosnian government and Muslim-held cities, has largely been neglected by moral analysts and modern military thinkers.

"Just Cause Revisited," in *Close Calls: Intervention, Terrorism, Missile Defense, and Just War Today.* Elliott Abrams, ed., Washington, D.C.: Ethics and Public Policy Center, 1998.

> In the opening chapter of a work containing many notable contributors (e.g., A. J. Bacevich, John R. Bolton, Robert Kagan, Margaret Thatcher, and R. James Woolsey), Johnson provides the foundation for subsequent chapters by providing an overview of just cause in the *jus ad bellum* portion of just war thought. He surveys the history of just cause and provides two arguments for why it needs to be reassessed and strengthened in contemporary thought.

"A Just War Argument for Ballistic Missile Defense," in *Close Calls: Intervention, Terrorism, Missile Defense, and Just War Today.* Elliott Abrams, ed., Washington, D.C.: Ethics and Public Policy Center, 1998.

> Johnson provides a second chapter (see above) in a work addressing just war thought a decade after the collapse of the Soviet Union. He looks specifically at the just war tradition and applies it to the duty of self-defense against missile attack.

"Bombing, Ethics of" and "Just War Theory," in *The Oxford Companion to American Military History.* John Whiteclay Chambers, ed., Oxford, New York: Oxford University Press, 1999.

These two entries in a standard reference work provide an introduction and synopsis of each of the topics. Each entry contains a brief bibliography and references other entries in the book.

"The Just-War Idea and the Ethics of Intervention," in *The Leader's Imperative.* J. Carl Ficcarrotta, ed., West Lafayette, IN: Purdue University Press, 2001.

See above under books (monograph) by date (1993).

"The Law of Nations: Religion, Ethics, and International Law Bearing on Conflict and Peace," in *Religion, Law, and the Role of Force.* Joseph I. Coffey and Charles T. Matthewes, eds., Ardsley, NY: Transnational Publishers, 2002.

Since the end of the Cold War, there has been a reshaping of the nature of religious debates and the role of religious belief with respect to conflict, peace, human rights, and protection of noncombatants. There have also been advances in international law. Johnson discusses the contemporary dialogue between religion and law over the problem of armed conflict and connects the dialogue to contemporary religious perspectives on peace. He also looks at four particular problems posed by armed conflict for religion and international law. Finally, he argues that if, as he believes, there are exceptional circumstances in which armed intervention by the U.N. and regional alliances are deemed necessary and just, then significant thought and planning must be given to post-conflict necessities.

"The Use of Force: A Justified Response," in *War as Crucifixion: Essays on Peace, Violence, and "Just War."* John M. Buchanan and David Heim, eds., Chicago: Christian Century Press, 2002.

This work comes from a collection of essays reprinted from *The Christian Century.* Included are essays from H. Richard Niebuhr,

John Howard Yoder, Reinhold Niebuhr, and Alan Geyer. See in articles below (1991).

"Can Contemporary Armed Conflicts Be Just? An Examination of Some Central Moral Issues," in *Gerechter Krieg.* Dieter Janssen and Michael Quante, eds., Paderborn, Germany: Mentis Verlag, 2003.

This chapter argues that much of the literature regarding war in the final decades of the 20th century was written with the expectation of World War III plus nuclear weapons. Such has not been the case of contemporary warfare. Instead, it has been waged with conventional weapons. Johnson looks at moral issues raised by contemporary warfare and does so from within the just war tradition.

"Just War Theory: Responding Morally to Global Terrorism," in *The New Global Terrorism: Characteristics, Causes, Controls.* Charles W. Kegley, Jr., ed., Upper Saddle River, NJ: Prentice-Hall, 2003.

The chapter presents a very strong moral argument against terrorism. Illustrating his argument from the September 11, 2001 attack, Johnson contends that terrorism is never morally or legally acceptable. In part, this is so because it deliberately chooses noncombatants as its targets. Additionally, terrorists often have a generalized animosity toward a whole group of people or culture and justify violence on that basis.

"Theoretical Context of Studies on Peace and Just War," in *Philosophies of Peace and Just War in Greek Philosophy and Religions of Abraham: Judaism, Christianity and Islam.* Mehdi Faridzadeh, ed., New York: Global Scholarly Publications, 2004.

Johnson presents a historical and political context for thinking about the relationship between religion and the pursuit of war and peace in Judaism, Christianity, and Islam. Each has a vision of peace at the end of days, but each also understands that war must be a possibility at times in the present age for the good of the political community.

"Lieber and the Theory of War," in *Francis Lieber and the Culture of the Mind.* Charles R. Mack and Henry H. Lesesne, eds., Columbia, SC: University of South Carolina Press, 2005.

The theme of the presentations in this book is the multi-faceted career of Francis Lieber (ca. 1800–1872). Johnson argues that Lieber's theory of war was more complex than his two best-known works from the American Civil War suggest (*Guerrilla Parties, Considered with Reference to the Law and Usages of War,* 1862 and *Instructions for the Government of Armies of the United States in the Field,* 1863). This book reflected his own experience of war as well as the major ideas in warfare during his era. Johnson contends that there is tension between how Lieber is remembered, usually in military ethics, and how he viewed the greater endeavor of warfare. Johnson notes that Lieber believed that making war short required great violence. Because of that, he allowed soldiers to follow "military necessity" to gain rapid victory; however, in so doing, they were permitted legitimately to inflict considerable suffering on noncombatants.

"The Just War Idea: The State of the Question," in *Justice and Global Politics.* Ellen Frankel Paul, Fred D. Miller, Jr., and Jeffrey Paul, eds., Cambridge and New York: Cambridge University Press, 2006.

See in articles below by date.

"Framing a Debate: Authority To Use Force in Just War Reasoning and International Law," in "What We're Fighting for ..." *–Friedensethik in der transatlantischen Debatte.* Gerhard Beestermoeller, Michael Haspel, and Uwe Trittmann, eds., Stuttgart: Verlag W. Kohlhammer, 2006.

Johnson acknowledges differences between continental Western Europe and Americans with respect to the use of armed force and how the authority to use such force by the United Nations and individual states is understood. Part of the differences rests in varied approaches to international law as well as renewed American interaction with the just war tradition. In Germany, the tradition is not as widely accepted. In the current century, some of this is evidenced in the 2001 statement "What We're Fighting For: A Letter from America" that was signed by 60 American intellectuals.

"Searching for Common Ground: Ethical Traditions at the Interface with International Law," in *Universalism vs. Relativism: Making Moral Judgments in a Changing, Pluralistic, and Threatening World.* Don Browning, ed., Lanham, MD: Rowman & Littlefield Publishers, Inc., 2006.

The interface between major ethical traditions and international law with the desire for highly stable, if not universal, values is presented in hopes of finding common ground for matters involving the law of armed conflict and human rights law. Johnson looks at the typology of international lawyer Georg Schwarzenberger and the ideas of the law of community, the law of power, and the law of reciprocity. He also looks at the just war tradition and the law of armed conflict as well as jihad in normative Islamic tradition. Further review and comparisons are made between human rights and Western culture and human rights and Islamic culture.

"Contemporary Just War," in *The Ethics of War.* Gregory M. Reichberg, Henrik Syse, and Endre Begby, eds., Oxford; Malden, MA; and Victoria, Australia: Blackwell Publishing, 2006.

The chapter by Johnson is one of 58 chapters of primary source writings about war through the centuries. This chapter focuses on just war thought in the face of nuclear war and in consideration of the lack of discrimination between combatants and noncombatants in contemporary warfare. Excerpts are taken from Johnson's "Does Defense of Values by Force Remain a Moral Responsibility?" (1989, see above) and "Maintaining the Protection of Non-Combatants" (2000, see below).

"Just War Thinking in Recent American Religious Debate Over Military Force," in *The Price of Peace: Just War in the Twenty-First Century.* Charles Reed and David Ryall, eds., Cambridge, New York: Cambridge University Press, 2007.

In the years between the publication of Paul Ramsey's two works, *War and the Christian Conscience* (1961) and *The Just War* (1968), Michael Walzer's *Just and Unjust Wars (1977)*, and with the United States Catholic Bishops' *The Challenge of Peace* (1983), there was a remarkable recovery of the just war idea in American public and religious debate. This continued in the last two decades of the 20th century and into the present. However, Roman Catholics, "mainline" Protestant denominations, and evangelicals have engaged, rejected, or gone beyond the tradition in a variety of ways such that there is no unified Christian American response to the use of military force and the just war tradition.

"Thinking Morally about War in the Middle Ages and Today," in *Ethics, Nationalism, and Just War: Medieval and Contemporary Perspectives.* Henrik Syse and Gregory M. Reichberg, eds., Washington, D.C.: The Catholic University of America Press, 2007.

In this brief chapter, Johnson argues that there is moral continuity between the medieval views of war and contemporary warfare, even though there are enormous differences between life in the Middle Ages and today.

"Maintaining the Protection of Noncombatants," in *Ethics, Nationalism, and Just War: Medieval and Contemporary Perspectives.* Henrik Syse and Gregory M. Reichberg, eds., Washington, D.C.: The Catholic University of America Press, 2007.

Johnson argues in this lengthy chapter for the necessity and primacy of the protection of noncombatants. Failure to do so negatively affects all concerned.

"Debates Over Just War and Jihad: Ideas, Interpretations, and Implications Across Cultures," in *Debating the War of Ideas.* Eric D. Patterson and John Gallagher, eds., New York: Palgrave Macmillan, 2009.

> Johnson addresses the questions of to what extent a clash of civilizations exists between the West and the world of Islam, how meaningful such a discussion is, and the differing interpretations of just war and jihad. He provides a comparison of the two traditions and offers a critique of radical Islam within the holy war tradition.

"Just War and Jihad of the Sword," in *The Blackwell Companion to Religion and Violence.* Andrew R. Murphy, ed., Oxford: Wiley-Blackwell Publishing, 2011.

> This chapter compares the historical traditions of the just war and jihad ideas of war. He argues that each tradition is embedded deeply in its respective culture, and each is simultaneously religious and political in nature.

"Contemporary Warfare and American Efforts at Restraint," in *From Jeremiad to Jihad: Religion, Violence, and America.* John D. Carlson and Jonathan H. Ebel, eds. Berkeley, CA: University of California Press, 2012.

> This chapter states that much of warfare in the last decade of the 1990s and the first decade of the 2000s intentionally sought to harm those whom the moral tradition of the just war sought to protect—noncombatants. In so doing, it rejected any idea of fundamental human rights. He believes that the recovery of the just war debate in the United States involved a re-interpretation of the idea that unintentionally led to the diminishment of noncombatant protection. Corrections can be made but not without concerted efforts.

"Moral Responsibility after Conflict: The Idea of *Jus Post Bellum* in the Twenty-First Century," in *Ethics beyond War's End.* Eric Patterson, ed., Washington, D.C.: Georgetown University Press, 2012.

> Johnson traces recent history and developments in the idea of *jus post bellum* and argues against standardization of rules governing it. Instead, he argues, there should be flexibility and decisions should be made based on moral and political considerations in each situation because each conflict is unique.

"Conclusion: A Look Back and a Look Forward," in *Just War, Holy War, and Jihad: A Comparative Study.* Sohail Hashmi, ed., Oxford and New York: Oxford University Press, 2012.

> Johnson presents a survey of earlier contributions in the book regarding the comparative ethics of war in Western and Islamic traditions. He places the current book in the evolution of the comparative studies and summarizes conclusions that can be gleaned from the development of the idea of holy war in each tradition. This is the concluding chapter of the book.

"The Right to Use Armed Force: Sovereignty, Responsibility, and the Common Good," pp. 19–34, in *Just War: Tradition, Authority, Practice.* Anthony F. Lang, Jr., Cian O'Driscoll, and John Williams, eds. Washington, D.C.: Georgetown University Press, 2013.

> This chapter emphasizes the importance of sovereign political authority in the just use of force as a last resort. Johnson presents the thinking from classical just war tradition regarding the just resort to war wherein the primary emphasis was that of sovereign authority with the purpose being order, followed by justice and peace, to a contemporary position in which there is less emphasis on authority and a primary emphasis placed on just cause. In the current construct as advocated by the U.S. Catholic bishops in their 1983 pastoral letter *The Challenge of Peace* and in the 1993 ten-year anniversary document

The Harvest of Justice is Sown in Peace, there is less weight given to the authority required for last resort. He argues that the shift has been detrimental to rectifying egregious violations of basic human rights and to the protection of noncombatants in asymmetric warfare.

"Enforcing and Strengthening Noncombatant Immunity," in *The Ashgate Research Companion to Military Ethics*. James Turner Johnson and Eric D. Patterson, eds., Farnham, Surrey: Ashgate Publishing, 2015.

See above under books by date.

"A Dialogue: Ethics, Law, and the Question of Detention in Non-International Armed Conflicts," in *Year Book of International Humanitarian Law,* Vol. 16 (2013). Terry D. Gill, gen. ed., Amsterdam/ Breda: Asser Press, 2015.

Non-international conflicts are difficult challenges for international law and ethical discourse. However, after providing an historical examination of the just war tradition, Johnson argues that it does provide a framework for ethical considerations regarding non-international armed conflicts.

"Foreword" to *Chinese Just War Ethics: Origin, Development, and Dissent*. Ping-cheung Lo and Sumner B. Twiss, eds., Abingdon, Oxon, and New York: Routledge, 2015.

Johnson provides a seven-page foreword that encourages a three-way dialogue among scholars of Chinese traditions and war, Islamic traditions and war, and Western traditions and war. He also notes the presence of multiple religious traditions in China.

"Then and Now: The Medieval Conception of Just War versus Recent Portrayals of the Just War Idea," in *Medieval Foundations of International Relations*. William Bain, ed., London and New York: Routledge, 2017.

This chapter provides a detailed study of the criteria for just war in medieval thought and how it has more recently been interpreted by Paul Ramsey, Michael Walzer, and the United States Catholic bishops. Johnson has often described these as the three pillars of the recovery of the idea of just war in contemporary thought. He articulates the differences between the understanding of just war in medieval thought and contemporary thought and presents his ideas regarding aspects of medieval thought that should be regained.

"War," in *The Oxford Handbook of Nineteenth-Century Christian Thought.* Joel D. Rasmussen, Judith Wolfe, and Johannes Zachhuber, eds., Oxford: Oxford University Press, 2017.

In a chapter that differs from many of his other writings, Johnson provides an historical overview of war in Christian thought in the "long" nineteenth century from American and British history. He looks at such conflicts as the Mahdist Rebellion in Sudan, the Indian Mutiny, and the American Civil War. The chapter has five sections: Setting the Stage; Christian Thought in the Form of Cultural Consensus: The Form Taken in Two Traditions; the Rise of Evangelical Christianity and Its Influence on War; Christian Sectarian Pacifism in the Nineteenth Century: The Case of the Mennonites; and The Rise of Catholic Opposition to 'Modern' War. He concludes that Christian attitudes regarding war spanned the spectrum of belief and that for many, the idea of restraint in war was lacking. Others advocated pacifism and the differing views were never reconciled as the new century dawned.

"St. Augustine: (354–430 CE)," in *Just War Thinkers: From Cicero to Today.* Daniel Brunstetter and Cian O'Driscoll, eds., London and New York: Routledge, 2017.

In a work designed to introduce the just war tradition and key figures in its development, Johnson provides an overview of the seminal thought of Augustine with respect to war and his unquestioned influence on the tradition.

"Foreword" to *Philosophers on War*, Eric Patterson and Timothy J. Demy, eds., Newport, RI: Stone Tower Books, 2017. Rev. ed. Stone Tower Press, 2022.

Johnson provides a brief foreword to a work that summarizes nineteen major thinkers of the West with respect to their ideas on war.

"Victory Though the Heaven's Fall? Unlimited Warfare as Theme and Phenomenon," 69–84 in *Moral Victories: The Ethics of Winning Wars*, Andrew R. Hom, Cian O'Driscoll, eds. New York: Oxford University Press, 2017.

Arguing within the just war tradition, Johnson looks at unlimited warfare and its relationship to ethics and victory. He discusses the classic tradition that coalesced in the twelfth and thirteenth centuries, was then overshadowed from the 17th to mid-20th centuries, and reinterpreted during the Cold War by Paul Ramsey, Michael Walzer, and the U.S. Catholic bishops. Johnson contends that in midst of a pluralistic and cross-cultural world it is possible to reach morally useful conclusions regarding the definition of, nature of, and means to victory even though there will not be unanimous agreement.

JOURNAL AND MAGAZINE ARTICLES (IN CHRONOLOGICAL ORDER)

"The Meaning of Non-Combatant Immunity in the Just War/Limited War Tradition," *Journal of the American Academy of Religion* 39:2 (June, 1971), 151–70.

This writing considers Christian just war doctrine, particularly regarding the distinguishing of combatants and noncombatants and engaging the works of Paul Ramsey and Robert W. Tucker.

"Ideology and the *Jus ad Bellum*: Justice in the Initiation of War," *Journal of the American Academy of Religion* 41:2 (June 1973), 212–28.

Johnson proposes a path to an adequate position on *jus ad bellum* and the right of a state to resort to war.

"Toward Reconstructing the *Jus ad Bellum*," *The Monist* LVII:4 (October 1973), 461–88.

This article addresses the inadequacies of current-day *jus ad bellum*, seeking to define moral doctrine limiting resort to war and to identify requirements for political application.

"Rationalizing the Hell of War: A Response to Gordon Zahn," *Worldview* 17:1 (January 1974), 43–46.

This response counters Gordon Zahn's criticism of just war tradition as not applicable to modern warfare, exemplified by the case of the Vietnam War.

"Natural Law as a Language for the Ethics of War," *Journal of Religious Ethics* 3:2 (Fall 1975), 217–42.

An evaluation of the utility of natural law as a common approach to analyze ethics and just war theory, this article incorporates thought from Paul Ramsey, Myers McDougal and Florentino Feliciano, and Franciscus de Victoria (also, Vitoria).

"Just War Theory: What's the Use?" *Worldview* 19:7–8 (July-August 1976), 41–47; discussion, November and December 1976 issues.

This seminal writing forms a foundational approach, applying just war tradition and ethics to current international affairs and politics.

"On 'No First Use' of Nuclear Weapons," *Worldview* 20:3 (March 1977), 43–44.

In a response to Bruce Russett's November 1976 *Worldview* article "No First Use of Nuclear Weapons" and Francis X. Winters' "The

Nuclear Arms Race: Man vs. War Machines" from the September issues of the same year, Johnson analyzes the concept of limited response and problems related to tactical nuclear weapons.

"The Cruise Missile and the Neutron Bomb: Some Moral Reflections," *Worldview* 20:12 (December 1977), 20–26; discussion, April 1978 issue.

Expositing on the technologies of the cruise missile and the neutron bomb as viable alternatives for planning and fighting wars—Johnson ties together the concept of charity, the question of discrimination of noncombatants, and the principles of civilization, humanity, limited warfare, and restraint.

"Moral Reflections on the New Civil Defense Debate," *Worldview* 22:1–2 (January-February 1979), 42–43.

Addressing debate on civil defense against nuclear weapons with Paul H. Nitze, Hans J. Morgenthau, John C. Bennett, Thomas J. Downey, Richard J. Barnet, David T. Johnson, and Paul Ramsey, Johnson prioritizes just war ethics, noncombatant protection, and defense against violence as applicable to U.S. missile defense in the President James E. Carter administration.

"On Keeping Faith: The Use of History for Religious Ethics," *Journal of Religious Ethics* 7:1 (Spring 1979), 98–116.

Johnson contends that individual moral identities are derived from a living history of both personal and communal religious practice and memory. As such, religious ethics should be treated as a baseline norm for contemporary decision-making and analysis.

"Marching as to War," *Matrix: Research at Rutgers* (Winter 1981), 9–11.

In this article, Johnson seeks to recover the Western just war tradition on the restraint of war, clarifying its history and development to stimulate public debate and application to contemporary issues.

"What Guidance Can Just War Tradition Provide for Contemporary Moral Thought about War?" *New Catholic World* 226:1346 (March-April 1982), 81–84.

> This article argues that just war tradition and moral theorists can adequately provide guidance for contemporary discussions of *jus ad bellum, jus in bello,* and the development of moral warfare technologies.

"The Moral Bases of Contingency Planning," *Hastings Center Report* 12 (1982), 19–20.

> This commentary emphasizes the importance of respecting noncombatant rights and caring for injured noncombatants in policy and war planning.

"Two Issues in Contemporary Defense: A Just War Critique," *Military Chaplains' Review* 7 (1982), 7–18.

> Prefaced by an introduction on the structure of the just war tradition and definitions of *jus ad bellum* and *jus in bello,* Johnson applies the framework to weapons strategy and use of force for intervention to protect the rights of others.

"Grotius' Use of History and Charity in the Modern Transformation of the Just War Idea," *Grotiana*, New Series 4:1 (1983), 21–34.

> Two criticisms commonly leveled at the just war tradition are that its history in Christianity and its development in previous centuries make it irrelevant for a secular world where realism often prevails in international relations. Johnson rebuts these criticisms arguing that neither is faithful to the history of the Western moral tradition. He does so by looking at the role of Grotius in the development of the just war tradition. In so doing, Johnson argues that the work of Grotius came at a time when the tradition was in transition for a distinctly Christian perspective in Western Europe to one that was becoming more international and secular. In this extensive article,

he demonstrates how Grotius set forth a historically and rationally grounded foundation for advocating restraint in war that was secular and became part of international law for the modern secular and pluralistic world.

"Ground for Nuclear Optimism," *Freedom at Issue* 72 (May-June 1983), 8–11.

Reviewing Lawrence Freedman's 1983 book, *The Evolution of Nuclear Strategy,* Johnson evaluates Freedman's contribution to understanding the general arc of U.S. nuclear strategy from 1945 to the early 1980s.

"The Idea of a Christian Soldier: A Historical Perspective," *Catholicism in Crisis* 2:4 (March 1984), 18–19.

In this article, the idea of the Christian soldier is examined from early days starting in the year 174 to the development of morality for the Christian soldier as a basis for application to modern military context.

"Two Kinds of Pacifism: Opposition to the Political Use of Force in the Renaissance-Reformation Period," *Journal of Religious Ethics* 12:1 (Spring 1984), 39–60.

This paper examines the opposition to political use of force by two types of pacifism in Western history. The first school, the pacifism of Erasmus, morally rejects violence, while the second, that of the Anabaptists of the Schleitheim Confession, accepts violence as an inevitable part of state affairs.

"Historical Tradition and Moral Judgment: The Case of Just War Tradition," *The Journal of Religion* 64:3 (1984), 299–317.

This paper evaluates the role of moralists as just war tradition information-bearers and educators. Additionally, it assesses the tradition of just war itself as morally prescriptive for addressing contemporary conflict.

"Threats, Values, and Defense: Does Defense of Values by Force Remain Morally Possible?" *Parameters: Journal of the US Army War College* 15:1 (Spring, 1985), 13–25.

> This article addresses the question of whether use of force to preserve values is ever morally permissible. Johnson reviews four ways that this is allowable in classic just war tradition, reflecting on the nature of and threats against values.

"Recent Strategic Developments: A Critical Overview from a Just War Perspective," *Analyse & Kritik: Zeitschrift fur Sozialwissenschaften* 9:1&2 (1987), 120–41.

> This essay applies just war tradition principles to three issues prominent in 1987: nuclear deterrence, strategic defense, and tactical nuclear weapons.

"Giudizio morale e questioni internazionali: i limiti del realism" ("Moral Judgment in International Affairs: The Limits of Realism"), *Teoria Politica* 5:1 (1989), 3–19.

> In this article, Johnson compares various forms of political realism, including the works of Reinhold Niebuhr, Hans Morgenthau, Robert Osgood, the American Catholic bishops, and Paul Ramsey, linking these to issues of war and peace.

"Is Democracy an Ethical Standard?" *Ethics & International Affairs* 4:1 (March 1990), 1–17.

> This article argues that family and religion form the basis of Western ethical standards, including the ideas of democracy and freedom.

"Just War Thinking and Its Contemporary Application: The Moral Significance of the Weinberger Doctrine," *Small Wars and Insurgencies* 1:2 (August, 1990), 146–70.

See book chapter above, "The Moral Significance of the Weinberger Doctrine," in Alan Ned Sabrosky and Robert L. Sloane, eds., *The Recourse to War: An Appraisal of the Weinberger Doctrine* (Carlisle Barracks, PA: U.S. Army War College, 1988).

"Just War Criteria," *World* 5:31 (January 19, 1991), 7–8.

This article assesses seven criteria that justify coalition use of force to counter Saddam Hussein's Iraqi aggressive invasion of Kuwait.

"The Use of Force," *The Christian Century* (February 6–13, 1991), 134–35.

The content in this article pairs with Johnson's book *Just War and the Gulf War.* With George Weigel, Washington, D.C.: Ethics and Public Policy Center, 1991 (see above). The author enumerates seven just war conditions he argues were met before the launch of US-coalition air attacks against Iraq after its invasion of Kuwait.

"Just War in the Thought of Paul Ramsey," *Journal of Religious Ethics* 19:2 (Special Focus Issue: The Ethics of Paul Ramsey) (Fall 1991), 183–207.

Focusing on Paul Ramsey's conception of just war, this paper covers three topics: Christian need to identify non-combatants, policy on discrimination and proportionality, and Ramsey's treatments of *jus in bello* and *jus ad bellum.*

"On U.S. Involvement in Bosnia," *The Christian Century* 110:17 (May 19–16, 1993), 543.

In a brief statement published alongside ethicist Alan Geyer (Wesley Theological Seminary, Washington, D.C.), Johnson argues that just war requirements did not exist for U.S. use of force in Bosnia.

"The Broken Tradition," *The National Interest* 45 (1996), 27–36.

This article traces the fundamental elements of and major changes in just war thinking during the 20th century, with an emphasis on the last three decades and policy implications.

"An Interest in Bosnia," *The Christian Century* 113:6 (February 21, 1996), 189–90.

Addressing developments as of 1996 regarding U.S. involvement in Bosnia, Johnson acknowledges that there are at least two reasons to support use of force: Christian moral tradition-based protection of neighbors from harm, and U.S. participation in support of NATO allies and international peace and order.

"The Question of Preemption," *Common Sense* 9 (Winter, 1996), 36–52.

In this essay, Johnson mines four reasons why the question of preemptive use of force is worthy of consideration. Establishing the answer in the positive, he then enumerates the necessary requirements to justify state use of preemption.

"Moral Traditions and Religious Ethics: A Comparative Enquiry," *Journal of Religious Ethics* 25:3 (25th Anniversary Supplement 1997), 77–101.

A comparative examination of three issues (political order, justified use of force, and claims of universality) using Augustinian and classical Islamic thought.

"Comment: 'Nonviolent Resistance: Trust and Risk-Taking Twenty-Five Years Later,'" *Journal of Religious Ethics* 26:1 (Spring 1998), 219–22.

Johnson critiques James Childress's approach to just war analysis while arguing for his own methods of placing moral historical thought in contemporary perspective.

"Human Rights and Violence in Contemporary Context," *Journal of Religious Ethics* 26:2 (Fall 1998), 319–28.

> This article addresses the post-World War II need to protect the individual rights of citizens as a moral obligation for the use of force under the international Law of Armed Conflict.

"Maintaining the Protection of Non-Combatants," *Journal of Peace Research* 37:4 (July 2000), 421–48.

> Johnson addresses the just war principle of identifying non-combatants and maintaining their protection in contemporary warfare. Johnson divides the article into five sections: 1) moral and just war analysis of non-combatants in war; 2) historical approaches and development of protection of non-combatants in war; 3) legal analysis of non-combatant protections, including the law of armed conflict and crimes against humanity; 4) the cases of Rwanda, Zaire, and Yugoslavia; and 5) moral arguments for maintaining non-combatant protections.

"Can a Pacifist Have a Conversation with Augustine? A Response to Alain Epp Weaver," *Journal of Religious Ethics* 29:1 (Spring 2001), 87–93.

> Johnson criticizes Alain Epp Weaver's comparative conversation on ethical wrongness between Augustine and Yoder. He argues that the two conversants do not make the same assumptions, as Augustine places wrongness with the actor's intent, whereas Yoder analyzes wrongness in terms of the objective character of the act itself.

"Comment: Just War Theory in Comparative Perspective," *Journal of Religious Ethics* 28:2 (Summer, 2000), 331–35.

> Commenting on Simeon Ilesanmi's "Just War Theory in Comparative Perspective" essay, this work prioritizes justice, peace, right authority, and "religio-cultural moral traditions on war."

"The Distortion of a Tradition," *Pacem* 5:1 (January 2002), 25–30.

Expanding on his work on just war and Islamic tradition, the author differentiates the defensive form of jihad from offensive jihad. Johnson has specific purposes: to educate readers on the last century of historic development of defensive jihad, to critique Osama bin Laden's appropriation of the idea in 1988, and to further discussion of Islamic traditional norms in the context of the 9/11 attacks in 2001.

"Jihad and Just War," *First Things* 124 (June-July 2002), 12–14.

In this essay, Johnson emphasizes the differences between traditional and extremist concepts of jihad. In the pursuit of using force in order to uphold high ideals of values and beliefs, both traditional Islamic and Christian just war thought aspire to protect the common good.

"Just War and Jihad: Two Traditions on the Use of Force," *Inquiries*, the publication of the Center for Free Inquiry, Hanover College 3:2 (Winter 2003), 1–7.

This article provides a comparative overview of the two traditions of just war and jihad, beginning with origins of each and culminating in a study along three central themes on justified use of armed force: authority, justice, and right conduct.

"Aquinas and Luther on War and Peace: Sovereign Authority and the Use of Armed Force," *Journal of Religious Ethics* 31:1 (Spring 2003), 3–20.

In this article Johnson examines the just war approaches of Aquinas and Luther for *jus ad bellum* regarding just cause and the use of force. Johnson places responsibility squarely with the sovereign leadership for moral assessment and action.

"Just War, as It Was and Is," *First Things* 149 (January 2005), 14–24.

This article seeks to reinvigorate and reconnect contemporary religious thought (especially Roman Catholic) with historical just war thinking in order to drive the theological and political debate on the use of force to achieve justice, order, and peace.

"Wojna sprawiedliwa—jaka byla i jaka jest," *Ethos* (the quarterly journal of the Instytutu Jan Pawla II, Lublin, Poland) 18 (Fall-Winter 2005), 71–72.

Polish version of "Just War, as it Was and Is," from *First Things*, January 2005 (see above).

"Aquinas and Luther on War and Peace," *Luther Digest*, vol. 13 (2005), 48–51.

Recent debate on resorting to armed force for humanitarian intervention focuses on the requirement of just cause. Johnson seeks, rather, to promote the classical views of Aquinas and Luther that sovereign authority is the correct primary assessor for *jus ad bellum.*

"Comment: 'Just War Theories Reconsidered,'" *Journal of Religious Ethics* 33:1 (March 2005), 599–606.

Johnson responds to criticism from H. D. Baer and J. E. Capizzi and critiques their work "Just War Theories Reconsidered."

"The Just War Idea: The State of the Question," *Social Philosophy and Policy* 23:1 (Winter 2006): 167–95.

This essay examines the concept of just war in both classical and contemporary contexts. The first half of the article applies the classical form in a post-World War II context to contemporary conflict from an American perspective; the second half critiques contemporary just war themes as tested against classical just war tradition.

"Humanitarian Intervention After Iraq: Just War and International Law Perspectives," *Journal of Military Ethics* 5:2 (2006): 114–27.

> In this essay, the author argues that future humanitarian intervention may follow customary practice as established in the 1990s rather than international law after the U.S. administration of President George W. Bush's invasion of Iraq in 2002–3.

"Torture: a Just War Perspective," *Faith and International Affairs* 5:2 (Summer 2007), 29–31.

> Johnson applies three classic just war elements to the case of torture, arguing against it.

"Thinking Comparatively about Religion and War," *Journal of Religious Ethics* 36:1 (March 2008), 157–79.

> This article reviews work related to religion and war, including authors Brekke, Sorabji, Perry Schmidt-Leukel, Bartholomeusz, Kelsay, and Reichberg et al.

"The Idea of Defense in Historical and Contemporary Thinking about Just War," *Journal of Religious Ethics* 36:4 (December 2008), 543–56.

> This work moves through three main stages of the development of just war thinking from classical to modern times: just cause as the justification for a sovereign's use of force in exercising the responsibility to maintain justice; sovereign state use of force as primarily a defense measure; and the continuation of state defense as a priority and the reinvigoration of just war thinking in contemporary context.

"Thinking Historically About Just War," *Journal of Military Ethics* 8:3 (Fall 2009), 246–59. Special Issue: James Turner Johnson and the Recovery of Just War Tradition.

> In this article, Johnson argues that ethicists must serve as scribes who educate the public and leadership on moral history and just

war tradition—a clarion call undergirded by a moral obligation to keep the lessons of the past contemporaneous.

"Tracing the Contours of the Jihad of Individual Duty," *Journal of Church and State* 53:1 (2011), 37–49.

Johnson interacts with chapter 4 of John Kelsay's landmark book *Arguing the Just War in Islam* (2007) and shows that Kelsay has advanced the understanding of the jihad of the sword from earlier interpretations such as that of Majid Khadduri's earlier standard *War and Peace in the Law of Islam* (1955). Johnson contends that even though Kelsay's writing is thorough, there is still work to be done with respect to jihad of the sword, especially with respect to what he considers to be distortions by present-day Islamist radicals.

"On Giving Birth to a New Organism and Helping to Shape a Discipline," *Journal of Military Ethics* 11: 1 (March 2012), 2–9.

This work reflects on ethics, war discourse and the founding of the *Journal of Military Ethics* to shape a new discipline.

"Holy War," *Nova et Vetera*, English Edition 10:4 (2012), 1099–113.

In this work, Johnson traces the idea of holy war from medieval times to the present day. He then contrasts medieval concepts with contemporary Roman Catholic social teaching.

"Religion, Violence, and Human Rights: Protection of Human Rights as Justification for the Use of Armed Force," *Journal of Religious Ethics* 41: 1 (March 2013), 1–14.

Johnson explores international human rights law and the use of force through two different lenses: 1) the Westphalian concept of sovereignty; and 2) the "Responsibility to Protect" (R2P) doctrine for the protection of citizens' human rights from violations by their own state governments.

"Contemporary Just War Thinking: Which is Worse, To Have Friends or Critics?" *Ethics & International Affairs* 27:1 (Spring 2013), 25–45.

> This article traces and breaks down various iterations of the just war concept, from its origins in the late twelfth century to modern reinventions. Influential thinkers appraised include contemporary philosophers Jean Bethke Elshtain, Jeff McMahan, David Rodin, and Brian Orend.

"*Ad Fontes*: The Question of Rebellion and Moral Tradition on the Use of Force," *Ethics & International Affairs* 27:4 (Winter 2013), 371–78.

> This essay considers the tension between traditional moral use of force by rulers and right of rebellion and natural law for the ruled.

"Ethics, Law, and Humanitarian Intervention: Biggar's Argument for the Precedence of Moral Order in the Dialectic with Positive Law," *Soundings* 97:2 (2014), 228–38.

> Johnston uses Nigel Biggar's work on morality, law, and the case of Kosovo as a starting point to analyze military use of force for humanitarian intervention since the 1990s.

"The Erosion of Noncombatant Immunity in Asymmetric War/*l'Érosion de l'immunité des noncombatants dans la guerre asymétrique*," *Air and Space Power Journal Africa and Francophonie/Afrique et Francophonie* 6:1 (1st Quarter 2015), English 53–64, French 61–74.

> This essay argues that law and moral discourse must adapt and protect noncombatant immunity in the cases of asymmetric and irregular warfare.

"Getting It Right," *Journal of Religious Ethics* 43:1 (March 2015, 170–77.

> In this article, Johnson critiques the accuracy of references made by Kristopher Norris in his article "'Never Again War': Recent Shifts in the Just War Tradition and the Question of "Functional Pacifism" in

Journal of Religious Ethics 42:1 (March 2014), 108–36. Johnson contends that Norris conflates Johnson's focus and concerns on just war with George Weigel's, which makes claims on the Roman Catholic Church position that Weigel terms "functional pacifism." Johnson argues use of the tradition of just war in recent times has been broken by deviation from its classic form as delineated by Aquinas and utilized by thinkers including Vitoria and Grotius.

"Christian Ethics and the Realm of Statecraft: Divisions, Cross-Currents, and the Search for Connections," *Providence*, Inaugural Issue (Fall 2015), 18–25.

In this inaugural issue, Johnson aims to turn the challenges faced by the integration of Christian ethics with political statecraft into opportunities for greater understanding of values, policy-making, and better-informed discourse and decision-making.

"Humanitarian Intervention, the Responsibility to Protect, and Sovereignty: Moral and Historical Reflections," *Michigan State International Law Review* 23:3 (2015), 609–34.

An article drawn from a 2014 work on the concepts of sovereignty and "Responsibility to Protect" (R2P). See the above entry under books, *Sovereignty: Moral and Historical Perspectives.* Washington, D.C.: Georgetown University Press, 2014. Specifically, readers will find exploration of these topics as applied to humanitarian intervention, moral thinking, and contemporary law application.

"The Tradition on Jihad of the Sword, Counter-Narratives, and Policy," *Soundings* 98:4 (2015), 440–48.

This article outlines two concepts as a baseline for possible engagement between Islam and the West regarding just war: tradition and context of jihad and the sword; and the intersection of Muslim religion, policy, and practice in contrast with just war doctrine in the West.

"Reading Augustine," *Providence* 8 (Summer 2017), 48–56.

Johnson directs the reader on how to read and understand Augustine and how his theological works, including *The City of God,* shaped Western doctrine and ethics.

"The Great War and International Law on War," *Soundings* 101:3 (2018), 255–72.

This article focuses on the first eighty years of positive international law to limit the destructiveness of war divided into three periods before, during, and after the First World War.

"Religion and the Human Rights Idea," *Journal of Religious Ethics* 46:2 (June 2018), 379–98.

In his comparative assessment of three works on the idea of human rights in relation to religion and ethics, Johnson evaluates various authors' works, including David Little; Sumner B. Twiss, Marian Simion and Rodney L. Peterson; and Linda Hogan.

"Armed Conflict And The Protection Of Populations: The Debate Over Humanitarian Intervention, Using Armed Force, And The Idea Of Sovereignty" *Brown Journal of World Affairs* 28:1 (Fall/Winter 2021), 1–15.

Johnson explores the development since the 1960s of the modern concept humanitarian intervention in the context of tensions and contradictions between this principle and the sovereign right of legitimate authorities to govern their territory without external interference. He identifies two main competing ideas of sovereignty: the first in terms of the "inviolability of state territory" as codified in the U.N. Charter (Article 2); and the second in terms of state and international "responsibility to protect" fundamental human rights. Johnson argues that, while both concepts are rooted in the idea natural law, the two concepts differ in the obligations and roles of state and international agents. Elucidating and exploring these definitions and differences, he offers baselines to continue discussion and debate on humanitarian intervention.

CHAPTER SOURCES

All essays and articles are reprinted with permission of the rights holder.

Chapter 1

New Catholic World 226:1346 (March-April 1982), 81–84. Reprinted with permission.

Chapter 2

First chapter, *Just War and the Gulf War,* with George Weigel. Washington, D.C.: Ethics and Public Policy Center, 1991. Reprinted with permission.

Chapter 3

First chapter, *Just War and Jihad: Historical and Theoretical Perspectives on War and Peace in Western and Islamic Traditions.* Edited with John Kelsay, Westport: CT, 1991. Reprinted with permission of the author.

Chapter 4

This lecture delivered to the United States Air Force Academy was published as a monograph in 1993. Subsequently, it was published as a chapter, "The Just War Idea and the Ethics of Intervention," in *The Leader's Imperative*, J. Carl Ficcarotta, ed., West Lafayette, IN: Purdue University, 2001. Reprinted with permission of the author.

Chapter 5

"The Question of Preemption," *Common Sense* 9 (Winter, 1996), 36–52. Reprinted with permission of the author.

Chapter 6

This chapter is a manuscript that was later published in a different format as "The Broken Tradition," *The National Interest* 45 (1996), 27–36. Reprinted with permission of the author.

Chapter 7

Annual Abraham Kuyper Lecture of the Center for Public Justice, "Can Force Be Used Justly?," given at Gordon College, Wenham, MA, November 2001. Reprinted with permission of the author.

Chapter 8

"Jihad and Just War," *First Things* 124 (June-July 2002), 12–14. Reprinted with permission.

Chapter 9

"Aquinas and Luther on War and Peace: Sovereign Authority and the Use of Armed Force," *Journal of Religious Ethics* 31:1 (Spring 2003), 3–20. Reprinted with permission.

Chapter 10

"Just War Theory: Responding Morally to Global Terrorism," in *The New Global Terrorism: Characteristics, Causes, Controls.* Charles W. Kegley, Jr., ed., Upper Saddle River, NJ: Prentice-Hall, 2003. Reprinted with permission.

Chapter 11

Unpublished lecture, "Catholic Just War Thought: The State of the Question," given at The Gregorian University, Rome, Italy, 2004; later appeared as an abbreviated article, "Just War As It Was and Is," *First Things*, 2005. Reprinted with permission of the author.

Chapter 12

"The Just War Idea: The State of the Question," *Social Philosophy and Policy* 23:1 (Winter 2006): 167–95. Reprinted with permission.

Chapter 13

"Torture: A Just War Perspective," *Faith and International Affairs* 5:2 (Summer 2007), 29–31. Reprinted with permission.

Chapter 14

Earlier version of an essay that later appeared as "Thinking Historically About Just War," *Journal of Military Ethics* 8:3 (Fall 2009), 246–59. Special Issue: James Turner Johnson and the Recovery of Just War Tradition. Reprinted with permission of the editors.

Chapter 15

"Just War and Jihad: Two Traditions on the Use of Force," *Inquiries,* the publication of the Center for Free Inquiry, Hanover College 3:2 (Winter 2003), 1–7. Reprinted with permission of the author.

Chapter 16

"Holy War," *Nova et Vetera,* English Edition 10:4 (2012), 1099–113. Reprinted with permission.

Chapter 17

"*Ad Fontes*: The Question of Rebellion and Moral Tradition on the Use of Force," *Ethics & International Affairs* 27:4 (Winter 2013), 371–78. Reprinted with permission.

Chapter 18

"Contemporary Just War Thinking: Which is Worse, To Have Friends or Critics?" *Ethics & International Affairs* 27:1 (Spring 2013), 25–45. Reprinted with permission.

Chapter 19

"Religion, Violence, and Human Rights: Protection of Human Rights as Justification for the Use of Armed Force," *Journal of Religious Ethics* 41:1 (March 2013), 1–14. Reprinted with permission.

Chapter 20

"The Erosion of Noncombatant Immunity in Asymmetric War/*l'Érosion de l'immunité des noncombatants dans la guerre asymétrique,"Air and Space Power Journal Africa and Francophonie/Afrique et Francophonie* 6:1 (1st Quarter 2015), English 53–64, French 61–74.

Chapter 21

Unpublished presentation at The Trinity Forum: "Evening Conversation: Just War and the Contemporary Security Environment, with James Turner Johnson," Washington, D.C., 2015. Reprinted with permission of the author.

Chapter 22

Unpublished presentation at annual McCain Conference, United States Naval Academy, 2015. Reprinted with permission of the author.

Chapter 23

"Christian Ethics and the Realm of Statecraft: Divisions, Cross-Currents, and the Search for Connections," *Providence* (Fall 2015), 18–25. Reprinted with permission.

Chapter 24

"Reading Augustine," *Providence* 8 (Summer 2017), 48–56. Reprinted with permission.

Chapter 25

"Paul Ramsey and the Recovery of the Just War Idea," *Providence* online (September 2019). Reprinted with permission.

Appendix B

"James Turner Johnson and the Dissemination of the Just War Tradition: An Annotated Bibliography," 269–310, by Timothy J. Demy and Gina G. Palmer in *Responsibility and Restraint: James Turner Johnson and the Just War Tradition.* Eric D. Patterson and Marc LiVecche, ed. Stone Tower Press, Middletown, RI, 2020. Reprinted and updated with permission.

ABOUT JAMES TURNER JOHNSON AND THE EDITORS

JAMES TURNER JOHNSON

James Turner Johnson (Ph.D., Princeton 1968) is Distinguished Professor emeritus of Religion and Associate of the Graduate Program in Political Science at Rutgers, The State University of New Jersey, where he has been on the faculty since 1969. His research and teaching have focused and Islamic moral traditions related to war, peace, and the practice of statecraft. Among his many writings are: *Ethics and the Use of Force: Just War in Historical Perspective* (Ashgate 2011), *The War To Oust Saddam Hussein* (Rowman and Littlefield 2005), *Morality and Contemporary Warfare* (Yale 1999), *The Holy War Idea in Western and Islamic Tradition* (Penn State 1997), and *Ideology, Reason, and the Limitation of War* (Princeton 1975).

ABOUT THE EDITORS

Eric Patterson, Ph.D., is executive vice president of the Religious Freedom Institute and scholar-at-large at Regent University and a Research Fellow at Georgetown University's Berkley Center for Religion, Peace, and World Affairs. He is the author and editor of numerous books, including *Responsibility and Restraint: James Turner Johnson and the Just War Tradition*, *Just American Wars*, *The Ashgate Research Companion on Military Ethics*, *Ending Wars Well*, *Ethics Beyond War's End*, *Politics in a Religious World*, *Debating the War of Ideas*, *Christianity and Power Politics*

Today, and *Just War Thinking: Morality and Pragmatism in the Struggle Against Contemporary Threats.*

He has twice worked at the U.S. Department of State's Bureau of Political-Military Affairs, served for over twenty years as an Air National Guard officer and commander, and was a White House Fellow. He holds a Ph.D. in Political Science from the University of California at Santa Barbara and a Master's degree in International Politics from the University of Wales at Aberystwyth.

Gina Granados Palmer, Ph.D., is a faculty member at the U.S. Naval War College, Newport, Rhode Island, and an entrepreneur with a background in mechanical engineering and production technology. She is co-author of *Religion and War: Exploring the Issues*. Focusing on leadership, ethics, technology, war, and the balance between diplomacy and defense, Palmer received a Ph.D. from Salve Regina University in Technology and Humanities, a Master of Liberal Arts degree in International Relations from Harvard University's Division of Continuing Education and a B.S. in Mechanical Engineering from California Polytechnic State University, San Luis Obispo.

Timothy J. Demy, Th.D., Ph.D., is Professor of Military Ethics U.S. Naval War College, Newport, Rhode Island and Honorary Fellow, Durham University (UK), Department of Theology and Religion. He is the author and editor of numerous articles, encyclopedias, and books on the subjects of ethics, religion, and security. Among his writings are *Christianity, War, and Peace: Questions and Answers from a Just-War Perspective.* Among his degrees, he earned the Th.M. and Th.D. from Dallas Theological Seminary, a Ph.D. from Salve Regina University, and Master's degrees from the University of Cambridge, the University of Texas at Arlington, and the U.S. Naval War College.